INTRODUCTION TO LEGAL NURSE CONSULTING

The West Legal Studies Series

Your options keep growing with West Legal Studies

Each year our list continues to offer you more options for every area of the law to meet your course or on-the-job reference requirements. We now have over 140 titles from which to choose in the following areas:

Administrative Law	Family Law
Alternative Dispute Resolution	Federal Taxation
Bankruptcy	Intellectual Property
Business Organizations/Corporations	Introduction to Law
Civil Litigation and Procedure	Introduction to Paralegalism
CLA Exam Preparation	Law Office Management
Client Accounting	Law Office Procedures
Computer in the Law Office	Legal Research, Writing, and Analysis
Constitutional Law	Legal Terminology
Contract Law	Paralegal Employment
Criminal Law and Procedure	Real Estate Law
Document Preparation	Reference Materials
Environmental Law	Torts and Personal Injury Law
Ethics	Will, Trusts, and Estate Administration

You will find unparalleled, practical support

Each book is augmented by instructor and student supplements to ensure the best learning experience possible. We also offer custom publishing and other benefits such as West's Student Achievement Award. In addition, our sales representatives are ready to provide you with dependable service.

We want to hear from you

Our best contributions for improving the quality of our books and instructional materials is feedback from the people who use them. If you have a question, concern, or observation about any of our materials, or you have a product proposal or manuscript, we want to hear from you. Please contact your local representative or write us at the following address:

West Legal Studies, 3 Columbia Circle, P.O. Box 15015, Albany, NY 12212-5015

For additional information point your browser at
www.westlegalstudies.com

INTRODUCTION TO LEGAL NURSE CONSULTING

Cynthia Weishapple

Chippewa Valley Technical College

WEST

THOMSON LEARNING

Australia Canada Mexico Singapore Spain United Kingdom United States

WEST
THOMSON LEARNING

Introduction to Legal Nurse Consulting
by Cynthia Weishapple

Business Unit Director:
Susan L. Simpfenderfer

Executive Editor:
Marlene McHugh Pratt

Acquisitions Editor:
Joan M. Gill

Developmental Editor:
Rhonda Dearborn

Editorial Assistant:
Lisa Flatley

Executive Production Manager:
Wendy A. Troeger

Production Editor:
Betty L. Dickson

Cover Designer:
Dutton and Sherman Design

Cover Image:
Digital Imagery©copyright 2000
PhotoDisc, Inc.

Executive Marketing Manager:
Donna J. Lewis

Channel Manager:
Wendy E. Mapstone

Library of Congress Cataloging-in-
Publication Data

Weishapple, Cynthia.
   Introduction to legal nurse consulting /
Cynthia Weishapple.
      p. cm.
   "West Legal Studies series."
   Includes bibliographical references and
index.
   ISBN 0-7668-1052-6
   1. Nursing—Law and legislation—
United States. 2. Nursing consultants—
Legal status, laws, etc.—United States.
I. Title.
   KF2910.N87 W45 2000
   344.73′0414—dc21   00-049944

NOTICE TO THE READER

PREFACE

Of the many innovations in the practice of law that emerged at the end of the twentieth century, legal nurse consulting is perhaps the most revolutionary. Substantial growth in the profession and interest in this new career field for registered nurses led to a proliferation of legal nurse consulting and nurse paralegal educational programs in postsecondary education institutions across the country, in Canada, and in England. This textbook was written in response to the need for specialized references addressing the unique learning concerns of legal nurse consulting students.

Written to the professional audience of educated and experienced registered nurses, this text inspires the student to explore unique talents, backgrounds, and interests that enhance personal qualifications and transcend the traditional boundaries of medical careers. The student is challenged to consider opportunities for using these unique qualifications and create new career paths for serving medical and legal needs.

CONTENT DESIGN

Introduction to Legal Nurse Consulting provides registered nurses with the information necessary to launch a career in legal services. Units of study include the following:

- the development of legal nurse consulting and how registered nurses can use their extensive medical backgrounds in this emerging career field

- an introduction to the American legal system

- an introduction to legal reasoning and legal analysis, which forms the foundation for all legal services

- an introduction to legal research, legal citation, and the tools for locating law

- an introduction to personal injury law, the area of practice in which most legal nurse consultants will engage

- medical-legal research and writing, including the typical documents that will be prepared by legal nurse consultants

- ethics pertaining to legal practitioners and legal nurse consultants.

These components form the fundamental knowledge that registered nurses will need to participate in the legal nurse consulting profession.

Unit and chapter objectives at the beginning of each chapter; and chapter summaries, key terms and phrases, and review questions at the end of each chapter aid students in retaining and internalizing information. A glossary at the end of the text, along with appendices included for ease of reference, provide instructors and students with additional resources. *Introduction to Legal Nurse Consulting* is designed to provide a stand-alone reference for nurses who are interested in the medical-legal process.

FEATURES

- *Ethics Bookmarks* appear throughout the textbook, reminding legal nurse consulting students of the importance of maintaining the integrity of the nursing profession, the legal profession, and the legal nurse consulting profession.
- *Net Results* features information about and access to resources available on the Internet.
- *Profiles* of currently practicing legal nurse consultants add a personal touch to the narrative. Legal nurse consulting students can read comments and suggestions from nurses in the field and can more fully recognize the various positions that legal nurse consultants fill in the delivery of legal services.
- *What LNCs Say . . .* includes tips and quotes from practicing legal nurse consultants. These comments give insight into the real world of legal nurse consulting.
- *Case Studies* following the major units of the textbook provide legal nurse students with the opportunity to read court opinions. Students examine legal theory and procedure and explore how legal nurse consultants have contributed to adjudication of claims.
- *Exercises* at the end of each chapter promote networking activities to acquaint registered nurses with professionals in the legal field. Portfolio activities assist registered nurses in preparing resumes and professional portfolios that promote their unique characteristics and qualifications and make them attractive components in the delivery of legal services.

HOW TO USE THIS TEXT

This book is designed to provide a survey of the legal concepts a registered nurse would be expected to know if the nurse were offering medical experience and education services to the legal community. As such, it can be used as a textbook for an introductory course in legal nurse consulting or nurse paralegal curricula or in continuing education classes or workshops. It can also be used as a resource in related courses, such as medical-legal research and writing or civil litigation. Chapters may be selected based on the syllabus of the course, the time available for the subject matter, and the extent to which the material or topic is of interest to the students.

If the textbook is used in a legal nurse consulting or nurse paralegal curriculum, it is recommended that it be used in conjunction with the supplements provided on the Interest at www.westlegalstudies.com. An actual medical malpractice case is used to develop assignments and exercises that will give the nurses practical experience developing medical-legal skills. If the textbook is used in a continuing education class or certificate workshop, it is recommended that the nurses be encouraged to complete the networking and portfolio exercises at the end of each chapter. These exercises will help nurses find opportunities for working in law and help them to market themselves in this new field.

TEACHING AIDS AND SUPPLEMENTS

The complete supplement package was developed to achieve two goals:

1. To assist students in learning the essential information needed to continue exploration into the exciting field of legal nurse consulting.

2. To assist instructors in planning and implementing their instructional programs with the most efficient use of time and other resources.

- **Instructor's Manual with Test Bank and Transparency Masters** West Legal Studies has provided a downloadable Instructor's Manual online at www.westlegalstudies.com in the Instructor's Lounge under Resource. Written by the author of the text the *Instructor's Manual* contains answers to text exercises and questions, suggestions for supplementing class material, ideas for class activities, assignments, and quizzes. The transparency masters can be found on the CD.

- **Computerized Test Bank (Thomson Testing Tools)** The Test Bank found in the Instructor's Manual is also available in a computerized format on CD-ROM. The platforms supported include Windows™ 3.1 and 95, Windows™ NT, and Macintosh. Features include:

  - Multiple methods of question selection
  - Multiple outputs—that is, print, ASCII, and RTF
  - Graphic support (black and white)
  - Random questioning output
  - Special character support

- **Web page** Come visit our Web site at www.westlegalstudies.com, where you will find valuable information specific to this book such as hot links and sample materials to download, as well as other West Legal Studies products.

- **WESTLAW®** West's on-line computerized legal research system offers students "hands-on" experience with a system commonly used in law offices. Qualified adopters can receive ten free hours of WESTLAW®. WESTLAW® can be accessed with Macintosh and IBM PC and compatibles. A modem is required.

- **Citation-At-A Glance**   This handy reference card provides a quick, portable reference to the basic rules of citation for the most commonly cited legal sources, including judicial opinion, statutes, and secondary sources. *Citation-At-A-Glance* uses the rules set forth in *The Bluebook: A Uniform System of Citation.*

- **Court TV Videos**   West Legal Studies is pleased to offer the following videos from Court TV. Available for a minimal fee:
  - *Fentress v. Eli Lilly & Co.,* et al—Prozac on Trial
    ISBN 0-7668-1095-X
  - *Flynn v. Goldman Sachs*—Fired on Wall Street: A Case of Sex Discrimination?
    ISBN 0-7668-1096-8
  - *Dodd v. Dodd*—Religion and Child Custody in Conflict
    ISBN 0-7668-1094-1
  - *In Re Custody of Baby Girl Clausen*—Child of Mine: The Fight For Baby Jessica
    ISBN 0-7668-1097-6

- **West's Paralegal Video Library** includes:
  - *The Drama of the Law II: Paralegal Issues Video*
    ISBN 0-314-07088-5
  - *I Never Said I Was a Lawyer: Paralegal Ethics Video*
    ISBN 0-314-08049-X
  - The Making of a Case Video
    ISBN 0-314-07300-0
  - Mock Trial Video—Anatomy of a Trial: A Contracts Case
    ISBN 0-314-07343-4
  - Mock Trial Video—Trial Techniques: A Products Liability Case
    ISBN 0-314-07342-6
  - Arguments to the United States Supreme Court Video
    ISBN 0-314-07070-2

These videos are available at no charge to qualified adopters.

ACKNOWLEDGMENTS

Many deserve my thanks and acknowledgment. Particularly, I would like to thank the following:

- Dan Kodatsky, the West sales representative who serves the college where I teach, who believed in this project, and promoted it with West editors.

- Marilyn Mason-Kish, RN, BS, LNCC, whose article " Finding the Needle in the Medical Records Haystack" (*Legal Assistant Today,* March/April, 1994) inspired me to develop an educational program for legal nurse consultants.

- Susan Brown, Dean of Instruction, Chippewa Valley Technical College, who said, "Let's do it!"

- The legal nurse students who embraced the curriculum and taught me.

- Rhonda Dearborn and Joan Gill at *West Legal Studies* who took a chance on a first-time author whose only qualification was enthusiasm.

- The legal nurse consultants whose profiles and comments have added so much to this textbook.

- Daniel Oran whose *Dictionary of the Law* is cited throughout the text.

- All those who reviewed the book and provided meaningful feedback, suggestions, and insights:

Stacey Barone
Hofstra University, NY

Katherine Belanger
National Institute for Paralegal Arts & Sciences, FL

Carol Bortman
Brockton Hospital of Nursing, MA

Mark Ciccarelli, Esquire
Kent State University, OH

Sandra DeLaGarza
University of Texas

Dora Dye
City College of San Francisco, CA

Fernaundra Ferguson
University of West Florida

Judith Gic, LA

Susan J. Howery
Yavapai College, AZ

Kathleen Mercer Reed
University of Toledo, OH

William Mulkeen
Essex County College, NJ

Barb Rodgers, RN CLNC, CEO MLR Medical Legal Review, LLC
Sullivan Business College, KY

Donna Schoebel
University of Cincinnati, OH

Toni C. Smith, EDD, RN
University of Rochester Medical Center, NY

Laura Stubblefield
Kaplan College

Anita Tebbe
Johnson County Community College, KS

I owe a deep debt of gratitude to my family—my husband, Timothy Weishapple, whose constant care and concern (and patience!) made it possible for me to complete this writing while teaching fulltime and pursuing my doctorate; my daughters, Jana and Chelsie; my late mother, Marguerite Aldrich, JD, and my father, James Aldrich, retired instructor (North Dakota State College of Science).

Cynthia Weishapple

TO THE STUDENT

What an exciting new career opportunity awaits you! Building on your medical education and experience, *Introduction to Legal Nurse Consulting* empowers you with legal theory, terminology, and procedural insight to enhance your qualifications for legal nurse consulting. It is intended as a learning tool and a desk reference. The information contained in this text is based on innumerable discussions with practicing legal nurse consultants, attorneys who value the contributions of legal nurse consultants, and others who believe that legal nurse consultants will play expanded roles in resolution of medical-legal claims in the twenty-first century.

Here are a few recommendations to help you get the most out of this textbook:

■ Read the text and study the margin definitions. Like medicine, the practice of law has its own language, and you should become familiar with it. Understanding and articulating *legalese* will facilitate your desire to become integral to the delivery of legal services.

■ Practice your new knowledge and skills by accessing the web site for this book at www.westlegalstudies.com. There you will find a true medical malpractice case from actual court documents and hypothetical scenarios you might face as a legal nurse consultants. Completing these assignments and exercises will hone your skills and reinforce your understanding of legal concepts and procedures.

- ▪ Use the exercises at the end of each chapter to develop your job-search techniques. Networking has been identified as the single most important factor in accessing the job market. The networking exercises provided in this text are designed to make you visible in the legal community and to promote your background. In addition, the portfolio exercises assist you in identifying special traits and characteristics you have and including these traits and characteristics in resumes, cover letters, and supporting materials in a way that will grab the attention of a potential employer.

- ▪ Retain this book as reference tool. No one can know all there is to know about the law or legal procedure. The glossary, appendices, and resources provided in this text give you access to information when you need it.

During the last decade, legal nurse consultants have forged career paths that capitalize on their medical experience and education, and require considerable investment in learning. *Introduction to Legal Nurse Consulting* assists you in learning about the intricacies of legal practice. The time you spend learning about legal theory, terminology, and procedure and developing legal skills will be rewarded with a challenging and satisfying career as a legal nurse consultant.

Please note the Internet resources are of a time sensitive nature and URL addresses may often change or be deleted.

Contact us at www.westlegalstudies@delmar.com

BRIEF CONTENTS

CONTENTS

CHAPTER 23

CLASS ACTION AND
MULTIDISTRICT LITIGATION   383

CHAPTER 24

INTRODUCTION TO EVIDENCE LAW   391

CHAPTER 25

THE BASICS OF CIVIL PROCEDURE   405

UNIT VI

MEDICAL-LEGAL WRITING   447

CHAPTER 26

INTRODUCTION TO LEGAL WRITING   449

CHAPTER 27

LEGAL CORRESPONDENCE   461

CHARTING A NEW COURSE

Challenging new opportunities exist for nurses in the legal profession. In this unit, you will find answers to these questions:

■ What exactly is a legal nurse consultant?

■ How did the profession get started?

■ What kind of work does a legal nurse consultant do?

■ What skills and abilities are needed to work effectively as a legal nurse consultant?

■ How is medical expertise valuable to the legal community?

■ What type of nursing experience is helpful?

■ How can I become part of this new profession?

CHAPTER 1

BUILDING THE BRIDGE BETWEEN MEDICAL AND LEGAL

OBJECTIVES

In this chapter, you will discover

- a definition for legal nurse consultant

- how the legal nurse consultant profession began

- what skills and characteristics are necessary to work effectively as a legal nurse consultant

- in what ways the legal nurse consultant profession has contributed to the cost-effective delivery of legal services and managed health care

- how the legal nurse consultant profession is expected to grow

OVERVIEW

Nurses are diligent workers who continually update their knowledge and skills. This characteristic, together with a commitment to integrity and a background rich in health care experience, qualifies nurses for roles as legal nurse consultants. Since 1985, legal nurse consultants have made a significant contribution to the practice of law and the administration of justice. Economic indicators suggest that legal nurse consultants will play an even greater role in the delivery of legal services in the twenty-first century.

HISTORY OF THE NEW PROFESSION

For many years, nurses have worked as claims administrators for insurance companies handling workers' compensation, disability, and rehabilitation claims. During the early and mid-1980s, the number of legal claims in medical negligence and products liability grew, and insurance companies and law firms benefited economically by employing nurses. These nurses assisted in processing medical-legal claims efficiently, testified on matters concerning nursing malpractice, and educated legal professionals on the subjects of medical indications and standards of care.

Isolated in an emerging and unique career track, legal nurse consultants began seeking the advice and support of other, equally isolated, legal nurse consultants. In the 1980s, three organizations of legal nurse consultants emerged at the grass roots level: the Arizona Nurse Consultants in Law, based in Phoenix, Arizona; the San Diego Association of Medical Legal Nurse Consultants, based in San Diego, California; and the Georgia Association of Legal Nurse Consultants in Atlanta, Georgia.

A National Steering Committee for the formation of a national organization was convened on June 1, 1989, and met in San Diego. In August of 1989, the American Association of Legal Nurse Consultants (AALNC) was incorporated, with headquarters in Phoenix, Arizona. The purposes of the national organization were to

- promote the professional advancement of registered nurses practicing in a consulting capacity in the legal profession
- provide a resource for information on matters related to legal aspects of nursing and health care laws
- establish recognition of legal nurse consultants as a professional group with their own skills and expertise in medical legal matters
- provide a forum for continuing education
- provide a communications network for mutual support and fellowship[1]

Network News, the newsletter of the American Association of Legal Nurse Consultants was first published in April 1990. The newsletter was later expanded to include scholarly articles and became part of the *Journal of Legal Nurse Con-*

sulting, published quarterly by the AALNC. As the journal grew in professional interest, *Network News* was severed. Since September, 1999, it has been published separately as the membership newsletter. The AALNC also sponsors an education conference annually to provide legal and medical updates.

The history of the AALNC mirrors the growth of the profession. From an initial membership of thirty in 1989, it has grown to a national membership exceeding 2000, with more than twenty-five chapters throughout the United States. Appendix B includes a list of AALNC chapters and Appendix D lists other professional organizations that may be beneficial for legal nurse consultants.

A NEW PROFESSIONAL

One of the most remarkable changes in the practice of law since the mid-1980s has been the emergence of this new career professional, the legal nurse consultant.

> "The primary role of the **legal nurse consultant** is to evaluate, analyze and render informed opinions on the delivery of health care and the resulting outcomes. . . . Distinct from the paralegal or legal assistant, the legal nurse consultant . . . brings specialized education and clinical expertise to the medically related issues of the litigation process."[2]

Legal advocacy is a service to which lawyers are committed for the pursuit of justice and equity. To provide legal services to injured persons in an efficient, effective, and profitable manner, lawyers are turning to nursing professionals as a way to minimize the ever-increasing costs connected with litigation, and to educate members of the litigation team regarding the medical issues in the claim. This is especially true at a time when increasing demands are being made on the legal services industry to provide cost-effective and affordable legal services.

In many states, **tort reform** legislation has been enacted that limits awards, attorney fees, and liability of joint **tortfeasors** in personal injury, products liability, and health care liability cases. National tort reform efforts, especially in the area of products liability, and the national concern for health care reform are indicators of additional limitations that may be imposed on law firms practicing in areas of personal injury, health care liability, and worker's compensation. Processing these actions at the facility, the insurance company, or the law firm requires substantial resources that may be reduced by employing a legal nurse consultant for initial medical-legal analysis.

Access to legal services is enhanced with the employment of a medical specialist. Legal nurse consultants may assist in the cost-effective delivery of legal services by

- reviewing and interpreting medical records
- rendering initial opinions (especially in health care liability cases where nursing standards are involved)

- acting as liaison among attorneys, clients, and medical specialists
- educating attorneys about the medical and pharmacological issues in legal claims
- supporting life-care, rehabilitation, or retraining plans
- assisting in **class action lawsuit** and **multi-district litigation** (especially products liability)
- assessing medical **damages** (past and future)
- researching medical literature[3]

In addition, many legal nurse consultants routinely draft litigation documents, research legal and medical issues, prepare trial exhibits, and summarize medical-legal documents.

Legal nurse consultants add value to the practice of law in other ways as well. Nurses are diligent workers, who pay keen attention to detail and organization. Injured persons may be more likely to provide complete information to a nurse, rather than to a legal professional. Timely communication between a legal nurse consultant and the injured client reassures the client that the case is progressing. In addition, nurses are educators and may assist clients in understanding the long and sometimes tortuous course of a lawsuit.

Many legal nurse consultants are self-employed and contract with attorneys, insurers, departments of health, and others requiring their expertise. These self-employed legal nurse consultants may assist in preparing courtroom exhibits, summarizing medical records and medical testimony, identifying standards of care for health care professionals, and assessing damages—especially future health care costs—for permanently injured clients.

Legal nurse consultants have found meaningful careers in personal injury litigation, medical negligence, products liability, and toxic tort litigation; criminal law practices; insurance companies; industrial and manufacturing operations; workers' compensation and Social Security Administration practices; health care facilities and health maintenance organizations. They are employed as risk managers, claims managers, case managers, compliance officers, investigators, expert witnesses, mediators in **alternative dispute resolution,** and life care planners.

DUTIES OF THE NEW PROFESSIONAL

The role of the legal nurse consultant extends two of the main functions of nursing: patient care and record keeping.

Patient Care

Whether the legal nurse consultant is training factory employees about devices and postures that may prevent repetitive motion injuries or evaluating the future needs of a person with spinal cord injury, the patient/client is the primary concern. The human element is what makes the nurse invaluable. While not active in the physiological healing process, legal nurse consultants may, nonetheless, monitor progress, make projections, and evaluate treatments in personal injury and medical negligence claims. They may work with employers and health care professionals to adapt the working environment for a returning employee in workers' compensation, personal injury, products liability, and medical negligence cases.

As a nurse educates a patient concerning disease characteristics and self-care, so, too, the legal nurse consultant educates legal staff on issues of pharmacology, diagnostic procedures, surgical standards, and clinical practices. Patient care is as integral to legal nurse consulting as it is to nursing. A thorough understanding of standards of care in health-related industries is the integrity of the legal nurse consultant profession.

This background makes legal nurse consultants ideally suited to employment in the legal offices of health care facilities, health maintenance organizations, and insurance companies. Initial analysis of patient care and potential liability will assist legal staff in resolving claims and disputes brought against the facility and will facilitate good patient relations.

Record Keeping   By far, the most productive use of legal nurse consultants in legal offices to date has been in the area of chart review, record summaries, and medical research.

Legal nurse consultants can expect to prepare **chronologies** of medical treatment, reviews of medical expenses, summaries of medical testimonies, and abstracts of medical literature. Because of their medical background, legal nurse consultants are well qualified to identify preexisting and related conditions that may have an impact on the value of an injured client's case. The condensed reports prepared by the legal nurse consultant provide legal staff with manageable guides to thousands of documents, thereby saving time, expense, and considerable stress in the course of litigation.

QUALIFICATIONS OF THE NEW PROFESSIONAL

To testify as an expert witness, the witness must possess expert qualifications. A registered nurse license may not be enough to qualify a nurse to testify as an expert in nursing care. The admission of expert testimony lies within the sound discretion of the trial court judge. The level of education sought for credible testimony at trial may be a bachelor's degree in nursing with several years of experience, a master's degree, or even a doctoral degree. The most compelling experts are those who also have considerable real life experience. While many legal nurse consultants got their start as expert witnesses in nursing malpractice cases,[5] advanced degrees are not required to adequately perform the duties of a legal nurse consultant.

Initial opinion on health care standards may be rendered by a registered nurse, whether that nurse has a bachelor's degree, is a graduate of a two-year (associate degree) nursing program, or is a graduate of a diploma school. Review and analysis of medical records, location of experts and medical literature, and assessment of damages does not require an advanced degree. Investigation of the workplace and recommendation of policies regarding **ergonomics** and workplace safety are within the expertise of a registered nurse. The investigation of a complaint made to a licensing board concerning the conduct of a nursing professional may be handled efficiently and effectively by a registered nurse.

In fact, the most important qualification of a legal nurse consultant is experience. Members of the AALNC believe that the expertise acquired after many years of clinical or surgical service provides the foundation for understanding and evaluating personal injury claims and health care liability. A minimum of two years of nursing practice is recommended by members of the AALNC in order to operate effectively as a legal nurse consultant.[6]

Other characteristics and qualifications for successful legal nurse consulting are consistent with the qualities that make for successful nursing.

- strong interpersonal skills
- excellent communication skills
- the ability to manage multiple priorities
- conscientious work ethic
- the ability to manage resources effectively
- technological literacy
- strong research skills
- willingness to continue learning

A skill that is essential in the legal office of the twenty-first century is computer literacy. While computer applications may be learned on the job, a nurse who is interested in pursuing a legal nurse consultant career, but is not fluent with basic computer functions, may consider enrolling in a computer applications class at a local college or university. With the increasing availability of legal and technical resources on the Internet, a course in navigating the World Wide Web would also be valuable training for a legal nurse consultant who is unfamiliar with these tools.

TRAINING PROGRAMS

The first college-based curriculum for legal nurse consulting was established in 1994 at the University of California at San Diego. This one-year, post-baccalaureate certificate includes courses in legal research, the legal nurse consultant profession, and workers' compensation. A short internship is required.

In 1995, the Wisconsin Technical College System initiated an advanced technical certificate–legal nurse program at Chippewa Valley Technical College, in Eau Claire, Wisconsin. It was moved to Northcentral Technical College in Wausau, Wisconsin, beginning in September, 1999. The National Center for

Paralegal Training in Atlanta, Georgia, offered its program for legal health care specialist in January 1996. Both the Wisconsin and the National Center for Paralegal Training programs offer courses in civil litigation, legal research, and legal writing. College-based curricula differ in the extent to which they expose students to substantive law, procedural law, and business aspects of legal nurse consulting. A list of colleges and universities offering legal nurse consulting programs and other training options for legal nurse consultants is included in Appendix C.

Additional seminar and workshop-based training programs have become available for legal nurse consultants, including Medical Legal Resources, which offers a home study program called "The Nuts and Bolts of Legal Nurse Consulting," written by Karen Wether, BSN, RN. Some legal nurse consultants customize their education by taking selected courses from paralegal or legal studies programs.

The American Association of Legal Nurse Consultants suggests that legal training may be obtained on the job. The professional status of an experienced nurse is the primary qualification for working as a legal nurse consultant. The legal intricacies, legal theories, and vocabulary of legal procedure may be assimilated quickly once a position in a legal office is secured.

Nurses who are considering a career change may feel more competent to apply for positions as legal nurse consultants if they have some legal education. Based on a recent survey by the American Association for Paralegal Education,[7] more educational options and college curriculum-based programs will be initiated to provide training that will meet the increasing demand for legal nurse consultants.

FUTURE TRENDS

Legal nurse consultants continue to explore challenging career options. As public awareness of the benefits of employing legal nurse consultants grows, demand for these services will increase. Economics may drive the insurance industry to require the use of legal nurse consultants, rather than physicians, in initial case development for health care liability claims and personal injury lawsuits.

A study was conducted in Pittsburgh recently by Dianne Alessio, a legal nurse consultant, and the results were reported in the *Journal of Legal Nurse Consulting*. Attorneys were surveyed concerning their awareness and use of legal nurse consultants. Of the 134 lawyers who responded, 59% were aware of the profession, but only 15% were aware of the Pittsburgh Chapter of the AALNC. These lawyers typically used paralegals and others to assist in medical litigation.[8] An inference of this study is that as attorneys become aware of the availability of legal nurse consulting services and are educated as to the added value and cost effectiveness of using legal nurse consultant services, the demand for qualified medical specialists employed as consultants to lawyers will grow.

Net Results

Professional Associations and Training

The AALNC maintains a home page with membership and seminar information, chapter directories, and links to medical and legal World Wide Web sources. Many of the colleges and training programs identified in this chapter also have web pages. The AALNC may be accessed via www.aalnc.org; The Wisconsin Technical College System advanced technical certificate–legal nurse may be accessed at www.northcentral.tec.wi.us; and The National Center for Paralegal Training may be accessed via www.ncpt.aii.edu.

The profession of legal nurse consulting is not, as of this writing, listed in the *Dictionary of Occupational Titles,* and the Department of Labor has no statistics or projections on the growth of the legal nurse consulting profession. The AALNC has, however, recently reported the results of a compensation survey. According to survey results, of the respondents who were being paid on a salary basis, 36.3% reported salaries between $30,000 and $50,000 and 36.1% received less than $30,000. It should be noted that the survey also indicated that 42.8% of respondents only worked between 1 and 20 hours per week on legal nurse consulting activities. Education level, years of experience, geographical location, full- or part-time status, and type of legal nurse consulting services rendered may influence the salary.

The survey showed that legal nurse consultants who provided independent services charged fees ranging between $14 and $200 per hour for professional services. The most frequently cited professional charge per hour was $75.[9] These data were collected by members of the AALNC and were intended for informational purposes only.

A list of the number of AALNC members working in particular legal specialties is provided in Figure 1-1.[10]

Although some of the responding nurses reported working in more than one area, if the data in Figure 1-1 were displayed in a pie chart, it would reveal that the greatest numbers work in personal injury (22%) and medical malpractice (19%). Approximately the same number of legal nurse consultants work in workers' compensation (11%), in products liability (10%), as expert witnesses (9%), and in risk management (7%). Fewer nurses reported working in rehabilitation (5%), case management (4%), toxic torts (4%), criminal law (3%), life care planning (2%), elder law (2%), and health-care administration (2%).

Several indicators suggest growth in the demand for legal nurse consultants.

- mergers of major health care facilities and subsequent demand for efficient disposition of patient claims
- growth in the area of managed care
- legislative trends toward mandatory alternative dispute resolution for medical claims
- continuing costs of fraudulent workers' compensation, Medicare, and Medicaid transactions
- legislative limits on damage awards and attorney fees, making it less profitable for attorneys to engage high-priced physician specialists early in the litigation
- increase in the number of health maintenance organizations, plans, and networks—contracts that generally require initial attempts to resolve medical-legal claims in-house
- increase in awareness of ergonomics and risk management to prevent workplace injuries

FIGURE 1-1 Number of Legal Nurse Consultants in Specialty Practice Areas by State

State	Admin Healthcare	Case Mgmt.	Criminal	Elder	Expert	Life-care Planning	Medical Malpractice	Personal Injury	Product Liability	Rehab	Risk Mgmt.	Toxic Torts	Workers' Comp.
AL	1	2		2	6	1	4	4	4	2	1		4
AK													
AR			4	3	3	1	4	4	3	2		1	4
AZ	5	8	35	3	12	4	30	28	15	7	20	9	11
CA	11	26	35	13	102	14	153	138	79	21	37	29	61
CO	4	4	2	1	6	3	13	16		7	7		11
CT	1	1	2	1	3		7	4	2	3	3	1	3
DE	1	2			3	2	6	6	4	3	3	1	3
DC	1												
FL	23	35	16	18	69	12	132	104	56	45	65	20	78
GA	8	6	4	1	11	2	32	33	18	9	18	5	25
HI						1		2		1			4
ID		1	2		3		3	2	1			1	3
IL	7	13	4	5	25	6	53	39	23	12	19	5	32
IN	2		2	1	5		11	15	9	1	5	4	15
IA	1	4	1		2		5	5	3	3	1	1	7
KS	4	7	5	3	4		12	9	9	7	4	3	8
KY	1	5	2	1	15	4	22	21	14	5	9	6	11
LA	1	6	6	1	4	3	27	24	14	7	11	7	17
ME		1					2	1	1	1			2
MD	5	3	2	1	8	3	23	19	12	6	7	4	14
MA	1	3	5		5	3	17	14	8	2	4	3	9
MI	2	10	4	4	13	3	24	20	11	7	6	5	13
MN	1	1			5		7	7	4	1		4	4
MO		2	2		11	1	21	23	15	2	5		22
MS			2		1		4	4	5	1	1	5	5

FIGURE 1-1 Number of Legal Nurse Consultants in Specialty Practice Areas by State (continued)

State	Admin Healthcare	Case Mgmt.	Criminal	Elder	Expert	Life-care Planning	Medical Malpractice	Personal Injury	Product Liability	Rehab	Risk Mgmt.	Toxic Torts	Workers' Comp.
MT		3	1		2	1	4	4	1	1	1		5
NE		1					1	3	1	1			2
NV			1		2		7	7	2		1	2	3
NH							1	2			1		1
NJ	6	7	5	4	15	2	36	28	19	6	14	3	12
NM		2		1	6	3	12	10	3	1	5		5
NY	4	9	14		14	3	43	35	17	6	16	12	21
NC	3	5	2	2	15	5	24	22	7	7	8	2	19
ND	1			1			1	2	1				2
OH	6	7	6	4	17	3	38	25	19	9	14	5	20
OK			1	1	2		4	6	3	2	2	1	5
OR	2	5	1	2	4	2	10	10	6	3	5	2	12
PN	12	23	8	5	37	10	74	65	34	32	11	8	48
RI	1	1	2	1	1		4	2	1	3	2	1	3
SD						1	2	2	1	2	1		1
SC		1	1		5		8	9	4	2	2	1	7
TN	1	2	2	3	7	1	12	14	9	4	5	3	13
TX	10	27	10	12	33	16	93	78	43	30	37	29	47
UT	1	2	1		4		6	5	3	1	3	1	5
VT	1		2				2	2	1				2
VA	3	9	3	1	12	6	29	27	15	14	5	5	18
WA		3	3	3	11	3	15	14	6	4	5	4	7
WV	1		3		1		10	9	7		2	1	7
WI	3	1	2	1	5	1	8	6	3	3	4	2	6
WY					1		2				2		
CANADA					2	1	4	3	2	1			

Nurses may have reported working in more than one area.

Portions of the 1998–1999 AALNC Membership Directory reprinted with permission of the American Association of Legal Nurse Consultants (AALNC), 4700 W. Lake Avenue, Glenview, IL 60025-1485, Copyright, 1998.

- societal demand to decrease the cost and the time involved in settling medical-legal claims
- recognition of governmental and industrial liability for exposure to toxic substances

CERTIFICATION

No state or federal licensure laws govern legal nurse consultants.

The AALNC commissioned a core curriculum, with multiple authors contributing to the organization's treatise on legal nurse consulting. This core curriculum, *Legal Nurse Consulting: Principles and Practice,*[11] was published in 1998 and is the basis for a certifying examination administered by the AALNC. This certification enhances professional status and promotes a standard of professional competence. The criteria that must be met to qualify for the certifying examination is discussed in Chapter Thirty-four. Preparatory seminars are available through the AALNC. Successful completion of the certifying examination allows a legal nurse consultant to add the LNCC (Legal Nurse Consultant Certified) designation to his or her name. This is a professional certification only. It does not preclude registered nurses from working as legal nurse consultants.

CHAPTER SUMMARY

- Legal nurse consultants provide medical expertise to the legal community.
- The legislative trend toward tort reform has promoted the use of legal nurse consultants for the cost-effective delivery of legal services in the areas of personal injury, health care liability, workers' compensation, and products liability cases.
- Patient/client care and record keeping are primary functions of the legal nurse consultant.
- The most important qualification of a legal nurse consultant is clinical or surgical experience.
- Many educational programs, including home study courses and curricula at colleges and universities, are emerging to provide legal training for registered nurses who are interested in becoming legal nurse consultants.
- The AALNC was founded in 1989. The *Journal of Legal Nurse Consulting* is published quarterly by the AALNC.
- *Legal Nurse Consulting: Procedures and Practice* is the core curriculum of the AALNC and is the basis for the LNCC examination, a professional certification.

■ Economic and political indicators suggest that legal nurse consultants will play diverse and increasing roles in the delivery of legal services in the future.

KEY TERMS

alternative dispute resolution	**damages**	**multi-district litigation**
chronologies	**ergonomics**	**tort reform**
class action lawsuits	**legal nurse consultant**	**tortfeasor**

REVIEW QUESTIONS

1. Write a definition of legal nurse consulting.
2. How does a legal nurse consultant assist in the cost-effective delivery of legal services?
3. What qualifications should a legal nurse consultant possess?
4. Identify trends that indicate growth in the legal nurse consultant profession.

INTERNET EXERCISES

1. Access the web page for this textbook at *www. westlegalstudies.com.* Read through the medical malpractice case and become familiar with the facts as they were presented in court documents.
2. Click on the assignments section of the web page and complete the assignment(s) for Chapter One.

EXERCISES

1. Networking. Refer to Appendix B. Contact the offices of a nearby chapter of the AALNC. Ask about a mentoring program. Determine if there are members in your area and interview a member legal nurse consultant. Find out about the legal nurse consultant's educational background, job description, usual job duties, and job satisfaction. If the legal nurse consultant is willing to share this information, discuss salaries, benefits, and other positions that may be available in the area. What advice would the legal nurse consultant give beginners in the field? Establish a networking file, system, or Rolodex. Keep a written record of the answers to these questions and the legal nurse consultant with whom you spoke.

2. Professional Portfolio. Look over your current resume. What special experience, training, and skills can you "sell" to the legal community? What personal characteristics qualify you for the position of legal nurse consultant? Why will attorneys want to hire you? As you evaluate yourself, jot down your unique qualifications, education, and personality traits. Keep these in a folder or portfolio. You will use these notes to develop power cover letters and resumes that will effectively market your abilities.

ENDNOTES

1. American Association of Legal Nurse Consultants, "The History of AALNC," *Fifth Annual National Conference Syllabus* (1994).

2. American Association of Legal Nurse Consultants, "What Is A Legal Nurse Consultant?" (1995) [Brochure].

3. C. Weishapple, "Working With A Legal Nurse Consultant," *The Practical Litigator* 7:5 (1996): 15–22.

4. American Bar Association, *Annotated Model Rules of Professional Conduct,* (1999) 4th Edition Rule 1.6. Copies of ABA *Model Code of Professional Responsibility, 1999 Edition* are available from Service Center, American Bar Association, 750 North Lake Shore Drive, Chicago, IL 60611-4497, 1-800-285-2221.

5. R. Janes, J. Bogart, J. Magnusson, B. Joos, and J. Beerman, "The History and Evolution of Legal Nurse Consulting," in *Legal Nurse Consulting: Principles and Practice,* ed. J. Bogart (Boston: CRC Press, 1998), 3–8.

6. American Association of Legal Nurse Consultants, *Legal Nurse Consultant Certification Handbook and Examination Application: April 1998–April 1999* (1998) [Brochure].

7. A. Tebbe, "Legal Nurse Consulting," *Paralegal Educator* 12:3 (1998): 26–27.

8. D. Alessio, BS, RN, "Increasing Attorneys' Awareness of the Legal Nurse Consultants' Services: A Study in Pittsburgh," *Journal of Legal Nurse Consulting* 7:2 (1996): 7–11.

9. American Association of Legal Nurse Consultants, *1999 Compensation Survey Results* (1999).

10. American Association of Legal Consultants, *Membership* Directory (1988).

11. J. B. Bogart, RN MN, ed., *Legal Nurse Consulting: Principles and Practice* (Boston: CRC Press, 1998).

CHAPTER 2

LIMITLESS OPPORTUNITIES

OBJECTIVES

In this chapter, you will discover

- diverse positions available to legal nurse consultants in legal offices

- what roles legal nurse consultants play in government, business, and industry

- how independent legal nurse consultants operate

- the expanding role of legal nurse consultants

OVERVIEW

The field of legal nurse consulting is open to the imagination, creativity, and determination of the registered nurse seeking employment in law. No single job description has been developed by the Department of Labor. However, legal nurse consultants have made significant contributions to the practice of law. This chapter will focus on six legal employers for whom legal nurse consultants have performed services and will identify the skills and education necessary to operate effectively in these legal arenas. There are many areas of opportunity for legal nurse consultants: elder law, healthcare administration, mediation, criminal law practices, and others. The six employers selected for this chapter represent the strongest employment potential for legal nurse consultants based on the professional information available[1] (see Chapter One). The six legal employers are listed in Figure 2-1, along with brief descriptions of how legal nurse consultants are used by these employers.

INDEPENDENT CONSULTING

Many successful legal nurse consultants are self-employed entrepreneurs. By contracting their services with area attorneys and others, they are afforded a flexibility not previously enjoyed in nursing. Two types of independent legal nurse consulting services will be profiled here: general legal nurse consulting and compliance consulting.

General Legal Nurse Consulting

The various duties of independent legal nurse consultants include medical reviews and summaries, and locating medical experts and medical literature. They may be asked to summarize and compare medical testimony in depositions, prepare timelines, or suggest trial exhibits. Independent contracting legal nurse consultants must deal with the stress of short deadlines, but are rewarded with a reliable reputation, as well as continued and expanded business. Legal nurse consultants who offer their services to attorneys must develop a system for checking **conflicts of interest** and must be aware of and abide by the ethical constraints of the legal profession.

Many independent legal nurse consultants offer their services to the public. They may be asked to investigate and recommend an appropriate facility for a victim of Alzheimer's or a disabled child. They may be asked to advocate on behalf of an elderly person who is confused about insurance, Medicare, and Medicaid benefits. They may be appointed as **guardians** for persons who need assisted living. In this capacity, the legal nurse consultant has a fiduciary duty to act in the best interest of the **ward,** the person under guardianship. Generally, all financial, health care, and personal decisions for the ward are the responsibility of the guardian. This type of advocacy requires that the legal nurse consultant comply with statutes prohibiting the unauthorized practice of law. Legal nurse consultants may not give legal advice or appear in court or before administrative agencies, with the exception of the Social Se-

FIGURE 2-1   Six Legal Employers of Legal Nurse Consultants

Legal Employer	Description
Independent Self-employed Legal Nurse Consultant	*General Legal Nurse Consulting:* Contracts with lawyers and others for delivery of legal nurse consulting services. *Compliance Consultant:* Works with health care facilities to ensure compliance with federal and state regulatory agencies.
Insurance	*Case Manager/Claims Administrator:* Oversees the processing of a medical claim filed with an insurance company.
Education	Develops curriculum for and teaches in legal nurse consulting educational programs.
Law Firm	*Expert Witness:* Renders expert opinion as to the standard of care of health care professionals. *Life-Care Planner:* Develops a plan for future care of a seriously injured person. *Medical-Legal Investigator:* Investigates a claim against a health care provider or supervises the investigation of a medical-legal claim. *Nurse Paralegal in Personal Injury Law:* Assists in the development or defense of a personal injury claim based in tort.
Government	Assists in processing claims, reports, and other actions in agencies such as the Food and Drug Administration or the Department of Justice.
Business and Industry	*Risk Manager:* Evaluates and establishes policies to minimize an organization's exposure to liability.

curity Administration, representing others. Legal nurse consultants operating in this capacity should consult with a lawyer whenever they are in doubt about the legal nature of the services they are performing.

The variety of cases, the freedom of being one's own boss, and the confidence of having considerable medical expertise that is marketable in business and legal environments are all advantages of being a self-employed, independent legal nurse consultant. Interpersonal and communication skills

Net Results

Certification

Credentials are extremely important in selling the services of a legal nurse consultant. Many certifying boards and organizations are accessible via the Internet. The American Health Information Management Association's home page has information concerning its certifying examinations. Access it at www.ahima.org. Additionally, certification in rehabilitation nursing is a generally accepted credential for defending a life care plan (discussed later in this chapter). Information about the Certified Registered Rehabilitation Nurse (CRRN) examination may be accessed at the home page of the Association of Rehabilitation Nurses, www.rehabnurse.org.

must be excellent. To successfully manage the business, a self-employed legal nurse consultant may consider taking an accounting class or a marketing class at a local university, or a community or technical college. Being able to sell medical information services and a general understanding of business are valuable assets of the independent legal nurse consultant.

Compliance Consulting

Preparing and keeping medical records is heavily regulated by state and federal health and human services agencies. To maintain state and federal funding, health care providers and facilities must conform to standards imposed. For instance, a nursing home whose records do not meet the requisite guidelines may be placed on probation or its license to operate may be suspended or withdrawn. The management of the facility may hire a legal nurse consultant to develop and implement policies on generating and retaining medical records that will put the facility back into compliance.

Certification in medical records is often acquired by nurses who act as compliance consultants. The American Health Information Management Association offers certifying examinations for Registered Health Information Administrator (RHIA) and Technician (RHIT) and for Certified Coding Specialist (CCS) and Specialist–Physician-based (CCS-P). Travel is usually necessary. Organizational skills, a thorough understanding of clinical procedures, and the willingness to accept a challenge and see a project through are important characteristics of the legal nurse consultant practicing as a compliance consultant.

INSURANCE

Legal nurse consultants who work with insurance companies often have the title of case manager or claims administrator. Case managers determine the potential cost of the claim to the insurance company and assist in the establishment of a **reserve**—the anticipated amount of money that is set aside for the settlement of a claim. Assigning the claim to outside counsel; assisting in investigation, discovery, and development of defenses; and monitoring the expenses of defense are all part of a claims manager's duties. In addition, the claims manager may assist in establishing a **structured settlement,** the purchase of an annuity to provide payments to the claimant for his or her lifetime or for a specified period of time.

The medical background of the claims manager facilitates evaluation of disability, personal injury, products liability, and health care liability claims processed by the insurance company. Legal nurse consultants who work with insurance companies may also be employed as workers' compensation case managers. In this capacity a legal nurse consultant reviews the medical disability claimed and monitors the progress of treatment for the injured worker. The workers' compensation case manager works with the injured worker to return to work either through retraining or adaptation of the workplace. Organizational skills, interpersonal skills, and resourcefulness are characteristic of case managers.

EDUCATION

According to the American Association for Paralegal Education, considerable growth is expected in the development of educational programs for legal nurse consultants.[2] To maintain certification through the AALNC and other certifying bodies, continuing education in nursing and legal or other standards must be documented.

Experienced legal nurse consultant educators are already at work in colleges and universities across the country. Legal nurse consultant educators may be required to create courses, develop objectives, organize advisory committees, supervise internships, and counsel students about academic and career options. The ability to work with a team, to follow a project through, and to meet internal and external educational standards is requisite for functioning as a legal nurse consultant educator.

With increasing educational programming, demands for affordable textbooks and treatises by and for legal nurse consultants will emerge. Coordinating medical and legal libraries to support these programs will provide additional opportunities for legal nurse consultants.

LAW FIRMS

Law firms employ in-house legal nurse consultants, sometimes called nurse paralegals, and contract for independent legal nurse consulting services. In this section, four areas of law firm employment for legal nurse consultants are profiled: expert witness, life-care planner, medical-legal investigator, and legal nurse consultant in personal injury litigation.

Expert Witness

Some legal nurse consultants confine their practices to acting as expert witnesses on nursing standards and/or clinical practices. To act as an expert witness, advanced education and many years of experience are generally necessary. A master's degree in nursing, nursing administration, or public health may be required before a judge will allow a nurse to express an opinion as to the ordinary and prudent care, or lack thereof, exercised by a defendant nurse or other health care provider. Expert legal nurse consultants often enhance their credibility by writing articles for professional periodicals and journals, and by presenting at workshops and seminars.

To act as an expert witness, the legal nurse consultant must be apprised of all relevant facts in the case. This will involve a review of all medical records, including nurses' notes and incident reports. The expert forms an opinion on whether the conduct of the health care professionals was reasonable under the circumstances existing then and there. The expert then writes a report explaining the opinion of the expert, the facts upon which it is based, and the standards of practice that apply. The expert legal nurse consultant may be deposed before having to appear in court, and the **deposition** may result in settlement of the matter without testifying at trial. An in-house legal nurse consultant does not testify as an expert for that employer, but provides expert analysis for case development. The legal nurse consultant who is an expert witness is independent of the parties and the law firms involved.

Legal nurse consultants who act as expert witnesses must be sensitive to ethical concerns, especially conflicts of interest. If a legal nurse consultant has been employed by or retained by a health care provider, it may be unethical for the legal nurse consultant to also provide services for the opposing side on the same case. Even after the employment is terminated or the services completed, it may be unethical for the legal nurse consultant to be retained by another party opposing the health care provider, since the legal nurse consultant may have inside information, which might be unfair to the health care provider.

Life-Care Planner

Many legal nurse consultants work in the area of rehabilitation consulting. Experience in home health care, orthopedics, and neurology provide a strong background for this type of work. Occupational therapy or vocational therapy and case management backgrounds are also valuable assets for life-care planning.

When a catastrophic injury occurs, especially brain or spinal cord injuries, future care for the injured party must include a projection of costs for medical, vocational, psychiatric, and pharmaceutical services. A nurse is uniquely qualified to assess these costs, investigate facilities that can provide the care outlined in the suggested **life-care plan,** and monitor the services provided.

To defend a life-care plan in court, that is, to testify to its validity, the nurse is required to be qualified as an expert. Qualification as an expert may be proven by the witness' experience, advanced education, specialty certifications or credentials, research, and published articles. Many life care planners are Certified Registered Rehabilitation Nurses (CRRN), Certified Case Managers (CCM), or Certified Life Care Planners (CLCP). While it is up to the discretion of the judge whether an expert is qualified to express an opinion, these credentials appear to be of great value to nurses who work with life-care planning.

Medical-Legal Investigator

A nurse employed as a medical-legal investigator previews claims and assists in the development of **products liability** or health care liability cases. Firms that employ nurses as medical-legal investigators are often referral firms only. They specialize in class action lawsuits, medical negligence, or products liability cases. The medical-legal investigator meets with the claimant and examines the circumstances that caused the harm. The investigator then makes a report to the attorney who meets with the claimant, decides whether or not that person has a **cause of action,** and accepts that person as a client. Once the retainer has been signed, the medical-legal investigator directs the fact development of the case. Frequent meetings are held with the attorney, the client, legal professionals, and experts. The medical-legal investigator may supervise the categorizing of evidence and the establishment of a records database for document control and retrieval.

Along with personal injury litigation, wrongful death, and health care liability cases, an emerging area of law for medical-legal investigators is **toxic torts.** Toxic torts deal with injuries resulting from exposure to substances such as herbicides, pesticides, plutonium, radiation, etc. Asbestos, tobacco, and latex glove litigation are widely known examples of legal claims based on toxic torts.

Criminal actions, especially those involving medical evidence and forensic/scientific investigation, such as sexual assaults and homicides, is another area of practice for medical-legal investigators with forensic nursing backgrounds. This may involve investigating medical, psychological, and social histories in a suspected child abuse case or it might involve analyzing and synthesizing medical records, forensic reports of trace evidence, and autopsy reports to match the accused with the alleged victim/crime.

Most medical-legal investigators are employed in law offices, but medical-legal investigators may also be employed by licensing agencies within state government. When a claim is made against a licensed health care professional, the medical-legal investigator is responsible for making an inquiry into the circumstances of the claim. This involves telephone contacts and meetings, document searches, and sometimes travel. The medical-legal investigator makes a recommendation to the inquiry board as to whether or not probable cause exists for the complaint. With this recommendation and the investigation records, the inquiry board determines whether to proceed with a hearing and potential disciplinary action against the health care professional.

Whether employed in a legal office or in the licensing agency, a nurse legal investigator enjoys considerable freedom in terms of scheduled time. To operate effectively as a medical-legal investigator, organizational skills and interpersonal skills are requisite. Knowledge of standards of practice and the legal system are also important. Discretion and integrity are especially important in investigations.

Personal Injury Litigation

Whether working in an insurance defense or in a plaintiffs' law office with attorneys who specialize in personal injury, health care liability, or products liability, legal nurse consultants contribute to the cost-effective resolution of lawsuits and claims made by people who have been physically or emotionally harmed. The harm may be caused by an automobile accident, medical negligence, exposure to toxic chemicals, product failure or defect, battery, or any number of incidents that result in physical pain and suffering.

Ethics BookMark

Conflicts of Interest

"(a) A lawyer shall not enter into a business transaction . . . adverse to a client. . . . (b) A lawyer shall not use information relating to representation of a client to the disadvantage of the client. . . ." Annotated Model Rules of Professional Conduct *Fourth Edition Rule 1.7 Copyright 1999.[3]* Courts have held that nonlawyer employees may have sufficient conflict of interest to compromise the fiduciary relationship between lawyer and client. The legal nurse consultant must be aware of interests that may be adverse to the client, for example ownership in a company against which the client is pursuing a claim. These conflicts must be made known to the attorney. The independent legal nurse consultant must keep accurate records of cases on which work is being done or has been completed and the parties involved so that future assignments may not be jeopardized by potential conflicts.*
*American Bar Association. Reprinted by permission of the American Bar Association. American Bar Association, *Annotated Model Rules of Professional conduct*, 4th ed. (1999) Rule 1.7. Copies of Model Code of Professional Responsibility, 1999 edition are available from Service Center, American Bar Association, 750 North Lake Shore Drive, Chicago, IL 60611-4497, 1-800-285-2221.

In addition to reviewing the medical records, interviewing health care providers, and assessing past and future medical expenses, the legal nurse consultant employed in personal injury assists in creating exhibits and preparing attorneys for depositions and trials. Legal nurse consultants work with medical illustrators, clients, health care professionals, experts, investigators, paralegals, and lawyers.

Knowledge of the legal system, civil procedure, and **tort** theories and defenses greatly enhances the contribution a nurse can make to the litigation team. Patience, strict attention to detail, and organizational skills are important to the legal nurse consultant working in personal injury law.

GOVERNMENT

Legal nurse consultants are employed in state and federal agencies. At the Department of Justice in Washington, D.C., legal nurse consultants help administer the Radiation Exposure Compensation Program. Legal nurse consultants are also employed to assist with Medicare fraud cases, the Vaccine Injury Compensation Program, and environmental case reviews and analyses. At the state level, legal nurse consultants are employed in the offices of district attorneys and attorney generals to assist in actions brought against corrections facilities and officers. These are claims brought by prisoners who have been injured or feel that their incarceration, treatment, or lack of treatment violates their civil rights. This may occur when a prisoner is refused medical or dental treatment he or she feels entitled to or when treatment is delayed in a way that the prisoner feels is unfair. A prisoner may also make a claim for personal injury resulting from personal contact, exercise, or work requirements. Personal injury actions involving government employees and highway accidents are also claims that legal nurse consultants may assist in processing. At local district attorney offices, nurses may assist with criminal actions involving child abuse, sexual assault, and homicide.

Nurses may be employed at the Social Security Administration as or claims reviewers, managers, and hearing officers. Workers' compensation divisions of state government agencies may also use legal nurse consultants to review workplace injuries and manage claims. In these capacities, the legal nurse consultant does many of the tasks already described: review and summarize medical, act as liaison with experts, meet with the parties involved, and research medical literature. Effective time and resource management is essential for the legal nurse consultant employed in government. Attention to detail, the ability to travel, and the willingness to continue learning are expected traits of the government legal nurse consultant.

BUSINESS AND INDUSTRY

Preventing repetitive motion injury; reducing workers' compensation claims; developing policies for disposing of toxic chemicals or handling water-, air-, and blood-borne pathogens; reviewing potential liability claims; analyzing liability;

Net Results

Factual Investigation

Many areas of factual investigation may now be efficiently handled by navigating the Internet. Businesses, executive profiles, pharmaceuticals, medical and legal literature, expert witnesses, government resources and documents, and locating lay witnesses are all within a fingertip's reach. Many university library card catalogs are now available via the Internet. Legal investigators may search the card catalog for literature and historical data, saving considerable time at the facility. The home page of the AALNC, www.aalnc.org, and the home page of the National Federation of Paralegal Associations, www.paralegals.org, provide excellent links to government, business, and other factual data.

and securing adequate liability insurance are all modern business demands that require strict attention to detail and medical accuracy. Whether the business is a brewery, a manufacturing facility, a resort, a health care facility, or a computer services company, all need the services of a skilled professional who will review the nature of the business and work to prevent situations of potential exposure. Risks of liability exist among and involve the workers, the facilities, the business property, the customers and visitors, transportation, materials, production processes, and products.

Risk management is an area where legal nurse consultants may assist business owners, corporations, hospitals, and other health care facilities. Recognizing potential risks, taking appropriate measures to minimize exposure to liability, and ensuring that the business has adequate insurance coverage to meet the risks are all part of the risk management function. Nurses who work as risk managers must combine knowledge of medicine with knowledge of the legal system and insurance concepts. They must be excellent educators, who are adept at interpersonal skills and communication techniques.

CHAPTER SUMMARY

- Imagination, courage, and self-understanding are all that are needed to forge a new path and create a professional identity as a legal nurse consultant.
- Career choices for nurses have been greatly enhanced with the entrance of nurses onto the legal scene.
- Rewarding careers in legal nurse consulting are emerging in the health care industry, manufacturing firms, insurance companies, legal offices, and governmental agencies.
- Many legal nurse consultants find fulfillment in self-owned consulting businesses.
- Opportunities are expected to grow for legal nurse consultants to serve as experts and teachers.
- Springboard careers will appear in writing and editing textbooks, professional publishing, and acting as medical-legal library reference aids or managers.

KEY TERMS

cause of action	life-care plan	structured settlement
conflicts of interest	products liability	tort
deposition	reserve	toxic tort
guardian	risk management	ward

REVIEW QUESTIONS

1. Why is it difficult to write a job description for legal nurse consulting?
2. Choose a career identified in this chapter. Explain the role of a legal nurse consultant engaged in that career. Where might the legal nurse consultant work? How is a nurse qualified for this position?
3. Identify and explain some ethical considerations to which an independent legal nurse consultant must be sensitive.
4. To act as an expert witness, what qualifications should a legal nurse consultant have? Why?

INTERNET EXERCISES

1. Access the web page for this textbook at *www.westlegalstudies.com*.
2. Click on the assignments section of the web page and complete the assignment(s) for Chapter Two.

EXERCISES

1. Networking. Call a local manufacturing firm or health care facility in your area. Ask to speak to the risk manager. If the risk manager is willing to share information with you, ask about the risk manager's educational background, how the position was obtained, job description, usual duties, job satisfaction, salary, benefits, etc. Ask about other opportunities for legal nurse consultants in the company. Add this information to your networking database, file, or Rolodex. Increase your networking database by selecting other career areas of interest and seeking professionals in those career areas who may share their stories with you.
2. Professional Portfolio. Identify career options in legal nurse consulting that appeal to you. How are you uniquely qualified to practice in that career? What additional training do you feel you need to be qualified? Establish goals for pursuing this career objective. Write down your goals and keep them in a folder or portfolio along with your current resume and the notes you made after completing Chapter One.

END NOTES

1. American Association of Legal Nurse Consultants, *1999 Compensation Survey, 1998 Member Directory.*
2. A. Tebbe, "Legal Nurse Consulting," *Paralegal Educator* 12:3 (1998): 26–27.
3. American Bar Association, *Annotated Model Rules of Professional Conduct,* (1999) 4th Edition Rule 1.7. Copies of ABA *Model Code of Professional Responsibility, 1999 Edition* are available from Service Center, American Bar Association, 750 North Lake Shore Drive, Chicago, IL 60611-4497, 1-800-285-2221.

ADDITIONAL REFERENCES

Bogart, J. B. RN MN, ed. *Legal Nurse Consulting: Principles and Practice.* Boston: CRC Press, 1998.

Connell, K. H., RN, BSN. "Career Alternatives for Legal Nurse Consultants." *Network News* 4 (1993): 3, 6.

Jarreau, C. C., RN. "Career Alternatives for Legal Nurse Consultants." *Network News* 4 (1993): 3, 6.

McHugh, J., RN. "Career Alternatives for Legal Nurse Consultants." *Network News* 4 (1993): 2, 4, 10.

Orr, M. J., RN, CIRS. "Career Alternatives for Legal Nurse Consultants." *Network News* 4 (1993): 1, 4.

Osmanski, P., RN. "Career Alternatives for Legal Nurse Consultants." *Network News* 4 (1993): 4, 10–11.

Pyle-Rodenbaugh, L., RN, MBA, ed. *Getting Started in Legal Nurse Consulting.* Glenview, IL: American Association of Legal Nurse Consultants, 1997.

Saber, M. A., RN. "Career Alternatives for Legal Nurse Consultants." *Network News* 4 (1993): 1, 4.

Sowers, R., RN. "Career Alternatives for Legal Nurse Consultants." *Network News* 4 (1993): 2, 4.

Spiegel, K. "Career Alternatives for Legal Nurse Consultants." *Network News* 4 (1993): 4, 11.

Van Allen, G. "Career Options: The Increasing Demand for Courtroom Nurses." *The Oklahoma Nurse* (July, August, September, 1996): 31.

Zaller, C., RN. "Career Alternatives for Legal Nurse Consultants." *Network News* 4 (1993): 4, 10.

CHAPTER 3

PLANNING FOR A CAREER IN LAW

OBJECTIVES

In this chapter, you will discover

- a system for analyzing experiences and education

- how to use self-assessment for planning a career change

- a total quality approach to tailoring skills and abilities for new career goals

OVERVIEW

Change is never easy, especially when it means giving up a secure position in a professional capacity. To better analyze whether a change in career will enhance self-image and self-confidence, increase profitability, and promote a healthier environment, it is wise to assess special skills and attributes that may be marketable in other professional areas. Focusing on unique personal characteristics, as well as education and experience, may bring alternative career options into sharper focus.

CHANGING CAREER PATHS

Mental health care professionals know that meaningful, challenging work is essential to a healthy lifestyle. People often experience similar stages in any career field: (a) the fresh enthusiasm of the newly inducted, (b) the mature competence of the seasoned professional, and (c) the routine continuum of a career that has hit the ceiling or is stalled.

Many professionals are able to continue in the second stage of their careers by adding new challenges to increase their expertise. Nurses seek certification in complementary fields; attorneys go from public to corporate or private practices; and engineers develop new designs, products, or projects. Legal nurse consulting may provide the new challenge that keeps vitality in a nursing career.

Nurses who are ready for a career change may capitalize on their education and experience by developing new career goals. Figure 3-1 provides a summary of the information presented in Chapter Two. It also describes some of the qualifications needed for the six legal employers that were described and that may be legal practice areas for registered nurses.

The table in Figure 3-1 may provide a starting point for isolating and analyzing the necessary background to develop new goals and career paths.

SELF-ASSESSMENT

The first step toward developing future goals is reviewing the past. The following questions may aid in the process of developing new career goals:

- How does my medical education prepare me for work in legal fields?
- What experiences will enhance the use of my medical background in legal fields?
- What personal characteristics make me valuable to legal professionals?
- How might I exploit intangibles (e.g., strong work ethic, team player, positive attitude, leadership abilities) to help me secure a position in a legal office?

Figure 3-2 illustrates a few of the ways that medical background may be used in specialty areas of the law.

FIGURE 3-1 Background and Skills for Working in Legal Positions

Legal Area	Helpful Background	Helpful Skills
Case Management	Medical background Legal knowledge Insurance knowledge	Organizational skills Interpersonal skills Resourcefulness
Compliance Consultant	Specialty certification Administrative law Clinical procedures	Ability to follow through Organizational skills Willingness to travel
Education	Education background Legal knowledge Legal nurse experience	Ability to work in teams Supervisory skills Teaching ability
Expert Witness	Advanced degree Specialty certification Knowledge of standards of practice	Detail oriented Communication skills Composure
Government	Medical background Legal knowledge	Detail oriented Ability to travel Willingness to learn
Life-Care Planning	Rehabilitation Orthopedics Neurology	Detail oriented Computer spreadsheet
Medical-Legal Investigation	Clinical or critical care Ob-Gyn Legal knowledge	Organizational skills Interpersonal skills Resourcefulness
Personal Injury Law	Clinical or critical care Legal knowledge Tort law	Patience Detail oriented Organizational skills
Risk Management	Medical background Legal knowledge Insurance knowledge	Teaching ability Interpersonal skills Communication skills
Self-employed	Medical background Business/marketing Legal knowledge	Entrepreneurial spirit Interpersonal skills Communication skills Ability to handle stress

FIGURE 3-2 Backgrounds Helpful in Law

Medical Background	Area of Law	Types of Cases
Ob-Gyn Pediatrics	Personal Injury	"Bad baby" cases "Bad birth" cases Failure to diagnose breast/ovarian cancer
Emergency Room Critical Care	Health care liability Risk management	Medical negligence (nurse, anesthetist, etc.) Failure of care
Neurology	Personal injury Law Health care liability Life-care planning	Spinal cord/brain injury Medical negligence Pharmaceutical
Orthopedics	Social Security Workers' Compensation Personal injury law Life-care planning Risk management	Accidental disability Workplace injury Negligence
Rehabilitation Home Health Case Management	Personal injury Law Health care liability Workers' Compensation Life-care planning	Medical negligence Automobile liability Workplace injury
Surgical Critical Care	Health care liability Personal injury law	Medical negligence Negligence
Geriatric Home Health	Elder law	Elder abuse Nursing home litigation
Forensic Critical Care	Criminal law Personal injury law	Child/spousal abuse Homicide Wrongful death

It is illustrative only and is not intended to limit or minimize options for registered nurses. Any background from gastroenterology to oncology may be put to use in the legal arena. It may be helpful to use the table as a starting point to list all personal educational and experiential background along with all of the legal areas where this background may be helpful. Then, consider a career path that provides the greatest potential for challenge and satisfaction.

CAREER GOALS

The second step toward achieving future goals is looking ahead. The following questions may aid in the process of ascertaining alternative career paths:

- What do I picture myself doing professionally five (three, two) years from now?
- Does this professional picture involve interaction with many people, working with computers, or analyzing documentation?
- Will this professional picture provide me with the security (salary, benefits) and flexibility I need?

Career goals are often vague: "I want to be a nurse" or "I want to be a lawyer." Once that vague professional idea is formulated, an educational process begins in which preferences are developed. These preferences (what the student is good at and what the student likes) are often areas a student could not have known about when embarking on the educational journey. Expect the same with legal nurse consulting. While traveling this new career path, important discoveries will be made about hidden markets for particular expertise.

Appendix B contains information about legal nurse consulting associations and Appendix D contains information about specialty nursing associations. Contacting members of these organizations may provide invaluable information about a specialty career track that is unique to specific personalities and professional backgrounds.

The more specific the career goal, the more accurately progress can be measured toward that goal. A general career goal, however, may allow flexibility and educational pursuits that might result in new and surprising twists in career fulfillment.

CAREER PLANNING

The total quality management (TQM) process is essential in career planning. Continuous process improvement are important watchwords of successful people. This process involves identifying barriers or situations that keep you from reaching your full potential and from adding value to your product or services.

Once a career goal is in mind, whether specific or general, the following questions may assist in identifying barriers and in planning how to achieve goals:

- What additional education and skills will I need?
- How can I acquire the education and skills I need to achieve my goal?
- How can I enhance the skills and abilities I already have?
- What other forces must I consider (family, financial, personal constraints)?

After identifying (and continually being on the lookout for) barriers, the quality process requires a creative approach to minimizing those barriers. For example, a registered nurse working in orthopedics has identified workers' compensation case management in an insurance company as a new career goal. The nurse knows little or nothing about workers' compensation and believes that it will add value to a resume if training in the field is listed. Several options exist:

- obtaining state and federal brochures about workers' compensation
- researching workers' compensation at the local library or on the Internet
- purchasing a book or seminar materials about workers' compensation
- attending a seminar on workers' compensation put on by a state agency, a professional organization, or the state bar association
- volunteering services in exchange for on-the-job education and training
- taking a class at a local college or university

All of these educational options will provide the nurse with enough background in workers' compensation to make a resume attractive and provide entry-level skill. A more thorough analysis of the options may reveal a hidden value gained from pursuing particular educational opportunities.

Obtaining state and federal brochures will involve only the cost of postage and sometimes printing, and the time involved in review. Research at the library will cost only time. Both will enable the nurse to include "basic knowledge of workers' compensation" in a highlights portion of a resume.

Purchasing a book or seminar materials has the added value of providing a ready reference for on-the-job use. This option will cost a little more than sending for brochures or doing research in the library and a little less than attending a seminar, at which the references and materials may be provided with the price of registration.

Attending a seminar or workshop on workers' compensation adds the invaluable asset of connections and networking. Meeting people who work in the field and being able to identify the influential speakers and authors of workers' compensation presentations may prove to be the ticket to employment.

One way that legal nurse consultants have gotten a foot in the door is by volunteering their services in legal offices where they can learn the procedural aspects of workers' compensation claims. Some legal nurse consulting and nurse paralegal programs provide students with this on-the-job experience through formal internships. The legal nurse consultant, albeit a volunteer, must abide by all ethical constraints of the legal and medical professions. During this internship, a legal nurse consultant may establish a professional legal nurse reputation and obtain recommendations from attorneys or claims managers for whom the volunteer work is performed. This type of on-the-job training is costly; valuable time is spent at the legal office for which no income is received. In the long run, however, this initial investment in training may prove profitable.

Registering for a class on workers' compensation or administrative law at a local college or university is generally more expensive than attending a seminar. For that additional expense, a good course will provide much more specific knowledge about the subject, additional resources and bibliographies, and guest speakers, along with the references and networking connections expected from meeting and learning with others on a regular basis.

A registered nurse may have the necessary medical background and desire to work as a case manager in workers' compensation. However, not having knowledge of the legal framework of workers' compensation may be a barrier to achieving this career goal. Enriching a medical background by learning more about the legal aspects of workers' compensation will add value to the nurse's qualifications. What option the nurse chooses for overcoming this barrier may have a direct impact on the nurse's ability to achieve the career goal.

Some barriers cannot be changed, for example, physical limitations, family commitments, and so forth. The total quality approach to career planning advocates a continual examination of the environment to identify ways in which the process of obtaining goals may be improved.

LEGAL NURSE CONSULTANT COMPENSATION AND BENEFITS

When contemplating a new career path, salary and benefits are a major consideration. It may be a decisive factor once the setting, type of work, culture of the work setting, and level of stress and skill demanded are determined.

The first compensation survey of the AALNC was published in 1999. Highlights of this survey are included in Chapter One. While 36.1% of the nurses responding reported earning less than $30,000 per year from legal nurse consulting activities, 58% earned between $31,000 and $75,000 per year.[1]

The *1999 Compensation Survey* by the AALNC also revealed that of the members responding, 54.1% worked between one and thirty hours per week on legal nurse consulting activities and 31.1% worked between one and ten hours per week on legal nurse consulting activities.[2] While the AALNC does keep a roster of the areas of work in which a legal nurse consultant performs (see Chapter Two), there is wide variance in job titles and descriptions for legal nurse consultants. This might make survey results incomplete or inadequate.

A general rule of thumb for nurses who are entering law firms, insurance companies, or risk management departments may be that the salary offered should be consistent with the salary the nurse is receiving or could expect to receive in the medical marketplace. This should take into account the nurse's years of experience, certifications achieved, benefits enjoyed, and educational background. Offering less than the nurse would be paid in a hospital or clinical setting fails to provide an appropriate incentive for the registered nurse to

Net Results

One of the most economical ways to communicate with other professionals is via the Internet. Listservs, chat rooms, and bulletin boards offer promising new avenues of communication for neophytes looking for mentors. One such listserv may be accessed at www.legalnurseconsultants.com/lncnurse.htm.* In addition, www.findlaw.com *provides a bulletin board for legal professionals. Browse this site to locate where other legal nurse consultants are talking.*
*E-mail discussion lists for legal nurse consultants may be accessed at www.mindspring.com/~ewriggs/lncpages.html.

venture onto the new career path and undervalues the medical expertise the nurse may bring to the legal environment. Still, an entry-level legal nurse consultant must recognize the economic reality. Lawyers will expect legal nurse consultants to prove to be trustworthy and capable and to add value to the legal service rendered before they will pay the legal nurse consultants salaries that approximate those received in a clinical setting. This proving ground is generally the first year of employment as a legal nurse consultant.

It may be important to note here that law firms also generally provide year-end bonuses or other incentives, such as professional wardrobe allowances. In this way, employees of the law firm often share in the financial success of the firm.

Another important consideration for nurses moving into law is the benefits offered by the new employer. Many small and mid-sized law firms do not provide complete benefits such as health insurance, disability and life insurance, or pension or profit sharing plans. Nurses who are employed in clinical or hospital settings may have these benefits paid by their employers. The cost of individually paid benefit packages is significant. Nurses should make certain that the salary offered is sufficient to cover any benefits that are lost due to a change in career goals, if benefits are not employer-paid.

Independent legal nurse consultants face a more complex problem. As self-employed entrepreneurs, they must bill an amount that will provide them with the costs of doing business, including self-employment tax, business and liability insurance, and office and overhead expenses, along with the individual cost of the benefit package that might have been available through a medical employer. The amount billed must also reflect the education and experience the nurse brings to the consulting situation. Certifications, graduate degrees, seminar presentations, publishing credits, and previous work in this medical-legal area are all integral to the billed hourly rate a nurse will charge for consulting.

The type of consulting work requested will also impact the amount billed by an independent legal nurse consultant. For example, reviewing and summarizing medical records may be billed at a different rate than testifying as an expert at a deposition or trial, and locating an expert may be billed at a different rate than locating medical literature. According to the *1999 Compensation Survey* of the AALNC, the most frequently cited rate for professional legal nurse consulting services was $75 per hour, and for expert testimony, $150 per hour.[3]

It is sometimes suggested that the independent legal nurse consultant request a **retainer** of 10 to 15% of the anticipated cost of consulting services or a flat-rate retainer. This will provide the independent legal nurse consultant with operating capital while completing the assignment and will ensure that at least partial payment is made, in the event the contract is dishonored. While it is unlikely that contracts with consultants will be dishonored by legal professionals, up-front money does add a measure of commitment to the relationship that may be important to both parties.

A legal nurse consultant may not charge a **contingency fee,** based on the successful outcome of the case. This practice is unethical for legal nurse consultants or any nonlawyer professional or expert. The danger of contingency fees is that the legal nurse consultant will be motivated by personal interest rather than by the best interest of the client or the interest of justice.

With little knowledge about salaries, benefits, or consultant fee rates, a registered nurse entering the field of legal nurse consulting must rely on a network of professionals with whom to discuss these important factors of employment and business. Using the connections available through professional associations and the medical community will provide some insight into the peculiar geographical considerations that impact compensation and benefits. It is not uncommon, especially among independent consultants, to confront an unwillingness to divulge fees charged. Experience is often the best indicator of what fees are appropriate in particular situations with particular parties.

REEVALUATING A CAREER

A registered nurse who has traveled down a career path in law should periodically revisit and revise career goals. Once experience and a reputation for excellence has been developed, the legal nurse consultant may reassess abilities and knowledge and refine career goals. The following questions may aid in reevaluating a legal nurse consultant career:

- Have I accomplished my initial career goals as a legal nurse consultant?
- What knowledge and experience can be added to my resume as a result of my experience as a legal nurse consultant?
- How can I capitalize on these skills?
- Am I in a position to (a) present a plan to my employer for increased responsibility and/or compensation, (b) strike out on my own as an independent legal nurse consultant, (c) consider a new career path, such as legal nurse educator or medical-legal **informatics** specialist?
- Where do I see myself in five (three, two) years, and where do I want to be?

Opportunities for nurses are limitless. The constant desire for new challenges and a professional approach to career goal development will provide nurses with the springboard to new and satisfying work.

CHAPTER SUMMARY

- Nurses interested in legal nurse consulting may capitalize on education, experience, and personal characteristics in defining future career goals.

- Career planning includes identifying barriers to achieving career goals and developing options for overcoming barriers that will be most likely to lead to success.
- Few statistics exist that report compensation and benefits for legal nurse consultants. This is an area that must be informally investigated by the nurse considering this career path.
- Career goal assessment is an ongoing process, and legal nurse consultants should reevaluate their careers and career goals periodically.

KEY TERMS

retainer   contingency fee   informatics

REVIEW QUESTIONS

1. How may nurses use their past education and experience to cross the bridge into legal work?
2. What are some considerations in determining the fee charged for independent legal nurse consulting?
3. What is a fair compensation for legal nurse consultants working in law firms, insurance companies, and risk management departments?
4. Identify or outline the steps in developing and reevaluating career goals?

INTERNET EXERCISES

1. Access the web page for this textbook at *www.westlegalstudies.com*. Review the medical malpractice case.
2. Click on the assignments section of the web page and complete the assignment(s) for Chapter Three.

EXERCISES

1. Networking. Contact your local or state bar association and ask for information on upcoming or annual continuing legal education seminars. Identify those that might be of help to you in advancing your career as a legal nurse consultant. If you are currently employed, ask your employer if these seminars qualify for tuition reimbursement. Do the same with the organizations you selected in Appendix B and with whom you completed Exercise One for Chapter Two.

2. Professional Portfolio. Begin assembling the documents that will sell you as a legal nurse consultant. Include the following: specialty certifications, educational transcripts, letters of commendation, agendas for conferences attended, copies of articles published, a list of professional references, and any other documentation that shows your ability to translate medical information into legal arenas. Contact the people on your list of professional references and secure their agreement to serve as references for you.

ENDNOTES

1. American Association of Legal Nurse Consultants, *1999 Compensation Survey Results* (1999).
2. Ibid.
3. Ibid.
4. American Bar Association, *Annotated Model Rules of Professional Conduct,* (1999) 4th Edition

Rule 5.4. Copies of ABA *Model Code of Professional Responsibility, 1999 Edition* are available from Service Center, American Bar Association, 750 North Lake Shore Drive, Chicago, IL 60611-4497, 1-800-285-2221.

ADDITIONAL REFERENCES

American Association of Legal Nurse Consultants. "Questions and Answers: Overcoming Isolation in Independent Practice." *Journal of Legal Nurse Consulting* 9:1 (1998): 24.

American Association of Legal Nurse Consultants. "Questions and Answers: Selecting Computer Equipment for a Legal Nurse Consulting Practice." *Journal of Legal Nurse Consulting* 8:3 (1997): 13.

Bogart, J. B., RN, MN, ed. *Legal Nurse Consulting: Principles and Practice.* Boston: CRC Press, 1998.

Davis, S. C., RN BSN. "For Better Business: Maximizing Your Professional Image." *Journal of Legal Nurse Consulting* 8:2 (1997): 19.

Magnuson, J. K., BSN RN LNCC and M. Garbin, PhD RN. (1999). "Legal Nurse Consultant Practice Analysis Summary Report." *Journal of Legal Nurse Consulting* 10:1 (1999): 10–18.

Pyle-Rodenbaugh, L., RN MBA ed. *Getting Started in Legal Nurse Consulting.* Glenview, IL: American Association of Legal Nurse Consultants, 1997.

Vermeer, M., RN. "For better business: A Billing System That Works." *Journal of Legal Nurse Consulting* 7:3 (1996): 21.

Wise, D., RN EdD. "Cultivating Your Business." *Network News* 4:4 (1993): 1, 3.

CHAPTER 4

CROSSING THE BRIDGE TO EMPLOYMENT

OBJECTIVES

In this chapter, you will discover

■ how to locate potential employers of legal nurse consultants

■ a method for customizing cover letters and resumes to a particular legal employer

■ the difference power resumes may have on potential legal employers

■ how to prepare for an interview with a potential legal employer or consumer

■ a system for marketing medical skills and expertise to the legal community

OVERVIEW

For registered nurses who would like to have full- or part-time employment in a law firm or in a legal office of an insurance company or government agency, it may be difficult to know where to start. Developing a portfolio, a power resume, a professional image, and a positive attitude will help bring success in the job market. For information on starting an independent legal nurse consulting business, please refer to Chapter Five.

MARKETING

Marketing in a new career field involves courage and stamina. Once experience and education are refocused toward the new career goal, locating potential employers and consumers of this expertise can be challenging and time-consuming.

Before beginning a search for new positions or employers, put together a portfolio. As standard features, include in the portfolio any licenses, specialty certifications, letters of commendation, honors, educational transcripts, registration receipts or agendas for conferences and workshops attended, a template resume, and a list of professional references. If you have taken training in legal nurse consulting and have generated reports, chronologies, summaries, or other documents, you may include these to sell your abilities. Use caution when including a document that has been generated on a previous legal case, as confidentiality may be breached, even if the names are cleansed from the document. Legal actions are unique, and the specific injury or other general information in the document may still provide clues to the identity of the claimant. If the document, such as a timeline, has been used as an exhibit in court, it is public record and may be freely displayed to others.

When you are called for an interview, customize the portfolio to the specific needs of the potential employer. If the interview is for a case manager in workers' compensation, include the syllabus from the course attended or the registration or agenda for the seminar attended, along with working papers from the seminar materials that indicate your understanding of the responsibilities of the position. Make two copies of the portfolio, in the event the employer would like to keep it and review it at a later time.

When seeking employment in a new career path, keep in mind the following questions:

- Why does this office need me?
- How will I do the job better than anyone else?
- What strong intangibles, such as work ethic, leadership, or resourcefulness, might sell me if my educational background is weak?
- What specific examples will show my ability to hit the ground running and see the project through?

Forearmed with answers to these questions that are customized to the position offered, an applicant may have the added advantage that is needed to secure employment. Remember the popular saying: It is not always the best athlete that wins the race, it is the best-prepared athlete.

FINDING POTENTIAL EMPLOYERS

Networking is considered one of the most important components of any search for employment.[1] Acquaintances who are already working in the field can be valuable links in the employment underground by providing information about potential positions before they are advertised. Contact members of the associations that promote your field of interest (see Appendix D for a listing of professional associations that may be helpful). Many of these associations have job banks and mentoring programs that may provide inside tracks to employment. The local library or the library at a nearby college or university will carry professional journals that may contain advertisements. The professional journals should become regular reading as the information contained in them will enhance understanding of the profession. Call the writer of an article or submit a resume to the writer, referring to the article and explaining how the writer or the writer's firm may benefit by employing you.

Locating Attorneys and Law Firms

Several directories are available to locate attorneys, including the following:

- *The Martindale-Hubbell Law Directory.* This directory is organized alphabetically by state, then city, then law firm. It profiles the members of the firm and identifies the specialty areas of law practiced by members of the firm.

- State Bar Directory. This directory is generally published annually by the state bar association and is usually organized in three ways: alphabetically by name; alphabetically by county, then city; and alphabetically by law firm. State bar directories may also have information concerning state offices, officers, and courts.

- West's Legal Directory on the Internet. This directory is organized by field and may be accessed by identifying a city and a specialty area of practice. The attorneys who practice in this area may be retrieved, listed, and profiled on screen.

These directories and local or county bar association directories are available in most law libraries. Computers with Internet access are available in most public, college, and university libraries.

What LNCs Say . . .

"At our firm, it is not unusual for a nurse paralegal to earn a higher salary than the other paralegals. Because our personal injury case load is so heavy, the attorney must rely on our nurse 'specialists' to perform the majority of the medical-related tasks associated with a case." Linda McGee, quoted in Career Options: The Increasing Demand for Courtroom Nurses, Oklahoma Nurse, July 1996.

Net Results

Legal Directories

Many resources are now available on the Internet. Locate Martindale-Hubbell at www.martindale.com. State bar associations may be accessed using a search engine or via www.findlaw.com. West's Legal Directory may be accessed at www.lawoffice.com. The Internet also has all of the telephone directories for every city in the United States. Use search engines such as www.yahoo.com or www.lycos.com to access attorneys in specific locations. Many search engines also provide mapping capability. Once an attorney and address are located, the computer will draw a map of how to get to that location from your location.

Locating Insurance Companies

State Commissioners of Insurance publish annual reports that generally list all of the insurance companies, including their home offices, that are licensed to operate in the state. These reports are available in local libraries, by contacting the Office of the Insurance Commissioner, and sometimes on the Internet. Phoning the insurance companies directly will provide information concerning who a resume should be directed to.

Locating Public Offices

Government positions are posted periodically in publications and on the Internet. For example, the official job bulletin for the State of Wisconsin is published on the seventh, the seventeenth, and the twenty-seventh of each month. It is available on the Internet through the Job Service links. Federal government positions are accessed by contacting the Office of Personnel Management (OPM) at one of its thirty-nine regional offices. These offices are listed in the phone book and generally provide a toll free number for information about prospective employment and examinations.

Most states publish Blue Books that identify all government offices and government officials of the state, along with demographic and economic information. These Blue Books contain information about the department of justice, attorney general, insurance commissioner, prison administration, university administration, and other potential employers of legal nurse consultants.

Locating Corporate Employers

Several directories are available for locating corporate employers, many of them with access, albeit limited, on the Internet.

- The *Corporate Technology Directory* is an annual publication that identifies technology corporations by company name, geographical location, and type of product. This directory provides information about corporate status, number of employees, annual sales, and names of executive officers. Nurses interested in risk management may find this resource an invaluable asset to seeking employment in the corporate world.

- *Standard and Poor's* and *Dun and Bradstreet* are corporate directories that may be used to access companies alphabetically by company name and alphabetically by state, then company name. These directories also provide corporate information, names of executive officers, and profiles of executive officers.

- *Hoovers Handbook of Business* identifies top corporations in the United States. The profiles in *Hoovers* are alphabetical by company name. The history of the company, its major products and markets, and its executives and departments are included in company profiles. *Hoovers* on the Internet provides links to any home pages of companies identified in its handbook; however, some information requires a subscription to access.

■ Every state has a *Manufacturers' Directory,* which is a compilation of the yellow pages of telephone directories throughout that state.

All of the directories described are available in most libraries. Once in this reference section of the library, several other individual directories may aid in locating potential employers.

Armed with little more than a telephone book, legal nurse consultants may access a wealth of potential employers, including consulting firms, insurance claims offices, health maintenance organization networks, hospital and clinic claims offices, and legal services organizations. Investigating these potential employers will provide legal nurse consultants with specific information for customizing their resumes and selling their expertise.

INITIAL CONTACT

The process of securing employment begins with contacting a potential employer. Depending on the type of employment desired, this contact may be in person or by mail.

An independent legal nurse consultant who is contracting with attorneys and other legal offices may wish to call for an appointment to explain the types of services the legal nurse consultant has to offer. Life-care planners often use this approach. After identifying the specific individual in the office most likely to be in need of the services offered, the legal nurse consultant calls to make an appointment, making it clear that the appointment is to market services and is not a potential client. A confirming letter identifying the specific services offered and containing some biographical information about the legal nurse consultant and a business card will make this clear. Keeping the appointment, arriving ahead of schedule, and preparing a concise and clear presentation will insure that, even if the legal nurse consultant is not hired, the prospective employer's time is well invested.

For traditional employment, the initial contact is generally with a cover letter and resume. It is extremely important, in today's competitive market, to customize cover letters and resumes to specific offices and specific areas of practice. Use any toehold to get in the door. If the firm has been in the news recently representing a party in a lawsuit, contributing to a charity, or participating in a civic activity, refer to it! Then explain how the firm may benefit by employing your services.

"Give it to me in one page!" is the demand of the information age. Keep the cover letter short and to the point. Resumes should be organized in a way that will draw attention to the most important attributes of the applicant. The person to whom this letter and resume is directed will want to feel that the time spent reading and considering this applicant is time well spent.

The initial contact should pique the interest of the potential employer, providing information about how the applicant can fill a need in the employer's organization. This interest will lead to an interview, which is the purpose of a cover letter and resume. A sample cover letter is included as Figure 4-1.

Net Results

Potential Employers
Many of the resources for locating employers, such as Hoovers Handbook of Business, are available on the Internet. Some resources may require subscriptions, but usually public information may be obtained without cost. Access Hoovers at www.hoovers.com, *access Standard and Poor's at* www.standardpoor.com, *and access Dun and Bradstreet at* www.dnb.com. *The Internet has also been used for job searches and information through the AALNC (*www.aalnc.org*) and the National Federation of Paralegal Associations (*www.paralegals.org*). In addition, resume preparation assistance may be provided through commercial vendors or without cost from college and university web pages.*

FIGURE 4.1   Sample Cover Letter

1010 First Building
Anytown, State 55556
1-800-111-1111

SUE N. WYNN, RN BSN LNCC
(date)

Potential Employer
111 First Street
One City, State 55555

Re: LEGAL NURSE CONSULTING

To enhance your professional image and potential for success, consider utilizing the medical-legal consulting services I offer:

- **Comprehensive medical records management** (*collecting, organizing, summarizing, evaluating, and translating medical histories and incidents, and developing database retrieval systems*)
- **Accurate and complete educational services** (*reviewing medical literature, locating and screening experts, developing exhibits and timelines that are clear to laypersons, and instructing on physiological concepts and practice standards*)
- **Thorough assessment of damages** (*calculating past and future medical expenses, medical appliances, adaptive devices, pharmacology needs, anticipated medical interventions, and psychiatric or psychological services*)
- **Complete trial preparation services** (*summarizing medical depositions; attending and reviewing adverse medical examinations; assisting in development of themes and educational evidence for jury understanding; arranging mock trial, focus group, or ADR options; and managing documents at trial*)

Whether the medical-legal claim is large or small, medical expertise in performing these tasks promotes a winning advantage! The work product I offer will simplify and expedite the efforts of your litigation team and will assist in strategy development for settlement and/or trial. I would be happy to show you sample documentation and describe how that documentation may be customized for your practice. Please call me at 1-800-111-1111 at your convenience.

Sue N. Wynn, RN BSN LNCC

Enclosures: [Resume]

FIGURE 4-2 Action Verbs for Use in Resume Preparation			
analyzed	established	interviewed	reported
assessed	evaluated	investigated	researched
briefed	examined	managed	reviewed
collected	expedited	modified	revised
consulted	formulated	originated	strategized
coordinated	generated	organized	summarized
demonstrated	implemented	prepared	taught
defined	initiated	presented	updated
designed	interpreted	recommended	validated
developed	introduced	reevaluated	verified

RESUMES AND CURRICULUM VITAE

Professionally prepared resumes indicate confidence in the applicant's abilities. A template resume will include education, experience, abilities, and references. This template will be the skeleton from which customized resumes may be created. For example, if the position description calls for knowledge of workers' compensation, then the workers' compensation education and experience of the applicant should be highlighted in a way that catches the reviewer's eye. If the applicant has little or no knowledge of workers' compensation, but is willing to learn, this intangible should be highlighted in the cover letter and resume.

"Keep it simple!" are the watchwords for resume preparation. However, varying type style, using bold, italics, boxes, dividing lines, or dividing symbols may work to draw attention to the specific qualifications that the applicant has for the position. Keep in mind also that employers in legal offices are, on the whole, conservative, and prefer traditional resumes with information that is easy to locate.

Power resumes describe those resumes that immediately attract the attention of the potential employer. The power resume is in a format that highlights the most important information and doesn't waste the potential employer's time with unnecessary, albeit laudable, characteristics. Vitality and interest in the position are communicated through the use of action verbs, describing education and experience with energy and enthusiasm. Action verbs suitable for resume preparation are listed in Figure 4-2.

Ethics Bookmark

Licensure

"The legal nurse consultant maintains professional nursing competence.

"The legal nurse consultant is a registered nurse and maintains an active nursing license. The legal nurse consultant is knowledgeable about the current scope of nursing practice and the standards of the profession. The legal nurse consultant does not practice law" (AALNC Code of Ethics and Conduct with Interpretive Discussion Rule 8, 1997).[2] *The obligation to comply with nursing licensure requirements continues even after the registered nurse becomes a legal nurse consultant. The integrity of the profession is medical expertise. A registered nurse should be careful not to compromise professional integrity by allowing licensure to lapse.*

When preparing the resume, whether template or customized, keep these guidelines in mind:

- Name, address, telephone, and fax and e-mail, if available, should be at the beginning of the page.
- Headings should be consistent in terms of placement and type style.
- List the education, degrees, licenses, certifications, and experience that specifically relate to the position applied for in the most conspicuous part of the resume.
- Avoid including personal information, such as marital status, parental status, race, hobbies, and so forth.
- Use action verbs! These dynamic words communicate your interest in the position, your most important capabilities, and your achievements.[3]
- Always proofread the resume before sending it out. Better yet, have someone else proofread it. If there is even the slightest error, it must be corrected! It is better to take the extra time and effort to correct the error than to appear careless to the potential employer.

Many word processing software packages include resume formats. These formats allow entry of data into an already existing resume design. The template resume may be saved and retrieved, along with each of the customized resumes that are prepared. A sample resume is included as Figure 4-3.

If the position calls for expert status or if expert status is something that is intended to be sold to the potential employer, prepare a **curriculum vita.** In addition to education, experience, and other qualifications, this vita should include every presentation made, books or articles written (even those written for local association newsletters), service on committees, leadership positions, focus groups, honors or grants/scholarships received, conferences organized or attended, guest lectures presented, and contributions to community service. The curriculum vita should be continually updated and may be as long as the professional qualifications demand. Figure 4-4 is a sample curricula vita.

INTERVIEW

Your cover letter has intrigued the potential employer. Your resume shows that you are qualified for the position. The interview will provide the potential employer with information about how well you will fit into the culture of the organization, how you handle stress and deadlines, and how you relate to others.

Many applicants for positions today are reviewed by screening committees or teams who will arrive at a consensus about whom to hire. Be prepared to explain why you are the right person for the position. Consider your unique attributes—those that set you apart from other nurses—and write down two examples of how you have used those attributes successfully in your employment or in volunteer situations.[4]

FIGURE 4-3   Sample Resume

1010 First Building
Anytown, State 55556
1-800-111-1111

SUE N. WYNN, RN BSN LNCC

Professional Characteristics:	Detail oriented
	Strong analytical and investigative skills
	Excellent communication skills
	Professional integrity
Professional Highlights:	Evaluated medical records in health care liability
	Researched and investigated liability in child restraint products liability cases
	Presented on medical negligence at Paralegal Conference
	Edited newsletter for local nurse's association
	Served on committee for continuing education of nurses
Education:	BSN, University of Wisconsin, 19____
	Professional Legal Nurse Consulting Course, 19____
	Numerous medical and legal seminars
Experience:	Independent consultant, 19____ to present
	U-W Medical Center, Madison, WI, 19____ to 19____
	Cardio-thoracic ICU nurse
	U-W Medical Center, Madison, WI, 19____ to 19____
	Medical-surgical nurse
Certifications:	Legal Nurse Consultant Certified
	Certified Critical Care Nurse
	Advanced Cardiac Life Support
Organizations:	American Association of Legal Nurse Consultants
	Chapter President, 19____
	American Society of Law and Medicine
	American Association of Critical Care Nurses
	Wisconsin Nurse's Association
Special Skills:	Computer proficiency, including Internet research

References and Writing Samples Available Upon Request

While qualifications will be part of the interview process, it may also be wise to prepare for the interview by recalling situations in which you have worked to resolve disputes, have gone the extra mile to see a project through, or have displayed leadership. Working in civic or charitable organizations, serving as an elected official in an association or on a governmental board, or

FIGURE 4-4   Sample Curriculum Vita

1010 First Building
Anytown, State 55556
1-800-111-1111

SUE N. WYNN, RN BSN LNCC

Professional Characteristics: Detail oriented
Strong analytical and investigative skills
Excellent communication skills
Professional integrity

Professional Highlights: Evaluated medical records in health care liability
Researched and investigated liability in child restraint products liability cases
Presented on medical negligence at Paralegal Conference
Edited newsletter for local nurse's association
Served on committee for continuing education of nurses

Education: BSN, University of Wisconsin, 19____
Professional Legal Nurse Consulting Course, 19____
Numerous medical and legal seminars

Experience: Independent consultant, 19____ to present
U-W Medical Center, Madison, WI, 19____ to 19____
Cardio-thoracic ICU nurse
U-W Medical Center, Madison, WI, 19____ to 19____
Medical-surgical nurse

Certifications: Legal Nurse Consultant Certified
Certified Critical Care Nurse
Advanced Cardiac Life Support

Organizations: American Association of Legal Nurse Consultants
Chapter President, 19____
American Society of Law and Medicine
American Association of Critical Care Nurses
Wisconsin Nurse's Association

Special Skills: Computer proficiency, including Internet research
Presentations: *Career Alternatives: Options for Nurses.* Wisconsin Health Management
Association, 19____

Informed Consent: The Nurse's Role. Oak Leaf Medical Center, 19____
When a Nurse Is Deposed. Wisconsin Bar Association, Mid-Winter Conference, 19____
Trends in Nursing Malpractice. Wisconsin Nurse's Association, Annual Conference, 19____
Reviewing Medical Records in Medical Negligence Cases. Springfield Paralegal Association, 19____

(Continued)

FIGURE 4-4   (continued)

SUE N. WYNN, RN BSN LNCC   Page 2

Presentations (cont'd):	*Medical Exhibits: Keep Them Simple!* Wisconsin Chapter of the Association of Trial Lawyers of America, Panel Discussion, Spring Conference, 19____
	Requisite References for the Legal Nurse Consultant. Meeting of local chapter of the American Association of Legal Nurse Consultants, 19____
	Using Computers in a Legal Nurse Consulting Practice. Meeting of local chapter of the American Association of Legal Nurse Consultants, 19____
Publications:	*The Nurse's Role in Informed Consent.* Newsletter of the Wisconsin Nurse's Association, 19____
	Nursing Malpractice Update. Monthly column in the newsletter of the local chapter of the American Association of Legal Nurse Consultants, 19____
	Reviewing Medical Records in Medical Negligence Cases. Newsletter of the Paralegal Association of Wisconsin, 19____
	Why I Became a Legal Nurse Consultant. Newsletter of the Wisconsin Nurse's Association, 19____
Honors and Appointments:	Advisory Committee, Legal Nurse Advanced Technical Certificate Program, Anytown, 19____
	Mayor's Task Force on School Safety, Anytown, 19____

References and Writing Samples Available Upon Request

---

being instrumental in leadership endeavors are important contributions to the interview discussion.

In addition, employers expect applicants to know something about their businesses. Prepare for the interview by researching any home page the company firm, or agency may have on the Internet. Then locate it in the directories already listed in this chapter and review its history, product lines or specialty areas, branch offices or subsidiaries, and sales or recent cases. News reports about the company should also be reviewed. An unfavorable impression is made if the applicant is asked, "What do you know about us?" and the applicant can only recite what is listed on the placard outside the office door.

Interviews are conducted in a variety of ways. Some employers interview the legal nurse individually; that is, the attorney for whom the legal nurse consultant would be working would hold a private interview with the applicant.

FIGURE 4-5   Frequently Asked Interview Questions

- Why don't you tell me about yourself?
- Why should I hire you?
- What are your major strengths?
- What are your major weaknesses?
- What sort of pay do you expect to receive?
- How does your previous experience relate to the position we have here?
- What are your plans for the future?
- What will your former employers (or references) say about you?
- Why are you looking for this sort of position and why here?
- Do you have any questions for me?

Reprinted with permission of Chippewa Valley Technical College, Career Planning and Placement, Copyright 1993.

Other employers, in larger firms, corporations, agencies, and educational institutions, may prefer a panel, group, or team interview. In this situation, the nurse is invited to an interview in which several involved people (even people not employed at the facility) will ask questions. The questions are generally the same for all applicants, but a team interview tends to be more stressful than a private interview.

Several questions will be asked at the interview that may seem to have nothing whatever to do with the job description or qualifications for the position. The interviewer wants to make certain that the applicant will fit into the culture of the workplace and will make a commitment to the employer. Some frequently asked interview questions are included in Figure 4-5.[5]

During the interview process, expect some uncomfortable questions, even questions you cannot answer. Remain poised and remind the potential employer that you are interested in this position and are confident that you have the ability to learn and perform the tasks required with integrity.

Unfortunately, some interviewers may still ask questions that may be considered discriminatory in nature. Refusing to answer the questions may eliminate your chances for placement in that position—although after hearing the question, the position may no longer be desirable. One way to answer illegal questions is to assure the interviewer that your age, family, disability, etc. will not interfere with your ability to perform the responsibilities of the position. If this is a position in which you are truly interested, your eagerness may successfully allay the interviewer's concerns about any potential discriminatory factors. Figure 4-6 provides some tips about illegal questions and how they may be asked.[6]

FIGURE 4-6 **Discriminatory Topics in Interviews**

- Height, weight, physical conditions, disabilities, record of disabilities, relatives with disabilities. You may be asked whether you are able to perform the job responsibilities with or without reasonable accommodations.
- Age, date of birth, marital status, children. You may be asked if relatives are employed at the company.
- Race, national origin, religious practices.
- Place of birth, citizenship. You may be asked if you are a United States citizen.
- Memberships in organizations. You may be asked about professional organizations; you may exclude any organizations that indicate the race, creed, color, or national origin of its members.

Reprinted with permission of Chippewa Valley Technical College, Career Planning and Placement, Copyright 1998.

The following guidelines may help to prepare for important interviews:

- Customize and organize your portfolio so that it may be referred to and accessed quickly.
- Do not ramble. Rehearse the questions that are expected to be asked so that you can answer them concisely and completely.
- Be honest.
- If the answer to a question is just not there, or it is difficult to think of a situation the interviewer would like to have described (such as, "Explain how you have worked with others to accommodate diverse points of view"), fall back on intangibles. Use interpersonal skills, work ethic, organizational skills, willingness to learn, ability to follow through, or other characteristics to prove leadership or qualifications in that area.
- Thank the interviewer(s).

FOLLOW-UP

Many job search professionals recommend that a letter be written following the interview, thanking the potential employer and reminding the employer of your interest in the position. This letter may also be used to expand on information discussed at the interview. A sample thank you letter is included in Figure 4-7.

While seeking a position or selling services as a legal nurse consultant, record-keeping is essential. Maintain a file for each employer with whom an interview is granted. In this file, keep copies of news articles and Internet printouts about the company, along with the position description and your

---

FIGURE 4-7   Sample Follow-up/Thank You Letter

1010 First Building
Anytown, State 55556
1-800-111-1111

SUE N. WYNN, RN BSN LNCC
(date)

Potential Employer
111 First Street
One City, State 55555

Re: LEGAL NURSE CONSULTING

Thank you for talking with me on (date) concerning the legal nurse consultant position you are currently seeking to fill.

(Name of firm, company, or agency) is a dynamic organization. I believe that my education, experience, and personal characteristics match well with the mission and goals of the organization. (Here add any specific follow-up information neglected at the interview, e.g., team processes, community involvements, etc.)

Working at (name of firm, company, or agency) would be challenging and rewarding! It was a pleasure to meet you (and the other members of the interview team).

Sue N. Wynn

---

customized resume. Keep a reminder, a calendar, or a **Tickler system.** If the perfect position wasn't offered to you, write the employer in three or six months, enclosing an updated copy of your customized resume. Perhaps the person hired is not working out and you may be in an advantageous position to meet the employer's needs. If a sales pitch was made to a particular law firm and that firm has not contacted you, after your follow-up letter, for three or six months, send another brochure, a Rolodex card with your services on it, or a packet of Post-it Notes with your company name and description of services on it. Keeping your name in front of potential employers is one of the key ingredients to successful marketing.

Professional courtesy and integrity are as important as professional competence. Your career depends on all three! When the position is secured, be careful not to sabotage your career by speaking ill of your employer or coworkers, being rude to clients, or wasting time. Self-defeating behaviors will ensure a dead-end position.[7]

The key ingredient in any successful career is faith!

- faith in yourself
- faith in your ability to translate your medical expertise into legal arenas
- faith in your teaching skills (attorneys and clients, especially, appreciate this)
- faith in your connections in the medical field
- faith in the certainty that you will succeed, even if previous attempts have been learning experiences

Careers, like all journeys, involve preparations, interruptions, connections, distractions, evaluations, re-evaluations, and self-actualizations. It is not a terminal process! Grow with it!

CHAPTER SUMMARY

- A marketing portfolio may include specialty certifications, letters of commendation, transcripts, agendas of conferences attended, resume, and a list of references.
- To have a competitive edge, resumes and cover letters should be customized.
- Many directories for locating potential employers in law firms, government, corporations, insurance companies, and manufacturing firms are available in local libraries and on the Internet.
- The initial contact with a potential employer, whether by letter or by appointment, should pique the employer's interest.
- Resumes should clearly identify qualifications and unique attributes of the applicant.
- Be prepared to demonstrate abilities with specific examples and to discuss cultural subjects at the interview, such as ability to work with others, ability to work under pressure, and so forth.
- Maintain a record-keeping system and follow up.
- Professional courtesy and integrity are as important as professional competence.

KEY TERMS

curriculum vita   power resume   Tickler system

REVIEW QUESTIONS

1. How may nurses use their past education and experience to cross the bridge into legal work?
2. Why is it important to customize cover letters and resumes?
3. What information should be in the most conspicuous part of the resume?
4. Identify the contents of a marketing portfolio.
5. What are some strategies for following up with potential employers after an interview?

INTERNET EXERCISES

1. Access the web page for this textbook at *www.westlegalstudies.com.*
2. Click on the assignments section of the web page and complete the assignment(s) for Chapter Four.

EXERCISES

1. Networking. Contact the associations listed in Appendix B that you have identified as valuable for your career development. Obtain information about potential job bank or mentoring services provided to members. Use the services that may advance your career.
2. Portfolio. Write a power resume using action verbs to bring your background and education to the attention of the reader. You may wish to consult a resume service for assistance. Develop several resumes, highlighting your unique experiences and attributes, from which you can draw to design customized resumes for particular employers. Keep these template resumes in your portfolio.

ENDNOTES

1. D. Helfgott, MPA, "Take Six Steps to Networking Success," *Planning Job Choices:* 38E 1995: 60–63.
2. American Association of Legal Nurse Consultants, *Code of Ethics and Conduct with Interpretive Discussion* (1997) Rule 8.
3. K. Wetther, BSN RN, "Creating a Resume for the Legal Field, Part II: The Anatomy of a Resume," *Journal of Legal Nurse Consulting,* 8:4 (1997): 19.
4. Ibid., 15.
5. Chippewa Valley Technical College, *Interview Questions* (1993).
6. Chippewa Valley Technical College, *Your Interview* (1998).

ADDITIONAL REFERENCES

Bogart, J. B., RN MN, ed. *Legal Nurse Consulting: Principles and Practices.* Boston: CRC Press, 1998.

Lena, E., BS RN LNCC. "The Power of Networking." *Journal of Legal Nurse Consulting* 10:2 (1999): 27–28.

McHugh, J., RN. "The Legal Nurse Consultant: The Newest Member of the Litigation Team." *Paralegal Reporter* (Summer, 1994): 18–19.

CHAPTER 5

CROSSING THE BRIDGE TO INDEPENDENT PRACTICE

OBJECTIVES

In this chapter, you will discover

- the entrepreneurial characteristics that facilitate success

- how to develop business goals and put them into a business plan

- options for financing for a small business

- marketing aspects of independent practice

- client relations policies that facilitate success

- a checklist for starting a small business

OVERVIEW

Many people dream of being their own boss. Owning and operating an independent practice requires the creation of a small service business. Whether the business is operated from home or from rented office space, the potential business owner needs to consider a variety of long- and short-term business options. These include how the business will be structured, what services will be offered and to whom, how the business will be financed, what goals the business owner aspires to achieve, and how the business will continue to thrive. There are also a number of state and local laws and regulations that may need to be considered. It takes stamina and courage to hang out the shingle of independent practice. Still, the freedom, the pride of developing a good business reputation, and the excitement of seeing a small business grow and develop often outweigh the difficulties of getting started.

ENTREPRENEURIAL SPIRIT

Business owners face uncertainty every day. It takes considerable character and commitment to venture into new enterprises, yet new ventures are the heart beat of the free enterprise system. Before making any business decisions, a potential independent business owner should engage in self-examination. The following questions may assist in determining whether the potential entrepreneur will become a *bona fide* business owner:

- Am I 100% committed to this idea?
- Am I self-motivated and self-disciplined?
- Am I willing to put up my assets and give up my regular income to turn this idea into a successful business?
- Am I willing to start over if my business fails?
- Am I realistic and objective about my business idea?
- Am I alert to opportunities?
- Am I optimistic and innovative?
- Am I willing to think and plan ahead, to develop goals and plans, to put them in writing, and to work hard to meet my goals and make my idea a reality?

There are bound to be setbacks and mistakes during the operation of a small independent practice. Learning from them is the mark of a truly successful person, for difficulties are often the stepping stones to success. Keep in mind the philosophy of Thomas Edison who believed that none of his experiments failed. He simply learned a great deal about what didn't work! This attitude is the true spirit of the entrepreneur. The person who prospers is the type of person who makes things happen, who consistently displays a positive attitude, and who is committed to business goals.

PRODUCTS AND SERVICES

Before becoming an independent business owner, you must have some idea of what need in the marketplace you can fill or create. The need for legal nurse consulting services may be similar, in marketing respects, to the need for anti-bacterial wipes and Post-it Notes. Consumers didn't know they needed them until they were available on the market.

There are many services that legal nurse consultants can provide to clients and consumers of medical information services. The AALNC, in preparing its certifying examination, surveyed members concerning time spent on professional activities. The results of that survey indicate that the responding legal nurse consultants spent approximately equal amounts of time on collecting records, literature, standards, etc. (20.5%); analyzing records, literature, standards, etc. (19%); and serving as communication liaison between lawyers and experts, clients, etc. (17.5%). The respondents also indicated that considerable time was spent drafting explanatory, initial opinion, and summary documents considered attorney work product (15%); educating themselves on medical issues (11%); and assisting in development of case strategy (10%).[1]

There are several legal nurse consulting services that are adaptable to independent practice:

- collecting, organizing, summarizing, and analyzing medical records and related documents
- performing medical research and medical literature reviews
- rendering initial opinion concerning causation, standard of care, and liability
- locating, interviewing, and evaluating potential expert witnesses
- assessing damages, especially medical damages
- developing trial exhibits to educate the jury
- summarizing, indexing, or digesting deposition transcripts or other litigation documents
- researching, writing, and/or evaluating life-care plans

The services listed above are not the only services legal nurse consultants may perform independently. They may be called upon to educate attorneys and others concerning medical issues involved, they may be asked to assist in developing trial strategy, or they may be asked to help design a computer system for tracking medical information in a class-action lawsuit. Imagination, background, and the owner's interests will provide insight into the services a legal nurse consulting business offers. You should expect to become an expert in the services you plan to sell.

In addition to products and services, the potential entrepreneur must ascertain who will be served by this business. Will the consulting services be offered to government agencies, to insurance companies, to private businesses or industries, to attorneys in private law practice, or to attorneys in general regardless of where they work? Legal nurse consultants who offer their services to the public must be mindful of the unauthorized practice of law statutes in their states (see Chapter Two).

Identifying the service to be performed and the potential client of that service is an important step in designing a business that will be successful. It is the foundation for organizing the business, determining the start-up costs, generating a business plan, formulating a marketing plan, and evaluating whether or not the business has been successful.

TYPES OF BUSINESS ORGANIZATIONS

There are several ways in which a business may be organized: **sole proprietorship, partnership, limited liability partnership, corporation,** and **limited liability company.** These organizations and their respective benefits and disadvantages are listed in Figure 5-1

To determine which organization and operational structure is right for your business, you should consult a commercial lawyer.

Sole Proprietorship

A sole proprietorship is uncomplicated and easy to create. It consists of one person who owns the business and is responsible for its debts. The business and the person have the same basic legal identity. No formal legal documents must be filed, unless there is a statute requiring a certificate of company name to be filed, or a license or permit to be acquired. The owner enjoys considerable freedom in decision-making. No board of directors or partners need to be consulted. A sole proprietor may react quickly to situations, since he or she has complete control over the business. And there is an additional incentive in sole proprietorship—success is credited entirely to the owner.

One disadvantage of a sole proprietorship is the owner's personal responsibility for all business debts and judgments against the business. Risk management may be important. While it is unlikely that a legal nurse consultant will be personally responsible for negligent acts since he or she is generally acting under the supervision or direction of an attorney or other employer, it may be valuable to have business liability and professional liability insurance. If the legal nurse consultant is joined in a lawsuit, the insurance company has the duty to defend.

A sole proprietorship has a limited life; if the owner becomes disabled or dies, the business terminates. If the sole proprietor employs others, the owner must apply for a federal tax identification number. Many legal nurse consultants who are sole proprietors are considered **independent contractors.** They may **subcontract** for overflow work or for work of a specialty nature about which the owner is not qualified to render an analysis. Independent contractors and subcontractors are not considered employees; their services are used for a limited time and purpose.

FIGURE 5-1   Types of Business Organizations and Their Distinguishing Characteristics, Benefits and Disadvantages

Business Organization	Characteristics	Benefits	Disadvantages
Sole Proprietorship	Owned by one individual Easy and inexpensive to create and operate	Inexpensive Exclusive control Owner reports income (or loss) on Schedule C of individual tax return	Owner pays self-employment tax Personal liability for all business debts
Partnership	Owned by two or more individuals Easy and relatively inexpensive to create and operate	Inexpensive Shared responsibility Partnership income (or loss) reported on individual partners' tax returns	Owners pay self-employment tax Partners personally liable for all business debts
Limited Liability Partnership	Owned by two or more individuals in the same profession (e.g., law, accounting, medicine) Partners are not responsible for negligence of other partners	Partnership income (or loss) reported on individual partners' tax returns	More expensive to create Must comply with statutory language May not be available in some states or for some professions Partners personally liable for all business debts
Corporation	Separate legal entity is created Owners are stockholders	Stockholders liability is limited to their investment	More expensive to create May be subject to regulatory compliance (annual reports) Corporation is taxed separately
Limited Liability Company	Separate legal entity is created	Owners' liability for business debts is limited Income (or loss) may be allocated differently than ownership interests May be taxed as partnership or corporation	More expensive to create

Sole proprietors report their income or loss on their personal income tax returns. A sole proprietorship is not taxed separately from its owner.

A legal nurse consultant considering an independent practice may start as a sole proprietor. As the business grows, the legal structure of the business may grow, too. The owner may add a partner, and later the owners might decide to change the legal status of their association and form a corporation.

Partnership

A partnership is a business association created by a contract between two or more persons. The partners agree to make investments in **capital** and labor in exchange for a share in the income (or loss) of the business. The partnership agreement may be oral or written, depending on the laws of the state in which the partnership is formed. Whether oral or written, the partnership agreement should be clear on the following points:

- name and address of each partner
- name, address, and purposes of the partnership
- capital contributions of each partner and how income and losses will be shared
- management of the partnership business

It is wise to have a partnership agreement reduced to writing so that future disputes may be more easily resolved. For example, if a partner wishes to withdraw from the partnership, how will his or her share be valued? How will income and losses be split between the partners? A partnership agreement often includes or is accompanied by a **buy-sell agreement,** which anticipates the death or withdrawal of a partner and makes appropriate provision for disposal of that partner's interest. Insurance may be purchased by the partnership to finance the buy-sell agreement.

Partnerships offer several advantages. Because there are more owners, there are more funds for expansion, improved credit potential, and increased potential for making sound business decisions. The stress of operating the business and the risks involved may be shared by the partners. Relative to liability, a partnership may be organized in one of two ways: as a general partnership or as a limited partnership.

General partnership. In a **general partnership,** the partners are considered to be fully and personally responsible for all business debts and judgments against the partnership. This is an important distinction because it means that the personal assets of each partner may be attached to pay partnership debts. All partners are considered to have equal rights of management and to have participated in the operation of the business.

Limited partnership. A **limited partnership** involves one or more partners who do not actively participate in the operation and management of the business. A limited partner's involvement in the partnership is only for purposes of investment. The limited partner provides no services, does not participate in management decisions, and is not included in the name of the partnership. A limited partnership must have at least one general partner who is personally liable for the partnership debts.

Because of the limited nature of limited partners' involvement in the business, their liability may not exceed their investment in the partnership. General partners are still personally liable for the debts of the business. The agreement establishing a limited partnership must be in writing and a partnership certificate or other formal document may need to be filed with the secretary of state or other state agency.

Limited Liability Partnership

Limited liability partnerships are not available in all states. In states where they are allowed, they may be restricted to partnerships of professionals such as lawyers, accountants, dentists, medical doctors, veterinarians, and so forth. State statutes should be consulted to determine whether limited liability partnerships are available for legal nurse consultants. (For information on how to research a statute, see Chapter Fifteen.)

In a limited liability partnership, all partners are personally responsible for business debts, but professional liability is limited. Partners are not personally responsible for the malpractice of other partners.

Corporation

Corporations are separate legal entities and, as such, they may own property, make contracts, sue others, and be sued. To form a corporation, **promoters** (potential corporate stockholders) must comply with state laws and file a charter or articles of incorporation with the secretary of state. The legal name of the corporation cannot be changed without amendment to the articles or dissolution of the original corporation.

Articles of incorporation include the names and addresses of the promoters; the purposes of the corporation; the duration of the corporation; the value, classification, and number of shares of stock authorized; and the name and address of the **registered agent** for the corporation. A registered agent is the person to whom all governmental communications will be sent and who is authorized to accept **service of process** on behalf of the corporation. State laws require that the corporate status be identified with Inc., Incorporated, Ltd., Corp., or other designation in the title of the corporation. In some states, it is possible for one person to form a corporation.

The owners of a corporation are stockholders who purchase shares of stock. The stock available is described in the articles of incorporation and may be **preferred** or **common.** The business of a corporation is managed according to the **by-laws** of the corporation. Generally, corporations are overseen by a board of directors elected by the stockholders. The board appoints officers to run the daily operations of the corporation.

There are several advantages to forming a corporation. The primary advantage is limited liability. Stockholders are not personally liable for the business debts of or judgments against the corporation. It is easy to transfer ownership; stock is bought and sold regularly and ownership is fluid. The corporation enjoys continuous life; that is, if one stockholder dies, becomes disabled, or sells his or her share, the corporation is not affected. Additionally, corporations may raise capital by issuing **debenture bonds** or authorizing the sale of additional stock.

The expense, time, and complexity of forming a corporation are disadvantages of this type of organizational structure. Corporations are subject to government regulation and are required to file annual reports, conduct annual stockholder meetings, and keep corporate records (minutes, resolutions, documents of corporate authority, stock certificates, etc.).

One of the major disadvantages of forming a corporation is taxation. The federal government, and most state governments, tax the income of a corporation before it is distributed to stockholders. Stockholders must pay income tax on the income received from the corporation. This double taxation may be avoided if the stockholders elect **S corporation** status. This status basically allows the income of the corporation to be passed through without taxation, similar to how a partnership is taxed. To elect S status, the corporation must be chartered in the United States; it must be based on unanimous agreement of the stockholders; there can be no more than 75 stockholders; there can be only one class of stock; and only individuals, estates, and trusts are allowed to be stockholders. Form 2553 (Election by a Small Business Corporation) must be filed with the Internal Revenue Service.

There are several other forms of corporations. Most are for-profit, but state laws allow incorporation as a nonprofit or charitable corporation. Professional, closed, and public service corporations are other types that have unique and specific rules for incorporation.

Limited Liability Company

A limited liability company is similar in some respects to a limited liability partnership. It is authorized by state statute and may not be allowed in every state. Approximately forty states have adopted limited liability company statutes, but the laws vary significantly.

Basically, a limited liability company is intended to provide limited liability to all investors, called members. Each member's liability for debts and judgments against the business is limited to his or her investment. Most states require that articles of organization, similar to articles of incorporation, be filed with the state. The name of the limited liability company must indicate its status with LLC, limited company, L.C., or limited liability company in the title. Some states restrict limited liability companies to professional services; in others, membership is not restricted.

Although state statutes vary, most laws authorizing the creation of limited liability companies have similar characteristics:

Net Results

Articles of Incorporation

Most states now have their government offices on the Internet. It is possible to download the standard form for articles of incorporation and other documents by accessing state web sites. An almost universal URL for state law is www.legis.state.XX.us. The XX in the URL is the two-letter postal abbreviation for the state you are researching. For example, if you are looking for Illinois law, you would find it via www.legis.state.il.us; California law would be www.legis.state.ca.us. These web sites will direct you to state statutes, administrative regulations, and case law. They will also have links to state governmental offices, which will provide links to downloadable forms.

1. Two or more members must form the limited liability company (except Idaho, Missouri, Montana, Arkansas, North Carolina, Colorado, and Texas, which allow one person to form a limited liability company).[2]

2. The duration of the limited liability corporation must be stated and may not exceed thirty years.

3. All members must have limited liability to the extent of their invested capital.

4. Membership shares are not freely transferable.

5. Members elect management.

The greatest advantage of limited liability companies is that member owners stand to lose only their initial investment and any later capital contributions made to the company. One disadvantage is that the Internal Revenue Service will determine how the organization should be taxed. If it has more characteristics of a corporation than a partnership, it will be taxed as a corporation. Thus, members may be subject to double taxation.

LEGAL CONSIDERATIONS

The legal structure of the business organization is only one of the difficulties that the entrepreneur must consider. Other legal considerations include name protection, licenses and permits, taxes, and risk management.

Name Protection

If the legal nurse consulting business is intended to include your name, you need not search to see if someone else already has rights to the name. For example, *Smith Consulting Service,* owned and operated by Juanita Smith, may invoke no legal requirements at all in some states and simply filing a certificate of business name in others.

If a fictitious name is used with the hope that a memorable logo will be developed and franchises established, it is important to ensure that using that fictitious name will not infringe on someone else's prior right to use that or a similar name. For example, *Smart Chart,* a business owned and operated by Juanita Smith, will invoke certain legal requirements depending on how the business is structured. If it is a sole proprietorship or a partnership, a certificate of fictitious name generally must be filed identifying the names and addresses of the owners of the business. If the business is a corporation or a limited liability company, the name must be checked by the secretary of state to ensure that no other business is incorporated under that name.

Logos, designs, and other distinctive marks of the business will be protected under common law if the owner uses those marks and maintains proof of the date of first use of the marks. It may be important, however, before designing logos, business cards, etc., to consult with a service that verifies that the design is available and will not infringe on prior rights in trademarks,

---

Net Results

Searching Trade Names and Trademarks

Although name searches on the Internet may not be complete, you may begin a search to see if there are any other companies on the Internet using the name you have considered. Simply use a search engine such as www.lycos.com, www.yahoo.com, www.infoseek.com, or www.excite.com and type the considered name into the search dialogue box. The computer will retrieve any and all matches to that name. There are also businesses on the Internet that specialize in searching trademarks and service marks. TrademarkScan is a database that contains trademarks that have been registered with the U.S. Patent and Trademark Office. The Patent and Trademark Office may be accessed directly at www.uspto.gov.

service marks, or copyright. It is advisable to consult a lawyer about issues of logo, trademark, and service mark protection.

Licenses and Permits

Although it may be generally assumed that businesses such as restaurants, liquor establishments, firearms dealers, pawn shops, and so forth are required to have licenses or permits, it may not be so obvious for legal nurse consulting services. It is imperative to check state and local laws regarding business licenses and permits. Failing to have an appropriate license or permit may subject the owner of the business to substantial penalties and may even result in the regulatory agency's prohibiting operation of the business.

Local zoning ordinances and restrictive covenants must be carefully checked. In many neighborhoods, residents are prohibited from operating businesses from their homes. These legal considerations are another reason it might be helpful to consult an attorney to help organize and start the business. A lawyer will verify that your potential business has filed all of the necessary documents, has acquired all of the necessary licenses and permits, and has met all requirements for location of the business.

Taxes

Because it is important to keep business and personal assets separate, it is recommended that a business owner apply for an Employer Identification Number.[3] Although a sole proprietor may use a personal Social Security number, if employees or independent contractors are engaged by the business owner, the Employer Identification Number is necessary. Similarly, if the state taxes income, it may be necessary to register with the state department of revenue and secure a state employer identification number.

It is essential for reporting and paying taxes that business records be accurate, complete, and clear. The services of an accountant or bookkeeper may be of value to help establish a bookkeeping system that will work for the business. In addition, the accountant or bookkeeper may assist in preparing or reviewing tax returns that must be filed by the business. Seeking the services of lawyers and accountants may seem like added expenses when starting a business, but the advice and services provided will be worth the expense in the long run.

There are several types of taxes about which business owners must be aware: income tax, employment tax, federal and state unemployment tax, and self-employment tax.

Income tax. Depending on how the business is organized, business owners must report income and losses and pay taxes on income from the business. Figure 5-2 identifies the tax forms that must be filed for particular types of businesses.

FIGURE 5-2   Forms to Report Income of Different Business
             Organizations

Type of Business	Tax Form
Sole proprietorship	Schedule C, Form 1040 (Profit or Loss from Business)
Partnership	Form 1065
Corporation	Form 1120 or 1120-A
S Corporation	Form 1120-S
Limited liability company	Form 1065, 1120, or 1120-A

Employment taxes. If the business will hire employees, federal (and most state) laws require employers to withhold employee income taxes. Each employee must complete a W-4 form identifying their filing status (single, married, etc.) and the number of dependents claimed. This form is necessary for computing the amount of federal, and usually state, income tax that must be withheld from the employee's paycheck. A payroll tax return must be filed quarterly. Withheld taxes must be deposited at authorized financial institutions regularly. Coupons from the Internal Revenue Service provide instructions on when these deposits must be made.

In addition to withholding the employee's estimated income tax, employers must withhold the employee's Social Security and Medicare taxes from the employee's paycheck. The employer's share of the Social Security and Medicare taxes must also be paid. Schedules for the amounts that must be withheld and paid are available in publications from the Internal Revenue Service. If the business organization is a corporation, you are considered an employee and must withhold the requisite income, Social Security, and Medicare taxes from your own paycheck.

Federal and state unemployment taxes. Employers are required to pay unemployment taxes based upon employee salaries. Those who must pay state unemployment taxes are given a credit for the taxes paid to the state. If the owners of a sole proprietorship or partnership are its only employees, federal unemployment tax need not be paid. Form 940 or 940EZ is used to report federal unemployment taxes.

Self-employment taxes. Sole proprietors and partners must pay self-employment taxes if they are not considered employees of the business. Self-employment tax is equivalent to the amount of Social Security and Medicare taxes that would be withheld from an employee and paid by an employer in an employment situation. Self-employment tax is reported and computed on Schedule SE.

Risk Management

You have already learned that risk management is an important aspect of every business (see Chapter Two). To be prepared for risks inherent in a business, take time to think through the following questions:

- How might people get hurt at, in, or near my business?
- What exposure do I have to professional liability?
- Will I be using my car for business?
- How could repetitive motions affect my health, and the health of my employees?
- As an independent contractor, what injuries might I sustain at the work site?
- As an independent contractor, what injuries might I be responsible for at the work site?

An insurance professional can help determine what types of coverage may be necessary. Fire, casualty, business, business liability, and malpractice insurance should be considered. Before purchasing an insurance plan, research the rates, coverage, and reputation of the insurance carrier.

MISSION, VISION, GOALS, AND STRATEGIC PLAN

Once you have made a preliminary assessment of your personal characteristics, determined the type of business organization that will best suit your idea, and considered the legal ramifications of starting your business, you should formulate a mission statement, a vision statement, goals, and a strategic plan to meet those goals. These documents will help keep the entrepreneur focused on the business idea and will provide a way to measure business success. The purposes of the mission, vision, goals, and strategic plan are summarized in Figure 5-3.

Mission

A mission statement addresses the business's reason for being. It describes the function of the business and creates internal focus. To formulate a mission statement, the following questions should be considered:

- Why does (or should) the business exist?
- What business (services provided) am I (or will I be) in?
- Who are (or will be) my major customers/clients?
- What want or need will I meet for them?
- What are my distinctive competencies and expertise?

Mission statements basically tell who you are, what you do, and for whom you do it. They should be general and flexible to allow for expansion and

---

FIGURE 5-3   Mission, Vision, Goals, and Strategic Plan

Mission	Why does the business exist?
Vision	What is the business's future?
Goals	What steps must be taken to achieve the vision?
Strategic Plan	What procedures and operations will help achieve the business's goals?

FIGURE 5-4   Examples of Vision Statements

Company	Vision Statement
Wal-Mart	*We exist to provide value to our customers*
Boeing	*Being on the leading edge of aeronautics, being pioneers*
3M	*Respect individual initiative*
Merck	*We are in the business of preserving and improving human life*

Source: Collins and Porras, *Built to Last*, 1997.

---

growth of the business. Reviewing the mission statement periodically (approximately every three years in a planning cycle) will help to keep the focus of the business in line with the vision and goals.

Vision

The vision statement may be the most important aspect of the business planning process.[4] It describes in a short statement what the business will be in the future. Examples of vision statements are included in Figure 5-4.

The vision statement should be dynamic and should reflect what you value most about your business idea. On discouraging days, the vision statement will remind you that you and your business exist on a core belief that will transcend crisis. It may be helpful to consider why you became a nurse in the first place. The vision statement comes from the heart and will seldom change.

Goals

Goals reflect those accomplishments that will place you firmly on the road to reaching your vision. They may be written in terms of work product provided or services performed or in terms of number of clients served. Goals may even deal with the number of employees you expect to hire within a particular period, or when you expect to be able to move into rented space instead of using your home office. Goals facilitate measurement of whether or not the business is succeeding. When you evaluate the results of your efforts after a month, a quarter, or a year of business, you may be surprised to find that the need you are actually filling in the marketplace is quite different from the need you expected to fill! That is why the mission statement and the goals must be general and flexible, offering you and your business an opportunity to reflect on what has succeeded and what lessons have been learned.

Strategic Plan

The strategic plan pulls together all of the processes, procedures, and operations necessary to accomplish the goals. Basically the strategic plan involves the following three elements:

- how the business will be structured; definition of the roles and relationships of people within the organization
- what processes will be involved; activities necessary for performing the organization's work
- what systems will be developed; how information will flow within the organization

Giving considerable thought to the mission, vision, goals, and strategic plan of the business will prepare you for one of the most critical tasks in the formation of an independent practice: writing the business plan.

THE BUSINESS PLAN

A **business plan** is a plan of action. It synthesizes all of the information already considered: the business design, legal framework, products or services, markets, and financial strategy. Besides providing direction and measurable goals for the business, it is generally necessary for obtaining a business loan. Excellent resources exist for writing business plans, including seminars conducted by local colleges and universities. The Small Business Administration provides printed materials on drafting business plans and online support on its website. Local libraries and libraries at colleges and universities have numerous books and publications, which include samples, on developing and drafting the business plan.

To be useful as a management tool and to convince others to invest in the business, the plan should contain certain features. It is important to consider the audience before finalizing the written document. Loan officers at banks may be looking for specific information concerning the planned product, market strategy, and financial projection. Potential partners or investors may be looking for information concerning management of the business, and expertise and qualifications of key personnel. Preparing a professional business plan not only puts your ideas about the business on paper, it reflects your pride and professionalism. The plan reveals your commitment to the idea, your enthusiasm and expertise, and your understanding of the business environment.

Business plans are composed of several sections, each providing critical information about how the business will be structured, financed, operated, marketed, and developed. A cover page generally is included with the company name and logo, if there is one, the names and addresses of the owners, and who to contact. Other portions of the business plan include an executive summary (which is actually written after all other sections of the business plan have been completed), business information (the business, background of the business, products or services, key people in the business), marketing strategy (market analysis, pricing strategy, promotion), and financial projections (start-up and operating expenses, profit potential).

Executive summary. This portion of the business plan is similar to an abstract in a professional journal. In concise language, it provides the reader with a basic idea of what the business is, how it will operate, what marketing strategies will be employed, and how and why the business will be profitable.

Business information. The business is described in this section. Its history is traced, its operating structure explained, and its management principles defined. What products and services will be offered and to whom are an important feature of this section of the business plan. The people who will be involved in the start-up of the business should be identified, along with their specific credentials for creating and running the business. The mission and vision of the business should also be included in this section.

The business information section of the plan should be realistic. It should include risks that the business may face and how those risks will be managed. Strategic goals of the business will help support the marketing strategy and financial projections.

Marketing Strategy. To clearly show how your product or service will be unique in the marketplace and to whom it will be marketed is the main objective of writing the marketing strategy section of the business plan. It is important to clearly show how your business will fill, or create, a need. Thus, an analysis of the market is a key ingredient in this section. Identify competitors and determine what share of the market competitors claim, how competitors' products and services are priced and marketed, and potential demand for your unique product or service. Detail a plan for promoting your products and services (television commercials, Yellow Pages, newspaper ads, advertisements in journals and periodicals, booths at conferences, etc.) and targeting your potential customer/client base.

Outline your pricing strategy and compare it to the competition. Exercise caution when considering the price for your products or services. Entrepreneurs often believe that they can produce and price their products or services cheaper than others in the business. This may be a business mistake that, once made, may be hard to correct. "You get what you pay for" is a common business adage. While it may be tempting to price products or services at a minimal profit margin to gain entry into the market, raising prices later may cause poor client relations.

Keep in mind that price conveys image. It capitalizes on the uniqueness of the business and conveys an idea about the quality of the product or service. If the price or rate set seems too high after some experience with it, it may easily be lowered. Then as business increases, your strategy may be to gradually reduce previously higher prices to attract more price-sensitive customers/clients, to meet competitors who enter the market (stimulated by your success!), and to reward long-term relationships with customers/clients.

Financial Projections. The business plan should explain how the business is expected to turn a profit; that is, how many customers/clients are expected to be served with what products or services and at what price. What expenses will be involved in providing those services and what portion of the profit will be turned back into the business. This section of the business plan requires the entrepreneur to clearly display on paper how the business idea will be turned into dollars. Cite statistics concerning the number of potential customers/clients that will be served. This information can be obtained from state offices such as the Bureau of Statistics. Use demographic information from the Commerce Department, the Census Bureau, or the Bureau of Labor Statistics and information from the state Department of Labor to show how the business will support other industries in the region. Use extrapolated data from professional journals to show how the business is expected to grow.

Expenses should be estimated in detail. You may want to consult an accountant for help in calculating ratio of gross profit to revenue and other projected revenue, expense, and **equity** calculations. This financial picture of the business will be scrutinized by potential funding sources.

It is sometimes suggested that the owners of the business include their personal financial statements in this section of the business plan.[5] If the business plan will be used to secure financing, the financial statements of the owners may be essential. Additionally, lenders will want to know what plans the business has to manage **cash flow.** A cash-flow plan is simply an outline or prediction of how much money the business will need to meet its daily operational expenses. This will involve establishing systems for invoicing clients, collecting bills, paying bills, and planning for purchases.

A sample business plan is included at the end of this chapter as Figure 5-12.

FINANCING A SMALL BUSINESS

The importance of keeping clear and accurate financial records cannot be stressed enough. An accounting system should be in place before business operations begin. Most entrepreneurs will need start-up capital. Locating sources for financing the business until it becomes profitable is an important activity.

There are several financing sources for small businesses, which are listed in Figure 5-5.

It may help to have the advice of an accountant to determine whether you will need to borrow money to start the business. Many legal nurse consultants begin their businesses while still in clinical practice, using their salaries to

---

FIGURE 5-5 Funding Sources for Small Businesses

- Personal investment
- Home equity loans
- Credit cards
- Loans from family and friends
- Banks
- Small Business Administration
- Community Development Grants

FIGURE 5-6 Example Start-up Costs for New Businesses

- Estimated cost of equipment, furniture, and supplies
- Cash for minimum income of six months
- Professional fees (attorneys, accountants, marketing specialists)
- Insurance
- Licenses or permits
- Deposits (telephone, utilities, rent, etc.)
- Rent (first six months)
- Remodeling or installation costs (for computer, fax, scan, phone, etc.)
- Loan fees, bank charges, etc.
- Signs, advertising, Yellow Pages, etc.
- Collateral materials
- Working capital, cash needed on hand, and cash for unexpected needs or miscellaneous items

---

fund the start-up business. A list of potential start-up costs for new businesses is included is Figure 5-6.

Home equity loans are often easy to obtain, since the loan is secured by a mortgage on a personal residence. If the funds needed to start the business are minimal, this funding source may be convenient. Alternatively, making business purchases on credit, using credit cards or revolving charge accounts, will help manage the obligations of the business without applying for a loan.

A business plan is helpful when obtaining loans from family and friends, and is essential when borrowing from a bank or from the Small Business Administration (SBA). The SBA is an independent government agency created by Congress to encourage, assist, and protect the interests of small businesses.

If you apply to a bank for a direct loan and are denied, ask the banker to give you a loan under the SBA's loan guaranty or to participate with the SBA in a loan. If you are still denied, go directly to the SBA.

The services provided by the SBA can be divided into three categories: management assistance, financial assistance, and procurement assistance. All three services are available at all SBA field offices around the country. These offices are listed in the government section of the telephone directory. The SBA can also be accessed via its website (see the *Net Results* section earlier in this chapter).

Special programs of the SBA provide for loans to women who own businesses or to minority women. These loans are guaranteed and generally have a lower interest rate than would be obtained from a bank.

MARKETING AN INDEPENDENT LEGAL NURSE CONSULTING BUSINESS

Marketing is essential to successful business. To build a strong client base, small business owners must maintain a marketing perspective. This involves a customer/client focus and knowledge of your business. Before beginning any marketing planning, consider why customers/clients would buy your products or services. Why would they need the products and services you offer? What makes your products and services unique? How can you add value in a way that will ensure continued business? Focus on these unique qualities of your business.

Reaching the customer/client is the first objective of a marketing plan, but penetrating the market can be a frustrating experience. (Please refer to Chapter Four for information on how to locate potential customers/clients.)

A marketing plan should include how to gain a toehold in the market and how to build market share. A carefully planned promotional strategy should be used to reach the maximum number of customers/clients at a minimal cost. This promotional strategy might include advertising, personal contact, attending conferences and seminars, and maintaining professional **collateral materials** (letterhead, business cards, etc.). Additional promotional strategies include publicity, free samples, and discounts.

Advertising

Commercials have become an integral part of our lives on television, on the radio, and on the Internet. Along with these, billboards, magazine ads, and infomercials all describe products and services that, hopefully, will be appealing. Determining which advertising media and message will best support the services and the image of the entrepreneur is a decision that may ultimately make or break the business.

Researching the market is critical to targeting potential customers/clients and reaching them in a way that will capture their attention. If attorneys are the target market, consider whether they are conservative or risk-taking types, how they market their services, and what their specialties are. It may be worthwhile to consult a public relations or marketing specialist to help design an advertising campaign that will maximize exposure to the types of customers/clients who will best be served by the business. For legal nurse consultants, advertising campaigns might include brochures, advertisements in professional journals, and web pages.

Brochures. Before considering the design of a brochure, determine what you intend to communicate. The message is the most important component of the brochure and you want the reader to focus on that message. It should be simple, clear, and to the point. Once the purpose and message are determined, decide how important each feature is—then design the brochure so that the most important information attracts the reader's attention first.

Collecting and studying brochures from other organizations might be a good first step in designing your own. Keep in mind the mission and vision of the business so the brochure aligns with the beliefs of the entrepreneur. The brochure may be the first introduction a potential customer/client has with the business; it should earn their respect.

Advertisements in Professional Journals. Because potential customers/clients of a legal nurse consulting service will probably be professionals, it may be wise to consider advertising in professional journals, such as state bar journals, publications of the Association of Trial Lawyers of America, and paralegal journals. Once again, this may be the first impression a customer/client has of the business so the ad should be designed in a way that fits the organization and the publication. A sample advertisement in a paralegal magazine is shown in Figure 5-7.

Web Pages. The Internet has become a marketing tool for many entrepreneurs. Legal nurse consultants have developed web pages that can be accessed using specific web addresses or via search engines. Developing a web page need not be expensive, but the design of the web page should be consistent with the advertising strategy and the mission and vision of the business. Local colleges and universities offer classes on web design that generally require only computer literacy as a prerequisite. It may also be wise to consult a web page designer to assist with this project. There are many new small businesses that offer web page design services. A profitable long-term partnership may be developed between a start-up legal nurse consulting business and a start-up web page design business. A sample legal nurse consulting web page is shown in Figure 5-8.

Personal Contacts

Many legal nurse consultants sell their services by personally contacting attorneys, law firms, and other potential clients. Chapter Four details ways to approach, follow up, and maintain contact with these potential clients.

Conferences and Seminars

Professional conferences and seminars offer an opportunity to network with other professionals and potential clients. Securing a booth in the exhibit hall

Net Results

Legal Nurse Consultant Web Pages

Before determining whether a web page is appropriate for your advertising campaign, you may wish to browse some of the web pages designed for legal nurse consulting businesses. Use any of the search engines (www.lycos.com, www.yahoo.com, www.infoseek.com, etc.) and enter legal nurse consulting as your search terms.

FIGURE 5-7

Do you need help
finding an
expert witness?

Is there a problem
with your
medical malpractice case?

Call us
for your free initial
telephone consultation.

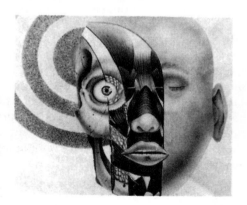

1302 Elmwood Avenue, Cranston, RI 02910
(401) 781-4290 • Fax (401) 781-2168
Circle No. 52 On Reader Response Page.

Reprinted with permission of New England Medical Legal Consultants, Inc.

FIGURE 5-8

Reprinted with permission of Kurt Zettlemoyer, Ginny Stegent, and Med-Legal Services, Inc.

and advertising your business's products and services may be expensive, however the contact cannot be undervalued. Name recognition is an important part of a marketing campaign. Keeping your business in front of potential customers/clients is a way to ensure that when they need your services, they will know where to turn. Attending and advertising at professional conferences indicates a commitment to the business and the profession.

Collateral Materials

Collateral materials include all of the paper products that support your business, such as stationery, invoices, business cards, envelopes, note pads, and so forth. These should be formatted in a way that aligns with the image of the business. Although it is tempting today to save money by simply using computer programs and clip art to design letterhead and logo, many experts believe that you cannot skimp on these collateral materials. A great design makes a great first impression.[6] A marketing, communications, or public relations specialist can help you design collateral materials that are right for your business.

At a minimum, letterhead, envelopes, and invoices should contain the name, address, telephone number, and e-mail address of the business. If the name of the owner of the business is not part of the title of the business, the name of the owner or president of the company may also be included. Many businesses today add their vision statements or mottos to their collateral materials.

The business card is the calling card of the professional. When designing it, just as in designing a brochure, it is important to first consider what message you mean to communicate. At a minimum, the business card should include name, name of the business, address, telephone number, and e-mail address. Additionally, the products or services provided by the business, or the vision statement or motto may be included.

Publicity

Some legal nurse consultants have consulted public relations or marketing professionals. These professionals might help you prepare a news release in which your new business and your expertise will be profiled or arrange for an interview with a local newspaper journalist to do an article on your enterprise. A sample news release/article is included as Figure 5-9.

Many local newspapers also provide space for business information highlighting people who have been named to important positions in banks, realty companies, and other businesses. Legal nurse consultants opening their own businesses might ask the newspaper what and how much information may be placed in these columns. A sample business information highlight is included as Figure 5-10.

There are many other ways to obtain publicity for a small business. Chairing a *walk for hunger,* participating in community and civic events, and being involved in professional organizations provide numerous opportunities for publicity. Legal nurse consultants sometimes write columns for newsletters, school publications, or local newspapers, or offer to make presentations to bar associations, insurance groups, or paralegal organizations.

Free Samples

One way for legal nurse consultants to get a foot in the door is to offer to perform a review without cost.[7] The purpose is to convince the customer/client that the services of the legal nurse consultant will enhance the legal work product, create an efficient and effective division of labor within the legal environment, capitalize on the expertise of legal staff (each works in the area in which he or she has been trained or specializes), and promote accurate and complete assessment.

FIGURE 5-9   Nurse Turns Knowledge, Talents to Legal Matters

By Susan Squires
Post-Crescent Staff Writer

Simply put, legal nurse consultant Laura Sinclair is an interpreter.

Sinclair, president of Sinclair Consulting in Appleton, translates medical jargon and mazes of patient history into tools her attorney clients can use in personal injury, medical malpractice and worker's compensation cases, whether they represent the plaintiff or the defendant.

"I can see what's not there as well as what is there," said Sinclair, 36 a registered nurse, who was fed up after 13 years of hospital nursing.

"Nurses have enormous responsibility, enormous accountability and no authority," Sinclair said.

During an exit interview, Sinclair told her former employer the hospital was more focused on its budgets than on its patients.

"I didn't quit lightly, and I was a good nurse," she said.

Legal nurse consulting is a comparatively new field, one of a growing number of careers absorbing nurses who want to use their education and experience outside the confines of hospitals and clinics.

Its professional association, the American Association of Legal Nurse Consultants, is only 9 years old. Sinclair is one of 3,000 members nationwide and may be the only independent practitioner in northeast Wisconsin.

Sinclair, who holds a bachelor's degree in nursing from the University of Wisconsin-Madison, opened shop last May, after she finished Chippewa Valley Technical College's five-semester curriculum in legal nurse consulting.

The 3-year-old program teaches registered nurses with at least one year experience how to adapt their medical experience to legal work. There are now 36 graduates.

Sinclair took CVTC's program through Fox Valley Technical College's distance learning program.

To date, Sinclair has worked on 40 cases, primarily for the Kaukaunna firm of McCarty, Curry, Wydeven, Peeters and Haak.

When a legal action is initiated, Sinclair sifts through the patient's medical histories, which may involve multiple hospitals and doctors. She identifies information relevant to the case or injury, summarizes the pertinent history, assesses the medical merits of the claim or case and delivers her opinion.

"I explain 'Here are the elements (of the injury) and this is how they could have occurred,' " she said.

Sinclair, who specializes in rehabilitation nursing, is able to forecast the future complications associated with an injury, like surgeries or prosthesis. The information is important to determining the financial impact of an injury or condition on the patient.

"In a lot of offices, paralegals or secretaries summarize the records. They don't understand the importance of arthritis five years ago," Sinclair said.

She also helps prepare her clients for court.

"In a lot of courtrooms, you'll see a lawyer with a stack of medical records pilled this high, and it takes 15 minutes for him to find what he needs. Meanwhile, opposing counsel has my summary," Sinclair said.

The summary, said attorney Gregg Curry, allows him to "put the medical records aside because I have a very clear, concise story of what happened to the client from time of injury to time of trial. It just makes the telling of the story that much more efficient.

"Instead of having reports arranged by physician, the records are woven together chronologically, which is how the patient saw them happen."

Curry sought out Sinclair's help for his personal injury cases.

"As the medical industry becomes more complicated, the legal profession becomes more complicated," he said.

Sinclair's services may not always win his cases, but they save Curry time and make him better prepared.

"When you are going to cross-examine the other party's doctor, you know which areas are maybe stronger than others, and which may need more explanation than others," Curry said.

If she is working for the plaintiff's attorney, Sinclair may accompany the patient to the independent medical examination to observe and reassure.

"They are very comfortable having a nurse with them when they go to a strange physician who they know is in an adversarial position," Sinclair said.

Sinclair hopes to work on medical and nursing malpractice cases. Her interest, she said, is more in the technical elements of the work than in ax-grinding.

"I think doctors need to be policed and nurses need to be policed. Do I want to reform health care? No," she said.

Product liability cases are another opportunity for growth in her field.

A 12-person legal nurse consulting firm summarized 750 women's medical histories in preparation for a class-action suit against a silicone breast-implant manufacturer.

On the horizon, Sinclair predicts, are products liability claims involving the diet drug Phen-fen, pulled from the market last year after some women who took it developed medical problems.

Though her practice has grown slowly, Sinclair has never regretted her decision to leave nursing.

"When you are a nurse, you have a lot of knowledge and a doctor gives you five minutes. With an attorney, you are dealing with someone who actually cares what you think," she said.

If area lawyers haven't embraced Sinclair's emerging practice, it may be because they don't know it is available, Curry said.

"I don't think the legal community is as aware of this service as they may be," he said. Also, consultants are more expensive on a "sheer-cost basis, but may be cheaper in the long run in that you are so much more efficient," Curry said.

Sinclair does not reveal her fees to nonclients—a covenant of her membership in the AALNC—but said they are much lower than the $60-$150-an-hour range some legal nurse consulting education programs promise.

The AALNC is in the process of establishing certification testing and criteria for the profession.

Sinclair hopes the current rarity of her specialty will work to her advantage.

"I feel like I've really got a jump on things because of those classes I took," she said.

FIGURE 5-10   Business

Sunday, March 29, 1998
Leader-Telegram
In Brief

Ken Vance Motors awarded

Ken Vance Motors of Eau Claire has won the state Department of Transportation's Right Way award, which recognizes vehicle dealers who set an example for others of the right way to do business in Wisconsin.

Ken Vance Motors participates in the DOT's Wise Buys program that helps customers make wise decisions when buying a new vehicle, and it complies with all laws, said Roger Cross, administrator of the Division of Motor Vehicles.

It sponsors training seminars and completes licensing paperwork correctly and on time.

Realty firm opens office

Woods & Water Realty has opened an office on Highway 10 East in Mondovi, its fifth office in the Chippewa Valley.

The office will offer realty services including residential, recreational, farm, commercial and new home construction.

Bruce Hayhoe is president of Woods & Water Realty, which has a sales force of 30 associates.

Lewis named manager

Mary Lewis has been named manager of Mutual Savings Bank's downtown branch at 319 E. Grand Ave.

Lewis, formerly a branch manager at First Federal Bank-La Crosse, will also be a consumer loan officer.

Mutual Savings Bank operates 53 offices in Wisconsin and Minnesota.

Inspection business opens

HouseMaster, a home inspection organization, has opened an office in Eau Claire.

The office, headed by Jeff Dueringer, offers pre-purchase and seller inspections in Eau Claire, Chippewa and Dunn County.

HouseMaster, with headquarters in Bound Brook, N.J., serves more than 270 cities in the U.S. and Canada.

Firm offers nurse consulting

Bonnie Phillips and Roxanne Westland have opened Phillips & Westland, Legal Nurse Consultants in Chippewa Falls.

The company's registered nurses assist attorneys and individuals with personal injury or general injury cases, medical malpractice, product liability and workman's compensation cases.

They have nursing experience and training in legal nursing, and they can review medical records to answer questions regarding care received. Other services offered include interviewing clients; obtaining, reviewing, summarizing and organizing medical records; completing medical expense reports; accompanying clients to medical examinations; interpreting medical reports and assisting with depositions and at trials.

Ranney opens new bakery

Sue's Deluxe Bake Shop, a bakery, has opened at 1319 Birch St.

Sue Ranney is owner. She formerly operated the Deluxe-Bakery downtown before selling it.

Short takes

- Norwest Corp. has been named the nation's "Most Admired" super-regional bank by Fortune Magazine in its Corporate Reputation Survey. Norwest Bank Wisconsin, which has offices in *Eau Claire, is a subsidiary of Norwest Corp.*, an $88.5 billion company providing banking and other financial services.
- West CAP Pleiades Project will sponsor a business workshop from 5 to 8 p.m. April 9 at the city offices in Cornell. Entitled "Look Before You Leap," the workshop will cover an overview of small business issues. The workshop is free. For more information or to register call 235-8525 or (800) 606-9227. Register by April 3.
- Michael D. Markin, senior vice president of investments for A. G. Edwards & Sons in Eau Claire, has been designated a Certified Investment Management Analyst through the Investment Management Consultants Association. Markin earned the designation following coursework and an examination at the Wharton School of Business.
- The University of Wisconsin-Eau Claire Small Business Development Center will put on a workshop on Fundamentals of Advertising Design from 8:30 a.m. to noon April 9 at the Quality Inn, Eau Claire. The session will offer tips on properly designing ads to sell your business. The fee is $59. For more information or to register, call 836-5637. *Register by April 6.*
- The UW-Eau Claire Small Business Development Center is offering counseling to small business owners and managers April 24 at the UW Center-Barron County Campus in Rice Lake. To make an appointment call 234-8176, ext. 0, by April 17.
- Mark Orgel and Tom Quigley, co-branch managers of Dain Rauscher's Eau Claire office, recently were named to the firm's Leadership Council. The Leadership Council Award annually recognizes Dain Rauscher's top managers in its 86 branch offices, based on leadership in client service and branch management. Minneapolis-based Dain Rauscher provides investment services to individual investors and small businesses.

From staff reports

Reprinted with permission of Eau Claire Leader Telegram.

Discounts

Another way to promote products or services is to offer them at a reduced or introductory rate for a specific period of time or for new customers/clients. Like the free sample described above, the purpose of the discount is to attract customers/clients and to show the prospective customers/clients that the services you have to offer will make their work easier, more efficient, and more profitable.

CLIENT RELATIONS

The Total Quality Management and Continuous Improvement concepts of business were discussed in Chapter Two. Adopting a quality approach to your business will greatly enhance your ability to meet the needs and expectations of customers/clients. The quality of service depends partly on the experience, knowledge, and ability of the entrepreneur to create opportunities for the customer/client to communicate specific needs.

The Total Quality Movement describes four types of products or services: generic, expected, augmented, and potential. The *generic* product or service is exactly what the customer/client wants—nothing more and nothing less. In fact, the product or service may even be a little defective (typographical errors or poor packaging), but it still meets the basic need of the customer/client. The *expected* product or service is exactly what the customer/client wants and meets his or her expectations as to image, packaging, neatness, etc. The customer, at this point, doesn't realize that he or she desires more than the expected product or service.

An *augmented* product or service has value added, which sets it apart from the expected product or service. For legal nurse consultants, this augmented product or service might be a table of contents, a cross-reference table, a narrative summary, headings, Post-it Notes flagging important entries, and so forth. The augmented product or service makes the customer/client see that this is better than the expected product and raises the bar of quality. Expectations and needs have been expanded.

The *potential* product or service *leads* the customer/client in expectation. Once the customer/client has received a potential product, he or she will accept nothing less. It goes beyond the augmented product or service because it adds value that was not anticipated. For legal nurse consultants, this potential product or service might consist of adding all of the features of the augmented product along with citations to medical literature on records analysis, suggesting experts within the field on chart reviews, or including a timeline that was not requested but which assists the legal staff in understanding the medical issues.

A commitment to quality principles will make client relations a priority. This commitment involves

- continually striving to think of ways to improve the product or increase the quality of service
- developing a process for completely understanding the customer/client's needs and expectations

- seeking to exceed client expectations
- becoming an expert and seeking training in areas that complement that expertise

Review the mission, vision, and goals of the business. Incorporate them into a customer/client relations policy statement by putting yourself in the position of the customer/client. Consider these questions:

- How and when will I give feedback to the customer/client?
- How and when will I ask for feedback from the customer/client?
- How will I manage customers/clients who are dissatisfied with my product or services?
- How will I manage customers/clients who are dissatisfied with my bill?
- What type of business image do I want to convey—friendly, professional, flexible?

Many client relations difficulties may be avoided by preparing a written document that outlines the expectations of the customer/client as you perceive them. This may be in the form of a contract for services or simply a confirming letter. If the perceptions outlined do not match those of the customer/client, unnecessary time, work, and headache may be averted by clearing up the discrepancies as soon as possible. This document may also provide for timely feedback; for example, the chronological summary may be expected within two weeks, the preliminary analysis within three weeks, and so on. On long projects, interim status reports may promote good client relations.

The product or service delivered is just as important as how it is delivered. Both will contribute to the reputation of the business. Word-of-mouth advertising is powerful. To ensure that your product is the best that it can be, you may want to develop a quality control system. If your business has more than one owner or employs others, you may wish to have someone else review the work you have performed to ensure that it meets the augmented and potential product or service requirements you have established. Accept their remarks and criticisms as healthy suggestions for improving the quality of the work performed. If you are a sole owner, you may wish to develop schedules that allow you to put the work away for a day or two to "cool." Later, when you review the work, you may see areas for improving its quality.

START-UP CHECKLIST

Dreams do not become reality without a great deal of preparation and hard work. A recent survey taken by the AALNC indicated that 53% of the respondents were owners of independent practices.[8] Each one of those respondents started with an idea.

Figure 5-11 provides an overview or checklist of the preparation necessary to start a business. This checklist may be modified or expanded depending on the nature of the business.

There is no substitute for planning well and for committing to paper what those plans are. These written documents will provide direction, keep you focused on your goals, and help you measure how successful you have been. It is important to revisit the plans (mission, vision, goals, etc.) of the business periodically. Looking forward to how your business will be situated in the market of the future will help to ensure continued success.

FIGURE 5-11 Checklist for Starting a New Business	
Preliminary analysis	Assess your entrepreneurial spirit
	Determine your expertise and decide what products or services you may provide
	Review business organizations and identify the structure that will work best for you*
	Consider the legal implications of starting your business (name protection, licenses, permits, taxes, and risks)
	Write a mission statement, a vision statement, a statement of business goals, and a strategic plan
Preliminary actions	Perform a market analysis (identify customers and competitors)
	Determine start-up costs and financial projections*
	Develop a marketing plan***
	Create the business*
	Write a business plan**
	Secure financing
Starting up	Obtain insurance, licenses, and tax ID number
	Install equipment (computer, fax, scanner, etc.)
	Get business cards and collateral materials
	Contract for supplies
	Write customer relations policy
	Market the business
	Work hard and prosper

*May require the services of a lawyer.
**May require the services of an accountant.
***May require the services of a marketing or public relations professional.

FIGURE 5-12   Sample Business Plan

BUSINESS PLAN

LNC ASSOCIATES, INC.

Bee Xiong, RN, CCM, CRN
Lorraine Jones, RN, BSN
Maria Sanchez, BSN, MBA

1111 2nd Street
Anytown, AS 44444
555.222.3333
e-mail: lncai@aol.com

October, 1999

Table of Contents

continued

FIGURE 5-12   Sample Business Plan   *continued*

EXECUTIVE SUMMARY

LNC ASSOCIATES, INC. will use a unique multidisciplinary approach to provide services to community businesses, manufacturing companies, government agencies and law firms in areas of risk management, legal nurse consulting, life-care planning, workplace safety, and health education.

    LNC ASSOCIATES, INC. will provide cost-effective, quality services and products to law firms who previously employed physicians (an expensive resource) and paralegals (lacking in medical background). To eliminate an expensive and time-consuming step in the medical records review process, **LNC ASSOCIATES, INC.** will evaluate medical information as it is being collected and summarized. In addition, **LNC ASSOCIATES, INC.** will assist attorneys in assessing future medical needs through life-care planning.

    Several indicators attest to a growing need for medical-legal expertise. There are more than 2,000 insurance companies and 17,000 attorneys in Anystate. In 1998, 9,590 personal injury and property damage lawsuits were filed in the state. There is a societal trend toward increased litigation involving health care issues. Among health care providers there is an increasing trend toward resolution of health care claims outside the courts. There is also a legislative trend toward limiting damages and attorney fees, decreasing the economic feasibility of utilizing expensive resources.

    LNC ASSOCIATES, INC. will provide evaluation, education, and coordination of risk management activities to business establishments to assist these businesses in maintaining costs and controlling negative environmental factors that may significantly reduce productivity.

    According to the 1996 County Economic Profile for Any County, there are 93 manufacturing establishments, 628 retail establishments, 156 wholesale establishments, and 543 service establishments. Risk management is an increasingly important factor in the growth and productivity of all businesses. Access to cost-effective consulting and education services for smaller businesses will assist those businesses in minimizing threats to health and safety on the job and reducing workers' compensation claims.

    The wide range of education, experience, and expertise of the management staff of **LNC ASSOCIATES, INC.** will enhance the quality of products and services provided. **LNC ASSOCIATES, INC.** will fill a need for linkages among legal, business, and health care professionals.

DESCRIPTION OF THE BUSINESS

LNC ASSOCIATES, INC., will offer medical expertise to community businesses, manufacturing companies, government agencies, and law firms. The business will

- secure, organize, and analyze medical records
- provide document control services
- locate expert witnesses
- offer initial expert opinion and expert testimony
- research medical and legal literature
- identify standards of care

- assist attorneys in the preparation of pleadings and discovery
- evaluate manufacturing environments relating to federal and state mandates
- promote industrial hygiene and reduce contaminant exposure
- educate managers and employees on issues regarding DILHR and OSHA regulations
- investigate business environments and develop plans to promote and enhance workplace safety and productivity
- coordinate activities of management and health care professionals for adapting the environment to comply with ADA regulations

LNC ASSOCIATES, INC. will act as a liaison in a variety of situations, providing linkages between legal and health care professionals, attorneys, and clients, employers and employees, management and regulatory agencies, and insurance customers and insurance providers. The firm will be unique in its multidisciplinary approach using nurses, legal nurse consultants, educators, and paralegal professionals.

ENVIRONMENTAL SCAN

Several indicators demonstrate a growing need for legal nurse consultants. There are more than 2,000 insurance companies in Anystate who employ nurses to investigate workers' compensation claims, personal injury lawsuits, and Social Security disability claims. Currently lawyers use paralegals, lacking in medical training, to gather the medical information. Physicians, an expensive resource, are employed to extract pertinent medical facts from the charts. A dilemma for the legal profession is finding nurses knowledgeable in both legal and medical issues. There are currently no Anystate legal nurse associations.

There are 200 attorneys in Anytown and 17,000 in Anystate. The number of cases involving personal injury, medical malpractice, Social Security disability, and workers' compensation is on the rise. In 1994, 9,590 personal injury and property damage lawsuits were filed in Anystate. In 1999, that number had risen to 17,442. These cases proceed through the judicial system for approximately one year. There is a societal trend reflecting increased litigation involving health care issues. There is also a legislative trend toward limiting damages and attorney fees, decreasing the economic feasibility of utilizing expensive resources.

Historically, physicians have performed chart review and medical summaries for lawyers. However, many physicians are no longer interested in providing this service because of the time constraints and the economic advantage of utilizing their expertise in private practice. In addition, physicians are costly and their reviews and opinions are limited to physician practices and standards of care. **LNC ASSOCIATES, INC.** will provide cost-effective, quality services and products to lawyers. Some legal nurse consultants, employed by large law firms, have been trained on the job by attorneys. Smaller law firms and businesses may contract with **LNC ASSOCIATES, INC.** to assess professional services in the medical-legal arena. Access to medical information services for those companies without resources or need to hire legal nurse consultants full time will be enhanced. In firms where paralegals have

continued

FIGURE 5-12   Sample Business Plan   *continued*

traditionally collected and summarized medical documents, however, **LNC ASSOCIATES, INC.** could evaluate the information as it is being gathered from medical charts, eliminating an expensive and time-consuming step in the review process.

According to the 1992 County Economic Profile prepared by the Department of Development, State of Anystate, 93 manufacturing establishments exist in Any County, employing approximately 5,000 workers. These figures were accumulated in 1987, when Triple T Tire, Inc., was still a significant employer. Since then new manufacturing interests have been established in Anytown, including Double U Technologies, Inc.

The Strategic Planning Statement of Anytown Community and Technical College, dated November, 1998, indicates that "although more new jobs continue to be created in the larger wholesale/retail and service sectors, new manufacturing jobs in the Anyriver Valley have grown at a faster percentage rate. This trend is expected to continue" (p. 8).

The Economic Profile indicates that there are 628 retail establishments in Anytown County, 156 wholesale establishments, and 543 service establishments. "Small business will continue to provide significant and growing employment in West Central Anystate" (p. 8 Strategic Planning Statement, Anytown Community and Technical College, November, 1998).

Risk management is an increasingly important factor in the growth and productivity of all businesses. Larger manufacturing and service industries may have in-house risk managers. **LNC ASSOCIATES, INC.** can provide smaller business establishments with cost-effective consulting services to assist these businesses in maintaining costs and controlling environmental factors that may significantly increase injuries and illness and reduce productivity.

Currently, the Any County Clerk's office contracts with agencies in southern Anystate and Illinois to evaluate workers' compensation claims. In addition, risk management training is contracted with outside sources. There are no resources available in northern Anystate to provide these services, according to the clerk's office. **LNC ASSOCIATES, INC.** will fill this need by providing evaluation, education, and coordination of risk management activities.

Opportunities for expansion from a local firm to a state, national, or world-wide consulting service provider exist with easy access to the Internet and World Wide Web. **LNC ASSOCIATES, INC.** could franchise the business and begin legal nurse consulting firms across the country. Since legal nurse consulting is a relatively new profession for nurses. **LNC ASSOCIATES, INC.** will capitalize on this novel idea. The firm is expected to flourish as satisfied customers return and refer their colleagues.

MARKETING STRATEGY

SELECTING TARGET MARKETS

Target markets include plaintiff and defense attorneys, nurse consultants, physicians, insurance companies, government agencies, workers' compensation cases, Social Security claims, corporate counsels, hospitals, clinics, long-term care facilities, and businesses. In the fiscal year ending June 30, 1998, there were 220 claims filed with the Patient Compensation Board, a mandatory mediation panel for claims against health care providers exceeding $600,000. **LNC ASSOCIATES, INC.** expects a growing market share as the reputation for quality, cost-effect services in medical/legal claims becomes known.

The business plans to use market research, needs assessment tools, and feasibility studies to aid in selecting other potential clients.

DEVELOPING MARKET STRATEGY

- Face-to-face contacts
- Business cards
- Internet
- Poster presentation at State Bar Conventions and lawyer groups
- Yellow pages

- Direct mail
- Educational seminars for attorneys and nurses
- Sample product portfolios
- Informational brochures
- Professional journals

Each of these strategies will be developed in more detail. For example:

Strategy	Timeline	Person Responsible	Evaluation	Contingency Plan
Face-to-face contacts with attorneys	Jan.-March	Xiong (Attorneys A-L in the Yellow Pages) Jones (Attorneys M-Z in the Yellow Pages)	Contract from 1 in 15 contacts	Direct mail to attorneys in Yellow Pages
Business cards	December	Sanchez	Name and design recognition	Post-It Notes and/or Rolodex cards
Internet	December	Sanchez	1 in 15 hits results in a request for information about services	Direct mail to attorneys in Yellow Pages and Yellow Pages ad
Poster presentation at Bar meetings and lawyers groups	ATLA in March and October; Bar Assn in June and Dec.	Xiong and/or Jones	Name recognition; 20 requests for information about services	Direct mail to attorneys in Yellow Pages and Yellow Pages ad
Yellow Pages	December	Sanchez	Name recognition and 40 requests for information about services	Direct mail and informational brochures; advertise in professional journals
Direct Mail . . . etc.	April-June	Sanchez	Contract for 1 of every 40 mailings	Samples

continued

FIGURE 5-12 Sample Business Plan *continued*

SALES FORECAST

Overhead expenses will include office supplies, computer, fax, and freight expenses. **LNC ASSOCIATES, INC.** is a service business, so profit will likely occur at end of first year and compound as more services are provided, such as life-care planning. The professional staff expect to initially process about 40 hours of cases per month at $80 per hour, expanding to 80 hours per month as the business grows, and eventually pursuing the consulting business full-time.

MANAGEMENT PLAN

Key managers (refer to resumes included in the Appendix):

Bee Xiong, RN, CCM, CRN	Clinical nursing experience (26 years):
	geriatrics (15 years)
	home health (7 years)
	pediatrics (2 years)
	medical-surgical (2 years)
	developmentally disabled (2 years)
	Advanced Certificate–Legal Nurse
	Life Care Planning Certification pending
Lorraine Jones, RN, BSN	Clinical nursing experience (4 years)
	long-term care (1 year)
	correctional health (4 years)
	mental health (4 years)
	administration (3 years)
	Advanced Certificate—Legal Nurse
	Risk management policy development: OSHA
Maria Sanchez, BSN, MBA	Nurse paralegal (8 years)
	Instructor (8 years):
	Nursing Program
	Legal Nurse

Staff development plans include training and certification in life-care planning, honing expertise in risk management, continuing development of software for nurse consultant documentation, and developing business contacts. **LNC ASSOCIATES, INC.** partnership collaboration will be fostered through scheduled weekly meetings and attending conferences sponsored by the American Association of Legal Nurse Consultant, Trial Lawyers of America, and Bar Associations.

Accounting, Internet marketing, and computer software will be developed (Sanchez) for the business. There will be monthly financial statements and quarterly status reports.

LNC ASSOCIATES, INC. will have weekly status case meetings and employ contracted legal nurse consultants. Eventually transcriptionists, paralegals, and more registered nurses may be employed.

FINANCIAL PLAN

ANALYZING CASH FLOW

Since this is a service business, overhead will include operating expenses only. Expenses will include marketing, office expenses (fax, phone, computer, misc.), and capital investment cost recovery.

The amount of annual sales is determined based on the following assumptions:

- 5% of the attorneys in Anytown will utilize the medical/legal services of **LNC ASSOCIATES, INC.** for ten hours per year.
- 5% of retailers in Anytown will utilize the risk management and education consulting services of **LNC ASSOCIATES, INC.** for eight hours per year.
- 5% of service establishments in Anytown will utilize the risk management and education consulting services of **LNC ASSOCIATES, INC.** for eight hours per year.
- 5% of wholesale establishments in Anytown will utilize the risk management and education consulting services of **LNC ASSOCIATES, INC.** for eight hours per year.

LNC ASSOCIATES, INC. will contract with legal nurses at $25.00 per hour. No workers compensation, withholding, FICA, or unemployment will be paid for these contracted nurses. **LNC ASSOCIATES, INC.** will bill at a minimum rate of $80 per hour.

Fixed monthly expenses will include:

• Office rental		$ 750.00
• Telephone		200.00
• Utilities		100.00
• Liability Insurance		200.00
• Reference materials		50.00
• Supplies		250.00
• Miscellaneous (freight, professional development)		200.00
• Amortized cost (1 year payoff) of:		
• 2 laptop computers	333.00	
• copy machine	166.00	
• desktop computer	333.00	
• laser printer	90.00	
• typewriter	45.00	
• conference/marketing	50.00	
• software	10.00	1,027.00
		$2777.00

continued

FIGURE 5-12   Sample Business Plan   *continued*

BREAK-EVEN ANALYSIS

$$\frac{\text{Fixed Expense} + \text{Variable Cost}}{\text{Sales}}$$

Variable Expense = $25/hour paid to legal nurse consultants × 638 hours = $15,950

Fixed Cost = $2,777 monthly expense × 12 = $33,324

Sales = $80/hour × 638 hours = $51,040

$$\frac{\$15,950 + \$33,324}{\$51,040} = 97\%$$

In approximately one year, **LNC ASSOCIATES, INC.** will reach the break-even point, and will begin to show a profit, which may be reinvested in the business or paid out as dividends to stockholders.

PROFIT MARGIN

The break-even analysis may also be calculated based on the contribution margin ratio; that is, the services that must be sold to recover fixed costs. This analysis is based on the following assumptions:

- **LNC ASSOCIATES, INC.** sells services at $80 per hour
- **LNC ASSOCIATES, INC.** pays the legal nurse $25 per hour (variable costs)
- Fixed costs are estimated at $2,777 per month; that is, $52 per hour

The contribution margin ratio is the money left after variable expenses are divided into the selling price. To determine the break-even point, the fixed costs are divided by the contribution margin ratio.

$$1 - \frac{\text{(Average variable cost}}{\text{(Selling price}} = \text{CMR (expressed as \%)}$$

$$1 - \frac{(\$55}{(\$80} = 68.75\%$$

$$\frac{\text{Fixed cost}}{\text{CMR}} = \text{BREAK-EVEN}$$

$$\frac{\$2,777}{68.75\%} = \$4,039.27 \text{ per month}$$

LNC ASSOCIATES, INC. must sell approximately 50.5 hours of service per month at $80 per hour to break even.

Sales $48,480 (50.5 × 12 months × $80/hour)

Variable Exp.   −$15,150 (50.5 × 12 months × $25/hour)

Fixed Costs   −$33,324 ($2,777 × 12 months)

Profits $ 6 (Break even)

START-UP COSTS

Fixtures and Equipment:

1 fax machine (no cost-PC to include fax capability)	- 0 -
2 laptop computers	$4,000.00
1 copying machine	2,000.00
1 desk top computer with laser printer	4,000.00
Telephone with conference features	150.00
Typewriter	500.00
Answering machine	100.00
File cabinets	1,000.00
Desk and chair	1,200.00
Reference materials	1,200.00
Client furniture and lamps	600.00
	$14,750.00

Office Supplies:

Paper	100.00
Bindings	50.00
Office miscellany (paper clips, stapler, pens, hole punch, etc.)	300.00
Computer software	300.00
Computer disks	300.00
	1,050.00

Insurance:

Business Liability	200.00

Deposits for Utilities:

Telephone	250.00
Utilities (gas, electricity)	300.00
Internet provider	100.00
	650.00

continued

FIGURE 5-12 Sample Business Plan *continued*

Travel Expenses:		
Professional Development	4,000.00	
Marketing Travel	500.00	
		$4,500.00
Advertising for the Opening:		
Display/presentation	400.00	
Newspaper advertising	75.00	
Brochure	200.00	
		675.00
Other Promotional Costs:		
Promotional gifts	300.00	
Models for court exhibits	100.00	
Business cards	60.00	
Flyers	200.00	
		660.00
		$22,485.00

APPENDIX

Table of Contents

CHAPTER SUMMARY

- Starting a business involves assessing one's personal characteristics and entrepreneurial spirit, and the need for products and services the business will deliver.

- There are several types of business organizations, including sole proprietorships, partnerships, limited liability partnerships, corporations, and limited liability companies.

- Sole proprietorships consist of one owner who controls the business. Sole proprietors are personally liable for all business debts and judgments against the business.

- Partnerships consist of two or more owners who have agreed to share the risks, work, and profits or losses of a business. A partnership may consist of general partners or, in limited partnerships, limited and general partners. General partners are personally liable for all business debts; limited partners are liable to the extent of their investment in the business.

- Limited liability partnerships may be formed in some states. These partnerships may be limited to certain professions. The partners in a limited liability partnership are not liable for the negligence of other partners, although all partners are personally liable for business debts.

- A corporation is a separate legal entity formed under the laws of the state in which it is incorporated. It is owned by stockholders who elect a board of directors to oversee the management of the company. The board of directors appoints the officers who are responsible for the daily operation of the business. Stockholders in a corporation are not personally liable for the debts of the corporation.

- Limited liability companies may be formed in some states and are also considered separate legal entities. Members in limited liability companies are liable for business debts only to the extent of their individual investments in the business.

- When starting a business, certain legal matters should be considered, including protecting the title or name of the business, obtaining any necessary licenses or permits, paying all necessary taxes, and insuring the business against risk.

- A mission statement, vision statement, statement of goals, and strategic plan should be formulated for the business.

- A business plan details the nature, structure, expenses, marketing analysis, projected profits, cash-flow analysis, and key personnel in the business.

- A small business may be financed through several sources including personal savings, home equity loans, credit card purchases of business equipment and supplies, loans from friends and family, loans from banks, and loans from the Small Business Administration.

- Marketing an independent practice may involve advertising, personal contacts, attendance at conferences and seminars, collateral materials, publicity, free samples, and discounts.
- Client relations are critical to success. A client relations policy should be written.

KEY TERMS

business plan	debenture bonds	preferred stock
buy-sell agreement	equity	promoter
by-laws	general partnership	registered agent
capital	independent contractor	S corporation
cash-flow	limited liability company	service of process
collateral materials	limited liability partnership	sole proprietorship
common stock	limited partnership	subcontractor
corporation	partnership	

REVIEW QUESTIONS

1. What personal characteristics are associated with entrepreneurs?
2. Distinguish between sole proprietorships, partnerships, limited liability partnerships, corporations, and limited liability companies. What are some of the advantages and disadvantages of these organizational structures?
3. Identify some preliminary legal considerations when starting a business.
4. What is a business plan and how is it used?
5. How may a legal nurse consulting business be marketed?

INTERNET EXERCISES

1. Access the web page for this textbook at *www.westlegalstudies.com.*
2. Click on the assignments section of the web page and complete the assignment(s) for Chapter Five.

EXERCISES

1. Networking. Contact your local chamber of commerce and ask if there are any programs or opportunities for networking with other small business owners. Many communities have "Business after Hours" evenings where local business owners and community leaders meet and talk. Interview a small business owner (web page developer, computer consultant, accountant) and ask how he or she got started, what organizational structure was used and

why, how the marketing plan was developed, and what advice he or she would give about writing a business plan. The chamber of commerce or the small business owner may have information about seminars and workshops of interest to entrepreneurs. Start to build business partnerships now.

2. Professional Portfolio. Draft a personal mission statement, vision statement, and statement of goals. Jot down potential names for your business and design potential business cards, letterhead, and logos. Keep these documents for later review if or when you decide to start your own business.

ENDNOTES

1. J. K. Magnuson, BSN RN LNCC and M. Garbin, PhD RN, "Legal Nurse Consultant Practice Analysis Summary Report," *Journal of Legal Nurse Consulting* 10:1 (1999): 10–18.
2. C. J. Miller and R. Bunn, "Limited Liability Companies—a Taxing Alternative," in D. V. Davidson, B. E. Knowles, and L. M. Forsythe, *Business Law: Principles and Cases in the Legal Environment,* 5th ed. (Cincinnati: South-Western College Publishing, 1994).
3. F. S. Steingold, JD, *Legal Guide for Starting and Running a Small Business,* vol. 1, Nolo.com:www.smallbiz.findlaw.com.
4. J. C. Collins and J. I. Porras, *Built to Last: Successful Habits of Visionary Companies* (New York: HarperCollins Publishers, Inc., 1997).
5. M. McKeever, *How to Write a Business Plan,* Nolo.com:www.smallbiz.findlaw.com.
6. C. Wolf, "Your Marketing Package: Creating Your Promotional Materials" (Presentation to 10th Annual Education Conference of the American Association of Legal Nurse Consultants, Reno, Nev., 1999)
7. A. Grogan, "Medical Bill Review" (Presentation to 5th Annual Education Conference of the American Association of Legal Nurse Consultants, Houston, Texas, 1994)
8. American Association of Legal Nurse Consultants, *1999 Compensation Survey Results* (1999).

ADDITIONAL REFERENCES

AALNC Greater Detroit Chapter. "Overcoming Isolation in Independent Practice." *Journal of Legal Nurse Consulting* 9:1 (1998): 24.

AALNC Greater Detroit Chapter. "Selecting Computer Equipment for a Legal Nurse Consulting Practice." *Journal of Legal Nurse Consulting* 8:3 (1997): 13.

AALNC Greater New York Chapter. "The Basic Principles of Contracts." *Journal of Legal Nurse Consulting* 10:3 (1999): 18–19.

Bogart, J. B., RN MN, ed. *Legal Nurse Consulting: Principles and Practice.* Boston: CRC Press, 1998.

Davis, S. C., BSN RN. "Maximizing Your Professional Image." *Journal of Legal Nurse Consulting* 8:2 (1997): 19–20.

Davis, S. C., BSN RN. "Organization: One of the Keys to Better Business." *Journal of Legal Nurse Consulting* 7:4 (1996): 19–20.

Lena, E., BS RN LNCC. "The Power of Networking." *Journal of Legal Nurse Consulting* 10:2 (1999): 27–28.

McKinley, L., RN. "Options for Organizing a Legal Nurse Consultant Business." *Journal of Legal Nurse Consulting* 10:2 (1999): 22–23.

Vermeer, M., RN. "A Billing System That Works." *Journal of Legal Nurse Consulting* 7:3 (1996): 21–23.

Wise, D., RN EdD. "Cultivating Your Business." *Network News* 4:4 (1993): 1, 3.

LEGAL NURSE CONSULTANT PROFILE

LeaRae Keyes, BSN, PHN, DCMS, CCM
Life Care Planning

LeaRae Keyes, BSN, PHN, DCMS, CCM, has worked as a legal nurse consultant since 1984. She has appeared in *Who's Who in American Nursing, Who's Who in American Education, Who's Who in Medicine and Healthcare, Who's Who in Sales and Marketing,* and *Who's Who in the World.* She founded the Minnesota Case Managers Network and has served as its president. She has been treasurer and president of the Minneapolis Chapter of the American Association of Legal Nurse Consultants, and has served as a contributing editor for its newsletter. Frequently, she is called upon to make presentations, particularly about cross-cultural case management. She is currently a nurse case manager, nurse consultant, trainer, speaker, and life care planner for Keyes & Associates, Ltd., in Minneapolis, Minnesota.

What do you like best about being a legal nurse consultant?

"I like knowing that I am contributing to the legal process and that there is a system for putting a dollar value on future medical costs. It is the sense of having a unique skill. This isn't something every nurse can do. It makes me feel like I'm contributing something that is valuable in terms of the resolution of medical-legal claims."

What challenges do legal nurse consultants face in your area of law?

"There is a limited need for life care planners. It's not something you can go into thinking that you'll just do life care plans. You have to have another line of business. For me, that's case management. For someone else, it might be different, but something that lends credibility to the process and that gives you something besides being a hired expert.

"Developing credibility and initially getting that first life care plan is a challenge! I was lucky; I fell into it. I worked for a company that had nurse consultants on staff and I was their marketing director. I worked for a company that had nurse consultants on staff and I was their marketing director. I was selling services to lawyers and one of the lawyers said he would only refer the case if I did the plan. That was more than twelve years ago!"

What advice would you give nurses who are interested in legal nurse consulting?

"Patience! Don't get frustrated if you don't get business right away. If you want to work as a life care planner, you need another position to help support you and give you credibility.

"I strongly recommend classes in life care planing. Also, it is important to network with other life care planners and other legal nurse consultants.

E-mail provides an easy communication system for dialogue with life care planners. I find that when I network with other legal nurse consultants around the country, not in competition with me, we can share information. It is helpful to network with others whose opinions you value.

"Be active in AALNC. The AALNC educational seminars are outstanding! It is a professional nurturing, but it also provides me with referrals and legal nurse consultants to whom I can refer cases.

"Attorneys look at your expertise and your credentials. Be prepared to explain what the credentials mean and what it took to get them."

What unique marketing strategy are you willing to share?

"Develop a niche. Cross-cultural case management has become my area of specialty. I do a fair amount of speaking and training in this area. It helps to promote my business because people get to know what I am and my knowledge base.

"Cross-cultural understanding is essential in case management today. This understanding helps build rapport. It helps to ask questions that others less sensitive to cultural issues may not be aware of. For instance, it is very common among Asian Americans and Native Americans to use traditional medicines in addition to prescribed medications. Knowing this cultural tradition may help in ascertaining the impact of prescribed medications on the health of the client. Sensitivity to cultural differences in body language, use of color, touching, and eye contact are critical in nurse consulting today.

"Whatever the nurse's niche, capitalizing on that specialty and networking with other professionals in the field will build credibility and business."

> "Attorneys look at your expertise and your credentials. Be prepared to explain what the credentials mean and what it took to get them."

THE AMERICAN LEGAL SYSTEM

Understanding the infrastructure of the American legal system is essential to working as a legal nurse consultant. In this unit, you will find answers to the following questions:

- What founding principles guided the governing structures of the United States?

- How does the Constitution impact today's laws?

- How are laws made?

- Why do we have so many courts and what exactly do they do?

- What is the difference between criminal, civil, and administrative law?

CHAPTER 6

THE FOUNDATION FOR THE AMERICAN LEGAL SYSTEM

OBJECTIVES

In this chapter, you will discover

- common threads of legal philosophy that link current practices to past legal practices

- the purposes of laws

- the concept of "natural law"

- how the articles and amendments of the United States Constitution impact law today

- what is meant by the "living document" interpretation of the United States Constitution

OVERVIEW

Law, whether written or unwritten, has been integral to every known society regardless of the level of civilization achieved by that society. Inherent in human nature is a strong sense of fairness and rightness, of possessory interests and personal dignity. In the United States, this is embodied in the Declaration of Independence, which states, "We hold these truths to be self-evident, that all men are created equal, that they are endowed by their Creator with certain unalienable Rights, that among these are Life, Liberty and the pursuit of Happiness." The Declaration of Independence effectively broke the ties between Great Britain and the Colonies and set the stage for the creation of a separate country. It was intended to convey the message that people living in the Colonies had the right to defend themselves against attack ("Life"), the right to criticize government, worship without persecution, and install a government that protected basic rights ("Liberty"), and the right to own and protect property and personal livelihood ("pursuit of Happiness").[1]

The Declaration of Independence was based on an underlying principle of justice that all men had basic characteristics in common, and that certain fundamental rights and freedoms were natural to individuals in society. This has become known as the concept of **natural law.**

ROMAN LAW

The foundation for much of the law in the American legal system can be traced to the Roman Empire and the Justinian Code. In A.D. 533, the Roman law was collected and classified into a uniform code, the *Corpus Juris Civilis,* meaning the body of civil law.[2] It was so powerful and unifying a system that it was resurrected during the time of Napoleon in 1807 and became the basis for much of the present law in Europe.[3]

Several tenets of the Roman law have influenced the later development of law in the Western world. Included among them is the concept of equity—that fairness should be controlling and that the circumstances of the case should be considered as (or more) important than the law. The right to appeal a judgment is considered one of the most important legacies of the Roman law.

ENGLISH COMMON LAW

The Roman law was adopted throughout most of Europe, and in England many of the tenets of Roman law were employed in a legal system known as common law, because it was derived from the customs and traditions of the people. This common law was not codified and was generally unwritten as a collective tool until it was compiled and published in Blackstones' *Commentaries on the Law of England* in 1765.[4] Judges in the English courts established several principles that made the common law uniform and consistent. These principles had a profound effect on the later development of the American legal system.

Net Results

Library of Congress

The Library of Congress catalog is available on the Internet. The catalog may be searched by title, author, or key words. Access the Library of Congress via www.lcweb.loc.gov.

Precedent was established when a ruling was made based on certain facts. This precedent (prior ruling) was applied in all later cases with similar facts. The concept of following precedent is known as **stare decisis** (let the decision stand). It is the precursor of the concept of equal protection, that all would be judged under the same standard.

In 1215 the *Magna Carta* (great charter) became the basis of modern English law.[5] It provided for free elections, civil liberties, and trial by a jury of peers. The courts evolved into two distinct systems, those actions that entitled the parties to a jury (legal relief) and those that could be decided without the assistance of a jury (equitable relief). Boundary disputes and questions about title to lands were heard in courts of equity; actions involving money damages or criminal allegations were heard in courts of law. The distinction is still important, as today we classify legal matters as equitable or legal. In the United States' legal system, courts may hear both **actions at law** and **actions in equity.** (It should be noted that Louisiana, Puerto Rico, and Guam are not common law jurisdictions. Practice in these areas may be dramatically different in substance and procedure.)

SOURCES OF MODERN LAW

Today in the legal system of the United States there are numerous avenues for creating law. These sources are summarized in Figure 6-1.

Treaties are contracts between nations that outline the rules countries will abide by in their dealings with one another and the responsibilities the nations have for maintaining their mutually beneficial relationship. Treaties

FIGURE 6-1	Sources of Law
Source	**Description**
Treaties	Agreements concerning the dealings and relationship between two or more nations
Constitutions	Fundamental law approved by the people creating a separate governmental entity; outlining its organizational structure; and granting powers, rights, and privileges
Statutes	Laws made by groups of people charged with that responsibility
Case law (common law)	Court- or judge-made law; judicial opinions concerning lawful conduct or interpretation of statutes or constitutional provisions
Administrative law	Rules and regulations promulgated by officials of administrative agencies charged with the responsibility
Executive orders	Orders by the president or governor within the scope of executive authority

are enforced according to the terms of the contract, usually through trade sanctions, embargo, or military force. Treaties and customary practices among nations create **international law.**

Constitutions serve several purposes. They create a separate legal entity (the United States or a separate state), they set up a structure of government, and they provide for general rights and liberties of the people within that nation. The Constitution is the primary source of law in the United States and takes precedence over all conflicting state constitutional provisions and conflicting state and federal laws.[6]

Legislative bodies enact **statute law.** Statutes are the written laws that provide for the protection of the people within that statutory jurisdiction. This body of law includes acts of the United States Congress and laws made by state legislatures, city councils, township boards, and other representative law-making groups.

Case law, sometimes called common law or judge-made law, includes the interpretation of the language and enforcement tactics of the statutory law and the rulings concerning rights and responsibilities of people in dispute. The decision of judges becomes the precedent upon which later cases are determined, thus creating law.

In an effort to create an efficient means of managing areas of social concern on a daily basis, administrative agencies have been created. These agencies, such as the Environmental Protection Agency on the federal level and the Department of Natural Resources on the state level, promulgate rules and regulations that have the force and effect of statutory law. These rules and regulations are known as **administrative law.** (For a more complete discussion of administrative agencies, see Chapter 16).

Executive orders are laws issued by the president of the United States or the governor of a state. They have the force and effect of law if they are within the scope of authority of the executive officer. For example, President Lyndon Johnson used the executive order to require all companies doing business with the United States government to take affirmative action to employ African Americans.[7] Failure to show affirmative action in hiring blacks could result in the loss of the government contract.

PURPOSES OF LAW

There are many reasons why laws are necessary in a civilized society. The most obvious one is to create the order and stability necessary to facilitate economic strength and growth. To provide a means for resolving disputes and to promote societal objectives, such as education and public health, are also important reasons why laws need to be enacted and enforced.

For legal professionals, there is a deeper, more profound reason for laws. This ideal is embodied in the statement that law is meant "to give power to the powerless."[8] Looking for the protection in the law provides a different perspective to legal professionals and helps them defend the laws others may find prohibitive or unnecessary.

CLASSIFICATIONS OF LAW

Law is classified in many different ways. The three most common classifications are criminal, administrative, and civil. **Criminal law** involves behavior that has been identified as opposed to the public good and has been prohibited by a statute. Administrative law, discussed earlier, is any rule or regulation involving an administrative agency, such as the Equal Employment Opportunity Commission. **Civil law** is anything that is not criminal or administrative and includes lawsuits involving torts, breach of contract, divorce, antitrust, and others. Some authorities classify administrative law within the umbrella of civil law. For purposes of this textbook, administrative law will be classified separately because of its unique processes.

The law is also classified as public or private. **Public law** is enacted by a legislative body and impacts the entire population served by that legislative body. Its intent is to promote safety and the public good. **Private law** is that which pertains to the rights and responsibilities of individual parties. It may involve a lawsuit for damages resulting from injury caused by the negligence of another, or it may involve remedies for breach of contract or antitrust.

Two important classifications of law for legal professionals are substantive law and procedural law. **Substantive law** involves the theory of law (its substance) and tends to outline rights and responsibilities. **Procedural law** involves the process by which rights are preserved or responsibilities are enforced. Both substantive and procedural law are part of any legal problem. For example, knowing that a person who, with intent, causes bodily harm to another is guilty of a criminal offense and liable for damages in civil battery is to recognize the substantive law. The procedural aspect of this situation would include criminal arrest, filing of a criminal complaint, and various hearings to determine guilt. In addition, in a civil action for damages to compensate for the harm suffered, the procedural law would include the time limits within which the lawsuit must be filed and the specific rules governing that civil lawsuit. Substantive and procedural law are inextricably intertwined, even though they are often studied separately. An important point to remember is that if the substance (merit of the claim) is lacking, following the procedure will gain nothing. Conversely, if the substance is compelling but the procedure is not followed, the claim may be dismissed regardless of how meritorious it is.

APPLICATION OF LAW

No one is expected to know all the intricacies of the law. Because the law is public, however, you are expected to know and understand the laws that affect you. "Ignorance of the law is no excuse," is a phrase often used to describe this demand on society. For example, if you own an apartment that is leased to another, you profit from that lease. You will be expected to know and understand the landlord/tenant laws of your state. The fact that you don't know them will not relieve you of liability or duty to abide by those laws. If it were otherwise, anyone could easily avoid the law by simply saying, "I didn't know that!"

Laws, however, are always secondary to the facts. In the American legal system, law is not stretched to encompass the facts. The facts must clearly show that the law is called into play or the law does not apply. This concept is meant to protect individuals from the strictly enforced power of legal authority. The following hypothetical law and a hypothetical fact situation may be used to illustrate this point.

The Facts

Barrett is a college student in a town thirty miles from where her best friend Lee is going to college. In January, the Friday before school resumes after winter break, Barrett goes to visit Lee. They attend a party where they lawfully consume alcoholic beverages. Barrett leaves her friend at 3 A.M. and begins to drive home. About halfway home, Barrett decides that she is too intoxicated to continue. She pulls into the parking lot of a closed fast food restaurant, parks the car but leaves it running for warmth, pushes her seat back, and falls asleep. A police officer patrolling the area, curious about the running vehicle, stops to investigate. Barrett nearly falls out of the car when the door is opened. She cannot find her driver's license; she is disoriented and exhibits the symptoms of intoxication. The officer performs the necessary sobriety tests and takes Barrett into custody. A breathalyzer test reveals a blood alcohol content of 0.2%. Barrett is cited for operating a vehicle under the influence of intoxicants in violation of statute 136.48.

The Law

136.01 (a) This chapter shall apply to all drivers of motor vehicles on public roads within the state. . . .

136.48 It shall be unlawful to . . . operate a motor vehicle . . . g) with a blood alcohol content equal to or greater than of 0.1%. . . .

Figure 6-2 shows the facts in relation to the law.

The law must be general so that it applies to the population of citizens, but in order to call the law into play, the facts must specifically match. If the match does not exist, the law does not apply.

Ethics Bookmark

Governing Authority

Although the American Bar Association has promulgated Model Rules of Professional Conduct, each state adopts its own ethical code. As a legal professional, you should become familiar with the code that has been adopted in your state. To find this quickly, use the Internet site for legal ethics at www.legalethics.com/states.htm.

FIGURE 6-2   Facts in Relation to the Law

Law	Facts
1) operate vehicle	1) keys in ignition, car running
2) blood alcohol content of ≥0.1%	2) blood alcohol content of 0.2%
3) public road	3) fast food parking lot, 3 A.M.

In Barrett's case, it is clear that she is operating a vehicle with a blood alcohol content that is greater than or equal to 0.1%. The issue (whether the fact fits the law) is whether the parking lot of a fast food restaurant is a public road at 3 A.M. The prosecutor would argue that it is a public road during regular business hours of the restaurant and for a reasonable time afterwards. This is because the fast food restaurant invites the public to transact business on its property, therefore holding its parking lot out for public use. But is it still a public road well after closing? The court in one state said no![9] Barrett was not endangering others; she was not operating a vehicle on a public road while under the influence of intoxicants. The court determined that the parking lot of the fast food restaurant at 3 A.M. was private property (see *City of Kenosha v. Phillips,* 142 Wis. 2d 549, 419 N.W. 236 [1988]).

This concept of general laws narrowly construed according to the circumstances is another result of the historical concern of protecting the less powerful (individuals) from the more powerful (government).

FORCES THAT IMPACT LAW

The American legal system is dynamic. It is meant to be flexible in order to accommodate justice in a way that will meet the ever-changing needs of a diverse citizenry. The United States Constitution is said to be a living document because as new issues and technologies become part of our social fabric, the law (with its roots in the Constitution) must adapt and provide direction for future relationships, and remedies that are equitable.[10]

Sometimes the law may seem contradictory. For example, a fourteen year old who is suspected of shoplifting will be tried in juvenile court and may be found delinquent (distinguished from guilty). The juvenile will be held in a restricted educational facility for the period of correction, or until the juvenile reaches majority or the age specified by state statute. However that same fourteen year old suspected of committing murder may be tried as an adult in adult court and be sentenced accordingly. How is it that a fourteen year old may be viewed as a child in one circumstance and as an adult in another? The only answer is in the evolving nature of the law itself and the lawmakers efforts to protect the people served by the law. There are numerous other illustrations of dichotomy in the law, yet the social good at the time demands a response from the law, and the law, created by people, simply does the best it can to balance and give credit to opposing points of view.

The law does not depend entirely on precedent to determine the future. For example, there are no prior rulings to assist courts in determining the rights, responsibilities, and relationships of parties who claim ownership in outer space or who have been involved in biogenetic engineering or cloning. In these situations, there is little to guide the court except the prevailing social, ethical, and economic forces of the day. Education, health care, and employment are all social issues that are reflected in legal determinations, along with the mores, norms, and religious thoughts of the people of the time.

Net Results

Constitutions on the Net

The United States government, under an initiative by Attorney General Janet Reno, has developed internet access to almost all government laws, including the United States Constitution. Additionally, most states provide access to their state constitutions via the World Wide Web. Subject searches are available using Boolean search techniques. Access the United States Constitution using the web site established for the White House at www2.whitehouse.gov. *The United States Constitution is also available at the web site for the American Civil Liberties Union,* www.aclu.org. *All state constitutions are available at* www.findlaw.com, *and individual state governments may be accessed using the almost universal address* www.legis.state.XX.us *where the XX is replaced by the two-letter postal abbreviation for the state being researched.*

In addition to responding to social change, the laws sometimes mandate social change. The abolishment of slavery, bigamy, and employment discrimination are examples of laws that lead society in its beliefs and economic structure. The changes are not always welcome, but if the law is just, the mandates are gradually accepted until eventually people cannot believe it could ever have been otherwise.

The United States Constitution is the infrastructure of the legal system. The courts in the United States have the mission of being the supreme protectors of rights identified in the constitution.

THE UNITED STATES CONSTITUTION

The Constitution is the original document that created the United States. It was approved by its citizens through the vote of delegates. A constitution has three functions: (a) it creates the new nation or state as a separate legal entity, (b) it outlines the system of government for that new nation or state, and (c) it provides for basic rights and privileges of the citizens of that nation or state.

Because it is the founding document, it is considered **primary law** (the first letter of the law), with which all other laws must be consistent. It is the yardstick against which all other government action is measured. In addition, the United States Constitution attempts to ensure a measure of dignity and power to every individual living in the United States. Although government is important to a civilized society, the Constitution made it clear that in American society, the government must not become more powerful than the people it serves.

THE TWO PARTS OF THE CONSTITUTION

The original Constitution, as adopted by nine colonies in 1787, contained only seven articles. The primary focus of those articles was the structure of the new government and a balance of power within the government that would work for the good of the people. Although many of the articles also contain provisions that protect the citizens of the United States, the original seven articles are generally viewed as the part of the Constitution that established the structure of government.

In 1791, the Bill of Rights was ratified and became part of the Constitution. These amendments articulate certain civil rights that provide the citizens of the United States with protection from the power of government. Although many of the amendments deal with the structure of government, they are considered to be the part of the Constitution that established civil liberties.

PURPOSES OF THE CONSTITUTION

The reasons for creating the Constitution are clearly articulated in the **preamble.** A preamble is often used in legal documents and provides the rationale for the action, agreement, or authorizing language that follows. Why this legal action is being taken which in the case of a constitution is why this legal entity, nation, or state must stand alone, is important for the interpretation of the remainder of the document.

The following are identified as purposes of the United States Constitution:

- to form a more perfect union
- to establish justice
- to ensure domestic tranquility
- to provide for the common defense
- to promote the general welfare
- to secure the blessings of liberty

THE ARTICLES OF THE UNITED STATES CONSTITUTION

The seven articles of the original Constitution were mainly concerned with the structure of the government and the powers to be exercised by each branch of government. The articles are summarized in Figure 6-3.

FIGURE 6-3	Articles of the United States Constitution
Article	**Description**
Article 1	Established the legislative branch comprised of two houses (the Senate and the House of Representatives) and empowered to make laws, coin money, collect taxes, establish a system of highways and a postal system, and regulate interstate commerce. All budget bills must start in the House of Representatives. This article prohibited *ex post facto* laws, *habeas corpus,* and *writs of attainder.*
Article II	Established the executive branch comprised of the president, the vice president, and the cabinet, and empowered the president to be commander in chief of the armed forces, to enter into treaties with other countries, and to appoint federal judges. Treaties and appointments to the judiciary must be approved by the Senate. The president has the power to veto laws passed by Congress (although the veto may be overridden by 2/3 vote of Congress).
Article III	Established the Supreme Court and authorized legislation to establish a court system. Federal courts are the supreme protectors of Constitutional rights.
Article IV	Provided that all states give full faith and credit to the laws of other states.
Article V	Provided the guidelines for amending or changing the Constitution.
Article VI	Provided that the Constitution, laws, and treaties of the United States shall be the supreme law of the land.
Article VII	Established ratification provisions for the Constitution.

FIGURE 6-4 Amendments to the United States Constitution

Amendment	Description
First	Freedom of religion, freedom of speech, freedom of the press, the right to peacefully assemble, and the right to petition the government to redress grievances (sometimes known as fundamental or primary rights)
Second	The right to keep and bear arms to ensure a free state
Third	Soldiers may not be quartered in private homes during peacetime without permission (sometimes referred to as the security of homeowners)
Fourth	Protection from unreasonable search and seizure; warrants must be based on probable cause
Fifth	"No person shall be . . . deprived of life, liberty, or property . . . without due process of law," protection from self-incrimination; protection from double jeopardy; the right to just compensation for property taken by the government for public purposes.
Sixth	The right to a speedy and public trial, the right to a jury in criminal matters, the right to confront witnesses, and the right to legal counsel
Seventh	The right to a jury trial in civil matters
Eighth	Protection from cruel and unusual punishment
Ninth	The rights enumerated under the Constitution shall not restrict or abridge other rights of citizens
Tenth	Restriction of powers of federal government to those identified in the Constitution; all others reserved to the states
Thirteenth	Abolishment of slavery and involuntary servitude
Fourteenth	"[n]o state shall make or enforce any law which shall abridge the privileges or immunities of citizens of the United States; nor shall any State deprive any person of life, liberty, or property, without due process of law; nor deny to any person within its jurisdiction the equal protection of the laws"
Fifteenth	The right to vote regardless of race, color, or previous condition of servitude
Twenty-fourth	The right to vote shall not be denied or abridged on the basis of failure to pay poll tax or any other tax
Twenty-sixth	The right to vote shall not be denied to anyone eighteen years of age or older
Twenty-seventh	Any pay raise Congress votes for itself shall not be effective until after the next election of representatives

THE AMENDMENTS TO THE CONSTITUTION

To date, there have been only twenty-seven amendments to the United States Constitution. Many of these additions concern the rights and privileges of residents of the United States. Important amendments, including the Bill of Rights, are summarized in Figure 6-4.

THE "LIVING DOCUMENT" INTERPRETATION

The United States Supreme Court has interpreted the Constitution to embody the spirit of liberty and a responsive government. It is not intended to be static; rather it is dynamic, changing with new technologies and new social concepts. Thus, the Supreme Court of the United States has adopted a "living document" philosophy about cases involving the interpretation of the Constitution. Certainly the framers of the Constitution could not have envisioned automobile or air travel, biogenetics or bioengineering. Because of the continuous nature of change in society, the courts must respond by recognizing the flexibility built into the language of the Constitution. The infrastructure of the Constitution is apparent in all other aspects of the legal system.

CHAPTER SUMMARY

- Roman law and English common law were powerful influences on the development of the American legal system.
- Natural law includes rights that people believe are inherent in human activities.
- There are several classifications of law including criminal law, civil law, administrative law, public law, private law, substantive law, and procedural law.
- The facts of the case control whether the law applies.
- Economic, social, religious, technological, and ethical forces impact the development of law.
- The Constitution is the founding document of the United States and is the supreme law of the land.
- The articles of the Constitution generally deal with the framework of government.
- The amendments to the Constitution generally deal with civil liberties.
- The United States Constitution has been interpreted as a "living" document, reflecting changes in society.

KEY TERMS

actions at law	executive orders	procedural law
actions in equity	international law	public law
administrative law	natural law	stare decisis
case law	preamble	statute law
civil law	precedent	substantive law
constitutions	primary law	treaties
criminal law	private law	

REVIEW QUESTIONS

1. What contributions did the Roman law and English common law make to modern American legal principles?
2. Distinguish between civil, criminal, and administrative law.
3. Why is it necessary to have laws?
4. What is meant by natural law?
5. What, in your opinion, is the difference between law and justice?
6. Why was it necessary to adopt the United States Constitution?
7. Why is the United States Constitution described as a "living document?"

INTERNET EXERCISES

1. Access the web page for this textbook at *www.westlegalstudies.com.*
2. Click on the assignments section and complete the assignment(s) for Chapter Six.

EXERCISES

1. Networking. For any organization of which you are a member (e.g., local or state nurses association or chapter of the AALNC), ask to see the constitution, charter, or articles of incorporation of that organization. Volunteer to serve on a by-laws committee or as a delegate to a state or national conference. The law-making activities of an organization on a small scale are similar to the law-making activities of state legislative bodies. Get involved!

2. Professional Portfolio. For each activity in which you have participated in any organization (e.g., nurses associations, civic and charitable organizations), document the nature of the activity (e.g., food bank, walk for hunger, etc.), the legalities necessary to complete the activity (e.g., governmental officials, permits, etc.), and the leadership role you played in organizing the activity. Maintain this list in your portfolio as evidence of service to the broader community.

ENDNOTES

1. D. Carper et al., *Understanding the Law,* 2nd ed. (St. Paul, Minnesota: West Publishing Company, 1995).

2. T. R. Van DerVort, *American Law and the Legal System: Equal Justice Under the Law,* 2nd ed. (Albany, NY: West Thomson Learning, 2000).

3. Ibid.

4. Ibid.

5. D. Carper et al., *Understanding the Law,* 2nd ed. (St. Paul, Minnesota: West Publishing Company, 1995).

6. U.S. Const. art. VI.

7. D. Carper et al., *Understanding the Law,* 2nd ed. (St. Paul, Minnesota: West Publishing Company, 1995).

8. Ibid.

9. *City of Kenosha v. Phillips,* 142 Wis. 2d 549, 419 N.W. 2d 236 (1988).

10. B. Walston-Dunham, *Introduction to Law,* 3rd ed. (Albany, NY: West Thomson Learning, 1999).

11. American Bar Association, *Annotated Model Rules of Professional Conduct,* (1999) 4th Edition Rule 1.6. Copies of ABA, *Model Code of Professional Responsibility, 1999 Edition,* are available from Service Center, American Bar Association, 750 North Lake Shore Drive, Chicago, IL 60611-4497, 1-800-285-2221.

CHAPTER 7

RESOLUTION OF LEGAL DISPUTES

OBJECTIVES

In this chapter, you will discover

■ the types of litigation in the American Legal System

■ the relief that is available in a civil action

■ how jurisdiction impacts litigation

■ the structure of the federal judiciary

OVERVIEW

The historical concepts of justice and natural rights that are embodied in the United States Constitution are the foundation upon which all other law in the country is built. The judiciary is responsible for ensuring that these basic tenets remain alive, preserving the best of our legal traditions in the current philosophies, technologies, and social patterns of the day. In addition, the courts of the United States are charged with being the supreme protectors of human rights, ensuring that due process is afforded every citizen and lawful resident of this country.

LITIGATION

Litigation is the most recognized vehicle for protecting legal rights. Litigation is simply the process of a lawsuit through the judicial system. It includes filing the complaint, serving the summons, responding to the complaint, discovery, pretrial hearings, trial, and post-trial activities.

TYPES OF LITIGATION

There are three basic types of litigation: criminal, administrative, and civil. An illustration of the differences among the three types of litigation is included in Figure 7-1. It is important to think of the three lanes or avenues to justice as separate and distinct. In a civil lawsuit, the wrongful party will be liable but will not go to jail. The conduct may be unlawful (meaning that it has been defined in case law or common law as a violation of duty), but it may not be illegal. The procedures and remedies for each type of litigation are unique and do not overlap.

FIGURE 7-1 **Comparison of Criminal, Administrative, and Civil Litigation**

	Criminal	Administrative	Civil
Party commencing the lawsuit	District (city or state) attorney on behalf of society	Agency official on behalf of agency	Injured party
Purposes	Protect society	Promote stability in area of social concern	Recover for economic losses
Burden of proof	Beyond a reasonable doubt	Greater weight of the evidence or clear and convincing evidence	Greater weight of the evidence; more likely than not
Remedies	Fines, imprisonment, rehabilitation, community service	Fines, orders to adjust or cease activities, enjoin activity	Compensatory damages, equitable remedies

Criminal

Criminal litigation involves offenses against society. It is based on the statutory law, usually called the Criminal Code, which identifies illegal activities and the classification of punishment for those persons found guilty of engaging in prohibited activities. In a criminal litigation, society is represented by a city attorney, district attorney, state's attorney, or United State's attorney. For most cases, the facts must be proved beyond a reasonable doubt in order to convict the accused. Because these offenses are deemed to be against the public good, a person convicted of violating the criminal code is often removed from society (jailed or imprisoned) for a period of time or is subject to alternative sentences such as probation or community service. The person is subject to fines and sometimes to court costs and defense fees. In addition, counseling, public service, or some rehabilitative requirements may be part of the consequences of being convicted.

Administrative

Administrative litigation involves conflicts with administrative agencies, such as the Internal Revenue Service or the Department of Natural Resources. A person who receives a notice of violation, often called a citation, of an agency regulation is not found guilty of a criminal offense even if the agency establishes the violation at a hearing. In fact, violations of administrative law are considered civil offenses, which result in fines or orders to cease the activity that violates administrative law.

Civil

Civil litigation involves any other action that is not criminal or administrative. Contract disputes, personal injury lawsuits, health care liability, antitrust, marital dissolution, and disputes involving property all fall within the realm of civil litigation. The parties involved in civil litigation are individuals or companies. The party seeking justice must generally prove by the greater weight of the evidence that the other party's wrongful conduct caused harm. The usual remedy in civil litigation is money in the form of compensatory damages. However, there are several other remedies that may be available to an injured party. These remedies are more fully described later in this chapter.

Another way to visualize the differences between the three roads to justice is to use an example. When a tenant writes a worthless check to a landowner, the landowner can turn the check over to the district attorney who will prosecute the tenant for violation of the criminal code. That prosecution (criminal litigation) will result in fines and jail time, but it will not get the rent paid unless the court orders restitution. To collect the rent, the landowner must sue the tenant in a civil lawsuit for the value of the unpaid rent and whatever other reasonable expenses were incurred as a result of the tenant's worthless check.

Similarly, if the tenant refuses to pay rent because the premises are not properly heated, the housing authority (administrative agency) may inspect

---

FIGURE 7-2   An Illustration of Criminal, Civil, and Administrative Litigation

	Criminal	Civil	Administrative
Worthless check for value of rent	Tenant is fined and may be jailed		
Civil lawsuit in small claims by landowner to collect value of worthless check (rent)		Tenant is found not liable for the rent, since premises were not adequately heated	
Housing authority notified of inadequate heat on premises			Landowner is cited for violating housing code

---

the property and issue a citation to the landowner (administrative litigation). This still does not get the rent paid, and the landowner may sue the tenant in a civil lawsuit for breach of the rental contract. In this case, however, the tenant may have a legitimate defense for not paying, which would be recognized by the court. This description of the difference between criminal, civil, and administrative litigation is summarized in Figure 7-2.

The difference between criminal and civil is often described by using certain types of wrongful conduct. For example, in most states the criminal act of battery requires proof that the person inflicting the battery intended to cause bodily harm and did cause bodily harm, and that the person injured did not in any way consent or permit the physical contact that caused the bodily harm. If someone deliberately punched another person in the nose, the elements of criminal battery would be relatively easy to discern, and the person charged would probably be found guilty of battery. This does not, however, pay for the medical expenses to have the injured party's broken nose treated. To recover for these expenses, courts may order restitution or the injured party may sue in a civil lawsuit. Here, the criminal act of battery and the civil action in battery arise from the same circumstances.

There are circumstances, however, that give rise to only one type of litigation. For example, an elderly woman is attempting to sit down in a lawn chair when it is pulled out from under her. She falls and breaks her hip. The act of pulling the chair out from under her would be sufficient to constitute a civil action in battery.[1] The physical contact results in harm to her and the intent, though only to play a prank and not to harm her, is sufficient to show that the conduct was wrongful and that there was reasonable certainty that harm would result. While this situation may give rise to a civil lawsuit, it would not be a criminal battery because there was no intent to cause bodily harm.

Because legal nurse consultants most often work in civil litigation, it will be the primary focus of this chapter.

REMEDIES IN CIVIL LITIGATION

In theory, courts mete out justice. It is a human attempt to right wrongs, to balance the scales, and to make the injured party whole. In civil litigation, there are basically two types of remedies: damages and equitable remedies.

Damages

Damages are money awards. The two categories of money damages are compensatory and punitive.

Compensatory damages are intended to repay the injured party for expenses that would not have been incurred but for the wrongful conduct of another. In contract disputes, these damages involve the expenses immediate to the breach of contract and the lost business that results as a foreseeable consequence of the breach of contract. In personal injury claims, compensatory damages include past and future medical expenses, past and future loss of income, and past and future pain and suffering. In addition, in personal injury claims, the family of the injured party may be entitled to a variety of separate actions as determined by state law, such as **loss of companionship.** This action is based on the recognized right of a spouse, children, or parents to the support, comfort, affection, and household maintenance services of the injured party, which are a natural part of familial living.

Punitive damages are sometimes called exemplary damages because they are intended to make an example of the defendant. The most important thing to remember about punitive damages is that this award of money has nothing to do with the losses of the injured party. Rather, this award is made to punish the outrageous conduct of the wrongful party. If the party causing the injury has acted with spite, malice, reckless indifference, or reckless disregard, or if the conduct of the party causing injury is heinous or especially reprehensible, the court may impose punitive damages. They are meant to act as a deterrent and to send the message that this conduct will not be tolerated by the courts.

Punitive damages have been awarded in cases against automobile manufacturers who were aware of dangerous defects in the automobiles when the automobiles were put on the market. More recently, punitive damages have been awarded in tobacco litigation and in litigation involving diet drugs.

Equitable Remedies

When the potential injury to the plaintiff cannot be prevented or recompensed, the laws of some states allow remedies in equity. **Equity** has a long history in English common law; in fact, there were separate courts of law for damages and for equity or non-money awards. Disputes about title or boundaries to land are good examples of cases that are in equity; that is, the rights of the parties to the property will not be satisfied with an award of money. The parties, instead, are interested in ascertaining and preserving their rights in the land. Thus, equity actions result in remedies based on fairness. In the

---

Ethics Bookmark

Frivolous Claims

"A lawyer shall not bring or defend a proceeding . . . unless there is a basis for doing so that is not frivolous," Annotated Model Rules of Professional Conduct, Fourth Edition, Rule 3.1 copyright 1999*[2] A frivolous claim is one that has no foundation in law or in fact. Attorneys are obligated to uphold the ideal of obtaining justice through the judicial system. A claim that has no foundation unduly ties up the system and the resources of the parties. In essence, a frivolous claim makes a mockery of the justice system, the parties, and the attorney as well as the attorney's firm and staff. Attorneys are subject to severe sanctions for misuse of the judicial system. Legal nurse consultants must be aware that all claims brought to court must have a reasonable basis in fact and law.*
*American Bar Association. Reprinted by permission of the American Bar Association. American Bar Association, *Annotated Model Rules of Professional conduct,* 4th ed. (1999) Rule 3.1. Copies of Model Code of Professional Responsibility, 1999 edition are available from Service Center, American Bar Association, 750 North Lake Shore Drive, Chicago, IL 60611-4497, 1-800-285-2221.

United States legal system, there are no separate equity courts. Rather, the courts hear both cases at law and cases in equity.

The most common example of a remedy in equity is the **injunction.** An injunction is a court order that prohibits certain conduct or requires that an activity cease, such as the sale of a parcel of land or the airing of an unauthorized version of a copyrighted song.

Another remedy in equity that is used in contract cases is known as **specific performance.** Specific performance is a court order that requires the parties to complete the transfer of certain unique property that has been bargained for. The order cannot be used to compel personal services, but where the subject matter of the contract is unique property that cannot be obtained otherwise in the marketplace, an order of specific performance may be the only remedy that is satisfactory.

JURISDICTION

Before any remedy at law or in equity is available, the action must be brought to a court that has the power to provide a remedy. This power is known as **jurisdiction.** While traditionally, this connotes a geographic territory, a more appropriate understanding of jurisdiction, when referring to the courts in the United States, is authority or power to act. This authority is derived from statutory or constitutional provisions and is not within the discretion of the individual courts. To be effective in administering justice, courts must have both subject matter jurisdiction and personal jurisdiction.

Subject Matter Jurisdiction

Subject matter jurisdiction is conferred by legislation. It authorizes the court to act on certain problems. If the court does not have the requisite power to hear and decide this type of controversy, any judgment rendered by that court is moot and cannot be enforced. There are several classes of subject matter jurisdiction, the most common of which are described in Figure 7-3.

To have the case begin in this court and the power of the court to make the first decision on the facts and law of the case is known as **original jurisdiction.** It is presumed that all state trial courts have original **general jurisdiction;** that is, that the courts can hear and decide any matter within their geographical territories. The federal trial courts, on the other hand, have **limited,** original **jurisdiction** and can only hear the types of cases that meet federal statutory guidelines. In almost all circumstances, a case brought in federal court may also be brought in state court. The courts have **concurrent jurisdiction,** meaning both courts have the power to resolve this problem. If one of the parties is not satisfied with the outcome of a court having original jurisdiction, the action may be appealed to a court having the power to review decisions of other courts. This is known as **appellate jurisdiction.**

FIGURE 7-3   Classes of Subject Matter Jurisdiction

Jurisdiction	Explanation	Court
Original	The first court to have power to hear and decide the facts and law	Trial courts
General	Power to hear and decide any matter within the geographic territory of the court	State trial courts
Limited	Power of the court is restricted to cases that meet statutory requirements	Federal trial courts
Appellate	Power to review the decision of courts to determine if the law was correctly applied	State and federal courts of appeals and supreme courts
Concurrent	Two or more courts have power to hear and decide the case	State courts and federal courts
Bankruptcy	This court is the ONLY court with power to hear and decide this case	Bankruptcy court, tax court, patent court, etc.

In cases involving bankruptcy, patent, and tax, **exclusive jurisdiction** is vested with adjunct federal courts. No other courts have the power to resolve these disputes, and the cases may not originate in any other court. The first consideration when commencing a lawsuit is to ensure that the court has subject matter jurisdiction.

Personal Jurisdiction

To make its decision enforceable upon the parties, the court must have **personal jurisdiction.** By filing the lawsuit with a particular court, the plaintiff voluntarily submits to the jurisdiction of that court. In order to bind the defendant to the jurisdiction of the court, personal jurisdiction must be established. Most state court rules or statutes provide for personal jurisdiction over residents of the state and those who do business within the state. But personal jurisdiction does not automatically vest simply because the defendant resides in the county where the lawsuit is filed. Personal jurisdiction on the defendant is said to be "perfected by **service of process.**" The due process requirements that a defendant be notified of the claims against him or her are met when the summons and complaint are delivered to the defendant. **Service** generally means delivery of a legal document to the other party or parties in the lawsuit. If service is in all respects fair, proper, and timely, the defendant cannot dispute the power of the court to resolve the dispute between the parties and to enforce the resolution against them.

Besides personally delivering the documents to the defendant, personal jurisdiction may arise under other circumstances. If the claim involves a property dispute and the property is situated in the geographical territory of the court, the court has *in rem* **jurisdiction.** Any decision regarding the property is binding on anyone with a claim on the property, regardless of where the party resides or does business.

Additionally, the "attachment" power of the court exists with what is known as *quasi in rem* **jurisdiction.** *Quasi in rem* jurisdiction is the power of the court to satisfy a money judgment with property located within its geographic territory. The court may constructively seize (attach) the property, have the property sold, and apply the proceeds of the sale to pay the unsatisfied money judgment. Even though the property was not the subject of the lawsuit, the court has the power to enforce the decision against anyone with a claim on the property.

FEDERAL COURT SYSTEM

An understanding of the structure of the dual court systems in the United States hinges on the concept of jurisdiction. Knowing which courts have power to determine the rights of the parties is critical to working within the system. Each state has its own system of courts that generally run parallel with the federal courts. The courts of the United States are depicted in Figure 7-4.

The Constitution established the Supreme Court and authorized Congress to establish such inferior courts as may be necessary. The Judiciary Act of 1791 set up the current structure of the federal courts.

The trial courts in the federal system are known as district courts. There is at least one United States District Court in each state, and several states have two or more. The jurisdiction of the district courts is outlined in the United States Code[3] and includes actions involving:

- admiralty
- commerce and antitrust litigation
- patents, copyrights, trademarks, and unfair competition
- civil rights
- United States as plaintiff or defendant

The limited original jurisdiction of the district courts is generally associated with **diversity jurisdiction** and **federal question jurisdiction.**[4] Diversity of citizenship, or diversity jurisdiction, arises when all of the parties on either side of the lawsuit are residents of different states and the amount in controversy exceeds $75,000. Federal question jurisdiction arises anytime a United States law or a constitutional issue arises in a case. The fact that the district courts have limited original jurisdiction does not prohibit state trial courts from hearing and deciding these same matters. In cases where courts have concurrent jurisdiction, the parties may determine in which court the action will be brought.

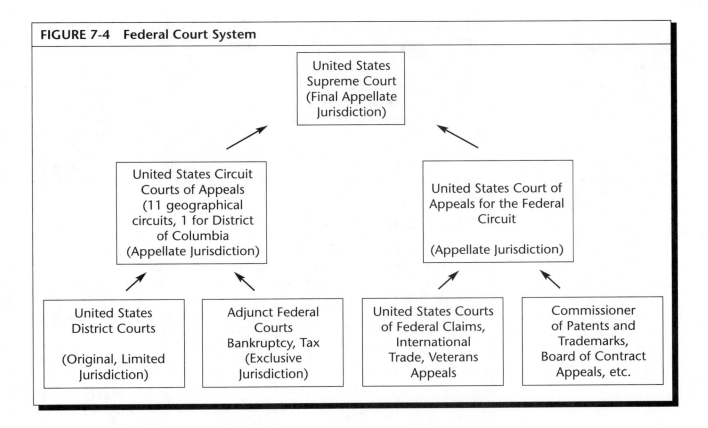

FIGURE 7-4 Federal Court System

There are eleven geographical circuit courts of appeals in the federal system. In addition, there is a court of appeals for the District of Columbia and a court of appeals for the federal circuit (hearing appeals from the Court of International Trade, the United States Claims Court, the Court of Military Appeals, and the Patent Court). The courts of appeals in the federal system have **appellate jurisdiction as a matter of right.** This means that the courts have no power to refuse an appeal. The due process rights of residents of the United States provides for at least one objective review of a previous decision. This appeal cannot be denied; therefore, the judges in the courts of appeals have no discretionary power over the cases brought before them.

The Supreme Court has limited original jurisdiction in rare cases in which one state sues another, a state sues the United States, or a claim involves a public ambassador. The primary function of the Supreme Court, however, is its appellate review. Since review is generally discretionary, the process for requesting review is known as **_certiorari._** Translated, _certiorari_ means to be more fully informed or to be more certain. A petition for _certiorari_ requests that one more objective review be made of the law in the case so that it will be more certain that the law was correctly and fairly applied.

Of the thousands of cases for which petitions for *certiorari* to the Supreme Court are made, fewer than one hundred are annually granted review.

The judges in the federal district courts, the federal circuit courts of appeals, and the Supreme Court are appointed by the president, approved by the Senate, and serve for life or until voluntary retirement (unless impeached).

In addition to the district courts, there are adjunct federal courts that have been created to shoulder the burden of numerous cases in specialized legal areas. These courts include bankruptcy courts, the Court of International Trade, the United States Claims Court, and the United States Patent Court. The judges who serve in adjunct courts are considered magistrates and do not have the privileges of federal judges. In bankruptcy court, for example, the judge is appointed by the president to serve a fourteen-year term.[5]

STATE COURT SYSTEMS

Most of the states follow a three-tiered system that is similar to the United States court system, including trial courts, intermediate courts of appeals, and a supreme court. Some states, such as North Dakota, only have two levels and the Supreme Court hears all appeals from the trial courts of that state. While the basic structure of the courts may be similar, the names of the courts may not. In New York, for instance, the superior court is the trial court, while in California, the highest court is the court of appeals.

In some states, trial courts may be limited to hearing only certain types of matters; e.g., family court, criminal court, civil court, etc. Most states now have small claims courts that allow parties to pursue claims having a minimal monetary value. The parties need not be represented by attorneys, and the procedures are simplified so as to facilitate justice without undue cost. The parties may present their cases to a court commissioner or justice of the peace rather than a judge, and they may be referred for mediation in an effort to settle the dispute. If a party is not satisfied with a decision at the small claims court level, there are procedural provisions for moving the case from the small claims court to the trial court.

The infrastructure of the court system, the makeup of the judges, and the prevailing philosophies of justice in each region are important components of successful litigation. Legal nurse consultants should become familiar with the state and federal courts in the areas in which they will be working. This knowledge will help equip nurses with the necessary background to assist in the cost-effective evaluation of claims and defenses.

CHAPTER SUMMARY

- Litigation is the process of resolving legal disputes.
- There are three separate and distinct classifications of litigation: criminal, administrative, and civil.

- Remedies in civil litigation include compensatory and punitive damages, and equitable remedies, such as injunctions.

- For a court to make and enforce a decision, it must have subject matter and personal jurisdiction.

- Subject matter jurisdiction may be original, general, limited, concurrent, appellate, or exclusive.

- Personal jurisdiction must be perfected by service of process.

- Federal trial court jurisdiction is generally based on diversity of citizenship and federal or Constitutional issues.

- *Certiorari* is the process for requesting review by an appeals court with discretionary appellate jurisdiction.

KEY TERMS

appellate jurisdiction	exclusive jurisdiction	loss of companionship
appellate jurisdiction as a matter of right	federal question jurisdiction	original jurisdiction
certiorari	general jurisdiction	personal jurisdiction
compensatory damages	*in rem* jurisdiction	punitive damages
concurrent jurisdiction	injunction	*quasi in rem* jurisdiction
diversity jurisdiction	jurisdiction	service of process
equity	limited jurisdiction	specific performance
	litigation	subject matter jurisdiction

REVIEW QUESTIONS

1. Explain the three types of litigation.
2. What remedies are available in civil litigation?
3. How are subject matter jurisdiction and personal jurisdiction different? Which must the court have?
4. Diagram the federal court system.

INTERNET EXERCISES

1. Access the web page for this textbook at *www.westlegalstudies.com*.
2. Click on the assignments section and complete the assignment(s) for Chapter Seven.

EXERCISES

1. Networking. Using the Blue Book (identified in Chapter Four), identify the following officials in the county court serving the county where you live: clerk of court, district attorney, judges, court commissioners or justices of the peace, sheriff, law librarian, court administrator, and any others with whom you may be dealing as a legal nurse consultant. Prepare a quick reference sheet including names, positions, and telephone numbers for these officials.

2. Professional Portfolio. Using the Blue Book, prepare or copy a diagram of the court system in your state. Include in the diagram the names and telephone numbers of officials within the system. Maintain the reference sheet prepared in Exercise One and this diagram in your professional portfolio.

ENDNOTES

1. *Garratt v. Dailey,* 46 Wash. 2d 197, 279 P. 2d 1091 (1955).

2. American Bar Association. *Model Rules of Professional Conduct,* (1994) 4th Edition Rule 3.1. Copies of ABA *Model Code of Professional Responsibility, 1999 Edition* are available from Service Center, American Bar Association, 750 North Lake Shore Drive, Chicago, IL 60611-4497, 1-800-285-2221.

3. 28 U.S.C. § 1333, 1337, 1338, 1343, 1345, 1346.

4. 28 U.S.C. § 1332, *et seq.*

5. Bankruptcy Reform Act of 1994, 11 U.S.C. §101 *et seq.*

ADDITIONAL REFERENCES

Bogart, J. B., RN MN, ed. *Legal Nurse Consulting: Principles and Practice.* Boston: CRC Press, 1998.

Carper, D., et al. *Understanding the Law,* 2nd ed. St. Paul, Minnesota: West Publishing Company, 1995.

Loecker, B., MSEd RN. "A Look at the U.S. Court Systems." *Journal of Legal Nurse Consulting* 7:3 (1996): 18–19, 23.

CHAPTER 8

THREE LANES: CRIMINAL, ADMINISTRATIVE, CIVIL

OBJECTIVES

In this chapter, you will discover

- the classifications of crimes

- the general process of criminal litigation

- what happens during a criminal trial

- how administrative litigation is generally conducted

- the process of civil litigation

- what options, besides going to court, are available for resolving legal disputes

OVERVIEW

The three roads to justice—criminal, administrative, and civil—were identified in Chapter Eight. Each process is intended to resolve a different type of legal dispute. Each has different processes with different remedies. Recognizing the differences is foundational to legal work. There are sometimes alternatives for resolving legal disputes other than following the traditional track. It is important to recognize when alternatives (discussed later in this chapter) may work in the best interests of the parties and the community.

CRIMINAL LAW

The area of law that is designed to provide a safe and respectful environment for community living is criminal law. Simply put, a **crime** is a wrong against the public good, for which a punishment is prescribed. The area of criminal law is founded upon legislation proscribing certain behavior.

To be guilty of any crime, two essential elements generally must be proven: ***mens rea*** (guilty intent) and ***actus reus*** (wrongful conduct). Criminal intent is sometimes referred to as evil knowledge or wrongful purpose. It is the knowledge that one is acting in violation of the law and the victim's rights in the desire or purpose of carrying out the act. The behavior that violates the law is the criminal conduct. To be found guilty of any crime, it must be proven that the accused acted in violation of the law and knew that the action was wrong.

Criminal negligence or negligent homicide is an exception to the *mens rea* rule. These criminal acts do not require strict proof of the state of mind of the actor; in fact, no state of mind need be proven at all. It is sufficient to show that the accused acted with reckless indifference or negligent disregard. Homicide by reckless use of a weapon and injury caused by driving while intoxicated fall within the criminal negligent exception to *mens rea*.

TWO CLASSES OF CRIMES

A **felony** is a crime that is designated by the legislature to be so serious that a person convicted of the act is imprisoned for one year or more. If the offense is such that the legislature says that punishment should be for less than one year, it is classified as a **misdemeanor.** A person convicted of a misdemeanor generally is incarcerated in the county jail and may be entitled to work or school release privileges. Additionally, the legislature may create a dividing line to distinguish which criminal act is a misdemeanor and which is a felony. For instance, many states identify theft as a misdemeanor so long as the value or the combined value of the items stolen is less than $1,000. If the value is $1,000 or more, the theft is classified as a felony.

Within each classification are several additional classes. Figure 8-1 identifies a typical felony classification structure.

FIGURE 8-1   Classification of Felonies

	Term of Imprisonment	Fine*	Example
Class A	Life imprisonment		Intentional Homicide
Class B	Not to exceed 60 years	$10,000	Reckless Homicide
Class BC	Not to exceed 30 years	$10,000	Second degree sexual assault
Class C	Not to exceed 15 years	$10,000	Homicide by negligent use of weapon
Class D	Not to exceed 10 years	$10,000	Homicide by intoxicated use of a vehicle
Class E	Not to exceed 5 years	$10,000	Homicide by negligent use of a vehicle

*A court may impose a prison sentence or a fine or both.

Source: Wisconsin Statutes, 939.50, 1998.

CRIMINAL PROCEDURE

There are many steps or stages to the process of a criminal action, including arrest, initial appearance, preliminary hearing, arraignment, plea bargaining, and trial.

Arrest

Criminal litigation or criminal procedure begins with an arrest. The arrest may be based on the witnessing of criminal conduct, or it may be based on a complaint made by someone who suspects that a crime has been committed. In either case, there must exist probable cause (the reasonable belief that a crime was committed by the accused). This is one of the protections written into the Constitution and built into the American legal system to prevent the government from detaining persons without legal justification (see Chapter Six).

Initial Appearance

Within a reasonable time, the accused must be brought before a judge or tribunal to know the reason for detention. This is commonly known as an **initial appearance.** If the accused is held in jail for too long without knowing what the pending charges are, a petition in *habeas corpus* may be filed. *Habeas corpus* is prohibited in the first article of the Constitution.

At the initial appearance, the accused is informed of the pending charges and, depending on the circumstances, may be released on **bail** or on **personal recognizance.** The posting of bail is meant to ensure that the accused will appear for trial. In the event the accused "jumps bail," and leaves the jurisdiction of the court, the bail (or pledge) is forfeited. If there is little reason to believe that the accused will leave the jurisdiction of the court, and depending on the nature of the criminal charges pending and the threat to society, the accused may be released without bond. This good faith release is known as personal recognizance.

Preliminary Hearing

After the initial appearance, a **preliminary hearing** may be held. The preliminary hearing is an opportunity for the judge to review the evidence available to determine whether there is probable cause to charge the accused with committing a crime. If the judge thinks there is insufficient evidence to support probable cause, the accused is released. If the judge determines that probable cause exists, the accused is bound over to the jurisdiction of the court. The preliminary hearing may be waived.

Arraignment

If probable cause is found at the preliminary hearing, the criminal charges are prepared and the accused is scheduled for an **arraignment.** At the arraignment, the formal charges are read to the accused and the accused is asked to enter a plea. If the plea is not guilty, the court will determine whether the accused has sufficient resources to hire an attorney or whether a public defender will be appointed for the accused. If the plea is guilty, the judge may order a presentence investigation or may immediately impose a sentence. If the plea is ***nolo contendere,*** the accused, while not admitting any wrongdoing, is sentenced as if a guilty plea had been entered. *Nolo contendere* is entered when the accused is unwilling to implicate others in criminal acts or is unwilling to risk a criminal conviction on the evidence that may then be available in a civil lawsuit. Even though the accused is sentenced as guilty, a *nolo contendere* plea cannot be used as evidence in a civil lawsuit based on the same circumstances.

Plea Bargaining

Plea bargaining may occur at any time during the criminal litigation, even after the case has gone to trial and has been submitted to the jury for deliberation. When a plea bargain is made, the accused agrees to plead guilty to a lesser charge. This agreement is deemed expedient for many reasons. First, it avoids the cost, time, and uncertainty of a criminal trial, thus conserving society's resources. Second, it has the effect of protecting society, because the accused faces the consequences of the wrongful act. Third, the accused generally negotiates a less severe sentence.

The judge always has the right to refuse to accept a plea bargain, but as a general rule, judges respect the integrity of the prosecutor's judgment and, in the interest of justice, carry through with the sentence agreement.

Trial

The defendant is entitled to a fair and impartial hearing on the evidence. This hearing in criminal litigation is the trial. There are several stages to the trial of a criminal matter.

Voir dire. The first part of a criminal trial involves selection of an impartial jury. **Voir dire** is a term that means "to speak the truth." It refers to the portion of the trial in which the judge and the attorneys question the jury to determine whether there exist any biases or strong opinions that may interfere with a person's ability to render a fair judgment.

Opening statements. Once the jury has been selected, the prosecutor and the defense attorney have the opportunity to address the jury in opening statements. Opening statements are not evidence and the judge will instruct the jury that the information presented is what the parties intend to prove. They are meant to set the stage for the delivery of evidence. The prosecutor gives the first opening statement. The defense attorney may follow immediately or may elect to reserve the opening statement for the period of time immediately preceding the defense's presentation of evidence. Defense attorneys sometimes prefer to reserve their opening statements because they may ask for dismissal after the close of the prosecutor's case. If the motion is granted, there is no need for an opening statement on behalf of the defense.

Presentation of evidence. The **burden of proof** in a criminal action rests with the prosecutor on behalf of the governmental authority against which the act was committed. Generally it must be proved beyond a reasonable doubt that the accused had the necessary intent and engaged in the proscribed conduct. Beyond a reasonable doubt does not mean beyond any doubt. Jurors are instructed to remember that doubt is often present, but that the facts must show an alternative explanation is reasonable. If the jury cannot find that an alternative explanation exists, they must find the accused guilty of committing the criminal act. When the prosecutor has submitted all the evidence that he or she believes will prove the criminal act by the accused, the prosecutor rests.

If the prosecutor has presented a *prima facie* **case;** that is, if the evidence presented appears on its face to indicate that the accused committed a crime, the accused is generally called upon to defend the action. If the prosecutor has not met the necessary elements to make a *prima facie* case, the defense may move for dismissal of the charges. If the judge determines, as a matter of law, that the prosecutor has failed to show evidence to establish the elements of the crime, the motion may be granted and the charges dismissed.

The accused need not defend the charges. If a motion to dismiss is not granted, defense counsel may bring proof to show that the accused had a legal excuse for acting or that there were circumstances that would allow for an exception or an alternative explanation for how the crime was committed.

There are generally two types of evidence: witness testimony and physical evidence. Witnesses are examined (questioned) about their knowledge of the circumstances that gave rise to the criminal charges. Witnesses are subject to **direct examination** by the attorney who called them; the opposing counsel will submit the witness to **cross examination.** Redirect and recross examination may go for as long as new evidence is being presented and clarified by the witness.

Closing arguments. After each side has submitted evidence in support of the respective claims, each party is entitled to summarize the evidence to the jury in what are known as closing arguments. Unlike the opening statements, which must be confined to the facts expected to be brought out by the evidence, closing arguments can be dramatic arguments and appeals to the jury. The prosecutor has the first right to argue the case and, after the argument closes or the time for argument expires, the defense counsel may respond with opposing arguments. If desired, the prosecutor has one more opportunity to appeal to the jury before the judge concludes the attorney's portion of the trial.

Jury instructions. Throughout the trial, the judge instructs the jury on the appropriate conduct and procedure for the trial. After closing arguments, however, the judge actually reads the elements of the criminal statute to the jury so they know what the law is. These **jury instructions** are the legal guidelines they must keep in mind while they deliberate. The jury's duty is to determine the facts. If they find that the accused did, in fact and beyond a reasonable doubt, have criminal intent and did, in fact and beyond a reasonable doubt, commit the illegal act, they must find the defendant guilty.

Jury deliberations. Once jury instructions have been read, the jury is excused, with instructions to elect a foreperson and to weigh the evidence to arrive at a verdict. If the jury finds that the accused is not guilty, the litigation comes to an end. The prosecutor generally does not have the right to appeal. If the case cannot be made against the defendant the first time, the prosecutor does not get a second chance. This is the protection against double jeopardy outlined in the Sixth Amendment to the Constitution. If the jury finds that the accused is guilty, the judge may order a presentence investigation or may immediately impose a sentence. The convicted party always has the right to at least one objective appeal to ensure that the law was correctly applied in the case.

ADMINISTRATIVE LAW

Administrative law and litigation involve controversies arising between individuals or companies and administrative agencies, such as the Internal Revenue Service on the federal level or the Department of Revenue on the state level. The procedures in an administrative litigation are peculiar to the agency and will vary in regard to the time constraints and the processes involved. Generally, administrative agencies have the power to require compliance through reports, on-site investigations, and additional inquiries. Agencies may employ the **subpoena** power of a court to ensure that the necessary compliance information is provided to the agency. If the agency finds that a party is not complying with agency regulations, administrative litigation and adjudication occurs within the agency.

Administrative Procedure

While each agency identifies different procedures and time requirements, there is basic uniformity in what to expect when engaged in administrative litigation. This is true because due process rights, guaranteed by the Constitution, cannot be violated or abridged by administrative action. Thus, the controversy must be litigated in a manner that affords protection to the person against whom the agency is taking action.

Notice of violation. Administrative litigation begins with a notice of violation. This notice must include the time, place, and purpose of a hearing concerning the alleged violation. It must also state the legal authority for issuing the notice and the jurisdiction under which it is operating. All matters of law and fact to be asserted at the hearing must be clearly identified in the notice of hearing.

Hearing. The first hearing in the administrative agency may be little more than a meeting of the parties. If resolution is reached through negotiation at the meeting, a letter confirming the agreement is sent to the party who is expected to comply with its terms. If the party alleged to have violated agency regulations is not willing to enter into an agreement or refuses to comply with the terms of the agreement, additional proceedings ensue.

It may be easier to discuss administrative litigation using an example. If a person asserts disability and applies for Social Security benefits, the application will be reviewed by Social Security personnel and a decision will be made concerning the alleged disability. If disability payments are refused, the applicant may petition the Social Security office for a hearing on this denial of benefits. At the hearing, the applicant will be given the opportunity to prove disability.

Written decision. If the hearing officer determines that the applicant does not qualify for benefits after the hearing, the officer must provide the applicant with a written decision citing the reasons for denying benefits. This written decision becomes the basis for all further proceedings in this matter.

Reconsideration. Appealing the written decision of the hearing officer is subject to very specific rules and time limits. Generally, the applicant may request reconsideration or rehearing before an **administrative law judge,** who may be an official in the agency. In federal agencies, they must be attorneys with at least seven years of experience. Although they work for the agency, they are not considered to be biased toward the agency but are charged with furthering the legislative intent and social concern of the agency. At the reconsideration hearing, the applicant may provide evidence of disability and may be represented by an advocate (legal nurse consultants may be employed in this area) in an effort to convince the administrative law judge that previous decisions by the agency were in error. The hearing generally ends with the judge reserving judgment and indicating the time within which the applicant may expect a written decision.

The decision of the administrative law judge, if contested by the applicant, does not become final but has the effect of a recommendation, which may be approved or rejected by a Board of Review.

Board of Review. Almost all agencies provide for a final review by a commission or board. The applicant is generally not allowed to provide additional factual evidence after a rehearing with an administrative law judge. Instead, the applicant or the advocate on behalf of the applicant may make a written appeal, and sometimes an oral argument, to the Board. The Board will ultimately rule on whether the applicant has provided sufficient proof of disability or whether the administrative law judge's denial of benefits will stand.

Judicial Review. If, after **exhausting administrative remedies,** the applicant is still not satisfied with the decision of the agency, the applicant may appeal to the courts. The courts, as supreme protectors of the rights of the people, may obviate the action of the agency if it finds that the applicant's due process rights were denied or abridged. Courts are generally reluctant to involve themselves too deeply in administrative matters. It is thought that doing so would undermine the autonomy of the administrative agencies and weaken their power in managing this area of social concern. In addition, judges often believe that the technical expertise of administrative law judges and review boards should not be compromised by judicial interference.

Basically, when an administrative action is brought for review by the courts, two questions are asked:

1. Were the due process rights of the parties protected?
2. Was the agency acting within its scope of authority?

The action is not retried. There are no new findings of fact. For federal agencies, judicial review is brought in the appeals courts, because only the law is subject to interpretation. If the court finds that there was insufficient factual evidence to support the finding of the agency, it will return the matter to the agency for further evidentiary proceedings. If the court finds that the agency acted outside its authority or that the constitutional rights of the applicant were abridged or denied, the court will reverse the decision of the agency.

CIVIL LAW

Anything that doesn't fall within the realm of criminal law or administrative law is classified as civil. The area that seems to get the most press is **tort law.** Tort law involves a wrong that causes harm to another for which the injured person may pursue a remedy in court. Civil law includes many other areas of law, such as commercial law, contract law, anti-trust, business law, probate disputes, real property disputes, and collections.

CIVIL PROCEDURE

It is often said that there are three stages in the civil litigation process: pleadings, discovery or disclosure, and trial. Each state has specific rules that guide the process in an orderly and uniform manner.

Pleadings

Pleadings, historically, were just that: pleas or requests to the court for justice. Today, pleadings are used to outline the problem—to identify the facts and the legal issues that are the subject of the controversy. Several important documents may be filed with the court during this stage, including the complaint, the summons, a motion to dismiss, an answer, a counterclaim, and others.

Complaint. The **complaint** or petition is the first document filed in a lawsuit. It outlines the plaintiff's claim against the defendant. The plaintiff must present a *prima facie* case (clear on its face that the facts as outlined would provide a remedy to plaintiff) showing plaintiff is entitled to relief. The complaint is filed with the court and a summons is issued.

Summons. Although a **summons** is said to issue from the court, it is prepared by the plaintiff's attorney. The **summons** notifies the defendant that a lawsuit has been commenced against him or her and that unless defendant submits an answer to the lawsuit, a default judgment will be taken against him or her. In state court proceedings, the summons is generally signed by the plaintiff's attorney.

Motion to dismiss. If the defendant believes that the claim does not establish a cause of action, the defendant may file a **motion to dismiss** the complaint. Arguments are made at a hearing on the motion and the judge will determine whether the complaint has met the necessary standards. If not, the action may be dismissed, or the judge may grant the plaintiff time to amend the complaint.

Answer. The defendant does not need to provide a defense when responding to the complaint. The defendant may simply admit or deny the allegations named in the complaint. When the **answer** is served and filed, the issues are said to be **joined.** This means that it is now clear which of the allegations in the complaint plaintiff must prove.

The plaintiff still has the burden of proof and defendant need not bear the expense of defense unless plaintiff proves his or her claim. In the answer, however, the defendant may set forth legal defenses to the claim. In some cases, the defendant must set forth certain defenses, such as lack of jurisdiction, or waive the right to bring those defenses later during the proceedings.

Other Pleadings. The pleadings usually filed are listed above. There are many others that may be filed, including counterclaims, cross-claims, and third party complaints.

A **counterclaim** is one that the defendant has against the plaintiff. It may or may not arise from the same circumstances that gave rise to plaintiff's claim, but the theory is that all disputes between the parties should be resolved at one time. By doing so, the parties do not burden the court and the witnesses with several different proceedings, nor are they required to maintain the evidence for other potential proceedings. Counterclaims are similar to complaints in that they must also establish a *prima facie* claim. The plaintiff then responds to the counterclaim in the same way that a defendant answers a complaint.

Cross-claims are generally filed by defendants against one another. For example, in a three-car pileup, the plaintiff in car 1 who was injured may sue both the defendants in cars 2 and 3. The defendant in car 2 may cross-claim against the defendant in car 3 claiming that if any liability attaches to defendant in car 2, defendant in car 3 is responsible for those damages. Cross-claims are sometimes filed by plaintiffs against one another in response to a counterclaim. More often, however, cross-claims are filed among the defendants, each alleging that the wrongdoing was the responsibility of the other defendant.

Third party complaints are used to bring additional defendants into the lawsuit who may be liable for all or a portion of the plaintiff's injuries. For example, in an intersection collision, plaintiff is injured and subsequently sues defendant—the other motorist involved. Defendant motorist had the brakes on the automobile involved in the collision adjusted the day before the accident. Defendant does not think it was his or her fault that the car did not stop at the stop sign but believes the mechanic who failed to repair the brakes is liable. Defendant may sue the company and/or the mechanic responsible for adjusting the brakes as a third party defendant. The third party defendant is now required to defend against the allegations of the plaintiff and the defendant. When a third party is joined in the lawsuit, the title of the lawsuit changes. Figure 8-2 illustrates the difference between the caption before and after the third party is joined.

The pleadings stage may end with a **motion for judgment on the pleadings.** This is a request to the court to study the complaint, the answer, and such other pleadings as have been filed and to determine whether one or the other party is entitled to judgment as a matter of law. This is not often done, since the pleadings will often identify a question that must be resolved by submitting evidence.

A **scheduling conference** generally occurs shortly after the pleadings are filed. The purpose of the scheduling conference is to establish a calendar for the lawsuit. The parties, through their representatives, meet with the judge and set deadlines for completion of activities prior to trial. Discovery dates are scheduled, a pretrial conference date is determined, and a tentative date for trial is established. Most judges are rather strict about keeping to this schedule and failure to comply may result in sanctions against the nonconforming party or even dismissal of the complaint, or entry of default judgment.

Discovery or Disclosure

There are no surprises in litigation. During **discovery,** the parties, through court-sanctioned requests, may obtain information about the witnesses and other evidence that will be used by the other party at trial. These court-sanctioned requests may include any of the devices identified in Figure 8-3.

Regardless of the discovery device used, the responding party must answer under oath, and the answers to discovery may be used at the trial if a

---

Net Results

Legal Forms

Many forms, including sample litigation documents, are now available at various web sites on the Internet. Many legal web pages provide links to specialty practice firms that may provide forms at no cost or for a fee. To examine some of the forms available on the Internet, check out these web pages:
www.westlaw.com, www.westlegalstudies. com, www.findlaw.com. *and* www.law.cornell.edu. *Legal forms are also available at this general site:* www.washlaw.edu.

FIGURE 8-2   Caption When a Third Party is Joined

Caption prior to joining third party.

United States District Court
Western District of Wisconsin

Pa Houa Lo,

Plaintiff,

v.

Yvonne Primeau,   COMPLAINT

Defendant.

Caption after joining third party.

United States District Court
Western District of Wisconsin

Pa Houa Lo,

Plaintiff,

v.

Yvonne Primeau,

Defendant and
Third Party   THIRD PARTY COMPLAINT
Plaintiff,

v.

A-1 Car Repair, Inc.,
a Wisconsin corporation,

Third Party
Defendant.

FIGURE 8-3   Discovery Devices

Device	Explanation
Interrogatories	Written questions to a party that must be answered under oath
Requests for Production of Documents or Things	Written requests for inspection of documents, records, entry onto land, or examination of an item
Depositions	Testimony under oath in response to questions from the parties of which a permanent record is made in the form of a deposition transcript
Requests for Admissions	A device requesting the other party to admit certain facts in order to avoid the cost of proof
Adverse Medical Exam	The defendant may schedule an examination by a physician of defendant's choosing in order to have an impartial opinion about plaintiff's injuries

discrepancy occurs. The only discovery device that can be used against a person who is not a party, such as a physician or a law enforcement officer, is the deposition.

New federal court rules require that the parties volunteer information without request. This is known as **disclosure.** Some states, including Arizona, have also adopted disclosure rules. The intent of disclosure is to reduce the cost of litigation and to promote the cooperation of the parties in a fair resolution of the claim. Before any discovery may be undertaken, the parties are required to meet and prepare a discovery plan. Certain information must then be passed back and forth within a strict time frame. Disclosure does not preclude the use of discovery devices; in fact, discovery devices may be necessary to obtain information that is not readily identifiable due to lack of specificity in the pleadings.

The discovery stage of civil litigation may conclude with a motion for summary judgment. **Summary judgment** is available to either party if the evidence relied upon indicates that there is no question of fact. Where there is no dispute about the events of the controversy, the judge may grant judgment as a matter of law to either party. Partial summary judgment may be used when liability is clear, but the damages must be proved. This reduces the caseload on the court and disposes of legal issues without the necessity of a trial.

Before the trial, a **pretrial conference** is convened. At the pretrial conference, the attorneys and the judge establish an agenda for trial. Agreements may be made on the number of jurors to impanel, any limitations on *voir dire,* and the number of strikes against potential jurors. The lay witnesses, expert witnesses, and physical evidence that will be brought to court is detailed and identified in the order in which it is expected to be presented. The estimated time for each witness is noted and stipulations on evidence may be made to avoid the expense of establishing facts that are undisputed.

Many judges view the pretrial conference as a last ditch effort to settle before going to trial and may facilitate negotiations between the parties. A **pretrial order** is issued that summarizes the agreements made during the pretrial conference and that serves as a "script" for trial. This pretrial order is so important that if a witness who is not identified in the pretrial order is called to the witness stand, the judge may refuse to allow that witness to testify and it may be grounds for mistrial.

Trial. Unlike popular television drama, trials are characterized by the calm, orderly presentation of facts and defenses. The purpose of a trial is to arrive at the truth. Civil trials do not differ greatly from criminal trials, which were discussed earlier in this chapter. The main point to remember about civil trial is that the burden of proof is less strict. Generally, a plaintiff must prove that it is more likely than not that the defendant's wrongful conduct caused plaintiff injury. This is known as the **greater weight of the evidence.** It is quite possible for a defendant who has been found not guilty of criminal charges to be found liable for civil damages based on the same circumstances.

What LNCs Say . . .

"I have considerable experience in investigation, negotiation, and arbitration of labor contracts. The skills and strengths I acquired in these areas have given me a broader outlook on health care than my nursing perspective. Alternative dispute resolution will be utilized more frequently in health care liability in the years ahead. This is my niche! Each nurse's background is unique; it is important to capitalize on that experience. This is what nurses interested in legal nurse consulting must do: find their niche and exploit it!" Connie Courtade, RN, BS, MAIR, Minneapolis, MN, used with permission.

POST-TRIAL ALTERNATIVES

If a party is not satisfied with the outcome of a trial, three options exist for a limited time after the trial has concluded. These are motion for a new trial, motion for judgment notwithstanding the verdict, and appeal.

Motion for New Trial

A **motion for new trial** must be based on an error of law that is so prejudicial to the jury that a fair trial was precluded. An example of an error of law would be a ruling by the judge on admission of evidence or on an objection to certain questioning. Sometimes called a motion for *trial de novo,* the motion requests that, in fairness to the party who may have been denied an impartial trial, the judge set aside the judgment of the court and begin again with a new jury.

Motion for Judgment Notwithstanding the Verdict

If it is clear from the record that the jury verdict is based in sympathy or horror and is not supported by the facts, the judge is obligated to overturn the jury. A **judgment** *non obstante verdicto,* judgment notwithstanding the verdict, or judgment NOV, results in a post-trial order that changes the jury verdict and enters a judgment consistent with the facts. No new trial is commenced and no new evidence is submitted.

Appeal

A fundamental due process right in the United States legal system is the right to at least one objective review of the proceedings. That is why intermediate courts of appeals are said to have appellate jurisdiction as a matter of right. The judges may not exercise their discretion, but are required to review cases brought before them. The right to appeal is intended to prevent the despotic use of judicial proceedings and to ensure the rights of the individual against the power of government. On appeal, the court will only review how the law was applied to the facts. No new determination of the facts will be made. In fact, the court will only look to see that there are sufficient facts on the record to support the judgment. If not, the case will be returned to the trial court for further evidentiary hearings.

ALTERNATIVE DISPUTE RESOLUTION

Because of the high cost of litigation, not just in monetary terms but also in terms of loss of time and production, and in psychological costs, trends are appearing that support alternatives to litigation. New legislation supporting resolution that is quicker and less painful may require the exercise of options other than, or before, court processes and trial. Health maintenance organizations frequently provide for settlement options in their contracts for services. Products liability laws include mandatory **alternative dispute resolution** attempts prior to going to court.[2] In Minnesota, court rules require some form of alternative dispute resolution in every civil case filed.[3] In Wisconsin and in other states, court rules allow judges, to require litigants to attempt alternative dispute resolution in good faith prior to scheduling trial of the matter.[4]

Alternative dispute resolution takes many forms and, as legislation and public sentiment continue to advance this trend, new methods for resolving disputes continually evolve. Among the most common are arbitration, mediation, negotiation, mini-trials, focus groups, and "hire-a-judge."

Arbitration

Arbitration involves an agreement between parties that their dispute will be resolved through **arbiters.** Generally, each party chooses an arbiter and those two arbiters choose a third. This three-member panel reviews a summary of the case, listens to testimony, reviews evidence, and makes a decision. The decision of the arbiters is final and cannot be appealed. That is what is bargained for in the agreement. The only time the parties can bring an arbitration matter to court is if one of the parties refuses to abide by the arbiters' decision.

Mediation

While arbitration is binding and final with the **condition precedent** of an agreement between the parties, **mediation** is a voluntary process entered into in the hope that the parties might reach a satisfactory middle ground. A neutral third party is chosen by the parties or the court. The third party may review a summary of the case and schedule a meeting. At the meeting, the parties may jointly present their sides or the mediator may choose to talk with each side separately to determine the potential for settlement. The mediator attempts to bring the parties from their polar positions to a middle ground where they can mutually accept resolution. The suggestions of the mediator are not binding. The cost of this procedure is minimal and the parties generally lose little by attempting this method of resolution. No part of the negotiations or conversation that occur during the mediation are admissible in court, so neither party is compromising legal strategy.

Negotiation

Negotiation is still the most frequently used form of alternative dispute resolution. It generally involves an attorney on adversarial terms, attempting to persuade the other side to a settlement that will be advantageous for his or her client. In almost all of the alternative dispute resolution options, with the exception of arbitration, negotiated settlement is the end result.

Mini-trials

Mini-trials may take several forms. In cases where liability may be extensive but where privacy may be advantageous, the parties might schedule a day to engage in an activity similar to a dress rehearsal for the trial. A neutral panel will be asked to serve as jurors, and members of the law firms will act as witnesses. The attorneys present the case as if it were being presented to a judge. In fact, a judge may be present! When the presentation is finished, the neutral panel deliberates and renders a verdict. The panel and the judge, if there is one, are free to discuss their perceptions with the attorneys. The objective is to be able to see more clearly what deficiencies exist in the case. Knowing this leads the parties toward a more realistic settlement negotiation.

Another form of mini-trial involves both attorneys presenting their opposing cases to a neutral panel, with or without a judge, in somewhat the same format. The panel and the judge do not offer comments about the strengths and weaknesses of the case, but the attorneys and the parties are provided with a true-to-life simulation of how their respective cases will be perceived at trial. Once the verdict is rendered, the parties are more likely to agree upon a fair settlement.

Focus Groups

Similar to the first described mini-trial, a **focus group** may be convened to assist the attorneys in developing trial strategies and trial exhibits. Because the focus group reviews only one side of the case, they often bring forth questions about defenses and weaknesses in the evidence that have the added effect of promoting negotiated settlement. Focus groups are generally convened in neutral settings such as hotel conference rooms by neutral moderators. The focus group is often instructed to refrain from indicating by nods or other gestures how they feel about the evidence. Witnesses may be called, but usually the focus group is given a written background of the case and a summary of what the witnesses will say. The focus group, then, pretends it is a jury in deliberation. They select a foreperson and proceed to question how they will arrive at a verdict. The verdict itself is not as important as the questions that are raised during deliberations. During this time, the attorneys are to be as inconspicuous as possible so as not to interrupt or interfere with the honest flow of dialogue among the focus group members. This process may be invaluable to the attorneys in assessing how their respective cases may be perceived by a jury.

Hire-a-Judge

Similar to the television programs that resolve disputes between neighbors and others, the **hire-a-judge** method of alternative dispute resolution came into vogue with the case of a television performer who was in dispute with a production company in California. The celebrity's position on a television sit com was terminated and a breach of contract claim was initiated. Rather than wait six years for the case to be heard in the civil courts, the parties agreed to hire a retired jurist, split the cost of the proceedings, and abide by the decision that was rendered. In many ways, hire-a-judge resembles arbitration. It requires a preceding agreement and it precludes the right to appeal. The advantage of using a retired judge is that the proceedings probably reflect more accurately the workings of a courtroom with the applicable rules of law.

ADVANTAGES AND DISADVANTAGES OF ALTERNATIVE DISPUTE RESOLUTION

There are numerous advantages to attempting alternatives to the litigation process. In all except arbitration and hire-a-judge, the parties retain their right to a day in court. Little is lost by trying. Alternative resolution is generally less expensive than going to court. It is often resolved more quickly and causes less emotional strain on the parties. Because it is resolved in private, the publicity of a court proceeding is avoided.

Perhaps the most important advantage is the psychological impact of having control over the resolution. Many people involved in the court system view it as a runaway train from which there is no escape. Having control over one's life is a major factor in psychological health and alternative dispute resolution, in most of its forms, returns power over the problem to the parties involved.

Disadvantages include the unwillingness of the parties to engage in alternative resolution in good faith and the potential of a greater award at trial. In addition, because alternative resolution is private, it prevents the establishment of precedent for future cases.

CHAPTER SUMMARY

- Crimes are classified as felonies or misdemeanors and each classification includes additional classes.
- Criminal procedure involves an arrest, an initial appearance, a preliminary hearing, an arraignment, and a trial.
- Plea bargaining may occur at any stage of a criminal litigation.
- Administrative procedure is less formal and includes hearings, rehearings or reconsiderations, appeal, and final review.
- Civil procedure is identified in three stages: pleadings, discovery, and trial.

- Alternative dispute resolution is a popular method of resolving legal disputes without going to court.
- Alternative dispute resolution may include arbitration, mediation, negotiation, mini-trials, focus groups, or hire-a-judge.

KEY TERMS

actus reus	exhausting administrative remedies	motion to dismiss
administrative law judge		*nolo contendere*
alternative dispute resolution	felony	personal recognizance
answer	focus groups	plea bargaining
arbiter	greater weight of the evidence	pleadings
arbitration	hire-a-judge	preliminary hearing
arraignment	initial appearance	pretrial conference
bail	joined	pretrial order
burden of proof	judgment notwithstanding the verdict	*prima facie* case
complaint		scheduling conference
condition precedent	jury instructions	subpoena
counterclaim	mediation	summary judgment
crime	*mens rea*	summons
cross-claim	mini-trials	third party complaint
cross examination	misdemeanor	tort law
direct examination	motion for judgment on the pleadings	*trial de novo*
disclosure		*voir dire*
discovery	motion for new trial	

REVIEW QUESTIONS

1. Identify and explain the steps in a criminal litigation.
2. What is involved in the pleadings stage of civil litigation? The discovery stage?
3. What options exist for a party who is not satisfied with the outcome of a trial?
4. Describe several options that may be used for alternative dispute resolution.

INTERNET EXERCISES

1. Access the web page for this textbook at *www.westlegalstudies.com.*
2. Click on the assignments section of the web page and complete the assignment(s) for Chapter Eight.

EXERCISES

1. Networking. Using the Yellow Pages, locate a law firm specializing in personal injury law that employs a nurse. Contact the office and interview the nurse. Determine what legal qualifications, if any, the nurse had prior to employment at the law firm. Ask the legal nurse consultant about his or her participation in the stages of civil litigation and in preparation for trial. If a trial is scheduled in the near future, plan to attend.

2. Professional Portfolio. Go to the local courthouse and ask to review a file on a medical negligence claim. Read through the pleadings and other documents in the file. Photocopy documents that impress you and begin to develop a systems file, folder, notebook, or computer system. Keep an index of the documents in this system in your professional portfolio.

ENDNOTES

1. American Bar Association, *Annotated Model Rules of Professional Conduct,* (1999) 4th Edition Rule 4.2. Copies of ABA Model Code of Professional Responsibility, 1999 Edition are available from Service Center, American Bar Association, 750 North Lake Shore Drive, Chicago, IL 60611-4497, 1-800-285-2221.

2. See, for example, the Magnuson-Moss Warranty Consumer Protection Act, 15 U.S.C.§ 2301.

3. Minn. Stat. Ann. §484.76.

4. Wis. Stat. 802.08 (1997–98).

ADDITIONAL REFERENCES

Bogart, J. B., RN MN, ed. *Legal Nurse Consulting: Principles and Practice.* Boston: CRC Press, 1998.

Carper, D., et al. *Understanding the Law,* 3rd ed. St. Paul, Minnesota: West Publishing Company, 1995.

Loecker, B., MSEd RN. "Alternative Dispute Resolution: Mediation and Arbitration." *Journal of Legal Nurse Consulting* 8:3 (1997): 10–12.

Ward-Collins, D., MSN RN. "Alternative Dispute Resolution: A Mediation Process for Conflict Resolution of Healthcare Issues." *Journal of Legal Nurse Consulting* 9:3 (1998): 2–7.

LEGAL NURSE CONSULTANT PROFILE

Kathleen Sullivan

Products Liability, Medical Malpractice, Personal Injury

Kathleen Sullivan is a registered nurse with a bachelor's degree in business administration. She is pursuing a master's degree in business-health care. After twenty years of clinical experience, Kathy responded to an advertisement in the newspaper and secured a position at a law firm in Madison, Wisconsin, that specializes in personal injury, including products liability and medical malpractice. Her background includes intensive care, general surgery, cardiovascular surgery, PACU, and operating room.

What do you like best about being a legal nurse consultant?

"I have the best of both worlds: I am able to use the medical knowledge I've accumulated and have also learned about different aspects of the law.

"The firm pays me to keep current in medicine! That's a real benefit of this position. I enjoy collaborating with the legal team, talking colleague to colleague on strategy and case evaluation. I still do a great deal of teaching, both with clients and the attorneys."

"I love the number of people I meet outside the legal profession—expert witnesses, vocational rehabilitation experts, life care planners. They help me keep current with what is happening in medicine and related fields."

What challenges do legal nurse consultants face in your area of law?

"We're seeing a tightening of what insurance companies are willing to pay for people who have been injured. As a legal nurse consultant, I have the responsibility of looking at all aspects of a client's injuries. This includes future prospects, treatment, and potential impact on employment and activities they may no longer be able to pursue. Knowing where and how to gather this information is critical."

"Maintaining good relationships with treating physicians and experts is a challenge. We always have great respect for their schedules so that we don't put them in a bind. For meetings and other requests we try to call at least two months in advance. Then, when we need something on short notice, it is more likely that that relationship will not be compromised."

What advice would you give nurses who are interested in legal nurse consulting?

"It is best to have several years of well-rounded experience. If you are working as an independent consultant, you have to be very aggressive to get business."

"Nurses must be very articulate to be able to convince the attorneys that they can help them and their clients. It is absolutely essential to keep current with medical practice."

"Another important aspect of the job is computer literacy. Many books are now available on CD ROM. Search engines on the Internet allow you to explore volumes of information. Get to know the web sites which will link you to important information. It would help to take a class on Medline searching or something equivalent to Medline."

"Keep in touch with teaching institutions. Take advantage of what is out in the community, especially if there is a teaching hospital nearby. Become familiar with the medical records departments and the people who work there. Relationships cannot be undervalued, especially when you need something on short notice."

What unique marketing strategy are you willing to share?

"Being able to use your resources may be your greatest strength. I located an expert witness, one of only five in this country, from a book on acetabular fractures. The book identified five doctors as members of an Acetabular Club! I called one of them and he became our expert witness. All of the resourcefulness you have acquired as a registered nurse will make you valuable to the legal community."

"All of the resourcefulness you have acquired as a registered nurse will make you valuable to the legal community."

CASE STUDY

State v. Mullins, 267 Kan. 84, 977 P.2d 931 (1999).

The following case involves a legal nurse consultant. As you read through the court opinion, consider the following questions:

- Was this a civil or criminal matter? Explain.
- What role did the legal nurse consultant play in resolution of this matter?
- What credentials, experience, and education qualified the legal nurse consultant to play a role in resolution of this matter?
- What controversy existed concerning the legal nurse consultant's testimony?

(Cite as: 1999 WL 219181 (Kan))

STATE of Kansas, Appellee,
v.
Thomas B. MULLINS, Appellant.
No. 80,022.
Supreme Court of Kansas.
April 16, 1999.
SYLLABUS BY THE COURT

(Cite as: 1999 WL 219181. *1 (Kan.))

LARSON, J.:
Thomas B. Mullins appeals his convictions of aggravated criminal sodomy, *K.S.A. 21-3506(a)(1)*, a severity level 2 person felony, and aggravated indecent liberties with a child, *K.S.A. 21-3504*, a severity level 3 person felony. Mullins contends the trial court erred (1) in denying his motion for a new trial, (2) in admitting ←**expert**→ testimony from Pat Phillips, a ←**registered nurse,**→ that the victim had not been coached, and (3) in sentencing him.

Facts

The prosecution was based on testimony of Mullins' biological child, B.M., that he had initially been subjected to his father's "lewd touching," which escalated to sodomy. B.M. had not reported this to his divorced mother until after contact with Mullins had ceased because he had feared for his safety.

The defense theories were that no abuse occurred, that B.M. had been coerced in his testimony by his mother to assist in a requested adoption by her new husband, or that if the acts testified to had occurred, B.M. was confused about the molester, who may have been one of several boyfriends his mother had affairs with after divorcing Mullins.

(Cite as: 1999 WL 219181, *2 (Kan.))

Because there were no visual indications of physical or sexual abuse, and no witnesses to the alleged offenses, Mullins was convicted primarily based upon the testimony of B.M.

In order to set the stage for the consideration of the alleged errors, we will set forth in more detail the testimony of various witnesses who appeared at trial.

B.M.

B.M. was born July 20, 1985, and was 11 years old at the time of the trial. He testified that beginning in the fall of 1992, Mullins began touching his "front privates" underneath his clothing with both hands. This occurred during visitations at Mullins' mother's house where Mullins lived. B.M. believed his father's threat that "if I told anybody he would kill me."

B.M. testified the abuse got worse after his 8th birthday. He testified he was punched and beaten, made to lay down on the bed, and Mullins would "get on top of me," where he "would move up and down with his front private in my back and it hurt." B.M. testified he was made to smoke cigarettes and drink beer and Mullins held a knife to his throat. This continued until B.M. was about 9 years old. He testified he was telling the truth and would not lie just to make his mom happy. He said he told his mother and the police what had happened to him because he felt safe once he moved away from Mullins. He said he loved his mother and wanted to be adopted by his stepfather.

continued

State v. Mullins   *continued*

A.R.

B.M.'s mother, A.R., testified he had lived with her during his entire life. Mullins' visitations were sporadic, sometimes weeks apart, and sometimes months apart. A.R. testified that on June 20, 1995, while having dinner with B.M. and her new husband, B.M. told them that Mullins had molested him. She said B.M. told her that Mullins would "hurt him and punch him and hold him down and say bad things to him." The day after this conversation, A.R. took B.M. to the Leavenworth Police Department where he was interviewed by and gave a statement to Detective Michael Jarowitz. She was not present in the room during this interview.

On cross-examination, A.R. admitted to a "fairly rocky relationship" with Mullins and his family. She denied several live-in arrangements, however, she admitted that she lived with several boyfriends when B.M. was younger. She denied leaving B.M. alone with any of her boyfriends.

She testified that prior to B.M.'s revealing he had been molested, B.M. would become violent and be subject to mood swings; however, his grades and behavior had improved dramatically since he told her about the abuse.

Officer Jarowitz

(Cite as: 1999 WL 219181, *3 (Kan.))

Officer Jarowitz testified he was the first officer to interview B.M. He indicated B.M. was scared and embarrassed. B.M. told him that when he was about 7 years old "sometimes his dad would play with his private parts." In Jarowitz' written report, it was stated that he had been told by B.M. that his dad would "stick his penis in his rear, and when he would scream he would push his face into the pillow until he would stop screaming." Jarowitz testified B.M. said he waited to tell "[b]ecause he . . . was scared and Tom told him if he would tell anybody he would kill him and his family."

Detective Pat Kitchens and Monica Mendoza

Monica Mendoza is a social worker who taped an interview of B.M. with Pat Kitchens present. B.M.'s mother was not there. Kitchens' testimony was that B.M.'s statements were consistent with those previously made. Essentially, the testimony was that Mullins fondled B.M.'s "front privates" when he was 7 years old and the acts changed from mere fondling to acts of sodomy after B.M.'s 8th birthday. Kitchens' stated B.M. said he had been threatened with a knife should he tell anyone. Kitchens admitted he did not interview any of B.M.'s teachers or counselors. He also said a search of Mullins' bedroom revealed a knife, but it was not the one involved.

Pat Phillips

Pat Phillips is a registered nurse who is the assistant director for the sexual abuse program at KU Medical Center, the children's center. She has B.S. in nursing from KU and a Masters in pediatrics nursing from the University of Florida. She was trained to be a pediatric nurse practitioner, has performed gynecological exams, and worked with Dr. Adams, a pediatrician an expert in the field of sexual abuse studies at KU. She is trained to take histories from families and children, as well as perform physical examinations. She has performed over a thousand sexual abuse examinations and has been qualified as an expert in all of the Kansas counties surrounding the Kansas City area. Phillips conducted a physical examination of B.M. in July 1995, took his history, and interviewed him regarding the allegations. She interviewed A.R. separately and generated a written report. Phillips testified B.M.'s physical exam was normal and showed no physical signs of sexual abuse. It was reported that B.M. suffered from constipation which resulted in large size and amount of stools. Phillips explained that physical indications of anal penetration were not present in 60 to 80 percent of the children sodomized. She indicated there were no signs that B.M. had been "coached," which is the basis for one of Mullins' allegations of error.

Marie Mullins

Marie Mullins is Mullins' mother. She testified her son lived at her house at the time the alleged events took place. She had observed her son and B.M. interact and there was nothing which caused her to be concerned about their relationship.

Thomas B. Mullins

The defendant testified and denied abusing B.M., either sexually or physically. He stated he would not give up his parental rights to B.M. and told this to A.R. Shortly after telling her that he would not consent to the adoption, he learned of the allegations that had been made against him.

The jury found Mullins guilty of both charges. He was sentenced to a pre- guidelines term of 15 years to life for the aggravated criminal sodomy consecutive to a post-guidelines term of 274 months for the aggravated indecent liberties conviction. Both parties agree the sentences were erroneously entered under the facts of this case. The trial court did not err in denying Mullins motion for a new trial.

The motion for a new trial resulted in several evidentiary hearings and was based on the prosecution's failure to furnish a medical report concerning B.M. until the time of trial. The factual basis for this report was a June 23, 1995, examination of B.M. at the Douglas Community Health Center by Dr. Smith who issued a written report. Included in this report was a statement that in 1993, B.M. had been seen by Dr. Lohrenz, a counselor in Leavenworth "because of a change in behavior" and numerous visits to Dr. Mills, a pediatrician, for other medical problems during the time of the alleged abuse.

(Cite as: 1999 WL 219181, *5 (Kan.))

On November 18, 1996, the day before testimony began in Mullins' trial, the prosecutor received Dr. Smith's report. It was furnished to Mullins' counsel immediately. Defense counsel objected that the report was late and highly prejudicial to Mullins because he had insufficient time to review the information. A continuance was requested for time to review the report and denial of Dr. Smith's testimony.

The trial court inquired of the prosecutor as to the delay. The response was that it had just been received. Dr. Smith had moved jobs from Douglas Community Health Center to KU Medical Center. When the State became aware that a report had been prepared, it had to get a signed release from B.M.'s mother, and that release had just been received. The prosecutor thought Dr. Smith had been endorsed as a witness but such was not the case.

The trial court agreed to grant a continuance but noted it would be at least February until the matter could be heard. The trial court also indicated it would favorably consider granting a mistrial if the defendant so moved. After defense counsel explained the situation to Mullins, they decided to decline a continuance and proceed for trial in order to avoid an additional 2 1/2 months of delay. The defense did not move for a mistrial, but the trial court excluded any testimony of Dr. Smith.

After the conviction, Mullins' new trial motion raised the fact he had been unable to present favorable evidence from Dr. Lohrenz and Dr. Mills. Dr. Lohrenz testified she had counseled B.M., but had no recollection of the meeting. Her ledger card showed appointments missed and she vaguely recalled discussing sexual abuse. For insurance purposes, she had diagnosed B.M. as having "an adjustment disorder and the child appeared to be both anxious and depressed, as best I could tell from such a brief contact."

continued

State v. Mullins   *continued*

At a later hearing, Dr. Mills, who was referenced in Dr. Smith's report, testified that he treated B.M. numerous times from March 10, 1992, through July 17, 1995. He testified that there were never any signs of sexual or physical abuse, although in March 1995, when treating B.M. for urination problems and large bowel movements, concern had been voiced that B.M. had been sexually abused. He made an entry on B.M.'s file reflecting the concern but said there was no physical evidence of sexual or physical abuse. He referred B.M. to Dr. Lohrenz for counseling. It clearly appears that the mother's concern about sexual abuse was not the reason for B.M.'s visit to Dr. Mills.

After the hearing, Mullins' counsel argued the testimony of Drs. Lohrenz and Mills was newly discovered and exculpatory, and in all probability his client would have been acquitted if this evidence would have been presented to the jury.

The prosecution countered that Dr. Smith's report was excluded from trial. All reports in their file were delivered immediately upon receipt and none of the information was exculpatory.

The trial court denied the motion for new trial, finding the State did not intentionally withhold any reports. Although the reports were late it was because they were discovered late, and the evidence discovered was not exculpatory.

(Cite as: 1999 WL 219181, *6 (Kan.))

On appeal, Mullins restates all of his arguments made in his motion for a new trial and contends we should reverse the trial court's determination.

The relevant portion of *K.S.A. 22-3501* relating to new trial states: "(1) The court on motion of a defendant may grant a new trial to him if required in the interest of justice." In deciding if a new trial is warranted, Mullins bears the burden of proving that (1) the evidence is new and could not have been produced at trial with reasonable diligence, and (2) the evidence is of such materiality that there is a reasonable probability it would produce a different result upon retrial. *State v. Matson, 260 Kan. 366, Syl. ¶ 6,921 P.2d 790 (1996).*

Mullins contends the prosecution had the obligation to obtain the medical reports for them at an earlier time. He also argues it is unfair to require him to abandon this issue by consenting to go ahead with the trial after he was offered a continuance or a mistrial.

Mullins asserts the many examinations by Dr. Mills of B.M. without any statement as to physical or sexual abuse or a showing of such abuse in the examinations would have made the difference in the trial. Additionally, he contends Dr. Mills' testimony could have impeached A.R. concerning the time when allegations of sexual abuse were discovered. The trial court properly found that Mullins has not met his burden of proving the evidence would have changed the result of the trial. The testimony of Dr. Lohrenz is sketchy and adds no support to the defense's contentions. In addition, the testimony of Dr. Mills, while relevant, would be cumulative to that of nurse Phillips who testified there were no signs of sexual or physical abuse. Dr. Mills' testimony might have been given greater weight than that of Phillips, but it is unclear that the outcome the trial would have been changed, because in essence, the decision of the jury was, in the final analysis, based upon whether the testimony of B.M. was believed. There was substantial competent evidence which the trial court heard to justify its decision. [The trial court's determination to deny the motion for new trial is not an abuse of discretion which this court will reverse on appeal. Mullins also makes a *Brady v. Maryland, 373 U.S. 83, 87, 83 S.Ct. 1194, 10 L.Ed.2d215 (1963),* argument that the prosecution suppressed evidence favorable to the accused. The factual situation is to the contrary; as soon as the evidence was available to the prosecution, it was made available to Mullins. There is no Brady violation.]

The trial court did not commit reversible error in allowing Phillips to testify she saw no evidence that B.M. had been coached to tell his story.

Mullins' contention is not that the trial court improperly allowed Phillips to testify as an expert witness under K.S.A. 60-456, but as to the extent of her expertise and in the answer of a single question, improperly gave an opinion as to the credibility of the alleged victim. Under these circumstances we held in *In re J.W.S., 250 Kan. 65, 71-72, 825 P.2d 125 (1992),* that the standard of review is as follows:

(Cite as: 1999 WL 219181, *7 (Kan.))

"The admissibility of expert testimony lies within the sound discretion of the trial court and its determination will not be reversed absent a showing of abuse of discretion. [Citation omitted.]

. . . .

"One who asserts an abuse of discretion bears the burden of showing such abuse. [Citations omitted.] Even if abuse of discretion is shown in a criminal case, the defendant has the burden of showing prejudice which requires reversal. [Citation omitted.]"

Phillips testified specifically as to her physical examinations of B.M. and she said she found no physical evidence of sexual abuse. She further testified concerning her separate interviews of both B.M. and his mother on two separate occasions. The line of questioning and the statement which gives rise to Mullins' objection occurred as follows:

"Q. [Mr. Cahill] Okay. Was there anything about that evaluation that caused you to be concerned that there might be coaching or that Brian in some way would be making this up? Anything inconsistent in his statements regarding that?"

"MR. REARDON: Your Honor, could we approach?"

"MR. REARDON: I object to this on the basis she can't be a human lie detector as to whether or not the child was telling the truth.

"MR. CAHILL: That's not what I am asking. Asking if anything led her to be concerned about the statements in that area that were inconsistent.

"THE COURT: I will allow it. Go ahead.

"Q. [Mr. Cahill] Go ahead and answer it.

"A. [Phillips] I thought he had been coached?

"Q. [Mr. Cahill] Right. Any indication of that kind of behavior? "A. [Phillips] No."

The prosecution was also allowed to admit Phillips' written report which stated that "the child gave a history of sexual abuse that meets [the] criteria for a valid allegation." This was objected to on the basis that it contained a statement referring to Dr. Smith and because the written report constitutes hearsay. This was overruled by the trial court.

Mullins complains on appeal that the coaching question calls for a psychological evaluation of B.M. which Phillips was not qualified to give. Mullins also argues the question itself was improper and allowing it to be answered constituted reversible error.

Mullins relies on *State v. Willis, 256 Kan. 837, 888 P.2d 839 (1995)* where we held that a licensed social worker was not qualified to diagnose medical and psychiatric conditions such as a rape trauma syndrome and post-traumatic stress disorder. Mullins additionally points to *State v. Jackson, 239 Kan. 463, 470, 721 P.2d 232 (1986),* where we held the trial court abused its discretion in allowing two social workers who possessed specialized training and experience in child abuse investigation to render their opinion that the victim was telling the truth.

continued

State v. Mullins *continued*

Phillips' qualifications and experiences clearly shows she possessed the education and background necessary to testify as an expert on the subject of child sexual abuse. The testimony given is not a psychological evaluation of B.M. The difficult question is whether asking if B.M. appeared to have been coached as to what to say was improper and, if it was, would it be considered to be harmless error or so egregious an error to require reversal and the granting of a new trial.

In *Arrington, 251 Kan. at 752, 840 P.2d 477,* we reviewed recent cases in this area in the following manner:

"[I]n *State v. Colwell, 246 Kan. 382, 790 P.2d 430 (1990),* . . . we stated:

" '. . . Although an expert may give an opinion on an ultimate issue as provided in K.S.A. 60-456(d), such witness may do so only insofar as the witness aids the jury in the interpretation of technical facts or assists the jury in understanding the material in evidence. An expert witness may not pass on the weight or credibility of evidence, or those matters are strictly within the province of the jury. *State v. Moore, 230 Kan. 495, Syl. ¶ 1, 639 P.2d 458 (1982).' 246 Kan. at 389, 790 P.2d 430."*

We further summarized in Arrington the cases relied upon by Mullins herein. We stated:

" 'In *State v. Lash, 237 Kan. 384, 699 P.2d 49,* the defendant was accused of sexually molesting his fifteen-year-old son. A psychologist who interviewed the son gave expert testimony. He was asked his opinion, based on testing and interviewing the son, whether the son had been sexually molested by the father. Over defendant's objection, the court permitted the psychologist to testify as to whether he had an opinion whether the son had been sexually molested but would not permit the expert to testify as to whether the son had been sexually molested by the father. *237 Kan. at 384-85, 699 P.2d 49.* The defendant was acquitted. The State appealed on a question reserved as to whether the trial court erred in not permitting the expert to testify that in his opinion the son had been sexually molested by the father. We affirmed the lower court's ruling, stating that the prosecutor's question was improper because it called for an opinion which would require the expert to pass upon the credibility of witnesses or the weight of disputed evidence. *237 Kan. at 386, 699 P.2d 49.*

" 'In *State v. Jackson, 239 Kan. 463, 721 P.2d 232 (1986),* the trial court permitted two expert witnesses, social workers with expertise in child abuse treatment, to testify that "in their opinions the child was telling the truth and in their opinions the defendant committed the acts of molestation with which he was charged." *239 Kan. at 470, 721 P.2d 232.* We reserved the conviction, stating that the experts attempted to serve as human lie detectors for the child and each told the jury that the child was truthful and the defendant was guilty as charged. We said, "We are convinced that it was the function of the jury to hear the testimony of the witnesses as to what the child said, and then to make a determination of the reliability of the child's statements." *239 Kan. at 470, 721 P.2d 232.' Colwell, 246 Kan. at 389-90, 790 P.2d 430." 251 Kan. at 752-753, 840 P.2d 477.*

We additionally summarized in Arrington, the case of *State v. Clements, 241 Kan. 77, 734 P.2d 1096 (1987),* in the following manner:

" 'In *State v. Clements, 241 Kan. 77, 734 P.2d 1096 (1987),* defendant was accused of sodomizing an eleven-year-old child. Defendant denied any act of sodomy had taken place. A mental health therapist, with expertise with sexually abused victims, saw the victim in counselling seven times. Over defendant's objection, he testified that the boy's progress in therapy was consistent with what he

would expect when a young boy was sodomized under such circumstances. *241 Kan. at 78-79, 734 P.2d 1096.* We found the testimony to be proper, reasoning:
"Although the complained-of testimony was close to the line of impermissibility, it does not cross the line. The witness did not give an opinion as to whether or not P. V. [the victim] was telling the truth."' *Colwell, 246 Kan. at 390-91, 790 P.2d 430." 251 Kan. at 753, 840 P.2d 477.*
Finally, we held in Arrington:
"In the present case, Ms. Inman was not asked and did not directly testify that in her opinion S. was telling the truth but merely testified that based upon her treatment of S. and considering his mental age and severe retardation, she did not think he was capable of being purposely deceitful. While the question may be a close one, we hold that when the testimony objected to is taken in its full context under the facts of this case, the trial court did not abuse its discretion in admitting the testimony." *251 Kan. at 753, 840 P.2d 477.*
There are subtle and not so subtle distinctions in the manner in which the questions leading to a suggestion of truthfulness of the victim are asked. When the trial court overruled defense counsel's objection, Phillips rephrased the question, "I thought he had been coached?" and answered, "[n]o." Technically, as prohibited by Lash and Jackson, the question asked of Phillips does not allow the giving of an opinion that B.M. had been sexually assaulted by Mullins or render an opinion that he was telling the truth. This does not, however, mean the question was proper, as it implies truthfulness. Arrington is factually distinguishable from our case, although it is a decision supporting the State's argument that the question asked did not end up with the witness vouching for the truthfulness of the victim as to the ultimate facts. In *State v. Clements, 241 Kan. 77, 734 P.2d 1096 (1987),* it was held that where the victim's therapist testified that the boy's progress in therapy was consistent with what he would expect of a young boy who had been sodomized, the testimony was deemed proper because the witness did not give an opinion as to whether the victim was telling the truth. A similarity between Clements and our case can be made.

(Cite as: 1999 WL 219181, *10 (Kan.))

In *State v. Smallwood, 264 Kan. 69, 955 P.2d 1209 (1998)* we found that expert testimony that a victim had died from child abuse was not improper because the expert was not testifying as to the ultimate question of the defendant's guilt or innocence. There, testimony that falling off a couch was one of the frequently heard standard excuses given in an instance of bringing an injured child to a hospital was improper, although it was harmless error. In our case, the prosecutor knew the theory of the defense was that B.M. had been induced to bring the subject up and coached in his testimony. As such, the question could have been interpreted by the jury to relate to the activity of the mother. If so interpreted, the question would not have been improper.
However, the question was directed to whether B.M. was coached, which is another way of asking if he was telling the truth. It is a close question, but we believe the line of inquiry to be improper, and the trial court erred in allowing the question to be answered.
This does not, however, require a new trial to be granted as we must determine if the harmless error rule applies. In discussing this rule in *State v. Sanders, 258 Kan. 409, 418, 904 P.2d 951 (1995),* Justice Lockett stated:
"The admission or exclusion of relevant evidence in a criminal case is governed by . . . the harmless error rule. . . . K.S.A. 60-261 sets out the harmless error rule. Error in the admission or exclusion of evidence by the court is not grounds for granting a new trial or setting aside a verdict unless refusal to

continued

State v. Mullins   *continued*

take such action appears to the court inconsistent with substantial justice. At every stage of the proceeding, the court must disregard any error or defect in the proceeding which does not affect the substantial rights of the parties. When reviewing the erroneous admission or exclusion of evidence, the error is harmless if no substantial right of the defendant is involved."

When we apply the directions of K.S.A. 60-261 to our determination, it is difficult to see how the answer to this single question examined in the light of all of the testimony and evidence introduced through 12 witnesses would constitute reversible error. We hold allowing this one answer is harmless error that does not cause prejudice to the substantial rights of Mullins so as to be inconsistent with substantial justice. See *State v. Clark, 263 Kan. 370, 376, 949 P.2d 1099 (1997).*

The conviction of aggravated criminal sodomy is affirmed. The conviction of aggravated indecent liberties with a child is restated pursuant to the rule of State v. Williams to be one of aggravated incest. The sentences for both convictions are vacated, and the case is remanded to the trial court for proper sentencing (under sentencing guidelines in effect at the time of the criminal activity).

Kan., 1999.

State v. Mullins

END OF DOCUMENT

LEGAL ANALYSIS

The examination of legal problems in light of precedents and current circumstances is the critical skill of legal professionals. While only attorneys may exercise legal judgment, the ability to work successfully in a legal environment requires an understanding of the components of the systematic and logical development of legal reasoning. In this unit, you will find answers to the following questions:

■ How does the law apply to a particular fact situation?

■ What tools of reasoning do legal professionals use?

■ How are issues of law formulated?

■ What is meant by the term legal brief?

CHAPTER 9

INTRODUCTION TO LEGAL REASONING

OBJECTIVES

In this chapter, you will discover

- how facts are analyzed

- how to isolate the elements in a particular law

- the process of legal analysis

- how legal professionals apply the steps in legal analysis to develop the issues in a fact situation

OVERVIEW

It is a paradox that legal reasoning theoretically begins with analysis of the law, when in reality legal analysis begins with a factual problem. This problem, a chronological recitation of facts that may or may not be proven, calls the law into play. The law does not expand to embrace facts that would otherwise not be consistent with the meaning of the law. It must be clearly shown that the facts are in accord with the letter of the law, or the law does not apply. This protection against the power of authority has been a stronghold of the United States legal system since its inception.

The steps used to determine whether a particular law will govern a fact situation are outlined below:

1. Isolate the relevant facts.
2. Identify the law.
3. Break the law down into its smallest **elements.**
4. Relate each fact to the elements.
5. Determine the **issues;** that is, whether the facts fit the law. If the facts call questions, these questions are legal issues that must be **adjudicated.**
6. Research the law or perform additional fact investigation to support a resolution.

It may be useful at this point to draw a distinction between questions of fact and questions of law. Generally, **questions of fact** are determined by a jury; **questions of law** are determined by a judge. Questions of fact have to do with who behaved in a particular way, how that person behaved, and whether that behavior caused harm to another. Many times the questions of law will have almost identical language to the questions of fact. One way to distinguish between questions of fact and questions of law is to apply the reasonableness standard. In negligence, if the conduct is not reasonable, it will generally be identified as negligent. What is reasonable depends upon what other prudent persons would do under similar circumstances. Whenever a question calls for a decision about the reasonableness of conduct, it is a question of fact for the jury. If the jury determines that conduct is unreasonable, the judge will generally instruct the jury to make a finding of negligence.

Questions that call for legal judgment are reserved for the judge. These questions arise during the legal proceedings and involve rulings on jury instructions, admission of evidence, and questioning of witnesses. Additionally, the legal conclusions at the close of the proceedings are considered questions of law. These questions (and conclusions) may contain words like responsibility, liability, or negligence.

It may help to examine a hypothetical situation. A second-floor tenant has repeatedly complained to the apartment building manager that the railing on the stairway is shaky and unsafe. According to the terms of the contract, the manager is responsible for maintaining the common areas of the building. The manager has repeatedly insisted that the railing will be fixed, but no work is done. One day, the second-floor tenant, while clutching groceries, grabs for the railing. The railing snaps; the second-floor tenant tumbles down fourteen stairs and is seriously injured.

This situation raises several questions of fact:

- Did the apartment building manager know, or should he or she reasonably have known, about the unsafe condition of the railing?
- Was the manager under a contract obligation to maintain the stairway railing?
- Did the manager have reasonable time and opportunity to repair the stairway?
- Did the disrepair of the railing cause the injury?
- What injuries were sustained?

These are all questions of fact because they have to do with the truth of the events giving rise to the legal dispute. Questions of fact may be submitted to the jury for determination; if there is no jury, these questions of fact will be determined by the judge.

The questions of law raised in this situation are similar:

- Is the apartment building manager negligent for failing to maintain the stairway?
- Is the manager liable for injuries to a tenant resulting from failing to repair a common stairway, the unsafe condition of which the manager knew or reasonably should have known?

It may seem as if the questions of fact and the questions of law are duplicitous. In fact, however, there is a fine distinction, which is consistent with the way matters are proved in court. If the jury finds that the manager had a duty to maintain common stairways, that the manager knew or should have known that the stairway was unsafe, that the manager had reasonable opportunity to repair the stairway and failed to do so, that reasonable apartment building managers would have repaired the stairway, and that the failure to repair the stairway was the cause of the tenant's injuries, those facts will give rise to a finding of negligence. The fact questions are central to the application of the law of negligence. The judgment of negligence is made by the court.

This is a basic illustration of the concept of legal reasoning and identifying the questions of fact (those that must be proved) and the questions of law (those that when the facts are proved, may be argued) are central to this process. This is consistent with the philosophy in American jurisprudence that the facts are controlling and that each action before the court must be judged on the totality of the circumstances then and there existing.

ISOLATING THE FACTS

When a legal problem is approached for the first time, it is difficult to know exactly what facts will be important unless one has a general understanding of the law. Before one can research, analyze, and apply the law, however, relevant facts must be tentatively identified.

This skill of identifying facts is fundamental to the process of legal analysis. It is disputes of fact that most often bring actions to court and it is on the facts that the courts will distinguish cases from previous or similar cases. The relevant facts guide research and provide the basis for additional investigation. Knowledge of the relevant facts assists in drafting pleadings such as complaints and answers. Finally, the facts ultimately determine whether the law applies.

Which facts are important and which are not is often a frustrating dilemma for beginning students of legal analysis. Each person will develop a unique system for initial analysis of the facts. To include more facts than are necessary is far better than overlooking a crucial fact. Recall the problem in Chapter Two involving the intoxicated student in an automobile parked at a fast food restaurant. Analyzing that situation gave rise to important questions of fact: Was Barrett operating a vehicle? Was Barrett's blood alcohol level over the legal limit? Isolating the facts revealed that Barrett had left the vehicle running while she slept and that her blood alcohol content exceeded the legal limit. The fact that the parking lot of the fast food restaurant was not considered public at 3 A.M. resulted in a ruling that the law did not apply, although the law was subsequently changed. The law at that time concerned only public roads. At first glance, the fact that Barrett was in a fast food parking lot at 3 A.M. may not have seemed like an important fact. But including the introductory law and its applicability only on public roads shifted the scales and resulted in a ruling in Barrett's favor. Thus, inclusion of facts may be preferable to exclusion of facts, at least until skill is developed in isolating relevant facts.

Developing skill requires practice. Several examples are provided in Figure 9-1, which will be used later in an analysis of the law. Use these examples to identify and list facts that may seem to be important. Keep in mind that these are abbreviated exercises and that in reality each situation will be replete with facts, both significant and insignificant.

Many legal professionals find it helpful to make a bulleted or numbered list of the facts, using short descriptors. These descriptors may later be matched with the elements of the law to determine what issues are presented. For example, in *Fact Situation 1,* the following may be a list of relevant facts:

- towel wrapped around twelve-year-old girl
- standing on dock
- sixteen-year-old boy snatches towel
- girl immediately dives into water
- suffers injury

There may be other facts that seem important to you. Each person analyzing the facts will "see" them differently, in the same way that people viewing the same room will see different objects. Get into the habit of writing the relevant facts, whether in bulleted lists, numbered lists, or narrative paragraph. Writing the facts will plant them firmly in your memory and will provide

---

FIGURE 9-1

Fact Situation 1

A twelve-year-old girl in a bikini is standing at the end of the dock. Because she is self-conscious about her developing body, she has wrapped a beach towel around herself. A sixteen-year-old boy, an acquaintance of the girl, walks out on the dock and playfully snatches the towel away from the girl's body. The girl, embarrassed, dives immediately into the water without ascertaining its depth. She hits the bottom, breaks her neck, and is rendered a quadriplegic.

Relevant facts: _____

_____

_____

_____

_____

Fact Situation 2

A farmer who is having marital difficulties moves out of his farmhouse and is staying with friends at a neighboring farm. While his friends are in town, the farmer commits suicide in the kitchen of their house by putting a shotgun into his mouth and pulling the trigger. When the friends return from town, the friend's wife enters the kitchen and immediately becomes hysterical. She suffers severe and lasting emotional distress as a result of having found the farmer's body.

Relevant facts: _____

_____

_____

_____

_____

Fact Situation 3

A man purchases a twenty-year-old 35 horsepower outboard motor that has been completely rebuilt. He installs the motor on his boat and, during an outing on the lake, the motor accidentally starts in gear. The man takes the motor to his brother-in-law, who owns a marina. The brother-in-law replaces the parts with like parts from the same manufacturer and returns it to the owner. The next time the owner of the outboard uses it, the motor starts in gear. The man is thrown from the boat, the boat runs over him, and severs his leg.

Relevant facts: _____

_____

_____

_____

_____

Ethics Bookmark

Due Diligence and Promptness

"A lawyer shall act with reasonable diligence and promptness in representing a client" Annotated Model Rules of Professional Conduct Fourth Edition Rule 1.3 Copyright 1999.[2]* *Clients do not often understand how much time is involved in the preparation of a claim. Still, the ethical rules require that an attorney process the legal matter as expeditiously as possible. This may be because the legal matter is one of the most important problems facing the client, and the client is anxious about its resolution. Legal nurse consultants must keep in mind the anxiety of the client and work with reasonable promptness to complete all assigned tasks. Where tasks cannot be completed in a timely manner, a note to the client will assure the client that the matter has not been abandoned by law firm personnel.*

*American Bar Association. Reprinted by permission of the American Bar Association. American Bar Association, *Annotated Model Rules of Professional conduct,* 4th ed. (1999) Rule 1.3. Copies of Model Code of Professional Responsibility, 1999 edition are available from Service Center, American Bar Association, 750 North Lake Shore Drive, Chicago, IL 60611-4497, 1-800-285-2221.

guidance when researching and analyzing the problem. Later, when memoranda are produced concerning this legal problem, your writing will save time and effort.

IDENTIFYING ELEMENTS IN THE LAW

Legal analysis continues with a look at the law. Once the law has been researched and a ruling appears to be on point, it must be analyzed in relation to the facts. To do this, the law must be broken down into its smallest parts, called elements. These elements are the points that must be proven in order to call the law into play. For example, in a court opinion the judge has described a battery as "an intentional infliction of a harmful bodily contact upon another."[3] It is relatively easy to identify what must be proven in order to establish liability for battery: a bodily contact that is intentional and results in harm.

To clearly identify the elements of the law, it is helpful again to make a bulleted or numbered list:

- physical contact
- intentional
- harm

The list is valuable for comparing the elements of the law with the facts and for later recollection of the analysis when preparing memoranda and other work papers.

The ability to identify elements is basic to all legal reasoning and is a springboard for all other legal activities. Element identification is essential for recognizing the issues that must be resolved. Drafting complaints and responsive pleadings is dependent upon the ability to meet each element of a legal claim or defense. Knowing what must be proven guides the investigation and the gathering of evidence. Being able to list the elements of a law is fundamental to legal procedure. Rules of law that may be applicable to the fact situations described in Figure 9-1 are included in Figure 9-2. List the elements that you believe must be proven in order to find liability.

COMPARING THE FACTS TO THE ELEMENTS

The next step in legal analysis is to compare the law with the facts. To do this, the bulleted or numbered lists may be employed effectively. Please note the comparison in the first fact situation with the law of battery illustrated in Figure 9-3.

Several questions come immediately to mind:

- Does snatching a towel constitute bodily contact?
- What is meant by intentional? Is it intent to harm or simply intent to cause a bodily contact?
- Could or should the boy have anticipated that the girl would panic and seek the first place that offered cover?

FIGURE 9-2

Law 1

"A definition (not all-inclusive but sufficient for our purpose) of battery is the intentional infliction of a harmful bodily contact upon another."[3]

Elements of the law: _____

_____

_____

_____

_____

Law 2

"Intentional infliction of emotional distress occurs when a person, by extreme or outrageous conduct, or with conduct in complete and reckless disregard for the rights of another, causes in that person severe emotional distress. Severe emotional distress is defined as distress which is disabling or results in the inability to function in work or relationships."[4]

Elements of the law: _____

_____

_____

_____

_____

Law 3

A warranty is a promise about the quality or characteristics of a product. Whenever a product is put on the market, the Uniform Commercial Code identifies an implied warranty that exists on the product. The implied warranty is that the product is safe for its reasonably anticipated use or consumption. A similar warranty exists when repair is made on the product. The person repairing promises that the product is fixed.[5]

Elements of the law: _____

_____

_____

_____

_____

FIGURE 9-3   Comparison or Fact and Law

Law	Facts
Physical contact	Boy snatches towel wrapped around girl's body
Intentional	Boy intended to cause girl embarrassment
Harm	Dive in shallow water results in broken neck and quadriplegia

The process of legal analysis does not immediately allow a conclusion; rather, it promotes questions that must be researched and argued. These legal questions that result from applying the facts to the elements of the law are called the legal issues. Issues cannot be legally resolved by simple or arbitrary decision. Resolution must be built upon a logical argument supported by precedent and other compelling foundation.

Look at *Fact Situation 2* and the law of intentional infliction of emotional distress. Make a comparison of the elements you have identified in the law of emotional distress and the relevant facts you selected from *Fact Situation 2.* Now try *Fact Situation 3* compared with *Law 3.*

To arrive at the issues, one must apply facts to the elements of law. Once the legal questions have been raised, additional analysis, usually based on additional factual or legal research, is required. In addition, to properly support an argued resolution, one must be prepared to rebut the opposing point of view. This is called **counteranalysis.**

Laws very often have been interpreted through the process of previous litigation. In order to determine the definition of intent, for instance, the case law in which intent is an issue would be researched. These cases would tell the legal professional how the court has defined intent. This definition would be broken down into its elements, and additional facts concerning the knowledge of the sixteen-year-old boy in *Fact Situation 1* would be investigated to see how the facts fit the law of intent.

The cycle continues until the analysis and the research lead to a logical, legally supportable argument with which to persuade the court.

CHAPTER SUMMARY

- ■ Legal analysis involves the relation of facts to elements of law.
- ■ Isolating relevant facts requires practice and an understanding of law.

- Isolating elements of a rule of law requires identification of what must be proven.
- Issues result when the facts do not exactly match the elements or when questions arise about how the facts fit.
- Legal analysis is often cyclical requiring additional research and analysis of the facts relative to different rules of law.

KEY TERMS

adjudication	elements	question of fact
counteranalysis	issues	question of law

REVIEW QUESTIONS

1. Identify the steps in legal analysis.
2. Why is it often difficult to isolate the relevant facts?
3. Explain why it is important to be able to identify the elements of a rule of law?

INTERNET EXERCISES

1. Access the web page for this textbook at *www.westlegalstudies.com.*
2. Click on the assignments section of the web page and complete the assignment(s) for Chapter Nine.

EXERCISES

1. Networking. Contact the law librarian at the county courthouse near you. Ask to make an appointment and tell the librarian that you are interested in pattern jury instructions. The pattern jury instructions identify what must be plead and proven in order to recover in an action at law. At the appointment, ask the librarian to explain to you how the pattern jury instructions are organized and spend some time reviewing the pattern jury instructions for the torts that interest you.
2. Professional Portfolio. Practice isolating relevant facts and identifying elements. Using the jury instructions, develop fact situations and show how the issues are determined. Include in your resume or cover letter that you understand the process of legal analysis or that you have acquired skill in legal analysis.

ENDNOTES

1. G. Van Allen, "The Increasing Demand for Courtroom Nurses." *The Oklahoma Nurse,* July, August, September, 1996, 31.

2. American Bar Association, *Annotated Model Rules of Professional Conduct,* (1999) 4th Edition, Rule 1.3. Copies of ABA *Model Code of Professional Responsibility, 1999 Edition* are available from Service Center, American Bar Association, 750 North Lake Shore Drive, Chicago, IL 60611-4497, 1-800-285-2221.

3. *Garratt v. Dailey,* 46 Wash. 2d 197, 279 P. 2d 1091 (1955).

4. *Harris v. Jones,* 281 Md. 560, 380 A. 2d. 611 (1977).

5. Uniform Commercial Code, s. 2-313.

ADDITIONAL REFERENCES

Oldham, R., RN, BS. *Medical Legal Internet Directory.* Peoria, AZ: R & G Press, 1997.

Statsky, W., *Essentials of Paralegalism,* 3rd ed. St. Paul, Minnesota: West Thomson Learning, 1998.

CHAPTER 10

LEGAL AUTHORITY

OBJECTIVES

In this chapter, you will discover

- what constitutes legal authority
- what is meant by primary authority
- how to analyze case law
- the sources of primary authority

OVERVIEW

Authority is generally defined as a power to act. When looking at legal analysis or legal reasoning, however, **authority** has a different meaning. Authority in the law is used to support an argument and usually refers to the legal basis for a position. When a judge asks, "What's your authority?" the response is generally expected to reveal a statute, a previous case, or an administrative regulation or ruling. There are several classifications of authority: primary, secondary, binding, and persuasive. Legal nurse consultants should be familiar with how these authorities are used in the process of analyzing legal problems.

TYPES OF AUTHORITY

There are basically two types of authority: primary and secondary. **Primary authority** is often called the "letter of the law," because it constitutes that which has been written and generally accepted as having the force of law (violation will result in a consequence). **Secondary authority,** on the other hand, includes the writings that explain or criticize the primary authority. Legal reasoning includes an examination of authority (legal research) in order to better understand the legal position and to develop sound arguments supported by nonarbitrary sources.

PRIMARY SOURCES

Primary authority is the preferred basis for an argument. It is called primary because it should be the first place one looks to determine the law governing a particular set of facts. Primary sources include statutory law, such as Constitutions, treaties and statutes; case law; and administrative rules and regulations.

Classes of Primary Authority

Primary sources may be **binding** (mandatory) or **persuasive.** A statute, which is primary authority, will be binding when the particular circumstances under examination occur within the geographical territory in which the statute was enacted and is in force. Similarly, case law will be binding in the geographical jurisdiction of the court issuing the opinion, while administrative rules and regulations will be binding in the geographical region in which they were made.

If a primary source is binding, it must be used by the court in making a decision. This is the strongest basis for an argument—binding authority. Only primary sources may be binding, but primary sources may also be persuasive. For example, a decision of the highest appeals court in Delaware will be a primary binding authority on all Delaware courts and a statute enacted by the legislature of Delaware will be a primary binding authority throughout the state. In Michigan, this Delaware court opinion and this Delaware statute will still be primary authority, but a court need not consider it in arriving at its decision. In Michigan, these laws are persuasive only.

The distinction between primary and secondary authority and between primary binding and primary persuasive authority is important to grasp. This distinction is what makes the difference in a concept called **hierarchy of authority.**

Hierarchy of Authority

When a legal problem is being analyzed, authority will have a graduating scale of importance in terms of how much consideration it will be given in the resolution of the matter. A decision of the United States Supreme Court is primary binding on all other federal and state courts; a decision of the Iowa Supreme Court is primary binding on all courts in Iowa alone. When there have been both state and federal statutes or rulings on a matter, which law takes precedence is a question that must be addressed.

Consider this hypothetical example: a statute in Kentucky states that medical treatment may not be provided without the consent of the patient or, if the patient is a minor or incompetent, the consent of the patient's guardian. An adult patient at a Kentucky mental health institution is suicidal and refuses food and drink. Parents of the adult patient may sue the mental health institution claiming that failure to provide intravenous feeding to the patient constitutes a denial of life, liberty, or property; a violation of due process of law; and the Constitutional provisions of equal protection.

Because the problem arose in Kentucky, the Kentucky statute is primary binding authority. The courts in Kentucky may declare the statute requiring consent of the patient to be constitutional and enforceable. Therefore, the health care facility cannot force the adult patient to eat. Suicidal depression, the court may reason (based on expert testimony), does not render the patient incompetent for purposes of giving consent to medical treatment. This ruling of the trial court may be appealed through the state court system. If affirmed, the parents may appeal to the United States Supreme Court. The United States Supreme Court may agree that the state statute is constitutional, but might still hold that the actions of the mental health facility are in violation of the due process clause of the Constitution. This ruling may seem contradictory, but there is solid reasoning for the court's determination.

It has long been held that a patient must be able to give an informed consent to the treatment offered by a health care facility.[1] It has also long been held that where emergency conditions do not allow for consent at the time of the life-threatening condition, it is incumbent upon the health care provider to act with reasonable care to save the life of the patient, even without consent.

In the case of a patient confined to a mental health facility being treated for suicidal depression, the court may conclude that the patient is indeed within the emergency exception to the statute. The patient is not willing to grant permission, and the mental health facility, by not employing means to save the patient's life, is denying that patient life, liberty, and property in violation of the due process clause of the constitution.[2]

Ethics Bookmark

Competence

"A lawyer shall provide competent representation to a client" Annotated Model Rules of Professional Conduct Fourth Edition Rule 1.1 Copyright 1999.* ³ Competency means that the professional providing service has the knowledge and skills to adequately serve the client. While attorneys may not know all there is to know about the law or legal procedure, attorneys must be cognizant of the resources for finding the law that applies to the client's problem. Likewise, legal nurse consultants employed by attorneys must be knowledgeable about the medical areas of practice for which they are employed.

*American Bar Association. Reprinted by permission of the American Bar Association. American bar Association, *Annotated Model Rules of Professional conduct,* 4th ed. (1999) Rule 1.1. Copies of Model Code of Professional Responsibility, 1999 edition are available from Service Center, American Bar Association, 750 North Lake Shore Drive, Chicago, IL 60611-4497, 1-800-285-2221.

Whenever a new legal problem presents similar facts, the hierarchy of authority must be established. In this case, the United States Supreme Court's decision is not acceptable to the people, Congress might enact a law that allows mental health facilities to honor the refusal of a patient to accept food and drink. This statute may supercede the earlier Supreme Court ruling. If, however, the Supreme Court determines that the statute is unenforceable and that a constitutional amendment would be needed to obtain a different result, the process for amending the constitution would have to be followed in order to overturn the Supreme Court. The decision of the Supreme Court is the most powerful in the ladder of reasoning. The court decision that interprets the statute will be placed higher in the argument than the general terms of the statute. A legislative override of the court decision will supercede that ruling and the original statute.

The concept of hierarchy of authority is sometimes complicated. An understanding of the concepts of primary authority and the circumstances in which primary authority will be binding or persuasive are critical to development of the argument. Sometimes determining which primary binding sources have greater weight in resolution of the legal problem will be a matter of professional legal judgment.

There are some general guidelines for establishing hierarchy of authority. Primary binding authority is always most important. Primary binding is always better than primary persuasive unless there are compelling reasons in the case why precedent should be overturned, and primary persuasive is generally considered better than secondary. If there is no precedent (binding authority), primary persuasive and secondary may be used to convince the court to adopt a particular ruling. A table of how primary authority affects courts in the United States is provided in Figure 10-1.

STATUTES

Any law written and adopted by the people or by delegates on behalf of the people falls within the category of statutory law. Statutory law is always primary authority—the letter of the law. It includes constitutions, treaties, Acts of Congress, state laws, county resolutions, city ordinances, and any other legislative act.

Statutes are read for their **plain meaning,** that is, what ordinary people would understand from the language of the law. Statutes are not meant to have hidden meanings and cannot be interpreted as such. Analyzing statutes requires reading the statute and selecting the elements of that statute that must be met with the facts in order to call that statute into governance over the legal problem.

Statutes are subject to interpretation by the courts. A judicial definition will supercede the plain meaning and will require additional legal analysis to determine whether the facts of the situation will fit into the judicial interpretation of the statute. Figure 10-2 gives an example of a client's problem and the statute that might apply. Select the relevant facts. Isolate the elements of the

---

FIGURE 10-1   Hierarchy of Authority

Type	Mandatory	Persuasive
US Constitution	All federal and state courts	
US Supreme Court Decision	All federal and state courts	
Federal Statute	All federal and state courts	
Federal Administrative Regulation	All federal and state courts	
US Court of Appeals Decision	All federal courts *within circuit*	All other federal and state courts
US District Court Decision	All specialized lower federal courts, if any, *within district*	All other federal and state courts
State Constitution	All state courts *within state*	
Decision of Highest State Court	All state courts *within state*	All other federal and state courts
State Statute	All state courts *within state;* Federal courts applying or interpreting	
State Administrative Regulation	All state courts *within state*	
Decision of State Appeals Court	All state courts *within jurisdiction*	All other federal and state courts

---

law. Compare the facts to the elements and identify the issues. The issues that arise from legal analysis are the legal questions. To answer the questions, additional authority must be found and studied through legal research. For a discussion of legal analysis, see Chapter Nine.

CASE LAW

Sometimes case law is referred to as common law or judge-made law. Because of the legacy of the English common law system (handing down precedent), the courts in the United States have continued to provide remedies in situations that are not governed by statute.

Negligence, for example, is not usually a criminal act and therefore is not generally included in the Criminal Codes (statutes) of most states. (There are some exceptions to this. Homicide by negligent use of a vehicle or by negligent use of a firearm or explosive are examples of criminal acts that arise out of a negligent standard of conduct.) Common law (case law) has identified four elements of negligence: (a) a duty to act with care for the safety of another, (b) a violation of that duty, and the violation of that duty (c) causing (d) harm to another. The injured person is recognized under common law as

What LNCs Say . . .

"A legal nurse consultant should have a permanent library for ease of reference. I recommend the following: Harrison's Internal Medicine (CD ROM), a good anatomy-physiology book, PDR, CPT & ICD-9 Code books, and Dorland's Medical Dictionary," Kathleen Sullivan, RN, BS, Habush, Habush, Davis & Rotier, Madison, WI, used with permission.

FIGURE 10-2   Hypothetical Case

After several visits to his family physician seeking relief from headache pain, Hasam Simsek underwent a CT scan. Based on the results of the scan, Simsek was referred to Carol Jackson, a neurosurgeon. Dr. Jackson diagnosed a basilar bifurcation aneurysm and recommended surgery as soon as possible. She indicated that the surgery to clip a basilar bifurcation aneurysm was relatively simple, that she had performed the surgery on a number of occasions, and that the risks involved were minimal. When Simsek asked how minimal, Dr. Jackson said the risks were equivalent to the risks involved in an appendectomy or a tonsillectomy. Dr. Jackson had, at the time, only once operated on a posterior aneurysm and had performed only twenty surgeries involving anterior circulation aneurysms. On January 17, Simsek underwent surgery after signing a standard informed consent form. As a result of the surgery, Simsek was rendered a quadriplegic.

FOR EDUCATIONAL USE ONLY W.S.A. 448.30

WEST'S WISCONSIN STATUTES ANNOTATED
REGULATION AND LICENSING
CHAPTER 448. MEDICAL PRACTICES
SUBCHAPTER II. MEDICAL EXAMINING BOARD

Copr. © West Group 1999. All rights reserved.
Current through 1999 Act 7, published 8/11/1999

448.30. Information on alternate modes of treatment

Any physician who treats a patient shall inform the patient about the availability of all alternate, viable medical modes of treatment and about the benefits and risks of these treatments. The physician's duty to inform the patient under this section does not require disclosure of:

(1) Information beyond what a reasonably well-qualified physician in a similar medical classification would know.
(2) Detailed technical information that in all probability a patient would not understand.
(3) Risks apparent or known to the patient.
(4) Extremely remote possibilities that might falsely or detrimentally alarm the patient.
(5) Information in emergencies where failure to provide treatment would be more harmful to the patient than treatment.
(6) Information in cases where the patient is incapable of consenting.

<<For credits, see Historical Note field.>>

<*General Materials (GM)*—References, Annotations, or Tables>

HISTORICAL AND STATUTORY NOTES
1997 Main Volume

Source:
L.1981, c. 375, § 2, eff. May 7, 1982.

LAW REVIEW AND JOURNAL COMMENTARIES

Pushing the limits of informed consent: Johnson v. Kokemoor and physician-specific disclosure. Richard A. Heinemann, Wis.L.Rev. 1079 (1997).

LIBRARY REFERENCES
1997 Main Volume

Physicians and Surgeons 15(8).

having a remedy against the wrongdoer, even though the conduct of the wrongdoer would not constitute a crime.

These court-made laws have as much weight in terms of primary authority as statutory law. Case law identifies rights, responsibilities, and remedies that are part of the natural heritage of human endeavors and are intended to be protected as such.

Reading Case Law

When reading case law, it is important to keep certain guidelines in mind. These guidelines are listed in Figure 10-3.

Court Rendering Opinion. The court writing the opinion will determine whether this court-made law is primary binding or primary persuasive. Since case law is only precedent in the geographic jurisdiction where the decision was made, this is one of the first considerations in determining how this case law will be used in resolution of the problem at hand. A United States Supreme Court opinion will be primary binding on all state and federal courts. However, a ruling of the United States Second Circuit Court of Appeals will only be primary binding in the second circuit. It may be highly persuasive in the other circuits, but the courts in those circuits are free to accept or reject the reasoning of the second circuit. Within the second circuit, however, the law (precedent) has been established, and it becomes binding on all later cases with similar facts, law, and issues.

FIGURE 10-3   Guidelines for Reading Case Law

Recognize . . .	Why
Court rendering the opinion	To determine whether the case law is binding or persuasive
Year of decision	To determine the point at which it is necessary to check for statutory override or later case rulings invalidating this opinion
Headnotes	To initially determine if the case is on point with the current legal problem
Facts	To determine whether the facts in the current problem are sufficiently similar to call the law into play
Issues	To determine if the legal question in the case is similar to the legal issue in the current problem
Decision	To determine the outcome or the rule of law established in the previous case
Reasoning	To identify the law and facts relied upon by the court in making its ruling; to identify additional sources of research

Trial courts generally do not establish precedent. While case law will always be primary authority, trial court rulings are not considered binding. In some states, trial court decisions will be binding only within the counties or districts in which those rulings are handed down. Trial court judgments are generally not published, with the exception of selected United States District Court cases reported by West Group in its *Federal Supplement* and *Federal Rules Decisions*. In order to have precedential value (primary binding) the case must have reached an appeals court for an objective review and determination of the law, and the opinion of the appellate court must have been designated for publication.

Year of Decision. Another important consideration when analyzing case law is the year of decision. Because the law is flexible and therefore changes with advances in technology and society, the ruling in the case you are analyzing may have subsequently been changed by a later opinion. Validation of the ruling requires a search of later law to determine that this ruling is still intact. In addition, because case law may be superceded by legislative act, later statutes must be reviewed in order to determine whether the court ruling is still good law.

Headnotes. More often than not, the court opinion being analyzed will have been reported in a way that provides editorial notes and research aids. It is important not to confuse these editorial features with the law that is expressed by the judges in the opinion. **Headnotes** often precede the court opinion. These are short descriptive paragraphs prepared by the editors of the publishing company identifying the facts and law that are at issue in the case. Because they are written by the editors and not the court, they cannot be relied upon as authority. In fact, to quote from the headnotes would be plagiarism and could be punishable as infringement of copyright. The court opinion itself is public domain so anyone can copy and distribute it. The headnotes help a researcher establish that the case is on point, but the opinion must be read in order to know what rulings of law were made.

All court opinions contain the same basic components: the facts of the case, the legal issues, an analysis of the law, and a decision of the court. When reading case law, the components should be given careful scrutiny.

Facts. Identification of relevant facts is a process that may require some practice, but it is essential to analysis. In the same way that the facts of consequence were isolated from the legal problem to be analyzed, the facts in a court opinion must be selected to determine whether there is sufficient similarity to the current problem to call the case law into play.

Issue. The legal question that is presented to the court must be similar to the legal question under analysis in order to use the court opinion as authority. This question is generally stated very early in the court opinion, sometimes in the first paragraph.

Decision. How the court ruled on the issue is critical to the analysis of the current legal problem. If the facts and issue in the court opinion are similar to the facts and issue in the problem being analyzed, the preceding court opinion will be given great consideration. It will be binding authority if the court opinion is in the geographical jurisdiction of the current problem; it will be primary persuasive if it is outside the jurisdiction.

Reasoning. The court will provide a foundation for its ruling by describing the law being relied upon and how the facts were related to the law. This analysis will assist in developing the argument in the current problem and may lead to sources of law that were not discovered or analyzed previously. Court decisions in the United States may not be arbitrary, capricious, or whimsical. It is critical for a court to support its ruling. Courts do this by showing relationship to precedent. When no prior law exists, they must demonstrate reasoning using sociological literature, medical literature, economic literature, or technological literature and the relationship between this new fact situation and an understanding of previous law.

Analyzing Case Law

Analyzing case law requires an examination of the case in terms of its similarities to the present situation, its differences to the present situation, and the need for additional information. To determine the factual similarities, look to the parties, places or things involved, the cause of action, and the remedies sought. The court opinion reproduced in Figure 10-4 relates to the facts and the statute provided in Figure 10-2.

If the parties are both surgical patients who have signed standard consent forms, and the language of the consent forms is virtually the same, it is safe to conclude that the previous case ruling applies to the present fact situation. The decision in the previous case should be adhered to as precedent.

If the previous case involves a patient undergoing sensitive neurosurgery, and the problem you are analyzing involves a patient undergoing relatively routine orthopedic surgery, the facts are somewhat dissimilar and the differences may indicate that the precedent is not applicable.

If the patient is undergoing neurosurgery, as in the precedent case, and records indicate that the patient watched a videotape, was given the opportunity to ask questions concerning the procedure, and was given general information about the risks involved, it may be important to know what specific information the neurosurgeon provided to the patient. This factual gap might have to be filled with investigation before a determination can be made as to the applicability of the precedent case to the new fact situation.

ADMINISTRATIVE RULES AND REGULATIONS

Administrative agencies are an extension of the legislative and executive branches of government. Experts within the agencies are expected to make regulations (legislative) and to enforce (executive) the purposes and intent of acts passed by Congress. For example, to implement the Civil Rights Act of 1964, Congress created the Equal Employment Opportunity Commission and vested it with powers to create, enforce, and adjudicate regulations consistent with the Civil Rights Act.[4]

Net Results

Primary Authority on the Internet

All federal statutes and most state laws are now available on the Internet at government web sites. A universal resource locator for state statutes can be found at www.legis.state.XX.us, where the XX is the two-letter postal abbreviation for that state. The laws of the United States can be found at the government web site, www.house.gov, at the web site for the Cornell Law School, www.law.cornell.edu/uscode, and at www.findlaw.com.

FIGURE 10-4

(Cite as: 199 Wis.2d 615, 545 N.W.2d 495)

Donna L. ←**JOHNSON**→, by her Guardian Ad Litem, Timothy J. ADLER, Plaintiff-Respondent-Petitioner,
v.
Dr. Richard KOKEMOOR, Physicians Insurance Company of Wisconsin and Wisconsin
Patients Compensation Fund, Defendants-Appellants-Cross Petitioners,
Sacred Heart Hospital, Wisconsin Healthcare Liability Plan, Wisconsin
Department of Health and Social Services and Healthcare Financing
Administration, Defendants.
No. 93-3099.
Supreme Court of Wisconsin.
Argued Nov. 1, 1995.
Decided March 20, 1996.

W.S.A. 448.30.

Milwaukee for the Wisconsin Academy of Trial Lawyers.
SHIRLEY S. ABRAHAMSON, Justice.
This is a review of a published decision of the court of appeals, *Johnson v. Kokemoor, 188 Wis.2d 202, 525 N.W.2d 71 (Ct.App.1994)*, reversing an order of the circuit court for Chippewa County, Richard H. Stafford, judge. We reverse the decision of the court of appeals and remand the cause to the circuit court for further proceedings on the question of damages. [FN1]

  FN1. The trial was bifurcated at the circuit court. The jury decided only the liability issue; the issue of damages has not been tried.

(Cite as: 199 Wis.2d 615, *620, 545 N.W.2d 495, **497)

Donna Johnson (the plaintiff) brought an action against Dr. Richard Kokemoor (the defendant) [FN2] alleging his failure to obtain her ←**informed consent**→ to surgery as required by *Wis.Stat. § 448.30* (1993-94). [FN3] The jury found that the defendant failed to adequately inform the plaintiff regarding the risks associated with her surgery. The jury also found that a reasonable person in the plaintiff's position would have refused to *621

(Cite as: 199 Wis.2d 615, *621, 545 N.W.2d 495, **497)

consent to surgery by the defendant if she had been fully informed of its attendant risks and advantages. [FN4]

  FN2. While there are other defendants in this case, in the interest of clarity we refer only to Dr. Kokemoor as the defendant.

  FN3. All future statutory references are to the 1993–94 volume of the Wisconsin Statutes.

  FN4. The parties agreed to a special verdict form requiring the jury to answer the following two questions:

(1) Did Dr. Richard Kokemoor fail to adequately inform Donna Johnson of the risks and advantages of her surgery?

(2) If you have answered Question 1 "yes", then and then only answer this

(Cite as: 199 Wis.2d 615, *621, 545 N.W.2d 495, **497)

question: Would a reasonable person in Donna Johnson's position have refused to consent to the surgery by Dr. Richard Kokemoor had she been informed of the risks and advantages of the surgery?

The jury answered "yes" to both questions.

The circuit court denied the defendant's motions to change the answers in the special verdict and, in the alternative, to order a new trial. In a split decision, the court of appeals reversed the circuit court's order. This case presents the issue of whether the circuit court erred in admitting evidence that the defendant, in undertaking his duty to obtain the plaintiff's ←**informed consent**→ before operating to clip an aneurysm, failed (1) to divulge the extent of his experience in performing this type of operation; (2) to compare the morbidity and mortality rates [FN5] for this type of surgery among experienced surgeons and inexperienced surgeons like himself; and (3) to refer the plaintiff to a tertiary care center staffed by physicians more experienced in performing the same surgery. *[**498*

(Cite as: 199 Wis.2d 615, *621, 545 N.W.2d 495, **498)

FN6] The **622*

(Cite as: 199 Wis.2d 615, *622, 545 N.W.2d 495, **498)

admissibility of such physician-specific evidence in a case involving the doctrine of ←**informed consent**→ raises an issue of first impression in this court and is an issue with which appellate courts have had little experience.

FN5. As used by the parties and in this opinion, morbidity and mortality

(Cite as: 199 Wis.2d 615, *622, 545 N.W.2d 495, **498)

rates refer to the prospect that surgery may result in serious impairment or death.

FN6. In a motion brought prior to trial, the defendant attempted to bar testimony and argument relating to his personal experience with aneurysm surgery and to the relative experience of other surgeons available to perform such surgery. The defendant argued that such disclosures are not material to the issue of ←**informed consent**→. The circuit court denied the defendant's motion and also ruled that the plaintiff could present expert testimony that the defendant should have advised her of and referred her to more experienced neurosurgeons.

The court of appeals concluded that the first two evidentiary matters were admissible but that the third was not. The court of appeals determined that evidence about the defendant's failure to refer the plaintiff to more experienced physicians was not relevant to a claim of failure to obtain the plaintiff's ←**informed consent**→. *Johnson, 188 Wis.2d at 223, 525 N.W.2d 71.* Furthermore, the court of appeals held that the circuit court committed prejudicial error in admitting evidence of the defendant's failure

continued

FIGURE 10-4 *continued*

to refer, because such evidence allowed the jury to conclude that the defendant performed negligently simply because he was less experienced than other physicians, even

(Cite as: 199 Wis.2d 615, *622, 545 N.W.2d 495, **498)

though the defendant's negligence was not at issue in this case. *Johnson, 188 Wis.2d at 224, 525 N.W.2d 71.* [FN7] The court of appeals therefore remanded the cause to the circuit court for a new trial. [FN8]

> FN7. Prior to trial, the plaintiff had voluntarily dismissed a cause of action alleging that the defendant was negligent in performing the surgery.

> FN8. Given the "overwhelming" evidence "that Kokemoor did not adequately inform Johnson," *Johnson v. Kokemoor, 188 Wis.2d 202, 227, 525 N.W.2d 71 (Ct.App.1994),* the court of appeals left to the circuit court's discretion whether it need retry the issue of the defendant's alleged failure to obtain the plaintiffs ←**informed consent**→ or whether it need retry only the causation issue.

The plaintiff's position is that the court of appeals erred in directing a new trial. The defendant's position ***623***

(Cite as: 199 Wis.2d 615, *623, 545 N.W.2d 495, **498)

in his cross-petition is that the circuit court and the court of appeals both erred in approving the admission of evidence referring to his experience with this type of surgery and to his and other physicians' morbidity and mortality statistics in performing this type of surgery.
We conclude that all three items of evidence were material to the issue

(Cite as: 199 Wis.2d 615, *623, 545 N.W.2d 495, **498)

of ←**informed consent**→ in this case. As we stated in *Martin v. Richards, 192 Wis.2d 156, 174, 531 N.W.2d 70 (1995),* "a patient cannot make an informed, intelligent decision to consent to a physician's suggested treatment unless the physician discloses what is material to the patient's decision, i.e., all of the viable alternatives and risks of the treatment proposed." In this case information regarding a physician's experience in performing a particular procedure, a physician's risk statistics as compared with those of other physicians who perform that procedure, and the availability of other centers and physicians better able to perform that procedure would have facilitated the plaintiff's awareness of "all of the viable alternatives" available to her and thereby aided her exercise of ←**informed consent**→. We therefore conclude that under the circumstances of this case, the circuit court did not erroneously exercise its discretion in admitting the evidence.

I.

We first summarize the facts giving rise to this review, recognizing that the parties dispute whether several events occurred, as well as what inferences should be drawn from both the disputed and the undisputed historical facts.
On the advice of her family physician, the plaintiff underwent a CT scan to determine the cause of her headaches. Following the scan, the family physician ***624***

(Cite as: 199 Wis.2d 615, *624, 545 N.W.2d 495, **498)

referred the plaintiff to the defendant, a neurosurgeon in the Chippewa Falls area. The defendant diagnosed an enlarging aneurysm at the rear of the

(Cite as: 199 Wis.2d 615, *624, 545 N.W.2d 495, **498)

plaintiff's brain and recommended surgery to clip the aneurysm. [FN9] The defendant performed the surgery in October of 1990.

> FN9. The defendant acknowledged at trial that the aneurysm was not the cause of the plaintiff's headaches.

**499

(Cite as: 199 Wis.2d 615, *624, 545 N.W.2d 495, **499)

The defendant clipped the aneurysm, rendering the surgery a technical success. But as a consequence of the surgery, the plaintiff, who had no neurological impairments prior to surgery, was rendered an incomplete quadriplegic. She remains unable to walk or to control her bowel and bladder movements. Furthermore, her vision, speech and upper body coordination are partially impaired. At trial, the plaintiff introduced evidence that the defendant overstated the urgency of her need for surgery and overstated his experience with performing the particular type of aneurysm surgery which she required. According to testimony introduced during the plaintiff's case in chief, when the plaintiff questioned the defendant regarding his experience, he replied that he had performed the surgery she required "several" times; asked what he meant by "several," the defendant said "dozens" and "lots of times." In fact, however, the defendant had relatively limited experience with aneurysm surgery. He had performed thirty aneurysm surgeries during residency.

(Cite as: 199 Wis.2d 615, *624, 545 N.W.2d 495, **499)

but all of them involved anterior circulation aneurysms. According to the plaintiff's experts, operations performed to clip anterior circulation aneurysms are significantly less complex than those necessary to clip posterior circulation aneurysms such as the plaintiff's. [FN10] ***625**

(Cite as: 199 Wis.2d 615, *625, 545 N.W.2d 495, **499)

Following residency, the defendant had performed aneurysm surgery on six patients with a total of nine aneurysms. He had operated on basilar bifurcation aneurysms only twice and had never operated on a large basilar bifurcation aneurysm such as the plaintiff's aneurysm. [FN11]

> FN10. The plaintiff's aneurysm was located at the bifurcation of the basilar artery. According to the plaintiff's experts, surgery on basilar bifurcation aneurysms is more difficult than any other type of aneurysm surgery.

> FN11. The defendant testified that he had failed to inform the plaintiff that he was not and never had been board certified in neurosurgery and that he was not a subspecialist in aneurysm surgery.

The plaintiff also presented evidence that the defendant understated the morbidity and mortality rate associated with basilar bifurcation aneurysm surgery. According to the plaintiff's witnesses, the defendant had told the

continued

FIGURE 10-4 *continued*

(Cite as: 199 Wis.2d 615, *625, 545 N.W.2d 495, **499)

plaintiff that her surgery carried a two percent risk of death or serious impairment and that it was less risky than the angiogram procedure she would have to undergo in preparation for surgery. The plaintiff's witnesses also testified that the defendant had compared the risks associated with the plaintiff's surgery to those associated with routine procedures such as tonsillectomies, appendectomies and gall bladder surgeries. [FN12]

> FN12. The defendant testified at trial that he had informed the plaintiff that should she decide to forego surgery, the risk that her unclipped aneurysm might rupture was two percent per annum, cumulative. Since he informed the plaintiff that the risk accompanying surgery was two percent, a reasonable person in the plaintiff's position might have concluded that proceeding with surgery was less risky than non-operative management.

***626**

(Cite as: 199 Wis.2d 615, *626, 545 N.W.2d 495, **499)

The plaintiff's neurosurgical experts testified that even the physician considered to be one of the world's best aneurysm surgeons, who had performed hundreds of posterior circulation aneurysm surgeries, had reported a morbidity and mortality rate of ten-and-seven-tenths percent when operating upon basilar bifurcation aneurysms comparable in size to the plaintiff's aneurysm. Furthermore, information in treatises and articles which the defendant reviewed in preparation for the plaintiff's surgery set the morbidity

(Cite as: 199 Wis.2d 615, *626, 545 N.W.2d 495, **499)

and mortality rate at approximately fifteen percent for a basilar bifurcation aneurysm. The plaintiff also introduced expert testimony that the morbidity and mortality rate for basilar bifurcation aneurysm operations performed by one with the defendant's relatively limited experience would be between twenty and thirty percent, and "closer to the thirty percent range." [FN13]

> FN13. The plaintiff introduced into evidence as exhibits articles from the medical literature stating that there are few areas in neurosurgery where the difference in results between surgeons is as evident as it is with aneurysms. One of the plaintiff's neurosurgical experts testified that experience and skill with the operator is more important when performing basilar tip aneurysm surgery than with any other neurosurgical procedure.

Finally, the plaintiff introduced into evidence testimony and exhibits stating that a ****500**

(Cite as: 199 Wis.2d 615, *626, 545 N.W.2d 495, **500)

reasonable physician in the defendant's position would have advised the plaintiff of the availability of more experienced surgeons and would have referred her to them. The plaintiff also introduced evidence stating that patients with basilar aneurysms should be referred to tertiary care centers—such as the Mayo Clinic, only 90 miles away—which contain the proper neurological intensive care unit and microsurgical facilities and ***627** which are staffed by neurosurgeons with the requisite training and

(Cite as: 199 Wis.2d 615, *627, 545 N.W.2d 495, **500)

experience to perform basilar bifurcation aneurysm surgeries.

In his testimony at trial, the defendant denied having suggested to the plaintiff that her condition was urgent and required immediate care. He also denied having stated that her risk was comparable to that associated with an angiogram or minor surgical procedures such as a tonsillectomy or appendectomy. While he acknowledged telling the plaintiff that the risk of death or serious impairment associated with clipping an aneurysm was two percent, he also claims to have told her that because of the location of her aneurysm, the risks attending her surgery would be greater, although he was unable to tell her precisely how much greater. [FN14] In short, the defendant testified that his disclosure to the plaintiff adequately informed her regarding the risks that she faced.

> FN14. The defendant maintained that characterizing the risk as two percent was accurate because the aggregate morbidity and mortality rate for all aneurysms, anterior and posterior, is approximately two percent. At the same time, however, the defendant conceded that in operating upon aneurysms comparable to the plaintiff's aneurysm, he could not achieve morbidity and mortality rates as low as the ten-and-seven-tenths percent rate reported by a physician reputed to be one of the world's best aneurysm surgeons.

The defendant's expert witnesses testified that the defendant's recommendation of surgery was appropriate, that this type of surgery is regularly undertaken in a community hospital setting, and that the risks attending anterior and posterior circulation aneurysm surgeries are comparable. They placed the risk accompanying the plaintiff's surgery at between five and ten percent, although one of the defendant's experts also *628

testified that such statistics can be misleading. The defendant's expert witnesses also testified that when queried by a patient regarding their experience, they would divulge the extent of that experience and its relation to the experience of other physicians performing similar operations. [FN15]

> FN15. The defendant's expert witness Dr. Patrick R. Walsh testified:
>
> In my personal practice, I typically outline my understanding of the natural history of aneurysms, my understanding of the experience of the neurosurgical community in dealing with aneurysms and then respond to specific questions raised by the patient. If a patient asks specifically what my experience is, I believe it is mandatory that I outline that to him as carefully as possible.
>
> FN24. See also Zaremski & Goldstein, supra, § 15.01 at 3 ("the scope of the disclosure is to be viewed in conjunction with the circumstances of each individual case").

continued

FIGURE 10-4 *continued*

III.

Before addressing the substantive issues raised by the parties, we briefly outline the standards of review which we apply to the circuit court's evidentiary ruling admitting the three items of evidence in dispute in this case.

[7] The defendant argues that the circuit court erred in admitting the evidence. He asks the court to declare that the three pieces of evidence at issue are not admissible as a matter of law in ←**informed consent**→ cases. [FN25]

FN25. Under Wisconsin's doctrine of ←**informed consent**→, whenever the

(Cite as: 199 Wis.2d 615, *634, 545 N.W.2d 495, **503)

determination of what a reasonable person in the patient's position would want to know is open to debate by reasonable people, the issue of ←**informed consent**→ is a question for the jury. *Martin, 192 Wis.2d at 172–73, 531 N.W.2d 70; Platta, 68 Wis.2d at 60, 227 N.W.2d 898;* see also *Canterbury, 464 F.2d at 788.*

In *Martin,* we upheld that part of a court of appeals decision reversing the circuit court's exclusion as a matter of law of certain evidence relating to the physician's failure to disclose a one-to-three-percent chance that the plaintiff might suffer intracranial bleeding following a serious head injury. The circuit court had determined that the disputed information involved "extremely remote possibilities" and was therefore not subject to disclosure under *Wis.Stat. § 448.30(4)* as a matter of law. Instead, we noted that while the undisclosed risk may have been small, "such risk may be significant to a patient's decision in light of the potentially severe consequences" and therefore should have been admitted. *Martin, 192 Wis.2d at 168, 531 N.W.2d 70.*

***635**

(Cite as: 199 Wis.2d 615, *635, 545 N.W.2d 495, **503)

[8][9] The general rule is that a circuit court's decision with regard to the relevance of proffered evidence is a discretionary decision. *State v. Pittman, 174 Wis.2d 255, 267, 496 N.W.2d 74 (1993).* Evidence is relevant when it "tends 'to make the existence of [a material fact] more

(Cite as: 199 Wis.2d 615, *635, 545 N.W.2d 495, **503)

probable or less probable than it would be without the evidence.' " *iN interest oF michaEL R.B., 175 wis.2d 713, 724, 499 N.W.2d 641 (1993)* (quoting *State v. Denny, 120 Wis.2d 614, 623, 357 N.W.2d 12 (Ct.App.1984)); Wis.Stat. § 904.01.* [FN26] Material facts are those that are of consequence to the merits of the litigation. *In Interest of Michael R.B., 175 Wis.2d at 724, 499 N.W.2d 641.*

FN26. *Wis.Stat. § 904.01* provides as follows:

Definition of "relevant evidence." " 'Relevant evidence' means evidence having any tendency to make the existence of any fact that is of consequence to the determination of the action more probable or less probable than it would be without the evidence."

[10] Evidence which is relevant may nevertheless be excluded if its probative value is substantially outweighed by the danger of unfair prejudice, confusion of ***636**

(Cite as: 199 Wis.2d 615, *636, 545 N.W.2d 495, **503)

the issues, or misleading the jury. *State v. Patricia A.M., 176 Wis.2d 542, 554, 500 N.W.2d 289 (1993); Wis.Stat. § 904.03.* [FN27] It is not enough that the evidence will be prejudicial; "exclusion is required only if the evidence is unfairly prejudicial." *Patricia A.M., 176 Wis.2d at 554, 500 N.W.2d 289.*

(Cite as: 199 Wis.2d 615, *636, 545 N.W.2d 495, **503)

FN27. *Wis.Stat. § 904.03* provides as follows:

Exclusion of relevant evidence on grounds of prejudice, confusion, or waste of time. Although relevant, evidence may be excluded if its probative value is substantially outweighed by the danger of unfair prejudice, confusion of the issues, or misleading the jury, or by considerations of undue delay, waste of time, or needless presentation of cumulative evidence.

[11] The question of whether otherwise admissible evidence is nevertheless unfairly prejudicial rests with the discretion of the circuit court. *Featherly v. Continental Ins. Co., 73 Wis.2d 273, 243 N.W.2d 806 (1976).* This court will not conclude that a circuit court erroneously exercised its discretion when there is a reasonable basis for the circuit court's determination. Finally, if the circuit court erred in admitting the evidence, reversal or a new trial is required only if the improper admission of evidence has affected the substantial rights of the party seeking relief. *Wis.Stat. § 805.18(2).* [FN28]

FN28. *Wis.Stat. § 805.18(2)* provides as follows:

No judgment shall be reversed or set aside or new trial granted in any

(Cite as: 199 Wis.2d 615, *636, 545 N.W.2d 495, **503)

action or proceeding on the ground of drawing, selection or misdirection of jury, or the improper admission of evidence, or for error as to any matter of pleading or procedure, unless in the opinion of the court to which the application is made, after an examination of the entire action or proceeding, it shall appear that the error complained of has affected the substantial rights of the party seeking to reverse or set aside the judgment, or to secure a new trial.

**504

(Cite as: 199 Wis.2d 615, *636, 545 N.W.2d 495, **504)

*637

(Cite as: 199 Wis.2d 615, *637, 545 N.W.2d 495, **504)

IV.

The defendant contends that the circuit court erred in allowing the plaintiff to introduce evidence regarding the defendant's limited experience in operating upon aneurysms comparable to the plaintiff's aneurysm. Wisconsin's law of ←**informed consent**→, the defendant continues, requires a physician to reveal only those risks inherent in the treatment. Everyone agrees, argues the defendant, that he advised the plaintiff regarding those risks: the potential perils of death, a stroke or blindness associated with her surgery.

continued

FIGURE 10-4 *continued*

The defendant argues that the circuit court's decision to admit evidence pertaining to his surgical experience confused relevant information relating to treatment risks with irrelevant and prejudicial information that the defendant did not possess the skill and experience of the very experienced aneurysm surgeons. Therefore, according to the defendant, the jury's attention was

(Cite as: 199 Wis.2d 615, *637, 545 N.W.2d 495, **504)

diverted from a consideration of whether the defendant made required disclosures regarding treatment to the question of who was performing the plaintiff's operation. Thus, the defendant contends, the circuit court transformed a duty to reasonably inform into a duty to reasonably perform the surgery, even though the plaintiff was not alleging negligent treatment.

The doctrine of ←**informed consent**→ should not, argues the defendant, be construed as a general right to information regarding possible alternative procedures, health care facilities and physicians. Instead, urges the defendant, the doctrine of ←**informed consent**→ ***638***

(Cite as: 199 Wis.2d 615, *638, 545 N.W.2d 495, **504)

should be viewed as creating a "bright line" rule requiring physicians to disclose only significant complications intrinsic to the contemplated procedure. The defendant interprets *Wis. Stat. § 448.30* as an embodiment of this more modest definition of ←**informed consent**→. In sum, the defendant urges that the statutory provisions require disclosure of risks associated with particular "treatments" rather than the risks associated with particular physicians. [FN29]

> FN29. The defendant also argues that the plaintiff is trying to disguise what is actually a negligent misrepresentation claim as an ←**informed consent**→ claim so that she might bring before the jury otherwise inadmissible evidence regarding the defendant's experience and relative competence.

The tort of negligent misrepresentation occurs when one person negligently

(Cite as: 199 Wis.2d 615, *638, 545 N.W.2d 495, **504)

gives false information to another who acts in reasonable reliance on the information and suffers physical harm as a consequence of the reliance. Restatement (Second) of Torts, § 311(1) (1965). An overlap exists between a claim pleading this tort and one alleging a failure to provide ←**informed consent**→. As the commentary to § 311 of the Restatement points out:

> The rule stated in this Section finds particular application where it is a part of the actor's business or profession to give information upon which the safety of the recipient or a third person depends. Thus it is as much a part of the professional duty of a physician to give correct information as to the character of the disease from which his plaintiff is suffering, where such knowledge is necessary to the safety of the patient or others, as it is to make a correct diagnosis or to prescribe the appropriate medicine.

Restatement (Second) of Torts, § 311(1) cmt. b (1965).

Because of this overlap between negligent misrepresentation and ←**informed consent**→, it is not surprising that allegations made and evidence introduced by the plaintiff might have fit comfortably under either theory. But this overlap does not preclude the plaintiff from making allegations and introducing evidence in an ←**informed consent**→ case which might also have been pled in a negligent misrepresentation case. This case was pled and proved under the tort of failure to procure ←**informed consent**→.

(Cite as: 199 Wis.2d 615, *638, 545 N.W.2d 495, **504)

639

(Cite as: 199 Wis.2d 615, *639, 545 N.W.2d 495, **504)

We reject the defendant's proposed bright line rule that it is error as a matter of law to admit evidence in an ←**informed consent**→ case that the physician failed to inform the patient regarding the physician's experience with the surgery or treatment at issue. The prudent patient standard adopted by Wisconsin in *Scaria* is incompatible with such a bright line rule.

As *Scaria* states and as *Martin* confirms, what a physician must disclose is contingent upon what, under the circumstances of a given case, a reasonable person in the patient's position would need to know in order to make an intelligent and informed decision. *Scaria, 68 Wis.2d at 13, 227 N.W.2d 647; Martin, 192 Wis.2d at 174, 531 N.W.2d 70.* The question of whether certain information **505

(Cite as: 199 Wis.2d 615, *639, 545 N.W.2d 495, **505)

is material to a patient's decision and therefore requires disclosure is rooted in the facts and circumstances of the particular case in which it arises. *Martin, 192 Wis.2d at 175, 531 N.W.2d 70.*

The cases upon which the *Trogun* and *Scaria* courts relied in fashioning Wisconsin's current doctrine of ←**informed consent**→ rejected the concept of bright line rules. The "scope of the disclosure required of physicians," stated the California Supreme Court, "defies simple definition" and must therefore "be measured by the patient's need, and that need is whatever information is material to the decision." *Cobbs v. Grant, 8 Cal.3d 229, 104 Cal.Rptr. 505, 502 P.2d 1, 10, 11 (1972).* "The amount of disclosure can vary from one patient

(Cite as: 199 Wis.2d 615, *639, 545 N.W.2d 495, **505)

to another," stated the Rhode Island Supreme Court, because "[w]hat is reasonable disclosure in one instance may not be reasonable in another." ***640***

(Cite as: 199 Wis.2d 615, *640, 545 N.W.2d 495, **505)

Wilkinson v. Vesey, 110 R.I. 606, 295 A.2d 676, 687–88 (1972). Finally, the *Canterbury* court's decision—which, as the *Martin* court underscored last term, provides the basis for Wisconsin's doctrine of ←**informed consent**→, *Martin, 192 Wis.2d at 173, 531 N.W.2d 70*—states explicitly that under the doctrine of ←**informed consent**→, "[t]here is no bright line separating the significant from the insignificant." *Canterbury, 464 F.2d at 788.*

Wisconsin Stat. § 448.30 explicitly requires disclosure of more than just treatment complications associated with a particular procedure. Physicians must, the statute declares, disclose "the availability of all alternate, viable medical modes of treatment" in addition to "the benefits and risks of these treatments."

The *Martin* court rejected the argument that *Wis. Stat. § 448.30* was limited by its plain language to disclosures intrinsic to a proposed treatment regimen. The *Martin* court stated that *Wis. Stat. § 448.30*

continued

FIGURE 10-4   *continued*

"should not be construed so as to unduly limit the physician's duty to provide information which is reasonably necessary under the circumstances." *Martin, 192 Wis.2d at 175, 531 N.W.2d 70.* [FN30] "There can be no dispute," the ***641***

(Cite as: 199 Wis.2d 615, *641, 545 N.W.2d 495, **505)

Martin court declared, "that the language in *Scaria* . . . requires that a physician disclose information necessary for a reasonable person to make an intelligent

(Cite as: 199 Wis.2d 615, *641, 545 N.W.2d 495, **505)

decision." *Id.*

FN30. Ruling before the publication of *Martin* on the admissibility of evidence pertaining to the defendant's experience, the circuit court made a similar point:

I've also looked at the ←**informed consent**→ instruction, 1023.2, and it says that the doctor or physician is under a duty to make such disclosures that will enable a reasonable person under the circumstances confronting the patient to exercise the patient's right to make a proper consent, so I don't think that—that we're limited to the references made in the statute. I think that anything that's necessary to a reasonable person to arrive at an informed and reasonable consent is allowable evidence, so clearly the six times [i.e. the six post-residency aneurysm operations which the defendant had performed] is allowable evidence and the fact that he made a statement that he had done this lots of time, there's nothing wrong with that [being admitted].

[12] In this case, the plaintiff introduced ample evidence that had a reasonable person in her position been aware of the defendant's relative lack of experience in performing basilar bifurcation aneurysm surgery, that person would not have undergone surgery with him. According to the record the

(Cite as: 199 Wis.2d 615, *641, 545 N.W.2d 495, **505)

plaintiff had made inquiry of the defendant's experience with surgery like hers. In response to her direct question about his experience he said that he had operated on aneurysms comparable to her aneurysm "dozens" of times. The plaintiff also introduced evidence that surgery on basilar bifurcation aneurysms is more difficult than any other type of aneurysm surgery and among the most difficult in all of neurosurgery. We conclude that the circuit court did not erroneously exercise its discretion in admitting evidence regarding the defendant's lack of experience and the difficulty of the proposed procedure. A reasonable person in the plaintiff's position would have considered such information material in making an intelligent and informed decision about the surgery.
We also reject the defendant's claim that even if this information was material, it should have been excluded because its prejudicial effect outweighed its probative value. The defendant contends that the admission of such evidence allowed the jury to infer that the plaintiff's partial paralysis was a product ****506***

(Cite as: 199 Wis.2d 615, *641, 545 N.W.2d 495, **506)

of the defendant's lack of experience and skill rather than a consequence of his alleged failure to inform. ***642***

(Cite as: 199 Wis.2d 615, *642, 545 N.W.2d 495, **506)

[13] We disagree with the defendant's claim that evidence pertaining to the defendant's experience was unduly and unfairly prejudicial. While a jury might confuse negligent failure to disclose with negligent treatment, [FN31] the likelihood of confusion is nonexistent or de minimis in this case.

(Cite as: 199 Wis.2d 615, *642, 545 N.W.2d 495, **506)

The plaintiff dismissed her negligent treatment claim before trial. It is thus unlikely that the jury would confuse an issue not even before it with the issue that was actually being tried. We therefore conclude that the defendant was not unduly or unfairly prejudiced by the admission of evidence reflecting his failure to disclose his limited prior experience in operating on basilar bifurcation aneurysms.

> FN31. See Marjorie Maguire Schultz, From ←**Informed Consent**→ to Patient Choice: A New Protected Interest, *95 Yale L.J. 219, 228–29 (1985).* One could only completely eliminate the potential that such confusion might arise by categorically prohibiting all actions predicated on an alleged failure to procure ←**informed consent**→.

V.

The defendant next argues that the circuit court erred in allowing the plaintiff to introduce evidence of morbidity and mortality rates associated with the surgery at issue. The defendant particularly objects to comparative risk statistics purporting to estimate and compare the morbidity and mortality rates when the surgery at issue is performed, respectively, by a physician of limited experience such as the defendant and by the acknowledged masters in the field. Expert testimony introduced by the plaintiff indicated that the

(Cite as: 199 Wis.2d 615, *642, 545 N.W.2d 495, **506)

morbidity and mortality rate expected when a surgeon with the defendant's experience performed the surgery ***643***

(Cite as: 199 Wis.2d 615, *643, 545 N.W.2d 495, **506)

would be significantly higher than the rate expected when a more experienced physician performed the same surgery. The defendant asserts that admission of these morbidity and mortality rates would lead the jury to find him liable for failing to perform at the level of the masters rather than for failing to adequately inform the plaintiff regarding the risks associated with her surgery. Furthermore, contends the defendant, statistics are notoriously inaccurate and misleading.

As with evidence pertaining to the defendant's prior experience with similar surgery, the defendant requests that the court fashion a bright line rule as a matter of law that comparative risk evidence should not be admitted in an ←**informed consent**→ case. For many of the same reasons which led us to conclude that such a bright line rule of exclusion would be inappropriate for evidence of a physician's prior experience, we also reject a bright line rule excluding evidence of comparative risk relating to the provider. The medical literature identifies basilar bifurcation aneurysm surgery as among the most difficult in neurosurgery. As the plaintiff's evidence indicates, however, the defendant had told her that the risks associated with her surgery were comparable to the risks attending a tonsillectomy, appendectomy or gall bladder operation. The plaintiff also introduced evidence that the defendant estimated the risk of death or serious impairment associated

continued

FIGURE 10-4   *continued*

(Cite as: 199 Wis.2d 615, *643, 545 N.W.2d 495, **506)

with her surgery at two percent. At trial, however, the defendant conceded that because of his relative lack of experience, he could not hope to match the ten-and-seven-tenths percent morbidity and mortality rate reported for large basilar bifurcation aneurysm surgery by very experienced surgeons.
***644**

(Cite as: 199 Wis.2d 615, *644, 545 N.W.2d 495, **506)

The defendant also admitted at trial that he had not shared with the plaintiff information from articles he reviewed prior to surgery. These articles established that even the most accomplished posterior circulation aneurysm surgeons reported morbidity and mortality rates of fifteen percent for basilar bifurcation aneurysms. Furthermore, the plaintiff introduced expert testimony indicating that the estimated morbidity and mortality rate one might expect when a physician with the defendant's relatively limited experience performed the surgery would be close to thirty percent.
Had a reasonable person in the plaintiff's position been made aware that being operated upon by the defendant significantly increased ****507**

(Cite as: 199 Wis.2d 615, *644, 545 N.W.2d 495, **507)

the risk one would have faced in the hands of another surgeon performing the same operation, that person might well have elected to forego surgery with the defendant. Had a reasonable person in the plaintiff's position been made aware that the risks associated with surgery were significantly greater than the risks that an unclipped aneurysm would rupture, that person might well have elected to forego surgery altogether. In short, had a reasonable person in the plaintiff's position possessed such information before consenting to surgery, that person

(Cite as: 199 Wis.2d 615, *644, 545 N.W.2d 495, **507)

would have been better able to make an informed and intelligent decision.
The defendant concedes that the duty to procure a patient's ←**informed consent**→ requires a physician to reveal the general risks associated with a particular surgery. The defendant does not explain why the duty to inform about this general risk data should be interpreted to categorically exclude evidence relating to provider-specific risk information, even when that provider-specific data is geared to a clearly delineated surgical procedure and identifies a particular provider ***645**

(Cite as: 199 Wis.2d 615, *645, 545 N.W.2d 495, **507)

as an independent risk factor. When different physicians have substantially different success rates, whether surgery is performed by one rather than another represents a choice between "alternate, viable medical modes of treatment" under *§ 448.30.*
For example, while there may be a general risk of ten percent that a particular surgical procedure will result in paralysis or death, that risk may climb to forty percent when the particular procedure is performed by a relatively inexperienced surgeon. It defies logic to interpret this statute as requiring that the first, almost meaningless statistic be divulged to a patient while the second, far more relevant statistic should not be. Under *Scaria* and its progeny as well as the codification of *Scaria* as *Wis.Stat. § 448.30,* the second statistic would be material to the patient's exercise of an intelligent and ←**informed consent**→ regarding treatment options. A circuit court may in its discretion conclude that the second statistic is admissible.

(Cite as: 199 Wis.2d 615, *645, 545 N.W.2d 495, **507)

[14] The doctrine of ←**informed consent**→ requires disclosure of "all of the viable alternatives and risks of the treatment proposed" which would be material to a patient's decision. *Martin, 192 Wis.2d at 174, 531 N.W.2d 70.* We therefore conclude that when different physicians have substantially different success rates with the same procedure and a reasonable person in the patient's position would consider such information material, the circuit court may admit this statistical evidence. [FN32]

> FN32. See Aaron D. Twerski & Neil B. Cohen, *Comparing Medical Providers: A First Look at the New Era of Medical Statistics, 58 Brook.L.Rev. 5 (1992).* Professors Twerski and Cohen note that the development of sophisticated data regarding risks of various procedures and statistical models comparing the success rates of medical providers signal changes in ←**informed consent**→ law. Specifically, they state:
>
> The duty to provide information may require more than a simple sharing of visceral concerns about the wisdom of undertaking a given therapeutic procedure. Physicians may have a responsibility to identify and correlate risk factors and to communicate the results to patients as a predicate to fulfilling their obligation to inform.
>
> Id. at 6.
>
> See also Douglas Sharrott, Provider-Specific Quality-of-Care Data: A

(Cite as: 199 Wis.2d 615, *645, 545 N.W.2d 495, **507)

> Proposal for Limited Mandatory Disclosure, *58 Brook L.Rev. 85 (1992)* (stating that it is difficult to refute the argument that provider-specific data, once disclosed to the public by the government, should also be disclosed to patients because the doctrine of ←**informed consent**→ requires a physician to inform a patient of both material risks and alternatives to a proposed course of treatment).

*646

(Cite as: 199 Wis.2d 615, *646, 545 N.W.2d 495, **507)

We caution, as did the court of appeals, that our decision will not always require physicians to give patients comparative risk evidence in statistical terms to obtain ←**informed consent**→. [FN33] Rather, we hold that evidence of the morbidity and mortality outcomes of different physicians was admissible under the circumstances of this case.

> FN33. For criticisms of medical performance statistics and cautions that provider-specific outcome statistics must be carefully evaluated to insure their reliability and validity when used as evidence, see, e.g., Jesse Green, *Problems in the Use of Outcome Statistics to Compare Health Care Providers, 58 Brook.L.Rev. 55 (1992);* Paul D. Rheingold, *The Admissibility of Evidence in Malpractice Cases: The Performance Records of Practitioners, 58 Brook.L.Rev. 75, 78–79 (1992);* Sharrott, supra, at 92–94, 120; Twerski & Cohen, supra, at 8–9.

continued

FIGURE 10-4   *continued*

(Cite as: 199 Wis.2d 615, *646, 545 N.W.2d 495, **507)

**508

(Cite as: 199 Wis.2d 615, *646, 545 N.W.2d 495, **508)

*647

(Cite as: 199 Wis.2d 615, *647, 545 N.W.2d 495, **508)

[15] In keeping with the fact-driven and context-specific application of ←**informed consent**→ doctrine, questions regarding whether statistics are sufficiently material to a patient's decision to be admissible and sufficiently reliable to be non-prejudicial are best resolved on a case-by- case basis. The fundamental issue in an ←**informed consent**→ case is less a question of how a physician chooses to explain the panoply of treatment options and risks necessary to a patient's ←**informed consent**→ than a question of assessing whether a patient has been advised that such options and risks exist.
[16] As the court of appeals observed, in this case it was the defendant himself who elected to explain the risks confronting the plaintiff in statistical terms. He did this because, as he stated at trial, "numbers giv[e] some perspective to the framework of the very real, immediate, human threat that is involved with this condition." Because the defendant elected to explain the risks confronting the plaintiff in statistical terms, it stands to reason that in her effort to demonstrate how the defendant's numbers dramatically understated the risks of her surgery, the plaintiff would seek to introduce other statistical evidence. Such evidence was integral to her claim that the defendant's nondisclosure denied her the ability to exercise ←**informed consent**→.

VI.

(Cite as: 199 Wis.2d 615, *647, 545 N.W.2d 495, **508)

The defendant also asserts that the circuit court erred as a matter of law in allowing the plaintiff to introduce expert testimony that because of the difficulties associated with operating on the plaintiff's aneurysm, the defendant should have referred her to a ***648**

(Cite as: 199 Wis.2d 615, *648, 545 N.W.2d 495, **508)

tertiary care center containing a proper neurological intensive care unit, more extensive microsurgical facilities and more experienced surgeons. While evidence that a physician should have referred a patient elsewhere may support an action alleging negligent treatment, argues the defendant, it has no place in an ←**informed consent**→ action.
The court of appeals agreed with the defendant that this evidence should have been excluded, and it further concluded that admission of this evidence created "a serious danger [that] the jury may confuse a duty to provide average quality care with a duty to adequately inform of medical risks." *Johnson, 188 Wis.2d at 224, 525 N.W.2d 71.*
We share the concern expressed by the court of appeals and underscored by the defendant, but their concern is misplaced in this case. Here, the plaintiff was not asserting a claim for negligent performance. Just because expert testimony is relevant to one claim does not mean that it is not relevant to another.
When faced with an allegation that a physician breached a duty of ←**informed consent**→, the pertinent inquiry concerns what information a reasonable person in

(Cite as: 199 Wis.2d 615, *648, 545 N.W.2d 495, **508)

the patient's position would have considered material to an exercise of intelligent and ←**informed consent**→. *Scaria, 68 Wis.2d at 13, 227 N.W.2d 647; Martin, 192 Wis.2d at 174, 531 N.W.2d 70.* Under the facts and circumstances presented by this case, the circuit court could declare, in the exercise of its discretion, that evidence of referral would have been material to the ability of a reasonable person in the plaintiff's position to render ←**informed consent**→.

The plaintiff's medical experts testified that given the nature and difficulty of the surgery at issue, the plaintiff could not make an intelligent decision or give an ←**informed consent**→ without being made aware that ***649**

(Cite as: 199 Wis.2d 615, *649, 545 N.W.2d 495, **508)

surgery in a tertiary facility would have decreased the risk she faced. One of the plaintiff's experts, Dr. Haring J.W. Nauta, stated that "it's not fair not to bring up the subject of referral to another center when the problem is as difficult to treat" as the plaintiff's aneurysm was. Another of the plaintiff's experts, Dr. Robert Narotzky, testified that the defendant's "very limited" experience with aneurysm surgery rendered reasonable a referral to "someone with a lot more experience in dealing with this kind of problem." Dr. Fredric Somach, also testifying for the plaintiff, stated as follows:

[S]he should have been told that this was an extremely difficult, formidable lesion and that there are people in the immediate geographic vicinity that are very experienced and that have had a great deal of contact with this type of

(Cite as: 199 Wis.2d 615, *649, 545 N.W.2d 495, **508)

aneurysm and ***509**

(Cite as: 199 Wis.2d 615, *649, 545 N.W.2d 495, **509)

that she should consider having at least a second opinion, if not going directly to one of these other [physicians].

Articles from the medical literature introduced by the plaintiff also stated categorically that the surgery at issue should be performed at a tertiary care center while being "excluded" from the community setting because of "the limited surgical experience" and lack of proper equipment and facilities available in such hospitals.

[17] *Scaria* instructs us that "[t]he disclosures which would be made by doctors of good standing, under the same or similar circumstances, are certainly relevant and material" to a patient's exercise of ←**informed consent**→. *Scaria, 68 Wis.2d at 12, 227 N.W.2d 647.* Testimony by the plaintiff's medical experts indicated that "doctors of good standing" would have referred her to a tertiary ***650**

(Cite as: 199 Wis.2d 615, *650, 545 N.W.2d 495, **509)

care center housing better equipment and staffed by more experienced physicians. Hence under the materiality standard announced in *Scaria,* we conclude that the circuit court properly exercised its discretion in admitting evidence that the defendant should have advised the plaintiff of the possibility of undergoing surgery at a tertiary care facility.

The defendant asserts that the plaintiff knew she could go elsewhere. This claim is both true and beside the point. Credible evidence in this case demonstrates that the plaintiff chose not to go elsewhere because the defendant gave her the impression that her surgery was routine and that it therefore made

continued

FIGURE 10-4 *continued*

no difference who performed it. The pertinent inquiry, then, is not whether a reasonable person in the plaintiff's position would have known generally that she might have surgery elsewhere, but rather whether such a person would have chosen to have surgery elsewhere had the defendant adequately disclosed the comparable risks attending surgery performed by him and surgery performed at a tertiary care facility such as the Mayo Clinic, only 90 miles away.

[18][19] The defendant also argues that evidence of referral is prejudicial because it might have affected the jury's determination of causation. The court of appeals reasoned that if a complainant could introduce evidence that a physician should have referred her elsewhere, "a patient so informed would almost certainly forego the procedure with that doctor." *Johnson, 188 Wis.2d at 224, 525 N.W.2d 71.* [FN34]

> FN34. The court of appeals expressed concern that the plaintiff's evidence regarding the defendant's failure to refer might cause the jury to confuse a physician's duty to procure a patient's ←**informed consent**→ with a separate and distinct tort establishing a physician's duty to refer. While acknowledging that other jurisdictions have recognized a distinct duty to refer, the court of appeals observed that Wisconsin has never done so. Nor does the court do so today. We merely hold that a physician's failure to refer may, under some circumstances, be material to a patient's exercise of

an intelligent and ←**informed consent**→.

651

The court of appeals concluded that admitting evidence regarding a physician's failure to refer was prejudicial error because it probably affected the jury's decision about causation in favor of the plaintiff. [FN35] Contending that a causal connection between his failure to divulge and the plaintiff's damage is required, the defendant seems to assert that the plaintiff has offered no evidence that the defendant's failure to disclose his relevant experience or his statistical risk harmed the plaintiff. Even had the surgery been performed by a "master," the defendant argues, a bad result may have occurred. [FN36]

> FN35. The dissenting opinion in the court of appeals determined the error to be harmless.

> FN36. For discussion of this aspect of causation, see Twerski & Cohen, supra.

The defendant appears to attack the basic concept of causation applied in claims based on ←**informed consent**→. As reflected in the ←**informed consent**→ jury instruction (Wis JI-Civil 1023.3 (1992)), which the defendant himself proposed

and which was given at trial, the question confronting a jury in an ←**informed consent**→ case is whether a reasonable person in the patient's position would have arrived at a different decision about the treatment or surgery had he or she been fully informed. As reflected in the special verdict question in this case, that question asked whether "a reasonable person in Donna Johnson's position [would] have refused to ****510**

(Cite as: 199 Wis.2d 615, *651, 545 N.W.2d 495, **510)

consent to the surgery by Dr. Richard Kokemoor had she been fully informed of the risks and ***652**

(Cite as: 199 Wis.2d 615, *652, 545 N.W.2d 495, **510)

advantages of surgery." If the defendant is arguing here that the standard causation instruction is not applicable in a case in which provider-specific evidence is admitted, this contention has not been fully presented and developed.

Finally, the defendant argues that if his duty to procure the plaintiff's ←**informed consent**→ includes an obligation to disclose that she consider seeking treatment elsewhere, then there will be no logical stopping point to what the doctrine of ←**informed consent**→ might encompass. We disagree with the defendant. As the plaintiff noted in her brief to this court, "[i]t is a rare exception when the vast body of medical literature and expert opinion agree that the difference in experience of the surgeon performing the operation will impact the risk of morbidity/mortality as was the case here," thereby requiring referral. Brief for Petitioner at 40. At oral argument before this court, counsel for the plaintiff stated that under "many circumstances" and indeed "probably most circumstances," whether or not a physician referred a

(Cite as: 199 Wis.2d 615, *652, 545 N.W.2d 495, **510)

patient elsewhere would be "utterly irrelevant" in an ←**informed consent**→ case. In the vast majority of significantly less complicated cases, such a referral would be irrelevant and unnecessary.

Moreover, we have already concluded that comparative risk data distinguishing the defendant's morbidity and mortality rate from the rate of more experienced physicians was properly before the jury. A close link exists between such data and the propriety of referring a patient elsewhere. A physician who discloses that other physicians might have lower morbidity and mortality rates when performing the same procedure will presumably have access to information regarding who some of those physicians are. When the duty to share comparative risk data is material ***653**

(Cite as: 199 Wis.2d 615, *653, 545 N.W.2d 495, **510)

to a patient's exercise of ←**informed consent**→, an ensuing referral elsewhere will often represent no more than a modest and logical next step. [FN37]

FN37. The *Canterbury* court included a duty to refer among its examples of information which, under the facts and circumstances of a particular case, a physician might be required to disclose in order to procure a patient's ←**informed consent**→. The court stated: "The typical situation is where a general practitioner discovers that the patient's malady calls for specialized treatment, whereupon the duty generally arises to advise the patient to consult a specialist." *Canterbury, 464 F.2d at 781 n. 22.*

(Cite as: 199 Wis.2d 615, *653, 545 N.W.2d 495, **510)

Given the difficulties involved in performing the surgery at issue in this case, coupled with evidence that the defendant exaggerated his own prior experience while downplaying the risks confronting the plaintiff, the circuit court properly exercised its discretion in admitting evidence that a physician of good standing would have made the plaintiff aware of the alternative of lower risk surgery with a different, more experienced surgeon in a better-equipped facility.

continued

FIGURE 10-4 *continued*

For the reasons set forth, we conclude that the circuit court did not erroneously exercise its discretion in admitting the evidence at issue, and accordingly, we reverse the decision of the court of appeals and remand the cause to the circuit court for further proceedings consistent with this opinion.
The decision of the court of appeals is reversed and the cause is remanded to the circuit court with directions.

BRADLEY, J., did not participate.
END OF DOCUMENT

These agency regulations, rules, and rulings constitute the body of law known as administrative law. Administrative law has the force of statutory law once it has been published and is primary authority. It becomes primary binding when the problem arises in the geographic jurisdiction from which that administrative law emanates.

Probably more than any other law, administrative law plays a part in our daily lives. When driving to work, maintaining a professional license, purchasing a home, dispensing controlled substances, developing a safe workplace environment, maintaining a checking account, and so forth, you are regulated by state and/or federal administrative agencies.

Because administrative law changes rapidly with changes in technology, privacy issues, and economic conditions, rules and regulations are generally not published in bound volumes, but are collected and maintained in loose-leaf format. In ringed binders, the law may be simply and efficiently updated; the outdated pages may be removed and replaced with pages containing the current law. Often, CD ROM services and Internet services provide up-to-date sources for administrative law.

Whether the law comes from statutory sources, case law, or administrative rules and regulations, the principles of legal analysis apply: isolate the relevant facts, break the rule of law down into its elements, apply the facts to each element, identify where questions arise, and conduct additional research to answer or argue the questions.

CHAPTER SUMMARY

- Primary legal authority refers to statutory, constitutional, court opinion, and administrative sources of law.
- Secondary legal authority explains and clarifies primary authority.

- Primary authority is binding within the geographic jurisdiction from which the law emanates.
- The hierarchy of authority refers to the weight or value of legal sources in resolving a current problem.
- Statutory law includes federal, state, and local law passed by legislative bodies.
- Case law refers to court opinions and is sometimes called judge-made law or common law.
- Administrative law includes those rules and regulations generated by federal and state administrative agencies.

KEY TERMS

authority
binding authority
headnote

hierarchy of authority
persuasive authority
plain meaning

primary authority
secondary authority

REVIEW QUESTIONS

1. Explain the difference between primary and secondary authority. Between binding and persuasive authority.
2. Why are secondary sources valuable?
3. When reading case law, what should be analyzed?
4. What is the plain meaning doctrine and how is it used in interpreting statutory language?

INTERNET EXERCISE

1. Access the web page for this textbook at *www.westlegalstudies.com*.
2. Click on the assignments section of the web page and complete the assignment(s) for Chapter Ten.

EXERCISES

1. Networking. Contact the local bar association to see if educational meetings are held. Volunteer to provide a short presentation on the expertise that registered nurses can bring to the practice of law and how attorneys can use nurses to expedite medical-legal claims. Have business cards prepared that describe your qualifications and hand them out freely. If you are invited to speak, use this book as a resource and be prepared for questions about the profitability of retaining nurses.
2. Professional Portfolio. Develop a cheat sheet to remind yourself about basic legal resources. Retain this in your portfolio in the event you are asked about legal research at an interview or in a business meeting. Include "understanding of legal resources" or "ability to read and analyze case law" in your resume or cover letter.

ENDNOTES

1. *Schoendorff v. Society of New York Hospital,* 105 N.E. 92 (1914).

2. See, for example, *Guardianship of Ruth E. J.,* 196 Wis. 2d 794, 540 N.W. 2d 213 (1995).

3. American Bar Association, *Annotated Model Rules of Professional Conduct,* (1999) 4th Edition Rule 1.1. Copies of ABA *Model Code of Professional Responsibility, 1999 Edition* are available from Service Center, American Bar Association, 750 North Lake Shore Drive, Chicago, IL 60611-4497, 1-800-285-2221.

4. *Johnson v. Kokomoor,* 199 Wis.2d 615, 545 N.W.2d 495 (1996).

5. Civil Rights Act, 42 U.S.C. s. 2000d et seq.

ADDITIONAL REFERENCES

Cannon, T. A. *Ethics and Professional Responsibility for Legal Assistants,* 3rd ed. New York: Aspen Law & Business, 1999.

Jacobstein, J., Mersky, R., Dunn, D. *Fundamentals of Legal Research,* 7th ed. Westbury, NY: The Foundation Press, Inc, 1999.

Statsky, W. *Essentials of Paralegalism,* 3rd ed. St. Paul, Minnesota: West Thomson Learning, 1998.

CHAPTER 11

PERSUASIVE APPLICATION OF AUTHORITY

OBJECTIVES

In this chapter, you will discover

- how traditional methods of reasoning are used to solve legal problems

- how legal authority provides a foundation for resolution of legal problems

- a general format for preparing a legal argument with authority

OVERVIEW

As has been noted in previous chapters, the legal analysis formula is rather like a spiral:

- isolating the relevant facts of the problem
- locating the law and breaking it into its elements
- applying the facts
- developing the issues
- refining the research and locating new law or sources of knowledge
- applying the facts, etc.

Eventually, additional sources of law or information will be repetitive or unavailable, and it will be necessary to synthesize the research and facts to arrive at a position that will facilitate justice in the situation. This position is what the attorney will eventually argue as appropriate and fair. While there may not be any law to guide this argument or support this position, it is necessary to use the tools available to make a convincing presentation of this position. In the United States legal system, decisions are not made arbitrarily or capriciously. Decisions must be based on authority, such as law or other social or behavioral science, and facts.

LEGAL REASONING

Attorneys basically use three types of reasoning when approaching legal problems: deductive reasoning, linear reasoning, and reasoning by analogy.

Deductive Reasoning

Deductive reasoning is a type of mathematical conclusion that begins with a proposition relating one concept to another concept. A third concept may be deduced because of the relationship of the other concepts. For example,

Proposition: All registered nurses must pass a licensure exam.

Statement: Arnold is a registered nurse.

Deduction: Arnold has passed a licensure exam.

To apply this to legal situations, consider this example:

Proposition: Failing to stop at a stop sign constitutes negligence.

Statement: Serina failed to stop at a stop sign.

Deduction: Serina is negligent.

The process of deductive analysis and reasoning must be carefully monitored, as it may provide inaccurate results. For example,

Proposition: All fish have fins and live in water.

Statement: Dolphins have fins and live in water.

Deduction: Dolphins are fish.

The deduction is erroneous because dolphins are mammals. In the same way, legal deductions may be inaccurate.

Proposition: All automobile drivers are licensed through the state.

Statement: Bethany drives an automobile.

Deduction: Bethany is licensed through the state.

Deductive reasoning is a process that is easy to follow and simple to explain. It must be used judiciously, however, to make certain that the conclusions are true and accurate.

Linear Reasoning

A more difficult reasoning concept is that of **linear reasoning,** or following a line of thought to its conclusion. Because it traces a trajectory of events, it requires that the analysis include human reactions and expectation. It is often used to contradict deductive reasoning. For example,

Proposition: Failing to stop at a stop sign is negligence.

Statement: Serina failed to stop at the stop sign.

Deduction: Serina is negligent.

Linear Reasoning: Serina failed to stop at the stop sign because she was attempting to reach a hospital as quickly as possible. Serina's passenger had unexpectedly suffered a seizure and Serina was responding to the emergency needs of the passenger. If this line of reasoning is followed, Serina has a valid reason for failing to stop at the stop sign and would, probably, not be found negligent.

Linear reasoning may be necessary in situations where there is no prior law to guide the reasoning process. Very often social, economic, medical, or scientific literature may be used to ground the argument and support the position.

Reasoning by Analogy

Reasoning by analogy may be the easiest process for attorneys and legal professionals to apply. It uses similar relational concepts as deductive reasoning, but its conclusion is based on a similarity of circumstances or a similarity of law.

Reasoning by analogy requires that the current facts be compared with facts in prior case law. This comparison includes a thorough examination of the similarities to, differences from, and gaps between the current fact situation and previously litigated cases. To facilitate this comparison, a four-stage analysis is often used: people, subject matter (places and things), legal theories and defenses, and remedies sought. The more similar previous cases are to the current fact situation in these four areas, the more likely that the rule of law adopted in the previous case will be adopted in the current fact problem. This is the basic premise of *stare decisis* (stand by the decision). It provides that precedent (rules of law in previous cases) will be followed if the facts in the current case are substantially similar.

Even if the facts are not similar, arguments may be made based on the legal theories or the remedies sought. For example, the fact that a summary judgment is granted in a civil lawsuit based on false imprisonment will not preclude that case from being used as a basis for argument where summary judgment is being sought in a case involving noncompetition clauses. Since the rule of law is the same, reasoning by analogy may effectively be used.

Because reasoning by analogy is the most consistent with the doctrine of *stare decisis,* it is probably the most often used type of reasoning applied by legal professionals.

Regardless of the kind of reasoning employed, it will be helpful to prepare a chart relating the current fact problem to prior case law. Figure 11-1 shows an example of a chart that may be employed for reasoning by analogy.

It is important to put this analysis down on paper for several reasons:

- writing clarifies thinking

- a written record helps ensure that no elements/similarities are overlooked that could result in a "sneak attack" by the opposition

- a written record provides direction for additional research or investigation

- a written record serves as a visual reminder by providing at-a-glance summaries that are invaluable in situations where schedules do not permit professionals to keep focused on only one task at a time

FIGURE 11-1   Synthesis of Facts and Law—Reasoning by Analogy

	Prior Case Law	Current Fact Problem
Similarities	Parties: (occupation, relationship) Subject matter: (situation) Legal theories: (negligence) Remedies: (punitive damages)	Does this problem involve a person in the same occupation or relationship as the prior case? Does the problem involve a similar situation (place or thing)? Are the legal theories similar? What remedies are being sought?
Differences	(use the same factors as similarities)	(use the same factors as similarities)
Gaps		What information do I need to fill the gaps? What don't I know that I need to know to synthesize this research with my current problem?

An alternative system such as a checklist, a diagram, or a process chart may work better for you. Take advantage of your natural organizational and relational skills to develop your own system.

A word of caution is appropriate: be prepared with a counteranalysis. What will be the opposing point of view? The opposing side will have access to all the same law and prior legal argument. It may be necessary to go back to the fact situation and reanalyze. Is there another way of looking at this problem? Are there gaps in the factual information that might work against your analysis? To diligently represent the interests of a legal client, it is essential to consider all of the arguments, both for and against.

PERSUASIVE ARGUMENT

Because the ideal of the American legal system is that the law is just and supportable and that no rulings will be made that are arbitrary, whimsical, or capricious, issue-specific arguments must always be supported with prior law or other authority. It may be well known that poor hygiene is related to incidences of infection, but in a legal argument, this "fact" must be supported with peer-reviewed studies in medical journals. The phrase "unreasonable conduct" must be used in connection with its judicial interpretation and referenced to supporting case law. Without this backing, argument is not convincing and not reliable. If the court cannot cite to the foundation for a position, the court will be reluctant to adopt it.

This is another important reason to chart the analysis and synthesis of legal problems. By chronicling the facts and law with notations, reference will be simplified when the argument is being prepared, and it will not be necessary to go through the entire court opinion again to locate the quote that applies.

SYNTHESIZING FACTS AND LAW

Synthesis is the process of putting together the pieces to make a logical and coherent whole. In law, synthesis involves collecting the statutes, cases, administrative rules and regulations, and other authority, and relating them to the issues of fact and law so that the common links between the past and the present emerge. Through synthesis, a persuasive argument is illuminated that favors the position that provides a just and fair solution to the problem.

It is unlikely that the current legal problem may be resolved using only one source of law or other learned literature. In fact, it is more likely that the research includes several sources, and that there are multiple issues involved. The process of synthesis brings connectedness to the myriad pieces of information that have a bearing on the problem.

Synthesis can be achieved using the same four-part analysis for reasoning that was employed in the analogy discussion and by bringing together all of the similarities or differences, depending on which side of the dispute is being represented. Another means of synthesizing is to arrange all of the

---

Ethics Bookmark

Adverse Authority

"A lawyer shall not knowingly . . . fail to disclose to the tribunal legal authority in the controlling jurisdiction known to the lawyer to be directly adverse to the position of the client and not disclosed by opposing counsel" Annotated Model Rules of Professional Conduct Fourth Edition Rule 3.3(a) Copyright 1999.*[1] Attorneys are required to complete a thorough research of the client's claim, including adverse authority. If the attorney knows of law that does not support the client's claim and this law is not brought up by the opposing side, the attorney is under an ethical obligation to disclose it. The common thread in all of the ethical rules is the concept of truth. The truth of the matter—and justice—are not possible if the parties are not fully apprised of the law and the facts.
*American Bar Association. Reprinted by permission of the American Bar Association. American Bar Association, *Annotated Model Rules of Professional conduct*, 4th ed. (1999) Rule 3.3(a). Copies of Model Code of Professional Responsibility, 1999 edition are available from Service Center, American Bar Association, 750 North Lake Shore Drive, Chicago, IL 60611-4497, 1-800-285-2221.

statutes, followed by the case law interpreting them, in an order that explains and expands the connection of these authorities to the facts of the case. This will outline a resolution that is consistent with existing and prior law.

An alternative is to start with the rules of law and identify their sources. Then follow up with issues and facts to lay the foundation for the reasoning that should be adopted by the court. Or begin by identifying the cause of action and then building the argument from general to specific (this is similar to the linear reasoning concept) using the law and the facts to support the position and promote understanding. Regardless of the synthesis technique employed, the result must be clear and convincing.

Proper synthesis depends on thorough legal analysis. Conscientiously reading and summarizing the law, and isolating and interpreting relevant facts are the building stones of legal argument. The synthesis is often reduced to writing in a memorandum of law, an interoffice memo, or a memo to the file. It may be helpful to identify a process for collecting and relating all of the bits and pieces that comprise a legal argument. This process may include restating the legal problem, organizing the legal issues, briefly answering the legal questions, and relating those answers to legal and other authority.

Restate the Problem

To begin with, the facts must be organized. The relevant facts will be applied to the rules of law to isolate the issues, but restating the problem will help keep in mind the client's goal and the result that will promote justice. Confine the statement of facts to those that are necessary to clearly describe the questions of law presented.

Organize the Issues

After identifying the facts that gave rise to the legal problem, write each issue succinctly and narrowly with a focus on the law that will be included later in the analysis. Writing issue statements is a difficult task, and it is often deferred to the attorney. Only with professional legal experience and judgment is it possible to coalesce the multifaceted aspects of a problem into the general, yet selective, jargon of legal specificity. Still, understanding the process of legal analysis, reasoning, and synthesis will arm the legal nurse consultant with tools to improve participation in the development of legal issues. Each issue must be clearly and narrowly stated so that the applicable law and reasoning illuminate the argument and the appropriate resolution of that issue.

Brief Answer

For each issue, a short recitation of the applicable law and expected outcome should be formulated. This serves the purpose of a topic sentence or **thesis statement,** allowing expansion of the principles of law and arguments relating to the issue in a way that clarifies the thesis statement.

Legal and Other Materials

The brief answer summarizes the conclusion and gives an answer to the problem. The supporting argument couched in law and learned materials provides an explanation of how the conclusion was reached (shows the work, as in a math problem). This approach to every issue may result in what seems to be excessive repetition. Do not be troubled by this; it is necessary to ensure that each point of the problem has been clearly resolved through a point of law or other learned source. It is also necessary to ensure that the decision is supported and not made arbitrarily or capriciously.

For this section of the memorandum or work paper, all the statutes and cases must be collected and organized. Here is where writing the legal analysis (see Chapter Nine), case briefs (discussed in Chapter Twelve), and the chart of similarities, and so forth will be of immeasurable value. Later, if a court document must be written on this problem, these documents will guide the writing with minimal reference to the original sources. By thoroughly and conscientiously completing these writings at the outset, you will save time, effort, and expense and minimize the cost of legal services to the client.

THE ROLE OF THE LEGAL NURSE CONSULTANT

This discussion has focused on legal analysis, particularly the synthesis of several sources of information to the application of law and facts. Many times the law alone will not be sufficient to arrive at resolution. Especially when the problem involves medical standards, the legal nurse consultant may play an invaluable role in analyzing the problem.

Standards of care created by the Joint Commission on Accreditation of Healthcare Organizations (JCAHO), the scope of practice for various roles in the medical profession, and the research of medical literature (treatises and journal articles concerning diagnosis and treatment) are all part of the analysis and evaluation process. These sources of authority are best researched and applied with the assistance of a qualified health care professional—a registered nurse. Synthesizing the results of this analysis and using proper medical and legal authority will give the attorney and the client a better grasp of the legal issues, the strengths or weaknesses of the claim, and potential resolution.

> **What LNCs Say . . .**
>
> *"Basically I go through everything for the attorneys to find out what's important and what's not important to the case," Laurie Entrekin, Long & Jaudon, Denver, CO, quoted in Discovery, June 1995. Reprinted with permission of Denver Paralegal Institute.*

CHAPTER SUMMARY

- Deductive reasoning, linear reasoning, and reasoning by analogy are used by legal professionals in analyzing current legal problems.
- Analysis of legal problems should be outlined or written.
- All conclusions in legal analysis must be supported by authority.

■ Synthesis is the process of collecting the authority, analyzing it in relation to the current legal problem, and arriving at a supportable conclusion.

■ A four-part analysis is often recommended: parties, subject matter, legal theories, and remedies.

KEY TERMS

deductive reasoning
linear reasoning

reasoning by analogy
synthesis

thesis statement

REVIEW QUESTIONS

1. Explain the concepts of deductive reasoning, linear reasoning, and reasoning by analogy. Which one is most often used by legal professionals?

2. Why is it important to record analysis in writing or in a table?

3. Explain the process of synthesis as it relates to legal problems.

INTERNET EXERCISES

1. Access the web page for this textbook at *www.westlegalstudies.com.*

2. Click on the assignments section of the web page and complete the assignment(s) for Chapter Eleven.

EXERCISES

1. Networking. Contact the state bar association and request information concerning upcoming continuing legal education seminars. If your resources permit (you may be able to attend at the reduced student rates), register and attend. At the sessions, pay particular attention to how the presenters relate changes in the law to existing practice. Bring your business cards and use this opportunity to promote your services to the attorneys and paralegals by whom you sit.

2. Professional Portfolio. Using your professional experience, think of a situation that you believe may have given rise to legal consequences. Use the case studies in this book to analyze the problem you selected using your professional experience. Develop a chart or table, or write an analysis and outline synthesizing the legal conclusion you believe would result. Be careful to ensure the privacy of the patients and others involved in the problem by identifying them with pseudonyms or general identifiers (e.g., patient, internist, etc.). Include this analysis and synthesis in your professional portfolio.

ENDNOTES

1. American Bar Association. *Annotated Model Rules of Professional Conduct,* (1999) 4th Edition Rule 3.3(a). Copies of ABA *Model Code of Professional Responsibility, 1999 Edition* are available from Service Center, American Bar Association, 750 North Lake Shore Drive, Chicago, IL 60611-4497, 1-800-285-2221.

ADDITIONAL REFERENCES

Barber, S. *Legal Writing* 2nd ed. Albany, NY: West Thomson Learning, 1997.

Statsky, W. *Essentials of Paralegalism,* 3rd ed. St. Paul, Minnesota: West Thomson Learning, 1998.

CHAPTER 12

WRITING A BRIEF

OBJECTIVES

In this chapter, you will discover

- what the terms legal brief, case brief, and trial brief mean

- the different methods for preparing case briefs

- the basic components of a case brief

- why it is important for legal nurse consultants to understand the case briefing process

OVERVIEW

A **brief** is a legal writing that can be used for many purposes. A **case brief** is used to summarize the findings of fact and law in a particular court opinion. A **trial brief** is a summary of the issues, the witnesses, and evidence that will be presented at trial. A brief in support of a motion is a summary of legal research supporting a legal position on a question of law that will be raised at a hearing or trial. An **appellate brief** is a formalized recitation of the alleged errors that occurred at the trial, together with a legally supported discussion of why the errors should invalidate the outcome and provide a basis for changing the judgment of the trial court. In addition, a brief is used to describe any **memorandum of law** on a particular issue.

The discussion about synthesis of law and facts in the previous chapter provides a strong backdrop for the thinking that occurs prior to writing a legal brief (memorandum of law). To facilitate that synthesis, this chapter will focus on writing case briefs. It will show how mastering this fundamental of legal work can facilitate learning how to prepare briefs of a larger scope, including appellate briefs.

CASE BRIEF

A case brief summarizes the facts and holding in a court opinion. It is basically a succinct description of the items identified in Chapter Ten that one must be cognizant of when reading case law. It includes the court writing the opinion, the date of decision, the facts, the issues, the decision, and the reasoning.

"Briefing" a case is valuable for several reasons:

- It assists in understanding the case.
- It provides a one-page summary of the issues and law.
- It records essential information about the case that may be used later in synthesizing the research, evaluating the claim, and drafting later documents.

Being able to brief a case, or understanding the process and importance of case briefing, is a fundamental skill of legal professionals. There are several ways to construct a case brief. The six-point method, the IRAC approach, and the opinion format are described in this chapter.

THE SIX-POINT METHOD

A common organizational method for briefing cases uses six points: facts, judicial history, issue, decision, reasoning, and procedural consequences. Although the case title and citation are critical and are always recorded at the top of the page, the title and citation are not considered part of the six points. A sample case brief using the six-point method is shown in Figure 12-1.

FIGURE 12-1　Case Brief Using Six-Point Method

State v. Sater
588 N.W. 2d 588 (Minn. 1999)

FACTS: Defendant Kelly Ruth Sater was tried on four charges of murder arising out of the same incident: first-degree, second-degree intentional, second-degree, and second-degree for the benefit of a gang. A jury found Sater not guilty on first degree murder and deadlocked on the lesser charges.

JUDICIAL HISTORY: After the trial, defendant moved for dismissal. Trial court denied motion, but certified the question to the Court of Appeals.

ISSUE: Does acquittal on one charge bar retrial of lesser charges?

DECISION: The court determined that statutory language did not, following acquittal on one charge arising from a single incident, bar retrial of lesser charges.

REASONING: The court looked to Minn. Stat. S. 609.035, which states that if a person's conduct constitutes more than one offense, the person may be punished for only one of the offenses, and a conviction or acquittal on any one of them is a bar to prosecution for any others. In *State v. Johnson,* 141 N.W. 2d 517 (1998), the court concluded that "no plea or dismissal of any offense charged will prevent the prosecution from continuing until all offenses charged are disposed of" (526). Because the lesser charges arising from the same offense remained unresolved after the trial, the court of appeals concluded that the unresolved charges would be subject to retrial.

PROCEDURAL CONSEQUENCES: The appeals court affirmed the decision of the trial court.

Facts

In this section of the case brief, the writer isolates the relevant facts. It is generally accepted that there should be enough facts that anyone not familiar with the case would understand why this matter came to court. In addition, any facts that have a bearing on the court's decision must be included.

Judicial History

Who brought the lawsuit and what happened in earlier judicial proceedings are included in this section. This explains to the reader where the lawsuit is in the court system and provides a frame of reference for the decision in the current appellate court.

Issue

The legal question that brought this case to the appellate court is recited here. It may be in the form of a question or it may be stated with alternatives. It is preferable to use a question format rather than a *whether or not* statement. For example, "Is 'anywhere' in the United States a reasonable territory restriction in a non-compete clause?" is preferable to "The question before the court was whether or not a non-compete clause defining the territory as 'anywhere in the United States' is reasonable." *Whether or not* statements are sometimes difficult to answer and may be ambiguous.

Decision

The decision is sometimes called the holding or the rule of law. It describes the conclusion of the court. "Yes" and "no" are insufficient as decisions in a case brief. It is not appropriate to merely identify that the court reversed or affirmed the decision of the lower court. The decision is a statement that includes the legal principle and the facts of this situation. For example, "The court concluded that 'anywhere in the United States' is an unreasonable territory restriction and declared the non-compete clause void and unenforceable" is appropriate wording for the decision section of a case brief.

Reasoning

There are two parts to the reasoning section of a case brief. First, the writer must point out the relevant statutory and case law used by the court as authority in arriving at its decision. It is important to identify the authority by its citation here (to be discussed later in Chapters Fourteen through Seventeen), so that anyone reading the brief can clearly see what precedent or other authority influenced the court. While the law must be cited accurately, the language of the law may be paraphrased.

The second part of the reasoning is the relation of the facts to the law. Here the writer of the brief shows that the facts clearly call the law into play. It is a causal relation concept; for example, "Because the employer conceded that 'anywhere in the United States' was an unreasonable territory restriction, the court concluded that the non-compete clause violated Sec. 103.465 of the state statutes. Section 103.465 states that if any part of a non-compete clause is unreasonable, the entire non-compete is rendered void and unenforceable."

Procedural Consequences

Contrary to popular belief, the ruling of the appellate court generally does not end the case. If the court of appeals finds that the trial court ruled with insufficient facts, it will send the case back to that court for further evidentiary hearings. Generally, whenever an appeals court reverses a decision, the case returns to the exact spot in the litigation process where the point of law was appealed. For example, if a defendant is granted **summary judgment,** meaning the court grants judgment prior to a trial because it appears that no facts are at issue, the plaintiff may appeal that ruling. If the appeals court reverses the summary judgment, the case returns to the point immediately before the summary judgment was entered. The case either continues through the trial process or is settled out of court.

If the case is affirmed, the parties still have the potential for appeal. In states where there is a three-tiered court system, the intermediate appeals court determination may be appealed, via *certiorari,* to the highest court and even to the United States Supreme Court.

IRAC

IRAC is an acronym for Issue, Rule, Application, and Conclusion. This organizational method has been used extensively in legal matters and provides for consistency and uniformity in brief writing and in legal analysis. All court opinions can be separated into these four components, which are described below. A sample case brief using the IRAC approach is shown in Figure 12-2.

FIGURE 12-2   Case Brief Using IRAC Approach

State v. Sater
588 N.W. 2d 588 (Minn. 1999)

ISSUE: Does acquittal on one charge bar retrial of lesser charges?

RULE: Minn. Stat. S. 609.035 states that if a person's conduct constitutes more than one offense, the person may be punished for only one of the offenses, and a conviction or acquittal on any one of them is a bar to prosecution for any others. In *State v. Johnson,* 141 N.W. 2d 517 (1998), the court concluded that "no plea or dismissal of any offense charged will prevent the prosecution from continuing until all offenses charged are disposed of" (526).

APPLICATION: Defendant Kelly Ruth Sater was tried on four charges of murder arising out of the same incident: first-degree, second-degree intentional, second-degree, and second-degree for the benefit of a gang. A jury found Sater not guilty on first degree murder and deadlocked on the lesser charges. Defense moved for dismissal based on Minn. Stat. S. 609.035. The motion was denied and the question certified to the Court of Appeals.

CONCLUSION: Because the lesser charges arising from the same offense remained unresolved after the trial, the court of appeals concluded that the unresolved charges would be subject to retrial.

Issue

The legal question presented in the case is the first part of the IRAC brief. An initial glance at the brief will tell the reader what was resolved in the court opinion and will help relate the case to the facts of the current problem. The issue, as outlined in Chapter Nine, is the question that arises when the facts do not exactly match the law. It is the crux of the legal problem.

Rule

Here the court synthesizes all statutory, administrative, and case law that applies to the question at hand. If the court interprets a statute in light of these facts, the statute citation is provided as part of the holding. If the court relies on precedent, the pertinent case is referenced. In this way, as in the six-point method, the brief makes clear what law was relied upon in arriving at its decision. It is important to keep in mind that the rule portion of the IRAC case brief is not the decision, holding, or rule of law established in the case, but the law used by the court in justifying its determination.

Application

In this section of an IRAC case brief, the writer applies the steps of legal analysis: breaking the rule into its elements and applying the facts. In this way, the reader clearly sees the relationship between the significant facts and the law cited in the rule section. This relationship lays the foundation for the court's conclusion.

Another important reason for using the IRAC method of case briefing is that it clarifies the analysis process. It creates a checklist to verify the accuracy of the legal reasoning and provides insight into how the court will react to the current fact situation or future problems.

Conclusion

The conclusion answers the legal question posed in the first section of the case brief, the issue. If the middle sections of the brief were eliminated, the reader would have a question and its answer, clearly stated and clearly related to each other. While the rule and application sections provide the reasoning of the court (as it is described in the six-point method earlier), the conclusion states the decision of the court in resolving the dispute brought before it. Here is where the holding or rule of law established in the case is identified.

OPINION FORMAT

The opinion format mirrors the technique used by justices writing the decisions of court cases. It includes similar component parts: issue, decision, judicial history, facts, reasoning, and disposition. A sample case brief using the opinion format is shown in Figure 12-3.

FIGURE 12-3 Case Brief Using Opinion Format

State v. Sater
588 N.W. 2d 588 (Minn. 1999)

ISSUE: Does acquittal on one charge bar retrial of lesser charges?

DECISION: The court concluded that acquittal on one charge arising from a single incident did not bar retrial of lesser charges.

JUDICIAL HISTORY: After a jury found defendant not guilty on first degree murder and deadlocked on lesser charges, defense moved for dismissal of the lesser charges. Trial court denied the motion and certified the question to the Court of Appeals.

FACTS: Defendant Kelly Ruth Sater was tried on four charges of murder arising out of the same incident: first-degree, second-degree intentional, second-degree, and second-degree for the benefit of a gang. A jury found Sater not guilty on first degree murder and deadlocked on the lesser charges.

REASONING: The court looked to Minn. Stat. S. 609.035, which states that if a person's conduct constitutes more than one offense, the person may be punished for only one of the offenses, and a conviction or acquittal on any one of them is a bar to prosecution for any others. In *State v. Johnson,* 141 N.W. 2d 517 (1998), the court concluded that "no plea or dismissal of any offense charged will prevent the prosecution from continuing until all offenses charged are disposed of" (526). Because the lesser charges arising from the same offense remained unresolved after the trial, the court of appeals concluded that the unresolved charges would be subject to retrial.

DISPOSITION: The appeals court affirmed the decision of the trial court.

Judicial History

Most justices will begin by describing the court proceedings that occurred in the lower court before the matter was brought to the appellate court. This section identifies who sued whom, what the trial court decided, and who is appealing. This sets the stage for the discussion of the case, which follows in the court opinion.

Issue

Following the judicial history, the court restates the question it is called upon to answer. In the same way, a case brief using the opinion format identifies the legal question following a description of the case history.

Decision

The jurist writing the court opinion will immediately answer the issue by declaring what the court concludes. This is the holding or the rule of law established in the case that becomes precedent in that jurisdiction.

Thus, the case brief written in opinion format, while following the judicial writing of case law, reveals immediately the crux of the problem and how it was resolved.

Facts

In a court opinion, the first paragraph is usually devoted a summary of the judicial proceedings that preceded this court's involvement. The second paragraph describes the issue and decision. The third paragraph outlines the relevant facts. These facts have significance to the outcome and are related to the reasoning of the court that the law relied upon.

Reasoning

Like the six-point method, the opinion format includes a section for outlining the statutory law and precedent used by the court in arriving at its decision. In addition, the facts described earlier are related to the law to show that the law is clearly called into play and that the decision of the court is justifiable.

Disposition

Similar to the procedural consequences section of a six-point brief, the disposition tells the reader what impact the court's decision has on earlier determinations and what will happen to the case now.

PROCESS OF WRITING CASE BRIEFS

Regardless of which method is used for briefing cases, the writer must carefully examine the court opinion in order to capture its essence in a one-page summary. To do this, several steps should be followed:

- Read the case through first to get a feel for the problem and the court's determination.
- Highlight the integral components of the brief-writing method to be employed:
  - for the six-point method: the facts, judicial history, issue, decision, reasoning, and procedural consequences
  - for IRAC: the issue, rule, application, and conclusion
  - for the opinion format: the issue, decision, judicial history, facts, reasoning, and disposition

---

Ethics Bookmark

Legal Nurse Consultant Competence

"The legal nurse consultant participates in ongoing educational activities pertaining to the health sciences and the law relevant to his or her practice area" AALNC Standards of Legal Nurse Consulting Practice, Standard 2.1 (1995).[1] While the integrity of the legal nurse consultant's position is the medical education and experience that is brought to the investigation and resolution of medical-legal claims, a legal nurse consultant cannot ignore the value of basic legal education. Particularly in areas of specialty practice, such as toxic torts and pharmaceutical negligence, legal nurse consultants should strive to seek out educational opportunities to keep them current with legal trends and decisions that impact their practice.

- Re-read the case to crystallize the important features before you begin to write.

- Write the case brief in your own words, quoting only where it will serve the reader to see the exact words used by the court.

- Use concise, but complete, sentences; add headings only if it will assist the reader in understanding the case brief.

- File and index the case brief in a research folder or document repository in the computer network, so that future researchers will not have to start over.

- Use the case brief to analyze the current legal problem and later to synthesize the results into a logical, coherent argument.

The case brief is a useful tool for analyzing current fact problems and recording research results. More than that, however, briefing a case is an invaluable exercise in understanding how court rulings are made and how the process of litigation operates. More than any other task, briefing cases provides insight into the difficulties of reconciling diverse points of view and interpreting past law in light of current circumstances.

There is probably no better way to understand law than to brief every case you read. The time and effort required will be rewarded with experience and skill in discerning court rulings and in analyzing legal situations.

Chapter Summary

- The word brief may refer to a case brief, a trial brief, a memorandum of law, an appellate brief, or any other summary of legal information.

- A case brief is used to summarize a court opinion.

- Case briefs may be organized using a six-point method, IRAC, or opinion format.

- Briefing a case provides valuable insight concerning the judicial system and the law of the case.

KEY TERMS

appellate brief	*certiorari*	summary judgment
brief	IRAC	trial brief
case brief	memorandum of law	

REVIEW QUESTIONS

1. Explain what is meant by the terms trial brief, appellate brief, and case brief.

2. Compare and contrast the components of a case brief using the six-point, IRAC, and opinion formats.
3. Why is it valuable to brief court opinions?

INTERNET EXERCISES

1. Access the web page for this textbook at *www.westlegalstudies.com.*

2. Click on the assignments section and complete the assignment(s) for Chapter Twelve.

EXERCISES

1. Networking. Contact a member of the AALNC who is employed in a legal office near you. (See Appendix B for help in locating association members.) Use previous contacts or identify a new contact and ask if and how legal briefs and case briefs are used in legal nurse consulting practice. If the legal nurse consultant is willing to share this information, ask which method is used for case briefing. Ask why this method works for the firm.

2. Professional Portfolio. Brief the case at the end of each of the Units in this textbook. Use any method that seems appropriate, or try briefing different cases using each of the methods outlined in this chapter. Include the case briefs in your professional portfolio. Add "ability to brief cases" in your resume or cover letter.

ENDNOTE

1. American Association of Legal Nurse Consultants. *Standards of Legal Nurse Consulting Practice.* (1995) Standard 2.1.

ADDITIONAL REFERENCES

Barber, S. *Legal Writing,* 3rd ed. Albany, NY: West Thomson Learning, 1997.

Bogart, J.B., RN, MN, ed. *Legal Nurse Consulting: Principles and Practice.* Boston, MA: CRC Press, 1998.

Yelin, A., Samborn, H. *The Legal Research and Writing Handbook.* Boston, MA: Little, Brown and Company, 1996.

LEGAL NURSE CONSULTANT PROFILE

Marilyn Mason-Kish

Toxic Torts

Marilyn Mason-Kish has a bachelor's degree in health services administration. Her nursing experience includes emergency room, medical-surgical nursing and nursing administration. She has been a legal nurse consultant since 1986, and has experience as an independent LNC as well as contributing to the legal team as an employee of a law firm. She was a founding member of the AALNC and served as president from 1993 to 1994. She has given numerous presentations on medical-legal aspects of litigation, has published several articles in national journals, and has authored the "References and Resources" column in *Journal of Legal Nurse Consulting*. She is an instructor in the legal nurse consultant program at San Francisco State University and is employed with a law firm specializing in complex litigation.

Photo used with permission of Paul Tsang, Master Photographer, Masterpiece Portrait and Wedding, San Carlos, CA.

What do you like best about being a legal nurse consultant?

"I like being able to benefit the legal community through my educational and experiential nursing background. As an LNC, I have been allowed to extend my career into a new area without making a complete career change.

"It is rewarding to have the opportunity to apply my nursing background to the legal field and to problem-solve in medical-legal matters. The whole process is fascinating! Attorneys, paralegals, and clients have been most appreciative of my contributions as a member of the legal team."

What challenges do legal nurse consultants face in your area of law?

"I believe the most significant challenge for legal nurse consultants working in complex litigation would be staying on top of the most current medical research available specific to their respective case work. Understanding the technical resources that are available and how they can be applied to complex litigation is mandatory but sometimes difficult to implement in view of budgetary constraints in the dynamic market of technical equipment.

"As LNC contributions continue to expand within the legal community, the development of educational programs for the LNC will become a key challenge for the LNC profession."

What advice would you give five nurses who are interested in legal nurse consulting?

"Make use of the marvelous collection of information that is available today specific to medical-legal issues and LNC practice: books, seminars, continuing education courses, LNC certification programs, networking, joining professional organizations such as AALNC, the International Society of Forensic Nurses, and the American College of Legal Medicine.

"In addition, develop or strengthen those skills that contribute to a successful LNC practice: computer literacy, articulation, and excellent writing skills. Commit to your desire for change and prepare for that change each day."

What unique marketing strategy are you willing to share?

"My first position with a law firm was the result of attending a continuing education course. I introduced myself to the person sitting next to me. She was a registered nurse working in a law firm in San Francisco and told me the firm had just advertised for a second nurse. I have her my business card and the next day she called me to schedule an interview. I was subsequently hired!

"My point in sharing this scenario is this: Opportunities may present themselves at those times and in those places when they are least expected. Be prepared to respond by maintaining a current curriculum vitae and *always* carry business cards. Entering the field of legal nurse consulting requires the ability to successfully market yourself as a professional, knowledgeable and capable. It is an investment in yourself and the legal nurse consultant profession with a full return!"

"Make use of the marvelous collection of information that is available today, from reading everything you can find on nurses and physicians and law to networking, attending seminars, and joining professional organizations."

LEGAL RESEARCH

Law books are the tools of the legal trade. A legal nurse consultant must understand the concept of citation and the fundamentals of locating law to work effectively in the legal environment. Whether statutory law, case law, or administrative law, these resources are critical to solving legal problems. In this unit, you will find answers to the following questions:

■ What is a legal citation and how is it used?

■ How are laws classified?

■ How are laws reported and made available to the public?

■ What techniques are employed to locate laws?

CHAPTER 13

STATUTORY
SOURCES OF LAW

OBJECTIVES

In this chapter, you will discover

- the source of statutory primary authority

- how statutory primary authority is cited

- where and how to locate statutory authority using legal citation

OVERVIEW

Legal sources are divided into two categories: **primary** and **secondary.** Primary is further divided into primary **binding** (mandatory) and primary **persuasive.** Primary law is the letter of the law; that is, it is the legislative enactments, case judgments, and agency rules and regulations that daily govern our lives. Please see Chapter Ten for a more complete discussion of authority. There are several types of primary authority. Figure 13-1 identifies the sources of primary authority. Any discussion of legal authority and sources of law involves the language of **legal citation.**

LEGAL CITATION

Legal citation is a universal language that accomplishes several purposes:

- Citations clearly identify the location of the material referenced.
- Citations indicate the source, date, and jurisdiction of the material referenced.
- Citations provide a quick and uniform language for referencing law.

There are two systems for legal citation. The most widely used is the *Uniform System of Citation,* developed by Harvard and commonly known as the *Blue Book of Citation.* The Blue Book system will be used throughout this text

---

FIGURE 13-1   Sources of Primary Authority

Source	Description of Law
Constitutions	Legal documents adopted by the people that identify a geographical area as a separate legal entity, outline its system of government, and describe the basic rights and duties of its citizens
Treaties	Legal contracts entered into between two or more nations; these contracts, together with customary practices, constitute international law
Statutes	Acts of Congress, laws made by state legislatures, ordinances adopted by city councils, and resolutions of township boards are all examples of statutory law
Case law	The judicial rulings made in legal disputes, sometimes called judge-made law or common law
Administrative rules and regulations	The law promulgated by agencies empowered by Congress or state legislatures to deal with problems of social concern; e.g., environment, transportation, etc.

as it is the citation system acceptable to the United States Supreme Court. A second system, known as the University of Chicago Style, uses a format similar to the Blue Book but more consistent with the American Psychological Association style of citation.

Rather like learning a foreign language, many of the rules of construction of legal citation must be memorized. Legal citation will be a component part of the sections in this chapter on primary sources of law including constitutions, statutes, and secondary sources of compiled legislative history.

CONSTITUTIONS

The Sixth Article of the Constitution of the United States reads "The Constitution, treaties, and laws of the United States shall be the supreme law of the land."[1] Constitutions and statutes are in the top tiers of the **hierarchy of authority.** (For a discussion of hierarchy of authority, please see Chapter Ten.)

A Constitution accomplishes many things:

- It creates a separate country or state.
- It outlines the governmental structure of that separate state.
- It empowers governmental officials.
- It establishes the limitations and scope of power of governmental bodies or officials.
- It describes the rights, liberties, and responsibilities of the citizens of the state.

There are fifty-one constitutions in the United States; the United States Constitution and one for each state in the union. If a state constitution (or a state or federal law) is in conflict with the United States Constitution, it will be declared void and unenforceable. The United States Constitution and its judicial interpretations is the highest law and takes precedence over all other sources of law.

PUBLICATION OF CONSTITUTIONS

Because the American legal system requires publication of the laws, the Constitution may be found in several sources, including the *United States Code*.

The Constitution of the United States of America

This publication of the Congressional Research Service of the Library of Congress contains each article, section, and clause of the Constitution and its amendments. Each of these is followed by editorial features, including analysis of the article, section, or clause in the United States Supreme Court. Citations to important Supreme Court cases are provided for ease of reference.

United States Code

The primary function of the *United States Code* (published by the United States Government Printing Office), the *United States Code Annotated* (published by West Group, a division of Thomson Learning), and the *United States Code Service* (published by Lawyer's Cooperative Publishing, a division of Thomson Learning) is to provide access to federal laws. The Constitution and its amendments are published in the first volume of each of these sources.

Citation

Regardless of where the Constitution is found, the citation to an article, a section, or a clause of the Constitution should refer to the original document.

U.S. Const. art. II, §1, cl. 2

This citation would immediately identify the preceding passage as a direct quote from the United States Constitution, article II, section 1 at clause 2. This citation format is the same when referring to the constitution of any state. For example, *Wash. Const. art. II, §2* refers to the Constitution of the state of Washington, article II, section 2.

The citation system is intended to be uniform, so that any legal professional, by looking at a citation, will know where to find the law and from what source the law originates.

TREATIES

Treaties are contracts between different nations. They codify mutual interests in trade, finances, security, and dispute resolution. Treaties are only one part of what is known as international law. International law also includes the customary practices between nations, and the industries and companies of different nations, which have established traditions of working together.

Because of the national interest in preserving Native American culture and self-governance, treaties have become more important in the transaction of legal matters in the United States. The Supreme Court has declared that tribal courts have concurrent jurisdiction with state and federal courts in matters concerning Native Americans.[2]

PUBLICATION OF TREATIES

Treaties are made by the president of the United States with the approval of the Senate.[3] There are many sources for locating treaties before and after ratification.

Congressional Index

The *Congressional Index* has a "Treaties" section that contains information about how to find a treaty that is pending before the United States Senate. Once that information is found, a request to a Senator from your state will generally provide you with a quick copy via fax or mail, if the source is not available in the library.

Treaties and Other International Acts Series

This series is a state department publication of treaties in pamphlet form. The pamphlets are numbered consecutively and the treaties are published in the order in which they are ratified or made.

United States Treaties and Other International Agreements

This publication is a series of bound volumes containing the authoritative text of the treaties of the United States. There are several other sources for locating international agreements and several commercial vendors of looseleaf publications that include the text of the law and interpretive notations and practice tips.

It is unlikely that legal nurse consultants will be expected to know the intricacies of locating international law. However, as the economy stretches globally and as immigration law becomes more prominent, all legal professionals should recognize the increasing importance of treaties and international concerns in the American legal system.

STATUTES

Statutes are one of the most critical sources of primary law. They include all Acts of Congress, state legislative acts, city ordinances, township resolutions, and all other laws adopted by a representative law-making body.

THE LAW-MAKING PROCESS

Most states follow the pattern of law making that exists in the federal congress. The steps that must be taken for a proposed bill to become a law are outlined in Figure 13-2.

Anyone may propose a law—the president, special interest groups, members of Congress, administrative agencies, or citizens. The proposed bill must be introduced to the floor of a house of Congress by a member of that house. If it is introduced in the House of Representatives, it is given an H.R. number; if it is introduced in the Senate, it is given an S. number. All bills are numbered sequentially during each session of Congress.

Once introduced and given a number, the bill is assigned to committee. In the committee, the wording of the bill is considered, hearings may be held to ascertain the importance and impact of the bill, and a report is issued explaining the importance of the bill and why it should be enacted.

If the bill originates in the House of Representatives, the bill is then sent to the Rules Committee for placement on the agenda before the entire House.

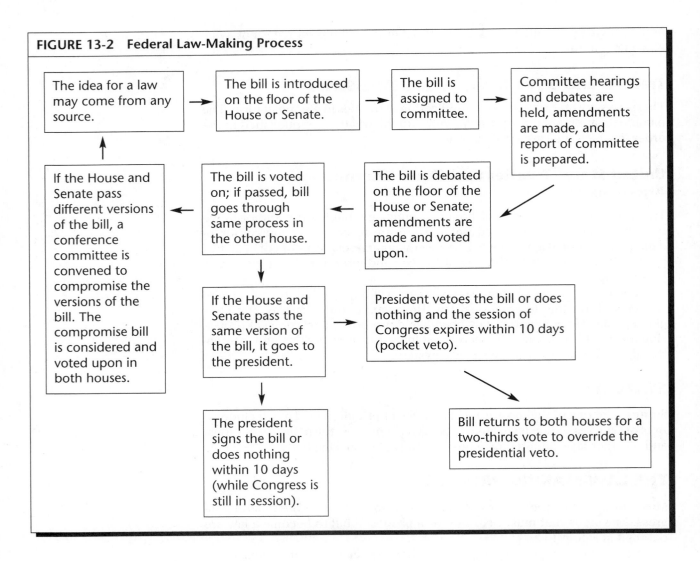

FIGURE 13-2   Federal Law-Making Process

On the floor of the House, the bill is debated, amendments may be made, and the bill is voted on. If it passes the House, it is referred to the Senate where the bill progresses through the same steps.

If the Senate, or second house, passes a version of the bill that is different from the one passed by the original house, the bill is referred to **conference committee.** The conference committee is made up of the chairs of the original committees and other interested members of both houses. Their charge is to compromise the differences in the legislation. The compromise bill must proceed through both houses again before it becomes law.

Once a bill has passed both houses in the same language, it goes to the president of the United States. The president has three options: sign the bill (after which it becomes law subject to its effective date), veto the bill, or refuse to sign the bill. If the president does not sign the bill within ten days, it becomes law as if the president had actually signed it. If the president does not sign the bill and the legislative session adjourns before the ten-day signing period is over, the bill dies. This is known as the **pocket veto.**

READING LAWS

Laws are read for their **plain meaning;** that is, they are interpreted to mean what ordinary citizens would understand them to mean. Sometimes, for the sake of precision, laws are written in lengthy and cumbersome sentences. It is often necessary to break the sentences down into fragments, isolate the important points, and then consider the points in order to arrive at the collective plain meaning of the statute section.

It is not uncommon to have to read statutory provisions more than once. Do not feel inadequate if the second reading still does not make the language clear. Even veteran legal scholars must often read and re-read statutory language to arrive at an understanding of the law.

Courts also interpret laws according to their plain meaning. Sometimes legislative materials, such as committee reports, Congressional debates, and transcripts of the committee hearings are used to help interpret the intent of the lawmakers. Whenever possible, however, the simplest construction of the statute is its plain meaning and the statute will generally be interpreted as such if it is tested in court.

PUBLICATION OF FEDERAL LAWS

United States laws are published both chronologically and by subject matter in several different sources.

Slip laws

The first publication of federal laws is chronological in pamphlet form called slip laws. Slip laws are available from congressional offices and from the United States Government Printing Office.

Statutes at Large

Slip laws are collected in the *Statutes at Large* and appear sequentially, as enacted during the legislative session. The *Statutes at Large* publication is generally considered to be the first public notice of the law.

> ### *What LNCs Say . . .*
>
> *"You will need a medical dictionary and* Black's Law Dictionary. *Current and older versions of the JCAHO (Joint Commission on Accreditation of Healthcare Organizations) standards for health care will come in handy, and you should have a book on nursing malpractice"* Connie Courtade, RN, BS, MAIR, Minneapolis, MN, used with permission.

United States Code

Because it is often difficult and time consuming to locate laws by their date of enactment, laws are **codified,** collected and arranged by subject matter. Codification provides ease of access via descriptive word indexes and topic outlines preceding each section of the code.

The official source for citing and locating United States laws is the *United States Code.* It is published by the United States Government Printing Office and is organized by topic into fifty titles, forty-eight of which are currently used. Each title is subdivided into sections. Every law passed by Congress is categorized under one of the forty-eight titles and is accessible using the index to the *United States Code.* The code is updated with pocket parts. There are two other bound publications, the *United States Code Annotated* and the *United States Code Service,* and several other sources for finding federal laws.

United States Code Annotated

The *United States Code Annotated* published by West Group, includes the **Key Number** index system peculiar to West resources and annotations about how the federal law has been interpreted in the courts. In addition, references are provided to the *Code of Federal Regulations.* Other legal research aids are also included, such as historical information and guides for using WestLaw.

United States Code Service

Published by Lawyer's Cooperative, the *United States Code Service* also provides the exact text of the United States law along with annotations and research aids. Valuable references in the *United States Code Service* include citations to the *American Law Reports* (see Chapter Sixteen).

Citation

The citation to a federal law includes the title number, the abbreviation for the series used, the section number, and the copyright year of the volume.

20 U. S. C. §1400 (1994)

Because the exact language of the law is published in the *United States Code Annotated* and the *United States Code Service,* the citation may also appear using one of these sources.

20 U. S. C. A. §1400 (1994)

20 U. S. C. S. §1400 (1994)

Each of these citations refers to the same law and may be found at title 20 of the *United States Code, United States Code Annotated,* or *United States Code Service,* at section 1400.

STATE LAWS

With the exception of Nebraska, state legislatures are **bicameral** (composed of two houses) and the law-making process in each of these states is similar to the law-making process in Congress. Most state laws must be submitted to the governor for signature in the same way that federal laws are submitted to the president.

PUBLICATION OF STATE LAWS

Like federal laws, state laws are published chronologically and by subject matter (in codes). The laws passed during the legislative session are collected chronologically in what are often called *Session Laws*. These **session laws** supplement and amend the existing codified laws of the state.

In addition to the session laws, each state collects its laws and organizes them by topic into a set of statutes that may be accessed by a descriptive word index or by topic outline. These sets of statutes go by various names. Figure 13-3 provides a list of the sets of statutes for each of the states.

FIGURE 13-3 Titles of State Statutes

State	Official Code	Abbreviation
Alabama	Code of Alabama	Ala. Code
Alaska	Alaska Statutes	Alaska Stat.
Arizona	Arizona Revised Statutes	Ariz. Rev. Stat.
Arkansas	Arkansas Code of 1987 Annotated	Ark. Code Ann.
California	West's Annotated California Code	Cal. [subject] Code
Colorado	Colorado Revised Statutes	Colo. Rev. Stat.
Connecticut	General Statutes of Connecticut	Conn. Gen. Stat.
Delaware	Delaware Code Annotated	Del. Code Ann.
District of Columbia	District of Columbia Code Annotated	D.C. Code Ann.
Florida	Florida Statutes	Fla. Stat.
Georgia	Code of Georgia Annotated	Ga. Code. Ann.
Hawaii	Hawaii Revised Statutes	Haw. Rev. Stat.
Idaho	Idaho Official Code	Idaho Code
Illinois	Illinois Compiled Statutes	Ill. Comp. Stat.
Indiana	Indiana Code	Ind. Code
Iowa	Code of Iowa	Iowa Code
Kansas	Kansas Statutes Annotated	Kan. Stat. Ann.
Kentucky	Baldwin's Official Edition, Kentucky Revised Statutes Annotated	Ky. Rev. Stat. Ann.
Louisiana	West's Louisiana Revised Statutes	La. Rev. Stat. Ann.

continued

FIGURE 13-3 **Titles of State Statutes** *continued*

State	Official Code	Abbreviation
Maine	Main Revised Statutes Annotated	Me. Rev. Stat. Ann.
Maryland	Annotated Code of Maryland	Md. Code Ann.
Massachusetts	General Laws of the Commonwealth of Massachusetts	Mass. Gen. Laws Ann.
Michigan	Michigan Compiled Laws	Mich. Comp. Laws
Minnesota	Minnesota Statutes	Minn. Stat.
Mississippi	Mississippi Code Annotated	Miss. Code. Ann.
Missouri	Missouri Revised Statutes	Mo. Rev. Stat.
Montana	Montana Code Annotated	Mont. Code Ann.
Nebraska	Revised Statutes of Nebraska	Neb. Rev. Stat.
Nevada	Nevada Revised Statutes	Nev. Rev. Stat.
New Hampshire	New Hampshire Revised Statutes Annotated	N.H. Rev. Stat. Ann.
New Jersey	New Jersey Statutes Annotated	N.J. Stat. Ann.
New Mexico	New Mexico Statutes Annotated	N.M. Stat. Ann.
New York	McKinney's Consolidated Laws of New York Annotated	N.Y. [subject] Law
North Carolina	General Statutes of North Carolina	N.C. Gen. Stat.
North Dakota	North Dakota Century Code	N.D. Cent. Code
Ohio	Page's Ohio Revised Code Annotated	Ohio Rev. Code Ann.
Oklahoma	Oklahoma Statutes	Okla. Stat.
Oregon	Oregon Revised Statutes	Or. Rev. Stat.
Pennsylvania	Pennsylvania Consolidated Statutes	Pa. Cons. Stat.
Rhode Island	General Laws of Rhode Island	R.I. Gen. Laws
South Carolina	Code of Laws of South Carolina 1976 Annotated	S.C. Code Ann.
South Dakota	South Dakota Codified Laws	S.D. Codified Laws
Tennessee	Tennessee Code Annotated	Tenn. Code Ann.
Texas	Vernon's Texas Codes Annotated	Tex. [subject] Code Ann.
Utah	Utah Code Annotated	Utah Code Ann.
Vermont	Vermont Statutes Annotated	Vt. Stat. Ann.
Virginia	Code of Virginia Annotated	Va. Code Ann.
Washington	Revised Code of Washington	Wash. Rev. Code
West Virginia	West Virginia Code	W. Va. Code
Wisconsin	Wisconsin Statutes	Wis. Stat.
Wyoming	Wyoming Statutes Annotated	Wyo. Stat. Ann.

Among other features, each codification of state law will include, at a minimum

- an index
- the text of the laws
- notations, usually concerning the history of the law, court interpretations of the law, and cross references or other research aids.

State codes are generally updated with **pocket parts.** It is critical to check for pocket parts and for the most recent session's laws to ensure that the law being researched is the most current.

CITATION

Citing to state laws varies, depending on the name of the statutory code for that state. Generally the code is identified by its abbreviation, followed by a chapter and section number. If the law is no longer in force, the copyright year of the volume in which the law was found may be included at the end of the citation. For laws currently in force, the year may be omitted. Several examples of citations to state laws follow:

Ark. Code Ann. §18-11-301

Idaho Code §36-1604

Neb. Rev. Stat. §37-1001

Wis. Stat. §104.365

MUNICIPAL LAW

In addition to the laws of the United States and each state, there are also laws enacted by municipalities. Municipalities generally derive their powers from the state, either by constitution or by state statute. In order to exercise that power, each municipality must adopt a founding document. This is generally known as a **charter,** but may also be called articles of incorporation. The charter establishes the municipality, outlines its form of government, and describes the rights and responsibilities of its officials and citizens. The charter is to a municipality as a constitution is to a state or to the United States.

Most municipalities and local governments create laws through **unicameral** legislative processes in city councils, county commissions, and township boards. The laws are often called ordinances and are maintained in the office of the attorney or auditor for that local government. They are published in the local newspaper and are codified for ease of reference. In larger cities, the codes may be published in bound volumes, but published municipal codes are the exception rather than the rule.[5]

Constitutions and statutes are primary tools of the legal trade. They empower the officials of each branch of government and provide the basic framework within which each official must act. Statutes may not conflict with the provisions of the Constitution, or the statute will be declared invalid and unenforceable.

Statutes create new law, amend existing law, or repeal laws no longer necessary. Understanding how laws are made, how they are reported, and how they are interpreted will enhance the contributions a legal nurse consultant makes to a legal environment.

CHAPTER SUMMARY

- Sources of primary authority include constitutions, treaties, statutes, case law, and administrative rules and regulations.
- Understanding legal citation is a critical skill of legal professionals.
- Constitutions are published in pamphlet form and in the *United States Code* (United States Constitution) and state codes (state constitutions).
- International law is increasingly important in a global legal marketplace.
- Statutes are read for their plain meaning; legislative histories may aid in interpretating statutory language.
- Federal, state, and municipal laws are published in codes.

KEY TERMS

bicameral	legal citation	primary authority
binding authority	municipal charter	secondary authority
codified	persuasive authority	session laws
conference committee	plain meaning	unicameral
hierarchy of authority	pocket parts	
Key Number system	pocket veto	

REVIEW QUESTIONS

1. In what sources are laws published?
2. Why is it important to understand the language of legal citation?
3. Describe the legislative process.

INTERNET EXERCISES

1. Access the web page for this textbook at *www.westlegalstudies.com.*
2. Click on the assignments section of the web page and complete the assignment(s) for Chapter Thirteen.

EXERCISES

1. Networking. If you are near the capital city of your state or can take a day to make a field study, attend a legislative session. Contact your representative and ask for a tour. Ask office staff about their responsibilities and how a nurse might be used in state offices. If you plan a day at the state capital, be sure to include the networking exercises outlined in Chapter Fifteen.

2. Professional Portfolio. Include the *Guide to Citation,* a supplement to this textbook, in your professional portfolio. This will emphasize to potential legal employers your commitment to understanding and correctly using the legal language of citation.

ENDNOTES

1. U.S. Const. art VI
2. *Fisher v. District Court of the Sixteenth Judicial District of Montana, in and for the County of Rosebud, Adoption of Firecrow,* 424 U.S. 382, 96 S. Ct. 943 (1976).
3. U.S. Const. art II, §2
4. American Bar Association. *Annotated Model Rules of Professional Conduct,* (1999) 4th Edition Rule 1.1. Copies of ABA *Model Code of Professional Responsibility, 1999 Edition* are available from Service Center, American Bar Association, 750 North Lake Shore Drive, Chicago, IL 60611-4497, 1-800-285-2221.
5. J. Jobstein, R. Mersky, D. Dunn, *Fundamentals of Legal Research* 6th ed. (Westbury, NY: The Foundation Press, Inc., 1994).

ADDITIONAL REFERENCES

Statsky, W. *Essentials of Paralegalism,* 3rd ed. Albany, NY: West Thomson Learning, 1998.

Walston-Dunham, B. *Introduction to Law,* 3rd ed. Albany, NY: West Thomson Learning, 1999.

CHAPTER 14

JUDICIAL SOURCES OF LAW

OBJECTIVES

In this chapter, you will discover

- what case law is

- the components of a court opinion

- how court opinions are reported

- how to read and write legal citations for court opinions

OVERVIEW

The opinions of judges in court cases are primary authority. Recall that primary authority is the letter of the law. It is binding authority in the geographic jurisdiction of the court, in the same way that statutory law is primary binding authority in the legislative jurisdiction in which it is made. A Colorado statute will be primary binding in Colorado, but it will only be persuasive in Wyoming. In the same way, a court opinion emanating from the Colorado Supreme Court will be primary binding in Colorado, but it will only be persuasive in Wyoming. United States laws and opinions of the Supreme Court are always binding on all lower courts and jurisdictions.

Case law refers to opinions of courts that are published. It is also referred to as judge-made law or common law because it is not codified like statutes, but is a declaration of historically recognized rights and practices.

The concept of **precedent** is part of the common law, or court-made law tradition. Precedent refers to the rule of law declared in a previous case. That precedent is followed in all later cases concerning similar facts. The following of precedent is known as *stare decisis.* It provides for uniformity and consistency in the practice of law. These foundational concepts in the court-made law tradition provide the infrastructure for the American ideal of equal protection of the laws.

In the hierarchy of legal authority, a court interpretation of a statute ranks higher than the statute itself. In other words, once the statute is identified as being important to the legal problem, the court decision concerning its interpretation will control its application, unless a later statute overrides the court decision. All court judges are sworn to uphold the United States Constitution and to interpret the cases that come before them in light of the Constitution.

THE COMPONENTS OF A COURT OPINION

Refer to Chapter Seven for the structure of the court system. A United States Supreme Court case will take precedence over a state supreme court case, and a state supreme court case will take precedence over an appeals court case within that state. Regardless of which court an opinion originates in, it will include certain identifiable components.

Title

The names of the parties are used to identify the court case. The Constitution of the United States prohibits the determination of hypothetical disputes; there must be two sides with opposite points of view on a particular problem. The plaintiff is generally identified first; however, in some states, when cases are appealed, the appellant (the party bringing the appeal) appears as the first party in the title.

A court opinion is reproduced as Figure 14-1. The title includes the complete names of the parties, and part of the name is in all uppercase letters. The name in capital letters becomes the name that is used for citation purposes, for example *Silkwood v. Kerr McGee Corporation.*

FIGURE 14-1   For Educational use Only

(Cite as: 464 U.S. 238, 104 S.Ct. 615)

78 L.Ed.2d 443, 20 ERC 1229, 14 Envtl. L. Rep. 20,077
Bill M. SILKWOOD, Administrator of the Estate of Karen G. Silkwood, Deceased,
Appellant,
v.
KERR-McGEE CORPORATION, etc., et al.
No. 81-2159.
Supreme Court of the United States
Argued Oct. 4, 1983.
Decided Jan. 11, 1984.

Administrator of estate of deceased laboratory analyst at federally licensed nuclear facility brought state law tort action against facility to recover for plutonium contamination injuries to analyst's person and property. Judgment was entered on jury verdict for plaintiff for compensatory and punitive damages. The United States District Court for the Western District of Oklahoma, Frank G. Theis, Chief Judge, *485 F.Supp. 566,* denied facility's alternative motion for judgment n.o.v. or for new trial, and facility appealed. The Court of Appeals for the Tenth Circuit, *667 F.2d 908,* reversed as to punitive damages, and appeal was taken. The Supreme Court, Justice White, held that: (1) decision was reviewable on certiorari but not

(Cite as: 464 U.S. 238, 104 S.Ct. 615)

appeal, and (2) award of punitive damages was not preempted by federal law.
Reversed and remanded.
Justice Blackmun filed a dissenting opinion in which Justice Marshall joined.
Justice Powell filed a dissenting opinion in which Chief Justice Burger and Justice Blackmun joined.

(Cite as: 464 U.S. 238, 104 S.Ct. 615)

Silkwood v. Kerr-McGee Corp.

[1] KeyCite this headnote
• *30* APPEAL AND ERROR
• *30I* Nature and Form of Remedy

• *30k2* k. Statutory provisions and remedies.
U.S.Okl., 1984.
Statutes authorizing appeals are to be strictly construed. *28 U.S.C.A. §§ 1252, 1254(2), 1257.*

continued

FIGURE 14-1 For Educational use Only   *continued*

(Cite as: 464 U.S. 238, 104 S.Ct. 615)

Silkwood v. Kerr-McGee Corp.
[1] KeyCite this headnote
- *170B* FEDERAL COURTS
- *170BVII* Supreme Court
- *170BVII(B)* Review of Decisions of Courts of Appeals

- *170Bk451* k. Appeal.
U.S.Okl.,1984.
Statutes authorizing appeals are to be strictly construed. *28 U.S.C.A. §§ 1252, 1254(2), 1257.*

(Cite as: 464 U.S. 238, 104 S.Ct. 615)

Silkwood v. Kerr-McGee Corp.
[2] KeyCite this headnote
- *170B* FEDERAL COURTS
- *170BVII* Supreme Court
- *170BVII(B)* Review of Decisions of Courts of Appeals

170Bk451 k. Appeal.
U.S.Okl.,1984.
Cases where a state statute is expressly struck down on constitutional grounds come within scope of jurisdictional grant of appellate jurisdiction in Supreme Court where Court of Appeals holds a state statute invalid as repugnant to the Constitution, but such is not the case where an exercise of authority under state law is invalidated without reference to the statute. *28 U.S.C.A. § 1254(2).*

(Cite as: 464 U.S. 238, 104 S.Ct. 615)

Silkwood v. Kerr-McGee Corp.
[3] KeyCite this headnote
- *170B* FEDERAL COURTS
- *170BVII* Supreme Court
- *170BVII(B)* Review of Decisions of Courts of Appeals

- *170Bk451* k. Appeal.
U.S.Okl.,1984.
Appeal from decision of Court of Appeals holding that award of punitive damages against federally licensed nuclear facility was preempted by federal law did not fall within Supreme Court's appellate jurisdiction as the Court of Appeals did not purport to rule on constitutionality of state punitive damages statute and the parties did not contest or defend constitutionality in their appellate briefs; however, decision was reviewable by certiorari. *28 U.S.C.A. § 1254(2).*

(Cite as: 464 U.S. 238, 104 S.Ct. 615)

Silkwood v. Kerr-McGee Corp.
[4] KeyCite this headnote
- *170B* FEDERAL COURTS
- *170BVII* Supreme Court
- *170BVII(B)* Review of Decisions of Courts of Appeals

- *170Bk453* k. Proceedings to obtain writ.
U.S.Okl.,1984.
Where case does not fall within Supreme Court's appellate jurisdiction, the jurisdictional statement may be treated as a petition for certiorari. *28 U.S.C.A. § 2103.*

(Cite as: 464 U.S. 238, 104 S.Ct. 615)

Silkwood v. Kerr-McGee Corp.
[5] KeyCite this headnote
- *360* STATES
- *360I* Political Status and Relations
- *360I(B)* Federal Supremacy; Preemption

- *360k18.11* k. Congressional intent.
Formerly 360k4.10
U.S.Okl.,1984.
If Congress evidences an intent to occupy the given field, any state law falling within that field is preempted.

(Cite as: 464 U.S. 238, 104 S.Ct. 615)

Silkwood v. Kerr-McGee Corp.
[6] KeyCite this headnote
- *360* STATES
- *360I* Political Status and Relations
- *360I(B)* Federal Supremacy; Preemption

- *360k18.3* k. Preemption in general.
Formerly 360k4.13
U.S.Okl.,1984.
If Congress has not entirely displaced state regulation over the matter in question, state law is preempted to the extent it actually conflicts with federal law, that is, when it is impossible to comply with both state and federal law or where state law stands as an obstacle to accomplishment of the full purposes and objectives of Congress.

continued

FIGURE 14-1 For Educational use Only   *continued*

(Cite as: 464 U.S. 238, 104 S.Ct. 615)

Silkwood v. Kerr-McGee Corp.
[7] KeyCite this headnote
- *360* STATES
- *360I* Political Status and Relations
- *360I(B)* Federal Supremacy; Preemption

- *360k18.31* k. Environment; nuclear projects.
Formerly 360k4.10
U.S.Okl.,1984.
Federal preemption of safety aspects of nuclear energy, as pronounced in Pacific Gas & Electric, does not extend to state-authorized award of punitive damages for conduct related to radiation hazards. Atomic Energy Act of 1954, §§ 1-236, as amended, *42 U.S.C.A. §§ 2011-2284.*

(Cite as: 464 U.S. 238, 104 S.Ct. 615)

Silkwood v. Kerr-McGee Corp.
[8] KeyCite this headnote
- *360* STATES
- *360I* Political Status and Relations
- *360I(B)* Federal Supremacy; Preemption

- *360k18.31* k. Environment; nuclear projects.
Formerly 360k4.10
U.S.Okl.,1984.
Award of punitive damages against federally licensed nuclear facility and on behalf of laboratory technician who was contaminated with plutonium was not preempted as conflicting with the federal remedial scheme under which Nuclear Regulatory Commission is authorized to impose civil penalties on licensees for violation of federal standards and did not hinder statutory purpose of encouraging widespread participation in development and utilization of atomic energy for peaceful purposes. *28 U.S.C.A. § 1254(2);* 23 O.S.1981, § 9; Atomic Energy Act of *1954, §§ 1-236, 3(d),* 11 (e, z, aa), 274(a)(1), (c)(4), as amended, *42 U.S.C.A. §§ 2011-2284, 2013(d), 2014*(e, z, aa), 2021(a)(1), (c)(4).

(Cite as: 464 U.S. 238, 104 S.Ct. 615)

Silkwood v. Kerr-McGee Corp.
[9] KeyCite this headnote
- *360* STATES
- *360I* Political Status and Relations
- *360I(B)* Federal Supremacy; Preemption

- *360k18.31* k. Environment; nuclear projects.
Formerly 360k4.10
U.S.Okl.,1984.
Where federally licensed nuclear facility was found to have violated Oklahoma tort law as regards plutonium contamination sustained by laboratory analyst, award of punitive damages was not preempted by federal law. 23 O.S. 1981, § 9; Atomic Energy Act of *1954, §§ 1-236,* as amended, *42 U.S.C.A. §§ 2011-2284.*

**616

Syllabus [FN*]

FN* The syllabus constitutes no part of the opinion of the Court but has been prepared by the Reporter of Decisions for the convenience of the reader. See *United States v. Detroit Lumber Co., 200 U.S. 321, 337, 26 S.Ct. 282, 287, 50 L.Ed. 499.*

*238

Appellant's decedent, a laboratory analyst at a federally licensed nuclear plant in Oklahoma operated by appellee Kerr-McGee Nuclear Corp. (hereafter appellee), was contaminated by plutonium. Subsequently, after the decedent was killed in an unrelated automobile accident, appellant, as administrator of the decedent's estate, brought a diversity action in Federal District Court based on common-law tort principles under Oklahoma law to recover for the contamination injuries to the decedent's person and property. The jury returned a verdict in appellant's favor, awarding, in addition to actual damages, punitive damages as authorized by Oklahoma law. The Court of Appeals, inter alia, reversed as to the punitive damages award on the ground that such damages were preempted by federal law.
Held:
1. The appeal is not within this Court's appellate jurisdiction under *28 U.S.C. § 1254(2).* The Court of Appeals held that because of the preemptive

effect of federal law, punitive damages could not be awarded. It did not purport to rule on the constitutionality of the Oklahoma punitive damages statute, which was left untouched. The decision, however, is reviewable by writ of certiorari. Pp. 620 - 621.
2. The award of punitive damages is not pre-empted by federal law. Pp. 621 - 627.
(a) The federal pre-emption of state regulation of the safety aspects of nuclear energy, see Pacific Gas & Electric Co. v. State Energy Resources Conservation and Development Comm'n, *461 U.S. 190, 103 S.Ct. 1713, 75 L.Ed.2d 752 (1983),* does not extend to the state-authorized award of punitive damages for conduct related to radiation hazards. There is ample evidence that Congress had no intention, when it enacted and later amended the Atomic Energy Act of 1954, of forbidding the States to provide remedies for those suffering injuries from radiation in a nuclear plant. Nor is appellee able to point to anything in the legislative history of the Price-Anderson Act—which established an indemnification scheme for operators of nuclear facilities—or in the implementing regulations that indicates that punitive damages were not to be allowed. Rather, it is clear *239

**617

that in enacting and amending the Price-Anderson Act, Congress assumed that state-law remedies were available to those injured by nuclear incidents, even though Congress was aware of the Nuclear Regulatory Commission's exclusive authority to regulate safety

continued

FIGURE 14-1 For Educational use Only   *continued*

(Cite as: 464 U.S. 238, *239, 104 S.Ct. 615, **617)

matters. Insofar as damages for radiation injuries are concerned, pre-emption should not be judged on the basis that the Federal Government has so completely occupied the field of safety that state remedies are foreclosed but on whether there is an irreconcilable conflict between the federal and state standards or whether the imposition of a state standard in a damages action would frustrate the objectives of the federal law. Pp. 622 - 626.

(b) The award of punitive damages in this case does not conflict with the federal remedial scheme under which the NRC is authorized to impose civil penalties on licensees for violation of federal standards. Paying both federal fines and state-imposed punitive damages for the same incident is not physically impossible, nor does exposure to punitive damages frustrate any purpose of the federal remedial scheme. The award of punitive damages does not hinder the purpose of *42 U.S.C. § 2013(d)* "to encourage widespread participation in the development and utilization of atomic energy for peaceful purposes," since Congress disclaimed any interest in accomplishing this purpose by means that fail to provide adequate remedies to those injured by exposure to hazardous nuclear materials. Finally, the punitive damages award does not conflict with Congress' intent to preclude dual regulation of radiation hazards, since, as indicated above, Congress did not believe that it was inconsistent to vest the NRC with exclusive regulatory authority over the safety aspects of nuclear development while at the same time allowing

(Cite as: 464 U.S. 238, *239, 104 S.Ct. 615, **617)

plaintiffs like appellant to recover for injuries caused by nuclear hazards. P. 626.
667 F.2d 908 (10th Cir.1981), reversed and remanded.
Michael H. Gottesman argued the cause for appellant. With him on the briefs were Arthur R. Angel, Robert M. Weinberg, Jeremiah A. Collins, James A. Ikard, Gerald L. Spence, and Daniel P. Sheehan.
C. Lee Cook, Jr., argued the cause for appellees. With him on the brief were William G. Paul, L.E. Stringer, **240

(Cite as: 464 U.S. 238, *240, 104 S.Ct. 615, **617)

Elliott C. Fenton, Larry D. Ottaway, William T. McGrath, Pamela J. Kempin, and Richard R. Wilfong. John H. Garvey argued the cause for the United States as amicus curiae urging affirmance. With him on the brief were Solicitor General Lee and Deputy Solicitor General Bator.*
*Briefs of amici curiae urging reversal were filed for the National Women's Health Network by Anthony Z. Roisman; for the State of Arizona et al. by Robert Abrams, Attorney General of New York, Peter H. Schiff, and Ezra I. Bialik, Assistant Attorney General, Robert K. Corbin, Attorney General of Arizona, and Anthony B. Ching, Solicitor General, Joseph L. Lieberman, Attorney General of Connecticut, and Peter J. Jenkelunas, Assistant Attorney General, Tany S. Hong, Attorney General of Hawaii, and Michael A. Lilly, First Deputy Attorney General, William J. Guste, Jr., Attorney General of Louisiana, and Kendall L. Vick, Assistant Attorney General, Francis X. Bellotti, Attorney General of

(Cite as: 464 U.S. 238, *240, 104 S.Ct. 615, **617)

Massachusetts, and Stephen M. Leonard, Assistant Attorney General, Brian McKay, Attorney General of Nevada, Irwin I. Kimmelman, Attorney General of New Jersey, and James J. Ciancia, Assistant Attorney General, Anthony J. Celebrezze, Jr., Attorney General of Ohio, and E. Dennis Muchnicki, Assistant

Attorney General, Leroy S. Zimmerman, Attorney General of Pennsylvania, T. Travis Medlock, Attorney General of South Carolina, and Richard P. Wilson, Assistant Attorney General, Jim Mattox, Attorney General of Texas, and David R. Richards, Executive Assistant Attorney General, and Jim Mathews, Assistant Attorney General, John J. Easton, Jr., Attorney General of Vermont, and W. Gilbert Livingston, Assistant Attorney General, Bronson C. La Follette, Attorney General of Wisconsin, and A. G. McClintock, Attorney General of Wyoming; and for the State of Minnesota by Hubert H. Humphrey III, Attorney General, and Jocelyn Furtwangler Olson, Special Assistant Attorney General. A brief of amicus curiae urging affirmance was filed by Harry H. Voigt, Michael F. McBride, and Linda L. Hodge for the Atomic Industrial Forum, Inc.

A brief of amicus curiae was filed by Joseph H. Rodriguez and Michael L. Perlin for the New Jersey Department of the Public Advocate.

Justice WHITE delivered the opinion of the Court.

Last term, this Court examined the relationship between federal and state

(Cite as: 464 U.S. 238, *240, 104 S.Ct. 615, **617)

authority in the nuclear energy field and concluded that states are precluded from regulating the *241

(Cite as: 464 U.S. 238, *241, 104 S.Ct. 615, **617)

safety aspects of nuclear energy. Pacific Gas & Electric Co. v. State Energy Resources Conservation & Development Comm'n, —— U.S. ——, ——, *103 S.Ct. 1713, 1724, 75 L.Ed.2d 752 (1983)*. This case requires us to determine whether a state-authorized award of punitive damages arising out of the escape of plutonium from a federally-licensed nuclear facility is preempted either because it falls within that forbidden field or because it conflicts with some other aspect of the Atomic Energy Act.

I

Karen Silkwood was a laboratory analyst for Kerr-McGee [FN1] at its Cimmaron plant near Crescent, Oklahoma. The plant fabricated plutonium fuel pins for use as reactor fuel in nuclear power plants. Accordingly, the plant was subject to licensing and regulation by the Nuclear Regulatory Commission (NRC) pursuant to the Atomic Energy Act, *42 U.S.C. §§ 2011-2284 (1976 ed. and Supp. V)*. [FN2]

> FN1. Silkwood was employed by Kerr-McGee Nuclear Corp., a subsidiary of Kerr-McGee Corp. The jury found that the former was the "mere instrumentality" of the latter. We therefore refer to both as Kerr-McGee.

> FN2. Under *42 U.S.C. § 2073*, the Commission is authorized to issue

(Cite as: 464 U.S. 238, *241, 104 S.Ct. 615, **617)

licenses to those who handle special nuclear materials like the plutonium processed in Kerr-McGee's plant. Section 2201(b) empowers the Commission to set standards and issue instructions to govern the possession and use of such materials. On April 2, 1970, Kerr-McGee obtained a license to receive and possess special nuclear materials at its Cimmaron plant. It closed the plant in 1975.

**618

continued

FIGURE 14-1   For Educational use Only   *continued*

(Cite as: 464 U.S. 238, *241, 104 S.Ct. 615, **618)

During a three-day period of November 1974, Silkwood was contaminated by plutonium from the Cimmaron plant. On November 5, Silkwood was grinding and polishing plutonium samples, utilizing glove boxes designed for that purpose. [FN3] In accordance with established procedures, she checked her hands for contamination when she withdrew them from the *242

(Cite as: 464 U.S. 238, *242, 104 S.Ct. 615, **618)

glove box. When some contamination was detected, a more extensive check was performed. A monitoring device revealed contamination on Silkwood's left hand, right wrist, upper arm, neck, hair, and nostrils. She was immediately decontaminated, and at the end of her shift, the monitors detected no contamination. However, she was given urine and fecal kits and was instructed to collect samples in order to check for plutonium discharge.

> FN3. A glove box is a supposedly impervious box surrounding the plutonium processing equipment which has glove holes permitting the operator to work

(Cite as: 464 U.S. 238, *242, 104 S.Ct. 615, **618)

on the equipment or the plutonium from outside the box.

The next day, Silkwood arrived at the plant and began doing paperwork in the laboratory. Upon leaving the laboratory, Silkwood monitored herself and again discovered surface contamination. Once again, she was decontaminated.
On the third day, November 7, Silkwood was monitored upon her arrival at the plant. High levels of contamination were detected. Four urine samples and one fecal sample submitted that morning were also highly contaminated. [FN4] Suspecting that the contamination had spread to areas outside the plant, the company directed a decontamination squad to accompany Silkwood to her apartment. Silkwood's roommate, who was also an employee at the plant, was awakened and monitored. She was also contaminated, although to a lesser degree than Silkwood. The squad then monitored the apartment, finding contamination in several rooms, with especially high levels in the bathroom, the kitchen, and Silkwood's bedroom.

> FN4. At trial, the parties stipulated that the urine samples had been spiked with insoluble plutonium, i.e., plutonium which cannot be excreted from the body. However, there was no evidence as to who placed the plutonium in the vials.

(Cite as: 464 U.S. 238, *242, 104 S.Ct. 615, **618)

The contamination level in Silkwood's apartment was such that many of her personal belongings had to be destroyed. Silkwood herself was sent to the Los Alamos Scientific Laboratory to determine the extent of contamination in her vital body organs. She returned to work on November 13. That night, she was killed in an unrelated automobile accident. *667 F.2d 908, 912 (CA10 1981).*
*243

(Cite as: 464 U.S. 238, *243, 104 S.Ct. 615, **618)

Bill Silkwood, Karen's father, brought the present diversity action in his capacity as administrator of her estate. The action was based on common law tort principles under Oklahoma law and was designed to recover for the contamination injuries to Karen's person and property. Kerr-McGee stipulated that the plutonium which caused the contamination came from its plant, and the jury expressly rejected Kerr-McGee's allegation that Silkwood had intentionally removed the plutonium from the plant in an effort to embarrass the company. However, there were no other specific findings of fact with respect to the cause of the contamination. During the course of the trial, evidence was presented which tended to show that Kerr-McGee did not always comply with NRC regulations. One Kerr-McGee witness conceded that the amount of plutonium which was unaccounted for during the period in question exceeded permissible limits. [FN5] **619

(Cite as: 464 U.S. 238, *243, 104 S.Ct. 615, **619)

485 F.Supp. 566, 586 (W.D.Okl. 1979). An NRC official testified that he did not feel that Kerr-McGee was conforming its conduct to the "as low as reasonably achievable" standard. [FN6] Ibid. There was also some evidence that the

(Cite as: 464 U.S. 238, *243, 104 S.Ct. 615, **619)

level of plutonium in Silkwood's apartment may have exceeded that permitted in an unrestricted area such as a residence. Ibid.

FN5. After allowing for hold-up (plutonium which remains in the equipment after a very thorough cleanout), the inventory difference (opening less closing) for the 1972-1976 period was 4.4 kilograms. This represented .522% of the 842 kilograms received by Kerr-McGee during that period. The NRC permits an inventory difference of .500%.

FN6. Federal regulations require that "persons engaged in activities under licenses issued by the Nuclear Regulatory Commission . . . make every reasonable effort to maintain radiation exposures, and releases of radioactive materials in effluents to unrestricted areas, as low as is reasonably achievable." *10 CFR 20.1(c) (1983).* In 1974, the regulation required reasonable efforts to maintain exposures and releases "as far below the limits specified [in other portions of the regulations] as practicable." The difference in the terminology is not significant. 40 Fed.Reg. 33029 (1975).

*244

(Cite as: 464 U.S. 238, *244, 104 S.Ct. 615, **619)

However, there was also evidence that Kerr-McGee complied with most federal regulations. The NRC official testified that there were no serious

continued

FIGURE 14-1 For Educational use Only *continued*

(Cite as: 464 U.S. 238, *244, 104 S.Ct. 615, **619)

personnel exposures at the plant and that Kerr-McGee did not exceed the regulatory requirements with respect to exposure levels that would result in significant health hazards. In addition, Kerr-McGee introduced the Commission's report on the investigation of the Silkwood incident in which the Commission determined that Kerr-McGee's only violation of regulations throughout the incident was its failure to maintain a record of the dates of two urine samples submitted by Silkwood.

The trial court determined that Kerr-McGee had not shown that the contamination occurred during the course of Silkwood's employment. Accordingly, the court precluded the jury from deciding whether the personal injury claim was covered by Oklahoma's Workers' Compensation Act, which provides the sole remedy for accidental personal injuries arising in the course of employment. Okla.Stat. tit. 85 §§ 11, 12 (1981). Instead, the court submitted the claims to the jury on alternative theories of strict liability and negligence. [FN7]

> FN7. In an effort to avoid a new trial in the event that the Court of Appeals disagreed with its ruling on the applicability of strict liability principles, the court instructed the jury to answer a special interrogatory as to whether Kerr-McGee negligently allowed the plutonium to escape from its plant. The jury answered in the affirmative.

(Cite as: 464 U.S. 238, *244, 104 S.Ct. 615, **619)

The court also instructed the jury with respect to punitive damages, explaining the standard by which Kerr-McGee's conduct was to be evaluated in determining whether such damages should be awarded: "[T]he jury may give damages for the sake of example and by way of punishment, if the jury finds the defendant or defendants have been guilty of oppression, fraud, or malice, actual or presumed. . . . "Exemplary damages are not limited to cases where there is direct evidence of fraud, malice or gross negligence. They may be allowed when there is evidence *245

(Cite as: 464 U.S. 238, *245, 104 S.Ct. 615, **619)

of such recklessness and wanton disregard of another's rights that malice and evil intent will be inferred. If a defendant is grossly and wantonly reckless in exposing others to dangers, the law holds him to have intended the natural consequences of his acts, and treats him as guilty of a willful wrong." *485 F.Supp. 566, 603 (W.D.Okl.1979)* (Appendix).

The jury returned a verdict in favor of Silkwood, finding actual damages of $505,000 ($500,000 for personal injuries and $5,000 for property damage) and punitive damages of $10,000,000. The trial court entered judgment against Kerr-McGee in that amount. Kerr-McGee then moved for judgment n.o.v. or a new trial. In denying that motion, *485 F.Supp. 566 (W.D.Okl.1979),* the court rejected Kerr-McGee's contention that compliance with federal regulations precluded an award of

(Cite as: 464 U.S. 238, *245, 104 S.Ct. 615, **619)

punitive damages. The court noted that Kerr-McGee "had a duty under part 20 of Title 10 of the Code of Federal Regulations to maintain the release of radiation 'as low as reasonably achievable.' Compliance with this standard cannot be demonstrated **620 merely through control of escaped plutonium within any absolute amount." *Id., at 585.* Therefore, the court concluded, it is not "inconsistent [with any congressional design] to impose punitive damages for the escape of plutonium caused by grossly negligent, reckless and willful conduct." Ibid.

Kerr-McGee renewed its contentions with greater success before the Court of Appeals for the Tenth Circuit. That court, by decision of a split panel, affirmed in part and reversed in part. *667 F.2d 908 (CA10 1981).* The court first held that recovery for Silkwood's personal injuries was controlled exclusively by Oklahoma's workers' compensation law. It thus reversed the $500,000 judgment for those injuries. The court then affirmed the property damage portion of the award, holding that the workers' compensation law applied only to personal injuries and that Oklahoma law permitted an award under a theory of strict liability in the circumstances ***246***

of this case. Finally, the court held that because of the federal statutes regulating the Kerr-McGee plant, "punitive damages may not be awarded in this case," *id., at 923.*

In reaching its conclusion with respect to the punitive damages award, the Court of Appeals adopted a broad preemption analysis. It concluded that "any

state action that competes substantially with the AEC (NRC) in its regulation of radiation hazards associated with plants handling nuclear material" was impermissible. Ibid. Because "[a] judicial award of exemplary damages under state law as punishment for bad practices or to deter future practices involving exposure to radiation is not less intrusive than direct legislative acts of the state," the court determined that such awards were preempted by federal law. Ibid.

Silkwood appealed, seeking review of the Court of Appeals' ruling with respect to the punitive damages award. We noted probable jurisdiction and postponed consideration of the jurisdictional issue until argument on the merits. *459 U.S. 1101, 103 S.Ct. 721, 74 L.Ed.2d 948 (1983).*

II

[1][2][3][4] We first address the jurisdictional issue. This Court is empowered to review the decision of a federal court of appeals "by appeal [if] a State statute [is] held by [the] court of appeals to be invalid as repugnant to the Constitution . . . ." *28 U.S.C. § 1254(2).* Silkwood argues that because the Court of Appeals invalidated the punitive damages award on preemption grounds and because the basis for that award was a state statute, Okla.Stat. tit. 23 § 9 (1981), [FN8] the Court of Appeals necessarily held that the state statute was unconstitutional, at least as applied in this case. Accordingly, Silkwood contends, this case falls within the confines of

§ 1254(2). We disagree.

> FN8. The Oklahoma statute authorizes an award of punitive damages "[i]n any action for the breach of an obligation not arising from contract, where the defendant has been guilty of oppression, fraud, or malice, actual or presumed."

247

continued

FIGURE 14-1 For Educational use Only   *continued*

(Cite as: 464 U.S. 238, *247, 104 S.Ct. 615, **620)

In keeping with the policy that statutes authorizing appeals are to be strictly construed, *Perry Education Ass'n v. Perry Local Educators' Ass'n, —- U.S. ——, ——, 103 S.Ct. 948, 953, 74 L.Ed.2d 794 (1983); Fornaris v. Ridge Tool Co., 400 U.S. 41, 42 n. 1, 91 S.Ct. 156, 157 n. 1, 27 L.Ed.2d 174 (1970),* we have consistently distinguished between those cases in which a state statute is expressly struck down on constitutional grounds and those in which an exercise of authority under state law is invalidated without reference to the state statute. The former come within the scope of § 1254(2)'s jurisdictional grant. *Malone v. White Motor Corp., 435 U.S. 497, 499, 98 S.Ct. 1185, 1187, 55 L.Ed.2d 443 (1978); Dutton v. Evans, 400 U.S. 74, 76 n. 6, 91 S.Ct. 210, 213 n. 6, 27 L.Ed.2d 213 (1970).* The latter do not. *Perry Education Ass'n, supra, 460 U.S., at ——, 103 S.Ct., at 953; Hanson v. Denckla, 357 U.S. 235, 244, 78 S.Ct. 1228, 1234, 2 L.Ed.2d 1283 (1958);* ***621

(Cite as: 464 U.S. 238, *247, 104 S.Ct. 615, **621)

Wilson v. Cook, 327 U.S. 474, 482, 66 S.Ct. 663, 667,

(Cite as: 464 U.S. 238, *247, 104 S.Ct. 615, **621)

90 L.Ed. 793 (1946). [FN9] See also *County of Arlington v. United States, 669 F.2d 925 (CA4 1982)* cert. denied, *459 U.S. 801, 103 S.Ct. 23, 74 L.Ed.2d 39 (1982); Minnesota v. Hoffman, 543 F.2d 1198 (CA8 1976),* cert. denied sub nom *Minnesota v. Alexander, 430 U.S. 977, 97 S.Ct. 1672, 52 L.Ed.2d 373 (1977).* The present case falls into the second category.

> FN9. Wilson and Denckla involve appeals from state court judgments under 20 U.S.C. § 1257 and its predecessor. However, such cases are relevant to the present issue because of "the history of . . . close relationship between" *§ 1254(2)* and *§ 1257. Calero-Toledo v. Pearson Yacht Leasing Co., 416 U.S. 663, 675-677 n. 11, 94 S.Ct. 2080, 2087-2088 n. 11, 40 L.Ed.2d 452 (1974).*

The Court of Appeals held that because of the preemptive effect of federal law, "punitive damages may not be awarded in this case." *667 F.2d, at 923.* It did not purport to rule on the constitutionality of the Oklahoma punitive damages statute. The court did not mention the statute, and the parties did not contest or defend the constitutionality of the statute in their appellate briefs. While the award itself was struck down, the statute authorizing such awards was left untouched. Cf. *Perry Education Ass'n, supra, 460 U.S., at ——, 103 S.Ct., at 953.* Therefore, the present appeal is not within our

(Cite as: 464 U.S. 238, *247, 104 S.Ct. 615, **621)

§ 1254(2) appellate jurisdiction. [FN10]

> FN10. Silkwood's reliance on *California v. Grace Brethren Church, 457 U.S. 393, 102 S.Ct. 2498, 73 L.Ed.2d 93 (1982)* is misplaced. Grace Brethren involved a direct appeal under *28 U.S.C. § 1252,* a statute which we have construed more broadly because of Congress' clear intent to create an "exception to the policy of minimizing the mandatory docket of this Court." Id., at 405, *102 S.Ct., at 2506.* See also *McLucas v. DeChamplain, 421 U.S. 21, 31, 95 S.Ct. 1365, 1371, 43 L.Ed.2d 699 (1975).*

*248

(Cite as: 464 U.S. 238, *248, 104 S.Ct. 615, **621)

Nevertheless, the decision below is reviewable by writ of certiorari. Ibid. The issue addressed by the court below is important; it affects both the states' traditional authority to provide tort remedies to its citizens and the federal government's express desire to maintain exclusive regulatory authority over the safety aspects of nuclear power. Accordingly, treating the jurisdictional statement as a petition for certiorari, as we are authorized to do, *28 U.S.C. § 2103,* we grant the petition and reach the merits of the Court of Appeals' ruling.

III

[5][6] As we recently observed in *Pacific Gas & Electric Co. v. State*

(Cite as: 464 U.S. 238, *248, 104 S.Ct. 615, **621)

Energy Resources Conservation & Development Comm'n, 461 U.S. 190, 103 S.Ct. 1713, 75 L.Ed.2d 752 (1983), state law can be preempted in either of two general ways. If Congress evidences an intent to occupy a given field, any state law falling within that field is preempted. *Id., at ——, 103 S.Ct., at 1722; Fidelity Federal Savings & Loan Ass'n v. de la Cuesta, 458 U.S. 141, 153, 102 S.Ct. 3014, 3022, 73 L.Ed.2d 664 (1982); Rice v. Santa Fe Elevator Corp., 331 U.S. 218, 230, 67 S.Ct. 1146, 1152, 91 L.Ed. 1447 (1947).* If Congress has not entirely displaced state regulation over the matter in question, state law is still preempted to the extent it actually conflicts with federal law, that is, when it is impossible to comply with both state and federal law, *Florida Lime & Avocado Growers, Inc. v. Paul, 373 U.S. 132, 142-143, 83 S.Ct. 1210, 1217-1218, 10 L.Ed.2d 248 (1963),* or where the state law stands as an obstacle to the accomplishment of the full purposes and objectives of Congress, *Hines v. Davidowitz, 312 U.S. 52, 67, 61 S.Ct. 399, 404, 85 L.Ed. 581 (1941). Pacific Gas & Electric, supra, at ——, 103 S.Ct., at 1722.* Kerr-McGee contends that the award in this case is invalid under either analysis. We consider each of these contentions in turn.

249

(Cite as: 464 U.S. 238, *249, 104 S.Ct. 615, **621)

A

In Pacific Gas & Electric, an examination of the statutory scheme and legislative history of the Atomic Energy Act convinced us that "Congress . . . intended that ***622***

(Cite as: 464 U.S. 238, *249, 104 S.Ct. 615, **622)

the federal government regulate the radiological safety

(Cite as: 464 U.S. 238, *249, 104 S.Ct. 615, **622)

aspects involved . . . in the construction and operation of a nuclear plant." *461 U.S., at ——, 103 S.Ct., at 1723.* Thus, we concluded that "the federal government has occupied the entire field of nuclear safety concerns, except the limited powers expressly ceded to the states." *Id., at ——, 103 S.Ct., at 1726.*
[7] Kerr-McGee argues that our ruling in Pacific Gas & Electric is dispositive of the issue in this case. Noting that "regulation can be as effectively asserted through an award of damages as through some form of preventive relief," *San Diego Building Trades Council v. Garmon, 359 U.S. 236, 247, 79 S.Ct. 773, 780, 3 L.Ed.2d 775 (1959),* Kerr-McGee submits that because the state-authorized award of punitive damages in this case punishes and deters conduct related to radiation hazards, it falls within the prohibited field. However, a review of the same legislative history which prompted our holding in

continued

FIGURE 14-1 For Educational use Only   *continued*

(Cite as: 464 U.S. 238, *249, 104 S.Ct. 615, **622), continued

Pacific Gas & Electric, coupled with an examination of Congress' actions with respect to other portions of the Atomic Energy Act, convinces us that the preempted field does not extend as far as Kerr-McGee would have it.

As we recounted in Pacific Gas & Electric, "[u]ntil 1954 . . . the use, control and ownership of nuclear technology remained a federal monopoly." *461 U.S., at ——, 103 S.Ct., at 1723*. In that year, Congress enacted legislation which provided for private involvement in the development of atomic energy. The Atomic Energy Act of 1954, Act of Aug. 30, 1954, ch. 1073, 68

(Cite as: 464 U.S. 238, *249, 104 S.Ct. 615, **622)

Stat. 919, as amended, *42 U.S.C. §§ 2011-2284* (1976 ed. and Supp. V). However, the federal government retained extensive control over the manner in which this development occurred. In particular, the Atomic Energy Commission (the predecessor of the NRC) was given "exclusive jurisdiction to license the transfer, *250

(Cite as: 464 U.S. 238, *250, 104 S.Ct. 615, **622)

delivery, receipt, acquisition, possession and use of nuclear materials." Pacific Gas & Electric, supra, at ——, *103 S.Ct., at 1724*. See *42 U.S.C. §§ 2014, (e), (z)*, (aa), 2061-2064, 2071-2078, 2091-2099, 2111-2114 (1976 and Supp. V).

In 1959 Congress amended the Atomic Energy Act in order to "clarify the respective responsibilities of the States and the Commission with respect to the regulation of byproduct, source, and special nuclear materials." *42 U.S.C. § 2021(a)(1)*. See S.Rep. No. 870, 86th Cong. 1st Sess. 8-12 (1959), U.S.Code Cong. & Admin.News 1959, p. 2872. The Commission was authorized to turn some of its regulatory authority over to any state which would adopt a suitable regulatory program. However, the Commission was to retain exclusive regulatory authority over "the disposal of such . . . byproduct, source, or special nuclear material as the Commission determines . . . should, because of the hazards or potential hazards thereof, not be disposed of without a license from the Commission." *42 U.S.C. § 2021(c)(4)*. The states were therefore still precluded from regulating the safety aspects of these hazardous materials. [FN11]

(Cite as: 464 U.S. 238, *250, 104 S.Ct. 615, **622)

FN11. At the time this suit was filed, Oklahoma had not entered into an agreement with the Commission under *§ 2021*. Even if it had, Kerr-McGee would have still been subject to exclusive NRC safety regulation because it was licensed to possess special nuclear material in a quantity sufficient to form a critical mass. See *42 U.S.C. § 2021(b)(4) (1976 ed., Supp. V)*.

Congress' decision to prohibit the states from regulating the safety aspects of nuclear development was premised on its belief that the Commission was more qualified to determine what type of safety standards should be enacted in this complex area. As Congress was informed by the AEC, the 1959 legislation provided for continued federal control over the more hazardous materials because "the technical safety considerations are of such complexity that it is not likely that any State would be prepared to deal with them during the foreseeable future." H.R.Rep. No. 1125, 86th Cong., 1st Sess. 3 (1959). If there were nothing more, this concern over the states' inability to formulate effective standards and *251

(Cite as: 464 U.S. 238, *251, 104 S.Ct. 615, **622)

the foreclosure of the states **623**

(Cite as: 464 U.S. 238, *251, 104 S.Ct. 615, **623)

from conditioning the operation of nuclear plants on compliance with state-imposed safety standards arguably would disallow resort to state-law remedies by those suffering injuries from radiation in a nuclear plant. There is, however, ample

(Cite as: 464 U.S. 238, *251, 104 S.Ct. 615, **623)

evidence that Congress had no intention of forbidding the states from providing such remedies. Indeed, there is no indication that Congress even seriously considered precluding the use of such remedies either when it enacted the Atomic Energy Act in 1954 and or when it amended it in 1959. This silence takes on added significance in light of Congress' failure to provide any federal remedy for persons injured by such conduct. It is difficult to believe that Congress would, without comment, remove all means of judicial recourse for those injured by illegal conduct. See *United Construction Workers v. Laburnum Corp., 347 U.S. 656, 663-664, 74 S.Ct. 833, 836-838, 98 L.Ed. 1025 (1954).* More importantly, the only congressional discussion concerning the relationship between the Atomic Energy Act and state tort remedies indicates that Congress assumed that such remedies would be available. After the 1954 law was enacted, private companies contemplating entry into the nuclear industry expressed concern over potentially bankrupting state-law suits arising out of a nuclear incident. As a result, in 1957 Congress passed the Price-Anderson Act, an amendment to the Atomic Energy Act. Pub.L. 85-256, 71 Stat. 576 (1957). That Act established an indemnification scheme under which operators of licensed nuclear facilities could be required to obtain up to $60 million in private financial protection against such suits. The government would then provide indemnification for the next $500 million of liability, and

(Cite as: 464 U.S. 238, *251, 104 S.Ct. 615, **623)

the resulting $560 million would be the limit of liability for any one nuclear incident. Although the Price-Anderson Act does not apply to the present situation, [FN12] the discussion preceding its enactment **252**

(Cite as: 464 U.S. 238, *252, 104 S.Ct. 615, **623)

and subsequent amendment [FN13] indicates that Congress assumed that persons injured by nuclear accidents were free to utilize existing state tort law remedies. The Joint Committee Report on the original version of the Price-Anderson Act explained the relationship between the Act and existing state tort law as follows:

> FN12. Under the Act, the NRC is given discretion whether to require plants licensed under § 2073 to maintain financial protection. *42 U.S.C. § 2210(a).* Government indemnification is available only to those required to maintain financial protection, id., *§ 2210(c),* and the liability limitation applies only to those who are indemnified. Id., *§ 2210(e).* The NRC did not require plutonium processing plants to maintain financial protection until 1977, 42 Fed.Reg. 46 (1977).

continued

FIGURE 14-1 For Educational use Only   *continued*

> (Cite as: 464 U.S. 238, *252, 104 S.Ct. 615, **623)

FN13. The 1957 version of the Price-Anderson Act was designed to expire in 1967. It was extended in 1965, Pub.L. No. 89-210, 79 Stat. 855, and again in 1975, Pub.L. No. 94-197, 89 Stat. 1111. In addition, several substantive changes were made through the years, most notably in 1966.

> (Cite as: 464 U.S. 238, *252, 104 S.Ct. 615, **623)

Pub.L. No. 89-645, 80 Stat. 891.

"Since the rights of third parties who are injured are established by State law, there is no interference with the State law until there is a likelihood that the damages exceed the amount of financial responsibility required together with the amount of the indemnity. At that point the Federal interference is limited to the prohibition of making payments through the state courts and to prorating the proceeds available." S.Rep. No. 296, 85th Cong., 1st Sess. 9 (1957), U.S.Code Cong. & Admin.News 1957, pp. 1803, 1810. See also H.Rep. 435, 85th Cong., 1st Sess. 9 (1957); S.Rep. No. 1605, 89th Cong., 2d Sess. 5 (1966), U.S.Code Cong. & Admin.News 1966, p. 3201.
Congress clearly began working on the Price-Anderson legislation with the assumption that in the absence of some subsequent legislative action, state tort law would apply. [FN14] This was true even though **624

> (Cite as: 464 U.S. 238, *252, 104 S.Ct. 615, **624)

Congress was fully aware of the *253

> (Cite as: 464 U.S. 238, *253, 104 S.Ct. 615, **624)

Commission's exclusive regulatory authority over safety matters. As the Joint Committee explained in 1965:

> FN14. In sustaining the Price-Anderson Act against a constitutional challenge, we echoed that assumption, noting that before the Act was enacted, the only right possessed by those injured in a nuclear incident "was to utilize their existing common-law and state-law remedies to

> (Cite as: 464 U.S. 238, *253, 104 S.Ct. 615, **624)

vindicate any particular harm visited on them from whatever source." *Duke Power Co. v. Carolina Environmental Study Group, 438 U.S. 59, 88, 89 n. 32, 98 S.Ct. 2620, 2638, 2639 n. 32, 57 L.Ed.2d 595 (1978).*

"The Price-Anderson Act also contained provisions to improve the AEC's procedures for regulating reactor licensees. . . . This manifested the continuing concern of the Joint Committee and Congress with the necessity for assuring the effectiveness of the national regulatory program for protecting the health and safety of employees and the public against atomic energy hazards. The inclusion of these provisions . . . also reflected the intimate relationship which existed between Congress' concern for prevention of reactor accidents and the indemnity provisions of the Price-Anderson legislation." S.Rep. No. 649, 89th Cong., 1st Sess. 4-5 (1965).
When it enacted the Price-Anderson Act, Congress was well aware of the need for effective national safety regulation. In fact, it intended to encourage such regulation. But, at the same time, "the right of the State courts to establish the liability of the persons involved in the normal way [was] maintained."

S.Rep. No. *296, supra, at 22,* U.S.Code & Admin.News 1957, p. 1823. The belief that the NRC's exclusive authority to set safety standards did not foreclose the use of state tort remedies was reaffirmed when the Price-Anderson

(Cite as: 464 U.S. 238, *253, 104 S.Ct. 615, **624)

Act was amended in 1966. The 1966 amendment was designed to respond to concerns about the adequacy of state law remedies. See, e.g., S.Rep. No. 650, supra, at 13. It provided that in the event of an "extraordinary nuclear occurrence", [FN15] licensees could be required to waive any issue of fault, any charitable or governmental **254*

(Cite as: 464 U.S. 238, *254, 104 S.Ct. 615, **624)

immunity defense, and any statute of limitations defense of less than 10 years. *42 U.S.C. § 2210(n)(1).* Again, however, the importance of the legislation for present purposes is not so much in its substance, as in the assumptions on which it was based.

> FN15. An "extraordinary nuclear occurrence" is "any event causing a discharge or dispersal of source, special nuclear, or byproduct material from its intended place of confinement in amounts offsite, or causing radiation levels offsite, which the Commission determines to be substantial, and which the Commission determines has resulted or will probably result in substantial damages to persons offsite or property offsite." *42 U.S.C. § 2014(j).* The Commission's criteria for defining an extraordinary nuclear occurrence are located at *10 CFR §§ 140.81- 140.85 (1983).*

Describing the effect of the 1966 amendment, the Joint Committee stated:
"By requiring potential defendants to agree to waive defenses the defendants'

(Cite as: 464 U.S. 238, *254, 104 S.Ct. 615, **624)

rights are restricted; concomitantly, to this extent, the rights of plaintiffs are enlarged. Just as the rights of persons who are injured are established by State law, the rights of defendants against whom liability is asserted are fixed by State law. What this subsection does is to authorize the [NRC] to require that defendants covered by financial protection and indemnity give up some of the rights they might otherwise assert." S.Rep. 1605, 89th Cong., 2d Sess. 25 (1966), U.S.Code Cong & Admin.News 1966, p. 3226. Similarly, when the Committee outlined the rights of those injured in nuclear incidents which were not extraordinary nuclear occurrences, its reference point was again state law. "Absent . . . a determination [that the incident is an 'extraordinary nuclear occurrence'], a claimant would have exactly the same rights that he has today under existing law—including, perhaps, benefit of a rule of strict liability if applicable State law so provides." Id., at 11, U.S.Code Cong. & Admin.News 1966, p. 3212. Indeed, the entire discussion surrounding the 1966 amendment was premised on the assumption that state remedies were available notwithstanding the NRC's exclusive regulatory authority. For example, the Committee rejected a suggestion ***625*

(Cite as: 464 U.S. 238, *254, 104 S.Ct. 615, **625)

that it adopt a federal tort to replace existing state remedies, noting that such displacement of state remedies would engender great opposition. Hearings before the Joint Committee On Atomic Energy on Proposed Amendments to Price- Anderson Act Relating to Waivers of Defense, 89th Cong.2d Sess. 31, 75 (1966);

continued

FIGURE 14-1   For Educational use Only   *continued*

(Cite as: 464 U.S. 238, *254, 104 S.Ct. 615, **625)

S.Rep. No. 1605, supra, at 6-9. If other provisions ***255**

(Cite as: 464 U.S. 238, *255, 104 S.Ct. 615, **625)

of the Atomic Energy Act already precluded the states from providing remedies to its citizens, there would have been no need for such concerns. Other comments made throughout the discussion were similarly based on the assumption that state remedies were available. [FN16]

> FN16. Atomic Energy Commission General Counsel Hennessey testified that "[i]t would appear eminently reasonable to avoid disturbing ordinary tort law remedies with respect to damage claims where the circumstances are not substantially different from those encountered in many activities of life which cause damage to persons and property." Hearings before the Joint Committee On Atomic Energy on Proposed Amendments to Price-Anderson Act Relating to Waivers of Defense, 89th Cong. 2d Sess. 35 (1966). See also id., at 41 ("the amendments would not actually change the structure of the tort laws of the various states. The legal principles of state law would remain unchanged, but certain of the issues and defenses . . . would be affected").

Kerr-McGee focuses on the differences between compensatory and punitive damages awards and asserts that, at most, Congress intended to allow the former. This argument, however, is misdirected because our inquiry is not

(Cite as: 464 U.S. 238, *255, 104 S.Ct. 615, **625)

whether Congress expressly allowed punitive damages awards. Punitive damages have long been a part of traditional state tort law. As we noted above, Congress assumed that traditional principles of state tort law would apply with full force unless they were expressly supplanted. Thus, it is Kerr-McGee's burden to show that Congress intended to preclude such awards. See *IBEW v. Foust, 442 U.S. 42, 53, 99 S.Ct. 2121, 2128, 60 L.Ed.2d 698 (1979)* (BLACKMUN, J., concurring). Yet, the company is unable to point to anything in the legislative history or in the regulations that indicates that punitive damages were not to be allowed. To the contrary, the regulations issued implementing the insurance provisions of the Price-Anderson Act themselves contemplate that punitive damages might be awarded under state law. [FN17]

> FN17. Following the 1966 amendment, the Commission published a form for nuclear energy liability policies and indemnity agreements. After reciting the waivers being made by the licensee in the event of an extraordinary nuclear occurrence, the form contains the following provision: "The waivers set forth above . . . do not apply to . . . Any claim for punitive or exemplary damages. . . ." 10 CFR § 140.91, Appendix A, para. 2(c) at 801 (1983).

> Had the Commission thought that punitive damages awards were precluded by earlier legislation, as Kerr-McGee suggests, there would have been no need

(Cite as: 464 U.S. 238, *255, 104 S.Ct. 615, **625)

to state that the waivers didn't apply to such awards. Since the waivers don't apply at all to the present situation, the clear implication is that punitive damages are available, if state law so provides.

(Cite as: 464 U.S. 238, *256, 104 S.Ct. 615, **625)

In sum, it is clear that in enacting and amending the Price-Anderson Act, Congress assumed that state-law remedies, in whatever form they might take, were available to those injured by nuclear incidents. This was so even though it was well aware of the NRC's exclusive authority to regulate safety matters. No doubt there is tension between the conclusion that safety regulation is the exclusive concern of the federal law and the conclusion that a state may nevertheless award damages based on its own law of liability. But as we understand what was done over the years in the legislation concerning nuclear energy, Congress intended to stand by both concepts and to tolerate whatever tension there was between them. We can do no less. It may be that the award of damages based on the state law of negligence or strict liability is regulatory in the sense that a nuclear plant will be threatened with damages liability if it does not conform to state standards, but that regulatory consequence was something that Congress was quite willing to accept.

We do not suggest that there could never be an instance in which the federal law ****626**

(Cite as: 464 U.S. 238, *256, 104 S.Ct. 615, **626)

would preempt the recovery of damages based on state law. But insofar as damages for radiation injuries are concerned, preemption should not

(Cite as: 464 U.S. 238, *256, 104 S.Ct. 615, **626)

be judged on the basis that the federal government has so completely occupied the field of safety that state remedies are foreclosed but on whether there is an irreconcilable conflict between the federal and state standards or whether the imposition of a state standard in a damages action would frustrate the objectives of the federal law. We perceive no such conflict or frustration in the circumstances of this case.

*257

(Cite as: 464 U.S. 238, *257, 104 S.Ct. 615, **626)

B

[8] The United States, as amicus curiae, contends that the award of punitive damages in this case is preempted because it conflicts with the federal remedial scheme, noting that the NRC is authorized to impose civil penalties on licensees when federal standards have been violated. *42 U.S.C. § 2282* (1976 ed. and Supp. V). However, the award of punitive damages in the present case does not conflict with that scheme. Paying both federal fines and state-imposed punitive damages for the same incident would not appear to be physically impossible. Nor does exposure to punitive damages frustrate any purpose of the federal remedial scheme. Kerr-McGee contends that the award is preempted because it frustrates Congress' express desire "to encourage widespread participation in the development and utilization of atomic energy for peaceful purposes." *42 U.S.C. § 2013(d)*. In Pacific Gas & Electric, we observed that "[t]here is little doubt that a primary purpose of the Atomic Energy Act was, and continues

(Cite as: 464 U.S. 238, *257, 104 S.Ct. 615, **626)

to be, the promotion of nuclear power." *461 U.S., at——, 103 S.Ct., at 1731*. However, we also observed that "the promotion of nuclear power is not to be accomplished 'at all costs' ". Id., at——, 103 S.Ct., at——. Indeed, the provision cited by Kerr-McGee goes on to state that atomic energy should be developed and utilized only to the extent it is consistent "with the health and safety of the public." *42 U.S.C. § 2013(d)*. Congress therefore disclaimed any interest in promoting the development and utilization of atomic energy by means that fail to provide adequate remedies for

continued

FIGURE 14-1   For Educational use Only   *continued*

(Cite as: 464 U.S. 238, *257, 104 S.Ct. 615, **626), continued

those who are injured by exposure to hazardous nuclear materials. Thus, the award of punitive damages in this case does not hinder the accomplishment of the purpose stated in *§ 2013(d)*. We also reject Kerr-McGee's submission that the punitive damages award in this case conflicts with Congress' express intent to preclude dual regulation of radiation hazards. See S.Rep. No. 870, 86th Cong. 1st Sess. 8 (1959). As we ***258**

(Cite as: 464 U.S. 238, *258, 104 S.Ct. 615, **626)

explained in part A, Congress did not believe that it was inconsistent to vest the NRC with exclusive regulatory authority over the safety aspects of nuclear development while at the same time allowing plaintiffs like Silkwood to recover for injuries caused by nuclear hazards. We are not authorized to second-guess that conclusion. [FN18]

FN18. The government cites no evidence to support its claim that the

(Cite as: 464 U.S. 238, *258, 104 S.Ct. 615, **626)

present award conflicts with the NRC's desire to avoid penalties which put "a licensee out of business . . . or adversely affect[] a licensee's ability to safely conduct licensed activities." 47 Fed.Reg. 9991 (1982). Thus, we need not decide whether an award could be so large as to conflict with that policy. Of course, Kerr-McGee is free to challenge the propriety of the amount of the award on remand. See text infra, at 626-627.

IV

[9] We conclude that the award of punitive damages in this case is not preempted by federal law. On remand Kerr-McGee is free to reassert any claims it made before the Court of Appeals which were not addressed by that court or by this opinion, including its contention that the jury's findings with respect to punitive damages were not supported by sufficient evidence and its argument that the amount of the punitive damages award was excessive. The judgment of the Court of Appeals with respect to punitive damages is therefore reversed, ****627**

(Cite as: 464 U.S. 238, *258, 104 S.Ct. 615, **627)

and the case is remanded to the Court of Appeals for proceedings consistent with this opinion. It is so ordered.

Reprinted with Permission of West Group, copyright 2000.

Citation

Following the title of the case, or sometimes above the title, is a citation to the location of the case in the **case reporters.** Case reporters are a series of volumes in which court opinions are reported. The reporters are generally restricted to cases within states, regions, or particular federal courts.

A citation to a court opinion follows a common format. The volume of the reporter series is listed first, followed by the standard abbreviation for the reporter series and the page number on which the opinion begins. The citation is followed by the year of decision in parenthesis. The year of decision is critical to understanding case law because the court opinion may be nullified by statutory override or by later case law.

In addition to the citation reported above or beneath the name of the case, parallel citations may also be provided. Please refer to Figure 14-1 and notice where the parallel citation is listed. **Parallel citations** are references to alternative sources of published court reporters where the same text of the case is reported. When citing to case law, it is recommended that all parallel citations be included, so that the court opinion can be located in any of the source reporters. Researchers may purchase alternative reporter services because of preferences for the research tools provided. Citing all parallel sources facilitates research.

Docket Number

When a case is filed at the trial court level, it is given a **docket number.** This number identifies the case as it progresses through the court system. The docket number is valuable for locating documents filed in the case, especially memoranda of law and legal briefs. Docket numbers also provide a means for locating case law via the Internet. Refer to Figure 14-1 to see where in the court opinion the docket number appears.

Date of Decision

The title, citation, and docket number are followed by the date of hearings on the court case and the date the opinion is rendered. The date is important to ensure that the opinion is still good law and has not been superceded by later case law or modified or nullified by statutory override. Locate the date of decision for the case reproduced in Figure 14-1.

Synopsis

A concise description of the case and the question of law presented is sometimes included in a short paragraph preceding the editorial features that are included with the court opinion. The **synopsis** will also include the court's determination as to the question of law presented. A synopsis is included in the court opinion reproduced in Figure 14-1.

Headnotes

In order to be able to locate case law by topic, editors of case law extract the major questions of fact and law in the court opinion and draft explanatory paragraphs about those questions. These **headnotes** are identified by topic and are reproduced in **digests** under that topic. Researchers interested in finding law about that point will be able to access all the law that is published on that point in the corresponding reporter service by finding that topic in the digest. All case reporters published by West Group include headnotes; many state reporters provide similar reference features.

Headnotes provide a quick look at the substance of the court case. Since they are not written by the court, they should be used for reference only. Rules of law established in the court opinion should be quoted directly from the opinion; the headnotes are not authority. The number of headnotes will depend on the number of legal questions presented in the case. Locate them preceding the court opinion in Figure 14-1.

Names of Counsel

The attorneys who appeared and argued on behalf of each party are listed following the headnotes. The names of counsel are valuable for accessing the research and the theories of the parties. With the advent of computer-assisted legal research, supreme court briefs are now available online. Considerable time and effort may be saved by discussing similar cases with counsel who have previously researched and presented on the points of law. Find the attorneys representing the parties in the case included in Figure 14-1.

Statement of Facts

Generally a short paragraph outlining the nature and the judicial history of the case is presented immediately before the court opinion. Refer to Figure 14-1 for a look at this brief paragraph.

Opinion

The decision of the court, along with an explanation of how that decision was made constitutes case law. The name of the judge authoring the opinion usually precedes the discussion. The opinion itself will contain all the components of a case brief, which was discussed in Chapter Twelve; that is, it will contain the issue, the decision, a statement of the facts, the judicial history of the case, the legal and factual basis for the decision, and the procedural consequences of the court's decision.

There are several types of court opinions. A **majority opinion** is written by a judge assigned to summarize the rationale of a majority of the judges who reviewed the case. The majority opinion is the portion of the reported case that constitutes primary case law.

A judge may agree with the majority but for different reasons, and may write a separate opinion expressing that legal reasoning. This opinion is called a **concurring opinion.** A concurring opinion is not precedent.

A **dissenting opinion** may be filed whenever a judge disagrees with the majority opinion and feels compelled to discuss the legal reasons why the majority decision may be faulty. A dissenting opinion is not precedent.

Per curium refers to an opinion of the entire majority, rather than the opinion of a judge assigned to write a decision. Generally, a per curium opinion simply reports the decision and provides little or no reasoning for the decision. In many cases, the point of law is well settled.

A **memorandum opinion** is a short decision of a court with no lengthy opinion as to the rationale for the decision.

Judgment

Following the opinion of the court is the disposition of the action. This is identified by the words **affirmed, reversed,** or **remanded.** If the case is affirmed, the decision of the previous court is good law. If the case is reversed, the decision of the previous court is nullified and the case returns to the trial court level for proceedings as if the judgment of the previous court had not been made. If the case is remanded, it is returned to the trial court for further hearings, usually on evidence, as the record before the appeals court may not be sufficient to support the factual findings of the previous court.

PUBLICATION OF CASE LAW

Case law is reported in **official** and **unofficial** case reporters. An official reporter is required by statute to publish the text of the court opinion. This is consistent with the concept in the American legal system that law must be made available to the public. The official source must be cited first in the legal citation. An unofficial source publishes the exact text of the court opinion, along with editorial features that the publisher hopes will make the unofficial source more attractive than the official one.

Because of the hundreds of thousands of court decisions made annually in the United States, not all appellate court opinions are designated for publication. The right to at least one appeal is a guarantee of due process in the American legal system. Appeals, therefore, may not result in any new or modified rules of law. If the question of law brought on appeal is well settled, the court may determine that it is not necessary to publish the opinion. An unpublished decision is available using online computer-assisted legal research databases. However, it should not be relied on as authority since it is not considered precedent.

An opinion will be designated for publication in the following circumstances:

- It establishes a new rule of law.
- It modifies an existing rule of law.
- It is a matter of continuing social concern in the United States or the jurisdiction of the court.
- It is designated for publication by the court.

What LNCs Say . . .

"Based on my experience in personal injury and medical malpractice, I recommend a fairly comprehensive library of reference material, particularly a 'core' text from each medical specialty for which the LNC must retrieve information or review for case-related medical information. Examples: Nelson's Textbook of Pediatrics; Harrison's Principles of Internal Medicine; Braunwald's Heart Disease; Schwartz's Principles of Surgery; Merritt's Textbook of Neurology; Taber's Cyclopedic Medical Dictionary" Marilyn Mason-Kish, BS, RN, LNCC, San Francisco, CA, used with permission.

PUBLICATION OF FEDERAL COURT CASES

Opinions of the federal courts are reported in official and unofficial reporters. All written decisions of the United States Supreme Court are published in an official source, but decisions of lower federal courts are reported in unofficial reporters only.

United States Supreme Court

The official reporter of the decisions of the United States Supreme Court is the *United States Reports* (abbreviated U. S.). It is published by the United States Printing Office and consists of several volumes for each term of the court.

Because of the often lengthy delay in publishing the *United States Reports,* two unofficial sources for opinions of the Supreme Court are generally included as parallel cites: The *Supreme Court Reporter* (abbreviated S. Ct.) and the *United States Supreme Court Reports, Lawyers' Edition* (abbreviated L. Ed.), now in its second edition (abbreviated L. Ed. 2d).

The *Supreme Court Reporter* is published by West Group and contains research tools including the **Key Number system,** the unit of organization for all West legal research tools. The *Lawyers' Edition* includes references to other Lawyer's Cooperative publications such as the *American Law Reports.* (See Chapter Seventeen for a discussion of the *American Law Reports.*)

When citing to a Supreme Court case, the title is followed by the official citation, the Supreme Court Reporter citation, the Lawyer's Edition citation, and the year of decision. The format for citing to case law is consistent: the volume number precedes the abbreviation for the reporter series, which is followed by the page number and the year of decision in parenthesis. The citation not only identifies where to find the law, but also where the law came from.

Refer to Figure 14-1 and note how the citation to that case is written:

> *Silkwood v. Kerr-McGee Corporation,* 464 U.S. 238, 104 S. Ct. 615, 78 L. Ed. 443 (1984)

The citation identifies that the case of *Silkwood v. Kerr McGee Corporation* can be found in volume 464 of the *United States Reports* (the official source) on page 238. The case can also be found in the *Supreme Court Reporter* in volume 104 on page 615, and in volume 78 of the Lawyer's Edition, second series, on page 443. This case was heard before the United States Supreme Court because the abbreviations for the reporters (U.S., S. Ct., and L. Ed. 2d) are reporters for supreme court decisions.

United States Circuit Courts of Appeals

Decisions of the circuit courts of appeals in the federal judiciary are not published in official sources. Rather, West Group publishes the *Federal Reporter* (abbreviated F.), which has been published in a second and third series (abbreviated F. 2d and F. 3d). The *Federal Reporter* also includes some decisions of the United States Claims Court and the Court of Customs and Patent Appeals. A case reported in the *Federal Reporter* is cited as follows:

Zimmerman v. North American Signal Co., 704 F. 2d 347 (7th Cir. 1983)

The circuit in which the case was decided is included in the parenthesis preceding the year of decision so that researchers will know the geographic impact of the precedent established in the case. The rule of law established in *Zimmerman* is only primary binding law in the 7th circuit; it is primary persuasive in all other circuit courts of appeals.

United States District Courts

There is no official reporter for the trial courts in the federal judiciary. Selected cases from the various districts are reported in West Group's *Federal Supplement* (abbreviated F. Supp.) and if the case involves interpretation of court rules, in the *Federal Rules Decisions* (F. R. D.). Not all federal appeals or district court cases are published; the editors at West Group determine whether a decision is sufficiently significant to warrant publication. A citation to a district court case follows:

Musser v. Mountain View Broadcasting, Inc., 578 F. Supp. 229 (E.D. Tenn. 1984)

This citation identifies that the case of *Musser v. Mountain View Broadcasting* emanates from the federal district court for the eastern district of Tennessee and was decided in 1984. The case may be located in volume 578 of the *Federal Supplement* beginning on page 229.

PUBLICATION OF STATE COURT CASES

Many states, by legislation, require certain publishers to print the opinions of the highest courts and the appeals courts of their states. These published volumes are referred to as official sources. Private vendors also publish state court opinions in unofficial sources with attractive editorial features. Because private publishers often provided the text of state court opinions faster than the official publisher, some states have abolished the official reporter and rely entirely on the unofficial source for publication of state court cases. If an official publication is required by state law, that source must be cited first, followed by the unofficial citation. The *National Reporter System* of West Group is the best-known unofficial source of state court decisions. It consists of reports for all fifty states published in regional reporters, which are identified in Figure 14-2. Figure 14-2 also lists the coverage for each of the reporters within West's *National Reporter System.*

In addition to the state reporters, West's *National Reporter System* includes reporters for the federal system and specialty reporters, are listed in Figure 14-3. The philosophy of West Group is to provide as much law as possible to practitioners. This allows the practitioners to use their own legal judgment as to the significance and application of the law.

Net Results

Federal and State Case Law

All recent federal court opinions and most state court opinions are now available on the Internet. Some of the web sites only contain opinions from the last few years and do not allow users to search for older case law. These web sites may be accessed through government home pages, through state bar association home pages, through West Group's home page for legal students (www.westlegalstudies. com) and through the legal links web sites: www.findlaw.com and www.law.cornell.edu. State court cases may be accessed using WestLaw or Lexis (paid Internet subscriptions) and current case law is often available at the state court web site. Access this site at www.courts.XX.us where XX is the two-letter postal abbreviation for the state you are researching.

FIGURE 14-2   West's Regional Reporters

Reporter	Coverage	Abbreviation
Atlantic	Connecticut, Delaware, Maine, Maryland, New Hampshire, New Jersey, Pennsylvania, Rhode Island, Vermont, and the District of Columbia	A. or A. 2d
South Eastern	Georgia, North Carolina, South Carolina, Virginia, and West Virginia	S. E. or S. E. 2d
Southern	Alabama, Florida, Louisiana, and Mississippi	So. Or So. 2d
North Eastern	Illinois, Indiana, Massachusetts, New York, and Ohio	N. E. or N. E. 2d
South Western	Arkansas, Kentucky, Missouri, Tennessee, Texas	S. W. or S. W. 2d
North Western	Iowa, Michigan, Minnesota, Nebraska, North Dakota, South Dakota, and Wisconsin	N. W. or N. W. 2d
Pacific	Alaska, Arizona, California, Colorado, Hawaii, Idaho, Kansas, Montana, Nevada, New Mexico, Oklahoma, Oregon, Utah, Washington, Wyoming	P. or P. 2d

FIGURE 14-3   Additional Reporters in the West National Reporter System

- Supreme Court Reporter
- Federal Reporter
- Federal Supplement
- Federal Rules Decisions
- West's Bankruptcy Reporter
- New York Supplement
- West's California Reporter
- West's Illinois Decisions
- West's Military Justice Reporter
- Veterans Appeals Reporter
- Federal Claims Reporter

A citation to a state court case with an official reporter is as follows:

Izazaga v. Superior Court, 54 Cal. 3d 356, 285 Cal. Rptr. 231, 815 P. 2d 304 (1987)

The case of *Izazaga v. Superior Court* was decided in California in 1987. It can be found in the official source, the *California Reports,* in volume 54 beginning on page 356. It can also be found in volume 285 of West's *California Re-*

porter beginning on page 231, and in volume 815 of West's *Pacific Reporter,* second series, beginning on page 304.

If there is no official reporter for the state, the citation would appear as follows:

Tussey v. Commonwealth, 589 S. W. 2d 215 (Ky. 1979)

The state in which the case was decided precedes the year of decision so that researchers will know the jurisdiction in which this case holds primary binding authority. *Tussey v. Commonwealth* can be found in volume 589 of West's *South Western Reporter,* second series, beginning on page 215.

It may be necessary to distinguish between a supreme court case and an appeals court case in states where no official reporters are required or in situations in which the official citation is not available. In those cases, the citation would appear as follows:

Thompson v. Economy Super Marts, Inc., 581 N. E. 2d 885 (Ill. Ct. App. 1991)

The case of *Thompson v. Economy Super Marts, Inc.,* was decided by the Illinois Court of Appeals in 1991 and can be found in an unofficial source, in volume 581 of West's *North Eastern Reporter,* second series, beginning on page 885.

The decisions of state trial courts are generally not published and are not considered precedent. They can be obtained from the court, but they do not provide the guidance that the appeals and highest state court opinions do.

Because court opinions are published chronologically, it would be difficult and cumbersome to research without a topical collection of case summaries. Headnotes are collected into just such a topical collection called digests. Digests of court opinions allow researchers to identify the subject matter of the legal problem and locate cases that deal with that subject matter. Digests are discussed in Chapter Sixteen.

Legal encyclopedias provide background about legal issues and citations to court cases in which those legal issues were discussed. Legal encyclopedias operate exactly like factual encyclopedias. They are arranged alphabetically by topic (from abatement to zoning) and begin with a brief and general statement of the law, followed by a complete discussion that gradually becomes more detailed and specialized. Like the footnotes in a factual encyclopedia, the statements in a legal encyclopedia are footnoted to legal citations. Legal encyclopedias are discussed in Chapter Sixteen.

CHAPTER SUMMARY

- Court opinions include consistent components: title, citation, date, docket number, synopsis, headnotes, names of counsel, opinion, and judgment.
- Case law is reported in official and unofficial case reporters.

■ Citations to case law should include the title of the case, the official citation, all parallel citations, and the year of decision in parenthesis.

■ West Group provides the most comprehensive system of federal and state case reporting services.

KEY TERMS

affirmed	Key Number system	precedent
case reporters	legal encyclopedia	remanded
concurring opinion	majority opinion	reversed
digests	memorandum opinion	*stare decisis*
dissenting opinion	official	synopsis
docket number	parallel citations	unofficial
headnotes	per curium	

REVIEW QUESTIONS

1. Give an example of when case law is primary binding and when it is primary persuasive.
2. Distinguish between official and unofficial publications of case law.
3. What can be learned from reading legal citation to case law?

INTERNET EXERCISES

1. Access the web page for this textbook at *www.westlegalstudies.com.*
2. Click on the assignments section, and complete the assignment(s) for Chapter Thirteen.

EXERCISES

1. Networking. If you are planning to spend a day at the state capitol, call ahead to see if the Supreme Court will be hearing oral arguments on that day. Sit in on the oral arguments and observe how they are conducted and the organizational techniques used by the attorneys.
2. Professional Portfolio. Brief the court opinion reproduced in Figure 14-1. Case briefing is discussed in Chapter Twelve. Maintain this case brief in your portfolio. Add "understanding of legal citation" to your resume or cover letter.

ENDNOTE

1. American Association of Legal Nurse Consultants, *Standards of Practice.* (1997) Standard 5.

ADDITIONAL REFERENCES

Jacobstein, J., Mersky, R., Dunn, D. *Fundamentals of Legal Research,* 6th ed. Westbury, NY: The Foundation Press, Inc, 1994.

Statsky, W. *Essentials of Paralegalism,* 3rd ed. Albany, NY: West Thomson Learning, 1998.

CHAPTER 15

ADMINISTRATIVE SOURCES

OBJECTIVES

In this chapter, you will discover

- how administrative agencies are created
- the powers of administrative agencies
- how administrative agencies promulgate rules
- where administrative law is published
- how administrative law is cited

OVERVIEW

Because it is impossible for Congress to continually monitor every area of social concern in the United States, administrative agencies are created to carry out the intent of certain legislation. For example, the Atomic Energy Act resulted in the creation of the Nuclear Regulatory Commission, which is responsible for the implementation and enforcement of this important legislation.

Administrative agencies exist only because the legislature authorizes the creation of the agency and provides the agency with basic powers. This authorization is identified in legislation called an **enabling act.**

ENABLING LEGISLATION

The founding document of an administrative agency is the law that created it. The powers and duties of officers within the agency can be traced back to this original document. Enabling legislation to an administrative agency is similar to the constitution of a state or country, or to the articles of incorporation of a business.

Basically, the enabling statute will

- create the administrative agency to carrying out the purposes of a particular act
- outline the governing structure of the administrative agency
- grant powers and responsibilities to the agency and its officers
- define guidelines within which the administrative agency must accomplish its purpose

Administrative agencies have considerable autonomous power. Courts are reluctant to interfere with the workings of administration agencies for several reasons. Agencies cannot accomplish their purposes if they are continually bird-dogged with judicial intervention. Also, these agencies are concerned with specialized and often technical matters and are viewed as having expertise that the court is generally unfamiliar with.

Administrative agencies impact almost every aspect of daily life and are critical to the operation of health care facilities and practices. Legal nurse consultants do well to understand the nature of administrative law, how to access and apply administrative law, and how to read and write proper citation to administrative law.

CLASSIFICATIONS OF ADMINISTRATIVE AGENCIES

Administrative agencies may be classified in several ways. Agencies are said to be executive, independent, social welfare, and regulatory.

Executive

Executive agencies are under the direct control of the president or chief executive. They are often referred to as the cabinet and are considered part of the executive branch of government. The president has direct power to appoint the heads of these agencies and these appointees may be removed from office at the will of the executive; that is, without due process or just cause.

Independent

Most federal administrative agencies are **independent;** that is, they operate without the specific control of the president. These agencies are created by legislation and, while responsible for enforcement of legislative intent, they are considered to be on the fence between the legislative and executive branches of government. Independent agencies may be known by any of a number of different titles including commission, board, authority, administration, bureau, or division. The name of the agency is not as important as the authority it is given in its enabling legislation.

Social Welfare

An agency dedicated to the health, education, and living conditions of society is considered a **social welfare agency.** These agencies include the Social Security Administration, Health and Human Services, Housing and Urban Development, Department of Education, and so forth.

Regulatory

Agencies that are used for "traffic control" are considered **regulatory** in nature. These agencies issue licenses, manage activities, set limits, and generally require compliance with standards that are deemed beneficial to an organized society. The Department of Transportation and the Interstate Commerce Commission are considered regulatory agencies. While it may be difficult to categorize an agency as being either for the social well being of residents or the orderly administration of activities, agencies are generally classified according to the original purpose of the enabling statute.

An excellent resource for information about administrative agencies is the *United States Government Manual*. This manual is published and revised annually and includes information about each agency and department of government. The enabling statute is referenced and a brief description of the agency is included, along with its functions and authority and the names of key officials within each agency.

POWERS OF ADMINISTRATIVE AGENCIES

Each administrative agency is empowered in the enabling statute with the authority necessary to carry out its purpose. Generally, agencies are given similar powers: rule-making power, investigative power, enforcement power, and adjudicatory power.

Rule-making power

The rule-making power of an administrative agency includes substantive and procedural rule making; that is, the agency can make **substantive rules** concerning the rights and responsibilities of parties, and **procedural rules** concerning the processes for preserving rights and enforcing responsibilities. These rules have the force and effect of law when they are published. The agency may also make **interpretive rules,** statements that explain how the agency interprets and intends to carry out its mission. Interpretive rules do not have the force of law.

The rule-making power of any agency must be exercised in ways that protect the constitutional privileges of residents of the United States. The regulations established by the agency cannot deny or abridge due process guarantees. For a more complete discussion of the due process concepts relative to administrative agencies, see Chapter Eight.

Investigative

To ensure compliance with regulations, agencies are empowered to investigate people and companies within their jurisdictions. Agencies may require compliance reports, inspections, and informational filings. Parties that do not cooperate with agency investigations may be compelled to do so with **subpoena** power.

The investigative power of the agency is limited to the scope of agency authority. To exceed that authority is to violate the rights of the party against whom the authority is exerted. For example, the IRS discovers that a taxpayer has unreported income from drug trafficking. The IRS can only prosecute the taxpayer on tax evasion. The information that is collected concerning the drug trafficking business may not be communicated to any other agency for any other purpose.

Enforcement

To ensure compliance with agency regulations, agencies are empowered to enforce those regulations with sanctions such as fines, suspension of licenses, cease and desist orders, and, as a final resort, the closure of a business. These actions cannot be taken, however, without protecting the due process rights of the suspected violator. A complaint, or notice of violation, must be made and the suspected violator must be notified of the suspected violation before any action can be taken.

Adjudicatory

After the notice of violation is filed and served on the party involved, the party is entitled to a hearing, to know the evidence that will be used, and to present a defense. Agencies are empowered to hold such hearings and to process claims in a manner similar to court proceedings. These adjudicatory powers charge the agencies with making determinations in disputes about agency actions. For a more complete discussion of the proceedings in an administrative adjudicatory action, please refer to Chapter Eight.

LAWS GOVERNING ADMINISTRATIVE AGENCY PROCEEDINGS

It may appear that agencies have unlimited power within their respective areas of social concern. The American people have always been conscious of the balance of power. To prevent agencies from wielding too much power in governmental operations, several laws have been enacted to ensure that the agencies are responsive to and protect the rights of those served by the agency.

Government-in-the-Sunshine Act[1]

This law requires that meetings of any governmental agency be noticed in advance, that the agenda of the meeting be publicly available, and that the meetings be open to the public. The law is intended to prevent clandestine operations. An agency open to public scrutiny is less likely to abuse power.

Administrative Procedures Act[2]

To provide an opportunity for the public to speak for or against proposed regulations, the Administrative Procedures Act requires that hearings be held on proposed regulations that could impact significant populations. This law, enacted in 1946, is intended to prevent arbitrary establishment of regulations that are in the interest of the agency rather than the citizens it serves.

Freedom of Information Act[3]

Intended to prevent agencies from keeping information secret that is ultimately intended and collected for public purposes, the Freedom of Information Act requires that agencies comply with requests to provide information. The agency may establish procedures for requesting information under the Freedom of Information Act but refusing to provide the information, unless it is a matter of national security, can be challenged in court.

PROMULGATION OF AGENCY REGULATIONS

Each agency is empowered to promulgate such substantive, procedural, and interpretive rules as may be necessary to accomplish its purpose. How these regulations are promulgated is peculiar to each agency. In general, however, if it will have significant impact, the agency staff drafts a tentative or proposed regulation. This proposal is published, along with the dates and times of public hearings at which individuals and business representatives have

What LNCs Say . . .

"I've researched everything from head to toe, including causes of disease, treatment, and outcome, cost of care, future care needs, and disabilities caused by injury. I use Medline (online) and textbooks to find my information. I also contact people I know (doctors, nurses, occupational therapists, physical therapists, etc.) to give me advice" Kathy Sullivan, RN, BS, Madison, WI, used with permission.

Net Results

Administrative Regulations

The Federal Register *and the* Code of Federal Regulations *are available on the Internet. While it is still a little troublesome to locate items in the* Federal Register *without having a citation or knowing which agency to search, the* Code of Federal Regulations *can be searched using key terms and phrases. Access the* Code of Federal Regulations *and the* Federal Register *via the legal web sites already identified:* www.findlaw.com *and* www.law.cornell.edu. *In addition, many of the federal agencies have home pages with links to regulations. Access the federal administrative agencies via a comprehensive listing site found at the Government Sources of Business and Economic Information:* www.whitehouse.gov/WH/Independent Agencies.

the opportunity to comment on the proposal. After the hearing and consideration of the public commentary, a final regulation is adopted by the agency and published. Administrative rules and regulations are made, revised, and repealed frequently.

PUBLICATION OF FEDERAL ADMINISTRATIVE LAW

There are two official sources for federal administrative law: the *Federal Register* and the *Code of Federal Regulations*.

Federal Register

The daily newspaper of federal administrative agencies is the *Federal Register*. It is published every Monday through Friday, except legal holidays and contains

- regulations adopted by federal agencies
- proposed regulations under consideration by federal agencies
- notices of hearings on proposed regulations
- notices of meetings and agendas that fall under the Government-in-the-Sunshine Act
- Executive Orders
- Presidential Proclamations

The *Federal Register* is organized alphabetically by agency and may be accessed by consulting the table of contents at the beginning of the Register or the index. The index is published monthly, so to ensure up-to-date information, it is necessary to consult the table of contents of any subsequent issues of the *Federal Register*.

Because the organization of the regulations published in the *Federal Register* is by agency, it is necessary to know what agency is responsible for the regulations being researched. This can be a difficult task and might require referring to the enabling legislation of the agency.

Code of Federal Regulations

The preferred source for citing federal administrative law is the *Code of Federal Regulations*. The *Code of Federal Regulations* (abbreviated C.F.R.) is organized into fifty titles that are similar to the titles of the *United States Code*. These titles do not necessarily correspond with the titles of the *United States Code;* instead, the titles are organized by agency. The C.F.R. is further subdivided into chapters, subchapters, parts, and sections.

At the back of each volume of the C.F.R. is a list of federal agencies and their respective titles. To search the C.F.R. by topic, it is first necessary to know which agency is responsible for that topic. Again one might need to consult the enabling legislation to determine which agency has the authority to promulgate rules concerning a particular topic.

A regulation found in the *Code of Federal Regulations* would be cited as follows:

21 C. F. R. pt. 101 (1992)

This 1992 regulation can be found at title 21 of the *Code of Federal Regulations* at part 101. If the citation is to a section, the section symbol would be used, and the citation would appear as follows:

21 C. F. R. § 101.62 (1993)

Note that the official citation does not include the agency promulgating this regulation.

LOOSELEAF SERVICES

Because the law of administrative agencies changes almost daily, it is not efficient to publish administrative law in bound volumes. Instead, many commercial vendors offer looseleaf services. These services not only contain the text of the rules and regulations, but also provide interpretive notes, practice tips, and sometimes sample documents. Looseleaf services are a convenient means for maintaining and updating an administrative law library. When the law changes, the outdated page is simply removed from the binder and the new page is inserted.

The rules and regulations of administrative agencies are primary authority and are binding in the jurisdiction in which they are promulgated. Because looseleaf services also provide commentary on the rules and regulations, they are considered secondary authority.

STATE ADMINISTRATIVE AGENCIES

There are numerous agencies within each of the fifty states of the United States and each state has a system for publishing the rules and regulations of those agencies. In some states, the entire body of regulations is codified in a fashion similar to the *Code of Federal Regulations*. In other states, each agency issues its own publication of rules and regulations. With the advent of the Internet, many of these agency regulations are available through state home pages. Often a quick call to the agency is sufficient to obtain a faxed copy of the desired regulation.

Each state publishes a book similar to the *United States Government Manual*. Several states offer a *Blue Book* that contains information about all branches of government and all levels; the names of state and county officials; and complete information about the agencies of the state and their functions and authority. The *Blue Book* is available in most libraries and copies are available from state offices and representatives. It is a valuable reference!

Ethics Bookmark

Professional Integrity

"A lawyer shall provide competent representation to a client" Annotated Model Rules of Professional Conduct Fourth Edition Rule 1.1 Copyright 1999.*⁴ This ethical rule has many facets and will be used several times throughout this textbook to illustrate different aspects of the word "competent." When activities get hectic at the law firm, which they are bound to do, the task that often gets neglected is updating the library. While putting pocket parts into the backs of books and changing out the pages in a looseleaf service is not intellectually stimulating, maintaining an up-to-date library is essential for competent representation of clients.
*American Bar Association. Reprinted by permission of The American Bar Association. American Bar Association, *Annotated Model Rules of Professional conduct*, 4th ed. (1999) Rule 1.1. Copies of Model Code of Professional Responsibility, 1999 edition are available from Service Center, American Bar Association, 750 North Lake Shore Drive, Chicago, IL 60611-4497, 1-800-285-2221.

CHAPTER SUMMARY

- Administrative agencies are created and empowered through enabling legislation.

- Agencies may be classified as executive, independent, social welfare, or regulatory.

- The powers of administrative agencies include promulgating rules and regulations, investigating compliance with and enforcing rules, and adjudicating claims.

- Several laws govern the rule-making power of administrative agencies, including the Sunshine Act, the Administrative Procedures Act, and the Freedom of Information Act.

- Federal administrative law is published in the *Federal Register,* in the *Code of Federal Regulations,* and in looseleaf services.

- State administrative law is published in state administrative codes.

KEY TERMS

enabling act	interpretive rules	social welfare agencies
executive agencies	procedural rules	subpoena
independent agencies	regulatory agencies	substantive rules

REVIEW QUESTIONS

1. What legislation controls actions within administrative agencies? How?

2. Distinguish between executive and independent administrative agencies. Between social welfare and regulatory agencies.

3. Explain the powers of administrative agencies.

INTERNET EXERCISES

1. Access the web page for this textbook at *www.westlegalstudies.com.*

2. Click on the assignments sections and complete the assignment(s) for Chapter Fifteen.

EXERCISES

1. Networking. Obtain a copy of the *Blue Book* for your state or find one in a local library. Review the pages that deal with administrative agencies in your state and identify any agencies that might employ legal nurse consultants. Call an agency and ask if there are any nurses on staff. If the nurse is available and willing to talk to you, conduct an informational interview. Ask about procedures for seeking employment with the agency. Maintain this contact and other information you learned about governmental agencies in your networking system, file, or Rolodex.

2. Professional Portfolio. Photocopy pages of the *Blue Book* (or download pages from web sites) about governmental agencies that may prove useful for the legal nurse consulting practice. Those of particular interest might be workers' compensation, the bureau of regulation and licensing, or others. Maintaining these with your professional portfolio will display an understanding of the interrelatedness of government structure and the resourcefulness of a good investigator.

ENDNOTES

1. Government-in-the-Sunshine Act, 5 U.S.C. s. 522(b).

2. Federal Administration Procedures Act, 5 U.S.C. s. 553(c).

3. Freedom of Information Act, 5 U.S.C. s. 551, et.seq.

4. American Bar Association, *Annotated Model Rules of Professional Conduct* Fourth Edition (1999) Rule 1.1. Copies of ABA *Model Code of Professional Responsibility, 1999 Edition* are available from Service Center, American Bar Association, 750 North Lake Shore Drive, Chicago, IL 60611-4497, 1-800-285-2221.

ADDITIONAL REFERENCES

Carper, D. L., et al. *Understanding the Law,* 3rd ed. St. Paul, MN: West Publishing Company, 2000.

Walston-Dunham, B. *Introduction to Law,* 3rd ed. Albany, NY: West Thomson Learning, 1999.

CHAPTER 16

SECONDARY AUTHORITY AND INDICES TO LAW

OBJECTIVES

In this chapter, you will discover

- what the sources of secondary authority are
- how secondary authority is useful in the practice of law
- the system of citation for secondary authority
- what indices to law are available
- how indices to find law are used

OVERVIEW

The previous chapters have introduced primary authority: statutes (including constitutions and treaties), case law, and administrative law. These sources provide the letter of the law. Practice as a legal nurse consultant invariably involves reading and examining legal principles. These principles are found in primary sources and in **secondary sources,** such as textbooks. Legal nurse consultants are not generally expected to be proficient at locating the law. However, legal professionals are expected to understand the universal language of citing to the law. Understanding the language of citation and recognizing the value of the legal authority is fundamental to understanding how the law works.

SECONDARY SOURCES

When there is no citation to primary authority concerning a legal question, many legal professionals recommend starting in secondary sources. Secondary authorities are writings that help explain and clarify the law. There are several reasons for consulting secondary authority:

- Secondary sources provide background and orientation to an unfamiliar topic of law.
- Secondary sources often provide quick answers to legal questions.
- Secondary sources provide citations and footnotes to primary authority.
- Secondary sources may suggest resolution of a problem.
- Secondary sources identify trends in the law.

   Many secondary sources are expositive; that is, they simply explain what the law is and how it has been applied. Other secondary sources are critical; they seek to show how the law should be applied. Some secondary sources provide exhaustive examinations of a legal topic; others provide only cursory discussions. In any case, secondary sources are valuable tools in the transaction of legal business.

CATEGORIES OF SECONDARY AUTHORITY

There are several ways that secondary authority contributes to an understanding of law. Secondary authority can be classified into four categories:

1. commentaries (discussions on the law)
2. dictionaries (legal definitions and interpretations)
3. restatements (past and future examination of common law concepts)
4. legislative history (documents that identify the intent of lawmakers at the time a bill was passed).

FIGURE 16-1   Commentaries on the Law

Commentary	Description
Textbook	General discussion of law intended for student use; sometimes called "hornbook".
Treatise	Comprehensive treatment of one legal topic.
Legal encyclopedia	Systematically covers every legal topic, arranged alphabetically.
Legal periodical	Law reviews and legal journals.
Looseleaf services	Thorough collection of legal materials in a highly regulated area of law.
Textual annotations	Editorially selected court decisions about which a complete memorandum of law is written.

These categories are not mutually exclusive and different authors use different classifications for secondary sources. Still, it is useful to categorize secondary sources and to examine each category more fully.

Commentaries

Commentaries on the law are probably the most useful for beginning researchers. Commentaries explain what the law is, how it has been applied, and what some of the exceptions and qualifications are concerning an area of law. The most common type of commentary is the legal textbook, but there are several other commentaries. Figure 16-1 identifies the commentaries commonly used by legal professionals. Commentaries range from basic generalizations about the law to critical and detailed examinations of how and why the law applies.

Textbooks

Written by legal scholars for use by students of law, textbooks, also called **hornbooks,** provide a survey of the law in a broad area such as torts, commercial law, or real estate. While textbooks provide valuable insight into the law on a given topic, there are more precise references for use in legal arguments. Wherever possible, primary sources should be used to resolve legal questions.

A citation to a textbook follows a format similar to that used in bibliographies:

Robert W. Hamilton, *Corporations,* 357 (2d 1981)

The citation clearly identifies that the source is a book written by Robert W. Hamilton. The quote can be found on page 357 of the book titled *Corporations,* second edition published in 1981.

Treatises

A thorough and comprehensive examination of one legal topic is provided in a **treatise.** Treatises are often multivolume sets and are highly respected secondary authority because they are written by legal experts. McCormick on *Evidence* and Larson on *Employment Discrimination* are examples of treatises. Legal treatises are similar to medical treatises; they are learned, in-depth analyses of specific subjects.

Treatises are cited in the same way as textbooks. If the treatise is a multivolume series, the volume number precedes the name of the author.

Legal Encyclopedias

In the same way that an encyclopedia such as the *World Book Encyclopedia* attempts to provide a complete collection of the body of knowledge, **legal encyclopedias** attempt to provide a complete collection of the body of law. Arranged alphabetically by topic, legal encyclopedia entries begin with general statements about the topic. As the article continues, the discussion becomes more precise. Legal encyclopedias are heavily footnoted with citations to primary authority. The encyclopedia entry is valuable for background and for orientation to the topic of law, but primary sources should be consulted and used to resolve legal issues.

Two major legal encyclopedias attempt to cover the entire body of law. *American Jurisprudence* (now in its second series and abbreviated Am. Jur. 2d) is published by Lawyer's Cooperative. It provides citations to primary authority along with research aids and references to other Lawyer's Cooperative tools, especially the *American Law Reports. Corpus Juris Secundum* (abbreviated C. J. S.) is published by West Group. The Key Number System of organization employed in West publications provides ready access to other law under that topic. *Corpus Juris Secundum* also provides footnotes to primary authority.

Citations to encyclopedias are not often used for anything other than reference. It is preferable to use primary authority, even primary authority that is persuasive only. A citation to a legal encyclopedia may be used to illustrate a common understanding of the law. The following is a citation to a legal encyclopedia:

76 Am. Jur. 2d *Trusts* § 75 (1975)

This entry may be found in volume 76 of the *American Jurisprudence* encyclopedia, second series, copyrighted in 1975, in section 75 of the topic Trusts.

Legal encyclopedias are updated with **pocket parts.** It is important to check the pocket part under the topic being researched to access the most current treatment of that topic.

Legal Periodicals

Legal periodicals like the *Harvard Law Review,* the *American Bar Association Journal,* and the *Wisconsin Lawyer* are valuable because they contain two basic types of works: lead articles and student works. The lead articles appearing in legal periodicals such as the *ABA Journal* are memoranda of law on current topics written by legal scholars, judges, and professors. These articles generally include all of the law on a particular topic and may be critical in nature.

Student works such as those appearing in the *Harvard Law Review* are exhaustive examinations of recent cases, statutes, or trends in the law. They are thoroughly referenced with citation to legal authority. Law review articles carry great weight in the resolution of legal issues, but are still secondary to primary sources.

Of course legal periodicals are valuable for many other reasons. They provide updates on court rules, statutes, and case law. Articles concerning the efficient and effective practice of law are also an important component of legal periodicals. Book reviews provide insight into recently published secondary sources. Bar journals are also a source of valuable information for licensed practitioners and associate members concerning the activities of the bar association.

A citation to an article in a legal periodical includes the name of the author, the name of the article, the volume number, the abbreviation for the periodical, and the page number of the article. The year of publication is in parenthesis.

A citation to an article would read as follows:

Muldowney and Shaw, *Environmental Cleanup Costs,* 63 Wis. Lawyer 22 (1990).

The article, "Environmental Cleanup Costs" by Muldowney and Shaw was published in 1990 in volume 62 of the Wisconsin Lawyer on page 22. Note that the citation to a periodical article does not include the month of publication.

Looseleaf Services

Looseleaf services are often used for administrative law, which tends to change rapidly. Because it is not profitable to continually republish bound volumes when the law changes, looseleaf services collect this information in removable binders. As the law changes, the page that has become obsolete is removed and a new page inserted. Looseleaf services generally provide the text of the law, along with commentaries, explanations, practice tips, and sample forms.

Textual Annotations

Publishers sometimes select important appellate court cases and develop **annotations** on the major point of law raised in the case. These annotations are actually complete memoranda of law, thoroughly analyzing the impact of the court ruling and providing footnotes to primary authority in other jurisdictions.

The most frequently used textual annotation is the *American Law Reports* (abbreviated A. L. R.), published by Lawyer's Cooperative. The original intent of the *American Law Reports* was to provide attorneys with only the cases that made significant additions to the body of law, rather than inundating them with all published cases, many of which simply reinforced existing principles.

There are currently six series of the *American Law Reports:* A.L.R., A.L.R. 2d, A.L.R. 3d, A.L.R. 4th, A.L.R. 5th, and A.L.R. Fed. To ensure that the annotation is still good law, Lawyer's Cooperative provides a toll-free hotline number for up-to-date additions or changes to the annotation. Legal professionals find the A.L.R. to be extremely valuable, not just for the research and the discussion, but for the logical development of ideas present in the annotations.

A citation to the A.L.R. is often seen in the usual format: volume number, A.L.R. series, and page number. A quotation from the annotation, however, requires additional information. The complete citation for an A.L.R. annotation is as follows:

> William B. Johnson, *Locating Easement of Way Created by Necessity,* 36 A.L.R. 4th 769 (1985)

The annotation "Locating Easement of Way Created by Necessity," written by William B. Johnson, may be found in volume 36 of the A.L.R., fourth series, copyrighted in 1985, beginning on page 769.

DICTIONARIES

It is surprising how often in court opinions, judges will refer to the common meaning of terms and phrases, as they are defined in everyday dictionaries such as *Webster's* and *New Collegiate.* There are many legal dictionaries, but the most prominent is *Black's Law Dictionary.* It provides definitions of all legal terms including Latin phrases used in law, often with citations to primary authority where the term has been judicially interpreted.

Legal dictionaries are not often cited in legal documents and are most commonly used as reference sources only. There are times, however, when it is critical to an argument that the dictionary be consulted. In a famous products liability case *Webster v. Blue Ship Tea Room,*[1] the court of appeals referred to *Webster's Dictionary* for a definition of fish chowder!

The correct citation to a dictionary entry is as follows:

> *Black's Law Dictionary* 724 (6th 1990)

The citation tells us that the definition quoted may be found in the sixth edition of *Black's Law Dictionary,* copyrighted in 1990, on page 724.

For legal nurse consultants, medical dictionaries provide additional sources of research and argument. Understanding how to properly cite those medical authorities for legal purposes will enhance the contribution a legal nurse consultant can make to the legal team.

RESTATEMENTS

For legal researchers, the importance of the *Restatements* cannot be overstated. Because they are commissioned and adopted by the American Law Institute and drafted by luminaries in their fields, they are considered heavyweight champions for a legal point of view. Courts are strongly influenced by citations to the *Restatements*.

In tort law, especially, almost every landmark case contains a reference to the *Restatement on Torts*. Legal nurse consultants are expected to be somewhat familiar with tort law and its development. The *Restatements* have provided an anchor for complex and uncertain applications of common law principles in personal injury litigation.

The function of the *Restatements* is to restate the law from its common law origins to its present day interpretation—its limitations and qualifications, and its potential for expansion to new situations. There are *Restatements* for agency, contracts, conflict of laws, foreign relations law, judgments, property, torts, and trusts.

A citation to the *Restatements* is properly written as follows:

Restatement (Second) of Torts § 481 (1964)

This citation refers to the second *Restatement* on Torts at section 481. It was adopted in 1964.

LEGISLATIVE HISTORY

A legislative history is a collection of materials used before and during the consideration of a bill. Courts may look to **legislative history** to understand the meaning of the law and the intent of the lawmakers at the time the law was passed. Several components of a legislative history are described below.

Bills

Each time the wording of a bill changes or is amended, the bill is rewritten. A legislative history includes comparing the language of the bill as it was introduced, and its amendments, to the final language of the law. The inclusion or deletion of language in these successive writings may give insight into legislative intent.

Committee Hearings

Committees are responsible for considering bills and deciding whether to recommend them for passage by the full house. To facilitate the committee's decision, hearings are often held on proposed legislation. Interested persons and experts testify for and against the proposed bill and provide useful information to committee members on the importance of the bill. Transcripts of these hearings are made and usually published. These transcripts aid in understanding why the committee adopted or did not adopt certain language in the bill.

Committee Reports

Whether or not hearings are held on the proposed bill, the committee's decision to recommend a bill for passage by the full house is contained in a committee report. This report includes the revised text of the bill, the changes

Net Results

Legislative Tracking

Many states now have legislative reference bureau web sites where it is possible to track legislation. This may be valuable for legal nurse consultants who deal with insurance or with a statutory cap on damages that is being considered by the legislature. By monitoring the legislation, and administrative regulations, legal nurse consultants are better able to assist in assessing claims that might be affected by the legislation. Access this information for each state using the uniform state law web address, www.legis.state.XX.us, where the XX is the two-letter postal abbreviation for the state being researched.

made by the committee, and the rationale for the committee's recommendation. There is a committee report from both houses if the bill has been passed. In addition, if the bill passed by one house is different from the bill passed by the other house, a **conference committee** is convened to reconcile the two versions of the bill. The report of the conference committee contains recommendations about the compromise bill.

Committee reports are usually considered the most important part of the legislative history, because they reflect the knowledge and understanding of the committee members who were most closely involved in the creation of the legislation.

Congressional Debates

After the bill has been reported out of committee, it is scheduled for consideration on the floor of each house. During the debates, amendments may be proposed and statements for and against the bill may be made. The debates are published in the *Congressional Record.*

Other Documents

The president (or governor) may send a message to the legislature concerning a particular bill, and executive agencies may file reports with the committees concerning pending legislation. These documents explain why the law is considered important in the eyes of key officials of government. In addition, when the president (or governor) signs or vetoes a bill, a statement may be made reflecting the executive's reasons for the action. This message should be included as part of the legislative history.

When the language of a statute is disputed and the court is called upon to determine the intent and impact of the statute, legislative history may be a valuable secondary source for supporting rationale in the interpretation of the law.

INDICES TO LAW

Because case law is published chronologically by date of decision, a system that allows topical access to the points of law in the published decisions is necessary. This system is provided in **legal digests** and other works that act as **indices to law.** These digests and other research aids are not authority and cannot be cited. They are finding tools for research purposes only.

Digests

Probably the quickest way to locate case law on a particular legal topic is to use the digests. Digests collect the major points of law (identified in the court opinion as editorial headnotes) and arrange them in alphabetical order under topic headings. Digests are organized like encyclopedias and are easy to use.

The *West Digest System* is generally considered the most comprehensive system for locating case law. It is organized around the Key Number system. Every case published by West is first analyzed by the editors, and then legal points are classified into one of seven categories: persons, property, contracts, torts, crimes, remedies, or government.

Each category is divided into subcategories and each subcategory is divided into topics. There are currently more than 450 topics corresponding to legal concepts in the West Key Number system. Each topic is further divided into the smallest unit of organization and assigned a Key Number. This key turns the lock and opens the door to all the published law on this point. All West publications are organized under this Key Number system; therefore the headnotes preceding a case in any of the National Reporter Series will correspond with the key in the digest for that series and with West's legal encyclopedia, *Corpus Juris Secundum*. Because of the universality of this system, researchers who have located a topic and key may turn to any West publication and find the law on that point. The Key Number system is an important feature of West Group publications.

Under each topic and key number in the West digests researchers will find abstracts (headnotes) of cases in which this point of law was discussed. These abstracts are organized by most recent case first; abstracts of federal cases appear first, then abstracts of state court cases, followed by treatments of this point of law in law review articles and other secondary sources.

Digests from other publishers are organized in similar fashion. Generally the unit of organization is a paragraph number or other indicator of a point of law under general topic headings. Once the paragraph or point of law is located, abstracts of cases in which that point of law is discussed follow.

To be certain that all of the law on a particular point has been found, researchers advise using the **descriptive word index,** a volume or series of volumes at the end of a series of digests. Because concepts may be expressed in many different ways (for example, shoplifting can be identified as retail theft, consumer theft, larceny, etc.), consulting the descriptive word index assures that alternative key terms and phrases have also been analyzed.

Digests are updated with pocket parts that contain the most current law. Once the key number or paragraph point of law is identified, the pocket part should be consulted for the most recent abstracts concerning that point of law.

Although it is of great value to have case law available on the Internet, the headnotes and abstracts used in digests are not public domain. Because these abstracts are written by the editors of the publishing house, they are copyrighted and cannot be accessed using the Internet unless the user has a subscription to WestLaw via the Internet. The Boolean searches currently available for finding case law on the Internet do not provide the precision that digests provide. Considerable time can be saved by consulting the digests.

Ethics Bookmark

Research

"The legal nurse consultant recognizes research as a methodology to further the legal nurse consultant's practice" AALNC Standards of Professional Performance Standard 7 (1995).[2] Medical and legal research are integral components of practice for legal nurse consultants. While legal nurse consultants may not be called upon to perform legal research, they may be expected to perform medical research and medical literature review, and to synthesize the results of their findings with legal principles.

Words and Phrases

Another index to law is *Words and Phrases*. Whenever a legal, or nonlegal, term or phrase is judicially defined in a court opinion, it is identified in a headnote in *Words and Phrases* published by West Group. Because it is a West publication, the Key Number system is used; this system allows researchers to locate other sources of authority on that judicial interpretation or legal definition.

Words and Phrases is arranged alphabetically and kept current by annual pocket parts. The judicial definition abstracted from the case is developed into a headnote by the editor of the publication; thus, *Words and Phrases* should not be relied upon as authority. The case in which the term was judicially defined should always be consulted and cited. *Words and Phrases* is simply a finding tool.

VALIDATING LAW

Shepard's Citations is the most well-known citator service. A **citator** traces the judicial history of the case, provides parallel citations, identifies how that case was used in later courts, and provides leads to secondary sources that have cited to that case. The process of validating a case (ensuring that it is still good law) using *Shepard's Citations* is called **Shepardizing.**

Shepardizing is critical to the success of a legal argument. A court ruling that has been overturned, reversed, or superceded by subsequent legislation is of no value. To rely on that court ruling will make the legal professional appear careless. While legal nurse consultants may not be expected to know the intricacies of verifying legal research, Shepardizing is so fundamental to the practice of law that it cannot be neglected in the vocabulary of legal tools.

Other case verification systems can be purchased via CD ROM or on the Internet. West Group offers *Key Cite,* a citation system available via a subscription to WestLaw, a computerized legal database. This system is more current than the published *Shepard's.*

COMPUTERIZED LEGAL RESEARCH

Access to legal research may be greatly expanded and simplified by using online computer services and CD ROM. This is not new to legal nurse consultants, as the same is true for medical research and online medical literature searches.

The two major online services for legal research are LEXIS and WestLaw. LEXIS was originally created by Mead Data Central, and is now owned by Little, Brown and Company. WestLaw, the legal database created and owned by West Group, is a division of Thomson Learning. Subscriptions to either (or both!) allow researchers to retrieve primary and secondary law, and factual and medical information using descriptive key terms. In addition to searching the databases by key terms, WestLaw employs an expert system that allows researchers to retrieve information by keying a question into the computer. The system automatically extracts the important terms from the question and searches the database for those terms. WestLaw has also announced plans to market a voice recognition system, which will allow researchers to retrieve documents simply by asking for them!

Legal professionals, whether or not they actually perform legal research must be familiar with law books, the tools of the trade. In addition, legal professionals must be able to recognize correct citation form and be able to identify the type of law being cited. Understanding this universal language of the law will help establish and solidify the legal nurse consultant's role in the delivery of legal services.

CHAPTER SUMMARY

- Secondary sources explain the law and may be classified as commentaries, dictionaries, Restatements, and legislative history.
- Commentaries include textbooks, treatises, legal encyclopedias, legal periodicals, looseleaf services, and textual annotations.
- Restatements are highly regarded secondary authority.
- A compiled legislative history includes different versions of a bill, committee reports, and congressional debates.
- Digests are useful for locating cases using the descriptive word index.
- *Shepard's Citations* is a system for verifying that law is still good.

What LNCs Say . . .

"Another important aspect of the LNC job is computer literacy. Many books are now available on CD ROM. Search engines on the Internet allow you to explore volumes of information. Get to know the web sites which will link you to important information. It would help to take a class on Medline searching or something equivalent to Medline, like Grateful Med" Kathy Sullivan, RN, BS, Madison, WI, used with permission.

KEY TERMS

annotation	indices to law	secondary sources
citator	legal digests	Sheparding
conference committee	legal encyclopedias	*Shepard's Citations*
descriptive word index	legislative history	treatises
hornbooks	pocket parts	

REVIEW QUESTIONS

1. List several reasons why it may be important to consult secondary sources of law?

2. What are the Restatements?
3. Why is Sheparding so important?

INTERNET EXERCISES

1. Access the web page for this textbook at *www.westlegalstudies.com*.

2. Click on the assignments section and complete the assignment(s) for Chapter Sixteen.

EXERCISES

1. Networking. Through the web site for the AALNC, legal nurse consultants have a source for networking on the Internet. Consider joining a chat group or a listserv. Develop professional contacts and maintain them in your system, file, or Rolodex.

2. Professional Portfolio. As you develop skill in legal research and use of the Internet, be certain to include these skills in your resumes and cover letters. Use the case on the web site for this textbook to conduct your own legal research. Include a copy of your research memorandum in your portfolio.

ENDNOTES

1. *Webster v. Blue Ship Tea Room,* 347 Mass. 421, 198 N.E. 2d 309 (1964).

2. American Association of Legal Nurse Consultants, *Standards of Professional Practice.* (1997) Standard 7.

ADDITIONAL REFERENCES

Bogart, J. B., RN, MN, ed. *Legal Nurse Consulting: Principles and Practice.* Boston, MA: CRC Press, 1998.

Jacobstein, J., Mersky, R., Dunn, D. *Fundamentals of Legal Research,* 7th ed. Westbury, NY: The Foundation Press, Inc., 1998.

LEGAL NURSE CONSULTANT PROFILE

James Fell

Independent Management–Corporate Defense

Photo reprinted with permission of Motophoto, Westlake, OH.

James Fell has dual bachelor's degrees in nursing and biology, dual master's degrees in nursing and business, and coursework toward a PhD. For many years prior to entering legal nurse consulting, Mr. Fell practiced as a nurse educator and nursing education administrator in Diploma, ADN, BSN, and ND programs. In addition, he serves in the Nurse Corps of the U.S. Naval Reserve where he presently holds the rank of Commander and is Officer in Charge of a fleet hospital medical detachment.

Mr. Fell began his legal nurse consulting career working part time for a medical litigation support company. In this role, he initially reviewed and summarized medical records in pharmaceutical, medical device, and toxic tort litigation. Later Mr. Fell entered the field full time and now functions as the firm's manager for corporate communications. In this capacity, Mr. Fell edits a medical legal newsletter that circulates to more than 2,600 attorneys. Articles authored by Mr. Fell have been published in a number of legal journals.

Mr. Fell has also taught legal nurse consulting and is a member of the Advisory Board for the Legal Nurse Consulting certificate program at a Cleveland, Ohio, college.

What do you like best about being a legal nurse consultant?

"Primarily, it's the variety of the work. Each case that one reviews is different. Each client has different needs. Legal nursing offers one the option to work on different types of lawsuits from the single case to a class action involving thousands of patients."

What challenges do legal nurse consultants face in your area of law?

"The most important thing that a legal nurse must remember, whether freelancing or working for a law firm or litigation support company, is that a high quality, 100% accurate work product is required by clients. The accuracy factor cannot be stressed enough. For example, the exact date of exposure to a particular toxic agent might be the critical element upon which an attorney may be structuring his/her case preparation.

"Furthermore, the legal nurse consultant's work products must not only be high quality, but must be produced at a cost reasonable to the client. Consequently, while 100% accuracy is essential, work products need to be completed within budgeted timeframes."

What advice would you give nurses who are interested in legal nurse consulting?

"First of all, a nurse must not rely on basic nursing education alone to prepare for entering the legal nurse consulting field. I believe that the best foundation can be attained through a multi-semester, college-based program incorporating coursework in medical legal research, torts and evidence, basic legal theory, business development and marketing, and, most importantly, a practicum in a law firm.

"Secondly, nurses interested in legal nursing should understand up front that this is a highly competitive field. It is the fortunate nurse who lands a job in a law firm where he/she will be mentored. I know of instances where legal nurse openings in law firms will generate fifty or sixty resumes from nurses. As a result, many nurses resort to freelance legal nurse consulting, with widely varying degrees of success.

"Involvement at both the national and local level of the American Association of Legal Nurse Consultants is one way for a beginning legal nurse to test the waters. Peers can be a valuable resource regarding jobs, salaries, etc., at the local level as one seeks to overcome barriers to entry into practice. Many times jobs in legal nurse consulting are not advertised. Nurses frequently obtain these positions through networking."

What unique marketing strategy are you willing to share?

"Without a doubt, it is writing for publication in the specialty legal journals. While it takes time to author a good article, it is excellent marketing and establishes one's expertise in the field."

"I believe that the best foundation can be attained through a multi-semester, college-based program incorporating coursework in medical legal research, torts and evidence, basic legal theory, business development and marketing, and, most importantly, a practicum in a law firm."

CASE STUDY

Keeth v. State Department of Public Safety and Transportation, 618 So. 2d 1154 (1993)

The following case involves a legal nurse consultant. As you read through the court opinion, consider the following questions and activities:

- Was this a civil or criminal matter? Explain.
- What role did the legal nurse consultant play in resolution of this matter?
- What credentials, experience, and education qualified the legal nurse consultant to play a role in resolution of this matter?
- What controversy, if any, existed concerning the legal nurse consultant's testimony?
- Consider briefing this case using any of the methods described in Chapter Twelve.

(Cite as: 618 So.2d 1154)

Buddy KEETH, et ux., Plaintiffs-Appellants,
v.
STATE of Louisiana, Through the DEPARTMENT OF PUBLIC SAFETY AND TRANSPORTATION,
Defendants-Appellees.
No. 24,720-CA.
Court of Appeal of Louisiana,
Second Circuit.
May 5, 1993.
Application Dismissed June 18, 1993.

SEXTON, Judge.

Plaintiff, Buddy Keeth, appeals the trial court's judgment rendered in his favor which found him 25 percent at fault and allegedly awarded him inadequate damages for personal injuries he received in an automobile accident caused by the defendants, Louisiana State Trooper James Pepper and the state of Louisiana, through the Department of Public Safety and Corrections. We reverse in part, amend in part, and affirm as amended.

FACTS

On November 20, 1990, at approximately 1:00 P.M., Louisiana State Trooper James Pepper was traveling from Homer to Shreveport on U.S. Highway 79 South. He was flagged down by Jeff Taylor, who wanted to talk to him about a traffic matter. The officer then proceeded to make a U-turn and he parked his car on the shoulder of U.S. Highway 79 North where Taylor was also parked on the shoulder of the road.

Meanwhile, Buddy Keeth was traveling at a speed of 55 miles per hour on U.S. Highway 79 South. As he crested and topped the hill approximately seven miles ***1158**

(Cite as: 618 So.2d 1154, *1158)

south of Homer, Mr. Keeth saw the trooper's car parked on the northbound shoulder of the roadway some 400 to 500 feet away. At that point, U.S. Highway 79 has two southbound lanes and one northbound lane. Mr. Keeth was driving in the inside lane, which is the lane closest to the northbound lane and the lane for ordinary traffic.

When Mr. Keeth was approximately 150 feet away, the state trooper's car suddenly pulled into the northbound lane of traffic and started to make a U-turn. Mr. Keeth immediately applied his brakes, but he was unable to avoid the collision. The accident occurred in the inside southbound lane as Mr. Keeth's vehicle slammed broadside into the passenger side of the state trooper's vehicle.

Officer Pepper testified that before he pulled back onto the road, he glanced in his rearview mirror and saw a northbound 18-wheel truck approximately 500 yards back. Officer Pepper then glanced ahead and saw no traffic approaching in the southbound direction. He looked back into his rearview mirror to check the 18-wheel truck again, and then proceeded out onto the highway and made his U-turn. Officer Pepper first noticed plaintiff's vehicle when he heard the brakes and tires squealing.

Mr. Keeth sustained multiple injuries from the accident. He was hospitalized at Schumpert Medical Center from November 20, 1990, until January 25, 1991, 28 days of which were spent in the intensive care unit. Mr. Keeth was later hospitalized again for surgery to his shoulder. Mr. Keeth has undergone substantial rehabilitation and physical therapy since being released from the hospital.

continued

Keeth v. State   *continued*

Mr. Keeth and his wife, Brenda, subsequently filed suit for damages against Officer Pepper and the state of Louisiana, through the Department of Public Safety and Corrections. On June 25, 1992, after a trial on the merits, the trial court found that Officer Pepper was negligent in not making sure the way was clear before commencing his U-turn and that the plaintiff was negligent in not maintaining control of his vehicle in order to stop before the collision or to take evasive action to avoid the collision. Officer Pepper and the state of Louisiana were assessed 75 percent of the fault and plaintiff was assessed the other 25 percent. The trial court awarded the following damages to Buddy Keeth:

1) Past and future medical expenses $255,000
2) Past and future physical pain, suffering, mental anguish, disability,
   enjoyment of life and disfigurement $250,000
3) Loss of wages: past and future...$225,000

Any other demands by the plaintiff were denied. Brenda Keeth was awarded $5,000 for loss of consortium and $3,200 for loss of earnings. A final judgment was signed on July 10, 1992, and it is from this judgment that plaintiff now appeals.

COMPARATIVE NEGLIGENCE

[1] On appeal, plaintiff contends the trial court erred in assessing him 25 percent fault. Plaintiff contends the sudden emergency doctrine should apply in the instant case, and he should not be faulted for applying his brakes instead of taking another course of conduct to avoid the accident. Defendants assert that Mr. Keeth had the last clear chance to avoid the collision and he failed to take any action other than jamming on his brakes. Defendants also contend that plaintiff failed to mitigate his damages because he was not wearing his shoulder seat belt when the accident occurred. Accordingly, defendants contend that plaintiff should be assessed a higher percentage of fault.

***1159**

(Cite as: 618 So.2d 1154, *1159)

[2][3][4] Contributory negligence is conduct on the part of the plaintiff which falls below the standard to which he should conform for his own safety and protection, that standard being that of a reasonable man under like circumstances. *Harris v. Pineset, 499 So.2d 499 (La.App.2d Cir.1986),* writs denied, *502 So.2d 114 (La.1987), and 502 So.2d 117 (La.1987).* LSA-C.C. Art. 2323 provides that a plaintiff whose negligence contributes to his own injuries for which he seeks damages shall have his claim reduced in proportion to his degree of fault. The determination and apportionment of fault are factual matters, and the trial court's findings in this regard should not be disturbed by a reviewing court unless they are erroneous. *Baugh v. Redmond, 565 So.2d 953 (La.App. 2d Cir.1990).*
[5] In assessing comparative fault, the trial court must consider the nature of each party's conduct and the extent of the causal relationship between the conduct and the damages claimed. Relevant factors concerning the nature of each party's conduct include: (1) whether the conduct resulted from inadvertence or involved an awareness of the danger; (2) how great a risk was created by the conduct; (3) the significance of what was sought by the conduct; (4) the capacities of the actor, whether superior

or inferior; and (5) any extenuating circumstances which might require the actor to proceed in haste, without proper thought. *Watson v. State Farm Fire and Casualty Insurance Co., 469 So.2d 967 (La.1985).* The record evidence in the instant case reveals that on November 20, 1990, Buddy Keeth was traveling at 55 miles per hour in his proper lane of travel on U.S. Highway 79 South. As he crested the hill approximately seven miles south of Homer, Mr. Keeth noticed two vehicles parked on the opposite shoulder of the road approximately 500 feet away. When Mr. Keeth was approximately 150 feet away from the vehicles, the state trooper's vehicle, without warning and unexpectedly, started to make a U-turn and block plaintiff's lane of traffic. Mr. Keeth immediately applied his brakes, but he was unable to avoid hitting the state trooper's vehicle.

[6][7] Under the doctrine of sudden emergency, a motorist without sufficient time to weigh all the circumstances and whose actions did not contribute to the emergency cannot be assessed with negligence if a subsequent review of the facts discloses he may have adopted a safer, more prudent, course of conduct to avoid an impending accident.

Hickman v. Southern Pacific Transport Co., 262 La. 102, 262 So.2d 385 (1972); Finley v. Bass, 478 So.2d 608 (La.App. 2d Cir. 1985); Jaffarzad v. Jones Truck Lines, Inc., 561 So.2d 144 (La.App. 3rd Cir.1990), writ denied, *565 So.2d 450 (La.1990).* Elements of a sudden emergency include a position of imminent peril; insufficient time to consider the circumstances and weigh alternatives; and the situation is not created by the driver's own negligence.

Ketchens v. Jones, 533 So.2d 127 (La.App. 4th Cir.1988).

[8][9] We find the sudden emergency doctrine applicable in the instant case. It is apparent that Buddy Keeth found himself in a position of imminent peril when the state trooper's vehicle suddenly started to make a U-turn when plaintiff was only 150 feet away. At 55 miles per hour, Mr. Keeth was traveling at a rate of 81 feet per second and therefore had less than two seconds to react once the state trooper turned into his lane. Although Mr. Keeth may have adopted a more prudent course of conduct to avoid the accident, such as swerving his vehicle to the right or left, it is clear that Mr. Keeth did not have sufficient time to consider these alternative courses of action. Mr. Keeth acted in a reasonable and prudent manner to avoid the collision by applying his brakes. This emergency situation was created entirely by the negligence of Officer Pepper. Therefore, the finding by the trial court that Buddy Keeth was at fault was clearly erroneous. We would also note that the failure to wear a seat belt should not be considered evidence of comparative negligence. *LSA-R.S. 32:295.1* E. Accordingly, the judgment of the trial court finding plaintiff 25 percent at fault will be reversed, ***1160***

(Cite as: 618 So.2d 1154, *1160)

and the defendants will be cast with 100 percent fault for the accident.

GENERAL DAMAGES

In the next assignment of error, plaintiff contends the trial court erred by awarding inadequate damages. Plaintiff contends that his general damage award

(Cite as: 618 So.2d 1154, *1160)

was below discretion in view of his devastating injuries. Defendants allege the trial court awarded an excessive sum for damages since all of the plaintiff's injuries have healed.

[10] General damages are those which may not be fixed with pecuniary exactitude. They instead involve mental or physical pain or suffering, inconvenience, the loss of intellectual gratification or physical enjoyment, or other losses of life or life-style which cannot be definitively measured in

continued

Keeth v. State   *continued*

monetary terms. *Anderson v. Bennett Wood Fabricators, 571 So.2d 780 (La.App. 2d Cir.1990)*, writ denied, *573 So.2d 1135 (La.1991)*.

[11][12] The assessment of monetary damages is discretionary with the trial court, and a judgment cannot be disturbed by a reviewing court absent a clear showing of abuse of discretion. The determination of whether the trial court abused its discretion in assessing damages must be based upon the peculiar facts of each case and with due regard for the fact that the trial court is in the best position to evaluate the credibility of the witnesses, including their testimony about the nature and extent of their injuries. It is only after an articulated analysis of the facts and circumstances peculiar to the case and the individual that a reviewing court may determine that an award is inadequate or excessive. *Lloyd v. TG & Y Stores Company, 556 So.2d 629 (La.App. 2d Cir.1990)*.

[13][14][15] The question for the appellate court is not whether a different award may have been more appropriate, but rather whether the trial court's award can be reasonably supported by the record. In testing whether the trial court abused its discretion by making an inadequate award, the evidence must be viewed in the light most favorable to the defendant. The appellate court must first reach a determination that the trial court abused its discretion before resort to prior awards is appropriate for purposes of determining what would then be an appropriate award. *Red v. Taravella, 530 So.2d 1186 (La.App. 2d Cir.1988)*.

[16] In assessing the plaintiff's award for general damages, we have considered the following factors. Through the testimony of Drs. Lloyd Whitley, Edward Anglin, and Eric Bicknell, plaintiff proved that he sustained the following injuries from the accident:

1) A fractured socket of the left hip;
2) A badly fractured right knee;
3) A fractured left shoulder;
4) Adhesive capsulitis in the right shoulder from extended immobility during overall treatment;
5) Facial lacerations;
6) Various abrasions and contusions;
7) Aggravation of existing neuropathy (a nerve disease which plaintiff suffered as a result of his diabetes).

Immediately following the accident, plaintiff was obviously in substantial pain. He was hospitalized from November 20, 1990, until January 25, 1991, 28 days of which were spent in the intensive care unit. Dr. Anglin performed surgery on plaintiff's right shoulder in August 1991 to correct the adhesive capsulitis caused by plaintiff's lengthy hospital stay. Dr. Anglin also testified that plaintiff will suffer severe arthritis in his left hip and right knee because of injuries received from the accident. Dr. Bicknell testified that the accident aggravated plaintiff's peripheral neuropathy condition and that plaintiff would now experience stiffness in his right hand.

Dr. Anglin and Dr. Bicknell also testified that plaintiff will have certain limitations in the future because of injuries received from the accident. Plaintiff will have difficulty getting in and out of vehicles or sitting in a vehicle for any length of time. ***1161**

(Cite as: 618 So.2d 1154, *1161)

Plaintiff will also have difficulty climbing stairs, standing on his feet for any significant period of time, and writing. Plaintiff testified that since the accident, he has been forced to abandon certain hobbies, such as riding horses and hunting. Plaintiff testified that he cannot play with his grandchildren like he used to. Plaintiff also stated that he is not physically able to travel long distances or attend church regularly.

In applying the standard of review noted above and having considered all the particular facts and circumstances in this case, we conclude that the general damage award of $250,000, while perhaps low, is not an abuse of discretion. This award is affirmed.

PAST AND FUTURE MEDICAL EXPENSES

Plaintiff contends that the trial court's award for past and future medical expenses was inadequate. Plaintiff asserts that Dr. Anglin's testimony indicates that plaintiff will need hip replacement surgery, knee replacement surgery, and right shoulder surgery in the future. Plaintiff points out that Dr. Bicknell testified that plaintiff would need future nerve conduction studies along with physical therapy. Plaintiff also contends he should be reimbursed for future medication expenses and future travel expenses. Therefore, plaintiff contends he is entitled to approximately $83,000 in future medical expenses. Defendants contend that plaintiff should not have received anything for future medical care. Defendants contend the doctors' testimony about plaintiff's future medical expenses is unreliable speculation without any objective medical findings. Therefore, defendants contend plaintiff is not entitled to an award for such alleged damages.

[17][18] An award for future medical expenses is in great measure highly speculative and not susceptible of calculation with mathematical certainty. However, like any other element of damages, future medical expenses must be established with some degree of certainty. Awards will not be made for future medical expenses which may or may not occur in the absence of medical testimony that they are indicated and setting out their probable costs.

Hunt v. Board of Supervisors of Louisiana State University, 522 So.2d 1144 (La.App. 2d Cir.1988).

[19] In the instant case, the trial court awarded plaintiff damages of $255,000 for past and future medical expenses. Exhibit P-21, which was entered into evidence without objection, sets forth plaintiff's medical expenses prior to trial. These expenses totaled $187,983.78. Although the trial court failed to detail its calculations, it appears that it awarded plaintiff approximately $67,000 for future medical expenses.

Our review of the record establishes the probability that plaintiff will need future medical care and was therefore entitled to an award for future medical expenses. Dr. Anglin testified that plaintiff would develop severe arthritis in his left hip and right knee. Because of this fact, Dr. Anglin stated it was more probable than not that plaintiff would need knee replacement surgery and hip replacement surgery in the future. Dr. Anglin also testified there was a greater than 50 percent chance that plaintiff would need additional surgery on his right shoulder. Dr. Bicknell testified that it was more likely than not that plaintiff would need several more nerve conduction studies along with periods of physical therapy.

As to the expense for each of these future medical procedures, each doctor suggested a possible cost range for each procedure. Ms. Glenda Dessommes, a ←**legal nurse consultant,**→ also testified regarding the average expected hospital, anesthesia, physical therapy, and medication expenses that plaintiff would encounter for his future medical procedures. After evaluating all of the factors in this record relating to the future medical expenses, we find the trial court's award of $67,000 for future medical expenses is within the lower range of estimated costs for these procedures and was not an abuse of the trial court's discretion. ***1162**

(Cite as: 618 So.2d 1154, *1162)

This assignment of error has no merit.

continued

Keeth v. State   *continued*

LOSS OF EARNINGS

Plaintiff contends that his $225,000 award for loss of earnings, past and future, was less than half of that projected by the undisputed testimony of Dr. Melvin Harju, an expert in finance, economics, and valuation of economic loss. Plaintiff asserts that the very lowest figure the trial court could have awarded was $400,000. Defendants allege that plaintiff should not have received an award for future wages since there was no showing of permanent disability. Defendants contend that Dr. Harju's report is not valid since it did not consider plaintiff's actual income as reflected in his tax returns for

(Cite as: 618 So.2d 1154, *1162)

the years 1988, 1989, and 1990. Defendants also contend that the financial information provided by the plaintiff's expert was highly speculative and unrealistic.

[20] Awards for loss of future income are inherently speculative and are intrinsically insusceptible of being calculated with mathematical certainty. Thus, the courts must exercise sound judicial discretion in determining these awards and render awards which are consistent with the record and which work an injustice on neither party.
Anderson v. Bennett Wood Fabricators, supra.

[21][22] The factors to be considered in determining loss of future income include the plaintiff's physical condition before and after his injury; his past work record and the consistency thereof; the amount the plaintiff probably would have earned absent the injury complained of; and the probability he would have continued to earn wages over the balance of his working life. A loss of future income award is not predicated upon the difference between the plaintiff's earnings before and after a disabling injury. Such an award is predicated, more strictly considered, upon the difference between the plaintiff's earning capacity before and after a disabling injury. *Anderson v. Bennett Wood Fabricators, supra.*

[23] In computing loss of future income, it is first necessary to determine whether and for how long a plaintiff's disability will prevent him from engaging in work of the same or similar kind that he was doing at the time of his injury. It is also necessary to ascertain whether he has been disabled from work for which he is fitted by training and experience. *Hunt v. Board of Supervisors of Louisiana State University, supra.*

[24] A review of the record indicates the injuries plaintiff received from the accident will prevent him from returning to work as a district manager for American Family Life Assurance Company (AFLAC). Dr. Richard H. Galloway, an expert in vocational disability and limitations, testified that plaintiff would not be able to engage in any substantial, gainful activity after the accident. Plaintiff also testified that he could not return to work. As previously mentioned, plaintiff has difficulty getting into and out of vehicles and he is unable to sit for any length of time. This, of course, prevents him from traveling to see clients. Plaintiff is also unable to write for any appreciable length of time, thus he is unable to fill out sales reports.

Plaintiff had been employed at AFLAC for six months and had been a district manager for only five days prior to the accident. In order to establish his projected loss of income, plaintiff presented the testimony of Alfred Kyle and Dr. Melvin Harju. Mr. Kyle, regional sales coordinator for AFLAC, used his 11 years experience with the company to project what plaintiff's income might have been for two years as a district manager. These projections were based upon the commissions plaintiff would make from his own personal production along with commissions he would receive from sales made by agents under his authority. Dr. Harju's calculations simply carried forward Mr. Kyle's projections for plaintiff's expected work life and provided for no productivity increases. Dr. Harju projected future lost earnings totaling $532,764.

Mr. Kyle testified that plaintiff's actual sales record was not reflected in the income *1163

(Cite as: 618 So.2d 1154, *1163)

projections which he made. Rather, these income projections were based on what he thought plaintiff was capable of selling. Mr. Kyle's projections of sales of $2,000 per week by plaintiff was, of course, speculative as plaintiff had only served as AFLAC district manager for a brief period. Plaintiff's actual income in the three years prior to the accident, as reflected by his income tax returns, was substantially lower than that projected for him as a district manager for AFLAC. Neither Mr. Kyle nor Dr. Harju considered plaintiff's previous income history as a car salesman or an insurance salesman when making their projections.

At the time of the accident, plaintiff had a life work expectancy of 8.5 years. Although plaintiff's income the prior three years was low, plaintiff had increased his earning capacity by going to work for AFLAC as a district manager. It is difficult to calculate plaintiff's projected loss of earnings, since he had only been employed in his new position as a district manager for five days. When all factors are considered, we find no abuse of discretion in the trial court's award of $225,000 for future loss of wages.

(Cite as: 618 So.2d 1154, *1163)

MRS. KEETH'S DAMAGES

Plaintiff contends the trial court's monetary award to Brenda Keeth, plaintiff's wife, was inadequate. Through the testimony of Brenda Keeth and her work supervisor, Mr. Scott, plaintiff contends that Mrs. Keeth should have been awarded $4,692.25 for missing work to be with her husband instead of the $3,200.00 awarded by the trial court. Plaintiff also asserts the trial court should have awarded Mrs. Keeth more than $5,000.00 for her loss of consortium claim.

[25] One may recover loss of earnings for attending to an injured spouse. *Mays v. American Indemnity Company*, 365 So.2d 279 (La.App. 2d Cir.1978), writ denied, 367 So.2d 392 (La.1979). Also, see *Nichols v. Hodges*, 385 So.2d 298 (La.App. 1st Cir.1980), writ denied, 386 So.2d 355 (La.1980). In the instant case, plaintiff clearly proved through the testimony of her supervisor, Mr. Scott, that Mrs. Keeth took five sick days and a four-month leave of absence in order to care for her seriously injured husband. Accordingly, we find the trial court erred in awarding $3,200.00 for Mrs. Keeth's loss of wages, when she showed a loss of $4,692.25. We will amend to so reflect.

[26] A claim for loss of consortium is broken down into several components including loss of: (1) love and affection, (2) society and companionship, (3) sexual relations, (4) the right of performance of material services, (5) the right of support from her husband, (6) aid and assistance, and (7) loss of felicity. Proof of any of these elements is sufficient for an award for loss of consortium. *Finley v. Bass, supra.* Mrs. Keeth testified that she visited the hospital every day after the accident and observed her husband in substantial pain. During this period, Mrs. Keeth obviously could not experience the same kind of love, companionship, affection, society, and comfort to which she was accustomed. Mrs. Keeth testified she had to fix her husband's meals, help him bathe, and help him dress for several months after he was released from the hospital. She testified that she and her husband were unable to have sexual relations for three months after the accident. Mrs. Keeth also stated that her sexual relationship with her husband has been significantly diminished since his accident. This fact was corroborated by

continued

Keeth v. State   *continued*

the testimony of the plaintiff. Mr. Keeth was also unable to support his wife since he cannot return to work. Finally, Mrs. Keeth testified that her husband is unable to ride horses, attend church, or play with his grandchildren like he used to.

[27][28] A judge or jury has much discretion in assessing damages in cases of offenses and quasi-offenses. *LSA-C.C. Art. 2324.1.* After finding that the lower court abused its discretion, the appellate court may raise (or lower) an award of damages to the lowest (or highest) point which is reasonably within the discretion afforded that court. *Coco v. Winston Industries, Inc., 341 So.2d 332 (La.1976);* ***1164**

(Cite as: 618 So.2d 1154, *1164)

Clark v. Ark-La-Tex Auction, Inc., 593 So.2d 870 (La.App. 2d Cir.1992), writ denied, *596 So.2d 210 (La.1992).*

[29] Based upon the foregoing, we conclude the trial court abused its discretion in awarding only $5,000.00 to Mrs. Keeth for loss of consortium. It is clear from the record that Mrs. Keeth's life-style was severely affected following the accident and she suffered a significant loss of love, companionship, affection, and sexual relations. A review of the jurisprudence, *Thomas v. Petrolane Gas Service Ltd. Partnership, 588 So.2d 711 (La.App. 2d Cir.1991); Peterson v. Western World Insurance Company, 536 So.2d 639 (La.App. 1st Cir.1988),* writ denied, *541 So.2d 858 (La.1989); Jaffarzad v. Jones Truck Lines, Inc., supra,* leads us to believe that the lowest loss of consortium award appropriate under the circumstances of this case is $8,500.00. Accordingly, the trial court's award to Mrs. Keeth will be amended to reflect $8,500.00 for loss of consortium.

DECREE

For the reasons assigned, the judgment of the trial court holding plaintiff 25 percent at fault is reversed and the defendants are recast with 100 percent fault. The trial court's awards to Mr. Keeth for general damages, past and future medical expenses, and loss of wages are affirmed. The trial court's award to Mrs. Keeth is amended to award her $13,192.25. All costs in this cause are assessed to the state insofar as the law allows, as may be determined by dollar amount hereinafter by the trial court. *LSA-R.S. 13:5112.*

REVERSED IN PART, AMENDED IN PART, AND AFFIRMED AS AMENDED.

END OF DOCUMENT

PERSONAL INJURY LAW

Legal nurse consultants are used primarily in personal injury law. There are many facets to this area of law and it comprises the greatest portion of this text. In this unit, you will find answers to these questions:

- What is a tort?

- How are torts classified?

- What is a class action lawsuit?

- How does the law of evidence work?

- What is involved in civil procedure?

- What is the role of the legal nurse consultant in personal injury litigation?

CHAPTER 17

INTRODUCTION TO TORT LAW

OBJECTIVES

In this chapter, you will learn

- a definition of tort
- the sources of tort law
- how torts are classified
- the basis for tort liability

OVERVIEW

The legal term **tort** comes from the Latin word *tortus,* which means to twist or to turn.[1] It may have evolved to include private wrongs in the sense that a person's plans or life's goals are twisted or turned by the wrongful act of another. Today a tort is defined as "a private wrong (other than a breach of contract) committed by one person (the **tortfeasor**) that injures another's (the victim's) person and/or property, for which the law allows the legal remedy of monetary damages."[2] Two or more persons acting together to cause harm to another are considered **joint tortfeasors.**

There are three distinct parts to the definition of a tort. First, it must be wrong. Second, it must cause injury. Third, it must be capable of judicial remedy. All three must be present for an action to constitute a tort. People are often negligent—failing to signal a lane change, exceeding the speed limit, and so forth. It is a failure of reasonable care to neglect to signal a lane change or exceed the speed limit. But unless that failure of care causes injury (some harm must occur) and the injured party sues, the action (or failure to act) does not take on the character of a tort for legal purposes.

CLASSIFICATION OF TORTS

In tort law, a distinction is made between conduct that is deliberate and conduct that is inadvertent or careless. That distinction results in a system for classifying wrongful conduct. **Intentional torts** are actions that are deliberate. **Negligent** torts (unintentional torts) are actions that are simply lacking in reasonable care. There are circumstances in which an actor will be liable even though the conduct was unintentional and all reasonable precautions were taken to protect others from harm. **Strict liability** in tort occurs when the nature of the activity (or product or thing) is so inherently dangerous to life and health that liability results, regardless of due care or lack of intent. Figure 17-1 provides examples of each of these classifications of torts.

In reality, torts and the lawsuits that result are seldom as simple as the examples provided in textbooks. While often it seems that there can be no disputable fact, the law allows for valid argument on both sides. For study purposes, the law is discussed as if few or very clear divergent views exist. But in reality there is no such thing as "black letter law," (universally accepted legal principles) with no confusing shades of gray. The circumstances will always control whether or not the law is called into play.

SOURCES OF TORT LAW

Tort law has its origins in judge-made law or common law. From the earliest recordings of history, it is clear that injured parties took their claims to a judge who ruled on whether or not another party was responsible for the in-

---

FIGURE 17-1 Examples of How Torts are Classified

Intentional Tort	Negligence	Strict Liability
A pointed a pistol at *B* and shot *B* in the chest.	*A* pointed a pistol into the air and fired. The shot hit *B* in the leg. *A* did not know that *B* was sitting in a tree.	*A* pointed a new pistol at the target of a firing range. The pistol misfired due to defective design and seriously injured *A*
A's action was deliberate; the purpose was to bring about the injury to *B*.	Without knowledge that *B* was in the tree, *A*'s conduct is merely negligent; it was not intended to cause harm to a particular person.	A firearm is inherently dangerous. The manufacturer of a defectively designed firearm is strictly liable for injuries resulting from the use of that product.

---

juries. Today, the foundation for tort law is still most frequently found in case law (common law), although there are statutes that provide for civil remedy in certain wrongful situations.

One of the most useful tools in understanding tort law is a state's pattern **jury instructions.** Jury instructions are guidelines that the judge reads to a jury before the jury is excused for deliberations. The jury instructions explain the law and identify what must be proved to establish liability. Whenever a tort action is brought to a law firm, the jury instructions provide a basis for drafting the complaint, for guiding the investigation, and for developing the evidence. Because the jury instructions are based on the case law in that state and usually include footnotes to primary authority, they are excellent sources for finding the law on that particular tort.

TORT LIABILITY

In order to hold a person liable for wrongs that cause harm to another, that person must have acted of his or her own free will. A person who is coerced with physical violence or threats of physical violence may not be held accountable for causing harm to another. For example, a passenger in a taxi suddenly puts a gun to the driver's head and demands that the driver run a stoplight. The driver does as told and runs the stoplight. As a result of the driver's failing to stop at the stoplight, someone is injured. The injured party can sue the taxi driver, but a reasonable jury will find that the driver is not at fault for the injuries, because the driver was not acting of his or her own volition.

In addition to tort liability being based on the volitional act of the wrongful party, the actor must be capable of understanding the consequences of his or her wrongful act. Mentally incompetent persons and minors are held to a

Net Results

Medical Malpractice and Health Care Liability

There are several sources on the Internet for researching and keeping up to date on the torts that comprise the area of medical malpractice and health care liability. A look at www.mcandl.com/ introduction.html will provide links to state medical malpractice laws; www.lectlaw.com/tmed. html will provide information about handling medical malpractice cases and the use of experts.

standard of care that is reasonable based on their age, level of education, experience, and intelligence. Children are held to the reasonable standard of children of similar age, education, and experience. However, there is case law to support an adult standard of care when children are engaged in hazardous activities generally reserved for adults (such as snowmobiling).[3]

There is almost always a discussion about the concept of intent or the lack of intent in court opinions involving tort law. For intent to exist, the conduct must be directed at an identifiable party (although injury may occur to someone else) with the substantial certainty that the conduct will harm that person. **Intent** for purposes of tort law is different from intent in criminal matters. In criminal matters the intent must be clearly unlawful, and the conduct must be done for the purpose of harming another or another's property. The definition of intent in tort is not as strict. Criminal intent and the intent to harm need not be proven, although criminal intent will generally result in civil liability. Recall the example of a person who pulls the chair out from under someone else. The purpose of the act is a practical joke. It is reasonably certain that the person whose chair is pulled out will fall on the floor (bodily contact). However no harm is intended. This will not result in a criminal charge of battery, but it would involve sufficient intent to result in liability for the tort of battery or the tort of assault and battery.

For liability to exist in intentional torts, the state of mind must be such that the actor knows with reasonable certainty that the conduct, directed toward another, will result in an invasion of that person's rights. In negligence, however, the state of mind is unimportant. Rather, the standard of conduct is the basis for the cause of action. Whenever conduct falls below a reasonable standard, and it is foreseeable that injury may result from that substandard conduct, liability will result for injury that does occur. In actions in negligence, the conduct is not directed toward a specific person. For example, a student remains in the library after the library closes. The security officer, without checking to determine whether anyone remains in the room, locks the library, imprisoning the student. This conduct would not result in the intentional tort of false imprisonment because the guard did not direct or intend imprisonment of the student. The officer's conduct would constitute negligence—the failure of care in inspecting the premises for remaining students. If the security officer actually knew that a student remained in the library and knew that locking the door would imprison that student, the requisite state of mind for the intentional tort of false imprisonment would exist. Without that knowledge, the officer's conduct is merely negligent.

In the area of strict liability, intent or failure of care need not be proven. In fact, in cases of strict liability, it is only necessary to prove that the activity or the product was unreasonably dangerous. For example, blasting with dynamite is an unreasonably dangerous activity. Regardless of the lack of intent to harm and regardless of the safety precautions, warnings, and care exercised to ensure that no one is harmed, liability will still attach to the actor when someone is injured as a result of the dynamite blasting.

Torts may invade the person, the property, or the peace of mind and dignity of the victim. Torts against the person include assault, battery, and false imprisonment. Torts against property include trespass and conversion. Torts against peace of mind and dignity include slander, libel, and intentional infliction of emotional distress. Regardless of the interests that are invaded, there must be a cause and effect relationship between the wrongful conduct and the harm that results. This is often described as **proximate cause.** A causal relationship must be established in the complaint, and it must be proven with the evidence.

Proximate cause is a matter of public policy and has been referred to as the limit of liability that is placed on the defendant for the consequences of the defendant's conduct.[4] Consequences that are directly related to the wrongful conduct are, of course, compensable. There are also times when the injury suffered is severe enough for the courts to require the defendant to be responsible. The unfairness of the burden on an innocent plaintiff requires the court to demand that the wrongful defendant bear the cost of plaintiff's injuries. In other circumstances, the courts are unwilling to trace a chain of events beyond a certain point. The classic discussion on proximate cause is the one used in *Palsgraf v. Long Island Railroad.*[5] In *Palsgraf,* the court described a situation in which a car fails to stop at a stop sign and crashes into an unmarked truck containing dynamite. The resulting explosion causes death to the parties involved in the crash and property damage to the surrounding buildings. Several blocks away, the sound of the explosion startles a nanny who drops a baby and the baby is injured. At what point will the court draw the line of liability?

This example illustrates the public policy behind the legal concept of proximate cause. Certainly all the harm described was *caused* by the driver of the car that ran the stop sign. The foreseeable harm that makes this action (running a stop sign) negligent is property damage to other vehicles and personal injury to other drivers and possibly pedestrians. The exploding truck was an unforeseeable consequence of the driver's wrongful conduct. Still, this devastating harm would not have occurred had the driver who ran the stop sign been operating the vehicle with reasonable care. The courts will demand that the driver answer for the death of the other driver and the property damage related to the explosion. The court in *Palsgraf* found that it was a matter of public policy to draw the line of liability at that point. The baby who is dropped and harmed because the nanny is startled by the blast would be too remote to result in liability. The cause of the injury is clear (the explosion caused by the driver who ran the stop sign), but public policy and reason suggest that to carry defendant's liability to the injury of the child would potentially create liability in any situation where unexpected noise occurs. This would not be in the public interest.

REMEDIES IN TORT

Damages are generally the expected result in a lawsuit based on tortous conduct. **Compensatory damages** are intended to "make the plaintiff whole." It is, of course, impossible to make the plaintiff whole, but requiring the defendant to bear the cost of the harmful consequences of the wrongful act is the human attempt to right the wrong. For a more thorough discussion on compensatory damages, see Chapter Seven.

In addition to compensatory damages, **punitive damages** may be awarded in situations where the conduct of the defendant has been in reckless disregard of the plaintiff's rights or where the conduct is so outrageous or reprehensible that additional damages are warranted as punishment. Punitive damages are also called **exemplary damages,** as the court attempts to make an example of this defendant so the conduct will not reoccur. Punitive damages have nothing to do with the pain or suffering of the plaintiff. Punitive damages are entirely dependent on the spiteful or reckless nature of the defendant's conduct. For a more complete discussion of punitive damages, please refer to Chapter Seven.

In addition to damages, there are torts that will allow for **equitable remedies.** The most frequently used equitable remedy in tort law is the **injunction.** For example, to prevent the continued trespass onto the land of another, an injunction might be ordered preventing this invasion. Similarly, a person who has been defamed by an untrue statement carelessly published in a newsletter may request a remedy in which the publisher makes a public retraction of the untrue statement.

LEGAL ANALYSIS OF TORTS

Whenever a tort claim is brought to a legal office, whether that claim involves personal injury, property damage, invasion of privacy or dignity rights, the legal professionals are required to thoroughly examine the facts and the law to determine whether a lawsuit is justifiable. To properly examine the claim, the following questions need to be asked and answered:

- Who has been injured?
- Who caused the injury?
- What injuries occurred?
- Who is responsible for compensating the injured party for those injuries?

Legal analysis skills provide legal professionals with a framework for determining which causes of action may be pursued based on the person injured, the injuries incurred, the cause of the injuries, and the party responsible. Applying tort law to specific facts requires a general knowledge of tort theory.

Each tort has unique **elements** (parts that must be proven in order to establish liability). The starting point in evaluating any claim is to identify the elements of the rule of law that comprises the tort. The facts of the claim must be investigated and must be matched with the elements of the tort to see if those elements are met with the evidence. If the elements are met, the tort has been committed, and the injured party is entitled to bring an action in court to recover damages. For a more complete discussion of legal analysis, see Chapter Nine.

CHAPTER SUMMARY

- Torts are private wrongs that result in harm and for which legal action may be brought.
- The three classifications of torts are: intentional torts, negligence, and strict liability in tort.
- Case law is the primary source for tort law, although statutes may provide for civil remedies.
- For tort liability to exist, the defendant's conduct must be volitional and there must be a cause and effect relationship between the wrongful act and the harm suffered.
- Proximate cause refers to the legal limit of consequences the defendant will be liable for.
- Legal remedies include compensatory and punitive damages and in some cases equitable remedies.

KEY TERMS

compensatory damages
damages
elements
equitable remedies
exemplary damages
injunction

intent
intentional tort
joint tortfeasor
jury instructions
negligence
proximate cause

punitive damages
strict liability
tort
tortfeasor

REVIEW QUESTIONS

1. Compare and contrast the three classifications of torts.
2. How is intent in tort different from criminal intent?
3. What is meant by proximate cause?

INTERNET EXERCISES

1. Access the web page for this textbook at *www.westlegalstudies.com.*
2. Click on the assignments section and complete the assignment(s) for Chapter Seventeen.

EXERCISES

1. Networking. Contact one of the judges who serves your local county court. Ask if the judge will consent to talk with you about tort claims in your area. The judge may be able to provide you with the titles of important cases. You may then review the file at the clerk of court's office. Ask the judge about the attorneys' strategies and how they developed their claims of liability (or defense) in tort. Talk about what experts were used and how those experts were perceived by the jury. Ask if the judge has a medical-legal claim on the calendar. If possible, attend the trial.

2. Professional Portfolio. If you are planning to start an independent business, it may be wise to contact a marketing firm or a public relations firm to help you establish professional materials. The business card, stationery, bills, and other documents that come from your office should promote confidence and professionalism. Start collecting samples of fliers, business cards, and professional stationery that appeal to you.

ENDNOTES

1. *New World Dictionary (Modern Desk Edition)* (New York, NY: Simon & Shuster, 1979).

2. D. Carper, et al., *Understanding the Law* 3rd ed. (St. Paul, Minnesota: West Publishing Company, 2000), 305.

3. *Robinson v. Lindsay,* 92 Wash. 2d 410, 598 P. 2d 392 (1979).

4. D. Oran, *Oran's Dictionary of the Law* 3rd ed. (Albany, NY: West Thomson Learning, 2000).

5. *Palsgraf v. Long Island R.R. Co.,* 248 N.Y. 339, 162 N.E. 99 (1928).

6. American Bar Association, *Annotated Model Rules of Professional Conduct,* (1999) 4th Edition Rule 3.3(a)(1). Copies of ABA *Model Code of Professional Responsibility, 1999 Edition* are available from Service Center, American Bar Association, 750 North Lake Shore Drive, Chicago, IL 60611-4497, 1-800-285-2221.

7. T. A. Cannon, *Ethics and Professional Responsibility for Legal Assistants.* (New York, NY: Aspen Law & Business, 1999).

ADDITIONAL REFERENCES

Brewer, J.B., RN, MS, ed. *Legal Nurse Consulting: Principles and Practices.* Boston, MA: CRC Press, 1998.

Richardson, E., Regan, M. *Civil Litigation for Paralegals,* 2nd ed. Albany, NY: West Thomson Learning, 1998.

CHAPTER 18

INTENTIONAL TORTS

OBJECTIVES

In this chapter, you will learn

- the definition of intent in tort

- about intentional torts against persons, privacy, property and dignity

- about defenses to intentional torts

OVERVIEW

The courts generally use common meaning when interpreting the language of the law. **Intent,** for purposes of tort law, is defined as deliberate conduct directed toward a particular person or group of people that causes injury to the person or the property of another.[1] As explained in the previous chapter, intent for purposes of tort liability does not need to meet the standard of *mens rea* (criminal intent), although many crimes are the basis for tort liability. Rather, the deliberate act of the defendant must be done with a substantial certainty that harm would result to the person at whom the conduct is directed.

The fact that an action directed toward one person results in injury to another does not relieve the defendant of liability. This is known as **transferred intent.** For example, A throws a stick at B intending to hit B, and with substantial certainty that the stick will cause injury to B. B ducks and the stick hits C instead, causing serious injury. A cannot escape liability by saying that A meant no harm to C. The fact that the act was done intentionally with the desire to bring about the result (that the stick should hit B and inflict injury) is sufficient to establish liability for the errant action causing harm to another.

There are numerous intentional torts. The danger in bringing a lawsuit in intentional tort is that intent is generally difficult to prove. Most people do not deliberately act in ways they are reasonably certain will cause harm to others. Most injuries result from negligent acts. Injuries resulting from negligence are generally covered by policies of liability insurance, but intentional torts may not be covered by insurance. Recovery in intentional tort might require court sanctioned execution on a judgment of damages. These collection procedures, such as garnishment or forced sale of property, may fetter the injured party to the judicial system and drain valuable resources. Still, the theory of intentional torts is central to a discussion of personal injury law and legal nurse consultants will be expected to know and understand the basic elements of the most common intentional torts.

Intentional torts may generally be classified as torts against persons, torts against peace of mind, torts against property, and torts against business. State laws differ in their definitions of, elements of, and defenses to intentional torts. Legal nurse consultants should always consult the law of the jurisdiction in which the incident occurred. This chapter is intended to briefly acquaint the legal nurse consultant with several of the most commonly discussed intentional torts.

TORTS AGAINST THE PERSON

Originally lumped into the universal category of trespass under English common law, torts against the person included any invasion of the rights of another. These intentional torts included battery, assault, assault and battery, and false imprisonment. A summary of these torts and their elements, and examples appear in Figure 18-1.

FIGURE 18-1   Torts Against the Person

Tort	Elements	Example
Battery	• Intentional • Bodily contact • Physical harm	A purposely pushes B down the stairs; B is injured.
Assault	• Intentional act • Arouses fear [of] • Imminent • Physical violence	A purposely picks up a stick and threatens B by waving the stick in B's face and yelling, "I'll hit you!"
Assault and battery	• Intentional • Offensive • Bodily contact	A purposely, in the presence of B's associates, snatches a plate from B and says, "We don't serve Negroes here!"[4]
False imprisonment	• Intentional • Unlawful • Restraint of physical liberty	A purposely, and without legal justification, tapes B in a restraint chair.[6]

Battery

Battery is generally defined as an intentional act that results in an unpermitted bodily contact that is harmful.[2] Clearly, someone who deliberately (and absent any legal defense) hits another in the face is liable in battery. (Because the criminal intent is also present, that person would be subject to criminal prosecution for battery, as well.) The example of pulling a chair out from under someone has been used to illustrate a battery. One of the key elements in battery is the unpermitted nature of the contact. If there is consent to the conduct, the defendant is not liable in battery. For example, an elderly person is exiting a vehicle and having difficulty. A passerby lends a hand, literally, but in doing so causes a fracture of the elderly person's wrist. The elderly person may sue (you can sue anyone anytime for anything!), but the courts will probably conclude that by acquiescing to the help of the passerby, the plaintiff gave consent to the contact. The passerby will not be held liable for battery.

It is useful to note here that lawsuits are not exclusive; that is, a lawsuit can be brought with many different causes of action based on the same circumstances. In the preceding example, the elderly plaintiff might sue in battery—which would probably not be successful—and in negligence. The fact that one of the theories does not succeed will not preclude establishment of liability on the basis of another theory.

Assault

An act that is intended to cause fear of imminent bodily harm is a civil **assault.**[3] Assault in tort is quite different from assault in criminal law. In criminal law an assault usually involves inappropriate touching of a person. Touch is not required for liability in the civil tort of assault. The tort of assault has no equivalent crime, although in some states terrorist threats may constitute a crime and a tort.

In tort, assault is the harm to the victim created by the threat or fear of physical violence from the actor. For example, *A* holds a gun to *B*'s head and says "I'm going to pull the trigger." If *B* reasonably believes the gun is loaded and that *A* intends to fire the gun, *B* may recover in assault, even if *A* never intended to pull the trigger and the gun was not loaded. *A* cannot defend the action by saying it was a joke or by saying that the gun was not loaded or by saying that *A* never intended to harm *B*. These are not defenses in an action based on assault if the victim is placed in reasonable fear of bodily violence.

If there is no means by which the threat can be carried out, or if the threat is made for sometime in the future, the elements of assault are not met. For example, *A* beats loudly on the locked and bolted door of *B*'s apartment and shouts, "I'm going to break every bone in your body!" Since *A* cannot enter *B*'s apartment, *A* does not have the means to carry out the threat. Without the present ability to carry out the threat, an assault cannot be established. Similarly, *A* is standing in the open doorway of *B*'s apartment with fists clenched and yells, "If you don't pay me, next time I see you, I'll break every bone in your body!" Because the threat is not imminent (it is not going to happen right now), assault cannot be established and the defendant would be relieved of liability for assault.

Assault and Battery

Whenever intentional conduct results in an unpermitted bodily contact that is humiliating or embarrassing, the actor may be held liable in the tort of **assault and battery.**[4] For example, *A* spits on *B* in the presence of *B*'s professional associates. *B* is humiliated and feels a loss of standing among peers. *B* may recover from *A* for assault and battery, an unpermitted bodily contact that is offensive and causes injury other than physical pain.

The crucial distinction between assault and battery and battery is that assault and battery does not result in physical pain and suffering. The crucial difference between assault and battery and assault is that the conduct does not threaten physical violence.

False Imprisonment

In order to establish a **false imprisonment,** the following elements must be met:[5]

- the actor must have intent
- the actor must confine or restrict the physical liberty of another

■ the actor must not have legal justification

■ the actor must not have the victim's consent

If these elements are met, damages need not be proven. In other words, the victim of the imprisonment need not show monetary loss resulting from the confinement. If the wrongful confinement exists, that fact alone gives rise to an award of damages. In this way, the courts have recognized the harmful mental and emotional impact a wrongful imprisonment creates upon human beings who are ordinarily free to move about at will.[6]

False arrest is a type of false imprisonment in which the wrongful confinement is effected under color of authority; that is, where the victim reasonably believes the defendant has the authority or the legal justification to place the victim in a confinement. This is the basis for lawsuits in situations where suspected shoplifters are detained by security officers or in medical situations where commitment to mental institutions or nursing homes is wrongfully effected or extended.

TORTS AGAINST PEACE OF MIND

The courts recognize that mental tranquility is a right that is generally equivalent to the right to bodily security. When this right is violated by intentional infliction of emotional distress, invasion of privacy, or defamation, the victim is entitled to seek recovery through an action at law. These torts against peace of mind are summarized in Figure 18-2.

Intentional Infliction of Emotional Distress

The elements of **intentional infliction of emotional distress** include a deliberate and outrageous act intended to cause the severe emotional distress of another that actually results in emotional distress.[7] Everyday vulgarity, poor manners, and unkind behaviors, even when repeated over extended periods of time, do not constitute intentional infliction of emotional distress. In order to meet the elements of this tort, the conduct must be such that it is not considered within the bounds of usual and customary conduct. The courts recognize that ridicule, though unfortunate and unkind, is not unusual or out of the ordinary and will not meet the requirement of outrageous conduct. In addition, to recover for intentional infliction of emotional distress, the emotional distress suffered must be extreme or severe. A few sleepless nights and an upset stomach will not be sufficient to establish severe emotional distress. In some states, the emotional distress required must be such that the victim is unable to function in work or social relationships; in other states, the emotional distress must be manifest in physical symptoms.

Intentional infliction of emotional distress is sometimes used in actions where there has been a misdiagnosis and the patient has suffered considerable stress believing that a health condition is more serious than it is, or vice versa. These claims have generally been unsuccessful as it is difficult to prove that the failure to properly diagnose the condition was an outrageous or heinous action.

FIGURE 18-2 Torts Against Peace of Mind

Tort	Elements	Example
Intentional infliction of emotional distress	• Outrageous conduct • Intended to cause emotional distress • Resultant emotional distress	A dresses like a security officer from the local college. A knows the prank will cause B emotional distress. A knocks on B's door and tells B that B's son hanged himself in the college dorm.
Invasion of privacy —intrusion	• Unreasonable intrusion [upon] • Solitude of another	A hides a video camera in B's bathroom and records B's activities.
Invasion of privacy —appropriation	• Unauthorized • Use for marketing purposes [of a] • Person's name or likeness	Without permission, A uses Mickey Mouse, an image owned by Walt Disney Co., to promote a car rental agency.
Invasion of privacy —unreasonable publicity	• Publication [that is] • Offensive and unreasonable [concerning] • A private matter	A posts a notice on the window of B's store. The notice says, "B has not paid his car repair bill."
Invasion of privacy —false light	• Publication [that places] • A person in a false light	B is photographed in front of a bank; this photo is printed in the newspaper above the headline: "Bank Robbed by Lone Gunman."
Defamation—libel	• Publication [of] • False statement [that results in] • Damage to a person's reputation or character	The school newspaper falsely reports that a student running for Student Senate recently suffered a complete breakdown and is on anti-depressants.
Defamation—slander	• False statement • Communicated in words or gestures [which results in] • Damage to a person's reputation or character	A, jealous of B's athletic talent, tells the coach that B is suffering from HIV, knowing that this is false information.

Invasion of Privacy

The right to solitude is a common law right, although the Fourth Amendment to the United States Constitution has been interpreted to provide a **right to privacy** in matters involving governmental action. The facets of the right to privacy in tort law are four-fold and include:

- unreasonable intrusion upon the solitude of another
- unauthorized appropriation of a person's name or likeness for marketing purposes
- unreasonable publicity concerning a private matter
- publicity that unreasonably places the victim in a false light

The intrusion aspect of invasion of privacy arises out of the reasonable expectation that certain places are private; that is, they are part of the necessary seclusion and solitude that are inherent in daily life. A bathroom or a bedroom, for instance, would be considered places where privacy is expected. To unreasonably intrude upon that secluded place violates the right to privacy and solitude. However, a person who leaves curtains open in the bedroom so the room is visible to passersby on the sidewalk cannot claim that privacy was invaded by those who looked in. Failing to protect one's privacy will effectively waive the right to solitude.

The appropriation aspect of invasion of privacy involves the use of a person's name or photograph, a drawing of that person, or any copyrighted creation of that person without permission and for the purpose of promoting the goods and/or services of another. For example, using a photograph of a football celebrity on a package of cereal without the celebrity's permission would violate the celebrity's right to privacy. Additionally, using a copyrighted cartoon figure to promote a computer software package without first obtaining the right to do so, would not only result in a lawsuit for copyright infringement, but would also unreasonably invade the right to privacy cartoon image's creator.

The unreasonable publication aspect of invasion of privacy occurs in the deliberate and unfair sensationalizing of a matter that would ordinarily be considered private. This tort requires proof that at the time of publication, the publisher intended to use the private information to diminish the respect and dignity afforded the person involved. A matter of public record, such as a criminal conviction, a bankruptcy, or a divorce is not considered private for purposes of this tort. The information must be such that it offends reasonable people. Unreasonable publication of a person's nervous condition and the medication taken to control the condition is information that would be considered private, unless voluntarily disclosed for public use, especially if it might give rise to an inference that the person was incapable of handling his or her work responsibilities.

The false light aspect of invasion of privacy is far more difficult to prove. It involves a situation in which the placement of a name or likeness of an individual would cause the public to associate the name or likeness with an unpleasant or criminal activity that is untrue. For example, *A* is pictured shoveling snow after an overnight record snowfall. Immediately below the picture appears the headline "Prisoner Freed from Federal Prison to Live in City." The association that *A*, innocently photographed shoveling snow, is the "man freed from prison" creates the false impression and invades *A*'s right to privacy.

The computerization of medical records and the increasing use of computer databases and the Internet create new problems in the protection of privacy. Increased statutory requirements, such as those outlined in the Federal Educational Right to Privacy Act and the Medical Records Confidentiality Act, are placed on users of computers to protect the rights of students, patients, and clients, and the information about them that is contained in computer databases.

Defamation

Defamation is a broad term used to identify an area of law having to do with the integrity of a person's reputation. In general, the courts have recognized that all persons are entitled to the enjoyment of a right and just reputation unless proven otherwise. There are several ways that defamation can occur; these defamatory actions are classified as either libel or slander.

Libel.   Whenever false statements are published, aired over radio or television, or otherwise available in print media, and those false statements harm the reputation of another, the defamation is known as **libel.** Whether or not the statements are read, heard, or otherwise received doesn't matter. The law only requires that the matter be published and that the defamatory nature of the matter be obvious. For actions involving the news media, libel may be proven by showing that the news agency failed to use reasonable care in ascertaining the truth of the matter prior to its publication. It is presumed that members of the news media do not act with malice or evil intent when publishing the news.

Slander.   False statements that are made orally or through gestures are slanderous. Anyone who repeats gossip, that is, untrue information about another that is damaging or results in a loss of association with that person is, theoretically, liable for **slander.** The law only requires that the false statement be communicated to one third party. It is not necessary to show that the matter was made public. It is necessary, however, to show that the person who made the false statement did so with malice; that is, with an intent to lessen the respect afforded the person about whom the untrue statement is made. A statement of opinion is not sufficient to support an action in slander. To say that someone is ugly and unmannerly is not slander; to falsely report that a person has a sexually transmitted disease is. Gestures may also constitute slander. For example, *A* is rumored to have AIDS; the rumor is untrue. At a tavern, *A* orders a drink. The barkeeper serves the drink and backs off. Later, when *A* has finished the drink, the barkeeper uses a napkin to pick up the glass that was used by *A* and drops the glass and napkin into the trash, in full view of the other patrons in the tavern. This gesture communicates to those present that there is something about *A* that is repugnant, revolting, or unsanitary. *A* has an action against the barkeeper and the tavern for the loss of reputation resulting from this conduct.

TORTS AGAINST PROPERTY

The United States Constitution and the courts in the United States have upheld a person's right to private ownership of property. In theory, this means that the exclusive right to possess and use the property lies with the owner or lawful possessor. Whether the property is **real** (land and anything permanently affixed to the land) or **personal** (tangible, movable objects such as jewelry, automobiles, and books), the owner is protected from unlawful violation of property rights. The exclusive right to possess and use real property may be violated by trespass and private nuisance. The exclusive right to possess and use personal property may be violated by conversion. Torts against property are summarized in Figure 18-3.

Trespass to Land

Entering or causing something to enter the land of another without permission is the invasion called **trespass.** Trespass is an intentional tort, but the intent required is not intent to injure, or the criminal intent (guilty knowledge) that the action violates another's rights. Rather, intent for purposes of trespass may arise out of mistake. If intent to enter the land is apparent, the fact that the person entered the land by mistake, without knowing that it violated the rights of another, is not a defense. For practical purposes, of course, it is unlikely that anyone would sue for a simple mistake, but, theoretically, the law protects the landowner from any unlawful invasion. For example, *A* has

Net Results

Torts on the Internet
There are several web sites dedicated to information concerning torts, including the American Bar Association's Tort and Insurance Practice Section, and a TortLaw listserv. Access these locations at www.abanet.org/tips/home.html *and* www.findlaw.com/01topics/22tort/mail_usenet.html.

FIGURE 18-3   Torts Against Property

Tort	Elements	Example
Trespass	• Intentional • Unauthorized • Entry onto land • Belonging to another	*A* throws a bag of trash onto *B*'s land.
Private nuisance	• Thing or activity [which] • Unreasonably or substantially interferes [with] • Use and enjoyment of land	*A* builds a horse barn on land next to an established restaurant; odor and flies from the horse barn interfere with restaurant patronage.
Conversion	• Intentional • Unauthorized • Taking or exercising of control [over] • Personal property • Belonging to another	*A* refuses to surrender the keys to *B*'s automobile.

permission to remove timber from *B*'s property. There are no markings to indicate where *B*'s property ends and *C*'s begins. Without meaning to invade *C*'s rights, *A* cuts timber that, in fact, belongs to *C*. *A* is still liable in trespass for invading *C*'s interest, even though *A* did not know the land belonged to *C* and believed that permission existed to remove the timber.

Private Nuisance

Trespass generally deals with entry onto land without permission or remaining on land after permission to be there has been revoked. A parallel tort is private nuisance. Whenever an activity or thing substantially interferes with the rights of a landowner to use real property (particularly for purposes of producing income) or to enjoy real property, a **private nuisance** may be actionable. For example, runoff from a field that has been treated with a herbicide contaminates the drinking water of the livestock on the next farm and causes harm. The livestock farmer, who uses land for purposes of raising livestock, can sue the field owner, who applied the herbicide that contaminated the water, for private nuisance, because the runoff from the herbicide substantially interfered with the livestock, the farmer's use of land. Noxious fumes, hazardous chemicals, noise, and interference with the sunlight needed for solar panels to generate alternative energy sources are examples of situations in which private nuisance has been the basis of a lawsuit. The nuisance need not be intentional, but can result from negligence or even strict liability. Considerations in determining liability in an action in private nuisance include which of the parties had a prior interest in the land, the nature and value of the investment in the land, and the extent of interference.

Conversion

The right to exclusive possession and enjoyment of personal property is equally protected. A person who exercises control over personal property without the authority of the owner is liable in **conversion,** sometimes still referred to as **trespass to chattels.** Conversion can occur under any of the following circumstances:

- failure to return personal property after reasonable demand has been made
- delivery of personal property to someone who has no right to receive it
- altering or destroying the personal property of another
- appropriating the personal property of another

The tort of conversion does not require an intent to steal the personal property of another. In other words, taking or exercising control over the personal property of another even by mistake will still, theoretically, result in liability. For example, this textbook is exactly like dozens of other textbooks belonging to students in a class. Believing a textbook belongs to her, *A* takes the textbook and puts it in her book bag. The textbook actually belongs to *B*. Even though *A* made an honest mistake, *A* exercised control over property that did not belong to her, and, theoretically, she will be liable to *B* for conversion of the textbook.

Equivalent crimes, that is crimes that will result in criminal prosecution and might also give rise to a civil lawsuit in the tort of conversion, are theft, embezzlement, and receiving stolen property, even if the receiver had no reason to believe that the property was stolen. Conversion occurs at the point at which unlawful possession or control is taken over the personal property.

The damages in conversion are the reasonable market value of the personal property. This does not mean the purchase price, nor does it mean the replacement cost of the item. Reasonable market value is what a reasonable seller would pay a reasonable buyer for the item in the condition it was in at the time of the conversion. Even if the property is returned without apparent damage, the owner is entitled to recover market value for the item as damages for the loss of exclusive possession and control.

TORTS AGAINST BUSINESS

Misrepresentation or bad faith, intentional interference with contract relations, and trade libel are examples of torts that involve harm to a person's business or profession. These torts are, in many respects, similar to torts against the person or against the peace of mind of the victim. Rather than direct the wrongful conduct against the person, however, the wrongful conduct results in loss of business, profits, customers, market share, or professional reputation in the community. Torts against business are summarized in Figure 18-4.

FIGURE 18-4   Torts Against Business

Tort	Elements	Example
Misrepresentation	• False statement [of a] • Material fact [that is] • Relied upon [to the] • Disadvantage of a party	A tells B that water on the property is safe to drink; B relies on the statement, drinks the water and is injured.
Intentional interference with contract relations	• Intentional • Inducement of a contract party [which results in] • Breach of contract	A offers a signing bonus to B if B will leave a three-year contract of employment and work for A.
Trade libel	• Intentional • False statements [about the] • Nature, quality, or title to goods [that results in] • Loss of business opportunities	Untrue statements about a voiceover on a recording (that it is not actually the artist identified on the jacket that is singing), which result in a major loss of sales.

Misrepresentation and Bad Faith

In contract law, **fraud** is described as a statement of material fact that is untrue and that is made for the purpose of enticing someone to enter into a contract that will be disadvantageous to that person.[8] Fraud in contract law is very similar to **misrepresentation** or **bad faith** in tort. Providing misinformation or failing to disclose the truth about certain facts, when an unsuspecting party relies on that misinformation or failure to disclose to his or her detriment, is the basis for a cause of action in misrepresentation in tort. For example, A wishes to hunt on the property of B and has been given permission to do so for many years. On the property is a tree stand often used by hunters with B's approval. B gives A approval to hunt on the property and to use the tree stand. A specifically asks B if the tree stand is safe and B replies that it is. When A climbs to the tree stand, it collapses and A is seriously injured. In this situation A may sue B for misrepresentation because A relied on B's statement about the condition of the tree stand when B knew or should have know of its unsafe condition.

Similarly, bad faith is apparent when someone deliberately refuses to carry out an obligation that is agreed upon. In the previous example, A has asked B about the tree stand. B says that the tree stand is in disrepair and agrees to fix it before A's scheduled hunting time. After A leaves, B thinks better of this agreement and decides that A may use the tree stand at his or her own peril. A, acting in good faith upon the promise of B, uses the tree stand and is seriously injured when it collapses due to disrepair. B's deliberate failure to fulfill a promise that is relied upon in good faith is actionable in bad faith, even where no contract existed between the parties.

Intentional Interference with Contract Relations

When parties enter into a contract, they have the right to expect that the contract will be fulfilled. Indeed, there would be no reason for the legal significance of contracts if the parties could back out of their promises at any time without consequence. The court provides remedies to parties who have been left with unfulfilled obligations in the form of breach of contract. This breach of contract may also be a tort when a third party induces the contract party to breach. For example, a well-known weather reporter has a contract with a local television station. A national television program recruits the weather reporter and offers a substantial financial incentive to accept a position with them. The weather reporter accepts the position in violation of the contract with the local television station. The local television station has a cause of action in the tort of **intentional interference with contract** relations against the national television program and a cause of action in breach of contract against the weather reporter.

Trade Libel

Trade libel is to business what defamation is to a person's character. It is based on untrue statements about the nature of a business that result in a loss of customers and profits. Disparagement of goods and slander of title are two examples of trade libel.

Disparagement of Goods.   Untrue statements about the quality or nature of the goods of a business, whether published or communicated verbally, are disparagement when the intent of the communication is to cause injury to the business. For example, a statement that the meat at a fast food restaurant is horsemeat rather than beef would be **disparagement** if the statement was untrue and made intentionally to harm the restaurant's business.

Slander of Title.   Similarly, untrue statements concerning the title or property interest in the goods of a business, whether published or communicated verbally, are **slander of title** when the intent of the communication is to injure the business's reputation. For example, a statement that some of the items sold at a particular store are stolen would be slander of title if the statement was untrue and intended to harm the store's business.

REMEDIES FOR INTENTIONAL TORTS

While all the intentional torts give rise to an action in compensatory damages, if the conduct is outrageous or in reckless disregard for the rights of the victim, punitive damages might also be available to the victim. In many of the intentional torts, the equitable remedy of injunction is also available. In the example given for private nuisance, the field owner who uses a herbicide may be required to pay compensatory damages for the diseases in the livestock due to their consumption of the contaminated water. It would be a considerable frustration for the livestock farmer to encounter the same problem the next spring when the field owner applies the herbicide again. Thus, the livestock farmer may request and be granted an order enjoining the field owner from using herbicides that may adversely impact the ground waters.

The intentional torts discussed in this chapter are generally well known. It is not intended to be a complete discussion of all intentional torts; there are many others, such as wrongful discharge, that are not included. The legal analysis required in claims of personal injury is the same regardless of the cause of action involved: isolating the facts, identifying the law of the jurisdiction, breaking the law into its elements, and applying the facts.

DEFENSES TO INTENTIONAL TORTS

Throughout this discussion of the major torts involved in personal injury litigation, there has been reference to situations in which the elements of the tort are not met. The first and foremost defense to any tort is the failure of the injured party to show that the facts constitute a tort. There are several other defenses to intentional torts: consent, self-defense, defense of others, defense of property, emergency or necessity, and the statute of limitations.

Consent

Almost all intentional torts require that the conduct be unauthorized or without permission. When the injured party **consents** to the conduct, the elements of the tort are not met. Consent may be express or implied. A victim who has the opportunity to prevent an unwanted touch, but does not do so, and is then touched, may not later expect to recover in tort. For example, *A*, a nurse practitioner wishes to examine *B*'s ear. *B* does not want *A* to conduct an examination, but says nothing and does not move away. *A* examines *B*'s ear. Unless the situation is accompanied by coercive threats or other manipulative tactics that would invalidate the consent, failing to stop *A* would be construed by the court to mean that the conduct was approved.

Consent may only be given by competent parties. Minors, legally adjudged insane persons, or persons who are incapacitated due to excessive substance abuse are not capable of understanding the consequences of consent; therefore, any consent given may be ineffective. In addition, consent can only be extended to the conduct that was the subject of the consent. This has been the basis of claims against health care providers. For example, a physician who has been authorized to perform an appendectomy discovers that the uterus is diseased and is a threat to the health of the patient. The physician performs a hysterectomy in addition to the appendectomy. The physician may be liable in battery (unauthorized bodily contact) because the consent for medical treatment extended only to the appendectomy. In some states the physician may be protected by the emergency or necessity defense discussed later in this chapter.

Self-Defense

When a victim does not have time to resort to legal means for protection, the victim may inflict harm to protect against threatened bodily contact or imprisonment. **Self-defense** is a complete defense, so the person who is harmed may not recover damages. To invoke the privilege of self-defense, it is not necessary for danger to exist. If reasonable people would believe themselves to be threatened with dangerous invasion of bodily security, the defense is available. Even if the danger can be avoided by retreating, the law still recognizes the right to defend oneself without penalty as long as the following conditions are met:

- the force used is reasonable
- the force used is not intended or likely to cause death or serious bodily harm
- the force is used to protect against threatened bodily harm or imprisonment

Reasonable force is the key. The courts have interpreted reasonable force to include proportionate force; that is, if an attacker is using fists, the victim may employ fists. To use a knife, a firearm, or other weapon would be disproportionate force and would not be reasonable. Lethal force to protect oneself may only be used in situations where lethal force is used against the intended victim and the intended victim reasonably believes that great bodily harm or death is intended. The defense of self-defense is generally a question of fact for the jury. The standard is an objective one: what a reasonably prudent person of average courage would have done under the circumstances existing then and there.

Defense of Others

The privilege of defense of others is only available in situations where the victim would be entitled to self-defense and intervention is necessary to save that person from bodily harm. **Defense of others** does not extend to insults or consensual fisticuffs; it must involve a real harm to someone who is unable to protect him or herself.

To invoke the privilege of defense of others, the following conditions must be met:

- There is reasonable belief that another, who is in a position of threatened bodily harm, is entitled to the defense of self-defense.
- Intervention is necessary to protect that person from harm.
- Reasonable force is used.
- The force used is not intended or likely to cause death or serious bodily harm.
- The force is necessary to protect another from threatened bodily harm or imprisonment.

For example, the driver of a loaded semi traveling on an interstate highway notices a pickup in front of the semi that is moving erratically from lane to lane. As the driver approaches, it becomes apparent that the pickup is actually following the driver in the vehicle ahead. Leaning out of the pickup truck is a man with a rifle, shooting at the vehicle. As the semi driver watches, the vehicle pulls over to the shoulder and a woman driver flees the vehicle, running into the ditch. The pickup truck screeches to a halt behind the vehicle. Believing the driver of the pickup, the man with the rifle, is still in the pickup, the semi driver rams the semi into the back of the pickup. The semi driver's reasoning is that unless the pickup truck is disabled, the woman in the ditch will be shot. If the man in the pickup truck is injured as a result of the semi driver's actions, and he sues the semi driver for injuries, a complete defense against the action would be defense of others.

Defense of Property

There are times when the court will allow bodily injury to another in order to protect an interest in property. Greater interest, however, is placed on life and health, and the courts will never allow property to be protected with lethal force. To invoke the privilege of **defense of property,** the following conditions must be met:

- The force used is reasonable.
- The force used is not intended or likely to cause death or serious bodily harm.
- The force is used only after a warning or demand to cease has been ignored.
- Force is the only means to prevent the threatened interference with property rights or to protect property (both real and personal).

The key components of this defense are the warning, or demand to cease the activity that threatens interference with property rights, and the existence of no other means to prevent the threatened interference. Without these, defense of property that results in injury, even to a trespasser, may result in liability for those injuries against the property owner.

Emergency or Necessity

An emergency may be defined in the law as anything sudden or unexpected that requires immediate response. As a result, a person in an emergency situation cannot be held to the same standard as someone who has sufficient time to consider the options and consequences of conduct.[9] Actors in emergency situations will be held to a reasonable standard under the emergency situation. The standard is an objective one—what persons of ordinary courage would have done under the circumstances.

Necessity, in the law, refers to "anything from an irresistible force or compulsion to an important, but not required action."[10] In situations of personal injury, necessity would be a defense when, without incurring the injury, more harm would have resulted. It is often associated with emergency events. For example, a threatened flash flood is forecast in a region of older homes. An elderly woman, whose home is already surrounded by water, is unwilling to leave. Knowing that the potential threat of flood would destroy the home and that her safety would be jeopardized, rescue workers come for her in a boat and physically remove her from her home. If the elderly woman suffers a broken rib as a result of this rescue and sues the rescue workers for battery, the defense would be necessity. Even if the threatened flood does not occur, if reasonable people would have acted to rescue the elderly woman, the rescue workers are protected from liability.

Statute of Limitations

For every tort action, there is a corresponding **statute of limitations.** A statute of limitations restricts the amount of time within which a lawsuit may be brought based on a particular occurrence. The statute is enacted for public policy reasons; it is unfair to expect people to have to answer for their actions forever. If an action is not brought within the time allowed in the statute of limitations, the victim is barred from recovery.

The statute of limitations for intentional torts varies from state to state, but in most states, the lawsuit must be brought within two years of the occurrence that constitutes an intentional tort. In a few states, a three-year statute of limitations exists. Sometimes the occurrence meets the elements of more than one cause of action and the statute of limitations on a second or third theory may not expire within the time specified for intentional torts. For example, in the state where the preceding example occurs concerning the elderly woman in the flash flood, the statute of limitations for intentional torts is two years, but the statute of limitations for personal injury resulting from negligence is three years. If the elderly woman does not bring her action in battery within two years, she can still pursue a remedy using a negligence theory, until the three years expire. This is one reason why investigation of the facts and research of all potential causes of action and defenses is critical at the outset of a personal injury claim.

Frivolous Claims

It is possible to sue anyone anytime for anything! Whether the lawsuit has merit is for the court to decide. If the lawsuit is brought for purposes other than justice; that is, for spite, harassment, or vengeance, the court will find that the lawsuit is not within the spirit of the law and may impose sanctions against the attorney and the party bringing the lawsuit. A **frivolous claim** is one that is without foundation in law or fact. Lawyers are ethically precluded from knowingly filing frivolous claims and may be disciplined or lose their licenses for violating the integrity of the court. If there is a reasonable basis in fact and law for the lawsuit, the lawyer files the complaint in good faith. The defense of frivolous claims is not available. The lawsuit may still be dismissed for failing to meet the elements of a cause of action or to establish liability, but the claim itself will not be labeled frivolous.

Intentional torts are an integral component of the study of personal injury litigation. While most personal injury lawsuits are based in negligence, intentional torts are often included as alternative theories in negligence claims. The exclusive defenses to intentional torts (consent, self defense, defense of others, defense of property) are not available as defenses to negligence. The failure to meet a cause of action or to establish liability, the statute of limitations, and frivolous claims are all defenses against personal injury claims. Because legal nurse consultants will be dealing with personal injury claims, an understanding of the legal concepts, consequences, and defenses to intentional torts is critical to understanding how the medical injuries correspond to the legal claims.

Ethics Bookmark

Frivolous Claims

"A lawyer shall not bring or defend a proceeding . . . unless there is a basis for doing so that is not frivolous" Annotated Model Code of Professional Conduct Fourth Edition Rule 3.1 Copyright 1999 American Bar Association.*[11] *Frivolous claims may arise when clients provide inaccurate information and attorneys do not take time to thoroughly investigate the claims, or when attorneys become too engaged in the energy of the argument. Sometimes attorneys advance claims or defenses simply to generate fees. These are unethical practices. Attorneys have a duty to uphold the integrity of the justice system. Claims without foundation may result in severe sanctions.* *American Bar Association. Reprinted by permission of the American Bar Association. American Bar Association, *Annotated Model Rules of Professional conduct,* 4th ed. (1999) Rule 3.1. Copies of Model Code of Professional Responsibility, 1999 edition are available from Service Center, American Bar Association, 750 North Lake Shore Drive, Chicago, IL 60611-4497, 1-800-285-2221.

CHAPTER SUMMARY

- Intentional torts are deliberate acts directed toward a person or group of people that cause harm.
- Intentional torts against the person include battery, assault, assault and battery, and false imprisonment.
- Intentional torts against peace of mind include intentional infliction of emotional distress, invasion of privacy, and defamation.
- Intentional torts against property include trespass, private nuisance, and conversion.
- Intentional torts against business include misrepresentation, bad faith, intentional interference with contract, and trade libel.
- Victims of intentional torts may recover compensatory and punitive damages and, in some cases, may seek equitable relief such as an injunction.
- Consent, self-defense, defense of others, defense of property, emergency or necessary, and the tolling of the statute of limitations are all defenses to intentional torts.
- A frivolous claim is one that has no foundation in law or fact.

KEY TERMS

assault	fraud	private nuisance
assault and battery	frivolous claims	real property
bad faith	intent	right to privacy
battery	intentional infliction of	self-defense
consent	emotional distress	slander
conversion	intentional interference with	slander of title
defamation	contract	statute of limitations
defense of others	invasion of privacy	trade libel
defense of property	libel	transferred intent
disparagement of goods	*mens rea*	trespass
false arrest	misrepresentation	trespass to chattels
false imprisonment	personal property	

REVIEW QUESTIONS

1. How is intent for tort different from criminal intent?
2. List and explain several intentional torts against persons. Against peace of mind. Against property. Against business.
3. What remedies are available to victims of intentional torts?

INTERNET EXERCISES

1. Access the web page for this textbook at *www.westlegalstudies.com*.
2. Click on the assignments section and complete the assignment(s) for Chapter Eighteen.

EXERCISES

1. Networking. By now, you should have a good start on a network of legal and professional sources to assist you in making the transition from nursing practice to legal nurse consulting practice. From this list, select those who may know about position openings or from whom you may seek a referral. When you feel ready to test the waters, call those you have selected and ask who a resume should be sent to or who to schedule a presentation with.
2. Professional Portfolio. The portfolio you have been collecting may be divided into two separate binders. In one binder, you will want to maintain all of the professional qualifications that will assist you in securing a position as a legal nurse consultant. In the other binder, you may wish to include the sample documents, lists, citations, etc., that will be of assistance to you in your practice. Make this binder a systems notebook and organize it so that you will be able to reference it quickly when you need information from it. For example, you may include sections for litigation documents, the court system in your state, case briefs, etc.

ENDNOTES

1. D. Carper, et al., *Understanding the Law,* 3rd ed. (St. Paul, Minnesota: West Publishing Company, 2000), 305.
2. *Restatement (Second) of Torts s. 18* (1964).
3. *Restatement (Second) of Torts s. 22* (1964).
4. *Fisher v. Carrousel Motor Hotel, Inc.,* 424 S.W. 2d 617 (Tex. 1967).
5. *Restatement (Second) of Torts s. 36* (1964).
6. *Big Town Nursing Home, Inc. v. Neuman,* 461 S. W. 2d 195 (Tex. 1970).
7. *Restatement (Second) of Torts s. 46* (1964).
8. D. Oran, *Oran's Dictionary of the Law,* 3rd ed. (Albany, NY: West Thomson Learning, 2000), 206.
9. *Ibid,* 167.
10. *Ibid,* 327.
11. American Bar Association, *Annotated Model Rules of Professional Conduct,* (1999) 4th Edition Rule 3.1. Copies of ABA *Model Code of Professional Responsibility, 1999 Edition* are available from Service Center, American Bar Association, 750 North Lake Shore Drive, Chicago, IL 60611-4497, 1-800-285-2221.

ADDITIONAL REFERENCES

Edwards, L., Edwards, J. *Tort Law for Legal Assistants.* Albany, NY: West Thomson Learning, 1999.

Lamb, D.L., BSN, RN. "Confidentiality of Medical Records, Part I and Part II: Electronic Patient Records." *Journal of Legal Nurse Consulting* 8:4 (1997) 16–17; and 8:2, 14–16.

Loecker, B.L., MSEd, RN. "Suits Against the Government." *Journal of Legal Nurse Consulting* 8:2 (1997) 18.

Shepard, S. "Whistle-blowing: Exposing Fraud Against the Government." *Journal of Legal Nurse Consulting* 9:2 (1998) 10–11.

CHAPTER 19

NEGLIGENCE

OBJECTIVES

In this chapter, you will learn

- what negligence is

- who is responsible for negligent acts

- how negligence is proven

- the defenses to negligence

OVERVIEW

Negligence is said to be an **unintentional tort.** This means that when the conduct occurred, it was not directed at a particular person to bring about a particular result. For example, if a person purposely steers a car to drive over someone and actually hits that person, it would be actionable in the tort of battery (intentional, unpermitted bodily contact, that results in harm). However, if a person fails to stop at a stop sign and hits a person entering the crosswalk, it would be actionable in the tort of negligence because the driver did not drive the car with the purpose of harming the person in the crosswalk. Still, the courts will not allow liability to be avoided simply because the driver (actor) did not intend to hurt anyone. The innocent person in the crosswalk is entitled to recover, because failing to stop at a stop sign is not reasonably prudent driving conduct.

FORESEEABILITY

Foreseeability is "the degree to which the consequences of an action should have been anticipated, recognized, and considered beforehand."[1] The tort of negligence is entirely dependent on the concept of foreseeability. Action that creates an unreasonable risk of harm to others is negligent. The risk created by a negligent act must be a foreseeable risk.

Foreseeability is a creation of public policy. It might not be in the best interests of society for negligent actors to be responsible for harm that no one could have anticipated as a consequence of that negligent act. The fact that it is a direct consequence may not be sufficient to invoke liability. For example, *A* is waiting on the platform as a train is pulling out. *B* is running to catch the train. As *B* nears the door, a porter inside the train reaches to assist *B* into the train and a porter on the platform reaches to push *B* into the train. In this attempt to assist *B,* a package *B* is carrying is dislodged and falls on the tracks. The package explodes and in the resulting confusion, weigh scales fall on *A* and cause her severe injury. In this case, the court concluded that the injury to *A,* weigh scales falling on her as she is waiting on the platform, was not a foreseeable risk associated with the action of the train's employees in assisting *B* to catch the train. Since this situation could not have been foreseen, no liability attaches to the train employees or the railroad company.[2]

Foreseeability may have less to do with the ability to anticipate harm than it does with the actual probability of harm. If harm is likely or intended, it is considered an intentional tort. If the harm is unusual, freakish, or bizarre, it is an **unavoidable accident** and no liability attaches. However, if harm is possible or probable as an ordinary and expected consequence of the conduct, it meets the test of foreseeability in the creation of an unreasonable risk.

There are many factors that may be applied to determine how foreseeable a particular injury is as a result of a particular conduct. Historical factors (previous experience with this particular occurrence), sensory considerations (light conditions, weather conditions), characteristics of the parties (children, adults, students), characteristics of the place (garage, schoolroom, park), common sense, and the ordinary and usual reactions of people are all factors to be considered in foreseeability. Foreseeability is the essence of negligence and the defenses to negligence. It permeates all of the elements necessary to establish liability for negligent conduct.

ELEMENTS OF NEGLIGENCE

To establish liability for negligence, the following four elements must generally be met with the facts:

- A relationship exists between the plaintiff and the defendant in which the defendant owes a duty of care for the protection of the plaintiff.
- A breach of the duty of care owed by the defendant to the plaintiff.
- The breach of duty is the proximate cause of injury to the plaintiff.
- The plaintiff must suffer some harm (damages must be provable).

In general, all of these elements are questions of fact for the jury. On some occasions, the courts have concluded that the evidence, in a light most favorable to the plaintiff, would cause reasonable minds to agree on the existence of the elements (the truth is clear) and have entered judgments as a matter of law.[3] This has occurred most often in cases where the relationship of care did not exist or the cause of the injuries was not the negligence of the defendant.

Duty Relationship

A driver on the highway owes a duty of care for the safety of passengers, other drivers, pedestrians, and property owners. There is no contract relationship, but the courts have recognized that the privilege of driving carries with it the responsibility to drive with care. The failure to do so that creates an unreasonable risk to passengers, other drivers, pedestrians, or property owners results in negligence when any are injured.

The duty relationship may exist because of a contract (builder and property owner, physician and patient), by common law (as in the case of driving and operating machinery), or by statute. Regardless, the duty of care owed to a particular victim must be foreseeable.

In the previous example, *A* is standing on the station platform while *B* is running to catch a train. The relationship foreseeable in this situation is the duty of care owed to the passenger who is attempting to catch the train. When the railroad employees assist *B* in getting on the moving train, the foreseeable risk is to *B*. In other words, by attempting to assist *B*, the train's employees create a duty relationship to act with reasonable care for *B*'s safety and the safety of *B*'s personal belongings.[4] A bystander, generally, is owed no duty of care.

Where children are concerned, the duty relationship is somewhat expanded. Much is to be expected of children that is not expected of adults.

Children are meddlesome and curious. They do not appreciate the risk to themselves when they enter unsafe property or explore unsafe conditions. One of the areas of negligence concerned with the safety of children is the **attractive nuisance** doctrine. Attractive nuisance occurs when children, because of their naturally curious natures, are drawn to an artificial condition on land that causes injury to the unsuspecting child. The landowner is liable even though the child is trespassing, if it is reasonably foreseeable that children in the neighborhood would be attracted to the artificial condition, and the landowner knew or should have known that the condition would be attractive and harmful to children.

Another instance of the expanded policy of safety for children is inherent in the **Pied Piper** cases. Vendors who make their profits from children by enticing them to take advantage of their goods or services will be responsible for the safety of the children. The driver and owner of an ice cream truck, for instance, that stops in a neighborhood in such a way that children will run across the street without heed to oncoming traffic may be liable for resulting injury or death of child patrons.

Standard of Care (Breach of Duty)

The general standard of care is based on an objective standard, that of the **reasonable person.** The law does not require that anyone guarantee the safety of others; the only requirement is to act with ordinary prudence and caution. This general standard becomes more and more specific, depending on the facts. A driver of an automobile must drive with reasonable care for the safety of others on the highway. That is a general standard of care. In addition, a driver must be cognizant of the parts of the automobile that might, as a result of continued use, become dangerous, such as the tires.[5] Because each case is decided on its facts, the circumstances will require that the general standard of care become specific to those circumstances. Road conditions, driver conditions, weather conditions, vehicle conditions, and distracting conditions along the roadway are all considerations in determining what the appropriate standard of care is for drivers.

The law does not cast a greater standard of care on any individuals.[6] Ordinary care is expected of everyone. A physical, emotional, or mental disability is only one consideration in determining ordinary care. Customary conduct (previous business dealings) and the standards of the community (what is usual and customary in that area) are also considerations.

Another concept in determining the specific standard of care is shifting of responsibility. Someone who knowingly creates an unreasonable risk of harm may safely expect that another will protect the unwary from that unreasonable risk. For example, *A* operates a machine that breaks up the concrete on a highway and digs the concrete out. *A* creates an unreasonable risk of harm to drivers on the highway. *A* reasonably expects that *B*, who previously set orange cones along the highway where *A* would be operating, and *C,* who follows behind *A* and puts up cautionary barriers, will take the necessary precautions to protect drivers from the risk of harm created by the broken highway. This shifting of responsibility may relieve *A* of liability if *B* fails to set orange cones along the highway and *C* fails to put up cautionary barriers.

In same cases, courts will not allow a shifting of responsibility. For example, a dangerous condition exists on land and the owner of the land contracts with the tenant to fix the dangerous condition. The tenant fails to fix the dangerous condition and a third party is injured. The courts have sometimes held that a landlord cannot escape liability by shifting it to the tenant, especially if the condition is unreasonably dangerous. This is also true in medical negligence claims based on lack of informed consent. Physicians may delegate to nurses and others the responsibility of obtaining informed consent from the patient. However, the courts will not allow the physician to shift responsibility for providing adequate information to the patient about the risks and alternatives to medical treatment. If the court finds that the patient did not have sufficient information to make a decision concerning medical treatment, the physician will be liable.[7]

Standard of care varies, too, with the activity that is involved. For example, children who operate snowmobiles (powerful motorized machines) may be held to an adult standard of care[8] because engaging in that activity is generally reserved for adults. In some states children are presumed, either through statute or by case law, to be incapable of negligence until they reach a certain age. If the child is under the age of 7, the child is presumed incapable of negligence; that is, the child cannot reasonably foresee the consequences of his or her conduct.[9] If the child is between the ages of 7 and 14, the child is presumed incapable of negligence, but the presumption is rebuttable with clear and convincing evidence. For children who are over 14, it is generally presumed that they are capable of negligence and should reasonably know the foreseeable consequences of their conduct. In any case, the factual circumstances and the foreseeability of the injury work together to determine the specific standard of care applied.

Causation

For liability to be established in negligence, there must be a link between the injuries suffered and the lack of ordinary care exercised by the defendant. This may be proven in several ways: *sine qua non,* direct consequence, and proximate cause.

Sine qua non. In legal terms, **sine qua non** refers to an essential prerequisite and often is used as the "but for" rule. The "but for" rule of causation states that "but for defendant's negligence, plaintiff would not have been injured." The *sine qua non* rule provides that the negligent defendant may be liable even for unforeseeable injuries, because the ordinary care of the defendant would have prevented plaintiff's harm.

Direct Consequence. The direct consequence rule of causation follows an unbroken chain of events from the negligent conduct to the injury. If the injury can be traced along this chain from the negligence to the injury without intervention, the defendant may be liable for the resulting injuries, regardless of whether or not they are foreseeable.

Proximate Cause. Causation is generally discussed in terms of **proximate cause.** Proximate cause is different from causation in fact and is influenced by public policy, which declines to trace liability beyond a particular point. See Chapter Eighteen for a more detailed explanation of proximate cause. There are several theories and arguments concerning the concept of proximate cause.

The *limiting-liability-to-risk* theory claims to simplify the problem of proximate cause because it makes the test for liability the same as the test for negligence. In other words, if the injury or harm was not foreseeable, there is no liability. The injury could not have been foreseen; therefore the actor could not have created an unreasonable risk of that injury and should not be liable.

There have been several arguments in favor of limiting liability to risk. One of those arguments is the **natural and probable** consequences of one's conduct. If the injury is not within the naturally occurring and expected range of anticipated results of conduct (if it is bizarre or unusual), it is unfair to impose liability. If the hazard is one that is outside the suspected hazard (no one could have reasonably anticipated it), it would, likewise, be unfair to impose liability. If the injury is too remote in terms of time and space (again, it could not have been anticipated at the time of the negligent conduct), liability would place an unfair burden on the defendant. These arguments have been adopted by some courts, however many courts are still of the opinion that careful conduct on the part of the defendant would have prevented injury to plaintiff. If liability places an unfair burden on the defendant, it is more unfair to place the burden for that injury on the shoulders of the innocent plaintiff.

Injury. Plaintiff must be able to prove that the harm suffered is compensable. There must be actual, monetary damages in order to establish liability for negligence. If plaintiff has suffered no harm, no claim will be allowed by the court, regardless of how errant the defendant's conduct was.

VICARIOUS LIABILITY

As part of the privilege of being able to delegate duties to employees, employers are generally held liable for the negligent torts of their employees. This is known as **vicarious liability,** the responsibility of one party for the conduct of another. In the case of employer liability, this concept is also known as ***respondeat superior*** ("let the master answer").

Parents are generally not responsible for the negligence of their children, however many homeowners insurance policies provide liability coverage for the negligence of children. In many states, too, parents who provide a motor vehicle to family members are responsible for injuries and harm caused as a result of the negligent use of that motor vehicle.

Vicarious liability in health care includes the "captain of the ship" doctrine. Nurses, who are hospital employees, and anesthetists, who are independent contractors, become the "borrowed servants" of the physician or surgeon and the physician or surgeon is generally answerable for their negligent conduct while acting under the direction of the physician or surgeon.

DAMAGES RECOVERABLE IN NEGLIGENCE

For actions in negligence, compensatory damages are divided into two categories: **special damages** and **general damages.** Special damages are those that are quantifiable; that is, there are receipts or bills that show the amount of money paid for these expenses. Examples of special damages include medical expenses, lost wages, medical appliances, environmental adaptations, and pharmaceuticals. General damages are damages that do not fall neatly behind a dollar sign. Pain and suffering, loss of companionship, and loss of enjoyment of life are examples of general damages.

In addition to compensatory damages, punitive damages are available in negligence actions if the plaintiff pleads and proves that the conduct of the defendant was in reckless disregard for the plaintiff's safety. The recovery of punitive damages in a negligence claim received national attention in the Ford Pinto case.[10] Litigation concerning injuries from tobacco and the diet drug known as Fen-Phen have also resulted in substantial punitive damages.

NEGLIGENCE PER SE

As previously mentioned, the standard of care in any given situation may be established by contract relationship, by case law, or by statute. When a statute prescribes conduct for the protection of other members of the community, conduct that violates that statute constitutes **negligence *per se.*** For example, a city ordinance requires that homeowners clear snow and ice from the sidewalks in front of their homes. The statute is to protect passersby on the public walkways of the city from foreseeable injuries if slippery snow and ice are not removed. *A* has reasonable opportunity to remove the snow and ice from the sidewalk of *A*'s home, but fails to do so. Failure constitutes a violation of the city ordinance. If *B*, walking on *A*'s sidewalk, is injured because of *A*'s failure to remove the ice and snow, *B* may sue *A* for negligence *per se.*

The elements of negligence *per se* are as follows:

- The duty of care is prescribed by statute.
- The statute is for the protection of the public.
- The statute intends to protect the public from a foreseeable harm.
- Defendant breached the statutory duty.
- Defendant's breach of the statutory duty caused injury.

What LNCs Say . . .

"I listened to the attorney each time he asked me about testifying as an expert witness. I told him I could not testify because it was a conflict of interest due to my employment. I assured him that I could do other things for him like prepare chronologies, analyze medical-related cases, research medical issues, find expert witnesses for him, etc. We had the conversation several times before he finally said, 'Well, maybe I can work through you to get an expert to testify' " Kay L. Scharn, RN, BSN, EdS, LNC, Eau Claire, WI, used with permission.

- The injury is provable.

Two questions arise in determining negligence *per se:*

- Who is protected by the statute?
- What harm is intended to be prevented by the statute?

If plaintiff falls within the class of people intended to be protected by the statute and the harm suffered by the plaintiff is of the type that was intended to be prevented by the statute, negligence *per se* applies. Once the statute is deemed to apply, the plaintiff need only establish the injuries. Most courts conclude that violation of the statute is **prima facie** evidence of negligence. Plaintiff need not establish a general standard of care or failure of care. Plaintiff need only establish that defendant violated the statute and that as a result of that violation, plaintiff was injured. Injuries that result from the operation of a vehicle while under the influence of an intoxicant fall within this category. If the defendant is proven guilty of being under the influence, or if the defendant defaults, violation of the OUI statute is evidence of negligence as a matter of law.

PROFESSIONAL NEGLIGENCE

There are no degrees in the standard of care for negligence liability; that is, there is no higher or lower standard of care. There is always and only *ordinary* care. Thus, even professionals who have attained advanced degrees and expertise through practice and research are held to the ordinary care that is usually exercised in that profession.

Professional negligence is often called malpractice. The great body of law on malpractice involves medical malpractice, but it can apply to any profession: law, dentistry, architecture, and so forth. Medical malpractice is seldom used as a category of professional negligence any more. Instead it is more often called health care liability or medical negligence. One of the most litigated areas of medical negligence has to do with the concept of **informed consent.** Courts have said that in order for a patient to make a decision concerning health care, the patient must be informed of the attendant risks and alternatives to the treatment prescribed. Failure to provide the patient with sufficient information to make an informed decision is a form of medical negligence.

RES IPSA LOQUITUR

Negligence is proved by establishing a duty relationship, a general standard of care, the specific standard of care under the circumstances, and the injuries resulting from defendant's failure to meet the standard of care. **Res ipsa loquitur** is a concept in negligence that shifts the burden of proof from the plaintiff to the defendant.

Literally translated, *res ipsa loquitur* means "the thing speaks for itself." In negligence law this means that the incident that caused the injury must have been a result of negligent conduct. It would not have happened if the defendant had been careful. The grandparent case in *res ipsa loquitur* involves a pedestrian in the 1800s who was innocently walking on the sidewalk when a barrel of flour rolled out of a warehouse window and hit him on the head causing substantial injuries.[11] In that case, the court determined that the innocent plaintiff minding his own business on the sidewalks of town need not show how the negligence occurred. Rather, it was up to the defendant to show that the defendant was not negligent. A barrel of flour, the court reasoned, does not roll out of a window without some negligence on the part of the warehouse employees; the plaintiff was not required to show where this negligence occurred.

There are three requirements for using a *res ipsa loquitur* theory of negligence:

- The incident must be of a kind that would not ordinarily occur in the absence of negligence.
- The injuries must be caused by an agency or instrumentality in the exclusive control of the defendant.
- The plaintiff must not in any way be a cause of the injury.

Airplane crashes are examples of incidences where *res ipsa loquitur* applies. A passenger passively enjoying the transportation cannot possibly have any control over the decisions of the pilot or the instruments or machinery necessary for flying the airplane. If the airplane crashes, the injured passenger need not show where or by whom the negligence occurred. Sometimes an additional requirement is needed for *res ipsa loquitur* to be invoked: the explanation for the injury is in the exclusive possession of the defendant. In the preceding example, the passenger cannot have access to the "black box" that contains recordings that assist investigators in determining the cause of an airplane disaster. The defendant airline company must prove that defendant's conduct was not negligent and did not cause the injuries. If defendant cannot make this proof, liability attaches.

In health care liability cases, *res ipsa loquitur* has been used when there appears to be negligence but the plaintiff is at a loss to understand who or what caused the injury, as when a shoulder is paralyzed during an appendectomy.[12]

DEFENSES TO NEGLIGENCE

Like intentional torts, a claim in negligence must be established in the facts. Even though a complaint may allege negligence generally, the court will look to see if all of the elements are met. Failing to prove the claim is always a defense in any personal injury action. There are several important historical defenses that have contributed to our current understanding of when liability does and does not attach. Because legal research often involves looking at past precedent, it is valuable to see how these historical defenses have shaped the modern defenses to negligence.

Net Results

Medical Negligence on the Internet

Numerous web sites exist with information concerning medical malpractice, health care liability, professional liability, and medical-legal news. The Health Care Liability Alliance web site provides legislative information and links to other sites. Access this web page at www.hcla.org. *Another site provides access to medical-legal news items at* www.afss.com/medical. *Information concerning medical malpractice can be found through the resources page of the National Federation of Paralegal Associations at* www.paralegals.org/LegalResearch/Practice. *Medical legal news may also be accessed using key word searches at sites such as* www.law.com/professional/litlaw.html *and* www.findlaw.com.

Historical Defenses

Historical defenses to negligence included contributory negligence, last clear chance, and assumption of risk. While some of these defenses still exist in language, these theories have been modified and integrated and, generally, fall under the current umbrella of comparative negligence.

Contributory Negligence. Historically, whenever the plaintiff was a cause of the plaintiff's own injuries, he or she was not entitled to recover. This doctrine can be traced to a "clean hands" theory adopted by the courts of common law. The "clean hands" doctrine stated that one who could not be proved blameless was not entitled to a remedy. Thus, historically, a plaintiff who was found **contributorily negligent** was completely barred from recovery, regardless of the degree of fault that was attributable to the plaintiff.

Last Clear Chance. The courts also tried to determine liability by identifying who the last person was who had the opportunity and the ability to protect the plaintiff from harm. If that person recognized the danger to the plaintiff, even if it was negligently created by the plaintiff, and that person could have taken steps to protect the plaintiff and did not, that person would be liable. Key in the **last clear chance** theory were the following elements:

- Defendant must have knowledge of the peril to plaintiff.
- Defendant must have opportunity to prevent harm to plaintiff.
- Defendant must have failed to take precautions to prevent harm to plaintiff.
- Reasonable people would have acted to prevent harm to plaintiff.
- Plaintiff is harmed.

Assumption of Risk. Historically, **assumption of risk** was the idea that the plaintiff recognized the danger to him or herself and voluntarily encountered that danger. Since the plaintiff did not take precautions to protect him or herself, the courts would not impose liability on someone else to provide plaintiff with greater protection. Assumption of risk is still recognized as a defense to negligence in some states.

Contemporary Defenses

The historical defenses of contributory negligence, last clear chance, and assumption of risk have generally been incorporated into the modern concept of comparative negligence. While comparative negligence is still sometimes called contributory negligence, it does not have the historical impact of barring plaintiff from recovery.

Comparative Negligence. **Comparative negligence** is the modern concept that recognizes that plaintiff's injuries might result from a number of causes including plaintiff's own negligence or knowledge of the risk. Basically comparative negligence statutes state that plaintiff's damages will be reduced in proportion to plaintiff's fault. If a jury decides that plaintiff is 30% negligent and that defendant is 70% negligent, plaintiff will be entitled to recover 70% of the damages awarded by the jury.

When a jury verdict results in 50% liability attaching to plaintiff and 50% to defendant, the state laws must be consulted. Some states like Florida and Wisconsin still allow the plaintiff to recover 50% of the damages, since plaintiff's fault was *not* greater than defendant's. In other states, plaintiff is precluded from recovery because plaintiff and defendant are equally at fault.

Failure to Take Precautions to Minimize Injury. The **seat belt defense** is a good example of the defense that requires plaintiff to take measures to minimize potential injury. This defense is not a defense to the act of negligence, but to the extent of liability for the damages caused by negligence. Plaintiff's failure to seek medical attention or to wear an available seat belt or motorcycle helmet are examples of this defense.

Many states now have statutes that limit the defense of failure to take precautions to minimize injury. For example, failure to wear an available seat belt may be proven by expert testimony to have caused injuries when the plaintiff was ejected from the vehicle. The state statute, however, may limit that defense to a maximum of 15% or 20% of the award of damages. The idea is that even if plaintiff could have avoided some injury to him or herself by wearing an available seat belt, plaintiff would not have been injured at all had defendant acted with reasonable care. Plaintiff, therefore, should not be punished for the wrongful conduct of defendant by being denied recovery for injuries because he or she was not wearing a seat belt.

Statute of Limitations. The statute of limitations is a complete defense to any action. In most states personal injury resulting from negligence carries a three-year statute of limitations. If a plaintiff does not bring a lawsuit within three years of the date of the occurrence, plaintiff is forever barred from bringing the lawsuit to court.

THE IMPACT OF NEGLIGENCE ON PERSONAL INJURY LITIGATION

Of all the personal injury lawsuits that are filed, negligence is the basis for the greatest share. Whether it is negligence *per se, res ipsa loquitur,* or professional negligence, this cause of action provides a broad framework within which to show the court that defendant's conduct fell below a reasonable standard. Nurses are not strangers to the law of negligence. For many years

---

Ethics Bookmark

Unwarranted Delay

"A lawyer shall make reasonable efforts to expedite litigation" Annotated Model Rules of Professional Conduct Fourth Edition Rule 3.2, Copyright 1999.*[13] *It is inexcusable for an attorney to allow the statute of limitations to toll without bringing a claim on behalf of the client. Attorneys attempt to ensure that this crucial date will not be overlooked by maintaining elaborate calendaring systems. Legal nurse consultants working in law firms should maintain separate calendars and note the statute of limitations date for each claim that the legal nurse consultant works on. Calendaring may prevent a file from falling through the cracks.*
*American Bar Association. Reprinted by permission of the American Bar Association. American Bar Association, *Annotated Model Rules of Professional conduct,* 4th ed. (1999) Rule 3.2. Copies of Model Code of Professional Responsibility, 1999 edition are available from Service Center, American Bar Association, 750 North Lake Shore Drive, Chicago, IL 60611-4497, 1-800-285-2221.

the courts have recognized the professional liability of registered nurses. While the liability has been borne by the health care facility or the physician whose instructions the nurse was carrying out, the failure to act with the ordinary and prudent care of other professional nurses has been well settled in the courts of the United States.

A legal nurse consultant is uniquely qualified to assist attorneys in the area of health care negligence. The nurse's background in hospital, clinical, or long-term care provides an invaluable educational advantage in the preparation of a case involving the alleged lack of care of a health care provider.

CHAPTER SUMMARY

- Negligence is conduct that falls below a reasonable standard and creates an unreasonable risk of harm to another.

- To establish liability in negligence, the following elements must be shown: one party is to act with reasonable care for the safety of another, the party fails in that duty, and injuries result from that failure of care.

- Vicarious liability is imposed upon one for the wrongful activities of another; *respondeat superior* is a type of vicarious liability.

- When a statute prescribes a duty for the protection of others, and the violation of that statute causes harm, an action in negligence *per se* may be available.

- *Res ipsa loquitur* involves an event that caused injury and that would not have occurred if the actor had been careful.

- The defenses to negligence include comparative negligence, statute of limitations, and failure to take precautions to minimize injury.

KEY TERMS

assumption of risk	natural and probable	seat belt defense
attractive nuisance	negligence *per se*	*sine qua non*
comparative negligence	Pied Piper cases	special damages
contributory negligence	prima facie	unavoidable accident
foreseeability	proximate cause	unintentional tort
general damages	reasonable person standard	vicarious liability
informed consent	*res ipsa loquitur*	
last clear chance	*respondeat superior*	

REVIEW QUESTIONS

1. How does negligence differ from intentional torts?
2. Distinguish between negligence *per se* and *res ipsa loquitur.*
3. Explain the defenses to negligence.
4. What constitutes professional negligence under the doctrine of informed consent?

INTERNET EXERCISES

1. Access the web page for this textbook at *www.westlegalstudies.com.*
2. Click on the assignments section and complete the assignment(s) for Chapter Nineteen.

EXERCISES

1. Networking. If possible, locate the headquarters for an insurance company in your area. Telephone the insurance company and ask to speak to a nurse in the claims department. If the nurse is available and willing to talk with you, conduct an informational interview. Ask about the process for seeking employment with that insurance company. Have the nurse identify the strengths and weaknesses of employment. If the nurse is willing to share this information, ask about compensation and benefits.

Maintain this information and this contact in your networking system, file, or Rolodex.

3. Professional Portfolio. As you become familiar with intentional torts and negligence, begin collecting news accounts about personal injury litigation. You can find these articles in nursing journals, professional journals, newspapers, newsletters, and on the Internet. Maintain these clippings in your separate systems folder and organize or identify them in a way that allows easy reference.

ENDNOTES

1. D. Oran, *Oran's Dictionary of the Law* (Albany, NY: West Legal Studies, 2000), 203.
2. *Palsgraf v. Long Island R.R. Co.,* 248 N.Y. 339, 162 N.E. 99 (1928).
3. *Tennessee Trailways v. Erwin,* 438 S.W. 2d 733 (Tenn. 1969).
4. *Palsgraf v. Long Island R.R. Co.,* 248 N.Y. 339, 162 N.E. 99 (1928).
5. *Delair v. McAdoo,* 324 Pa. 391, 188 A. 181 (1936).
6. *Hill v. City of Glenwood,* 124 Iowa 479, 100 N.W. 522 (1904).
7. *Robinson v. Lindsay,* 92 Wash. 2d 410, 598 P. 2d 392 (1979).
8. *Johnson v. Kokomoor,* 199 Wis. 2d 615, 545 N.W. 2d 495 (1996).
9. W. Prosser, J. Wade, V. Schwartz, *Torts: Cases and Materials,* 8th ed. (Westbury, NY: The Foundation Press, Inc., 1988), 168.
10. *Grimshaw v. Ford Motor Company,* 119 Cal. App. 3d 757, 174 Cal. Rptr. 348 (1981).
11. *Byrne V. Boadle,* 2 H. & C. 722, 159 Eng. Rep. 299 (1863).

12. *Ybarra v. Spangard,* 25 Cal. 2d 486, 154 P. 2d 687 (1944).

13. American Bar Association, *Annotated Model Rules of Professional Conduct,* (1999) 4th Edition Rule 3.2. Copies of ABA *Model Code of Professional Responsibility, 1999 Edition* are available from Service Center, American Bar Association, 750 North Lake Shore Drive, Chicago, IL 60611-4497, 1-800-285-2221.

ADDITIONAL REFERENCES

"Can a Legal Nurse Consultant Be Sued for Malpractice?" *Journal of Legal Nurse Consulting* 7:4 (1996) 16.

"Chart Review: Allegations of Negligent Pain Management." *Journal of Legal Nurse Consulting* 10:4 (1999) 20.

Loecker, B., MSEd, RN. "The Doctrine of Informed Consent." *Journal of Legal Nurse Consulting* 7:4 (1996) 17–18.

Patton, M.J., CRNA, JD. "The Standards for Disclosure of Risk in Informed Consent." *Journal of Legal Nurse Consulting* 11:1 (2000) 17–19.

CHAPTER 20

MEDICAL NEGLIGENCE

OBJECTIVES

In this chapter, you will learn

- what medical negligence is

- who is responsible for medical negligence

- the defenses to medical negligence

- how legal nurse consultants play an invaluable role in processing a medical negligence claim

OVERVIEW

Negligence is the failure to act with reasonable care, the care that is exercised by the great majority of ordinary, prudent people. There have been medical negligence claims based on almost every aspect of health care from diagnosis to recovery and rehabilitation. This chapter cannot provide information about every aspect of this area of law, but will introduce the most common causes of medical negligence claims, the most common defenses to medical negligence claims, and the most common roles of legal nurse consultants in processing medical negligence claims.

There are four elements in a cause of action based on negligence: (a) duty (b) breach of duty (c) causation (d) injury. When discussing medical negligence, the elements take on specific interpretations.

Duty

The health care provider-patient relationship must be established first. Without that relationship, no liability can attach. This relationship might be established by contract, either express or implied; by **quasi contract** as in the case of emergency treatment when the patient is unconscious; or by statute, which requires health care providers to render assistance in certain circumstances such as traffic accidents.

Standard of Care

In order to find liability in a medical negligence case, a health care provider must have failed to act with the requisite standard of reasonable care for the safety of the patient. Generally this standard of care is the skill, knowledge, and degree of care ordinarily exercised by the average health care provider of the same specialization. Specifically, the standard of care depends upon the circumstances of the case and may also involve several other generally accepted concepts that provide insight as to the reasonable care that should have been provided.

Licensing Regulations. In many states, failing to have the requisite license to practice in the scope of the health care provided is *prima facie* evidence of negligence. These regulations establish a minimum standard of education and experience without which the provider is not qualified. Licensing regulations for health care professionals are intended to protect the public from unqualified practitioners; therefore, failing to meet licensing requirements may constitute negligence.

Policies and Procedures. Hospitals, clinics, nursing homes, and other health care facilities have policies and procedures for surgical, emergency, and routine activities. Failure to abide by the facility's policies and procedures may be evidence of a lack of ordinary and prudent care.

State Laws and Administrative Regulations. Failing to meet certain statutory requirements of care may constitute negligence. For example, the Emergency Medical Treatment and Active Labor Act[1] (part of the Comprehensive Omnibus Budget Reconciliation Act) requires that health care providers render medical assistance to anyone on facility grounds who has medical concerns. Failing to provide assistance may result in a finding of negligence. Nursing homes are heavily regulated by administrative agencies that may prescribe standards that must be met in order to maintain federal or state funding. These standards may be used as evidence of the reasonable care necessary to avoid liability.

Tort Law. Considerable case law exists identifying situations of health care liability and the specific standard of care involved. These cases establish precedent in the jurisdiction where the case is appealed. It is important to remember, however, that the facts of each case are unique. While case law provides guidelines for evaluating a current problem, arguments will be made on both sides and the court may arrive at a different ruling. Still, case law does establish some general expectations and standards with which to measure the care provided.

Scope of Practice. Most professional specialties identify a scope of practice within which professionals may serve. National organizations often establish ethical codes and standards of practice that may help identify what the reasonable care should have been in a given situation.

Manuals, Textbooks, and Treatises. Use and maintenance manuals for medical equipment may provide standards of care when that equipment is involved in alleged medical negligence. Textbooks describe procedures and detail standards for the reasonable care of patients in various situations. Treatises are scholarly works written by experts that study one aspect of a discipline. If the health care provider is considered an expert in that field, a treatise may establish the degree of care to which that health care provider should have conformed.

Joint Commission on Accreditation of Healthcare Organizations. The JCAHO provides standards of practice for healthcare facilities that are generally accepted nationally as the ordinary and prudent standard for providing reasonable care to patients and clients.

Causation

While it is often easy to identify the negligent conduct or failure of care that caused injury to a patient, there are times when it is obscure. Health care providers may be found liable under the negligence theory of **res ipsa loquitur** if the injury suffered by the patient must have been the result of negligence—as when a surgeon operates on the wrong patient.

There might be intervening actions that cause the injury and for which the health care provider, even though negligent, will not be liable. For example, a patient consults a physician who negligently prescribes a drug to which the patient is allergic. The patient refuses to take prescribed medication and subsequently dies. The estate of the deceased patient might sue

Net Results

Standards of Practice

Standards of practice and information on standard of care for some medical professionals may be accessed via the Internet. The American Medical Association can be accessed at www.amaassn.org. The American College of Emergency Physicians can be found at www.acep.org and the Emergency Nurses Association can be accessed at www.ena.org. For links to boards of nursing, go to www.ncsbn.org. For links to nursing resources in general, access the school of nursing at the University of Wisconsin at www.son.wisc.edu. The Joint Commission on Accreditation of Healthcare Organizations, is available at www.jcaho.org.

the physician, but will not be able to establish causation. Even though the physician has been negligent, the physician's negligence did not cause the injury. Whenever causation is an issue, the determination is facilitated by removing the act that is claimed to have caused the injury. In the preceding case, the patient would have died regardless, because the patient did not take personal care to prevent harm. The fact that the physician prescribed incorrect medication, when removed from the scenario, does not affect the result.

Injury

Generally, damages in negligence include past and future medical expenses, past and future wage loss, and past and future pain and suffering. Future expenses usually must be reduced to present day values using a formula that takes into consideration inflationary rates and cost of living changes. Additional injuries in medical negligence cases include loss of enjoyment of life; loss of chance of life or loss of chance for a better life; loss of quality of life; and other holistic, sometimes called **hedonic damages,** that result in loss of the pleasure of life.

SPECIAL FEATURES OF MEDICAL NEGLIGENCE

Negligence is a very broad category of tort law; it always depends upon the circumstances, and the law prescribes only the general standard of reasonable care. For medical negligence, there are several specific aspects of negligence law with which legal nurse consultants should become familiar.

Vicarious Liability

Similar to the *respondeat superior* doctrine, **vicarious liability** imposes responsibility for the actions of others on a party not involved in the wrongdoing. This may include an employer's responsibility for the actions of employees and **borrowed servants.** Whenever a nurse is found negligent while acting within the scope of employment with a hospital or clinic, the hospital or clinic, as employer, is financially responsible for the losses suffered as a result of the nurse's negligence. Similarly, if a nurse employed by the hospital is under the direction of a surgeon or other physician who is not a hospital employee, the surgeon or physician is responsible for the nurse's negligence under the borrowed servant rule.

Vicarious liability may also extend beyond employers. Manufacturers of medical devices and equipment who fail to properly instruct the users of the devices or equipment or who sell defective equipment that is unsafe may be liable for negligence. This doctrine is more fully explained in Chapter Twenty-three.

Captain of the Ship Doctrine

Historically, the doctrine of **captain of the ship** relates to the physician's responsibility for the actions of all those who give care to the patient under the physician's direction. It is based on the legal concepts of maritime law, extended now to airline travel as well. The captain, or pilot, is the chief executive officer aboard and is vested with the duty to bring the "ship" safely home. The captain may make such rules as are necessary and carry them out as needed in order to protect passengers from danger.

Historically, the captain of the ship doctrine was applied to protect hospitals as charitable immunities. Public policy in previous years demanded that the services offered by the hospital, a nonprofit organization, be precluded from liability. It was thought that the funds used to operate the hospital and provide healing services, particularly when those hospitals were subsidized by religious and charitable organizations, should not be subject to the high cost of litigation and potential liability. Because of this historic **charitable immunity** concept, injured patients were forced to look to other sources for losses suffered as a result of negligent care.

The captain of the ship doctrine has been eroded in recent years, particularly with the proliferation of policies and procedures adopted by hospitals for their staff and the abolishment of the charitable immunity doctrine. If the hospital provides policies for the safe implementation of the procedure, even though it was ordered by the physician, who is not a hospital employee, the hospital may be liable since the procedure is being carried out according to the instructions in the hospital policies and procedures manual.

In addition, **independent contractors** have become more prominent in medical environments. Anesthesiologists and physical therapists, though working under the general direction of a physician, are not, in fact, employees or borrowed servants and are responsible for their own conduct in carrying out the directives of the physician. This is because independent contractors generally have specialized knowledge and are free to select appropriate measures for completing the directive of the physician. The physician does not directly control or supervise independent contractors, therefore, they are liable for losses sustained when they perform negligently.

Borrowed Servant Doctrine

A borrowed servant is one who is temporarily loaned to another master, or employer. The temporary master, or employer, is responsible for the acts of borrowed servants when they are carrying out the directives of the temporary master, or employer. This is often the case in surgical procedures when the hospital loans staff to the surgeon for the performance and term of the surgery. The surgeon then becomes the temporary master, or employer, and is responsible for the actions of the borrowed staff while they are acting under the surgeon's direction. Here again, however, the courts have found that if policies and procedures exist governing the conduct of the staff during the surgical procedure, the hospital and not the surgeon, may be liable when staff violate the existing policies and procedures.

Informed Consent

One of the most frequent claims in medical negligence is that of failing to adequately inform the patient. Courts have said that the **doctrine of informed consent** arises from and reflects the fundamental notion of bodily integrity. This natural right exists only if the patient is adequately informed about the positive and negative aspects of prescribed medical treatment. If physicians fail to provide sufficient information about risks, benefits, and feasible alternatives, they may be found negligent in the care and treatment of a patient. Although in practice, physicians sometimes delegate to nurses the responsibility of providing information to the patient and obtaining from the patient the written consent to treatment, the courts have consistently held that the physician is liable, rather than the nurse or facility, for failing to obtain an informed consent.

Several factors are involved in the disclosure process, but courts have generally concluded that the physician must provide information that is material to the patient's decision to accept or reject treatment. Material facts are those that would influence the decision. The "scope of disclosure required by physicians defies simple definition" and "must be measured by the patient's need."[2] Negligent failure to disclose must be proven with expert testimony. Only other physicians have the professional degree of care and skill necessary to identify what disclosure would have been reasonable under the circumstances.

Physicians and health care providers will not be liable simply for a bad result if the requisite care is provided to the patient and the patient is given sufficient information to understand the risks and alternatives to the treatment prescribed. However, at least one court has held that failure to provide information to a patient about the risks of not undergoing a routine examination resulted in a judgment of medical malpractice. In that case, a woman refused a PAP smear because of an inability to pay for the test. She was later diagnosed with uterine cancer and died. The estate and survivors claimed that if the physician had adequately informed the deceased of the importance of the examination and the risk of failing to undergo the procedure, she would have submitted to the test, the cancer would have been detected earlier, and she would have had a greater chance of survival. The decision in favor of the physician was reversed.[3]

Failure to Diagnose or Misdiagnosis

Like failing to adequately inform, failing to diagnose or failing to diagnose correctly are also common in medical negligence claims. When a diagnosis is missed, the loss of chance for survival, for quality of life, and for enjoyment of life are often claimed as damages.

Failure to Refer

At least one source has interpreted JCAHO standards to indicate that a physician should refer a patient to a specialist if any of the following conditions exist:

- The diagnosis is obscure.
- The patient exhibits psychiatric symptoms.
- The patient is a poor risk.
- Doubt exists about appropriate treatment.
- The patient requests referral.[4]

This JCAHO interpretation, however, may not constitute the reasonable standard of care under the circumstances and may not be relied upon as *prima facie* evidence of medical negligence. Still, failure to refer constitutes a significant portion of the medical negligence claims brought to court.

DAMAGES IN MEDICAL NEGLIGENCE CASES

Compensatory damages in medical negligence claims may be of two kinds: special or general. Special damages are those damages that may be quantified and are usually backed up with receipts or bills. Special damages include all past medical expenses, all past lost wages, all past pharmaceuticals, and all other medically-related expenses paid by the injured party. General damages are those that deal with the wholeness of life. They include pain and suffering, loss of companionship, loss of chance, mental anguish, hedonic damages, and loss of dignity. These damages are difficult to prove and are subject to the discretion of the jury. Punitive damages are available to a patient if the patient proves that the health care provider acted with reckless disregard of the patient's rights. Although punitive damages may be alleged in the complaint, the outrageous conduct justifying an award of punitive damages is generally difficult to prove in a medical negligence claim.

When it is claimed that the medical negligence results in the death of the patient, **wrongful death** damages are supportable. These include the potential lifetime earnings of the deceased, based on actuarial tables, and other benefits and losses resulting from the untimely death of the patient. Future damages generally must be reduced to present values using a formula based upon the rate of inflation and the cost of living index.

DEFENSES TO MEDICAL NEGLIGENCE

The defenses to negligence (contributory negligence, statute of limitations, and failure to take precautions to minimize the damages) are also defenses to medical negligence. There are, however, other defenses to medical negligence claims that are based in public policy. It is important to the public that medical facilities and medical treatment be available. Too many lawsuits resulting in high

Ethics Bookmark

Professional Referrals
"The legal nurse consultant may collaborate with legal professionals, health care professionals, and others involved in the legal process. . . . The LNC makes referrals as needed" AALNC Standards of Professional Performance Standard 6 (1995).[5] *Legal nurse consultants must not hold themselves out as experts in all aspects of nursing or medical care. For assignments involving analysis and evaluation of specialized medical cases about which the legal nurse consultant has little medical background, the nurse may have an ethical duty to refer that assignment to another medical professional with the appropriate background to competently complete the assignment.*

awards to plaintiffs result in escalating costs for health care. In many states, legislatures have established limits for the amounts of money that may be recovered in medical negligence claims. These statutory caps operate to balance the needs of an injured patient with society's need for affordable health care.

Statute of Limitations

While the statute of limitations for negligence in most states is three years, in medical negligence, a distinction may be made between the date of injury and the date of discovery of the injury. In addition, the basis for the claim (intentional tort, breach of contract, etc.) of medical liability may result in a difference in the tolling of the statute of limitations.

Intentional Tort. If the claim is based in an intentional tort, such as battery, assault, or intentional infliction of emotional distress, the statute of limitations is generally two years. Each state enacts its own statute of limitations, however, so the law of the state in which the action is to be commenced must be checked.

Date of Wrongdoing. The statute of limitations generally begins to toll on the date of the act or omission that is claimed to be negligent. If the action is based on medical negligence, the statute generally runs for three years after the incident causing injury. However, if the action is based on breach of contract or breach of promise or warranty, most states provide a six-year statute of limitations. Remember, while many state laws are parallel, it is important to check the specific state law to determine what the time limitation is and whether the claim has been brought within that time. Many states preclude this juggling of time limitations by providing specific statutes of limitations for medical malpractice or health care negligence. These statutory provisions require lawsuits against medical providers, *regardless of the claim upon which liability is based,* to be brought within the time specified.

Date of Discovery. Because medical negligence may not be apparent at the time of the incident that caused the injury, many states allow claims to be brought within a specific time after the injury is discovered or should reasonably have been discovered. States that allow the statute of limitations to run from the date of discovery generally also provide for a protection to the health care provider. In Wisconsin, for instance, a claim in medical negligence may be brought within three years of the incident, or within one year from the date the injury was discovered or reasonably should have been discovered. In any case, though, the lawsuit may not be brought later than five years after the event that caused the injury.[6]

Wrongful death. If the medical negligence results in death, a question arises as to whether the statute of limitations runs from the date of injury that caused death or the date of death. For example, a patient is diagnosed with a stroke. This diagnosis is erroneous and negligent and six months later the patient is properly diagnosed with malignant glioblastoma. Eleven months later, the patient dies. Whether the statute of limitations runs from the date of the missed diagnosis or from the date of the patient's death is a matter to be determined by the court, if it is not clear in the statutes.

Errors of Judgment

Health care providers are not liable for errors of judgment if the requisite skill, care, and knowledge were present in the treatment of the patient. The fact that a physician selected one of several medically acceptable treatments, and that treatment failed or caused injury, does not make the physician liable if he or she exercised reasonable care in ascertaining all of the relevant facts to base a diagnosis on.

Employment Retirement Income Security Act

The Employment Retirement Income Security Act (ERISA) of 1974 provides a defense to claims made against health maintenance organizations that are managed and owned by employees for the benefit of employees and their families. If the HMO meets the elements outlined in the act, some courts have concluded that federal law preempts claims made under state tort (personal injury) law.

In order to meet the ERISA defense, the health care provider must be

- a plan, fund, or program
- established or maintained by an employee organization
- for the purpose of providing medical, surgical, hospital care, etc.
- to participants or beneficiaries.

Recently, courts have held that certain health maintenance organizations fall within the federal domain created by ERISA.[7]

Constitutional Defenses

The Ninth Amendment clearly states that the rights identified in the United States Constitution are not meant to be exclusive; that is, that the people of the United States are entitled to natural rights that are not enumerated in the Constitution. This amendment has been interpreted to mean that natural rights may not be diminished simply because they were not specifically included.

The right to reject or accept medical treatment (the natural right to determine what is to be done with one's body) is critical in medical negligence claims. In one case, a patient signed a "Refusal to Permit a Blood Transfusion" prior to surgery. During surgery, the surgeon negligently lacerated the uterus and the patient bled to death. It was established at the trial that the patient's hemorrhage was caused by the negligent act of the surgeon, but that death would have been averted had the patient been given a blood transfusion. A lawsuit in wrongful death was not successful. Although there are times when a medical professional can use the implied consent doctrine to administer treatment in exigent circumstances, in this case, the medical staff could not prevent the patient's bleeding to death because of the written, signed order that was on the record. Because expert testimony established that death would have been prevented had the patient accepted blood transfusion, the court found that the physician was protected by the patient's constitutional right to refuse treatment, even for a medical condition caused by the negligence of the surgeon.[8]

Contributory Negligence

In most situations, contributory negligence occurs when a patient refuses to comply with the directives of the treatment or fails to maintain a timely follow-up schedule. Additionally, if a patient is not honest about the condition or fails to provide the physician with complete information, the patient may have contributed to his or her own injuries. In most states, the comparative negligence rule applies. Plaintiff's damages are reduced in proportion to the plaintiff's contribution or fault. See Chapter Nineteen for a more complete discussion of the defense of contributory negligence.

Contributory negligence is not a defense in a claim based on lack of informed consent.[9] Clearly the patient cannot have access to information concerning the risks and alternatives to the treatment prescribed and cannot be held contributorily negligent for failing to ask about such risks and alternatives. To allow a contributory negligence defense in a claim based on lack of informed consent would be to place the patient in the equivalent position of the physician.

Charitable Immunity

As stated earlier, the historical concept of charitable immunity involved the public policy of not attaching liability to religious, educational, and nonprofit organizations dedicated to charitable purposes. The doctrine of charitable immunity has been abolished in most states and limited in others.

THE ROLE OF THE LEGAL NURSE CONSULTANT IN MEDICAL NEGLIGENCE

The medical expertise, the analysis and evaluation, and the network of professional contacts and quick access to medical literature that the legal nurse consultant brings will greatly enhance the legal services provided. Legal nurse consultants should ensure that the attorney has relevant records. A professional with medical competence should review, summarize, and evaluate the records and search for gaps and potential missing records. The legal nurse consultant should also identify and calculate damages, particularly medical damages, and scrutinize medical bills for unrelated or unnecessary treatments.

Once the records have been analyzed and the legal nurse consultant has made a preliminary evaluation, experts may need to be located and retained to provide testimony and opinion concerning the medical negligence. Information sent to the expert will include the summaries and analysis made by the legal nurse consultant.

As the case progresses, legal nurse consultants may be involved in

- drafting and responding to medical discovery
- attending independent (adverse) medical examinations
- consulting with graphic artists and other members of the litigation team concerning visual aids and exhibits for trial
- attending and assisting in medical depositions
- attending and assisting at trial

Perhaps more than in any other area of legal practice, legal nurse consultants will provide essential services and education to the litigation team in medical negligence claims. With increasing reliance on alternative dispute resolution for claims against health care providers, legal nurse consultants provide cost-effective, value-added services to attorneys, insurance companies, and health maintenance organizations for timely and fair disposition of medical negligence claims.

CHAPTER SUMMARY

- The standard of care in medical negligence may be established by licensing regulations, policies and procedures, state statutes, tort law, professional associations, statements on scope of practice, manuals, textbooks, treatises, JCAHO, and other sources.
- Vicarious liability is imposed upon physicians or facilities employing health care professionals and directing the activities of those health care professionals.
- Common bases for medical negligence claims include lack of informed consent, failure to diagnose, misdiagnosis, and failure to refer.
- Damages in medical negligence include compensatory damages (special and general) and punitive damages.
- The defenses to medical negligence include the statute of limitations, ERISA, contributory negligence, and constitutional defenses.
- Health care providers are not liable for errors in judgment when ordinary and reasonable care and skill are exercised.
- Legal nurse consultants may assist in medical negligence claims by providing initial evaluation; locating the appropriate standards of care; computing damages; locating experts; and assisting in the general maintenance of the case file, discovery, and communication with the client.

KEY TERMS

borrowed servant	hedonic damages	*respondeat superior*
captain of the ship	independent contractor	vicarious liability
charitable immunity	quasi contract	wrongful death
doctrine of informed consent	*res ipsa loquitur*	

REVIEW QUESTIONS

1. How may the statute of limitations in medical negligence be different from the statute of limitations in a regular negligence claim?
2. Explain some of the more common bases for medical negligence claims.
3. What defenses are available in medical negligence?
4. How may the requisite standard of care be established?

INTERNET EXERCISES

1. Access the web page for this textbook at *www.westlegalstudies.com.*
2. Click on the assignments section and complete the assignment(s) for Chapter Twenty.

EXERCISES

1. Networking. An invaluable way to learn about the process and end-product of medical negligence litigation is to observe a medical negligence trial. Contact the local courthouse. Usually a clerk of court, a person in charge of jury trials, the law librarian, or other administrator will be willing to help you schedule this observation. While at the trial, which may take several days, take notes about the exhibits used, the themes developed, and the styles and personalities of the attorneys and their methods of organization. Consider how you might assist the attorney in the courtroom.

2. Professional Portfolio. Consider all of the specialized professional associations for health care professionals, such as the American College of Radiology and the American Society of Anesthesiologists. Almost all of them have standards of practice and codes of ethics. Some may have web sites where this information is readily available. Research some of the major professional associations on your list and copy their particular standards of practice. Keep these standards in your systems file, binder, or folder. Organize or index them in a way that allows for easy reference.

ENDNOTES

1. *Emergency Medical Treatment and Active Labor Act,* 42 U.S.C. s. 1395dd.

2. *Cobbs v. Grant,* 502 P. 2d 1 (Ca, 1972).

3. *Truman v. Thomas,* 27 Cal. 3d 285, 611 P. 2d 902, 165 Cal. Rptr. 308 (1980).

4. E.S. Calloway, "Understanding Hospital Records." *The Practical Lawyer* 30:1 (1984): 11—22.

5. American Association of Legal Nurse Consultants, *Standards of Professional Performance,* (1995) Standard 6.

6. Wis. Stat. 893.55 (1997–98).

7. *Butler v. Wu,* 853 F. Supp 125 (1994).

8. *Shorter v. Drury,* 103 Wash. 2d. 645, 696 P. 2d. 115 (1985).

9. *Brown v. Dibbell,* 227 Wis. 2d 28, 595 N.W. 2d 358 (1999).

ADDITIONAL REFERENCES

AALNC Greater Detroit Chapter. "Standard of care." *Journal of Legal Nurse Consulting* 7:3 (1998): 20.

Bogart, J.B., RN, BSN, MS, ed. *Legal Nurse Consulting: Principles and Practice.* Boston: CRC Press, 1997.

Brown, T.A., RN. "Victims of Domestic Violence: What Is the Standard of Care?" *Journal of Legal Nurse Consulting* 10:4 (1999): 25, 27.

Fedorka, P., PhD., RNC. "Court Decisions Involving Standards of Care." *Journal of Legal Nurse Consulting* 10:2 (1999): 17–21.

Fedorka, P., PhD, RNC. "Defining the Standard of Care in Nursing Practice." *Journal of Legal Nurse Consulting* 10:2 (1999): 11–16.

Gibson, L.Y., PhD, RN, CPNP and K.C. Malley, RN, CEN. "A Case Study of Pediatric Nursing Standards in the Acute Care Setting and Strategies for Reducing Litigation Claims." *Journal of Legal Nurse Consulting* 9:4 (1998): 3–9.

CHAPTER 21

STRICT LIABILITY

OBJECTIVES

In this chapter, you will learn

- what constitutes strict liability

- circumstances and activities that give rise to actions in strict liability

- defenses to strict liability

- the role of the legal nurse consultant in actions based on strict liability

OVERVIEW

Strict liability is imposed upon a defendant when the activity the defendant engages in is abnormally dangerous to life and health. It does not matter that the defendant took due care and reasonable precautions to prevent injury, because the activity itself demands responsibility for the consequences. Perhaps the easiest example is blasting. Because the use of explosive devices is abnormally dangerous to life and health, it is immaterial that the company employing the explosives took precautions to seal off the area and took due care to ensure that the explosive was of the proper type and quantity. If someone is injured as a result of the blast or if property is damaged, the company employing the explosive devices will be liable for the damages.

Courts have identified several areas in which strict liability will be imposed. These are not universal rules, however, and it is important to check individual state court rulings and statutes to determine what activities and circumstances give rise to strict liability in a specific state.

STRICT LIABILITY CIRCUMSTANCES

The Restatement (Second) of Torts §520 identifies the factors that might be used to determine what constitutes an abnormally dangerous activity giving rise to an action in strict liability. Those factors are

- existence of a high degree of risk of some harm to the person, land, or **chattels** of others
- likelihood that the harm that results from it will be great
- inability to eliminate the risk by the exercise of reasonable care
- extent to which the activity is not a matter of common usage
- inappropriateness of the activity to the place where it is carried on
- extent to which its value to the community is outweighed by its dangerous attributes.[1]

All of the factors need not be present to establish strict liability. The critical question is whether the risk of harm created is of such significance that reasonable precautions cannot reduce the risk or prevent harm. Without engaging in any activity, a defendant may be liable under a strict liability theory of tort if the defendant creates a circumstance that is dangerous to life and health. Among these circumstances are exposure to toxic chemicals, leaking underground storage tanks, and owning and keeping animals.

Exposure to Toxic Chemicals

Courts have almost consistently held that exposure to toxic chemicals will result in strict liability against the defendant responsible for maintaining or disposing of the chemicals. The fact that the defendant did not intend to harm or did not even realize the risk of harm created is not a defense. The circumstances of the situation are always most important and the facts of each case must be reviewed to determine whether a strict liability theory may be applied. In addition, state law and state statutes must be reviewed to see if authority exists for a strict liability claim.

Leaking Underground Storage Tanks

Similarly, damages for injuries resulting from the disposal of hazardous waste have been granted under the theory of strict liability. Leaking underground storage tanks and hazardous disposal sites are major areas of practice for researchers, environmental specialists, and legal services. Laws are just beginning to determine the responsibility for harm that results from waste that, because of time and decay, become abnormally dangerous to life and health.

Animals

Most states have enacted statutes declaring that injuries caused by animals are the strict liability of the animal's owner. Most states have "dog bite" statutes that require dog owners to be responsible for injuries suffered when a dog attacks or bites another. Additionally, if a wild animal is kept as a pet, the animal's owner is, by statute and common law in most states, strictly liable for the harm that animal causes.

STRICT LIABILITY ACTIVITIES

Most strict liability cases involve products. Products liability is discussed in Chapter Twenty-three. When the action does not arise as a result of a dangerous product, it most often arises out of an activity that results in an abnormally dangerous risk of harm. These activities include crop dusting, storing gases and chemicals, and nuclear transport and testing.

Use of Pesticides or Herbicides

Many courts, although this is not universal, have held that using pesticides and herbicides that have the potential to drift and cause harm to the property or crops of another results in strict liability against the user. The use of pesticides and herbicides are advantageous for some, but their application and use may cause harm or death to others. While not every case will result in strict liability and not every injured party's risk of harm will be so abnormal as to call strict liability into play, it is generally held that in order to balance the responsibility for use of dangerous products, the actor must be liable for the consequences of such use.

Net Results

Internet Information on Toxic Chemicals and Environmental Issues

Information about toxic chemicals may be accessed by using the Toxic Tort Defense Connection web site. This web site allows searches for chemical, allergen, and pathogen information using the Toxlaw Chem-Tracker. Access this web site at www.toxlaw.com. In addition, the United States Environmental Protection Agency provides information regarding leaking underground storage tanks. Access the EPA at www.epa.gov.

Storage of Explosive Gases or Chemicals

Courts have held that storing or leaving poisonous gases or flammable liquids in areas where residents may be exposed to an abnormally dangerous risk of inhalation, explosion, or fire will result in strict liability. In one case, the defendant left hydrocyanic acid gas in the basement of an apartment building that was unoccupied. The gas was used to kill insects that had invaded the building. The next morning, plaintiff, unaware of the defendant's activities, was nearly fatally poisoned because he had a head cold and was unable to smell the fumes. The court found the defendant strictly liable for creating an abnormally dangerous condition for anyone who entered the building.[2]

Nuclear Transport and Testing

Nuclear testing and accidents that occur during the transport or maintenance of nuclear materials present abnormal risks of harm. These potential hazards are regulated by federal legislation, but the United States Supreme Court has ruled that injuries resulting from plutonium contamination may result in punitive damages under state tort theories.[3] Radiation injuries suffered by residents of certain areas of Nevada and Arizona are covered under federal legislation that calls for compensating the victims of diseases related to radiation fallout from nuclear testing.[4]

DEFENSES TO STRICT LIABILITY

Some legal theorists claim that if strict liability is responsibility for all consequences, then there are virtually no defenses to employ to relieve the defendant of liability. The courts, however, have identified behaviors and causes that counter the normally dangerous risk created by defendant, and statutes have imposed limitations on the extent of defendant's liability in certain situations.

Assumption of Risk

A plaintiff sees an area that is sealed off, and signs that identify the area as a "blasting zone." Plaintiff enters the sealed area anyway, fully recognizing the risk to him or herself and is injured when the explosive detonates. Courts will recognize that the plaintiff assumed the risk of injury and defendant's liability may be reduced or eliminated. The theory behind **assumption of risk** is that if plaintiff voluntarily proceeds to encounter a danger, fully cognizant of the risk to him or herself, plaintiff cannot look to another for responsibility. A plaintiff who does not protect him or herself cannot expect someone else to provide greater protection. In some states, the defense of assumption of risk has been abolished or incorporated into the defense of contributory or comparative negligence. As with other areas of discussion in this textbook, reference to specific state law should be made.

Contributory Negligence

Contributory negligence is generally not a defense to strict liability (it is a defense to negligence, the failure of reasonable care); however, courts have allowed the defense in certain circumstances. For example, a plaintiff taunts and teases a dog, throws sticks at the dog, pokes it, or otherwise provokes it. The dog finally bites the plaintiff. State law makes owners of dogs strictly liable for the injuries caused by the dog; however, the court may allow evidence to be admitted to show that the plaintiff was not completely innocent in the incident. This evidence may not relieve the defendant of liability, but it may be a defense to the extent of the damages. Plaintiff's own conduct contributed to the injuries, and plaintiff's award of damages may be reduced by the percentage of fault ascribed to plaintiff. State case law and statutes should be consulted to determine what defenses may be employed against an action based on strict liability.

Statute of Limitations

Every state has a statute of limitations that should be consulted to determine whether a general time limit exists within which actions based on strict liability must be brought. The Uniform Product Liability Act[5] provides for a ten-year statute of limitations following delivery of the product. This is an area of defense law that is heavily dictated by public policy. How long is it reasonable for a manufacturer to be liable for a product? According to this federal legislation, a presumption is created that after ten years, any harm suffered is a result of something that creates an abnormal risk of harm other than a defect in the product.

State statute and case law may provide greater protection to an injured plaintiff. For example, in Wisconsin, a plaintiff purchased a used 1957 35-horsepower outboard motor that started in gear. He took the motor to a marine repair where it was rebuilt with parts from motors of the same type. Afterwards, the plaintiff was seriously injured when the motor started in gear. Plaintiff sued the manufacturer of the outboard motor. The Court of Appeals in Wisconsin held the manufacturer liable under the **stream of commerce doctrine.** Even though the motor was thirty years old, purchased used, and completely rebuilt, the manufacturer had placed the motor on the market in a dangerously defective condition, and the manufacturer was strictly liable for the injuries suffered by plaintiff.[6]

Intervening Causes

Most courts have held that defendant will not be liable if the injuries are not within the scope of danger that the abnormal risk creates. For example, owners of wild animals are strictly liable for the injuries caused by them. If the wild animal gets loose and frightens a day care provider who then runs into the path of a car that has failed to stop at a stop sign, should the owners of the wild animal be liable? Most courts will find that the driver who failed to stop at the stop sign would be the cause of the injury to plaintiff, rather than the activities of the uncaged wild animal.

In addition, **acts of God** or **acts of nature,** which are unforeseeable, may also relieve the defendant of liability. For example, a farmer sets a fire to burn off a stubble field. Before setting the fire, the farmer checks the weather forecast and learns that there will be mild winds (0–5 mph) from the north and northeast. While the fire is burning, a sudden wind shift occurs and winds increase substantially. Smoke from the burning field is trapped close to the ground by a temperature inversion and is blown over a nearby highway. Drivers on the highway are blinded and have trouble breathing because of the smoke. One driver pulls her car over to the side of the road, exits the vehicle in search of clear air, is hit by another vehicle, and is killed. Is it fair to hold the farmer liable for creating an abnormal risk of harm to drivers on the highway? Courts may conclude that the farmer's fault was superceded by the unforecast, unforeseen change in winds, and the farmer might not be liable.

ROLE OF LEGAL NURSE CONSULTANTS IN STRICT LIABILITY ACTIONS

Lawsuits based in strict liability involve collection of factual data, interaction with governmental agencies, and assessment of injuries and damages. Legal nurse consultants may assist in the development of the case by interviewing the injured party, acquiring the necessary records, summarizing and evaluating the records, assessing damages, performing medical research, locating and working with experts, and assisting in preparation for trial.

Interviewing

The primary function of the legal nurse consultant is to apply medical knowledge and experience to the demands of the legal field. When interviewing clients, legal nurse consultants will pay particular attention to the medical aspects of the claim. Identifying preexisting conditions is critical to a successful outcome. Nurses are adept at eliciting information concerning past and current medical treatment that will help the legal team to properly evaluate the claim and secure all medical records.

Acquiring Records

Acquisition of records may be the responsibility of the legal assistant or the paralegal on the litigation team. However, the legal nurse consultant, based on information obtained during interviews and updates with the client, will be able to identify records that might otherwise be overlooked. Once records have been obtained, legal nurse consultants will recognize when records are missing or when there are gaps in treatment. This will lead to additional fact gathering from the client and, possibly, the acquisition of additional records. These records may include accident reports not previously identified by the client, work-related injuries for which incident reports have been filed, and insurance claims.

Summarizing and Evaluating Records

No one on the litigation team is in a better position to review the assembled records than the legal nurse consultant. A general summary will provide the nurse with a broad overview of causal issues, complaints, medical treatments, the client/patient's history of following prescribed activities, and related facts. More specific summaries will detail necessary facts for review by an expert and for use in related medical and legal research. Summaries that are prepared for purposes of cross referencing will assist the litigation team in ascertaining the specific areas of proof and damages that must be presented to the court. For more information about what summaries may be prepared by legal nurse consultants and how those summaries are used, refer to Chapters Twenty-six, Twenty-seven, and Twenty-eight.

Assessing Damages

Medical bills, collected as part of the records, establish proof of past medical expenses. These include all medical bills, such as hospital bills, physician services, pharmaceutical records, radiology expenses, and the cost of appliances as well as travel for medical treatment. These bills must be examined carefully to ensure that the treatment rendered is directly related to the injury claimed.

Future medical expenses are best estimated by someone with experience in the medical field. Whether medical treatment will continue and for how long is generally based on expert testimony. The legal nurse consultant may prepare a damages worksheet for future medical expenses that might be submitted as part of a settlement package or used by an expert to support a demand for future medical expenses at trial. These future medical expenses must generally be reduced to present value. Ultimately the amount allowed for future medical expenses rests with the jury. However, the legal nurse consultant, by virtue of experience, is more likely to incorporate all aspects of medical treatment in assessing future medical expenses. On the defense side, the legal nurse consultant is equipped to dispute potential expenses that may not be warranted or justified.

Performing Medical Research

If the lawsuit is based on exposure to toxic chemicals, pesticides, or herbicides, the legal nurse consultant may be called upon to do medical research concerning the long-term effects of exposure. Medical research may also identify symptoms and disabilities that are likely to occur and the degree of likelihood that they will. Studies may support the need for continuing treatment, the success ratio for continued treatment, and increased morbidity or mortality rates resulting from exposure.

Legal nurse consultants may be asked to find literature about practitioners and experts in the field. Governmental agency records concerning the use, warning, and safety standards of the activity, chemical, or product that caused injury may be easily accessed. FDA records, records from the Center for Disease Control, and other specifically related medical resources may be acquired by the legal nurse consultant. All of these records help the litigation team understand the medical issues, recognize the extent of medical damages, and prepare for the advocacy of these claims at trial. For a more complete discussion of medical research, please see Chapter Thirty-one.

Locating Experts

By virtue of the legal nurse consultant's networking in the medical field, he or she is in the best position to locate reliable experts. Especially in strict liability, expert witnesses are necessary because of the technical nature of the abnormal danger to which the injured party allegedly has been exposed. The legal nurse consultant may locate and interview medical experts to determine whether they are qualified and able to describe causes and conditions in ways a jury can understand. These medical experts may be compiled in a database containing their curriculum vitae, their areas of specialty, previous cases on which they have worked, and the success or failure of the cases in which they have testified.

Legal nurse consultants may be responsible for compiling the case materials to be sent to the expert. These case materials will provide the basis for the expert's opinion. Detailed records should be kept of what documents, summaries, and other materials were sent to an expert for review. In addition, the legal nurse consultant may locate learned treatises and articles in medical journals that will assist in preparing the expert or corroborating his or her opinion.

Assisting in Preparation for Trial

Educating the medical team will provide a dress rehearsal for educating the jury. The legal nurse consultant will be invaluable in identifying appropriate trial exhibits, models, charts, or diagrams to help the jury understand the medical issues. Helping to draft appropriate questions for eliciting medical facts and opinions will enhance the litigation team's trial technique.

The legal nurse consultant will be intimately familiar with the medical records and potential future medical treatment of the client. Therefore, he or she will provide valuable assistance at the trial by taking notes on medical testimony and relating the testimony to the fact records. Strict liability is a growing area of law and one in which legal nurse consultants may enhance the delivery of legal services and the just resolution of claims.

CHAPTER SUMMARY

- Strict liability is a cause of action in which defendant has created an abnormally dangerous risk of harm that cannot be alleviated by precautions or due care.

- Circumstances giving rise to actions in strict liability include exposure to toxic chemicals, leaking underground storage tanks, and owning or controlling animals.

- Activities giving rise to actions in strict liability include use of pesticides and herbicides, storage of explosive gas or chemicals, and nuclear transport and testing.

- Defenses to strict liability include assumption of risk, statutes of limitations, intervening causes, and sometimes contributory negligence.

- Legal nurse consultants may assist in the development of strict liability claims by interviewing clients, acquiring records, summarizing and evaluating records, assessing damages, performing medical research, locating experts, and assisting in preparation for trial.

KEY TERMS

act of God	chattels	strict liability
act of nature	contributory negligence	
assumption of risk	stream of commerce doctrine	

REVIEW QUESTIONS

1. Explain the concept of strict liability.
2. In what specific ways can a legal nurse consultant enhance the delivery of legal services in a strict liability claim?
3. Identify circumstances and activities that give rise to actions in strict liability.

INTERNET EXERCISES

1. Access the web page for this textbook at *www.westlegalstudies.com*.
2. Click on the assignments section and complete the assignment(s) for Chapter Twenty-one.

EXERCISES

1. Networking. There are several listservs available on the Internet for professionals who need to talk with one another. Some assess a minimal charge, but many are free with your Internet service provider. Consider joining a listserv. The AALNC provides a listserv at a minimal cost to its members. Locate this information at www.aalnc.org. Findlaw.com provides chat rooms and bulletin boards to post questions to other legal professionals. Access this site at www.findlaw.com. Listservs are an excellent source of dialog and help professionals keep up to date on important aspects of their area of expertise.

2. Professional Portfolio. Collect journal and newspaper articles concerning recent strict liability cases. Check the Internet to see if there are sites available that provide more complete information about these strict liability circumstances or activities. Maintain these clippings in your systems file, folder, or binder. Organize or index them in a way that will allow easy access.

ENDNOTES

1. Restatement (Second) of Torts §520.
2. *Luthringer v. Moore,* 31 Cal. 2d 489, 190 P. 2d 1 (1948).
3. *Silkwood v. Kerr McGee,* 464 U.S. 238, 104 S. Ct. 615, 78 L.E. 2d 443 (1984).
4. Radiation Exposure Compensation Act, 42 U.S.C. s. 2210
5. 44 Fed. Reg. 62732
6. *Mulhern v. Outboard Marine,* 147 Wis. 2d 890, 436 N.W. 2d 31 (1988).
7. American Association of Legal Nurse Consultants, *Code of Ethics and Conduct with Interpretive Discussion Code No. 2* (1995).

ADDITIONAL REFERENCES

Lamb, D.L., BSN, RN. "Expert Affidavits." *Journal of Legal Nurse Consulting* 10:1 (1999): 19–20.
Lamb, D.L., BSN, RN. "Who Qualifies as an Expert?" A Review of a Case in Pennsylvania and Cases in Florida." *Journal of Legal Nurse Consulting* 7:4 (1996): 14–15, 20.

CHAPTER 22

PRODUCTS LIABILITY

OBJECTIVES

In this chapter, you will learn

- what theories of recovery are available in products liability lawsuits

- the warranties that are established by law for consumer protection

- how strict liability is applied to consumer products

- the defenses to products liability

- the role of the legal nurse consultant in products liability

OVERVIEW

Manufacturers and sellers are liable for defective products and products that fail to perform adequately when proper use results in injury. If the user of the product is not injured, there may still be a claim in breach of contract (the product purchased was defective), but the action would not fall under the umbrella of products liability. To commence a lawsuit in products liability, the user of the product must have been injured in some way.

THEORIES OF RECOVERY IN PRODUCTS LIABILITY

Products liability is not a cause of action; it is an area of the law. To sustain an action in products liability, the action may be brought under any or all of three basic theories of recovery: breach of warranty, negligence, and strict liability.

Breach of Warranty

A **warranty** is a promise that the product will live up to certain standards. Any assertion of fact about the characteristics, quality, or performance of a product is a warranty. If a warranty is untrue, or is dishonored, the party to whom the warranty was given may recover in **breach of warranty.** Breach of warranty is similar to breach of contract and is based on the idea that a warranty, or promise, is essential to the integrity and performance of the contract. Even if the user of the product was unaware of the warranty or the warranty was made after the sale, courts have held that the failure of the warranty results in failure of the contract, and the seller will be liable.

Punitive damages are generally not available in an action based on breach of contract. This is also true for products liability actions based in breach of warranty. For all practical purposes, however, attorneys will commence a lawsuit in products liability based on all three theories, thus preserving punitive damages through the negligence and strict liability theories.

There are two basic types of warranties under law: express and implied.

Express Warranties. Promises that are communicated in writing, documentation, catalogs, sales brochures, pictures, drawings, specifications, and so on are **express warranties.** Express warranties may also be communicated verbally on television, in radio commercials, and in person. Any statement of fact about the product constitutes a warranty. For example, a statement that a cosmetic is fragrance free, that a sweater is 100% wool, or that a blanket is all new polyester fiber are warranties (promises) about the product. If the warranty is untrue and the user of the product is harmed as a result, the injured user may sue in breach of warranty.

Implied Warranties. In order to protect consumers, the Uniform Commercial Code established several warranties that exist as a matter of law.[1] These warranties cannot be voided by the manufacturer or seller without specific notification to the consumer. **Implied warranties** include the warranty of merchantability and the warranty of fitness for a particular purpose.

Warranty of Merchantability. The reasonable expectations of the consumer when purchasing the product are the essence of the **warranty of merchantability.** This warranty has several components:

- The product is of fair and average quality.
- The product is fit for its ordinary intended purpose.
- The product is adequately packaged.
- The product conforms to its label.

If any of these inherent promises about the product are untrue and the consumer is injured as a result, a breach of warranty claim is available to the injured user. For example, a carbonated beverage packaged in a glass bottle explodes and the consumer is cut by shattering glass. Because the product was not adequately packaged, the consumer who was injured can sue the manufacturer for breach of implied warranty of merchantability.

Warranty of Fitness for a Particular Purpose. When a seller knows the specific use intended by the consumer and makes a recommendation to the consumer about which product to purchase for that specific use, the seller has made a warranty of fitness of the product for that use. If the product, in fact, cannot perform according to the recommendation of the seller and the consumer is injured, the injured party may sue the seller under the **implied warranty of fitness for a particular purpose.** For example, a consumer explains the need for a bicycle that will withstand rugged terrain and unfinished roads. The seller warrants and recommends a particular brand of bicycle, which the consumer ultimately purchases. When the consumer uses the bicycle on gravel, it spins out of control and the consumer is thrown from the bicycle and severely injured. The consumer may maintain an action in breach of implied warranty of fitness for a particular purpose because the consumer relied upon the expertise of the seller when the consumer selected and used the product.

Negligence

In previous chapters, you learned that an action in negligence consists of four components: a duty relationship, a breach of that duty, causation, and injury. The duty relationship exists whenever one party owes to another party ordinary and reasonable care for his or her safety. This duty relationship may arise by contract, as in a sales contract; by statute; or by common law, as in a court ruling. Most of the duties owed by the manufacturer to a consumer exist as a result of common law. Because of advances in technology and information, courts have held that manufacturers are in a better position to know and understand the dangerous aspects of products. Unwary consumers may expect that manufacturers will act with reasonable care for their health and safety.

The duties owed by the manufacturer to the consumer include all of the following:

- compliance with safety regulations
- use of the best available safety devices

- affirmative testing and inspecting of the product
- warnings about hazards of use
- instructions concerning assembly and use in language and drawings that consumers can understand
- reasonable care in design, manufacture, packaging, and distribution of the product
- protection from tampering

If the manufacturer fails to use reasonable care in any of these areas of responsibility and the consumer is injured as a result, a claim of negligence may be made against the manufacturer. For example, a brand of aspirin is advertised in Spanish on a television station that serves a Spanish-speaking community in the United States. The aspirin contains a label, written entirely in English, with a warning concerning the risk of Reyes Syndrome. A Spanish-speaking mother, who sees and hears the television commercial saying that this aspirin will reduce fever, purchases the aspirin and administers it to her three-year-old child. The child dies of Reyes Syndrome. The manufacturer of the product, by advertising in Spanish and providing the product to a Spanish-speaking community, owed a duty to Spanish-speaking consumers to provide the label information in Spanish.[3]

In order to hold the seller (other than the manufacturer) liable for negligence, it is necessary to prove that the seller failed to disclose essential information about use of the product or that the seller failed to store, inspect, or advertise the product with reasonable care.

In recent years, a trend has emerged prescribing a duty on the part of manufacturers to protect consumers from dangers that result because of product aging or excessive use. This requires that manufacturers, aware that a product may become hazardous as it ages or is used extensively, has a duty to disclose the potential hazards that result from the wear and tear and age of the product. Failure to warn current users of old or worn products about such hazards may be negligence.

Another aspect of negligence law that applies in products liability is the doctrine of **res ipsa loquitur.** This doctrine is applied in situations that would not occur unless negligence were present. The courts reason that consumers who are injured under these circumstances need not prove where or by whom the negligence occurred. The exploding carbonated beverage bottle is a good example. The bottle would not explode if it had been carefully packaged, tested, distributed, and stored. The injured plaintiff need not explain where the negligence occurred; the burden of proof effectively shifts to the defendant.

Whenever the manufacturer acts with reckless disregard for the rights and safety of the consumer, the injured consumer can claim punitive damages. Sometimes called exemplary damages, punitive damages in products liability are meant to punish the defendant manufacturer for the manufacturer's conduct, which the court finds to be unacceptable. By awarding punitive damages, in addition to compensatory damages, the court attempts to make an example of the defendant so the conduct that gave rise to the lawsuit will not be repeated. Recent Fen-phen litigation has resulted in punitive damage awards.

Strict Products Liability

Strict liability exists where the defendant creates an abnormally dangerous risk of injury to the plaintiff. Strict products liability has six elements:

- The product was defective.
- The defect makes the product unreasonably or abnormally dangerous.
- The defective product is expected to reach the consumer without substantial change.
- The defective product causes injury.
- The consumer properly used the product.

In strict products liability, the manufacturer may be strictly liable if the product is inherently unsafe for its intended use through a defect in the design of the product, a defect in the manufacture of the product, or a defect in the warnings and instructions concerning the product.

Defects in Design. One of the best examples of defects in design is the three-wheel all-terrain vehicle. The sale of three-wheelers has been banned throughout the United States because the vehicles were basically unstable for their intended purpose. Advertisements that three-wheelers were able to handle rough terrain and to take steep inclines at high speeds conflicted with design capabilities. Several people, many of them young, were killed and thousands injured.

A medical appliance that was found to be defectively designed and unreasonably dangerous for users was the Dalkon Shield IUD. This intrauterine device, intended to prevent pregnancy, was shown to be associated with internal hemorrhaging, perforation of the uterus, and, in some cases, death.[4]

Defects in Manufacture. When the manufacturing process results in an abnormal risk of harm to the consumer, the manufacturer will be strictly liable for the injuries that result. For example, in an attempt to reduce the risk of harm, it is determined that a protective cover must be attached to a product. There are two ways to attach the protective cover; it may be welded, or it may be screwed on. Welding the cover would make it permanent. Because of the cost differential, the manufacturer elects to screw the covers on. The protective covers are removed by consumers because they make operation of the product cumbersome. As a result of removing the protective cover, consumers are injured. This defect in the manufacture of the product may result in the imposition of strict liability upon the manufacturer of the product if it is reasonably foreseeable that a nonpermanent cover will be detached, increasing the risk of harm to consumers.

Net Results

Products Liability on the Internet

The Alexander Law Firm in California has created a web site called "The Consumer Law Page," which provides access to online resources concerning products liability. Access this web site at http://consumerlawpage.com. *Other resources on the Internet provide information about tobacco products liability and silicone breast implants. See a web site devoted to products liability at* www.productslaw.com *or check out products liability at* www.paralegals.org/LegalResources/Practice. *Another important web site for products liability is the United States Consumer Product Safety Commission located at* www.cpsc.gov.

Defects in Warnings. Warnings and instructions that do not adequately address the risk associated with assembly and use of a product may create an abnormal risk of injury to the consumer. For example, a warning states that risk of injury will be reduced if the user of the product replaces the cover before starting the machine. If the court determines that this warning does not adequately inform the user of the fire hazard associated with starting the machine, the manufacturer will be strictly liable for injuries that result. Again, the court rationalizes that the manufacturer is in the best position to know about the dangers associated with use of the product and has an affirmative duty to adequately warn the unwary consumer about those risks. A medically-related strict products liability action based on defective warnings and instructions involved silicon breast implants.

DEFENSES TO PRODUCTS LIABILITY

The defenses to products liability are similar to the defenses for negligence and strict liability generally. These defenses may be categorized under the topics of plaintiff's conduct, and disclaimer or recall. Statutes of limitations and statutes restricting recovery are also defenses to products liability.

Plaintiff's Conduct

The usual defenses of contributory negligence and assumption of risk fall under the umbrella of plaintiff's conduct. If plaintiff misuses the product or if the product is used in an unforeseeable manner, the manufacturer may avoid liability. However, if the product is misused in a way that is foreseeable, the manufacturer, cognizant of that risk, has a duty to warn consumers about the risks of the *foreseeable misuse* of the product. For example, a toy comes wrapped in plastic. Stamped on the plastic is a warning that the plastic is not a toy and should not be used for play. This is to avoid the foreseeable risk of misuse of the plastic and the potential for suffocation or choking injuries. The injured party's contributory negligence (misuse of the product) may preclude recovery from the manufacturer.

Similarly, a product that is altered by the plaintiff in a way that makes the product unsafe for its intended use may relieve the manufacturer of liability. In these cases, the courts may determine that the plaintiff, by altering the product, created the abnormal risk and generally cannot shift blame back to the manufacturer. For example, the owner of a compact car replaces the factory-installed tires with large truck tires. If the compact car becomes unstable as a result of the excessively large tires, the manufacturer will not be responsible for any harm that results. The plaintiff's contributory negligence, that is, altering the product in a way that makes it unsafe, may preclude the manufacturer's liability.

The traditional defense of assumption of risk also applies to products liability cases. For example, if a consumer discovers that a product is defective but uses it anyway, the manufacturer may be relieved of liability. Consumers generally have a duty to inspect products before use. Failure to do so may result in a finding of contributory negligence. However, it is unreasonable to expect that all products will be inspected before use. For example, everyday at lunchtime, a businessperson purchases a newspaper and a candy bar at a nearby newsstand and goes to the park to read the newspaper and eat the candy. The practice of the businessperson is to unwrap the candy while reading the paper. After several bites of the candy bar, the businessperson decides that it tastes decidedly "funny" and looks at the candy bar. It is covered with worms and webbing. Immediate, violent illness ensues. In a products liability lawsuit against the manufacturer and the newsstand, the defense of reasonable inspection was brought forward. The court determined that it was not reasonable to expect that wrapped products, advertised as ready for consumption, should be unwrapped and inspected prior to use.[5] Similarly it is not reasonable to pour out and inspect a package of dry soup prior to emptying it in boiling water.

Disclaimer of Warranty

The Uniform Commercial Code and other legislation specifies what steps must be taken by a manufacturer or seller to disclaim a warranty. If a warranty and a disclaimer are made in the same communication, the warranty will be enforced and the **disclaimer** will be nullified.

To disclaim the implied warranty of merchantability, the UCC requires a seller to use language that is conspicuous and uses the word merchantability.[6] If the product is sold **as is,** the buyer is put on notice that the buyer assumes the risk of any defect in the goods and the manufacturer and seller may be relieved of liability. A manufacturer of consumer goods having a value of $15 or more and providing a written warranty concerning those goods is governed by the Magnuson-Moss Warranty Act.[7] This law specifically prohibits the disclaimer of the implied warranty of merchantability.

Statutes of Limitations

Statutes of limitations will govern the cause of action employed by the plaintiff. Generally, a negligence claim will hold a three-year statute of limitations and a claim based on breach of warranty will hold a four-year statute of limitations.[8] Statutes of limitations are specific to each state, and state statutes should be consulted to identify the specific statute of limitations in question.

Where the defect or injury could not have been discovered within the usual statutory limit, some states have identified a period of time after which the plaintiff knew or should reasonably have known about the defect or injury. For example, a construction worker is exposed to toxic chemicals as a result of working in an area that was previously used as a waste dump site. The construction worker develops leukemia many years later. Courts in some states have believed that the law was unfair to the construction worker who could not have known about the exposure or the related risk of leukemia until years after the statute of limitations had expired. Because these laws are made by state courts, it is important to check the precedent in the jurisdiction where the lawsuit is filed to determine whether the courts have adopted a statute of limitations based upon discovery or whether this law has been codified in the state statutes.

Statutes of repose impact strict liability actions. A statute of repose fixes the statute of limitations from the date of sale rather than from the date of occurrence causing injury. These statutes are heavily influenced by public policy to protect manufacturers. For example, federal law prohibits a consumer from filing a lawsuit against the manufacturer of a small airplane after fourteen years has elapsed from the date of sale of the aircraft.[9]

Limitations on Liability

Statutes sometimes provide specific immunity or limitation on the liability for certain defective products. For example, the National Vaccine Injury Act[10] created a program that protects both the person injured by a vaccine and the manufacturer of the vaccine. The injured party has a more efficient process for obtaining compensation, even though the actual amount of damages is capped.

THE ROLE OF THE LEGAL NURSE CONSULTANT IN PRODUCTS LIABILITY CASES

Strict products liability involving drugs or medical devices is a challenging area of law. Legal nurse consultants interested in this field will be valuable to attorneys for several reasons:

- their knowledge of drug interactions and contraindications
- their knowledge of the standard of care required of health care providers when prescribing and employing drugs and devices
- their familiarity with the process of approving drugs and devices through the Food and Drug Administration
- their ability to educate the litigation team on the medical aspects of a strict liability action

Certainly, there is inherent danger in the application of any drug or device. The risk of danger must be weighed against the benefit of its use in the specific situation to determine whether a strict products liability action is warranted or whether the prescribing provider has been negligent in making the prescription. Additionally, if the manufacturer provides appropriate and adequate warnings and instructions concerning the use of the drug or device, a strict products liability action may not be viable. The warnings and instructions should be sufficient to alert the health care provider, sometimes called the **learned intermediary,** of the potential risks to the patient. If the learned intermediary fails to convey adequate warnings and instructions provided by the manufacturer, the fault or liability may rest with the learned intermediary. Warnings and instructions for over-the-counter drugs must be easily understood by the consuming public. Legal nurse consultants, because of their experience and education, are in a position to determine whether labeling and product inserts are easily understood or whether the health care provider prescribed drugs or devices without providing adequate information to the patient/client.

In addition, legal nurse consultants may, after review of FDA documentation, provide insight into whether manufacturers of drugs and devices adequately tested and inspected the products or provided sufficient notification of hazards that came to light after the drug or device was approved and marketed. The manufacturer is considered to be in the best position to know all of the inherent aspects of the drug or device and is under a continuing duty to investigate, report, and warn against risks that become apparent. FDA regulations require revision of the label or insert materials whenever there is reasonable evidence that a serious hazard is connected with use of the drug or device.

Legal nurse consultants who are familiar with the process for approval of drugs and devices through the FDA will be able to acquire information that will assist the litigation team evaluate the claim. Before an application for approval is submitted to the FDA, the manufacturer of the drug or device must test it in a three-phase process. During Phase I, the drug is tested on healthy subjects who are given dose escalations and watched for side effects. During Phase II, the drug is tested for its efficacy on the target population. Phase III is the comparison testing phase, where half of the sample population is randomly treated with the drug and the other half is not treated or treated with placebo. The results of all three testing phases are submitted to the FDA where conditions of the testing and the results of testing are scrutinized. If the FDA finds the research and testing adequate, and labeling requirements met, approval is granted.

It may be clear to the legal nurse consultant that the three-phase process of testing new drugs may be inadequate for certain populations, such as the elderly, and for long-term effects of continued use. Still, public policy demands that an effective medical treatment not be withheld because of risks that may be impractical to discover. Thus, the manufacturer is under a continuing duty to monitor literature and heed letters of complaint concerning the drugs and devices manufactured and to warn of the side effects identified as soon as is reasonably appropriate.

Since 1976, medical devices have come under the authority of the FDA. There are three categories of medical devices. Class I medical devices are not deemed to be of high risk, and manufacturers are only required to meet good manufacturing practices prior to marketing the device. Class II medical devices are subjected to special quality control requirements during manufacturing to ensure that they are safe for their intended purpose. Class III medical devices are defined as "critical" devices implanted within the body that, if defective, would be life threatening. Class III medical devices must be tested under the regulatory scheme of the FDA prior to application for approval.

Manufacturers of a drug must report any adverse event associated with use of a drug to the FDA within fifteen days of learning of the event. The FDA's Spontaneous Reporting System is critical in a medical products liability lawsuit. The reports may be from physicians, patients, or the manufacturer. They provide important information about the risks associated with the drug or device and the point in time when the manufacturer should reasonably have become aware of the association of that risk with the drug or device.

The legal nurse consultant working on an action based in strict products liability will need to collect and analyze

- FDA regulations regarding testing and labeling
- FDA records concerning approval of the drug or device
- FDA reports of adverse events associated with use of the drug or device
- medical literature concerning the drug or device
- all records concerning the plaintiff, including medical, AODA, employment, education, criminal, and military

Legal nurse consultants may assist in accumulating the product, client medical, and FDA records; summarizing, analyzing, and correlating the records; identifying appropriate experts for use in the case; and assisting the litigation team in evaluating the appropriate actions or defenses suggested by the evidence collected.

CHAPTER SUMMARY

- Products liability lawsuits may be based in breach of warranty, negligence, and strict liability.
- Warranties are promises concerning the product that may be expressed or implied.
- Strict liability encompasses defects in design, defects in manufacture, and defects in warning and labels.
- Defenses to products liability include the conduct of plaintiff, disclaimers of warranty, statutes of limitations, and statutory caps on damages.
- Legal nurse consultants may be valuable in cases of strict medical products or pharmaceutical liability by collecting and analyzing client and FDA records and educating the litigation team on the medical aspects of the claim.
- The FDA requires a three-phase testing process for a drug before an application for approval may be submitted.
- Medical devices are under the authority of the FDA, and Claim III devices (critical) must meet the three-phase testing scheme.

KEY TERMS

as is	implied warranty	*res ipsa loquitur*
breach of warranty	implied warranty of fitness for	statutes of repose
disclaimer	a particular purpose	warranty
express warranty	learned intermediary	warranty of merchantability

REVIEW QUESTIONS

1. Identify and explain the difference between express warranties, the implied warranty of merchantability, and the implied warranty of fitness for a particular purpose.

2. List several duties owed by a manufacturer of products to the consumer.
3. How may a legal nurse consultant assist in the development of a products liability case?

INTERNET EXERCISES

1. Access the web page for this textbook at *www.westlegalstudies.com.*

2. Click on the assignments section and complete the assignment(s) for Chapter Twenty-two.

EXERCISES

1. Networking. Contact a law firm in your area identified in the Yellow Pages as working with or specializing in products liability. Ask if they employ legal nurse consultants and, if so, ask to speak to one. If the firm does not employ a legal nurse consultant, ask to speak with the paralegal who works with products liability claims. If someone at the firm is willing to talk with you, ask about the investigation that is done concerning the products that are claimed to cause injury. If you are a member of a nurse's association or have joined a local chapter of the AALNC, invite this person to speak to your organization. You may also wish to invite this person to lunch to talk about products liability and legal careers in general.

2. Professional Portfolio. Begin collecting news articles concerning medical products, pharmaceuticals, and devices that have been the subject of products liability lawsuits. Having these articles in your portfolio or keeping a separate news scrapbook will display a keen interest in this area of law. Additionally, the news articles may provide networking opportunities with professionals from other law firms who have worked on cases that are similar to cases you might eventually work on.

ENDNOTES

1. UCC s. 2-314

2. American Bar Association, *Annotated Model Rules of Professional Conduct,* (1999) 4th Edition Rule 1.4(a). Copies of ABA *Model Code of Professional Responsibility, 1999 Edition* are available from Service Center, American Bar Association, 750 North Lake Shore Drive, Chicago, IL 60611-4497, 1-800-285-2221.

3. *Ramirez v. Plough, Inc.,* 6 Cal. 4th 539, 863 P. 2d 167, 25 Cal. Rptr. 2d 97 (1993).

4. See, for example, *In re Northern District of California "Dalkon Shield" IUD Products Liability Litigation,* 526 F. Supp. 887 (N.D. Cal. 1981)

5. *Kassouf v. Lee Bros. Inc.,* 209 Cal. App. 2d 568, 26 Cal. Rptr. 279 (1963).

6. UCC § 2-316

7. *Magnus Moss Warranty—Federal Trade Commission Improvement Act,* 15 U.S.C. § 2301, et seq. (1975).

8. UCC § 2-725

9. 49 U.S.C. s. 44112

10. *Vaccine Injury Compensation Act,* 26 U.S.C. s. 9510, 42 U.S.C. 201

ADDITIONAL REFERENCES

Peterson, A.M., EdD, RN, CS. "Fen-Phen/Redux Litigation: History and Status." *Journal of Legal Nurse Consulting* 10:3 (1999): 11–17.

Peterson, A.M., EdD, RN, CS. "The Rise and Fall of Fen-Phen and Redux." *Journal of Legal Nurse Consulting* 9:3 (1998): 8–13, 19.

Pippin, P.L., BSN, RN. "Pharmaceutical Products Liability, Part I: Legal Concepts." *Journal of Legal Nurse Consulting* 8:3 (1997): 2–6 (1997): 12.

Pippin, P.L., BSN, RN. "Pharmaceutical Products Liability, Part II: Clinical Research and the Role of the FDA." *Journal of Legal Nurse Consulting* 8:4 (1997): 2–7.

Pippin, P.L., BSN, RN. "Pharmaceutical Products Liability, Part III: The Role of the Legal Nurse Consultant." *Journal of Legal Nurse Consulting* 9:1 (1997): 2–6.

Woodward, P.K., JD, BSN, RN, LNCC. "Do Patients Still Have a Learned Intermediary?" *Journal of Legal Nurse Consulting* 10:4 (1999): 17–19.

CHAPTER 23

CLASS ACTION AND MULTIDISTRICT LITIGATION

OBJECTIVES

In this chapter, you will discover

- what is involved in a class action litigation

- what is meant by multidistrict litigation

- how complex litigation is classified

- the role of the legal nurse consultant in complex (class action and multidistrict) litigation

OVERVIEW

When a lawsuit involves many parties in related cases pending in different jurisdictions, the case may be identified as **complex litigation.** In addition, whenever litigation involves large numbers of witnesses, documents, and extensive discovery, as is typical in class-action lawsuits based in medical products liability, the action may be designated as complex. This designation allows the judicial officers to use special authority in managing the case. This authority is outlined in the Federal Rules of Civil Procedure. Specifically, Rule 16(c)(12) authorized judges in federal court to adopt "special procedures for managing potentially difficult or protracted actions that may involve complex issues, multiple parties, difficult legal questions, or unusual proof problems."[1]

CASE MANAGEMENT

It is the judge's responsibility to identify complex litigation and to develop management techniques that will ensure a just, efficient, and inexpensive disposition of the case. Successful management requires that unnecessary and unproductive activity be minimized and that the coordination of activities and the cooperation and management of counsel reduce judicial and time pressures so that the case is not unduly protracted. To that end, attorneys are required to comply with the management authority granted to judges in complex litigation. Failure to comply may result in sanctions.

A judge in complex litigation must scrutinize the judicial record to ensure that he or she is qualified to manage and hear the matter. Judges must **recuse** whenever "impartiality might reasonably be questioned."[2] If a conflict of interest arises that would substantially interfere with the outcome of the case, the case must be reassigned as expeditiously as possible, with the new judge making a scrutiny of the record for potential conflicts.

Complex litigation usually involves two or more related cases filed in the same court. These cases are generally consolidated for purposes of coordinating hearings and proceedings on the same issues. Consolidating the cases under one judge promotes efficiency and uniformity in the proceedings and minimizes the costs to respective parties. How the case is managed will depend on the nature of the complex litigation and the experience and skill of the judge and the attorneys. The judge generally develops a plan that prescribes the procedural steps, with time limits and deadlines, to give direction and order to the necessary pretrial activities. This plan may be developed at the outset, or it may be developed and integrated in successive stages of the litigation. If the plan is developed with the participation of counsel, it is more likely that counsel will adhere to the plan, sanctions will not be imposed, and the ultimate goal of timely and efficient disposition will be realized.

CLASS-ACTION LAWSUITS

Whenever a claim is made by or against a class of parties, the litigation tends to be complex, and judicial management is required. "Whether a class is certified and how its membership is defined can often have a decisive effect not only on the outcome of the litigation but also on its management."[3] Generally a **class-action** will be certified if it is brought by individuals representing a large group of identifiable members. For example, the class-action lawsuit involving silicon breast implants was brought on behalf of all women who received silicon breast implants during a specified time period.

Four Requirements for Class-Action Status

To be certified as a class-action lawsuit under the Federal Rules of Civil Procedure, four requirements must generally be met.[4]

- The class must be so numerous that joinder of all members of the class is impracticable.
- There must be questions of law or fact that are common to the class.
- The claims of the representative parties must be typical of the claims of the class.
- The representative parties must fairly and adequately protect the interests of the class.

In a class-action lawsuit, the attorneys and the representative parties assume a **fiduciary responsibility** to act in the best interests of the class members rather than in their own best interests. In addition, the court bears the responsibility of protecting the interests of the class members through appropriate notifications.

Procedure in a Class-Action Lawsuit

Rule 23(a) also governs the procedure for class-action lawsuits. The first two steps are the most important. The first step is for the court to determine as soon as practicable if the claim may be brought as a class-action; that is, to certify the class. This determination will depend on whether the four requirements outlined in the preceding section are met, what issues can be tried as a class, and the definition of the class. The second step is to determine the best notice practicable under the circumstances, which includes "individual notice to all members who can be identified through reasonable effort."[6] This has generally been interpreted to mean via first class mail to identified members of the class and via public notice (in newspapers, journals, etc.) for unknown members.

Class Definition

To be certified as a class, a class definition must be developed. This definition must be sufficiently precise to clearly identify a group of people. For instance, definitions that identify "those persons who have been discriminated against" are too vague to provide sufficient detail and may frustrate the efforts of a class-action litigation. The class definition must identify persons who are entitled to relief, who will be bound by a final judgment, and who will be entitled to notice. Thus the class definition may be qualified by adding descriptions of the claims made on behalf of the class, such as "those persons employed at [a particular company] who have been denied employment or promotion on the basis of race."

Notice Requirements

Communication with class members is a critical aspect of class-action lawsuits. It is also a costly component of litigation. Notice is required when a class is certified and when parties propose to dismiss or settle a class-action lawsuit.[7] The notice must explain the right of class members to **opt out** and the procedures to follow if a class member elects to opt out. Generally, a simple form is attached to the notice that will allow a class member to do so. In addition, the notice must explain the binding nature of the judgment in the lawsuit on all class members who choose not to opt out and the right of any class member to be represented by counsel.

Settlement notices should detail the important terms of the proposed settlement, provide information about attorney fees, explain how the settlement will be distributed, and identify the time and place of the hearing on settlement and the procedures for objecting to or opting out of the settlement. The names, addresses, and phone numbers of counsel should be clearly displayed on the notice so that class members will have access to counsel for questions concerning the settlement proposal. Notice must also be given to class members whenever the judge determines that it is needed for the protection of the class members.[8] What is included in the notice and which party will bear the cost of notice will depend upon the circumstances that require notification of class members.

Duties of Counsel

The court has the duty of selecting the class representative and the **lead counsel** from among the pool of clients and attorneys making up the class. The judge has wide discretion in making this selection, which is not limited to those appearing for the class representatives. Experience, reliability, and resources of attorneys will influence the judge's appointment of lead counsel, as this will help ensure an efficient and economical disposition of the action. The court may appoint other counsel, such as a **liaison counsel** and a **trial coun-**

sel, to assist the lead counsel as may be needed under the circumstances of the class-action lawsuit. The lead counsel has the duty to formulate and present positions on substantive and procedural law. The liaison counsel has the duty to manage the litigation and to perform the administrative functions of the case management plan. Trial counsel has the duty to develop trial strategy and present the evidence on behalf of the class at the trial, if trial becomes necessary. The primary concern in appointing a class representative is that the representative be free of conflicts of interest and be best suited for the fiduciary role. In addition, the court may appoint a **steering committee** for tasks assigned by the court or lead counsel. These tasks may include the preparation of legal briefs or the management and conduct of discovery.

RELATED FEDERAL CIVIL CASES

Whenever it appears that cases involving common questions of law or fact are pending in the same federal court, the judge assigned to those related cases may issue an order to consolidate them. This order will establish a master plan coordinating the proceedings in order to save time and expenditures involved in adjudicating related matters. Relieving the parties of multiple filings of the same documents substantially reduces duplication of effort and increases the potential for timely resolution.

MULTIDISTRICT LITIGATION

Related civil cases that are pending in several different federal courts may be consolidated under the rules of **multidistrict litigation.** The Judicial Panel on Multidistrict Litigation is authorized to transfer civil actions to any district for coordinated proceedings when it determines that transfer "will be for the convenience of the parties and witnesses and will promote the just and efficient conduct of such actions."[9] The objectives of consolidating cases under multidistrict litigation are to

- eliminate duplication in discovery
- avoid conflicting rulings and schedules
- reduce litigation costs
- save time and effort for parties, witnesses, attorneys, and the court.

There are no specific guidelines for determining which district the consolidated actions will be transferred to. The panel will give consideration to the federal court where the largest number of cases is pending, the federal court where discovery has occurred, the federal court where cases have progressed the farthest, the site of the occurrence or where facts common to the consolidated cases exist, or a location where costs and inconvenience will be minimized.

The Judicial Panel on Multidistrict Litigation has broad discretionary powers. They may select the district and select the judge. The transferee

Net Results

Federal Rules on the Internet

The Federal Rules of Civil Procedure are available on the Internet, including the rules specific to class actions, related consolidated cases, and multidistrict litigation. Access these rules using the web site for the Cornell Law School Library, www.law.cornell.edu/ rules/frcp. *This site may also be accessed through links found at* www.findlaw.com.

judge has authority to develop a management plan for the litigation of the consolidated claims. This is the major value of multidistrict litigation: it affords the parties an opportunity to negotiate a global settlement and dispose of the claims without the extensive cost and delay of multiple trials.

THE ROLE OF THE LEGAL NURSE CONSULTANT IN COMPLEX LITIGATION

When a lawsuit involves a class action or complex litigation, the law firm handling it is generally experienced in such claims and has developed expertise in managing them efficiently. Legal nurse consultants may be required to carefully analyze the facts and medical records of actual parties to determine whether they are representative of a definable class. Additionally, legal nurse consultants may be required to develop summary reports of similar injuries or claims of harm resulting from a particular activity, drug, or medical device. These similarities may be important in the consolidation of cases or the designation of complex litigation. Duties similar to those described in the preceding chapter may fall upon the legal nurse consultant if the claims involve products liability.

Legal nurse consultants may also be involved in **mass tort claims** that result in a complex litigation designation. Mass tort claims may involve airline crashes, exposure to toxic chemicals, or fires. While the injuries usually occur in a single incident, the diversity and dispersion of claims may require the coordination and consolidation available under the complex litigation designation. In these cases, legal nurse consultants may perform management functions in terms of acquiring documents, developing and maintaining a database, and selecting information necessary for the appropriate disposition of claims.

Whether the litigation is a class action, consolidated related cases, or multidistrict litigation, the legal nurse consultant must work closely with the attorneys, the investigators, the paralegals, and other professionals to ensure that the case management plan is complied with and that the collection, review, analysis, and synthesis of the documentation is thoroughly and efficiently completed.

CHAPTER SUMMARY

- ■ Whenever a case involves numerous parties, extensive documentation, and related cases, it may be designated as complex litigation.
- ■ Class-action lawsuits involve individuals representing a large identifiable group with similar claims.
- ■ Judges have wide discretion in complex litigation and class-action lawsuits to develop case management plans for the expedient processing of the case.

- Multidistrict litigation involves related claims filed in several federal district courts but joined in one proceeding.
- Mass tort claims may involve airline crashes, exposure to toxic chemicals, explosions or fires.
- Legal nurse consultants may assist in complex litigation and class-action lawsuits by coordinating the collection, analysis, and evaluation of medical information.

KEY TERMS

class action	liaison counsel	recuse
complex litigation	mass tort claims	steering committee
fiduciary responsibility	multidistrict litigation	trial counsel
lead counsel	opt out	

REVIEW QUESTIONS

1. What types of cases may be designated as class-action lawsuits? As complex litigation? As consolidated related cases? As multidistrict litigation?

2. How may legal nurse consultants assist in the management of complex litigation?

INTERNET EXERCISES

1. Access the web page for this textbook at www.westlegalstudies.com.

2. Click on the assignments section and complete the assignment(s) for Chapter Twenty-three.

EXERCISES

1. Networking. If you are near a large city, check the Yellow Pages to see if any of the attorney offices advertise class-action representation. Phone the law office and ask if a registered nurse is employed there. If the nurse is willing to talk with you, conduct an informational interview. Ask about the specific responsibilities of a nurse in class-action lawsuits that may be different from responsibilities of general personal injury litigation. If the nurse is willing to share this information, ask about compensation, benefits, and working conditions. Maintain this information in your networking system, file, or Rolodex.

2. Professional Portfolio. To get a better idea of how complex litigation operates, check out the web sites for tobacco litigation identified in the Net Results section of this chapter, or perform your own Internet research on a litigation of interest to you, such as Fen-Phen or asbestos. If

you might be applying to a law firm that has been involved in complex litigation, add "Understanding of complex litigation" or "Familiarity with concepts related to class-action lawsuits and multidistrict litigation" to your resume or cover letter.

ENDNOTES

1. Fed. R. Civ. P. 16(c)(12).
2. 28 U.S.C. § 455 (a); Code of Judicial Conduct for United States Judges, Cannon C3(c)(1) *reprinted in* 69 F.R.D. 273, 277.
3. Federal Judicial Center, *Manual for Complex Litigation Third* (St. Paul, Minnesota: West Publishing Company, 1994), 212.
4. Fed. R. Civ. P. 23(a).
5. American Bar Association, *Annotated Model Rules of Professional Responsibility,* (1999) 4th Edition Rule 1.8(e). Copies of ABA *Model Code of Professional Responsibility, 1999 Edition* are available from Service Center, American Bar Association, 750 North Lake Shore Drive, Chicago, IL 60611-4497, 1-800-285-2221.
6. Fed. R. Civ. P. 23(b)(3).
7. Fed. R. Civ. P. 23(c)(2), 23(e).
8. Fed. R Civ. P. 23(d)(2).
9. 28 U. S. C. § 1407.

ADDITIONAL REFERENCES

Bogart, J.B., RN MN, ed. *Legal Nurse Consulting: Principles and Practice.* Boston: CRC Press, 1998.

Federal Judicial Center. *Manual for Complex Litigation Third.* St. Paul, Minnesota: West Publishing, 1994.

CHAPTER 24

INTRODUCTION TO EVIDENCE LAW

OBJECTIVES

In this chapter, you will discover

- the difference between direct and circumstantial evidence

- what requirements evidence must meet in order to be admissible in court

- the rules regarding witness testimony

- what hearsay is and what some of the major exceptions to the hearsay rule are

- the rules regarding expert witness opinions

- the rules regarding physical evidence

- how the legal nurse consultant may assist attorneys in the area of evidence law

OVERVIEW

Evidence law is a special area of law that deals with what testimony and physical evidence will be allowed to be presented in court. A working knowledge of the laws of evidence guides the investigation, facilitates evaluation of the claim, and allows the litigation team to be better prepared for argument for and against the admission of certain evidence.

The Federal Rules of Evidence govern the admission and exclusion of evidence in federal courts. Similar rules have been adopted for state courts, but it is important to verify evidentiary rules with the state statutes or rules of procedure if the action is litigated in state court. The rules of evidence are complex. This chapter is intended to provide an overview of the commonly accepted rules of evidence. Citations to the Federal Rules of Evidence will be provided. The legal nurse consultant should always consult the rules of evidence for the jurisdiction in which the action will be tried.

CLASSIFICATIONS OF EVIDENCE

There are two broad classifications of evidence: direct and circumstantial. **Direct evidence** is what a witness sees, hears, smells, touches, or otherwise has direct knowledge of. **Circumstantial evidence,** on the other hand, consists of facts and occurrences that suggest the existence of other facts.

Direct Evidence

Witnesses generally are required to have knowledge of the facts they testify about. Direct evidence would allow a lay witness to testify to the fact that one of the parties smelled of alcohol, if the witness actually smelled liquor on the party. Direct evidence is usually considered the most compelling. Without direct knowledge, the testimony of the witness may be classified as hearsay, which is discussed later in this chapter.

Circumstantial Evidence

Although there has been no direct observation or witnessing of a wrongful act, the law allows evidence that will establish that the wrongful act did occur and by whom. It is important to recognize that circumstantial evidence may be almost as compelling as direct evidence. Consider the following fictional dialogue during trial:

Defense counsel to witness: "Did you actually see the defendant bite off the plaintiff's ear?"

Witness: "No, I didn't actually see the defendant bite off the plaintiff's ear."

Defense counsel: "Then how do you know that the defendant bit off the plaintiff's ear?"

Witness: "I saw defendant spit it out!"

Although no direct evidence is available, the circumstantial evidence is convincing. The totality of the circumstances is always the controlling factor in law.

RELEVANCE

For evidence to be admissible, it must be **relevant.**[1] Relevance generally means that the testimony or object to be admitted in evidence must be important to the outcome of the case; that is, the testimony or object must help to arrive at the truth of the matter. Likewise, relevance may include testimony or an object that tends to disprove or corroborate a material fact, that is, a fact that is necessary to arrive at the truth.

The ability of an item of evidence to prove what it purports to prove is known as its **probative value.** Probative value means its weight or credibility as proof of the fact in question. Although an item of evidence may be relevant to the action, the probative value of that evidence may be outweighed by circumstances that would prevent one of the parties from getting a fair trial. These circumstances are sometimes called limitations on relevance.

LIMITATIONS ON RELEVANCE

It is relevant to know what injuries resulted from a particular wrongful act. It is, however, improper to display those injuries in bloody, gory, or horrifying ways. Thus, while photographs of the victims at the scene of an accident may be relevant, if the injuries are such that they would unduly shock the jurors, the photographs may not be allowed at trial. Jurors may be swayed by the visions of bloody carnage, rather than by the evidence of liability. Therefore, the court may deem the probative value of the photographs to be outweighed by their ability to prejudice the jury. The injuries of the parties must then be identified in ways other than the accident scene photographs.[2]

Additionally, if the evidence is repetitious or distracting, the court may disallow it. For example, defense counsel calls witness after witness to testify to the violent relationship that existed between the plaintiff and the defendant. While the violent relationship may be relevant to the determination of the truth, belaboring the point, and subjecting the jury to the same testimony from different witnesses without proving new facts, may have the effect of unfairly influencing the jury—or putting them to sleep! The judge may disallow further testimony concerning the same fact.[3]

Evidence of character, though relevant under some circumstances, is not admissible to prove a fact. The fact that defendant is trustworthy and honest is not admissible to prove that defendant did not appropriate money from a trust fund. However, the same testimony, that defendant is trustworthy and honest, may be admissible if the credibility of defendant's testimony is called into question.[4]

Prior convictions are generally inadmissible during the course of a trial. Unless the conviction is directly related to the incident that gave rise to injury, the conviction is irrelevant. For example, the fact that defendant has been convicted on three previous charges of arson may be inadmissible in a civil lawsuit for damages resulting from a fire alleged to have been caused by defendant. Only if the defendant has been convicted of arson in the incident that gives rise to the civil lawsuit will the conviction be admissible. No other prior record may be used to prove or disprove that defendant caused the fire that resulted in harm.[5]

WITNESS TESTIMONY

The general rule regarding the testimony of witnesses is that they must have knowledge of the facts to which they testify.[6] For lay witnesses, this usually means that there has been some direct observation of facts bearing on the case. Opinion testimony by lay witnesses is generally not permitted, with the exception that anyone may testify to opinions that are generated as part of common knowledge, such as height, weight, distance, and so forth.

Lay Witnesses

The testimony of lay witnesses is limited to the actual knowledge of the witness and the opinions that are formed based on common understanding. Lay witnesses may also express opinion on facts to which they have been repeatedly exposed. For example, a witness may testify that in the witness's opinion, the voice on the other end of the telephone was the plaintiff, even though the plaintiff was not identified during the telephone conversation. If this opinion is based on the witness having known plaintiff for a number of years and having talked with the plaintiff on the telephone on numerous occasions, the opinion will be allowed into evidence, based on the repeated observations of the witness.

Similarly, a witness may express an opinion as to the handwriting of an individual based on having seen that handwriting on a number of occasions. For example, the accountant in the office may testify that in the accountant's opinion, the signature on the will is that of the accountant's employer. That opinion is based on seeing the employer's signature on checks, deposit receipts, and other accounting documents. The opinion testimony by this witness will be admissible to prove that the signature on the will is the signature of the employer.[7]

Privilege

In general, **privilege** refers to a defense or a justification in the law for a certain action or failure to act. Certain relationships give rise to the privilege: attorney-client, physician-patient, clergy-parishioner, husband-wife.[8] Some states include a privileged relationship between social workers and clients. Relative to witness testimony, the concept of privilege is inviolate; that is, one party may not be compelled to testify concerning the other without permission.

Privilege exists only where the relationship is preserved through private communication. Therefore, the conversations of the attorney or attorney's staff with the client are privileged as long as the attorney and client are talking in the privacy of the attorney's offices. If the attorney and the client are discussing the case over lunch at a public restaurant, the privileged communication may be impaired, as it is possible that the conversation could be overheard. Similarly, the privilege that exists between husband and wife is confined to communications between them when they are alone. Clergy-parishioner communications are privileged when they take place in the clergy's office and in private. The clergy's testimony that a parishioner is honest will be admissible if character is an issue; however, the information confided to the clergy by the parishioner at a private meeting will be inadmissible.

Privilege is not the same concept as confidentiality. While many relationships are confidential, such as banker-depositor or teacher-student, the parties may still be compelled to testify about their communications without the permission of the other. A subpoena is generally required in order to get this testimony.

Expert Witnesses

In order to express an expert opinion, the witness must be qualified as an expert.[9] This requires that the credentials of the witness be brought into evidence to prove that the witness is capable of rendering an expert opinion. This recitation of the credentials of the expert is known as **qualifying the witness.**

In addition to qualifying the expert, all of the facts upon which the expert's opinion is based must be presented to ensure that the opinion has sufficient basis to be accurate. Failure to inform the expert of a material fact may result in an objection to the expert's opinion and the possibility of its being excluded from consideration in the outcome of the trial.[10]

To prevent the risk of junk science being admitted into factual evidence, federal courts are required to determine that the opinion expressed by the expert witness is reliable. In *Daubert v. Merrell Dow Pharmaceuticals, Inc.,* the United States Supreme Court held that in order for scientific evidence and opinion to be reliable, it must have been appropriately tested or researched using generally accepted methodology, subjected to peer review, and published in reputable journals.[11] This ruling has been extended in some state courts and demands that the expert be prepared to explain how the scientific evidence and opinion was generated and made public.

Hearsay

The Sixth Amendment of the Constitution allows for parties in a lawsuit to confront witnesses against them. Parties may not be able to properly defend themselves unless they have all the information about the claims made against them. **Hearsay** is generally inadmissible because it is unreliable; that is, it cannot be verified.[12] To allow hearsay in evidence would allow the courts in the United States to convict parties on the basis of what someone said someone saw or heard. There are more exceptions to the hearsay rule than

Net Results

Rules of Evidence on the Internet

The Federal Rules of Evidence are available on the Internet, along with the Federal Rules of Civil and Criminal Procedure. Locate the Federal Rules of Evidence at www.law. cornell.edu/rules/fre/over view.html. State rules of evidence may also be available by accessing state bar association web sites or state court web sites. To find these rules through the legislative home page or the home page for the courts, use the universal URL www.legis.state.XX.us or www.courts.state.XX.us, where the XX is the two-letter postal abbreviation for the state being researched.

FIGURE 24-1   *Res Gestae* **Statement**

Res Gestae Statement	What Is Included
Excited utterances	Exclamations made immediately before, during, or after the incident
Present sense impressions	Statements recognizing the sequence of events or activities immediately before, during, or after the incident
Then-existing physical of mental conditions	Comments detailing the condition of the vehicles, the party's lack of sleep or attention, etc., made immediately before, during, or after the incident.

can be discussed in this overview, but those that appear frequently are identified below.

Res Gestae. Statements that are made "in the heat of the moment" are sometimes referred to as **res gestae** ("things done") and are admissible in evidence.[13] Comments that are immediate to the incident in question are made without conscious thought of protecting oneself. Those comments are considered to be true, and anyone who overhears those comments can testify to their substance. *Res gestae* statements can be any of three varieties as shown in Figure 24-1.

Admissions Against Interest. If a party admits wrongdoing or claims to be at fault, anyone overhearing that statement may be called to testify to it.[14] Admissions against interest are not considered hearsay because it is believed that a person would not admit fault unless the admission were true. As time progresses, stories about the incident change in ways that favor the parties telling the story. Thus, *res gestae* and admissions against interest allow the court to be privy to comments that are made at times or under circumstances that prevent the declarant from revising the story to his or her advantage.

Statements to Secure Medical Attention. The treating health care providers probably did not witness the incident that gave rise to the injuries. Their testimony, therefore, is hearsay; it depends on what the patient said about how the injuries occurred. Because it is a generally accepted notion that patients want to receive appropriate treatment for their injuries, it is unlikely that they would lie about the origins of their symptoms. Therefore, if a patient's statement changes as time progresses, medical staff may be called to testify as to the description of the events given at the time medical treatment was sought.[15]

Recorded Recollection. Whenever a recording is made relatively soon after an incident occurred, that recording may be entered in evidence if the recollection of the witness is unclear. The recording may be in a diary, a letter, a note on the calendar, or any other written or audio recollection of the event in question.[16]

Records Kept in the Ordinary Course of Business. Businesses routinely keep records, receipts, and work orders. These documents may be offered in evidence, even though the person who actually completed the records is not available to testify. Since documentation is an essential function of business, it would be unproductive for the court to require testimony to prove all of the entries that exist on a business record. Examples of records kept in the ordinary course of business are records of telephone calls, hotel stays, vehicle maintenance, and appliance repair.[17] In some states, a separate rule exists for medical records. Medical records are generally admissible without testimony when they are certified to be true and correct copies of the actual medical records that exist at the health care facility.

Public Records. Public records; records of criminal proceedings; marriage, birth, and death certificates; and driving records are also exceptions to the hearsay rule and are admissible to prove that the event occurred. Even though some of these documents are protected by privacy laws, they are government documents maintained for public purposes. As such, they are deemed to be reliable and are an exception to hearsay.[18]

Prior Statement. When the credibility of a witness is called into question, hearsay evidence may be admissible to show that the witness made a previous statement concerning the matter. If the prior statement was different from that offered into testimony, the witness's veracity may be dubious. If, however, the prior statement is the same as that offered into testimony, the witness's veracity may be enhanced.[19]

Unavailability of Declarant. There are mixed decisions concerning the exception to hearsay that allows second-hand evidence when the declarant is unable to testify due to death, stroke, senility, or other circumstances.[20] It is always important to check the rules and case law for the jurisdiction in which the action is brought to determine whether and how this exception to hearsay has been employed.

It's Not for Its Truth. Hearsay is also admissible when the context of the testimony is to prove something other than the ordinary meaning of the words used.[21] For example, E.T. rushes into a room at 8:50 P.M. and announces, "B.J. just tried to kill me!" A person in the room who hears E.T.'s announcement may testify to that statement if it is not to prove that B. J. is the killer. If the hearsay is offered to show that E.T. was alive and well at 8:50 P.M., it is admissible. Thus, "it's not for its truth" is an often-used backdoor for getting hearsay into evidence.

PHYSICAL EVIDENCE

In addition to witness testimony, physical evidence may be offered to prove the facts of a case. Physical evidence is sometimes called demonstrative evidence or documentary evidence. It is, in fact, anything that is tangible and not witness testimony. Physical evidence may include photographs, diagrams, medical reports, records or bills, soil samples, and so on. There are special

Ethics Bookmark

Falsifying Evidence

"A lawyer shall not knowingly . . . offer evidence that the attorney knows to be false" Annotated Model Rules of Professional Conduct Fourth Edition, Rule 3.3(a)(4) Copyright 1999.*[22] Legal nurse consultants are sometimes confronted with records that appear to have been altered, deliberately destroyed, or falsified. The legal nurse consultant has a duty to bring these records to the attention of the attorney (whether plaintiff or defendant). Failing to bring this suspicion to the attention of the attorney may result in severe sanctions.

*American Bar Association. Reprinted by permission of the American Bar Association. American Bar Association, *Annotated Model Rules of Professional conduct,* 4th ed. (1999) Rule 3.3(a)(4). Copies of Model Code of Professional Responsibility, 1999 edition are available from Service Center, American Bar Association, 750 North Lake Shore Drive, Chicago, IL 60611-4497, 1-800-285-2221.

FIGURE 24-2 Authentication of Physical Evidence

Method of Authentication	What It Proves
Chain of custody	The item offered in evidence is the same item that was involved in the incident
Testimony of someone with knowledge	The item offered in evidence is the item about which the witness has knowledge
Unique characteristics	The item offered in evidence is the item in question because it is easily identifiable by unique characteristics
Expert testimony	The item offered is exactly similar to the item destroyed in the incident because of identifying product labels, batch numbers, etc.

---

rules regarding the admission of physical evidence. Generally, physical evidence requires the testimony of a witness having knowledge of that evidence. This testimony is intended to establish that the item is what it purports to be. Proving that the physical evidence is what it is said to be is the process of **authentication.**[23]

Authentication

There are many ways that physical evidence may be authenticated. Figure 24-2 shows various ways to prove that an item is what it is said to be.

Establishing a **chain of custody** is another way to prove that physical evidence is what it is claimed to be. For example, a defective outboard motor is removed from the boat immediately after an unfortunate water skiing incident. The motor is maintained in the boathouse and never used again. When the lawsuit begins, the owner of the outboard motor delivers the motor to a member of the law firm and gets a receipt. The motor is continuously maintained at the law firm until the action goes to trial. Testimony concerning the storage and maintenance of the outboard motor (physical evidence) shows a chain of title that will effectively authenticate the item.[24]

Items that have unique characteristics may be authenticated by testimony concerning those unique characteristics. Items that have been destroyed, such as through a fire or explosion, may be presented in evidence using an item that was manufactured at the same time, from the same materials or formula, from the same facility, and with the same quality control standards along with expert testimony confirming those facts.[25]

Best Evidence Rule

Whenever physical evidence is offered, the original item involved in the dispute is preferred. This is known as the best evidence rule and is meant to avoid the possibility of fraudulently altered copies or destruction of original items in bad faith—to avoid having them produced in a litigation. There are times, however, when the best evidence rule is not practical. For example, in an automobile collision, it is not practical to have the automobiles present in the courtroom, nor is it always feasible to provide the jury with a view of the vehicles at an impound lot or other location. Therefore, photographs of the automobiles are generally admissible in evidence to show damages and to support an expert witness's reconstruction of the incident.

There are also circumstances when copies of documents will be admissible as evidence. If the authenticity of the original document is not in question and the admission of the copy will not be unfair to a party, the copy may be admitted. If the original no longer exists, unless it has been destroyed in bad faith, and the parties agree that the copy accurately depicts the original, a copy is admissible.[26]

Self-authenticating Documents

Certain documents are admissible without testimony that they are what they are claimed to be. Commercial paper, such as checks or promissory notes; newspapers and magazines; governmental publications; certified documents, such as medical records; and documentation containing the signature and seal of a notary public are all deemed to be admissible without further proof that they are what they are claimed to be. These documents are said to be **self-authenticating.**[27]

OTHER EVIDENTIARY CONCEPTS

Additional evidentiary devices are important for developing the investigation, assessing the case, and presenting materials at trial. These devices include presumption, judicial notice, stipulation, and the learned treatise rule.

Presumption

Presumption is an evidentiary mechanism that serves to establish a fact by the existence of other facts.[29] For example, the fact that two people are married to each other may give rise to the presumption that the property owned by them is marital property, acquired during the marriage. In order to show that the property is not part of the marital estate, the party wishing to preserve individual property must prove, with clear and convincing evidence, that the property was individually owned, kept separate, and intended to remain separate from the marital estate.

Judicial Notice

Whenever a fact is commonly known or easily verifiable, the judge may take **judicial notice** of it; that is, no further proof is required to show that the fact exists.[30] Items that fall within the judicial notice rule are geographic and historical facts of the region, local ordinances, or other facts that are readily verifiable through a reliable source. As with business records and self-authenticated documents, it would be unproductive for the court to require proof of a fact that is common knowledge.

Stipulations on Evidence

The parties may agree to facts that need not be proved. For example, if the parties agree that the experts are qualified to testify and render opinions, they may stipulate to that and need not spend time in court proving that the experts have attained expert status. This is an area that is heavily influenced by attorney strategy, and attorneys will not stipulate to what they want to prove with testimony and exhibits, even where there is no dispute about the facts. If the parties enter into a stipulation on evidence, the judge will instruct the jury that the fact exists and does not require proof.

Learned Treatise

To avoid the sometimes excessive cost of having experts testify in court, many jurisdictions have adopted a **learned treatise** rule. This rule allows a party to bring in a scholarly journal article or a treatise that provides information important to the case. If any expert testifies that the scholarly journal or treatise is reliable as to its content or usage, it may be allowed into evidence without additional testimony concerning the scientific or technical facts contained within it.[31]

HOW EVIDENCE LAW IMPACTS THE ROLE OF THE LEGAL NURSE CONSULTANT

There are many more rules of evidence, and specific applications and cautions concerning evidence law. Law schools and colleges that provide paralegal and legal assistant training offer entire courses on the subject. It is unlikely, however, that legal nurse consultants will be involved in the intricate arguments concerning pieces of evidence. It is more likely that they will assist in the development of those pieces of evidence and in the development of expert testimony and testimony about damages. It is incumbent upon the legal nurse consultant to be familiar with the major and most universal of the evidentiary rules.

While the conduct of the trial, the presentation of evidence, and the arguments for and against admission of evidence are the exclusive domain of a licensed attorney, legal nurse consultants who assist in the investigation and preparation of a case for trial will be expected to have a working knowledge of evidence law. Recognizing what may or may not be allowed in evidence to prove a fact will facilitate the development of appropriate courtroom exhibits and the preparation of witnesses. In addition, understanding the rules of evidence will give the legal nurse consultant the necessary background to ensure that experts are qualified to testify and that the testimony is based upon complete access to the facts. Legal nurse consultants might be employed to research medical literature that may be admissible under the learned treatise rule. The medical background and experience of the legal nurse consultant is what is needed in the legal office. Familiarity with the rules of evidence will be value added!

CHAPTER SUMMARY

- There are two classifications of evidence: direct and circumstantial.
- There are two categories of evidence: witness testimony and physical evidence, or exhibits.
- Lay witnesses may testify to what they have witnessed and may offer opinion based on observations or repeated observations.
- Experts must be qualified before rendering an opinion in court.
- Hearsay is generally inadmissible, although there are several exceptions to the hearsay rule.
- Physical evidence must be authenticated and courts usually employ the best evidence rule.
- Legal nurse consultants must have a working knowledge of evidence law to ensure that exhibits are admissible and that experts are qualified to testify.

KEY TERMS

authentication	judicial notice	qualify the witness
chain of custody	learned treatise	relevant
circumstantial evidence	presumption	*res gestae*
direct evidence	privilege	self-authentication
hearsay	probative value	

REVIEW QUESTIONS

1. Identify some of the major exceptions to the hearsay rule. Why are these exceptions allowed?
2. Distinguish between direct and circumstantial evidence. Witness testimony and physical evidence.
3. Why is it important for a legal nurse consultant to understand the basics of evidence law?

INTERNET EXERCISES

1. Access the web page for this textbook at *www.westlegalstudies.com.*

2. Click on the assignments section and complete the assignment(s) for Chapter Twenty-four.

EXERCISES

1. Networking. Now that you have learned a great deal more about the civil process and the rules of evidence, make plans to attend another civil jury trial. If possible, attend a medical negligence trial. Most courthouses have personnel who schedule field studies for local schools who would be willing to let you know when the next medical negligence case is going to trial, or you may be able to find out about cases from your contacts in previous networking assign-ments. During breaks in the trial, talk casually with the litigation teams, observe the evidence that is used, and pay attention to any objections raised about the evidence.

2. Professional Portfolio. Prepare a table for your own use identifying the major rules of evidence as they appear in this textbook. Keep this table with your systems file, folder, or binder, and organize or index it for easy access.

ENDNOTES

1. Fed. R. Evid. 401.
2. Fed. R. Evid. 403.
3. Fed. R. Evid. 403.
4. Fed. R. Evid. 404(a).
5. Fed. R. Evid. 404(b).
6. Fed. R. Evid. 602.
7. Fed. R. Evid. 701, 901(b)(2), 901(b)(5).
8. Fed. R. Evid. 501.
9. Fed. R. Evid. 401.
10. Fed. R. Evid. 703, 705.
11. *Daubert v. Merrell Dow Pharmaceuticals, Inc.,* 113 S. Ct. 2786, 125 L. Ed. 2d. 469 (1993).
12. Fed. R. Evid. 802.
13. Fed. R. Evid. 803(1).
14. Fed. R. Evid. 801(d)(2).
15. Fed. R. Evid. 803(4).
16. Fed. R. Evid. 803(5).
17. Fed. R. Evid. 803(6).
18. Fed. R. Evid. 803(8).
19. Fed. R. Evid. 803(9).
20. Fed. R. Evid. 613, 801(1).
21. Fed. R. Evid. 804(b).
22. American Bar Association, *Annotated Model Rules of Professional Conduct,* (1999) 4th Edition Rule 3.3(a)(4). Copies of ABA *Model Code of Professional Responsibility, 1999 Edition* are available from Service Center, American Bar Association, 750 North Lake Shore Drive, Chicago, IL 60611-4497, 1-800-285-2221.
23. Fed. R. Evid. 901.
24. Fed. R. Evid. 901(b)(1).
25. Fed. R. Evid. 901(b)(1), 901(b)(3), 901(b)(4).
26. Fed. R. Evid. 1002.
27. Fed. R. Evid. 902.
28. G. Van Allen, "Career Options: The Increasing Demand for Courtroom Nurses." *The Oklahoma Nurse* July, August, September, 1996, p. 31.

29. Fed. R. Evid. 301.

30. Fed. R. Evid. 201.

31. Fed. R. Evid. 803.18.

ADDITIONAL REFERENCES

Lamb, D. L., BSN, RN. "Who Qualifies as an Expert?: A Review of a Case in Pennsylvania and Cases in Florida." *Journal of Legal Nurse Consulting* 7:4 (1996): 14–15, 20.

Loecker, B. L., MSEd, RN. "Attorney-Client Privilege and Confidentiality." *Journal of Legal Nurse Consulting* 9:1 (1998): 14–15.

Loecker, B. L., MSEd, RN. "Exclusionary Rules of Evidence." *Journal of Legal Nurse Consulting* 7:1 (1996): 13–14.

Stopp, Margaret T. *Evidence Law in the Trial Process.* Albany, NY: West Thomson Learning, 1999.

CHAPTER 25

THE BASICS OF CIVIL PROCEDURE

OBJECTIVES

In this chapter, you will discover

- what is meant by civil procedure

- the steps involved at each stage of civil procedure

- how motion practice and especially dispositive motions may expedite litigation

- how the rules of civil procedure govern litigation

- the role of the legal nurse consultant in civil procedure

OVERVIEW

The process of a lawsuit through the court system is governed by the rules and practices that are developed by the legislature or the courts to facilitate the efficient and expeditious management of legal claims. This procedure guides the lawsuit through the judicial system the same way speed limits and controls guide traffic on the highway. Failure to abide by the rules and practices of the court may jeopardize the claim, regardless of the merit of that claim.

Federal trials are governed by federal rules. There are separate rules for criminal and civil procedure, and there are rules of evidence and appellate procedure. In addition, each court has the power to establish individual rules for the jurisdiction served by the court.

State courts are governed by state rules and practices, and the local rules imposed by individual courts. This chapter will focus on the federal rules of civil procedure. Many state court rules parallel the federal rules. It is critical, however, to know and abide by the rules and practices for the court in which the action is taken.

There are three stages in the litigation process: pleadings, discovery, and trial. These stages will be used as the organizational framework to explain the rules of civil procedure that impact activities during each stage.

PLEADINGS

The Federal Rules of Civil Procedure identify several **pleadings** that are allowable in federal courts: complaints, answers, counterclaims, cross-claims, motions, and third-party complaints. The pleadings introduce the parties and the problem to the court. The legal and factual foundation for the legal claim or defense is set forth in the pleadings.

Complaint

The initial document in a civil lawsuit is the complaint. The caption of a complaint identifies the court, the venue, the parties, the title of the document, and so forth. There are basically three parts to the main body of the complaint: jurisdiction, claim, and prayer for relief.

After the caption, the complaint must explain to the court that the court has **subject matter jurisdiction** over the problem and **personal jurisdiction** over the parties. Subject matter jurisdiction is governed in federal court by the limited jurisdiction outlined in the United States Code. The limited subject matter jurisdiction of the federal district courts is outlined in Figure 25-1.

Figure 25-1 is not intended to be an exhaustive list of the subject matter jurisdiction of the federal courts, but to identify those that are most frequently used. Federal courts will often have **concurrent jurisdiction** with state courts, so the action may be brought in either. One exception, of course, is bankruptcy, which must be brought in federal bankruptcy court.

FIGURE 25-1   Subject Matter Jurisdiction of Federal Courts[1]

Jurisdiction	Types of Cases
Diversity jurisdiction	Plaintiff and defendant reside in different states and the amount in controversy exceeds $75,000
Federal question jurisdiction	Actions involving any federal laws, federal crimes, constitutional questions, civil rights, and treaty disputes
Federal interpleader act	Disputes concerning the ownership of property held by a third party when the value of the property exceeds $10
Intellectual property	Actions concerning copyright, patent, trademark, and plant variety
Bankruptcy	Exclusive jurisdiction in the adjunct federal bankruptcy courts

---

FIGURE 25-2   Personal Jurisdiction of the Federal Courts[2]

Personal Jurisdiction	How Personal Jurisdiction Is Applied
Defendant resides in the district of the federal court	Residence is determined by where the defendant lives, maintains a driver's license, or is registered to vote
Defendant does substantial business in the district of the federal court	This includes mail order businesses and internet sales; if the defendant advertises and does business within the district, the defendant is bound by the jurisdiction of the court
The incident occurred in the geographic jurisdiction of the federal court	If the incident giving rise to the litigation occurred within the geographical boundaries of the federal court, the parties, regardless of where they reside or do business, will be bound to the jurisdiction of the court—subject to being properly served with process

Personal jurisdiction is vested in the federal courts under conditions identified in Figure 25-2. Personal jurisdiction is perfected by **service of process;** that is, the papers must be delivered to the defendant in order to bind the defendant to the jurisdiction of the court.

Figure 25-2 only highlights the major considerations about the personal jurisdiction of the federal court—There are many others. It is important to always monitor the rules to be certain that the activities involved in processing the litigation conform to the rules.

In addition to the subject matter jurisdiction and personal jurisdiction of the court, **venue** is a major consideration. Venue means neighborhood and it

FIGURE 25-3 Venue in Federal Court[3]	
Venue	**Rationale**
The district in which defendant resides	Because the defendant generally has little or nothing to gain from the lawsuit, the court seeks to make the expense of defending the action as minimal as possible
The district in which the cause of action arose	Because the witnesses and physical evidence is located in this district, it will be less costly to bring the witnesses and other evidence to court
The district in which the property that is the subject of the litigation is located	Again, because the witnesses and facts concerning the property are located in this district, it will be the most convenient for the parties

refers to the geographical forum that is the most convenient for processing the lawsuit. There are several considerations under federal rules for determining where appropriate venue is for the lawsuit. These considerations are identified in Figure 25-3.

The first paragraphs of the complaint will identify the jurisdictional foundation for the lawsuit and will identify the plaintiff and the defendant, and where each party resides or does business. This should be sufficient to establish that the court has subject matter and personal jurisdiction, and that the venue for the lawsuit is proper. Strict adherence to the rules of construction for complaints is critical. Paragraphs in complaints must be numbered sequentially and limited to a single set of circumstances. Each claim must be founded upon a recognized theory of recovery and must show that plaintiff is entitled to recovery from the defendant.

The **prayer for relief** (sometimes called the wherefore clause or the **ad damnum** – "to the damages") must clearly state what the plaintiff is seeking from the defendant. The exact amount of money damages need not be specified. The damages sought may be described as "in an amount to be determined by the Court."

A sample complaint is included in Figure 25-4. Sidebar comments identify the specific rules that apply to the construction of the complaint. A jury demand is often included in the complaint, although the rules provide that a jury trial may be demanded in writing anytime after filing the complaint, but not later than ten days after service of the last pleading.[4] Many attorneys will routinely demand a jury trial on behalf of their clients in order to preserve the right to a jury. If a demand is not made within the time specified in the court rules, the right to a jury trial is waived. If the action is commenced in state court, it is necessary to check state court rules to comply with the time requirements for requesting a jury.

FIGURE 25-4   Sample Complaint with Explanatory Rules

IN UNITED STATES DISTRICT COURT
FOR THE WESTERN DISTRICT OF
WISCONSIN

*****

Hasam Simsek,
      Plaintiff, File No. _____
   v.
Carol Jackson   COMPLAINT
     Defendant.

*****

Plaintiff, for his complaint against
Defendant, states:
JURISDICTION
1. Plaintiff resides at 111 2nd Street, Anytown, Any County, Wisconsin.

2. Defendant, Carol Jackson, is a neurosurgeon, licensed to practice medicine in the state of Minnesota, with offices at 222 3rd Street, Someplace, Some County, Minnesota.
3. Because the plaintiff and defendant reside in different states and the amount in controversy exceeds $75,000.00, the court has jurisdiction pursuant to 13 U.S.C. § 1332.

CLAIM I—MEDICAL NEGLIGENCE

4. On January 17, —-, Defendant performed surgery on Plaintiff to remove a basellar bifurcation aneurysm diagnosed by Defendant.
5. Defendant failed to exercise the degree of skill, care, and judgment usually exercised by neurosurgeons when performing this procedure.
6. Defendant acted with reckless disregard for plaintiff's health and safety in the negligent performance of this surgical procedure.

FRCP 10(a)—caption shall contain the name of court

FRCP 10(a)—caption shall contain the title of the action, file number, names of parties

FRCP 9(b)—allegations in numbered paragraphs; contents of paragraphs limited to single set of circumstances

FRCP 8(e)(1)—each averment shall be simple, concise, direct; no technical form of pleadings

FRCP 9(f)—averments of time and place are material

FRCP 8(a)—the complaint shall contain a short, plain statement of claim showing plaintiff is entitled to relief

continued

FIGURE 25-4   Sample Complaint with Explanatory Rules   *continued*

7. As a result of Defendant's negligence, Plaintiff has suffered grievous bodily harm, has lost all motor ability, and has lost sight and speech.

8. As a direct result of Defendant's negligence, Plaintiff has incurred expenses for medical care, hospitalization, medication, medical appliances and devices, adaptation of the living environment, home health care, loss of income, and other expenses that will continue into the future.

   FRCP 9(g)—special damages shall be specifically stated

9. As a further result of Defendant's negligence, Plaintiff has suffered emotional and physical pain that will continue into the future.

CLAIM II—LACK OF INFORMED CONSENT

Plaintiff realleges all preceding paragraphs.

10. Defendant was under a duty to adequately inform Plaintiff of the risks attendant to the surgical procedure and any alternatives to the procedure.

11. Defendant failed to adequately inform Plaintiff of the risks of this type of surgery or the alternatives available.

12. Had Defendant provided information to Plaintiff concerning the risks attendant to this type of neurosurgery and the alternatives available, Plaintiff would not have submitted to the surgical procedure.

13. As a result of Defendant's negligent failure to adequately inform Plaintiff, Plaintiff has suffered grievous bodily harm, has lost all motor ability, and has lost sight and speech.

14. As a direct result of Defendant's negligent failure to adequate inform Plaintiff, Plaintiff has incurred expenses for medical care, hospitalization, medication, medical appliances and devices, adaptation of the living environment, home health care, loss of income, and other expenses that will continue into the future.

15. As a future result of Defendant's negligent failure to inform, Plaintiff has suffered emotional and physical pain that will continue into the future.

CLAIM III—TORTIOUS MISREPRESENTATION

Plaintiff realleges all preceding paragraphs.

16. In preparation for the surgical procedure described in this complaint, Defendant made the following misrepresentations of fact to the Plaintiff:
    A. That the risks attendant to the removal of a basellar bifurcation aneurysm were similar to those attending an appendectomy or a tonsillectomy.
    B. That Defendant had performed this surgery on numerous occasions.
    C. That the morbidity and mortality rates were minimal.
17. At the time these misrepresentations were made, Defendant knew or reasonably should have known that the statements were false.
18. At the time these misrepresentations were made, Defendant claimed expertise in neurosurgery and had an economic interest in making the misrepresentations.
19. Defendant's misrepresentations were made with reckless disregard for the health and safety of Plaintiff.
20. As a result of Defendant's tortious misrepresentation, Plaintiff has suffered grievous bodily harm, has lost all motor ability, and has lost sight and speech.
21. As a direct result of Defendant's tortious misrepresentation, Plaintiff has incurred expenses for medical care, hospitalization, medication, medical appliances and devices, adaptation of the living environment, home health care, loss of income, and other expenses that will continue into the future.
22. As a future result of Defendant's tortious misrepresentation, Plaintiff has suffered emotional and physical pain that will continue into the future.

continued

FIGURE 25-4 Sample Complaint with Explanatory Rules *continued*

WHEREFORE, Plaintiff demands judgment against Defendant for:

    A) Special and general damages in an amount to be determined by the court;
    B) Punitive damages in an amount to be determined by the court;
    C) Plaintiff's costs and disbursements of this action;
    D) Such other and further relief as to the Court seems appropriate.

TRIAL BY JURY OF TWELVE IS DEMANDED.	FRCP 38—jury demand with or after complaint but not later than 10 days after service of last pleading
Dated: _____	
_____ Jeremy Johnson Attorney for Plaintiff 234 5th Street Anytown, WI 55555	FRCP 11(a)—every pleading shall contain a signature and the name of the party or attorney signing

According to federal rules, an action is commenced when the complaint is filed with the clerk of court, provided service of the summons and complaint is made upon the defendant within 120 days of the filing of the complaint. Complaints must be filed within the time limit imposed by the statute of limitations for that type of action.

Summons

Once the complaint is filed, a summons is issued from the court. The summons notifies the defendant that a lawsuit has been commenced against the defendant and specifies the amount of time within which the defendant must answer the complaint. Although the summons is said to issue from the court, it is prepared by the plaintiff's attorney and signed by the clerk of court.

The rules require that the summons and complaint be served together within 120 days of the filing of the complaint. There are several options for serving the defendant: personal service, substituted service, service at the residence of the defendant, service by mail, service by publication, and admission of service. While the plaintiff is generally free to select the method of service, the rules require that certain attempts at service be made before service at the residence of the defendant or service by publication will constitute sufficient delivery of process.

Personal Service. The marshal is the chief law enforcement officer of the federal district in which the court has jurisdiction. As such, it is the marshal's office that has the official responsibility for service of process on defendants residing in that district. In order to have **personal service** made by the marshal, plaintiff must complete and file a Request for Service and Process Record.

To have someone other than the marshal serve process on the defendant, it is necessary to file a petition for appointment of alternative process server. This petition is signed by the judge and allows anyone over the age of eighteen, who is not a party to the lawsuit, to deliver the documents to the defendant. Proof of personal service is established by filing the affidavit of service signed by the marshal, deputy marshal, or other process server.

Substituted service. Whenever the defendant is represented by an attorney or has appointed an agent with the power to accept service on behalf of the defendant, **substituted service** will be allowed. In that case, the attorney or agent may be personally served in lieu of serving the defendant. Similarly, if the defendant is a minor or incompetent and a legal guardian, a **guardian *ad litem,*** or a **conservator** has been appointed for that defendant, the law allows service upon the guardian, guardian *ad litem,* or conservator. Substituted service may be proved by filing with the court an affidavit of service signed by the process server.

Service at the Residence of the Defendant. If the process server has made diligent effort to serve the defendant personally and has been unable to do so, the law allows service by leaving a copy of the summons and complaint at the residence of the defendant. The documents must be delivered to a member of the household, fourteen years of age or older. In addition, the process server must explain to the person accepting the documents the nature of the process and the consequences of failing to respond to the complaint. The affidavit proving service should include a paragraph indicating that the process server tried to serve the defendant personally before leaving the summons and complaint at the residence of the defendant.

Service by Mail. In order to reduce the cost of litigation, federal rules allow the summons and complaint to be served by mail.[5] To be effective, plaintiff must mail, via regular mail, two copies of the summons and complaint; two copies of a waiver of service; and a notice of the defendant's responsibility to accept service of process by mail, along with a postage-paid return envelope. Samples of the waiver of service and the notice of defendant's responsibility to accept service of process by mail are included in Figure 25-5.

If the defendant accepts service and returns the waiver to plaintiff, defendant has sixty days to answer the complaint. The waiver is filed with the court and constitutes proof of acceptance of service of process. Failing to accept service and to return the waiver will result in the defendant's being taxed the costs of alternative service.

Service by Publication. If it has been impossible to serve the defendant personally or to determine a residence at which to leave the summons and complaint, the law allows service by publication. Service by publication requires that the summons and complaint be published in a legal newspaper in the county in which the defendant was last known to reside. The summons and complaint must be published once a week for three successive weeks. To prove service by publication, an affidavit of the publisher must be filed with the court. In addition, an affidavit of mailing must be filed stating that the plaintiff mailed a copy of the summons and complaint via registered mail to the last known address of the defendant. Proof of service by publication is not effective unless both affidavits are filed with the court.

Admission of service. Under certain circumstances, the defendant may be anticipating the lawsuit and may be willing to admit service without the necessity or expense of personal service. This often happens in divorce and is

---

FIGURE 25-5   Waiver of Service and Notice of Defendant's Responsibility to Accept Service of Process by Mail

NOTICE OF LAWSUIT AND REQUEST FOR WAIVER OF SERVICE OF SUMMONS

To: [Defendant]

A lawsuit has been commenced against you. A copy of the complaint is attached to this notice. It has been filed in the United States District Court for the [district] and has been assigned docket number [docket number].

This is not a formal summons or notification from the court, but rather my request that you sign and return the enclosed waiver of service in order to save the costs of serving you with a judicial summons and an additional copy of the complaint. The cost of service will be avoided if I receive a signed copy of the waiver within [at least 30] days after the date designated below as the date on which this Notice and Request is sent. I enclose a stamped and addressed envelope [or other means of cost-free return] for your use. An extra copy of the waiver is also attached for your records.

If you comply with this request and return the signed waiver, it will be filed with the court and no summons will be served on you. The action will then proceed as if you had been served on the date the waiver is filed, except that you will not be obligated to answer the complaint before 60 days from the date designed below as the date on which this notice is sent.

If you do not return the signed waiver within the time indicated, I will take the appropriate steps to effect formal service in a manner authorized by the Federal Rules of Civil Procedure and will then, as authorized by those Rules, ask the court to require you to pay the full costs of such service. In that connection, please read the statement concerning the duty of parties to waive the service of summons, which is set forth at the foot of the waiver form.

I affirm that this request is being sent to you on behalf of plaintiff, this _____ day of _____ , 20 _____ .

_____
Signature of Plaintiff's Attorney

WAIVER OF SERVICE OF SUMMONS

TO: [name of plaintiff's attorney]

I acknowledge receipt of your request that I waive service of a summons in the action of [caption of action], which is case number [docket number] in the United States District Court for the [district]. I have also received a copy of the complaint in the action, two copies of this instrument, and a means by which I can return the signed waiver to you without cost to me.

I agree to save the cost of service of a summons and an additional copy of the complaint in this lawsuit by not requiring that I be served with judicial process in the manner provided by Rule 4.

I will retain all defenses or objections to the lawsuit or to the jurisdiction or venue of the court except for objections based on a defect in the summons or in the service of the summons.

I understand that a judgment may be entered against me if an answer or motion under Rule 12 is not served upon you within 60 days after [date request was sent].

Dated: _____

_____
Signature
Printed/typed name _____

DUTY TO AVOID UNNECESSARY COSTS OF SERVICE OF SUMMONS

Rule 4 of the Federal Rules of Civil Procedure requires certain parties to cooperate in saving unnecessary costs of service of the summons and complaint. A defendant who, after being notified of an action and asked to waive service of a summons, fails to do so will be required to bear the cost of such service unless good cause be shown for its failure to sign and return the waiver.

It is not good cause for a failure to waive service that a party believes that the complaint is unfounded, or that the action has been brought in an improper place or in a court that lacks jurisdiction over the subject matter of the action or over its person or property. A party who waives service of the summons retains all defenses and objections (except any relating to the summons or to the service of the summons), and may later object to the jurisdiction of the court or to the place where the action has been brought.

A defendant who waives service must within the time specified on the waiver form serve on the plaintiff's attorney a response to the complaint and must file a signed copy of the response with the court. If the answer or motion is not served within this time, a default judgment may be taken against the defendant. By waiving service, a defendant is allowed more time to answer than if the summons had been actually served when the request for waiver of service was received.

available as an alternative to service in any civil action. To prove admission of service, the defendant will sign a document admitting service at the time the defendant picks up the summons and complaint. This admission of service is filed with the court.

Responding to the Complaint

Once the summons and complaint have been served, the defendant has twenty days to respond to the complaint or forty days to respond to a complaint that is served by publication. If the defendant fails to respond or make an appearance in the action, the plaintiff is entitled to petition for **default judgment.**

There are several ways that a defendant can respond to a complaint. The defendant can move for dismissal of the complaint, which historically is called a **demurrer,** although demurrers as pleadings have been abolished under federal court rules and many state court rules. A defendant can also answer the complaint by admitting or denying the factual allegations of the complaint, or the defendant might bring in a third party who is responsible for all or a portion of the plaintiff's injuries.

Motion to Dismiss. A motion to dismiss the plaintiff's complaint is generally based on some procedural defect and does not usually attack the merits of the claim. For example, a motion to dismiss may be filed if the defendant was not properly served. If the forum court does not have personal jurisdiction over the defendant, any judgment or order emanating from that court will be unenforceable. If the complaint was not properly served and the time for service has expired, the complaint will be dismissed. In that case, plaintiff must refile the action, assuming that time remains in the tolling of the statute of limitations. The Federal Rules of Civil Procedure identify several grounds for a motion to dismiss. These grounds are listed in Figure 25-6.[6]

The list of grounds for motions to dismiss identified in Figure 25-6 is not inclusive. Whenever a complaint is received in the law office, it is important to review the grounds available for dismissal to determine whether the lawsuit might be removed from the system before the necessity of a defense.

When the defendant moves for dismissal, it may be necessary to consolidate defenses. **Affirmative defenses** will relieve a defendant of liability regardless of defendant's fault. These defenses, however, must be brought forward in the first responsive pleading. The motion to dismiss must include every affirmative defense to which the defendant is entitled, otherwise that defense will be deemed waived. That defense cannot be brought up in a later pleading nor can proof of that defense be offered at trial.

A motion to dismiss must be filed within the time for answering the complaint (usually twenty days). If the motion to dismiss is denied, defendant has ten days from the denial of the motion to dismiss to answer the complaint.

Answer. The most frequent response to a complaint is an answer. The answer simply admits or denies the factual allegations of the complaint. In ad-

---

FIGURE 25-6   Grounds for a Motion to Dismiss[5]

Basis for Motion to Dismiss	Procedural Explanation
Lack of subject matter jurisdiction	If the court does not have the power to make a determination on this type of controversy, any judgment or order of the court will be moot
Improper service or untimeliness of service	If the personal jurisdiction has not been perfected through service of process, the court has no power to enforce any judgment or order against the defendant
Lack of capacity to be sued	If the defendant does not exist, or if the defendant is a minor or an incompetent, the action cannot be maintained against that party
Res judicata	If the matter has already been tried to conclusion or has been settled and a stipulation for dismissal with prejudice has been filed, the action may not be brought back to court
Statute of limitations	If the lawsuit was not brought within the statutory period for maintenance of actions of that kind, it is barred and the action will be dismissed
Failure to state a claim upon which relief may be granted	This is also the basis for a demurrer; that even if all of the facts alleged in the complaint are proven, they do not establish liability against the defendant

---

dition, the defendant may assert that he or she has insufficient knowledge to determine the truth of the allegation. A response claiming lack of knowledge has the effect of a denial. The allegations that are denied or to which defendant claims a lack of knowledge, then become the points that plaintiff must prove. It is said, therefore, that the issues are **joined** when the answer is filed. Additionally, any defenses available to the defendant should be brought in the answer. These defenses may include contributory negligence in a negligence claim, or consent or self-defense in an action based in intentional tort. A sample answer is included in Figure 25-7.

The answer must be served on the plaintiff. Service of litigation documents, after the summons and complaint, is generally completed via mail. A certificate of mailing is attached to the original document and filed with the court. The defendant, in addition to answering the complaint and outlining any potential defenses, may file a counterclaim, a cross-claim, or a third-party complaint.

Counterclaim. If the defendant has a legal claim against the plaintiff, whether or not it arises from the same circumstances that gave rise to plaintiff's complaint, the defendant may join that claim in the present lawsuit. The

FIGURE 25-7   Sample Answer

IN UNITED STATES DISTRICT COURT
FOR THE WESTERN DISTRICT OF WISCONSIN

*****

Hasam Simsek,

                    Plaintiff,   File No._____

   v.

Carol Jackson,   ANSWER

                   Defendant.

*****

Defendant, for her answer to Plaintiff's complaint, states:

FIRST DEFENSE

1. Plaintiff's complaint fails to state a cause of action upon which relief may be granted from this defendant.
   ANSWER
2. Defendant admits the allegations contained in paragraphs 1, 2, 3, and 4 of Plaintiff's complaint.
3. Defendant denies the allegations contained in paragraphs 5 and 6 of Plaintiff's complaint.
4. Defendant is without sufficient information to form a belief as to the truth of the allegations of injury and damage contained in paragraphs 7, 8, and 9, and denies that those damages arose as a result of defendant's negligence.
5. Defendant admits the allegations contained in paragraph 10 of Plaintiff's complaint.
6. Defendant denies the allegations contained in paragraph 11 of Plaintiff's complaint.
7. Defendant is without sufficient information to form a belief as to the truth of the allegations in paragraph 12 of Plaintiff's complaint and, therefore, denies those allegations.
8. Defendant is without sufficient information to form a belief as to the truth of the allegations of injury and damage contained in paragraphs 13, 14, and 15 and denies that those damages arose as a result of defendant's conduct.
9. Defendant denies the allegations contained in paragraphs 16 and 17 of Plaintiff's complaint.
10. Defendant admits that neurosurgery is her medical specialization, but denies a claim of expertise or an economic interest in Plaintiff's decision.
11. Defendant denies the allegations contained in paragraph 19 of Plaintiff's complaint.
12. Defendant is without sufficient information to form a belief as to the truth of the allegations of injury and damage contained in paragraphs 20, 21, and 22 and denies that those damages arose as a result of defendant's conduct.

AFFIRMATIVE DEFENSES

13. Plaintiff was adequately and fully informed of the risks inherent in this surgical procedure and freely consented to the procedure.
14. Plaintiff's injuries are a direct and proximate result of his own negligence and lack of care.

WHEREFORE, Defendant demands judgment as follows:

A) Dismissing Plaintiff's complaint;
B) For Defendant's costs, disbursements, and attorney fees incurred in this action; and
C) For such other relief as this Court deems appropriate.

Dated: _____

_____

Irek Spacek
Attorney for Defendant
678 9th Street
Someplace, MN 56666

rationale for this is simple. As long as the parties are in court, it is expedient to resolve all of their differences at one time. A **counterclaim** is similar to a complaint in that it must meet the elements of a cause of action and must establish a claim for relief. The relief demanded by the defendant against the plaintiff need not be the same relief demanded by the plaintiff in the original lawsuit. For example, plaintiff demands compensatory damages in an action against defendant. Defendant counterclaims demanding an injunction against plaintiff. Despite the difference between these remedies at law and in equity, the courts will allow defendant to bring the counterclaim.

The Federal Rules of Civil Procedure identify two types of counterclaims: compulsory and permissive.[7] A **compulsory counterclaim** is one that arises out of the same circumstances as the plaintiff's claim. If the defendant has a claim against plaintiff and does not join it in the present action, the claim is forever barred. A compulsory counterclaim may not be brought by the defendant in a separate lawsuit against the plaintiff.

A **permissive counterclaim** is any claim, regardless of its basis, that defendant has against plaintiff and for which the statute of limitations has not expired. Resolving all of the differences between the parties at one time, lessens the burden on the court calendar and the time and cost to the parties.

Cross-claim. Whenever a party, usually a defendant, believes that a codefendant is liable for the injuries to plaintiff, the defendant may enter a **cross-claim** against the codefendant. This usually appears in cases where employees are the parties alleged to have been negligent. The employee files a cross-claim against the employer claiming that the employee was acting within the scope of employment and that the employer is responsible for any negligence assigned to the employee-party under the legal doctrine of *respondeat superior.* Cross-claims are also filed in actions involving automobile accidents where several defendants are involved.

Third Party Complaint. Sometimes the defendant believes that his or her actions are not the cause of the injuries to plaintiff and that another, not a party to the lawsuit, should answer for those injuries. For example, on Monday defendant's vehicle is in the shop for repair of the brakes. Monday evening, employees at the shop tell defendant that the brakes are fixed. Tuesday morning, on the way to work, defendant rear-ends another vehicle causing injury to the driver. The driver sues the defendant. Defendant believes that the accident was caused by faulty repair of the brakes and brings the brake shop in as a third party to answer for the injuries to plaintiff. When defendant brings in a third-party defendant, the caption of the lawsuit changes. Where previously the caption read *Plaintiff v. Defendant,* after filing a third-party complaint, the caption will read, *Plaintiff v. Defendant and Third-Party Plaintiff v. Third-Party Defendant.* The third-party defendant is entitled to the same defenses as the defendant.

Motion for Judgment on the Pleadings

When all of the pleadings are filed, either party may petition the court for judgment on the pleadings. If there appears to be no issue of fact, the court may grant judgment in favor of either party. The court is restricted to a study of the pleadings, however, and no other information, evidence, or testimony may be relied upon.

Scheduling Conference

The pleadings stage of the litigation generally ends with the scheduling conference. The scheduling conference is for the purpose of establishing a timeline for the disposition of the case. A date for discovery to be complete will be identified, the pretrial conference will be scheduled, and the date for trial will be set. The conference is generally attended by attorneys and may be completed via telephone conference.

Once the scheduling order has been entered, it is critical to ensure that all dates and reminder dates are put on the office calendar system. A legal nurse consultant would be wise to maintain a separate reminder system so that necessary procedures on the case do not fall through the cracks in the exigency of day-to-day office activities.

DISCOVERY

Discovery is the part of the litigation process in which the parties provide one another with the evidence they intend to rely on at court. There are many functions of discovery:

- Discovery ensures adequate preparation, to avoid surprises at trial.
- Discovery aids in accurate assessment of the case.
- The information discovered may provide the basis for a negotiated settlement.
- The information discovered may provide the basis for a motion for **summary judgment.**
- Discovery preserves evidence.

Discovery is similar to pretrial investigation in that it allows the parties access to all the evidence. In addition, because discovery is courtsanctioned, it allows the parties access to information not obtainable without a subpoena. If a party fails to comply with a discovery request, that party may be sanctioned by the court and may even have his or her action dismissed or a default judgment entered against him or her. Courts have a great deal of discretion in assessing monetary sanctions against parties who refuse to comply with discovery.

There are five devices for obtaining information that is in the possession of the other party: interrogatories, requests for production or inspection, depositions, requests for admission, and physical and/or mental examinations. Legal nurse consultants should be familiar with these devices. Legal nurse consultants might be expected to assist in the drafting or defending of these devices when medical issues are concerned.

Interrogatories

Written questions to a party, which require answers under oath, are known as **interrogatories.** Because interrogatories have been used indiscriminately by some attorneys (innumerable questions with innumerable subparts concerning information of questionable relevance), some state courts have limited the use of interrogatories or, as in Oregon, have eliminated them altogether. Answers to interrogatories are useful for narrowing the issues of fact and law, and for acquiring information about the physical evidence that will be used at trial. Answers to interrogatories thus aid in the drafting of additional discovery and may provide the basis for a motion for summary judgment.

Requests for Production of Documents and Things

Having learned from the interrogatories that certain documents exist and the name of the custodian of those documents, they may be inspected using the discovery device of a **request** (or demand or motion) **for production.** This device allows parties to enter land, test appliances, and review documents in the possession of the other party. Of particular importance to legal nurse consultants working in defense is the request for production of medical records, medical reports, and medical bills. Once these documents are received, the legal nurse consultant will be charged with their review and analysis in light of the claims made in the complaint. Alternatively, defense counsel may request an authorization for release of medical records signed by the plaintiff. Then the legal nurse consultant will acquire the records directly from the health care provider using the signed authorization.

A request for production of documents or things, generally asks the opposing party to provide the documents at a time and place that is convenient for copying and inspecting. The responding party is required to respond under oath that the documents will be made available but may change the date, time, and place and require that review be at a time convenient for the responding party.

Depositions

The only discovery device that may be used against a nonparty is the **deposition.** A deposition is the sworn testimony of a **deponent,** that is, a witness or party, in answer to direct and cross examination questions by the attorneys for the parties. This testimony is recorded in a manner similar to court testimony and a written transcript is provided to the parties. A judge is not present at a deposition. If there is an objection to the questioning, the parties may agree to continue with the questioning or may interrupt the deposition until a judge has the opportunity to rule on the objection.

To ensure the attendance of a witness who is not a party to the lawsuit a **subpoena** must be served on that witness along with the appropriate witness and mileage fees. A subpoena is a court order to appear and testify. If the witness has possession of documents that may be important in the litigation, a **subpoena *duces tecum*** may be served. The subpoena *duces tecum* is a court order that requires the witness to appear and bring identified documents.

Typically several depositions are taken during the course of a lawsuit. Depositions allow attorneys to assess how witnesses will be perceived at trial, and the testimony provided will assist them in more accurately assessing the case. Medical depositions and depositions of expert witnesses may be used at trial to avoid the high cost of experts testifying in person. Depositions are the best way to preserve the evidence of a witness or party who is or may become elderly, ill, or disabled.

The legal nurse consultant will undoubtedly be involved in preparation for medical depositions. All of the following activities of a legal nurse consultant will be valuable aids to the attorney during a deposition involving medical issues:

- drafting questions
- providing summaries and chronologies
- indexing or tabbing important medical records, reports, or bills
- identifying potential medical exhibits to which the witness will testify
- educating the attorney on the medical intricacies of the case
- taking notes at the deposition and keeping track of follow-up questions that the attorney may overlook

Many nurses have been witnesses in depositions and are familiar with the procedure. Legal nurse consultants who have never been part of a deposition process may ask to ride along with the attorney they are working with at his or her next deposition to acquire a better understanding of the strategies and techniques used.

Legal nurse consultants may be called upon to summarize depositions. This may involve a thorough summary of the testimony of a witness or it may involve extracting exact testimony in a digest or abstract form. At a minimum, legal nurse consultants should index depositions and/or tab critical testimony. An index is similar to the index at the back of a book. The important topics, such as names, treatments, and medical indications, are identified in alphabetical order. Each page of the deposition that contains a reference to that topic, name, treatment, or medical indication is listed next to it, so the attorney can locate all references to that topic by looking in the index.

The most frequently used devices during discovery are interrogatories, requests for production, and depositions. Requests for admission and adverse medical examinations (AMEs) are often used toward the end of the discovery phase as the case progresses toward trial.

Requests for Admission or Denial

In order to save time and expense at trial, one party may demand that the other party admit the truth of a fact or the genuineness of a document. **Requests to admit** medical records is one example of a frequently used request for admissions. Requests to admit the qualifications of an expert are also frequently used. A request to admit, or deny, is a useful tool of strategy for the attorney. If no response to the request for admissions is received within the thirty-day response period, the facts listed in the request for admission are deemed conclusively established for purposes of trial and proof may not be brought later to disprove those facts. In addition, a responding party may not simply deny the listed items. A diligent inquiry must be made to ascertain the truth of the facts alleged. If a responding party denies an item requested to be admitted and that item is later proved true at the trial, the responding party may be taxed the costs of proof, including reasonable attorney fees.

The legal nurse consultant may be instrumental in determining the truth of medical records and medical bills that are sought to be admitted or denied. Because the legal nurse consultant is the one most familiar with the medical issues of the claim, these documents will, more than likely, be delivered to the legal nurse consultant for evaluation.

Adverse Medical Examination

It would be unfair to have only the opinion of the plaintiff's treating physician. The court rules allow defendant to select a physician to examine and evaluate the condition of the plaintiff. The **adverse medical examination** (AME) is

Net Results

Disclosure Rules on the Internet

The Federal Rules of Civil Procedure, the Federal Rules of Criminal Procedure, and the Federal Rules of Evidence are all available on the Internet. Access these rules by using the web site established for the Cornell Law School: www.law.cornell.edu/ rules/frcp.

a way to provide the defense with access to plaintiff's medical condition and to establish alternative diagnoses, prognoses, and treatment options.

Legal nurse consultants on either side of the case may be involved in the adverse medical examination. For plaintiff, the legal nurse consultant may accompany the plaintiff to the adverse medical exam. While the nurse may not be allowed into the examining room with the plaintiff, questioning the plaintiff afterwards will provide the nurse with information to put into a memo or summary for use by the attorney. If he or she is allowed in the examining room, notes may be taken either during or immediately after the exam about the questions that were asked by the examining physician and the extent of the examination.

A defense legal nurse consultant may be instrumental in selecting the physician who will conduct the adverse medical examination. In addition, the nurse may interview the physician afterwards and may correlate the adverse medical report with the other medical records, the medical literature, and other discovery.

Disclosure

Federal rules were recently changed to include voluntary **disclosure.** The rationale for this change was that parties should cooperate to keep the expense and time involved in discovery to a minimum. Rather than demanding information from the parties, disclosure rules require that parties voluntarily disclose information without the necessity of a request. The major features of disclosure are outlined in Figure 25-8.

Arizona state courts have adopted disclosure rules; however, not all federal districts, nor state courts, have adopted disclosure rules. It is incumbent upon the legal professionals to ascertain the discovery and disclosure rules that apply in the jurisdiction in which the lawsuit is brought.

Motion for Summary Judgment

Discovery and/or disclosure should be undertaken with the view that the information obtained will facilitate the negotiated settlement of the action. Most attorneys believe that settlement is in the best interest of the client, as it avoids undue publicity, delays of trial, and the potential for retrials or appeals, and generally eases the emotional burden on the parties. If it is apparent from discovery, and disclosure that there are no facts in dispute, either party may seek to dispose of the case through summary judgment.

A motion for summary judgment requests that the court review the information contained in the pleadings and obtained through discovery and enter judgment as a matter of law without a trial on the case. If the judge determines that there is no factual issue to present to a jury, the judge is free to apply the law to the situation described by the parties and enter judgment in favor of either party.

FIGURE 25-8   Federal Disclosure Rules[8]

Rule Number	Required Disclosure	Purpose and Intent
F.R.C.P. 26(f)	Meeting to plan disclosure	Counsel must meet fourteen days before the scheduling conference to develop a discovery plan. A written plan must be presented to the court within ten days after the meeting.
F.R.C.P. 26(1)	Disclosure	As part of the plan presented to the court, the parties must voluntarily disclose names and addresses of individuals likely to have discoverable information, copies of documents and things relevant, a computation of damages, and copies of insurance policies.
F.R.C.P. 26(a)(2)	Disclosure of experts	At least ninety days before trial, the parties must disclose information about the experts who are expected to testify at trial. This information must include a report written by the expert and information concerning fees paid to the expert.

There are very specific rules governing the motion and process of a summary judgment. For example, a summary judgment must allow the opposing party at least twenty days to respond and the responding party must specifically reference the record to show that a genuine contradiction about the facts appears and that the issue should be submitted to a jury. A hearing is generally held giving the parties an opportunity to present arguments for and against the summary judgment. The judge relies on written briefs submitted by counsel that outline and apply the law to the arguments presented.

Summary judgment is a very useful tool for disposing of a case without going to trial, especially if the parties are unwilling to settle. The Federal Rules of Civil Procedure allow partial summary judgment as well, so the issue of liability may be summarily disposed of, while the issue of damages may have to be proven.

Pretrial Conference

The discovery and disclosure phase of litigation generally ends with the **pretrial conference.** The pretrial conference is viewed by some judges as a last ditch effort to settle the case before trial. Therefore, they may attempt to promote settlement negotiations during the conference. The rules require that the pretrial conference be attended by an attorney who has the authority to settle on behalf of the client.

The pretrial conference is to determine whether the case is ready for trial and to prepare an agenda for the proceedings. Matters that might be discussed and agreed upon at the pretrial conference are

- the number of jurors to be impaneled
- limitations on *voir dire*
- the number of challenges available to the attorneys during jury selection
- the order of proof
- the number of witnesses and the anticipated time for their testimony
- limitations on the number of expert witnesses
- the physical evidence that is expected to be offered
- stipulations on evidence
- the anticipated length of the trial
- the final trial date

In federal court, the parties are required to prepare a pretrial report, which must be filed with the court before the pretrial conference. The pretrial report generally reports the undisputed facts; the disputed facts; the witnesses expected to be called and the exhibits to which they will testify, if any; deposition testimony to be offered; physical evidence; expert witnesses, including their qualifications; and questions of law that will be presented at the trial. State and local court rules may also require a pretrial report; it is important to verify the necessary documentation prior to the pretrial conference.

Once the pretrial order is issued, the script for trial is set. Most federal judges use the pretrial order as the final word on matters brought at the trial. If a witness is introduced who is not identified on the pretrial order, that witness will generally not be allowed to testify. It is critical to include all potential witnesses and evidence in the pretrial report, which is incorporated into the pretrial order, to ensure that they will be available to the attorney at trial. It is far better to have listed the witness and not use him or her, than to have not listed the witness and later discover that that witness's testimony is necessary.

Every step of the litigation process, if carried out correctly, should prepare the attorney for the next step. Investigation will provide the basis for a settlement brochure; the settlement brochure will provide the basis for the pretrial report; and the pretrial report will provide the basis for the trial.

TRIAL

The ancient saying "All roads lead to Rome" may be applied to the activities in litigation. All activities lead to trial, the ultimate destination. The trial is generally for the benefit and education of the jury. This jury of peers is re-

---

Ethics Bookmark

Resource Management

"The legal nurse consultant considers factors related to ethics, effectiveness, and cost in planning and delivering client services. . . . The LNC assists legal professionals and others in identifying and securing appropriate services available to address issues pertaining to the case or the claim" AALNC Standards of Professional Performance Standard 8 (1995).[9] While trial is the ultimate objective of all of the planning in any lawsuit, trial may not be in the best interests of the client. Legal nurse consultants can provide valuable insight into solutions that may work for clients, other than legal solutions. The client's best interest must always be the goal.

sponsible for making a determination on the questions of fact presented in the claim. Examples of questions of fact may be

- Did the physician exercise the degree of skill and knowledge exercised by the average physician having due regard for the state of medical science at the time of the incident?
- Did the failure to diagnose plaintiff's cancer cause plaintiff's death?
- Was plaintiff's failure to seek medical attention a cause of plaintiff's injuries?

These questions are not generally within the knowledge of lay persons, so expert witnesses will be necessary to prove these facts. Still, the issues of fact are resolved by the jury. A trial without a jury is known as a **bench trial.** In a bench trial, the judge acts as the finder of fact and makes determinations on both issues of fact and how the law applies to those facts. A trial is played out in many scenes, including voir dire, opening statements, presentation of evidence, presentation of defense, closing arguments, jury instructions, and jury deliberation.

Voir Dire

The trial begins with jury selection. Translated, **voir dire** means "to speak the truth" and the questions to the jury are intended to ensure that the jury is objective and qualified to make impartial decisions that will impact the plaintiff and defendant. Attorneys are invited to submit voir dire questions to the judge, who begins the questioning. Jurors are asked if they know the plaintiff and defendant, if they know the attorneys for plaintiff and defendant, and if they are aware of the circumstances giving rise to the claim through newspaper articles, television news, and so forth. If a potential juror is friendly with the plaintiff or defendant, the juror may be biased in favor of the friend and will be excused from the trial. In that case, another potential juror is selected who must answer all of the questions. After the judge has completed the voir dire, the attorneys are invited to ask questions of the potential jurors. After this questioning, the attorneys make their strikes to arrive at the number of jurors requested for the trial.

Opening Statements

After the voir dire, the attorneys may make **opening statements.** Opening statements are not evidence. The attorneys tell the jurors what they expect the evidence to prove. Opening statements are simply ways for the attorneys to introduce the jurors to the case and the issues at bar. At this point in the trial, attorneys are not allowed to argue or to be demonstrative in their presentations. The attorney for plaintiff speaks first. The attorney for defendant may speak immediately after plaintiff's attorney, or may reserve the right to make an opening statement at the beginning of the defendant's evidence.

Presentation of Evidence

Plaintiff has the burden of proof and presents evidence in support of the claim. Plaintiff's attorney calls witnesses and examines them in an effort to establish a *prima facie* case. Defense counsel has the opportunity to cross-examine these witnesses. The purpose of a trial is to arrive at the truth in a calm and orderly fashion. Plaintiff's attorney will try to organize the evidence so that it unfolds as a logical and unfortunate story that clearly implicates the defendant as the cause of plaintiff's injury.

Motion for Directed Verdict

If plaintiff has failed to establish a *prima facie* case, the defendant's attorney may petition the court for **directed verdict** in favor of the defendant. If the judge also feels that plaintiff's evidence does not meet the elements of the claim or does not implicate the defendant as the responsible party, directed verdict may be entered in favor of the defendant.

Whether or not plaintiff has established a case, it may be important for a defendant to move for directed verdict. A motion for directed verdict that is denied may provide the basis for appeal. In addition, in federal court, a party is precluded from petitioning for new trial if a motion for directed verdict has not been made during the original proceedings.

Presentation of Defense

After the close of plaintiff's evidence, and if directed verdict is not granted in favor of defendant, defendant may offer evidence to prove that the defendant's conduct was excusable; was not the cause of the injuries; or that others, including plaintiff, contributed to plaintiff's injuries. At this time, defendant's attorney will call witnesses for direct examination—plaintiff's attorney may cross-examine—and present physical or demonstrative evidence to support exculpating the defendant. Defendant is not required to present a defense and failing to defend may not be construed as an admission of guilt. At the close of defendant's evidence, either party may move for directed verdict.

Closing Arguments

Sometimes called the **summation, closing arguments** are allowed to both parties at the close of all the evidence. This is the point at which the attorneys may become argumentative and theatrical. They attempt to remind the jurors of what evidence was presented and what the only possible conclusion from that evidence is. Closing statements or arguments are not evidence; they are a final opportunity for the attorneys to impress their ideas on the minds of the jurors.

Jury Instructions

Before the jury is excused for deliberations, the judge will read them the **jury instructions.** These are the legal guidelines, or elements of the law, that must be used by the jury in making its decision. The jury instructions are used throughout the process of the litigation, as they clearly explain what must be plead and proved in order to establish liability in a claim. The jury instructions read by the judge are contributed by the attorneys, and each attorney has the opportunity to object to the other's request for jury instructions. These arguments are heard outside the presence of the jury and the final decision about what jury instructions will be read belongs with the judge.

Jury Verdict

The jury is charged with making a decision about liability in a civil lawsuit. The burden of proof for actions of this kind is generally the greater weight of the evidence. The jury must find that it is more likely than not that defendant caused the injuries sustained by plaintiff. Whether the jury must be unanimous in their decision depends on the court rules governing the procedure.

The first duty of the jury is to elect a chairperson who presides over the deliberations and presents the verdict to the judge. In most jurisdictions, it is permissible to poll the jury after the trial to find out how they voted. Post-trial jury investigation may also reveal why they voted as they did, what evidence was most influential, and what their understanding of the law is or was at the time of trial.

POST-TRIAL ALTERNATIVES

A party who is not satisfied with the outcome of a civil trial has several opportunities to have the case reviewed or the outcome changed. These alternatives include a new trial, a judgment NOV (notwithstanding the verdict), and appeal.

Motion for New Trial

If there has been an error of law so significant that it has denied a party the right to a fair and impartial trial, that party may move the court for a *trial de novo* or a new trial of the issues. Errors of law include improper voir dire; improper opening or closing statements; improper rulings on evidence; or improper conduct on the part of the judge, the attorneys, or the parties involved in the trial.

Under the Federal Rules of Civil Procedure, a motion for new trial must be brought within twenty days of entry of judgment. Since it is unlikely that a transcript of the proceedings will be made within that time period, the notes of those in attendance at the trial are invaluable. A legal nurse consultant who assists in the trial may be asked to submit materials in support of a motion for new trial based on notes taken and observations made at trial.

Motion for Judgment Notwithstanding the Verdict

Whenever the jury verdict is not supported by the evidence, the judge has an obligation to overturn the verdict and enter a **judgment NOV.** A motion for judgment *non obstante verdicto* must be made within twenty days of the entry of judgment in federal court and must clearly explain, by reference to the record and to the law, that the verdict was contrary to the evidence. The rules allow a motion for new trial and a motion for judgment NOV to be combined and disposed of at one hearing.

Appeal

As previously mentioned, due process in the United States includes, at a minimum, the right to notice of the claim, a hearing to defend against the claim, and the right to appeal. The party who decides to appeal becomes known as the **appellant,** and the opposing party becomes known as the respondent or **appellee.** In some jurisdictions, the title of the case will change to reflect the party who is appealing to be entered as the first-named party. This may be different from the party who was identified as plaintiff.

Notice of appeal in federal court must be served on the responding party not later than thirty days after entry of judgment. The appellant is responsible for submitting the transcript and records to the appeals court. The order for transcript must be made within ten days of filing the notice of appeal, and the transcript must be submitted within thirty days of that order. The appeal must be perfected by the filing of a brief within forty days after the date on which the record is filed. The responding party has thirty days to file an opposing brief. In addition, nonparties may submit briefs in an attempt to educate the court on the impact that the decision will have on special interest groups and other populations. These briefs are known as *amicus curie* (friend of the court) or intervener briefs.

There are definite rules concerning the presentation of briefs on appeal, and the rules of appellate procedure must be consulted to ensure that the briefs are prepared appropriately. Each brief is restricted to a specific length, depending on what type font is used in the document. The briefs must be bound, served on all parties, and filed with the court of appeals.

THE ROLE OF THE LEGAL NURSE CONSULTANT IN CIVIL PROCEDURE

The legal nurse consultant may play a crucial role in the progress of a lawsuit through the court system. From assisting with drafting pleadings and **dispositive motions,** to drafting and summarizing discovery and assisting at trial, the legal nurse consultant's medical background adds value to the litigation team at every stage of civil procedure.

CHAPTER SUMMARY

- There are generally three stages in civil procedure: pleadings, discovery or disclosure, and trial.

- Pleadings include documents that explain the problem (complaint, answer, counterclaim), and that must be served on the parties and filed with the court.

- Discovery involves the exchange of evidence prior to trial and is accumulated through the use of interrogatories, requests for production, depositions, requests for admissions, and adverse medical examinations.

- At the trial, jury selection (voir dire) is conducted, the parties make opening statements, they present their evidence, the parties make closing arguments, the judge reads the jury instructions, and the jury is excused for deliberation and arrival at a verdict.

- Parties not satisfied with the outcome of a trial may use post-trial options such as motions for new trial, motions for judgment NOV, and appeal.

KEY TERMS

ad damnum	deponent	pretrial conference
adverse medical examination	deposition	opening statements
affirmative defense	directed verdict	request to admit
amicus curie	disclosure	request for production
appellant	dispositive motions	service of process
appellee	guardian ad litem	subject matter jurisdiction
bench trial	interrogatories	subpoena
closing arguments	joined	subpoena *duces tecum*
compulsory counterclaim	judgment NOV	substituted service
concurrent jurisdiction	jury instructions	summary judgment
conservator	personal jurisdiction	summation
counterclaim	personal service	*trial de novo*
cross-claim	permissive counterclaim	venue
default judgment	pleadings	voir dire
demurrer	prayer for relief	

REVIEW QUESTIONS

1. For what purpose are dispositive motions, especially motions to dismiss and motions for summary judgment, used?
2. How do disclosure rules differ from discovery?
3. How might a legal nurse consultant assist in the three phases of a lawsuit: pleadings, discovery, and trial?

INTERNET EXERCISES

1. Access the web page for this textbook at *www.westlegalstudies.com.*
2. Click on the assignments section and complete the assignment(s) for Chapter Twenty-five.

EXERCISES

1. Networking. If you have not seen the movie *Twelve Angry Men,* this would be a good time to rent the videotape. It is an old movie, but it very clearly depicts the dynamics of a jury deliberation. Watching this will provide you with insight into the workings of a jury, what influences them, and how they react to each other. This will be extremely valuable to you when employed as a legal nurse consultant and prepare for trial.

2. Professional Portfolio. Diagram the stages of a civil lawsuit, including the activities that occur and the documents that are used at each stage (pleadings, discovery, and trial). Maintain this diagram in your systems file, folder, or binder and organize or index it for easy retrieval.

ENDNOTES

1. 28 U.S.C. § 1332, et seq.
2. Fed. R. Civ. P. 4(k)(2).
3. 28 U.S.C. ; st 1391.
4. Fed. R. Civ. P. 38.
5. Fed. R. Civ. P. 4(c).
6. Fed. R. Civ. P. 12(b)(6).
7. Fed. R. Civ. P. 13(a), 13(b).
8. Fed. R. Civ. P. 26.
9. American Association of Legal Nurse Consultants, *Standards of Professional Performance* (1995) Standard 8.

ADDITIONAL REFERENCES

Franzen, S., BA. "The Role of the Legal Nurse Consultant in Discovery." *Journal of Legal Nurse Consulting* 8:1 (1997): 2–5.

Loecker, B.L., MSEd, RN. "Adjudication Without Trial: Summary Judgment." *Journal of Legal Nurse Consulting* 8:1 (1997): 24–25.

Pollock, D.A., BS, RN, CNOR, LNCC. "The LNCs Vital Role in a Defense Medical Examination." *Journal of Legal Nurse Consulting* 11:1 (2000): 8–13.

Weishapple, C.L. "Deposition Summaries." *Journal of Legal Nurse Consulting* 9:3 (1998): 14–16.

LEGAL NURSE CONSULTANT PROFILE

Yolanda Smith

Independent Consulting—Risk Management

Yolanda G. Smith completed her master of science degree in nursing in 1990 from Hunter College in New York City. The degree was as a Clinical Nurse Specialist: Medical-Surgical Nursing, with a specialization in Cardiothoracic Surgery. She received a bachelor of science degree in nursing in 1982 from Downstate School of Nursing in Brooklyn, New York. In June 2000 Ms. Smith was appointed an auxiliary member of the New York State Board for Nursing, which focuses on professional misconduct and licensing issues. She is certified in adult critical care and is an advanced cardiac life support and basic life support provider. Ms. Smith is the founder and president of YGS Medical-Legal Consulting, established in June 1997 and located in Brooklyn, NY. She is an independent legal nurse consultant, nurse educator, seminar speaker, and Associate Director of Nursing: CNS Cardiothoracic Services at Downstate Medical Center. She was named in *International Who's Who of Professional Management* in 1997 and *Who's Who in American Nursing* in 1993.

Ms. Smith completed two home study programs in 1997 for legal nurse consulting offered by the Medical-Legal Consulting Institute, Inc., Houston, Texas and Medical Legal Resources, Carlsbad, California. To stay current with liability issues affecting nursing and healthcare, she subscribes to *Capital Update: The Legislative Newsletter for Nurses* by the ANA. She has attended numerous seminars and workshops on medical malpractice and risk management.

What do you like best about being a legal nurse consultant?

"I like the investigative aspect of recreating the alleged negligent act through medical chart analysis/interpretation, synthesizing research findings into the chronological chart summary, and interviewing the medical experts. I truly enjoy being part of the litigation team from the initial claim to settlement or trial and educating the attorney on the merits of the case and the medical-legal issues presented. It has been extremely gratifying for me to earn the respect and appreciation of my attorney clients when they review my work product, including my recommendations for strategy development. They show their support by continuing to utilize my consulting services and by referring me to their colleagues."

What challenges do legal nurse consultants face in your area of law?

"One of the biggest challenges for legal nurse consultants is to feel comfortable with their professional nursing skills and then being able to confidently articulate to attorneys the many benefits of utilizing their services. Many attorneys do not realize how to locate nurse experts or how important nurses can be to the development of their cases. Most attorneys use doctors at the onset, which could prove to be quite costly. If you ask a doctor to review a medical chart, the doctor usually focuses on the specific incident. A nurse would be more comprehensive in examining the records and explaining the strengths/weaknesses of the case. Attorneys could obtain a more in-depth opinion and description surrounding the alleged circumstances involved in the case from a nurse."

What advice would you give nurses who are interested in legal nurse consulting?

"I would advise nurses to be realistic in their goals, to persevere, and to have a support system in place. Starting an independent legal nurse consulting business takes start-up capital, a tremendous amount of time, dedication, and sacrifice. Spend time learning your individual strengths and what services you can provide that are different from other legal nurse consultants. Concentrate on getting your name known by marketing yourself through public speaking, publishing, volunteering to participate on task forces/projects in your chosen specialty. Most of all have confidence in yourself and your abilities to be successful. You must be able to accept 'no' for an answer without taking it personally. Sometimes it is easy to become discouraged when you do not receive a response from an attorney after mailing your marketing materials or when your follow-up call is handled by a secretary who is not courteous.

"I would also recommend that you join professional organizations and read a variety of journals from different disciplines. This will give you a more global and current viewpoint on medical-legal issues. Also, take a computer class and become proficient in navigating the World Wide Web. This is extremely helpful when performing medical research and literature searches.

"I had an additional advantage by having teaching experience and a nursing education background. I developed 'Legal Issues in Nursing: Charting with a Jury in Mind,' which was approved for 7.5 contact hours from the New York State Nurses Association (1998). I have marketed this seminar to local hospitals and supplemental staffing agencies. I have always received excellent evaluations and a good turnout of nurses. This has put me in touch with risk management departments and attorneys. The seminar focuses on regulatory agencies, common liability issues for nurses, standards of care, documentation errors, and corrective action plans for documentation issues. Presenting this seminar has led to other opportunities (local and national) for other nursing seminars and has given me exposure to medical-legal professionals.

"I also served as a consultant, advisory board member, and teacher in the Legal Nurse Consultant program at Long Island University. Being involved in teaching educational programs adds to your knowledge credibility and potential as an expert witness. Take advantage of opportunities to speak about your area of specialty. You will be surprised at the positive feedback and opportunities that result from those engagements.

"I am a member of the American Association of Legal Nurse Consultants and I had a wonderful opportunity to be a member of a task force which developed, *Getting Started in Legal Nurse Consulting: An Introduction to the Specialty* (2d ed., 1999)."

What unique marketing strategy are you willing to share?

"I had applied for membership in the Association of Trial Lawyers of America. If you are not an attorney, an attorney member must sponsor you to become a member. I was given the names of three attorneys in the area who sponsor potential members. I randomly selected an attorney from the list. I sent him a cover letter stating why I wanted to become a member of ATLA, the membership application form, a copy of an article I co-wrote on legal nurse consulting for *Nursing Spectrum,* and my marketing material. He signed my ATLA application form, and I was called for an interview. I met with three members of the firm and got a contract to perform chart reviews, assist with trial preparation, and cross-reference deposition testimony with the medical record."

"Spend time learning your individual strengths and what services you can provide that are different from other legal nurse consultants. Concentrate on getting your name known by marketing yourself through public speaking, publishing, volunteering to participate on task forces/projects in your chosen specialty."

CASE STUDY III

Moore v. Willis-Knighton Medical Center, 31,203 (La. App. 2 Cir. 10/28/98), 720 So. 2d 425 (1998)

The following case involves a legal nurse consultant. As you read through the court opinion, consider the following questions:

- Was this a civil or criminal matter? Explain.
- What role did the legal nurse consultant play in resolution of this matter?
- What credentials, experience, and education qualified the legal nurse consultant to play a role in resolution of this matter?
- What controversy, if any, existed concerning the legal nurse consultant's testimony?
- Consider making a diagram or process chart of the legal proceedings in this matter. Use your knowledge of legal procedure to fill in information not clearly specified in the court opinion; for example, complaint served and filed, or answer served and filed. Be as specific as possible by trying to identify what allegations might have been made in the complaint.
- Consider writing a case brief on this opinion using any of the formats outlined in Chapter Twelve.

(Cite as: 31,203 (La.App. 2 Cir. 10/28/98), 720 So.2d 425)

Madeline MOORE, Plaintiff-Appellant,
v.
WILLIS-KNIGHTON MEDICAL CENTER, et al., Defendant-Appellee.
No. 31203-CA.
Court of Appeal of Louisiana,
Second Circuit.
Oct. 28, 1998.

(Cite as: 31,203 (La.App. 2 Cir. 10/28/98), *1, 720 So.2d 425, **426)

GASKINS, Judge.

The plaintiff, Madeline Moore, appeals from a jury verdict rejecting her claim that the defendant, Willis-Knighton Medical Center, was negligent in issuing her a toilet seat to use at home while recuperating from right hip repair surgery which did not clamp down on the toilet. Two months after her discharge, the plaintiff claims the toilet seat

(Cite as: 31,203 (La.App. 2 Cir. 10/28/98), *1, 720 So.2d 425, **427)

slipped during use and the plaintiff fell, breaking her left hip. For the following reasons, we affirm the jury verdict and trial court judgment.

FACTS

In 1984 the plaintiff was 67 years old and was employed as a salesperson in a local millinery shop. In December of that year, she slipped and fell at work, breaking her right hip. The plaintiff was hospitalized and the hip was surgically repaired by Dr. M.E. Milstead. On December 18, 1984, she was released from the hospital. Because Dr. Milstead was not on duty, his colleague, Dr. Lewis Jones, discharged the plaintiff from the hospital. Dr. Jones, who had also treated the plaintiff in the past, ordered an elevated toilet seat to be sent home with the plaintiff. The hospital supplied the plaintiff with a toilet seat like the one she used in the hospital. The device was designed to raise the normal level of the toilet seat in order to lessen the strain on a joint post-operatively. The seat had metal extensions that pressed down onto the rim of the bowl, but it did not clamp down. It was delivered to the plaintiff in a box and under the bottom of the toilet seat was the following warning:

This product is designed to safely support 250 lbs. When weight exceeds this, transfer patients, or when patients with balance problems are involved, "CLAMP LEG" models should be used. SIDE RAILS are also recommended for certain conditions. CAUTION: Patient should never be left alone when using this device.

(Cite as: 31,203 (La.App. 2 Cir. 10/28/98), *2, 720 So.2d 425, **427)

Due to complications with the healing process, Mrs. Moore was initially told not to place weight on the right foot and shortly thereafter, she was told to only use toe touch weight bearing on her right side and to continue to use her walker. On February 26, 1985, while at home alone, she attempted to use the elevated toilet seat and she claims that the seat tipped with her and she fell, breaking her left hip. She was again hospitalized and the left hip was surgically repaired by Dr. Jones.

On May 1, 1985, Dr. Jones deemed the plaintiff to be sufficiently recovered from the right hip injury to return to work. However, she was still being treated for the left hip and did not return to work. The plaintiff continued to see Dr. Jones for pain in her left hip until June 18, 1985. At that point Dr. Jones released the plaintiff from his care and felt that she could have returned to work in September or October of 1985. The plaintiff claims that as a result of the second hip injury, she never recovered sufficiently to return to work and she required assistance in cooking, cleaning, and bathing. However, with assistance, she was able to live at home alone for ten years after this injury. The plaintiff contended that the toilet seat given her was designed to be used only by persons who required no assistance in walking and not by those with balance problems. She asserted that, because her right hip was still healing, requiring the continued use of a walker, she had a mechanical balance problem. She further asserted that she received either no instructions or incorrect instructions in the hospital in the use of the walker in conjunction with the toilet seat and that she received no instructions in the use of the walker and toilet seat upon her release from the hospital. She contended that Dr. Jones and Willis-Knighton Medical Center were negligent in providing her with a commode *3

> (Cite as: 31,203 (La.App. 2 Cir. 10/28/98), *3, 720 So.2d 425, **427)

extension not designed for her type of disability, in failing to warn of the instability of the extension and in failing to instruct her or instructing her improperly in its use.

A medical review panel was convened and on February 6, 1989 determined that the evidence did not show that Dr. Jones or Willis-Knighton Medical Center failed to meet the applicable standard of care. The plaintiff then filed suit in district court on May 5, 1989, naming Dr. Jones and Willis-Knighton Medical Center as defendants. The plaintiff reached an agreement with Willis-Knighton to accept $75,000.00 and half the costs in settlement of all her claims against the hospital, reserving her right to seek damages in excess of the sum paid by Willis-Knighton from the Louisiana Patients' Compensation Fund and Dr. Jones. However, under the terms of the agreement, Willis-Knighton was required to remain in the case as a nominal defendant. Accordingly, Willis-Knighton was represented at trial by the **428

> (Cite as: 31,203 (La.App. 2 Cir. 10/28/98), *3, 720 So.2d 425, **428)

Louisiana Patient's Compensation Fund and Oversight Board. Dr. Jones was dismissed from the suit after jury selection, but before the testimony began.

The case was tried before a jury. On July 11, 1997, the jury returned a 9-3 verdict finding that Willis-Knighton did not breach the standard of care owed by the hospital to the plaintiff in this case. The plaintiff filed motions for judgment notwithstanding the verdict and for new trial which were denied by the trial court. The plaintiff then appealed the jury verdict.

   ARGUMENTS ON APPEAL

The plaintiff first argues that the jury erred as a matter of law in finding that the hospital did not breach the standard of care owned to her. Mrs. Moore contends that the jury failed to apply the national standard of care as instructed by
*4

continued

Moore v. Willis-Knighton Medical Center   *continued*

the trial court and, instead, applied Willis-Knighton's own standard of care to the facts presented. The plaintiff contends that she presented ample uncontradicted evidence that the applicable standard of care was breached in her case. The plaintiff argues that she established that she was given a toilet seat extension not appropriate for a person with her disability. She also claims that she received erroneous instructions from the nursing staff to place her weight completely on the walker while sitting and rising. She further claims that the hospital records show that on discharge, she was given no instructions on the use of the toilet seat extension.

The plaintiff urges that, because the jury failed to apply the law as instructed, the jury erred as a matter of law in denying her claim and this court should reverse the verdict and conduct a de novo review. The plaintiff asserts that on de novo review, we should make determinations as to causation and comparative fault and should award her damages.

   Legal Principles

[1][2][3] Malpractice claims against a hospital are subject to the general rules of proof applicable to any negligence action. A plaintiff must prove that the defendant had a duty to protect against the risk involved, that the defendant breached its duty and that the plaintiff's injury was caused by the defendant's conduct. *Smith v. State, through Department of Health and Human Resources, 523 So.2d 815 (La. 1988); Roberts v. Cox, 28,094 (La.App.2d Cir.2/28/96), 669 So.2d 633.* However, a hospital is not an insurer of a patient's safety and is not required to guard against or take measures to avert a situation which a reasonable person would not anticipate as likely to happen under the given circumstances. *Bossier v. DeSoto General Hospital, 442 So.2d 485 (La.App. 2d Cir. 1983),* writ ***5**

denied *443 So.2d 1122 (La. 1984).* The mere fact that an injury occurs or an accident happens raises no presumption or inference of negligence on the part of the hospital. *Galloway v. Baton Rouge General Hospital, 602 So.2d 1003 (La. 1992).*

[4][5][6][7] Hospitals are held to a national standard of care. The locality rule does not apply to hospitals. *Keyworth v. Southern Baptist Hospitals, Inc., 491 So.2d 15 (La. 1986).* Hospitals are bound to exercise the requisite amount of care toward a patient that the particular patient's condition may require. *Hunt v. Bogalusa Community Medical Center, 303 So.2d 745 (La. 1974); Borne v. St. Francis Medical Center, 26,940 (La.App.2d Cir.5/10/95), 655 So.2d 597,* writ denied *95-1403 (La.9/15/95), 660 So.2d 453; Parker v. Centenary Heritage Manor Nursing Home, 28,401 (La.App.2d Cir.6/26/96), 677 So.2d 568,* writ denied *96-1960 (La.11/1/96), 681 So.2d 1271.* It is the hospital's duty to protect a patient from dangers that may result from the patient's physical and mental incapacities as well as from external circumstances peculiarly within the hospital's control. A determination of whether a hospital has breached the duty of care it owes to a particular patient depends upon the facts and circumstances of the case and is a question of fact for the jury. *Borne v. St. Francis Medical Center, supra.* In finding or refusing to find a breach of duty, the finder of fact has great discretion. *Borne, v. St. Francis Medical Center, supra; Parker v. Centenary Heritage Manor Nursing Home, supra.*

[8][9][10] In a medical malpractice case, a reviewing court will give great deference to a jury's findings when medical experts express ****429**

different views, judgments and opinions on whether the standard of care was met in any given case. *Maxwell v. Soileau, 561 So.2d 1378 (La.App. 2d Cir. 1990),* writs denied ***6**

567 So.2d 1123 and 1124, (La. 1990). Such opinions are necessary sources of proof whose views are persuasive, though not controlling, and any weight assigned to their testimony by the jury is dependent upon the expert's qualifications, experience, and studies upon which his testimony is based. *Alello v. Smith, 94-103 (La.App. 5th Cir. 7/26/94), 641 So.2d 664,* writ denied *94-2231 (La. 11/18/94), 646 So.2d 382.* Where there are two permissible views of the evidence, the fact finder's choice between them cannot be manifestly erroneous or clearly wrong. *Rosell v. ESCO, 549 So.2d 840 (La. 1989).*

[11][12] It is well settled that the testimony of each witness qualified and accepted as an expert should be given effect if and when it appears to be well grounded from the standpoint of sincerity and common sense. *Quinones v. U.S. Fidelity and Guaranty Company, 93-1648 (La. 1/14/94), 630 So.2d 1303.* The weight to be given to the testimony of experts is largely dependent upon their qualifications and the facts upon which their opinions are based. However, the sincerity and honesty of opinions expressed are matters in which the trial court is in a particularly advantageous position to determine. It is, in effect, a question of credibility, and when the experts are widely disparate in their conclusions, the rule has special relevance. *Quinones v. U.S. Fidelity and Guaranty Company, supra.*

[13] The finding of fact by a jury should be upheld unless it is shown to be clearly wrong or manifestly erroneous. *Martinez v. Schumpert Medical Center, 27,000 (La.App.2d Cir.5/10/95), 655 So.2d 649.* The Louisiana Supreme Court has announced a two-part test for the reversal of a fact finder's determinations:

1) The appellate court must find from the record that a reasonable factual basis does not exist for the finding of the trial court, and

2) the appellate court must further determine that the record establishes that the finding is clearly wrong (manifestly erroneous).

*7

Stobart v. State, Department of Transportation and Development, 617 So.2d 880 (La.1993), citing *Mart v. Hill, 505 So.2d 1120 (La.1987).*

[14] Even though an appellate court may feel its own evaluations and inferences are more reasonable than those of the fact finder, reasonable evaluations of credibility and reasonable inferences of fact should not be disturbed upon review where conflict exists in the testimony. *Rosell v. ESCO, supra; Stobart v. State, Department of Transportation and Development, supra.*

Evidence Presented at Trial

The plaintiff contends that she presented ample evidence to establish the duty owed to her by the hospital, breach of that duty, causation and damages. The plaintiff, who was 67 years old at the time of the accident and 80 years old at the time of trial, testified that in the hospital she was instructed in using the walker but not in using the walker with the toilet seat extension, nor was she given instructions about using the seat at home when she was discharged from the hospital. On the

continued

Moore v. Willis-Knighton Medical Center   *continued*

morning of the accident, the plaintiff claims that she sat straight down and the toilet seat then tipped with her. She stated that she was 100% sure that she sat straight down on the seat.

Katherine Moore, the plaintiff's granddaughter, testified that she lived with the plaintiff during the time in which this accident occurred. She stated that her grandmother was not given any instructions regarding the use of the toilet seat extension when she was discharged from the hospital in December 1984. Her grandmother went to her son's house (the witness' father) after her discharge from the hospital, and remained there approximately one week. The plaintiff used the toilet seat extension at that residence without mishap. When the plaintiff returned to her own home, Katharine stated that she installed the toilet seat extension at the ***8**

(Cite as: 31,203 (La.App. 2 Cir. 10/28/98), *8, 720 So.2d 425, **429)

house and stated that it was not unsteady or loose and was not removed from the toilet for any purpose after its installation. Katherine testified that she used the ****430**

(Cite as: 31,203 (La.App. 2 Cir. 10/28/98), *8, 720 So.2d 425, **430)

device, as did guests to the home and no problems were encountered. Katherine testified that on the day of the accident, she left the house to go to her job which began at 8:00 a.m. Shortly thereafter, she received a call that her grandmother had fallen. According to Katherine, when she looked in the bathroom, the toilet seat extension was tilted.

At trial the plaintiff's treating physician, Dr. Lewis Jones, testified that he ordered a toilet seat extension for the plaintiff to take home. He stated that he thought the plaintiff requested the toilet seat. The seat provided was identical to the one used by the plaintiff in her hospital room during her twelve-day hospital stay. However, Dr. Jones stated that he did not specify this particular type of seat for the plaintiff. Dr. Jones testified that regardless of the warning on the seat, in his practice he has found that patients can safely use this device with the assistance of a walker and that the seat was adequate and proper for the plaintiff's use two months following hip surgery. He testified that he has never had any other patient who reported any difficulty with the use of this toilet seat. Brenda Ross, a registered nurse on the orthopedic floor at Willis-Knighton Medical Center, stated that she was employed at the hospital during the plaintiff's original hospitalization in 1984. She testified that she did not recall if she ever assisted the plaintiff in using the restroom. She stated that when she did aid patients, she instructed them to use the walker as their sole support in getting up and down. Ms. Ross signed the plaintiff's discharge papers when she checked out of the hospital in December 1994. She was questioned about a page in the plaintiff's hospital chart which was to be checked "yes" or "no" as to whether ***9**

(Cite as: 31,203 (La.App. 2 Cir. 10/28/98), *9, 720 So.2d 425, **430)

discharge instructions were given. In the plaintiff's chart, this item was left blank. She testified that she could not remember what instructions were given to the plaintiff on discharge. She stated that the usual procedure was to instruct a patient during his or her hospital stay how to use a walker and toilet seat extension and that on discharge, a patient would be shown how to install the toilet seat, reinforced on how to use it with a walker, and how to ambulate with a walker. The patient would also be instructed as to the amount of weight to put on the limb and proper wound care. She testified that she had seen toilet seat tipping problems, but this was due to improper patient usage and the patient was asked to sit down and then stand up straight.

Maude McCart, a licensed practical nurse employed at Willis-Knighton testified that she was part of the staff on the orthopedic floor that cared for Ms. Moore during her hospitalization. Ms. McCart did not recall ever assisting the plaintiff in using the bathroom. She stated that when she did assist patients they were instructed to use their walkers as their sole support in getting up and down. She testified that at that time, the practice was to chart only those things out of the ordinary, therefore, the chart did not contain a notation every time the plaintiff was assisted in using the bathroom in the hospital. It was also established that many times, nurses' aids assist patients in getting to the bathroom and aids were not allowed to make chart notations. Ms. McCart testified that this type of toilet seat extension was the only one in use at the hospital during the plaintiff's hospitalization. She also testified that the protocol on the orthopedic floor was to instruct patients in how to use walkers and in how to sit on the toilet with their walkers and this instruction was reinforced each time the patient went to the bathroom.
10

(Cite as: 31,203 (La.App. 2 Cir. 10/28/98), *10, 720 So.2d 425, **430)

Ms. McCart testified that if a patient didn't sit on the toilet seat straight, it could tip forward. She stated that she had seen this happen, but the patient was not harmed and was told to sit down on the seat and try again to stand up straight. She stated that the physician determined the type of device to be used by patients and if a patient slowly and carefully uses this type toilet seat, there should be no problem in its use.

Illa Rogers, an expert in nursing, testified that she was employed at Willis-Knighton as the director of nursing in 1984-85 when the plaintiff was a patient there. She stated that the nursing staff and physical therapists would be involved in training patients to use walkers and bathroom facilities. She stated that the toilet seat extensions were utilized because they provided both comfort and safety
****431***

(Cite as: 31,203 (La.App. 2 Cir. 10/28/98), *10, 720 So.2d 425, **431)

for post-operative orthopedic patients. She was questioned regarding the deficiencies in the plaintiff's hospital chart as to whether instructions in the use of the seat, while in the hospital or on discharge, were given. She stated that the patient would have been given verbal instructions at discharge but could not recall if, in 1985, written instructions were also issued. Ms. Rogers testified that the deficiencies in the chart represented a deviation in the charting policy of the hospital and not a deviation in the standard of care given the patient.

Paula Click Fenter, an expert in physical and rehabilitative therapy, testified that she was employed at Willis-Knighton in December 1984 and at that time patients were instructed in the use of their walkers and in making transfers. Ms. Fenter testified that the proper method for sitting down using a walker is to keep one hand on the walker and to reach back to the seat with the other hand.

(Cite as: 31,203 (La.App. 2 Cir. 10/28/98), *10, 720 So.2d 425, **431)

Dr. Lee Etheridge, an orthopedic surgeon and a member of the medical review panel which found that neither Willis-Knighton nor Dr. Jones breached any ***11***

continued

Moore v. Willis-Knighton Medical Center   *continued*

(Cite as: 31,203 (La.App. 2 Cir. 10/28/98), *11, 720 So.2d 425, **431)

standard of care in this case, testified that elevated toilet seats began to be used in the early 1980s and the type used in this case was the only kind he had seen. He testified that the plaintiff should have had some assistance while using this device and that, according to the standard of care today, this seat would be inappropriate. However, it was not inappropriate at the time this accident occurred, because they had just become available and "there was a learning curve going on." He stated that he had never heard of any other problems in using a toilet seat extension. Dr. Etheridge testified that after 70 days, the plaintiff would have recovered somewhat from her surgery and should be responsible for her own safety to some degree. He also stated that he felt that the plaintiff bears some responsibility for her fall.

To establish her claim that Willis-Knighton breached the applicable standard of care in giving her this toilet seat, the plaintiff introduced the testimony of numerous experts. These experts testified that the toilet seat was unstable and was not suitable for use by the plaintiff due to her balance problems caused by the use of a walker. They also testified that the plaintiff was not given correct instruction in the hospital as to how to make transfers from the toilet seat to the walker. They further testified that Willis-Knighton breached the applicable standard of care in failing to give the plaintiff instructions on discharge as to how to use the toilet seat extension.

The plaintiff presented the testimony of Dr. George Shoedinger, III, an expert in orthopedic surgery, who testified that the applicable standard of care in 1984 required the hospital to provide patients with appropriate medical devices consistent with their condition. He testified that it would constitute a deviation in the standard of care if a nurse fails to inform a patient that she must have assistance when using the seat extension and that it was inappropriate *12

(Cite as: 31,203 (La.App. 2 Cir. 10/28/98), *12, 720 So.2d 425, **431)

to provide this device to a patient without warning of its instability. His understanding of the accident was that the plaintiff did not sit straight down on the toilet seat and consequently, it tipped. The gist of this testimony was that the defendant breached its standard of care, not necessarily in providing this toilet seat, but in failing to properly instruct the plaintiff in how to use it and in not warning of its dangers. When questioned about the warning on the toilet seat, Dr. Shoedinger testified that he would agree that if there were any instructions or warnings on a medical device provided to a consumer for their use, the consumer is required to read the warning. He also stated that there was no doubt about the fact that someone should have been able to look at this device and determine that it is not stable because it could be easily removed from the toilet bowl.

Jeannine Onge, a ←**registered nurse** → presented by the plaintiff as an ←**expert**→ in nursing care and hospital procedures, testified that this type of nonclamping toilet seat was not appropriate for use by a patient such as the plaintiff who had a balance problem due to hip surgery. She stated that the plaintiff needed a clamp down model and grab bars. If nurses instructed the plaintiff to use the walker as her sole support in seating herself and rising from the toilet seat, that would be **432

(Cite as: 31,203 (La.App. 2 Cir. 10/28/98), *12, 720 So.2d 425, **432)

incorrect. Ms. Onge stated that a breach of the standard of care occurred in this case because the plaintiff's hospital chart does not show that discharge instructions were given including no instructions in the use of the toilet seat. Ms. Onge testified that the device could be safely used by patients with a walker if they were properly instructed. She also stated that she was not always aware that the plaintiff had used this type toilet seat throughout her hospital stay and she also assumed that the accident occurred when the plaintiff did not sit straight down on the toilet seat. *13

(Cite as: 31,203 (La.App. 2 Cir. 10/28/98), *13, 720 So.2d 425, **432)

Barry Bates, an expert in biomechanical engineering with expertise in human performance, testified that the toilet seat given to the plaintiff was basically a dangerous device for the circumstances under which it was used. He stated that the plaintiff had a balance problem due to her walker. He also testified that the plaintiff must not have seated herself straight on the toilet seat because asymmetrical forces caused the accident.

Joan Seifert, a registered nurse who had worked at P & S Hospital and Louisiana State University Medical Center, testified that in 1984, various types of toilet seat extensions were available, including a model that clamped down on the toilet bowl, as well as an extension with arms and a bedside commode. She stated that the nonclamping model in this case was not appropriate for use by a patient such as the plaintiff was using a walker. Ms. Seifert testified that, due to problems with the nonclamping model, P & S Hospital discontinued its use and began using the model that clamped down. Contradicting the instructions given by Ms. Ross and Ms. McCart, this witness stated that if a patient was instructed to use a walker as the sole support for getting up and down from the toilet seat, this would be incorrect and would be a deviation in the standard of care. She also testified that it was a breach in the standard of care to fail to document discharge instructions and in dispensing this toilet seat to the plaintiff.

Sharon Kelly, an expert in physical therapy, testified that the hospital was careless in providing the plaintiff with a nonclamping toilet seat, given her balance problems caused by using a walker. According to Ms. Kelly, in 1984, clamping seats were available as well as bedside commodes that could also be used in conjunction with a toilet.

*14

(Cite as: 31,203 (La.App. 2 Cir. 10/28/98), *14, 720 So.2d 425, **432)

Discussion

[15] It is not disputed that the trial court correctly instructed the jury that "the standard of care that a hospital owes to a patient is a national standard of care and is not governed by the locality rule." The plaintiff contends that, in finding that the defendant did not breach the standard of care owned to her, it must have rejected the instructions regarding a national standard of care and must have evaluated the evidence under a standard of care prescribed solely by the defendant, Willis-Knighton. Therefore, the plaintiff urges that the jury erred, as a matter of law, in rejecting her claim against the defendant requiring that this court conduct a de novo review of the record. After an extensive review of the record in this case, we are not persuaded that the jury failed to follow the trial court's instructions. We find that the jury evaluated the facts and circumstances of this case and made a factual finding to reject the evidence and testimony offered by the plaintiff regarding whether the defendant breached the national standard of care. Accordingly, we find that the jury did not err as a matter of law.

The plaintiff presented extensive expert evidence in an effort to establish her claims that the toilet seat extension was inappropriate because of her disability, that she was improperly instructed in the use of the seat and that, upon discharge, she was given no instructions in its use. The plaintiff claims that

continued

Moore v. Willis-Knighton Medical Center   *continued*

these factors prove that the defendant breached the standard of care owed to her. However, the record contains evidence and testimony which contradicts the plaintiff's claims.

As stated above, a hospital is required to exercise the amount of care toward a patient that the particular patient's condition may require. The plaintiff's contention is that the toilet seat given to her in this case was not appropriate for her use because she had a balance problem. However, Dr. Etheridge testified that in *15

(Cite as: 31,203 (La.App. 2 Cir. 10/28/98), *15, 720 So.2d 425, **432)

1984, this was the type of toilet seat was commonly used and that he **433

(Cite as: 31,203 (La.App. 2 Cir. 10/28/98), *15, 720 So.2d 425, **433)

never heard of any other patient being injured while using this type seat. Dr. Jones, the physician who issued this seat to the plaintiff, stated that the seat was adequate for the plaintiff's use, that patients with the plaintiff's disability could safely use the device and that he had never heard of any other patient having a problem using the seat. In addition, Dr. Jones stated that he thought the plaintiff requested a raised toilet seat to take home with her from the hospital.

Further, the seat had a warning label on it that was as readily visible to the plaintiff as to hospital personnel. Dr. Shoedinger, the plaintiff's own expert testified that the toilet seat required a warning to the plaintiff of its dangers but also stated that, because there was a warning on the seat, the consumer would be required to read that warning. He further stated that any instability the seat might have should be readily apparent to any user who looked at it due to the fact that it was not permanently attached to the toilet.

Nurses Ross and McCart testified that the only problems they observed in using the toilet seat occurred when patients used it improperly by failing to sit down and stand up straight. However, the seat was safe if used slowly and carefully by the patient.

Barry Bates, the plaintiff's expert in biomechanical engineering, stated that this accident could not have occurred unless the plaintiff failed to sit down on the seat straight. The plaintiff testified that she was 100% certain that she sat straight down on the toilet seat.

Katherine Moore testified that she installed the toilet seat in the plaintiff's home and that was not unsteady or loose. Further, it was used for approximately *16

(Cite as: 31,203 (La.App. 2 Cir. 10/28/98), *16, 720 So.2d 425, **433)

two months, not only by the plaintiff, but also by Katherine and by visitors to the home, without any difficulty. Also, Dr. Etheridge, a member of the medical review panel, stated that seventy days following her surgery, the plaintiff should have been responsible for her own safety to some extent and bore some responsibility for her fall. Even though the plaintiff presented testimony by numerous experts to support her claims, the record also shows that the plaintiff used the seat for twelve days in the hospital, asked to take one home, and then used the seat for seventy days in her own home without mishap. The warnings on the seat were as readily discoverable by the plaintiff as by personnel at the hospital. Further, the record contains testimony that, if used slowly and carefully, the toilet seat was safe for use even by persons on walkers. Therefore, there is a basis in the record for the jury to conclude that the toilet seat extension provided to the plaintiff was not inappropriate for her to use seventy days following her original surgery.

Regarding the claim that she received improper instructions in the use of the walker with the toilet seat, the record show that, although the nurses on the orthopedic floor who cared for the plaintiff during her 1984 hospitalization did not relate the proper method for making transfers, it is not clear that these nurses ever assisted the plaintiff in using the bathroom and gave her the improper instructions. Further, the record shows that the main responsibility for such instruction comes from the physical therapists. Paula Click Fenter testified as to the proper method for making transfers and stated that hospital patients were given such instruction. Therefore, there was a basis in the record for the jury to conclude that the hospital did not breach its standard of care to the plaintiff by improperly instructing her in using a walker to transfer from a walker to the toilet seat extension. *17*

(Cite as: 31,203 (La.App. 2 Cir. 10/28/98), *17, 720 So.2d 425, **433)

Finally, the plaintiff contends that the hospital breached its standard of care in failing to give her instructions upon discharge in how to use the toilet seat. The record shows that hospital personnel could not remember if written discharge instructions were given to patients in 1984 or whether only oral instructions were given. Brenda Ross, the plaintiff's discharge nurse, testified as to what instructions are usually given a patient upon discharge. Regarding the fact that the plaintiff's chart did not indicate whether discharge instructions were given, Illa Rogers, director of nursing, testified that this was a deviation in the charting procedure and not a deviation in the standard of cared owed to this patient. Therefore, there is a reasonable basis in the record for the jury to conclude that Willis-Knighton **434*

(Cite as: 31,203 (La.App. 2 Cir. 10/28/98), *17, 720 So.2d 425, **434)

did not breach the applicable standard of care in failing to give the plaintiff discharge instructions. In this case, even though the plaintiff presented expert testimony which conflicted with the defendant's position, the issue of whether a breach in the standard of care occurred is a factual question over which the jury had great discretion and the resolution of which turns upon the evaluation of the credibility of the testimony by experts and others. Although there may be two permissible views of the evidence, the jury here made a choice and we do not find that their choice is manifestly erroneous or clearly wrong. Even though a reviewing court might feel that other evaluations and inference may be more reasonable than those of the jury, the jury in this case made reasonable evaluations of credibility and reasonable inferences of fact which will not disturb upon review.

CONCLUSION

For the reasons set forth above, the jury verdict and trial court judgment, finding that the defendant, Willis-Knighton Medical Center, did not breach the *18*

(Cite as: 31,203 (La.App. 2 Cir. 10/28/98), *18, 720 So.2d 425, **434)

applicable standard of care owed to the plaintiff, Madeline Moore, is affirmed. Costs in this court and in the court below are assessed to the plaintiff.

AFFIRMED.

END OF DOCUMENT

UNIT VI

MEDICAL-LEGAL WRITING

Legal nurse consultants are expected to draft documents using their medical background and their knowledge of the law. In this unit, you will find the answers to these questions:

■ What is involved in legal writing?

■ What correspondence will legal nurse consultants prepare?

■ How do legal nurse consultants synthesize medical and legal issues into legal documents?

■ How do computer programs and software facilitate the drafting of medical-legal documents?

■ How does the legal nurse consultant assist in developing documents in preparation for trial and trial exhibits?

CHAPTER 26

INTRODUCTION TO LEGAL WRITING

OBJECTIVES

In this chapter, you will discover

- the precision necessary in legal writing

- the "stages" of writing legal documents

- the mechanics of effective written communication

- what documents a legal nurse consultant will be expected to draft

OVERVIEW

Probably one of the most difficult transitions for nurses entering the legal profession is in the area of writing. While both the medical and legal industries are paper-intensive, the type of writing that is traditionally done by a nurse in a clinical setting is a far cry from the writing expected of a legal nurse consultant. This does not mean that nurses don't have the skills to write well; it simply means that without use, writing skills tarnish. This chapter will focus on pulling unused writing abilities out of storage and buffing them into a professional shine.

Legal nurse consultants will be expected to draft a variety of legal documents. Many of these documents are working papers that will be used within the legal office: medical summaries, medical bill analyses, life-care plans, medical deposition summaries, interoffice memoranda, evaluation of claims in light of medical standards, and summaries of expert opinions. In addition, legal nurse consultants may be expected to assist in the development of pleadings, such as complaints, answers, and motions to dismiss; discovery documents, such as interrogatories; requests for production; and questions in preparation for depositions.

Effective legal writing must be clear, concise, and well organized. The trend in the American legal system is toward **plain English;** that is, to avoid legalese wherever possible and to refrain from making simple concepts sound complex. The plain English movement has been codified in some states, so attorneys and court personnel are required to draft documents in language that ordinary citizens can understand.[1] Because of the deluge of information available in this age of technology, it is imperative that consultants keep in mind the value of brevity and clarity.

STAGES OF LEGAL WRITING

Legal scholars have identified three stages of legal writing: prewriting, writing, and postwriting. By developing skill at each stage in the writing process, nurses will be better prepared to present medical information in a legal format. In addition, they will find that they are more marketable and more confident in their ability to communicate well in the professional sphere of law. The three stages of writing are identified in Figure 26-1.

Prewriting

The first step in effective communication is considering why the communication is needed, who will be reading the communication, and the value that will be attached to it. Although it may seem tempting to skip some essential information (the attorney already knows it; there are other documents in the file with this information), many other people may have to work on this file (experts, for instance) who may not be familiar with the facts. If the lead at-

FIGURE 26-1 Three Stages of Writing	
Stage in the Writing Process	**Questions to Consider**
Prewriting	Why is the communication necessary? Who will read the document? What constraints must be considered (time, money, client circumstances)?
Writing	What information must be communicated (reduced to an outline)? How can the information be communicated simply (clearly, coherently, and completely)?
Postwriting	How can the communication be improved (headings, tables)? What can be left out? Is the document grammatically correct and in proper format?

torney on the case suddenly dies or becomes ill, it is valuable to have a complete document for the person who takes over. In addition, the document may become part of a master file system within the office. Master file systems are often maintained for legal memoranda, so that attorneys who work on later cases need not start research from scratch. Litigation firms maintain expert file systems, where curriculum vitae and summaries are maintained for reference in later cases. If the office maintains such a system, it is necessary to ensure that all documents prepared are complete enough to provide future practitioners with a thorough understanding of the circumstances under which the documents were drafted.

Perhaps a written document is not necessary. Before writing, consider whether the communication may be accomplished over the telephone or via e-mail, or whether it is necessary at all. For example, the attorney has recently seen a potential client who has a claim in health care liability based on an incident that occurred six years ago. The legal nurse consultant recognizes that the statute of limitations in health care liability, regardless of the theory under which it is brought, expires five years after the incident. It will not be prudent for the legal nurse consultant to continue work on the claim if it is clear from the tolling of the statute of limitations that the action is barred. A simple phone call or e-mail, including a reference to the statute citation, may be sufficient.

Most of the documents prepared by the legal nurse consultant will be read by attorneys, paralegals, investigators, and experts. This is a highly literate audience and the legal nurse consultant must write in a way that makes the communication understandable, yet does not insult the reader. If a communication is for a client, the language, structure, and content of the document may be completely different from a communication prepared for an expert. Client communications require an approach that is educational and helpful.

Before writing, consider the constraints under which the communication is being made. Legal nurse consultants may be requested to complete work for the attorney at the eleventh hour. This may not be due to lack of diligence on the part of the attorney, but rather to an honest belief that the case would settle before trial. Thus, a week before trial, the legal nurse consultant may be asked to summarize depositions, prepare a chronology or timeline, or evaluate an expert's opinion. The limited amount of time available to complete the project may be a major factor in how the communication is prepared.

Writing

Once consideration has been given to why the document is needed, who will be reading it, and what constraints impact its preparation, the actual writing begins. The most difficult part of any written project is beginning. To help get started, write what must be communicated. It doesn't matter what the writing starts with; it is always easier to change the contents to reflect greater coherence once a draft has been prepared.

Paralegals who draft documents for attorneys often feel frustration because the documents that are returned to them are red lined, crossed out, and scribbled on. As a result, paralegals often think they have not accomplished the task they were assigned to do. This is generally not the case. For the attorney, looking at a draft is far easier than generating a new document. The attorney can immediately see any faults in the reasoning or construction of the document and can identify areas for additional explanation, even when the paralegal included everything that the attorney requested. It is always easier to start with something and change it. So, start writing!

It may be helpful to begin with an outline. This is useful for isolating information that is essential and for developing a logical flow of information within the document. The outline need not be formal; jotting down ideas may serve as a useful guide for the preparation of the document. Outlines also provide a basis for the use of headings or titles that may simplify access to the information in the document.

Postwriting

Once a working draft has been prepared, give it a cooling off period. If there is sufficient time, the document should be set aside for twenty-four hours. When you come back to the document, you will have a clearer perspective on how to improve the organization of the document, the writing, and the image of the communication. Many techniques can help improve the organization of a document. Headings are often used to indicate important divisions in the information. If headings are used, make them consistent by using the same

---

FIGURE 26-2 Parallel Construction

	Examples of Parallel Construction	Examples of Writing Without Parallel Construction
Headings	Memory of accident Use of medical appliance Cost of medical care	Remembering the accident Medical appliances The bills for medical care
Lists	• Inability to write • Sensation of "tingling" • Loss of feeling	• Impaired writing ability • Client feels "tingling" • Radial nerve damage

---

grammatical pattern. Consistency in writing is called **parallel construction,** which means that there is a uniform system for communicating the information. Figure 26-2 shows the difference between writing that uses parallel construction and writing that does not. If the first heading begins with an active verb (e.g., using), make certain that all later headings begin with an active verb. Parallel construction should be used throughout the document as it provides a clean, professional appearance and promotes organization.

Graphs may provide easy reference to quantifiable information. Bulleted lists are often used as an alternative to writing a narrative series of ideas. Tables, timelines, and charts can also provide the reader with information at a glance, saving time and promoting comprehension. In the postwriting or rewriting stage, writers should consider using whatever tools and techniques will help the reader quickly access and understand the information communicated.

Many legal offices have specific formats for chronologies, summaries, evaluative reports, and other documents. Check with office personnel to see if a sample is available and make certain the document being written conforms to the sample provided. This format has been designed to provide the attorney and other professionals with a quick glance at the most important information. If no format has been developed, consider developing one and asking for feedback as to its design and usefulness.

Finally, in the postwriting stage, always proofread. Another reason the cooling off period is important is that too often typographical errors are overlooked when the document is hot off the press. Typographical errors leave an impression of carelessness that a consultant cannot afford.

CAUTIONS CONCERNING LEGAL WRITING

It is easy to get stuck in the potholes of the legal writing highway. Traditional legal documents have sometimes been used to display extensive vocabularies, to evade certainty and promote ambiguity, and to be so purposely vague as to defy comprehension. Reading these traditional documents provides a frame of reference for writing in a similar fashion. Legal nurse consultants should be careful to avoid this tendency. Additionally, as a medical professional working in a legal field, legal nurse consultants should avoid legalese, avoid persuasive language, and avoid gender-specificity.

Avoid Legalese

Unless it is necessary to be precise in the communication, it is better to avoid these archaic legal phrases:

- To-wit
- Insofar as
- Hereinabove
- Aforementioned
- Party of the first part
- On his part
- Notwithstanding the foregoing

In addition, legal terms and medical terms should be avoided where possible. Use the names of the parties, rather than plaintiff and defendant. Use heart muscle instead of myocardium. The simpler the communication, the easier it will be for everyone to understand.

Avoid Persuasive Language

The intent of the communication prepared by a legal nurse consultant is to educate the attorney or other readers, not to argue the case. It may be the assignment of the legal nurse consultant to evaluate whether a medical negligence claim exists considering the facts in the documentation provided. An opinion will be made by the legal nurse consultant and should be communicated to the attorney. However, that communication should not begin with a statement like "I think we can win this one!" Whether or not the case can be won is a matter for legal judgment; it is not within the sphere of the legal nurse consultant's evaluation. Rather, the legal nurse consultant should clearly and in a straightforward manner describe the incidents that gave rise to the claim of negligence compared with the appropriate standards of medical care. This comparison will provide the attorney with the information necessary to make a legal judgment and to inform the client about what action can be taken.

Avoid Gender-specificity

In legal work, gender-specific language is inappropriate and may be ambiguous. For example, "The specialist met with the patient and he told him about his symptoms." It is not clear from this statement whether the specialist or the patient did the talking, nor is it clear whose symptoms were discussed. It is far better to replace the gender-specific language: "The specialist met with the patient and told the patient about the symptoms." Once in the habit of avoiding gender-specificity, it becomes much easier to write in clear language that is less likely to be misinterpreted or offensive. Similarly, it is a good idea to avoid using gender-specific pronouns, even when the person is known. For example, "Mary Walker was the floor nurse. She should be called as a witness." Instead, write, "Mary Walker was the floor nurse. The floor nurse should be called as a witness." If possible, avoid using pronouns altogether.

FUNDAMENTALS OF WRITING WELL

It may be necessary to return to some basic tenets of writing in order to buff up tarnished writing skills. In the following paragraphs are tips that may facilitate clear writing. It is not intended that this chapter will take the place of an English composition class, but that it will serve as a review of good writing skills in the areas of grammar, sentence structure, and paragraph structure.

Grammar

There are several rules of grammar that should be followed in order to produce a professional document that is clear and coherent.

- A sentence must always have a noun and a verb.
- The noun and the verb should be in close proximity to each other.
- The noun and the verb should match in terms of tense.
- The tense should not change within the sentence.
- Prepositional phrases may not stand alone; prepositional phrases are not sentences.
- Objects should follow prepositions.

These rules are illustrated in Figure 26-3. In addition to these basic rules of good grammar, writers should also be careful not to use adjectives and adverbs unnecessarily. Adding too many modifiers or qualifiers to a sentence may make it clumsy and difficult to understand. Adhering to basic rules of grammar will enhance the communication and its ability to be understood by those who read it.

Grammar also includes the proper use of punctuation. This may be an area in which review and practice are needed. While capitalization, periods, and question marks may be easily mastered upon review, commas, semicolons, colons, and hyphens may require additional practice.

Commas. A comma is used to identify a pause in a sentence, to separate two separate ideas that are joined into one sentence, to identify a parenthetical phrase, and to separate a list of items. These rules are illustrated in Figure 26-4.

What LNCs Say . . .

"If we want attorneys to hear us, we need to talk in a language they understand. In nursing education programs, nurses learn how to write problem-related information in charting formats that do not require sentences or the formalities of professional writing. In the legal field, these writing skills are not sufficient—a legal nurse consultant must be able to communicate logically, courteously, and coherently, and must be able to present information appropriate to the legal audience" Kay L. Scharn, RN, MSN, EdS, LNC, Eau Claire, WI, used with permission.

FIGURE 26-3   Grammar Rules

Rule	Illustration
A sentence must always have a noun and a verb.	*Incorrect:* Going to court. *Correct:* The attorney is going to court.
The noun and the verb should be in close proximity to each other.	*Incorrect:* The attorney, because of having to attend a hearing on behalf of indigent clients who could not afford an attorney, is going to court. *Correct:* The attorney is going to court to attend a hearing on behalf of indigent clients.
The noun and the verb should match in terms of tense.	*Incorrect:* The jury (collective noun) were in deliberation. *Correct:* The jury was in deliberation.
The tense should not change within the sentence.	*Incorrect:* Everyone should have their cholesterol checked. *Correct:* Everyone should have a cholesterol screening.
Prepositional phrases may not stand alone; prepositional phrases are not sentences.	*Incorrect:* Due to difficulty in finding an attorney. *Correct:* The defendant did not respond timely due to difficulty in finding an attorney.
Objects should follow the preposition.	*Incorrect:* It was coincidence that, whether intentionally or unintentionally and regardless of how caused, the driver spotted the accident. *Correct:* It was coincidence that the driver spotted the accident. It does not matter whether it was intentional or unintentional or how it was caused.

FIGURE 26-4   Use of Commas

Rule	Illustration
A comma is used to identify a pause in the sentence.	When the medical report is received, evaluation of the client's claim may be thoroughly analyzed.
A comma is used to separate two separate ideas that are joined into one sentence.	I will request the medical report, and the investigator will interview the witnesses.
A comma is used to identify a parenthetical phrase.	The Defendant, XYZ Health Care Facility, adopted a policy of charting by exception.
A comma is used to separate a list of items.	To properly evaluate the claim, we will need to acquire the medical records, the medical bills, and a medical report from the treating physician.

FIGURE 26-5 Use of Hyphens and Dashes

Rule	Illustration
A dash is used to add emphasis to a sentence.	The client was not being totally honest—truth was not important.
A hyphen is used to connect a two-word adjective.	Interviews often begin with open-ended questions.

Semicolons. Semicolons are used to separate complete sentences that are closely related, but which, when written in separate sentences, would create disjointed or choppy reading. Consider this example: *Patients are not products off an assembly line; they are human beings with hearts and souls.*

Colons. A colon is used to identify that an important qualifier, explanation, or list follows an idea that can stand alone as a sentence. Consider this example: *The patient was given two prescriptions: Hydrocodone and Penicillin.*

Hyphens and Dashes. Dashes are used to add emphasis to a sentence, and hyphens connect a two-word adjective. These rules are illustrated in Figure 26-5. Using a variety of punctuation adds a professional quality to the communication, but only if the punctuation is used properly.

Punctuation can impact the interpretation of legal documents. For example, a will has the following clause: "All of the rest, residue, and remainder of my estate, I give to my children, Ann, Marguerite, and Glenn." Interpretation of this clause would be that Ann, Marguerite, and Glenn each receive an equivalent one-third share of the remaining estate. However, this might not be the result if the punctuation had been different. Consider the difference in this clause: "All the rest, residue, and remainder of my estate, I give to my children, Ann, Marguerite and Glenn." Because the comma is placed between Ann and Marguerite, and because only one comma is used in this clause, the effect may be that Ann would receive one-half of the estate, and Marguerite and Glenn would receive the other one-half.

Sentence Structure

A sentence is a single idea or set of circumstances. It should be simple and straightforward. Because most writing specialists believe that active voice should be used (rather than passive voice), it may be well to consider action verbs as the primary component of a sentence.

Active voice. When it is important to know who is doing what, active voice with action verbs should be used. For example, "The treating physician read the patient's record." It is immediately clear that the physician read the record and that the physician is the important character in the sentence.

Net Results

Legal Forms on the Internet

There are number of legal and business forms on the Internet. Most of the forms can be downloaded without cost, although some web sites charge a fee for using documents. One of the most useful web sites for legal professionals is www.findlaw.com. This location provides links to virtually every area of law on the Internet and provides a collection of forms at www.findlaw.com/16forms/index.html. West Legal Studies also provides a web page for legal students, which includes a collection of forms. Access this web page at www.westlegal studies.com. State bar associations' web pages may also provide forms specific to state law. Attorneys who maintain their own web sites may provide access to forms, although some of them charge a fee for using the forms.

Passive voice. On the other hand, when the actor is not the important component of the sentence, passive voice may be used. For example, "The patient's record was read by the treating physician." Here the key importance is on the patient's record.

Sentences should be kept short. Many authors suggest that a sentence having more than twenty-five words is too long. Varying the length of sentences aids the communication by providing it with simplicity and complexity, emphasis and diminished importance. Using a variety of sentences, like using a variety of punctuation, is an indication of professionalism and confidence in the ability to communicate well.

Paragraph Structure

Paragraphs collect sentences that are related to the same theme or topic. Each paragraph should have a topic sentence that identifies the theme that will be explored in that paragraph. The length of paragraphs varies with the amount of information needed to complete the discussion of that theme or topic.

Writers often face the problem of combining paragraphs into a coherent and logical flow of information. For readability, paragraphs should use a **transition sentence** that leads the reader from the previous paragraph's topic or argument into the succeeding paragraph's topic or argument. With transitions, the writer is allowing the reader to follow the thought process from the beginning point to the final point. One way to visualize the transition sentence is to think of the infrastructure of a skyscraper. The steel and concrete frame girding is necessary so that one floor can be built upon the next. Even though each floor (paragraph) may be decorated differently, the floors are held together by strong links to each other. The transition sentence connects the previous thought to the next.

TYPICAL DOCUMENTS PREPARED BY LEGAL NURSE CONSULTANTS

Legal nurse consultants may be responsible for drafting any or all of the following legal documents:

- client intake memoranda
- correspondence for acquiring medical records
- correspondence with the client
- medical authorizations
- summaries, chronologies, and chart reviews
- evaluative reports
- correspondence with experts
- medical literature reviews
- summaries of medical depositions
- life-care plans

These legal documents are discussed in greater detail in later chapters, and sample documents are included.

Legal nurse consultants may assist in the preparation of many other litigation documents, including complaints, answers, motions to dismiss, interrogatories, answers to interrogatories, requests for production, settlement demands, pretrial reports or briefs, affidavits, and legal memoranda and briefs. Because legal nurse consultants will be most familiar with the medical issues in the claim, legal professionals will depend on that medical expertise for drafting numerous documents and reports during the course of the litigation.

CHAPTER SUMMARY

- Writing well is a critical skill of legal professionals.
- The three stages of writing include prewriting, writing, and postwriting.
- Legal nurse consultants should avoid legalese, persuasive language, and gender-specific language.
- Good writing requires skillful use of grammar, sentence structure, and paragraph structure.
- Legal nurse consultants draft many different kinds of medical-legal documents and assist legal staff in drafting other litigation documents.

KEY TERMS

parallel construction   plain English   transition sentence

REVIEW QUESTIONS

1. What are the three stages of writing and what questions are considered during each stage?
2. Why must legal nurse consultants be conscious of grammar, sentence structure, and paragraph structure?
3. What types of documents do legal nurse consultants prepare?

INTERNET EXERCISES

1. Access the web page for this textbook at *www.westlegalstudies.com*.
2. Click on the assignments section and complete the assignment(s) for Chapter Twenty-six.

EXERCISES

1. Networking. If you are currently employed in a health care facility, locate a standard of care from the policies and procedures manual of the facility. Draft a summary of the standard of care as if an attorney had requested that you identify that particular standard of care.

2. Professional Portfolio. Photocopy the forms that are provided in this textbook. Maintain them in your systems file, folder, or binder, and organize or index them for easy reference. Having sample documents available will provide you with greater confidence at an interview and on the job.

ENDNOTES

1. Steve Barber, *Legal Writing,* 2nd ed. (Albany, NY: Delmar Publishers, 1997), 8.

2. American Bar Association, *Annotated Model Rules of Professional Conduct,* (1999) 4th Edition Rule 7.2. Copies of ABA *Model Code of Professional Responsibility, 1999 Edition* are available from Service Center, American Bar Association, 750 North Lake Shore Drive, Chicago, IL 60611-4497, 1-800-285-2221.

ADDITIONAL REFERENCES

AALNC Greater Detroit Chapter. "Writing for a Professional Journal—Step by Step." *Journal of Legal Nurse Consulting* 11:1 (2000): 20–21.

Lamb, D. L. BSN, RN. "Expert affidavits." *Journal of Legal Nurse Consulting* 10:1 (1999): 19–21.

CHAPTER 27

LEGAL CORRESPONDENCE

OBJECTIVES

In this chapter, you will discover

- what letters are most frequently written by legal nurse consultants

- the mechanics of letter writing

- formats for legal correspondence

- how legal nurse consultants may enhance professionalism by enhancing letter-writing skills

OVERVIEW

Legal correspondence is an integral component of fact gathering for litigation. Legal nurse consultants can expect to develop a working relationship with those employed in medical records departments through their correspondence and telephone calls. In addition, letters will often provide the introduction between the legal nurse consultant and the medical experts in the case. To be able to craft legal correspondence that is clear, concise, and respectful of the time of the recipient is an important skill for legal nurse consultants to develop.

Legal nurse consultants can expect to prepare the following types of correspondence:

- letters requesting medical records, bills, and opinions
- letters to experts supplying information and requesting opinions
- letters to insurance companies or clients regarding the status of the case
- letters to clients requesting and supplying information
- letters to manufacturers, government agencies, and other sources for information about medical products
- letters to licensing bureaus, professional associations, and health care facilities for records concerning the competence of health care providers
- portions of the settlement demand letter dealing with the medical issues

This list is not exhaustive. Legal nurse consultants may also be asked to correspond with employers concerning adaptive environments for returning workers who require accommodation. Letters may be written to research specialists concerning articles appearing in medical journals, or letters may be written to legal associations such as the Association of Trial Lawyers of America for information concerning products liability claims that are being brought across the country. Regardless of the matter that requires correspondence, legal nurse consultants must be skilled at effective letter-writing.

PURPOSES OF LEGAL CORRESPONDENCE

Letters are written for any number of reasons. They may be written to confirm appointments or understandings, request information, provide information, persuade the other party to settle, or record information. Litigation practice promotes the establishment of a systems file or folder where routine documents prepared during a litigation are located. These documents may be stored in a network repository and called up on the computer screen to be used as each case requires. Form letters should be adapted to the circumstances of the case. Customizing the form letters ensures that the information communicated is done so at a minimum of expense and without duplication of effort.

The purpose of the letter must always be kept in mind and the tone should be adapted to match the desired outcomes. Honoring the time and expertise of a medical specialist will go a long way toward eliciting a response from that professional. A gentle reminder to the client about information that is needed may promote a more trusting relationship than a threatening or demanding letter.

THE COMPONENTS OF A LETTER

There are several components of a legal business letter: date, inside address, reference, salutation, body, complimentary closing, signature, and end notations. These components are identified in the illustration in Figure 27-1.

Date

The date of the letter should be the date on which the letter is actually prepared. If there is a gap between the dictation of a letter and the date when the letter has been processed, the date of processing should be the date indicated at the top of the letter.

If there are any special notations concerning the delivery of the letter, these notations should be made in bold or underlined text immediately under the date. These notations might be "**Via Facsimile**" or "EXPRESS MAIL."

Inside Address

The inside address indicates the name and address of the recipient of the letter. This part of the letter should be separated from the date or delivery notation by three or four line spaces. The name of the recipient should be on the first line; title, company name, address, and city-state-zip code should each be on a separate line. If the recipient is an individual, title and company name are omitted and the address is usually the residence of the individual.

While it is still proper within the body of the letter to include a comma between the city and the state in the last line of the address, the address on the envelope should include no punctuation. Eliminating punctuation marks on the envelope will facilitate processing at the post office.

Questions often arise concerning the proper way to address an individual. Whether to use Mr. or Ms. will be apparent from a review of previous correspondence. Many firms omit these designations altogether and simply identify the recipient by first and last name.

Reference Line

The reference line is valuable for several reasons: it serves to alert the recipient to the subject of the communication, it aids in filing and retrieving information needed for the correspondence, and it may indicate the importance to be attached to the correspondence. In a traditional business format, the reference

FIGURE 27-1   Components of a Legal Business Letter

Downing & Pavelski, S.C.
Attorneys at Law
101 Main Street
Madison, Wisconsin 53606

Patrick Downing, J.D.   602.781.1234
Barbara Pavelski, J.D.   fax: 602.781.1245

June 17, —— *(date)*

Federal Express *(mailing notations)*

Robert Silver, Claims Attorney   *(inside address)*
General Insurance Company, Inc.
One GIC Road
P.O. Box 2002
St. Charles, IL 60174

Re: *Simsek v. Jackson*   *(reference line)*
         Your File No. 00-107-MED
         Your Insured: Carol Jackson
         Date of Occurrence: January 17, ——

Dear Mr. Silver: *(salutation)*

We continue to investigate this matter, but due to the extensive nature of the injuries to my client, we are enclosing our settlement brochure and demand at this time. We have little doubt that your client will be found totally at fault if this matter goes to trial. A prompt and fair settlement will be beneficial to both parties.

Because of the suffering my client endures daily, we are unwilling to engage in prolonged settlement negotiations. If we do not hear from you on or before July 1, ——, a lawsuit will be filed.   *(body of the letter)*

Sincerely,   *(complimentary closing)*

DOWNING & PAVELSKI
                              (signature)
Barbara Pavelski

BP/cw

Enclosure   *(end notes)*
cc: Hasam Simsek

line is separated from the city, state, and zip code of the inside address by one line space. In letters where the salutation is omitted, there may be two line spaces separating the reference line from the inside address and the reference line may be bolded or underlined.

Salutation

The **salutation** is sometimes called the greeting and in traditional business correspondence begins with "Dear M__._____:" It is separated from the reference line by one line space. The potential for a letter to be received by the proper party and to be responded to in a timely manner is enhanced by directing the letter to a particular person. For example, if the name of the custodian of records is not known, it may expedite results in the case to call the facility and ask who is in charge of the records. Addressing the letter to that person and naming him or her in the salutation will begin to build a relationship that may be useful for many years.

Because of the trend toward non–gender-specific correspondence, the salutation may be eliminated. For an example of this newer style of letter, see Figure 27-2. If the person to whom the letter is written is well-known to the writer, a friendly first name followed by a comma may begin the first paragraph of the letter. This is one way to eliminate the problem of how to properly address a recipient.

Body of the Letter

The body of the letter is where the real skill of writing is apparent. Here it is especially important to keep in mind the recipient of the letter. If the letter is being written to a medical specialist, the legal nurse consultant should use medical professional language and avoid legal terms. If the letter is being written to a legal specialist, with minimal medical background, medical terminology may need to be simplified in order to convey the message without sounding condescending. If the letter is being written to a client both medical and legal terminology should be kept to a minimum.

The body of the letter should be separated from the salutation by a line space and begin with a topic sentence that explains the purpose of the letter. In a short letter, paragraphs (usually two or three) are of approximately the same length. In longer letters, such as settlement demands, paragraphs may be lengthy and separated by titles or headings. Keep the purpose of the letter in mind and to use language specific to that objective.

Complimentary Closing

The **complimentary closing** will follow the body of the letter, with a line space between. Law firms often have a pattern closing that is already a component of the computer system and is automatically displayed using macros or other

FIGURE 27-2 Business Letter Omitting Salutation and Closing

Downing & Pavelski, S.C.
Attorneys at Law
101 Main Street
Madison, Wisconsin 53606

Patrick Downing, J.D.   602.781.1234
Barbara Pavelski, J.D.   fax: 602.781.1245

June 17, ——

Federal Express

Robert Silver, Claims Attorney
General Insurance Company, Inc.
One GIC Road
P.O. Box 2002
St. Charles, IL 60174

Re: *Simsek v. Jackson*
        Your File No. 00-107-MED
        Your Insured: Carol Jackson
        Date of Occurrence: January 17, ——

Mr. Silver, we continue to investigate this matter, but due to the extensive nature of the injuries to my client, we are enclosing our settlement brochure and demand at this time. We have little doubt that your client will be found totally at fault if this matter goes to trial. A prompt and fair settlement will be beneficial to both parties.

Because of the suffering my client endures daily, we are unwilling to engage in prolonged settlement negotiations. If we do not hear from you on or before July 1, ——, a lawsuit will be filed.

Barbara Pavelski

BP/cw

Enclosure
cc: Hasam Simsek

codes. Variations of "Very truly yours," and "Sincerely," are closings that are often used.

Signature

At least three or four line spaces should be left for the handwritten signature of the party writing the letter. Following these line spaces should be the typed name of the individual who signed the letter. In addition, the status of that individual should be noted. For example, the letter may be signed "Very truly yours, Vera Evans, Legal Nurse Consultant." This clearly indicates to the reader that the person signing the letter is not a practicing attorney working in the firm identified in the letterhead. This is an ethical concern that must always be honored. Non-lawyer professionals must never allow a client or others to assume that they are practicing attorneys. See Chapters Thirty-three and Thirty-four for a further discussion on ethics.

End Notes

If the letter has enclosed documents, end notes may be important references. These notes appear after the last line of the typed signature and are separated from the signature by a line space. End notes include enclosure notations, carbon copy notations, and blind carbon copy notations.

LETTER STYLES

All letters have the same basic components. How the components are structured is determined by the style or format of the letter. Typically, legal business letters may be prepared in block, modified block, and modified semi-block. A review of previous correspondence by the firm will identify which style should be used. Several computer programs, such as Microsoft's Letter Wizard, will automatically format your letter in the appropriate style.

Full Block

Full block letters are the most efficient because they do not require any indentations. All components of the letter begin at the left margin. Figure 27-3 shows a letter in full block letter style.

Modified Block

In a **modified block** letter style, all components of the letter are flush left with the exception of the date, the complimentary close, and the signature, which begin in the middle of the page. See Figure 27-4 for an example of a letter in modified block style.

Modified Semi-block

In a **modified semi-block** letter, the date, complimentary close, and signature are indented to the center of the letter. The reference line and all paragraphs are indented about five spaces (1/2 inch) from the left margin. The letter in Figure 27-5 illustrates the modified semi-block style of letter-writing.

FIGURE 27-3   Letter in Full Block Style

Downing & Pavelski, S.C.
Attorneys at Law
101 Main Street
Madison, Wisconsin 53606

Patrick Downing, J.D.   602.781.1234
Barbara Pavelski, J.D.   fax: 602.781.1245

June 17, ——

Robert Silver, Claims Attorney
General Insurance Company, Inc.
One GIC Road
P.O. Box 2002
St. Charles, IL 60174

Re: *Simsek v. Jackson*
       Your File No. 00-107-MED
       Your Insured: Carol Jackson
       Date of Occurrence: January 17, ——

Dear Mr. Silver:

We continue to investigate this matter, but due to the extensive nature of the injuries to my client, we are enclosing our settlement brochure and demand at this time. We have little doubt that your client will be found totally at fault if this matter goes to trial. A prompt and fair settlement will be beneficial to both parties.

Because of the suffering my client endures daily, we are unwilling to engage in prolonged settlement negotiations. If we do not hear from you on or before July 1, ——, a lawsuit will be filed.

Sincerely,

DOWNING & PAVELSKI

Barbara Pavelski

BP/cw

Enclosure
cc: Hasam Simsek

FIGURE 27-4 Letter in Modified Block Style

Downing & Pavelski, S.C.
Attorneys at Law
101 Main Street
Madison, Wisconsin 53606

Patrick Downing, J.D.   602.781.1234
Barbara Pavelski, J.D.   fax: 602.781.1245

June 17, ——

Robert Silver, Claims Attorney
General Insurance Company, Inc.
One GIC Road
P.O. Box 2002
St. Charles, IL 60174

Re: *Simsek v. Jackson*
       Your File No. 00-107-MED
       Your Insured: Carol Jackson
       Date of Occurrence: January 17, ——

Dear Mr. Silver:

We continue to investigate this matter, but due to the extensive nature of the injuries to my client, we are enclosing our settlement brochure and demand at this time. We have little doubt that your client will be found totally at fault if this matter goes to trial. A prompt and fair settlement will be beneficial to both parties.

Because of the suffering my client endures daily, we are unwilling to engage in prolonged settlement negotiations. If we do not hear from you on or before July 1, ——, a lawsuit will be filed.

Sincerely,

DOWNING & PAVELSKI

Barbara Pavelski

BP/cw

Enclosure
cc: Hasam Simsek

FIGURE 27-5   Letter in Modified Semi-Block Style

Downing & Pavelski, S.C.
Attorneys at Law
101 Main Street
Madison, Wisconsin 53606

Patrick Downing, J.D.   602.781.1234
Barbara Pavelski, J.D.   fax: 602.781.1245

                                                          June 17, ——

Robert Silver, Claims Attorney
General Insurance Company, Inc.
One GIC Road
P.O. Box 2002
St. Charles, IL 60174

        Re: *Simsek v. Jackson*
               Your File No. 00-107-MED
               Your Insured: Carol Jackson
               Date of Occurrence: January 17, ——

Dear Mr. Silver:

    We continue to investigate this matter, but due to the extensive nature of the injuries to my client, we are enclosing our settlement brochure and demand at this time. We have little doubt that your client will be found totally at fault if this matter goes to trial. A prompt and fair settlement will be beneficial to both parties.

    Because of the suffering my client endures daily, we are unwilling to engage in prolonged settlement negotiations. If we do not hear from you on or before July 1, ——, a lawsuit will be filed.

                                        Sincerely,

                                        DOWNING & PAVELSKI

                                        Barbara Pavelski

BP/cw

Enclosure
cc: Hasam Simsek

LETTER-WRITING TIPS

Many of the tips for enhancing writing in general apply to letter-writing also. The effectiveness of the communication will be greatly enhanced—and additional time, expense, and frustration will be avoided—if the following guidelines are kept in mind when writing letters:

- Write simply. Do not try to impress the reader by using words not in common usage or by drafting long and eloquent sentences. Writing simply will ensure that the communication will be understood.

- Visualize the reader. Even if you have never met the person to whom the letter is written, it is likely that the person's work environment is much like your own. Respect the time and responsibilities of the person to whom you are writing.

- Add personal touches to client letters. Because a relationship of trust is one of the most critical aspects of the relationship between the attorney and staff, and the client, building rapport with the client through correspondence will make the client feel part of the team. These personal touches should relate to the mission of the correspondence or the case. For example, in a letter confirming the scheduling of a deposition, a paragraph may be added that states: "Please remember to maintain your personal journal and let me know if you experience any new difficulties in using your fingers."

- Don't assume the reader knows what you need. When requesting information, be specific. X-rays, emergency room records, autopsy reports, and operating room records may not be included if the request simply asks for hospital records.

- Proofread the letter. If the letter is written on the computer, it is difficult to locate mistakes. To ensure that the correspondence of the firm promotes a professional image, it may be a good idea to set all letters aside until a certain point in the afternoon. Then proofread them, since typographical errors will more likely be discovered if the letters cool for a period of time, and send them out.

- Enclose enclosures. Time is wasted when the recipient of the letter has to call the firm to say that the enclosure is missing from the letter. This is another good reason to set aside all letters and review them later.

- Monitor correspondence. Maintain a calendar system. For every letter sent out requesting information, place a notation on the calendar to check whether a response was received. This check may be made twenty or thirty days after the letter is sent out. If no response has been received, a reminder letter or a follow-up telephone call may be appropriate. For every client experiencing a medical problem, place a notation to check with the client periodically. If the client has not communicated with the legal nurse consultant within twenty or thirty

Net Results

Writing Resources on the Internet

Web sites for assistance in writing include medical and legal dictionaries, legal citation, and legal forms. Access the Hosford Medical Terms Dictionary at www.ptcentral.com/university/medterms_zip.html. *An online search engine that includes more than 675,000 words in 120 dictionaries can be accessed at* www.onelook.com. *The Real Dictionary of the Law may be accessed at* www.law.com/students/index.html. *Additionally the World Wide Legal Information Association has a dictionary online that claims to explain legal terms in plain language. Access this site at* www.duhaime.org/dictc.htm. *Proper legal citation can be found in the resources section of* www.findlaw.com *and at* www.law.cornell.edu/citation/citation.table.html. *Links to legal forms are at* www.findlaw.com *and* www.westlegalstudies.com.

Ethics Bookmark

Fees

*"A lawyer's fee shall be reasonable" Annotated Model Rules of Professional Conduct Fourth Edition Rule 1.5(a) Copyright 1999 *[1] Many factors are considered in determining whether a fee is reasonable: the attorney's experience and reputation, the time involved, the case involved, and what is usually and customarily charged for similar services in the area where the attorney is located. Clients often complain about the high cost of a simple letter prepared by the attorney. Unless the bill has been padded or unless the item has been double billed, the fee to the client may be justified, based on the factors considered. If the attorney was traveling to a deposition on a case involving another client, billed that client for travel time, dictated the letter while traveling, and billed a second client for the time involved in dictating the letter, the attorney has engaged in unethical double-billing practices.*
*American Bar Association. Reprinted by permission of the American Bar Association. American Bar Association, *Annotated Model Rules of Professional conduct,* 4th ed. (1999) Rule 1.5(a). Copies of Model Code of Professional Responsibility, 1999 edition are available from Service Center, American Bar Association, 750 North Lake Shore Drive, Chicago, IL 60611-4497, 1-800-285-2221.

days, the legal nurse consultant may wish to write a letter inquiring about the injury, medical treatment, or condition of the client, or informing the client about the status of the case.

BUILDING RELATIONSHIPS THROUGH CORRESPONDENCE

Legal nurse consultants will find that they correspond regularly with the same individuals. To ensure that the business relationship between them is a positive one, legal nurse consultants should strive to draft letters with professional respect. When the treating physician must be deposed, it is far better to call the physician's office and request information about the physician's schedule two to three months in advance. Allowing the physician's office to reserve time for the deposition will show respect for the practice. Physicians are often scheduled for several months in advance and sending a notice only thirty days prior to the deposition will not enhance a working relationship between the law firm and the physician.

Medical records custodians will be more likely to respond quickly and kindly to an emergency request if the legal nurse consultant has developed a past practice of providing them with specific requests and sufficient time to respond. Respecting the time of medical librarians will also provide a foundation of professional courtesy that may be honored at a time when the legal nurse consultant is suddenly desperate for a certain piece of medical literature.

In the legal field, as in other areas of business, it is a good idea to avoid burning bridges. Becoming angry or belligerent will do little to advance the client's claim and may impede progress on future cases. Threatening, demanding, or offensive letters should always be avoided. Legal nurse consultants should strive to build working relationships based on mutual consideration. This will ensure that the future needs of the law firm will be accommodated with ease. Correspondence that is clear, to the point, and respectful of the recipient is the hallmark of a true professional.

TYPES OF LEGAL CORRESPONDENCE

Many different kinds of letters are written by lawyers and their staff. These letters have many purposes, including acquiring information, disclosing information, confirming information, rendering an opinion, and requesting settlement of a matter.

Acquiring Information

Numerous letters are written requesting information. These letters may be sent to the client, to health care providers, to treating physicians, to government agencies, to opposing attorneys, and to insurance companies. A letter may be written to the client asking for pre-injury photographs or to a health care facility requesting copies of medical records. Treating physicians are asked for reports on the condition of the patient/client. Letters to government agencies request copies of compliance reports and statistical reports. Information may be needed from opposing counsel concerning convenient times and places for depositions. Letters may be written to the insurance companies of the client to access the adjuster's investigation or the claims paid by insurance companies.

Disclosing Information

Status reports are often sent to the client and if the law firm is engaged in defense, to the insurance company. These letters update interested parties on the proceedings. Because it may take several months to complete the investigation of a personal injury claim, it is advisable to communicate regularly with the client, so the client doesn't think that his or her claim is being neglected. Sometimes it takes as long as six months to obtain medical records. Monthly communications with the client indicating that the firm is still waiting to receive those records and is pursuing other activities will enhance client relations.

Confirming Information

There are several reasons why it is advisable to write letters of confirmation. Letters provide a paper trail of verbal communications. Confirmation letters may also provide a checklist of the matters discussed and agreed to at a meeting or over the telephone. Confirmation letters remind clients and others of important meetings and what their responsibilities are in preparing for those meetings. A sample confirmation letter is included as Figure 27-6.

Rendering an Opinion

Attorneys render legal judgment and give advice and recommendations concerning legal action. Legal nurse consultants may assist attorneys in drafting letters that deal with medical-legal issues. An opinion letter is usually drafted from an interoffice memoranda, routinely prepared by the attorney's staff, concerning the law and the facts. The purpose of the opinion letter is to assist the client in making a decision about his or her legal rights. Thus, the letter rendering a legal opinion must be signed by the attorney.

Requesting Settlement of a Matter

It is usually in the best interests of the parties to try to settle the matter before going to court. Since plaintiff has started the action and has the burden of proof, the plaintiff is usually the one who initiates settlement negotiations. This is done through a vehicle known as the settlement demand letter. This letter may include a concise recitation of the liability issues, a brief description of the damages, and the amount of money that the plaintiff would be willing to accept in settlement of the matter.

When cases are complex or involve extensive damages, a **settlement brochure** may be prepared to support the claims of the plaintiff. A settlement brochure is based on full disclosure and expands on the demand letter. Included with the demand letter may be the accident report, medical reports, photographs, expert evaluations, and legal and medical authority supporting

---

FIGURE 27-6   Sample Confirmation Letter

Downing & Pavelski, S.C.
Attorneys at Law
101 Main Street
Madison, Wisconsin 53606

Patrick Downing, J.D.   602.781.1234
Barbara Pavelski, J.D.   fax: 602.781.1245

June 17, ——

Marie Lopez
1415 16th Street
Madison, WI 53606

Re: **CLAIM AGAINST A-1 MANUFACTURING**
      Our File No. 2000-CIV-167

Thank you for talking with me today concerning your injuries resulting from the use of the product manufactured by A-1 Manufacturing. This letter is to confirm your appointment to meet with Attorney Pavelski and me on Tuesday, July 28, ——, at 9:30 A.M. in our office.

To more fully evaluate your claim, please bring the following items (if available) to your appointment:

- The product that caused injury
- Insurance policies covering your medical expenses
- Names, addresses, and phone numbers of anyone who has knowledge of the incident or product causing injury
- Any photographs of the product or injuries
- Any newspaper reports concerning the incident or product causing injury
- Medical bills
- Employment information

We look forward to meeting with you. If you have any questions, please call me.

Erica Cheng, BSN, RN
Legal Nurse Consultant

the plaintiff's claim. Many attorneys believe that the settlement brochure communicates to the insurance company a strong faith in the foundation for the claims of liability against the defendant. Both the simple settlement demand letter and the settlement brochure are written in persuasive language. A sample settlement demand letter is included in Figure 27-7.

FIGURE 27-7 Sample Settlement Demand Letter

Downing & Pavelski, S.C.
Attorneys at Law
101 Main Street
Madison, Wisconsin 53606

Patrick Downing, J.D.   602.781.1234
Barbara Pavelski, J.D.   fax: 602.781.1245

February 23, ——

Robert Silver, Claims Attorney
General Insurance Company, Inc.
One GIC Road
P.O. Box 2002
St. Charles, IL 60174

Re: My client: Thao Von Dang
      Your Insured: Samuel Klein
      Date of Occurrence: August 4, ——
      Your Claim No. 00-4367

Dear Mr. Silver:

On August 4, ——, your insured's German Shepherd attacked my client, Thao Von Dang while Thao was in the park, playing with other children, and chasing a ball. The German Shepherd caught Thao by the hand and maintained a grip on Thao's hand, attempting to shake the child. If help had not been immediately available, it is believed that the dog would have bitten off Thao's fingers.

    The law in this state is well settled regarding liability of dog owners for injuries inflicted by their pets. Enclosed is a summary of cases involving unprovoked and unexpected attacks made by dogs against children. Your insured is liable for the actions of the dog and the resulting injuries to my client.

    Thao was taken to Local Hospital and treated in the emergency room by Dr. Brooks. The x-rays showed a displaced fracture. An IV was started. Increasing doses of intravenous Demerol were required in order to manage Thoa's pain. Thao was taken to surgery. Dr. Ackerman, an orthopedic surgeon, performed an open reduction; repair required placement of two pins.

continued

FIGURE 27-7   Sample Settlement Demand Letter   *continued*

Robert Silver
February 23, —
Page Two

Thao suffered a "Salter-Harris II" fracture of the proximal phalanx of the left long finger. The operative notes point out that the neuro vascular bundle on the ulnar side of the left long finger was intact but had been markedly stretched and irritated by the dog bite. In addition, there were crushing injuries at the base of the little ring and index finger secondary to teeth marks and lacerations over those regions.

On August 6, ——, Dr. Ackerman noted that Thao had some post surgical nausea and ran a temperature of 101 degrees on his first postoperative day. On the fourth day after the incident, Thao was discharged from the hospital and sent home with a cast on his hand. He was given medication for continued pain relief.

Thao was again seen by Dr. Ackerman at Orthopedics Unlimited on August 31, ——. At that time, the pins were removed. On September 1, at Local Hospital, Thao was seen for initial evaluation and a splint. On September 5, Thoa was seen by Celia Burnley at Local Medical Center Therapy Unit where it was noted that Thao was in the initial stages of recovery. Thao was again seen at Local Medical Center Therapy Unit where it was noted that his home therapy was successful and good compliance was reported.

On October 4, ——, Thao was seen again by Dr. Ackerman who noted that he had a good range of motion but that he still suffered from triggering in his left long finger. Thao received injections of Marcaine and Aristocort. Thao had intermediate visits to Dr. Ackerman where continued triggering of his left long finger was noted. Office notes indicate that Thao may need to have a trigger finger release at some future date. It was noted that there was good functional return of Thao's fingers with no growth plate difficulty. Dr. Ackerman's report is enclosed.

Enclosed is a summary of Thao's medical specials to date, totaling $13,976.20. Future treatment to deal with the triggering is anticipated, along with future plastic surgery to reduce the scarring to his hand. Thao recently consulted with a plastic surgeon, Dr. Longfellow. A copy of his analysis is enclosed.

In addition to the physical pain and disfigurement of my client, the treatment and anticipated future treatment, Thao has suffered lasting fear and emotional distress due to the vicious nature of the German Shepherd's attack. Thao was only seven years old at the time of the attack, and it is believed that his nightmares and his fear of dogs (and pets in general) will continue well into his adult life.

Considering the substantial trauma of the attack, the discomfort and duration of Thao's rehabilitation, the permanency and visibility of his scars, and the potential future medical intervention required, we would be willing to settle this matter for $70,000.00 Should this matter be settled through negotiation, we also demand that the necessary filing fees and other costs involved in obtaining court approval for this settlement on behalf of a minor be borne by your insured.

Robert Silver
February 23, —-
Page Three

We are ready to proceed with a lawsuit if we do not hear from you by March 15, ——.

Sincerely,

DOWNING & PAVELSKI

Barbara Pavelski

BP/cw

Enclosures
cc: Bee Von Dang

CORRESPONDENCE WRITTEN BY THE LEGAL NURSE CONSULTANT

In the previous chapter, you learned that legal nurse consultants engage in a great deal of legal correspondence. While not exhaustive, this correspondence is typically to communicate with or about the client, to acquire medical records, and to communicate with physicians and experts.

Communication With or About the Client

If the legal nurse consultant is employed in a referral firm, it may be the responsibility of the legal nurse consultant to meet initially with the client and communicate the client's potential claim to the attorney. A memorandum of the client interview may also be called an intake memo. The memorandum is drafted from notes taken during the interview, sometimes using a client questionnaire. The memorandum should include all of the information necessary for the attorney to make a judgment about whether the client has a justiciable claim. A form for an interoffice memorandum concerning an initial interview with a client is included in Figure 27-8.

Once the interview is complete, the legal nurse consultant should immediately draft the memorandum, along with a letter to the client thanking him or her, confirming later appointments, and identifying any additional information needed from the client.

What LNCs Say . . .

"Writing skills are generally not part of a nursing curriculum. This is an area where nurses are at a disadvantage and need to refine their skills" James Fell, RN, BSN, MSN, MBA, LNC, Bay Village, OH, used with permission.

FIGURE 27-8   Sample Interoffice Memorandum of Initial Consultation

Name:
Address: Daytime phone:
                                              Home phone:
Date of birth: SS#:
Spouse's name: Date of marriage:
Child(ren):   Date of birth:

Occupation:
Employer:

Date started employment with this employer:
Previous employers (if necessary):

Date of incident:
Parties involved, addresses, and phone numbers (if available):

Description of incident:

Weather (if appropriate):

Witnesses, addresses, and phone numbers (if available):

Factors affecting incident (traffic controls, conditions of parties, conditions of vehicles, road conditions, etc.):

Medical information:

Emergency treatment (at scene, transport, hospital, emergency room, etc.):

Postincident treatment:

Current symptoms, restrictions, pain, etc.:

Pre-incident health:

Insurance information:

Comments about client:

Notes for investigation:

If the attorney accepts the case and is retained by the client, the legal nurse consultant may enhance client relations by maintaining a calendar system and communicating regularly with the client. A phone call may be sufficient, but if the client has not received any correspondence from the firm for more than one month, a status letter should be written.

CORRESPONDENCE FOR ACQUIRING MEDICAL RECORDS

Once the client is brought on board, the legal nurse consultants will be expected to compile the medical records. To obtain medical records, the client/patient must sign an authorization to release medical information. Some health care providers will accept photocopies of this authorization, but it is a good idea to have the client sign several so original signed authorizations will be available if needed. A general medical authorization may not be sufficient to obtain records concerning sensitive information, such as alcoholism, drug addiction, or AIDS. Separate forms must be signed by the client to obtain these medical records. A sample medical authorization is included in Figure 27-9.

FIGURE 27-9   Sample Authorization for Release of Medical Records

AUTHORIZATION TO RELEASE MEDICAL RECORDS

I authorize the release of all medical records and bills relating to my health care, including any records involving alcohol and drug abuse, to

DOWNING & PAVELSKI, S.C.
Attorneys at Law
101 Main Street
Madison, Wisconsin

This authorization shall remain in effect until revoked by me in writing.

Dated:_____

_____
[signature]
[name of patient]
[date of birth]
[Social Security number]

It may be a good idea to phone the medical records librarian of the facility from whom you are requesting records to determine what fees will be charged and what information is necessary to acquire the records. Some states have regulatory or statutory language limiting the amount health care providers may charge for copies of medical records. At a minimum, the request for medical records should contain the following information:

- the complete name of the patient
- the date of birth or Social Security number of the patient
- the inclusive dates of treatment or hospitalization
- the records requested
- a check for the copy fee or a promise to pay upon receipt of an invoice

While many letters to health care records librarians request "any and all records" pertaining to the patient/client, it is often recommended that the letter identify and request all potential records that may be kept separate from the hospital record. These records may include emergency room records, surgical records, anesthesia records, pathology reports, and radiology reports. To avoid duplication of effort, it is wise to specify all potential records.

CORRESPONDENCE WITH PHYSICIANS AND EXPERTS

When the client/patient has been discharged by the physician or when the client's condition has stabilized, it will be necessary to obtain a report from the treating physician. This letter should be based on a detailed review of the medical records and the complaints of the client. Basically, the physician's report should deal with the prognosis, permanency, and pain or impairment associated with the client's injuries. A sample request for physician's report is included in Figure 27-10.

Additionally, legal nurse consultants often communicate with medical experts. The purpose of this correspondence is to provide the medical expert with all the relevant facts, usually through chronologies and summaries of documents, and to request an opinion concerning the medical-legal issue. The expert rendering the opinion may or may not be called to testify. If the expert is expected to testify, he or she must be a skilled educator. The jury will rely on expert testimony to make determinations of fact in medical negligence claims. Legal nurse consultants, through their correspondence and communication with experts, may help the litigation team decide which experts will be most able to clearly explain a medical protocol to a lay jury.

FIGURE 27-10   Sample Request for Physician Report

Downing & Pavelski, S.C.
Attorneys at Law
101 Main Street
Madison, Wisconsin 53606

Patrick Downing, J.D.   602.781.1234
Barbara Pavelski, J.D.   fax: 602.781.1245

December 14, ——

Lucia Ackerman, MD
Medical Arts Building, Suite 200
404 Harvey Lane
Madison, WI 53606

Re: Patient: Thao Von Dang
          Patient's date of birth: March 18, ——
          Date of first treatment: August 4, ——

Dear Dr. Ackerman:

Thao Von Dang was viciously attacked by a dog in the city park on August 4, ——. You subsequently treated Thao for injuries to his hand as a result of the attack. His father has retained our office to investigate the circumstances surrounding the attack and Thao's injuries.

To properly evaluate Thao's claim, we would appreciate a report from you concerning the following:

- The initial diagnosis of Thao's injuries
- A description of the treatment rendered
- Your prognosis for Thao's recovery and the likelihood of future medical intervention
- Your opinion as to any restrictions in movement, permanent scarring, or impairment of Thao's hand or physical abilities, and how this restriction, scarring, or impairment will impact Thao's life
- A description of the pain or discomfort associated with this injury

An authorization to release medical information is enclosed.

Please bill our office for your services in preparing this report. If you have any questions, feel free to contact us. Thank you for your cooperation in this matter.

Sincerely,

DOWNING & PAVELSKI

Barbara Pavelski

BP/cw

Enclosure
cc: Bee Von Dang

CHAPTER SUMMARY

- Before drafting correspondence, the legal nurse consultant should take time to consider the purpose of the communication and who will receive it.
- Most business letters include the date, inside address, reference line, salutation, body of the letter, closing, signature, and end notations, although contemporary style allows omission of the salutation and closing.
- Letter styles include full block, modified block, and modified semi-block.
- Legal nurse consultants will be appreciated for their letter-writing skills.

KEY TERMS

full block
complimentary closing

modified block
modified semi-block

salutation
settlement brochure

REVIEW QUESTIONS

1. Identify the component parts of a business letter.
2. What tips will help legal nurse consultants draft effective business communications?
3. How may legal nurse consultants build relationships using letters?

INTERNET EXERCISES

1. Access the web page for this textbook at *www.westlegalstudies.com.*
2. Click on the assignments section and complete the assignment(s) for Chapter Twenty-seven.

EXERCISES

1. Networking. Using the standard of care you located for Chapter Twenty-seven, draft a letter to the fictional attorney who requested that information. If you have time, cross check this standard of care with textbooks or other medical literature to support your description of the standard of care.
2. Professional Portfolio. Make copies of the sample documents in this chapter or draft letters of your own using the different styles of letter writing. Use computer aids to make this process easier. Maintain these copies in your systems folder, file, or binder, and organize or index them for easy reference.

ENDNOTES

1. American Bar Association, *Annotated Model Rules of Professional Conduct,* (1994) 4th Edition. Rule 1.5(a). Copies of ABA *Model Code of Professional Responsibility, 1999 Edition* are available from Service Center, American Bar Association, 750 North Lake Shore Drive, Chicago, IL 60611-4497, 1-800-285-2221.

ADDITIONAL REFERENCES

Barber, S. *Legal Writing, Second Edition.* Albany, NY: West Thomson Learning, 1997.

Bogart, J. B., RN MN, ed. *Legal Nurse Consulting: Principles and Practices.* Boston: CRC Press, 1998.

CHAPTER 28

MEDICAL SUMMARIES

OBJECTIVES

In this chapter, you will discover

- the purposes of medical summaries

- why medical summaries are considered attorney work product

- the steps in the medical summary process

- the types of medical summaries that are prepared by legal nurse consultants

OVERVIEW

The primary function of the legal nurse consultant is to assimilate medical information into a legal format. For the beginning legal nurse consultant facing stacks and stacks of medical information, this may seem a monumental task. Approached in a systematic fashion, acquiring, assembling, summarizing, and customizing medical summaries is relatively easy to manage. The first step is a review of the file in order to understand the issues in the claim. If the lawsuit has begun, this may involve a review of the pleadings, that is, the complaint and answer. If the lawsuit has not yet commenced, a review of the intake memo or an initial conference with the claimant will provide the background necessary to initiate a records search and summary. If the legal nurse consultant is working as an independent contractor, it may be useful to request copies of these documents before approaching the medical summaries.

There are many reasons why the medical records must be organized and summarized:

- to condense mountains of information into logical format
- to access medical information quickly
- to see at a glance the medical facts and treatments of the client/patient
- to educate the legal team on the medical issues in the claim
- to establish a chronological flowchart of incidents following the injury and preceding the injury to determine if there are any preexisting conditions
- to identify issues that require a review of medical literature or the evaluation of experts
- to provide medical specialists and vocational experts with complete information in a format that is easily verifiable
- to facilitate the correlation and comparison of medical information, such as physicians orders, medication, graphic sheets, diagnostic procedures, and medical bills
- to assist in the development of exhibits for depositions and at trial
- to evaluate the claim

Once the legal nurse consultant is familiar with the case, the purpose of the medical summary should be ascertained. If the summary will be used by experts, it may be more technically precise than if it will be used to educate the legal team. If it is to be used as an exhibit at trial, it may be prepared in a way that educates a lay jury. Knowing how the summary will be used will facilitate its efficient and cost-effective preparation.

The circumstances of the legal situation will determine how extensive the medical summaries must be. For example, in a personal injury action involving an automobile accident, the attorney may be interested in the medical injuries and in the past and future medical treatment. The attorney might also want to know about other losses sustained by the client and their relationship to any previous health conditions. It may not be necessary to acquire hospital policy documents; pharmaceutical records, for potential drug interactions; or informed consent information. In a claim involving health care negligence, however, considerably more documentation may be required. What medical records to request will be apparent from a review of the file and a discussion with the attorney. The legal nurse consultant is the expert concerning the medical information and may recommend to the attorney that certain records be acquired in addition to the ones that the attorney has identified. Many attorneys give legal nurse consultants *carte blanche* in deciding which medical records must be acquired.

ATTORNEY WORK PRODUCT

The medical summaries and other documents the legal nurse consultant prepares for a case are considered **attorney work product.** Attorney work product is loosely defined as theories, conclusions, and working papers that help the attorney develop strategies for a case. If a document is classified as attorney work product, it is generally not available to the other party during discovery. This privilege extends to all lay staff and independent contractors of the attorney. The attorney work product rule does not apply if the summary is going to be used at trial as a trial exhibit.

To ensure the nondisclosure of attorney work product, some firms use a heading on those documents. The heading may read "ATTORNEY WORK PRODUCT—DO NOT DISCLOSE CONTENTS OF THIS DOCUMENT." The beginning legal nurse consultant might want to ask whether this protective heading should be included on documents he or she prepares.

STEPS IN THE MEDICAL SUMMARY PROCESS

There are four basic stages in the process of developing medical summaries and several steps the legal nurse consultant must take in order to have complete and comprehensive medical information. The four stages are acquiring the records, assembling them, analyzing and summarizing them, and following up on matters identified during the record review. Figure 28-1 shows the stages and steps in the medical summary process.

Acquisition

It is well established that medical records are owned by the facility in which they were prepared, but the patient has a right to the information contained in those records. As a result, authorization to release medical records is essential to their acquisition or review. See Chapter Twenty-seven for a sample authorization. Even though the patient/client signs a release of all medical information,

---

Ethics Bookmark

Withdrawal

"[A] lawyer . . . shall withdraw from the representation of a client if: the representation will result in violation of the rules of professional conduct of other law" Annotated Model Rules of Professional Conduct, Fourth Edition Rule 1.16(a)(1) Copyright 1999. *[1]* *Sometimes clients exaggerate their medical illnesses, believing that by continuing to seek treatment they will enhance their chances of a considerable settlement. Attorneys must counsel clients that to fabricate disability or illness is fraudulent. Attorneys are prohibited from participating in fraudulent conduct. If a legal nurse consultant finds that the client is not being altogether straightforward regarding his or her medical claim, the legal nurse consultant must bring this to the attention of the attorney.*

*American Bar Association. Reprinted by permission of the American Bar Association. American Bar Association, *Annotated Model Rules of Professional conduct*, 4th ed. (1999) Rule 1.16(a)(1). Copies of Model Code of Professional Responsibility, 1999 edition are available from Service Center, American Bar Association, 750 North Lake Shore Drive, Chicago, IL 60611-4497, 1-800-285-2221.

FIGURE 28-1   Stages and Steps in the Medical Summaries Process

State of Process	Steps Taken
Acquisition	• Identify records to acquire • Ensure that the records are comprehensive and complete • Watch for altered and missing records • Note needed document that may only be acquired through discovery
Assembly	• Separate by health care provider • Organize for ease of review • Tab and paginate • Code for ease of reference
Analysis	• Draft chronological overview • Prepare interoffice memo with analysis • Note additional summaries, analysis, or medical research that may be undertaken
Follow up	• Compare treatment with textbook or standards of care • Review medical literature • Locate medical experts

---

health care providers may not release certain sensitive information without the patient/client's specific authorization. These sensitive areas include alcohol and drug treatment, HIV testing, testing for sexually transmitted diseases, and mental health records.

Certain records may only be obtained during discovery and certain records may not be obtainable. Incident reports by health care professionals concerning accidents, departures from routine, or mistakes may be obtained after litigation has begun. Upon receipt of a request, or demand, to produce the document, the health care facility must comply or face court sanctions. If the document was prepared for the legal department of the facility, it might not be discoverable. It would be considered attorney work product—a document prepared in anticipation of litigation. Documents related to peer review are generally not obtainable, nor is it possible to obtain information from the National Practitioner Data Bank. Health care facilities are required to report adverse licensure or professional review actions to the data bank, as well as any payments made as a result of health care negligence claims. While health care facilities are required to consult the data bank before granting privileges to a health care practitioner, this information is not available to the public.

The legal nurse consultant has two options for acquiring medical records: review the records personally at the facility, making copies of those that he or she considers critical, or requesting the facility to provide certified copies of the records. Requesting copies from the facility is the most frequently used

---

FIGURE 28-2   Sample Certification

State of ————)
) ss.
County of ———)

     I certify that I am the records manager at [health care facility]. The attached are true and correct copies of the medical records relating to [name of patient] prepared and maintained in the ordinary course of business by [health care facility].

Dated: _____

                                     _____
                                     [signature]
                                     [name of records manager]

     Subscribed and sworn to before me this _____ day of _____ , _____

                                     _____
                                     Notary Public
                                     My commission expires: _____

---

option and may be the most convenient way to acquire the medical records. If the copies are certified to be true and correct copies of the original documents in the facility, they are admissible in court. Thus, it is advisable to request certified copies. Many records managers in large health care facilities are Registered Records Administrators (RRAs) through the American Health Information Management Association. They are familiar with certification and will provide the appropriate certificate with the copies. For other health care facilities, it may be necessary to include a certificate for signature by the provider of the records. A sample Certification of Medical Records is included in Figure 28-2.

The Joint Commission for the Accreditation of Healthcare Organizations requires two components of hospital records: the admission record and the clinical record. The admission or administrative record may include consent forms, admission information, and a statement indicating the diagnosis and procedures performed. The clinical record may include a summary sheet, patient history, physical examination, physician order sheets, physician notes, diagnostic reports, nurses notes, graphic sheets, and medication and treatment sheets.

It is incumbent upon the legal nurse consultant to ensure that the medical records acquired are comprehensive. The initial conference with the client or a review of the file will identify the facilities from which records should be

FIGURE 28-3   Sample Health Care Record Checklist

SINCLAIR CONSULTING
Laura M. Sinclair, RN, BSN, LNC
1419 South Midpark Drive
Appleton, Wisconsin 54915
(920)954-6859

HEALTHCARE RECORD CHECKLIST
(PATIENT NAME)
(CASE NUMBER)
(DATE OF INJURY/CLAIM/ACCIDENT)

INJURIES
1. Right wrist fracture
2. Bruised left knee
3. Whiplash injury

FACILITY:	DATES OF SERVICE:	REQUESTED:	RECEIVED:
1. Clinic	09/27/83 to 05/01/98		
2. Dr. G	12/22/87 to present		
3. Dr. F	07/07/97 to 08/07/97		
4. Clinic of	12/01/87 to 09/26/96		
5. Dr. H	12/01/87 to 09/26/96		
6. Dr. L	09/15/97 to present		
7. Medical center	10/13/95 to 02/26/98		
8. Medical center	06/25/95 to 07/25/97		

Reprinted by permission of Laura M. Sinclair, President, Sinclair Consulting.

sought. A quick review of these records, as they come in, will provide clues to additional health care providers that records should be obtained from. Additionally, legal nurse consultants should be alert to the possibility that the records provided by the facility may not be complete. Certain records may not be maintained with the other records or may have been completed and filed after the records manager complied with the request. Monitoring this comprehensive record collection may be the responsibility of the legal nurse consultant. A valuable aid to monitoring the collection of medical records may be a checklist of health care providers. This checklist will provide the legal nurse consultant with an overview of which records have been requested and which have been received. A sample checklist is included in Figure 28-3.

Some records may not be obtained from the facility because they are not owned by them. Ambulance records, outpatient therapy or rehabilitation, autopsy reports, pharmaceutical records, home health care records, and original radiography films are examples of records that may not be included in response to a request for medical records from a health care facility. The legal nurse consultant may have to make additional or separate requests for these documents.

As the records are accumulated and initially reviewed, the legal nurse consultant may become aware that certain records appear to be altered or that certain records are missing. Clues suggesting a record has been altered include

- long, narrative written descriptions that purport to cover a considerable period of time but appear to have been written at the same time by the same person
- late entries that do not appear to conform to policies for late entries
- typewritten additions to the record that do not seem to conform to standard record preparation or that bear dates that do not conform to the remainder of the record
- notes that are written over

Legal nurse consultants should approach every set of records with a certain amount of healthy suspicion. If it appears that records have been altered, this suspicion should be brought to the attention of the attorney and the original records should be reviewed. Altering records is a serious legal offense for which court sanctions and sometimes criminal penalties may be applied.

Before concluding that a record is missing, the legal nurse consultant should carefully page through the entire record. The record that appears to be missing may simply have been misplaced in the file. The stray record may be found later in the file, retrieved, and properly placed without making an additional request to the health care facility. Because the record is not included does not give rise to an inference of negligence or bad faith. The missing record may have been the result of a misfiling at the health care facility or an inadvertent copy error. If after requesting the missing record that the legal nurse consultant believes must have been prepared, the records manager denies the existence of the record, the nonexistence of this record should be documented. The absence should also be reported to the attorney. Destruction of records is another serious legal offense for which sanctions and criminal penalties may be applied.

Some medical records that do not contain information concerning the patient's health care are still pertinent to the action. These documents are prepared in the regular course of business but are not part of the patient record. Emergency room logs and operating room logs are two examples. If the legal nurse consultant believes that these records are important to evaluation of the claim, a note should be made to obtain these documents during discovery.

Assembly

Prior to any review, the necessary medical records must be assembled into a logical sequence. It is often recommended that the records of health care providers be maintained separately. All records are tabbed and paginated but the physician's or HMO's records are separated from the hospital records, the physical therapy records, and so forth.

Organizing the records to facilitate review is critical. Besides arranging the records chronologically, they may be sequenced or grouped in a way that aids analysis. You may find it easiest to organize records using the financial statements first and cross checking documents with bills. Alternatively, you might organize and analyze by type of report, so you would review all the laboratory tests, pathology reports, or office calls at the same time. Hospital records may be organized in the order identified in the section on acquisition of medical records. Each legal nurse consultant will find a system of organization that facilitates his or her personal analysis style.

The first look at the records should be to ensure that all the information requested has been received. Additionally, as the first review progresses, it may become apparent that certain records must exist but were not initially requested. These records should be obtained and placed in the collection in an order that facilitates a logical and sequential review. How the records are ordered may depend on the issues in the claim. For example, in a case involving an automobile accident that caused injury to a client, medical records may be organized to include the important records concerning diagnosis, prognosis, and impairment. Anesthesia records and surgical records may not be critical and may be placed later in the collection. After the summaries are prepared, the attorney might want to have these noncritical documents removed from the collection as not bearing on the issue of damages.

Three-ring binders are often used for collection and assembly of medical records. Because three-hole punching may remove critical information, some legal nurse consultants prefer to collect records in file folders fastened with Acco two-hole-punch metal fasteners at the top of the documents. Divider tabs are used to distinguish the records of one provider from the records of another provider. If the records are voluminous, it may be wise to keep the records for each provider in a separate three-ring binder or folder. The binders/folders may be color-coded and the pagination may identify the binder and the record. For example, the medical summary might refer to the location of the record as R-26, which would be interpreted to mean the red binder on page 26.

Once the records have been collected and determined to be complete, they should be paginated for ease of reference. The records may already have page numbers on them, so it may be necessary to identify the law firm's pagination system by circling the page number or using a Bate stamp system to distinguish it from the provider's system of pagination. Paginating is necessary for referencing the medical documents in the summaries prepared by the legal nurse consultant, for retrieval of the appropriate record during a deposition or at trial, and for supplying complete information to the medical specialists or other experts that may be needed in the case.

By collecting, tabbing, and paginating the records, the legal nurse consultant will gain an initial insight into critical components of the client's claim.

This first impression will assist the legal nurse consultant in the second step of the process, which is to review the record and draft the medical summaries.

Analysis

The medical summaries must be organized in a way that will be useful for the legal team, particularly the attorney. Having a general overview of the records from the process of collecting, tabbing, and paginating them, the legal nurse consultant will already have an idea of how to organize the information. The office may have used a spreadsheet-type organization in previous cases. The beginning legal nurse consultant should review the documents generated in closed files to see how this medical information has been formatted.

At a minimum, the medical summaries will include a chronological overview of the medical records, an interoffice memo to the attorney providing the analysis required, and notations concerning the legal nurse consultant's recommendations and additional information. These notations may also be in the form of a memo to the file or to investigators, paralegals, or the attorney. The notations might include the need for medical literature review or expert opinion, suspicion of alteration of records, or investigation of potential defenses, such as patient noncompliance or use of cultural remedies.

Chronological Overview. The **chronological overview** of the medical records should include the date (and the time in cases where surgical procedures went wrong or in bad birth or bad baby cases), a reference to the facility record, and a short summary of the medical information in that record. This overview may include extraneous entries, such as a visit to the physician because of cold or flu symptoms. Still, all information contained in the medical records should be noted in the chronology. The physician may have prescribed Tylenol Codeine for the cough and cold symptoms of a patient with a history of drug or alcohol abuse. This may have indications for potential causation or contributory negligence in an automobile collision case. If the legal nurse consultant does not include all aspects of the record in the initial summary, it is certain that the other side will! Once discovered, the opposing side will use every means to develop that information into an issue. The legal team needs to be prepared for such tactics.

The chronological overview is important for developing a timeline of the damages or injuries in question, for extracting critical information for use in later summaries, for educating the legal team on the progression and outcomes of the treatments, and for developing exhibits for use at depositions and trial. It is a necessary first step in the writing of medical summaries. A sample chronological overview is included in Figure 28-4.

Included with the chronological overview or any medical record summary should be a list of abbreviations. This will save the attorney and other legal professionals considerable time since they will not have to go to another source to decipher the abbreviations. A sample list of abbreviations is included in Figure 28-5.

FIGURE 28-4 Health and Record Summary

SINCLAIR CONSULTING
Laura M. Sinclair, RN, BSN, LNC
1419 South Midpark Drive
Appleton, Wisconsin 54915
(920)954-6859

HEALTHCARE RECORD SUMMARY
(PATIENT NAME)
(CASE NUMBER)
DATE OF INJURY: 06-25-95

Prepared by: L. Sinclair, RN, LNC   Date: 01-04-00

DATE:	FACILITY:	DOCUMENTATION:
09/27/83 to 12/02/85	Clinic	Chronic depression, alcohol abuse, Xanax overdose, suicidal ideation, migraines. H/O right scapular discomfort treated with ASA and Motrin. Obesity. Iron deficiency anemia following gastric bypass surgery. Mild DJD right ankle. Pedal edema. Recurrent groin cysts. Dr. N. (1036-35).
07/18/86	Clinic	EMG to rule out lumbar disc disease. Within normal limits. Dr. M. (1045-46).
09/04/86 to 11/06/87	Clinic	Left knee F/U after steroid injection. Temporary relief. Early DJD. Moderate tenderness along lateral aspect of left knee. B12 shot for anemia. Dr. M. (1024-25).
12/01/87	Dr. H	Left knee pain positional. Peroneal nerve entrapment. Recommend arthroscopy and release. (4009, 5006).
12/22/87	Dr. G	Second opinion on left knee surgery. Chronic pain involving lateral side of left upper tibial region. Burning sensation, worse at night. Can't lie on left side. PE negative. Symptoms point to nerve entrapment. Recommend arthroscopy. (2003).
01/11/88	Dr. H	Pre-op H+P. Dr. N. (5014-16).
01/14/88	Dr. H	OR report. Peroneal nerve entrapment syndrome. (4006, 5022).
01/26/88	Dr. H.	F/U surgery. Has not had a dramatic response but is as expected. F/U in 4 more weeks. (4008, 5007).
02/19/88	Dr. H	Doing well until increased activity. Probable irritation only. Motrin. (4008, 5007).
12/16/88	Dr. H	Pain in the right foot, TTP. Recommend bone scan. (4008, 5007).
12/27/88	Dr. H	Bone scan negative for stress fracture. Pain right foot, mild DJD bilaterally. (4005, 5021)
01/06/89	Dr. H	Right foot pain continues. Steroid injection. No further diagnosis can be made at this time. (4009, 5007).

05/14/92	Dr. H	Right heel pain, plantar fascitis, steroid injection. (4010, 5007).
08/11/92	Dr. H	Plantar fascitis recurred with pain in mid foot and ankle. Ankle swollen, heel very tender, repeat injection. Ankle and foot pain probably secondary to positioning to relieve heel pain. (4010, 5008).
10/12/93	Dr. H	Continued heel pain. Refer to Dr. Mitchell. (4011, 5009).
06/25/96	Med. Ctr.	County rescue report. A+O driver in 55 mph MVA. Hit by car pulling out from stop sign. Complained of neck, right wrist, and bilateral knee pain. No deformity noted. CMS checks WNL. Transported to Medical Center. (8000).
06/25/95	Med. Ctr.	ER assessment. Complained of right wrist and neck pain. Impact on driver's side front and car spun around. Complained of H/A, left knee pain. Immobilizer on, right wrist splinted. Discharged to home with husband. (8001).
06/26/95	Med. Ctr.	ER report. Head atraumatic. Chest and abdomen negative. C-spine XR negative. Diagnosis: mild right wrist trauma. Treatment for right wrist included splint and ice. Immobilizer and crutches with TTWB for the left knee. Off work until see by Dr. B. Dr. H. (8002-3).
06/25/95	Med. Ctr.	XR left knee shows moderate degenerative arthritis of patellar femoral joint with effusion. (8006). XR C-spine negative. (8007). XR right wrist shows chip fracture at dorsum of wrist and moderate degenerative narrowing of the first carpal metacarpal joint. (8007).
06/29/95	Dr. G	47 yo nursing assistant. MVA this past weekend. Someone pulled out in front of her. Neck pain better. Pain right hand and left knee. Bruising and crepitus in front of left patella. Diffuse swelling right wrist. XR shows degenerative arthritis at base of thumb, carpal metacarpal joint with small avulsion fracture. Also small avulsion fracture at dorsal aspect of the lunate. Treated with pop-up wrist splint. XR left knee shows degenerative arthritis in the lateral facet of the patella, aggravated by the dashboard injury. Off work one additional week, PT. (2003).
07/17/95	Dr. G	Gradually improving. Soreness anterior aspect of left knee, particularly with stairs and kneeling. Wrist somewhat sore. RTW. RTC in 3 months. (2002).
08/29/95	Dr. H	MVA. Initially remembers injuries to the right wrist, left knee and whiplash. Small fracture right wrist. Knee symptoms persist with stair climbing. Right wrist improved. ER films of left knee show degenerative changes of the lateral facet of the patella. Accident could not have caused all injuries present in the patella. Previous patellar dysplasia present. Has developed whiplash symptoms over the last 2 mos. Burning cervical pain radiating to the right scapula. Difficulty looking up. XR today (−). C-spine strengthening exercises. MRI if symptoms persist. (4011, 4013, 5009-10).
09/11/95	Med. Ctr.	Outpatient PT eval. for neck pain. Complained of burning intermittent spasms aggravated by lifting head. Occasional H/A. MVA in June. Pain increased one mos. later. Decreased flexion and pain with extension of neck. HEP given. (8013-15).

continued

FIGURE 28-4   Health and Record Summary   *continued*

10/03/95	Dr. H	Neck unchanged. Radiculopathy at C6-7. MRI to rule out pathology on C6-7 left side. Has had tennis elbow symptoms in the past. XR did not show pre-existing cervical disk disease. Any abnormal findings of MRI at C6-7 would be accident related. (4013, 5010).
10/13/95	Dr. H	MRI negative at C6-7. Minimal disc bulging at C5-6. No surgery warranted. (4013, 5010, 7027).
10/30/95	Clinic	Physical. MVA this summer. Fractured right wrist and whiplash. MRI abnormalities. PT ineffective. Slowly improving on own. 60# weight loss on protein sparing diet. Weight regained. Occasional recurrence of depression. Prozac. Iron and B12 deficiency. Arthroscopy and exploration of peroneal nerve entrapment 1988. Weight 232#. Residual cervical whiplash symptoms. Left arm symptoms. Labs: hemogram, B12, TSH, chem panel. Dr. N. (1022-23).
11/16/95	Clinic	F/U on labs. Low hemoglobin. Oral iron and B12 started. Dr. N. (1021-22).
11/21/95	Dr. H	MRI negative. Still has symptoms of left shoulder and elbow pain. XR to R/O rotator cuff damage negative. Continued trouble with patella. Accident 3–4 mos. ago. Premature to investigate further. Allow time to heal. (4012-13, 5010-11).
02/06/96	Dr. H	Symptoms unchanged. EMG. (4012, 5011).
02/13/96	Dr. H	EMG. MVA 1995. Cervical muscle spasms with pain into left tricep area, approximately 1 month after MVA. Numbness and tingling to left hand. Occasional symptoms to right hand but to a lesser degree. Results of EMG show no evidence of cervical radiculopathy. Carpal tunnel syndrome left, mild carpal tunnel syndrome right. (4003-4, 5018-19).
03/01/96	Clinic	Lab repeat, migraines, no other complaints. Dr. N. (1021).
03/07/96	Clinic	Lab F/U. Microcytic anemia. Most likely malabsorption secondary to gastric bypass. Also irregular prolonged menses. Menopausal. Colonoscopy scheduled to R/O cancer. Dr. N. (1020-21).
04/09/96	Clinic	OB physical. Discussed gynecological surgery to help with menses. PE WNL. Dr. L. (1019-20).
04/29/96	Clinic	Family MD visit. Discussed gynecological surgery. Carpal tunnel surgery with Dr. H. Dr. N. (1018-19).
05/02/96 to 07/17/96	Clinic	Endometrial ablation procedure. OB F/U visit. Dr. D. (1017-18).
05/02/96	Dr. H	EMG suggests carpal tunnel as reason for left arm symptoms. No cervical radiculopathy found. Surgery for carpal tunnel release recommended. Right wrist may improve on own if left is done. Difficult to call carpal tunnel syndrome work related. Patient will wait a couple of months and decide on surgery. (4012, 4014, 5011-12, 7022-23).

09/17/96	Clinic	Depression. Resurfacing symptoms in the past year. Decreased self-esteem. Not suicidal. Resume Prozac. Dr. N. (1016-17).
09/24/96		Continue iron and B12 supplements. Dr. N. (1016).
09/26/96	Dr. H	F/U left arm. Surgery recommended for carpal tunnel release. (4014, 5012).
10/22/96	Clinic	Depression improved. Pain right elbow increased with gripping and lifting arm. Lateral epicondylitis (tennis elbow). Splint, ice, and conservative measures. Steroid injection possible. Dr. N. (1015-16).
01/07/97	Clinic	OB checkup. WNL. Dr. D. (1015).
02/10/97	Clinic	F/U depression. Needs to address alcoholism. F/U with Dr. G. Prozac. Trazadone for sleep. Menopausal. Dr. N. (1014-15).
03/10/97	Clinic	Depression, alcoholism, wheezing. Sleeping better, gastritis improved. Appointment with alcohol counselor. Slight asthma. Inhaler. Dr. N. (1012-14).
07/14/97	Dr. F	Left lateral epicondylitis. Pain radiates to left bicep and forearm. Work involves a lot of use of these muscles and aggravates symptoms. Also carpal tunnel syndrome with surgery recommended. Patient looking for non-surgical treatment. Steroid injection given. Off work until next week. (3008).
07/17/97	Med. Ctr.	XR left elbow negative. (8017).
07/21/97	Dr. F	F/U left elbow. Much relief. Full ROM. Begin PT, including heat and US. RTW but no use of the left arm. RTC 1 wk. (3007).
07/24/97	Dr. F	Increased intensity and frequency of migraines. Worse since MVA. Has snapping sensation in the neck. Denies radiating pain. H/A exacerbated by stress and caffeine. TTP in trapezius muscle and occipital nerve bilaterally. MRI 1995 shows no herniation but bulging at C5-6. H/A is migraine and tension in nature. Pain coming from neck. Repeat MRI. (3005-6).
07/25/97	Med. Ctr.	MRI of the brain. Questionable MS. Need clinical correlation. MRI of the C-spine notes degenerative changes at the epifacet joint of C5-6. Negative disc herniation. (8018).
07/28/97	Dr. F	F/U chronic neck pain and H/A. H/O migraine with aura. Neck pain with radiation to triceps and shoulders bilaterally. Occasional N+T of fingers bilaterally. H/O carpal tunnel syndrome. MRI 7/97 shows possible multiple sclerosis and degenerative changes at C5-6. No disc herniation noted. PE reveals full ROM, TTP over trapezius. Treatment: stretch techniques to trapezius muscle. TPI ×2 with excellent pain relief. F/U with Dr. B. regarding MRI findings. (3002-3).
08/07/97	Dr. F	F/U. Overall much better. Feels neck pain leads to H/A. Stretched left trapezius and tricep. TPI ×4. RTW may exacerbate symptoms. Patient wishes to RTW without restrictions. (3011-12).

continued

FIGURE 28-4   **Health and Record Summary**   *continued*

08/18/97	Clinic	Neuro clinic visit. H/O H/A for past 30 yrs. Left arm pain. Increased frequency since June 1997. Tylenol decreases intensity. Caffeine aggravates. LUE pain for the past year, a dull ache. Left hand is weak and falls asleep. Pt. is left-handed. Orthopedic surgeon recommended carpal tunnel release. Sister-in-law had had experience with such and ended up with disability. Pain goes down posterior forearm. Also c/o bilateral neck and shoulder aches. Some TPI with relief in the past. Cervical ROM is slightly painful. Denies radiating pain. No aggravation with coughing or sneezing. Internal rotation and abduction increase pain. Tennis elbow left side diagnosed previously. Cortisone shot ineffective. Medical history includes nervous person with depression, esophageal reflux, migraines, mild asthma, arthritis, rheumatic fever. PE: Wt. 242#, Tinel and Phalen sign positive bilaterally, worse on left than right. Diagnosis: migraines with aura, bilateral carpal tunnel syndrome with referred pain to LUE, possible analgesic abuse, questionable C6 radiculopathy. Treatment for migraines. Carpal tunnel release surgery. Dr. M. (1010-12).
09/15/97	Dr. L	PT therapy note. Bilateral medical epicondylitis. Bilateral carpal tunnel syndrome. US, heat. Evaluation for orthosis. Patient c/o high pain level to left elbow rating 8/10. Right elbow 2/10. Full ROM. Numbness in digits at night, difficulty with heavy ADL tasks. Nursing assistant and elbow pain increases when turning or transporting patients. Plan therapy at clinic closer to home. (6010).
09/15/97	Dr. L	Letter from Dr. L to Dr. M. States bilateral wrist and arm pain is not due to the right wrist fracture in the MVA. Unable to state conclusively that the MVA did not contribute to the current problems. PE: decreased sensation in the medial nerve distribution. Positive Tinel and Phalen sign. Full ROM to neck, shoulder, elbow and small joints of the hand. No evidence of proximal radiculopathy or compression neuropathy. Bilateral carpal tunnel syndrome and medial epicondylitis. Therapy with splinting, surgery and steroid injection prn. (6005-6).
10/13/97	Dr. L	F/U carpal tunnel syndrome. Also has CMC joint osteoarthritis and medial epicondylitis. Feel surgery is warranted but epicondyle pain would not improve. N+T of hands would. Possible steroid injection at time of surgery to lateral epicondyle. (6004).
11/20/97	Clinic	Depression. Increase Prozac. Dr. B. (1009).
01/29/98	Dr.L	F/U. Wishes to have carpal tunnel surgery. Lengthy discussion regarding causation. MVA but unclear if this lead to underlying condition. Fractured right wrist in MVA, now has carpal tunnel syndrome. Cannot comment on causation. Scheduled for surgery. (6004).

02/20/98	Dr. L	H+P. Left carpal tunnel syndrome and medial epicondylitis. N+T in hand with pain in left elbow. Conservative treatment ineffective. EMG positive for carpal tunnel syndrome. Decompression of medial nerve with injection of the medial epicondyle. Scheduled for surgery. (6008, 7010).
02/26/98	Dr.L	OR report. No complications. (6007, 7012).
02/26/98	Med. Ctr.	Day surgery. D/C instructions, Vicodin for pain. (7006). MD notes. (7007-9). Perioperative records (7013-18).
03/12/98	Clinic	H/O gastritis, esophageal reflux, gastric bypass for obesity, possible NIDDM, ruptured tendon right foot, cervical muscle spasm, alcoholism. Current meds include Prilosec, Prozac, Prempro, Atenolol, Trazadone and Flexeril. Dr. B. (1007-8).
03/13/98	Dr. L	F/U. Much improvement. N+T much better. RTC 6–8 wks. (6003).
04/02/98	Clinic	OB GYN F/U. WNL. Dr. D. (1010).
05/01/98	Clinic	Facial rash. Synalar cream. MVA 1995 "side-swiped," MRI revealed bulge in the disc. Repeat MRI normal. C/O discomfort in the LUE, shoulder and neck region since MVA. Left carpal tunnel release surgery. Off work for a number of weeks. Two orthopedic surgeons confirmed diagnosis. Patient denies pain in the wrist or fingers. RTW. Return of left lateral neck and posterior scapular pain and left lateral epicondyle pain. Taking Darvocet at HS. Low blood sugar episode. Family H/O NIDDM. Past medical history of depression, eczema, possible NIDDM. Patient to continue weight loss and diet restrictions. Suggest orthopedic re-evaluation, possible repeat injection for LUE pain. Referral to Dr. L. Dr. B. (1004-5).
05/08/98	Dr. L	F/U. Happy with results. Complains now of neck and upper shoulder and arm pain. Referred to primary physician. Suggest ortho or neurosurgical eval. (6003).

Reprinted by permission of Laura M. Sinclair, President, Sinclair Consulting.

Analysis Memo. Once the chronology has been prepared, the legal nurse consultant will draft a memo to the attorney containing a preliminary **analysis** of the medical condition, for purposes of damages, or the errors and omissions of diagnosis and/or treatment, for purposes of health care liability. Because this memo will be the springboard for everything else that is done relative to the medical issues in the claim, it must be drafted with precision and professional integrity. A sample analysis memo is included in Figure 28-6.

It is often suggested that the opening paragraph of the memo identify the issue and the brief analysis made by the legal nurse consultant. This will allow the attorney to see immediately what the legal nurse consultant has to report. The remainder of the memo should detail how that analysis was made.

FIGURE 28-5   Medical Abbreviations

HEALTHCARE RECORD SUMMARY
(PATIENT NAME)
(DATE OF INJURY)

Prepared by: Laura M. Sinclair, RN, BSN, LNC   Date: 01-04-00

Abbreviation	Meaning	Abbreviation	Meaning
H/O	History of	RTW	Return to work
ASA	Aspirin	RTC	Return to clinic
EMG	Electromyography—test that measures nerve function of certain muscle	MVA	Motor vehicle accident
		MRI	Magnetic resonance imagery—detailed x-ray of a part of the body, particularly soft tissue
F/U	Follow up		
DJD	Degenerative joint disease	HEP	Home exercise program
PE	Physical exam	R/O	Rule out
H+P	History and physical	US	Ultrasound
OR	Operating room	MS	Multiple sclerosis
TTP	Tender to palpation	N	Nausea, numbness
A+O	Alert and oriented ($\times1$ = to person, $\times2$ = to person, place, $\times3$ = person, place, time)	T	Tingling
		ROM	Range of motion
		TPI	Trigger point injection
CMS	Circulatory, musculoskeletal, sensation	LUE	Left upper extremity
WNL	Within normal limits	RUE	Right upper extremity
H/A	Headache	LLE	Left lower extremity
ER	Emergency room	RLE	Right lower extremity
XR	X-ray	C/O	Complains of
C-spine	Cervical spine	CMC	Carpometacarpal
T-spine	Thoracic spine	D/C	Discharge
L-spine	Lumbar spine	NIDDM	Non-insulin dependent diabetes mellitus
PT	Physical therapy		

Reprinted by permission of Laura M. Sinclair, President, Sinclair Consulting.

FIGURE 28-6 Analysis Memo

Sinclair Consulting
Laura M. Sinclair, RN, BSN, LNC
1419 South Midpark Drive
Appleton, Wisconsin 54915
(920)954-6859

January 11, 2000

Ms. Nancy Smith
ABC Insurance Company—Legal Department
3232 North Main Street
Appleton, Wisconsin 54911

Dear Nancy,

Enclosed is a medical record summary for Mrs. M. who was involved in a motor vehicle accident on June 25, 1995 with your insured, Mr. K.

There are several issues involved here so I will try to address each claim as it appears in the complaint.

Mrs. M. claims the following injuries:

1. *Avulsion fracture of the right wrist at the dorsal aspect of her lunate, thumb, and carpometacarpal joint.* XR report from the time of the injury states that Mrs. M. had a chip fracture at the base of her hand as well as moderate degenerative changes at the first carpometacarpal joint. There is no documentation of complaints regarding the right wrist after 8-25-95. At that time, Mrs. M. had begun to complain of whiplash symptoms with cervical pain radiating to her right scapula and, subsequently, she developed pain in the left upper extremity and elbow. An MRI done 10-95 was negative for cervical radiculopathy. An EMG done 2-96 ruled out cervical neuropathy also but it demonstrated that Mrs. M. had bilateral carpal tunnel syndrome. Dr. H. stated that the carpal tunnel syndrome was the reason for the upper extremity symptoms. Mrs. M. saw Dr. L. in January of 1998. He had a lengthy discussion with her at that time regarding the cause of her problems. In a letter to Dr. M., Dr. L. states that he was unable to comment on whether or not the MVA led to Mrs. M's. current trouble with carpal tunnel syndrome. He does note that she had a mild fracture to her right wrist and then later developed bilateral carpal tunnel syndrome. It should be noted also that the carpal tunnel syndrome was worse on the left, the wrist that was NOT injured. In general, carpal tunnel syndrome is caused by repetitive action of the wrist or hand, not a fracture.

2. *Aggravation of pre-existing condition of the right and left wrists and arms.* Medical documentation from 1983 to 1993, two years before the accident in question, contains no documentation of symptoms of carpal tunnel syndrome or epicondylitis. Mrs. M. was not diagnosed with carpal tunnel syndrome until 8 months following the accident. It is possible that the carpal tunnel syndrome did exist but was asymptomatic. It would appear that neither

continued

FIGURE 28-6   Analysis Memo   *continued*

Dr. H. nor Dr. L. can say with confidence that this syndrome is independent of the MVA. It is possible that the injury aggravated the syndrome. It should be noted, however, that the carpal tunnel syndrome was worse on the left wrist and the fracture occurred on the right wrist. Mrs. M. was also left-handed and would have used this hand more frequently. In February of 1996, she complained of occasional numbness and tingling of the fingers of both hands, the left being worse than the right. It is possible that these symptoms of carpal tunnel syndrome were simply manifesting at this point in time. There is no definite documentation by any doctor stating that the MVA exacerbated the carpal tunnel syndrome or the epicondylitis. This should be clarified at deposition. In October of 1995, Dr. H. noted that x-rays done before the accident had not shown any pre-existing cervical disc disease, therefore, any abnormal findings of the MRI done on 10/13/95 would be a result of the accident and that MRI was normal.

3. *Injuries to both knees.* There is documented history of left knee discomfort for Mrs. M. in 1986–87. She was diagnosed with a peroneal nerve entrapment and surgery by Dr. H. corrected that problem. There is no further documentation of knee pain, right or left, until the time of the accident. At that time, Mrs. M. complained of pain in the left knee in the emergency room. The x-ray taken at that time showed moderate degenerative arthritis of the patellofemoral joint with effusion. Dr. H. documents clearly in August of that year that the MVA was not responsible for all of the patient's knee problems. There was notable bruising and swelling of the knee, but arthritis was present before the accident. There was no evidence of a fracture. There is no documentation, current or otherwise, of any problems with right knee.

4. *Aggravation of pre-existing arthritic conditions.* There is documentation from Dr. M. in 1986–87 of early degenerative joint disease of the left knee. Mrs. M. had previous steroid injections to treat this problem. There was also moderate degenerative arthritis noted on the x-ray at the time of the accident in both the left knee and the right hand. It should be noted that after the accident, in early 1996, Mrs. M.'s complaints were centered on her cervical pain and the pain in the left upper extremity, which were eventually attributed to the carpal tunnel syndrome and epicondylitis. The left knee pain is last mentioned in documentation of 8-95.

5. *Soft tissue injuries to the neck and cervical spine.* There is documentation of soft tissue "whiplash" type injury in the records from the ER immediately following the accident. This injury was treated by physical therapy in September of 1995 and recurred in July of 1997, when the patient was treated by Dr. F. This type of whiplash injury, as you know, can persist off and on for several years without every being completely eliminated. As of August 1997, following several trigger point injections, Mrs. M. reported feeling "much better." MRI and EMG ruled out any physical injury to the spine itself or the surrounding nerves.

6. *Severe pain and suffering.* As you know, this can be difficult to quantify. It is apparent from the records that Mrs. M. did have quite a bit of discomfort from the carpal tunnel syndrome and the epicondylitis. Whether the MVA contributed to or aggravated these syndromes is a matter of argument. Depositions of both Dr. H. and Dr. L. should clarify this issue.

7. *Adverse emotional response: anxiety and depression.* There is a long history of anxiety and depression documented in the records. Mrs. M. is a recovering alcoholic and has been treated for depression as far back as 1983, when the records begin. She has suffered from suicidal ideation and has tried several antidepressant medications in the past. Her depression has been episodic and an MVA with its subsequent injuries would certainly cause increased stress. Mrs. M. did

remain out of work as a result of her injuries, which certainly could contribute to depression. Whether her need for surgery for carpal tunnel syndrome was a direct result of the MVA is again, a matter of debate.

I hope this clarifies some of the issues in this case. The outcome will depend on the testimony of both Dr. H. and Dr. L. as to causation. If you have questions regarding this summary or would like help in preparing for depositions, please do not hesitate to contact me. I have included illustrations of the hand and knee, as well as the carpal tunnel syndrome and avulsion fractures. Thank you for your continuing requests for my services.

Sincerely,

Laura M. Sinclair

Laura M. Sinclair, RN, BSN, LNC
Sinclair Consulting

Reprinted by permission of Laura M. Sinclair, President. Sinclair Consulting.

A memo concerning a health care liability claim should include paragraphs for the following:

- medical issue(s)
- analysis, or brief answer
- facts
- relevant standards of practice
- comparison of the facts to the standards of practice
- conclusion, or expansion on the brief answer
- follow up identifying additional investigation or research that should be undertaken

A memo concerning a personal injury resulting from an automobile accident would include paragraphs for the following:

- issues, or causation and damages
- analysis
- facts of the case
- foundation for determining causation or damages, such as medical literature or medical records
- comparison of injuries or damages to the foundational literature or record
- conclusion, or expansion of the brief answer
- follow up—additional investigation or medical research that must be completed in order to fully evaluate the client's claim

The analysis memo educates the attorney as to the preliminary medical issues, whether they are health care claims or claims of damages or causation. The more thorough and conscientious the legal nurse consultant is in preparing this initial memo, the more likely it is that later development of the medical issues of the claim will be comprehensive.

Follow-up

Once the medical chronology and analysis memo have been prepared, the legal nurse consultant may be required to complete some follow-up activities. These may include a review of the medical literature (see Chapter Thirty-one), or a comparison of the client's treatment with the textbook, policy, or professional standard of practice to more clearly identify errors and omissions. In addition, the legal nurse consultant may be asked to **audit the medical bills** to determine whether the patient was billed for a procedure that was omitted in the medical record. Medical bill review is discussed in the next chapter.

One of the most frequently requested follow-up activities is the location of expert witnesses. Expert witnesses may be used to build the case or they may be used to testify at trial. If they are used to help understand the case, they are generally not discoverable (as attorney work product). Therefore, if a legal nurse consultant has no background in obstetrics and cannot provide an educated review of fetal heart monitor strips, this review should be referred to an expert in the field. To attempt to make an assessment of the fetal heart monitor strips would not serve the best interests of the client. In fact, the AALNC has an ethical rule concerning this topic: "The legal nurse consultant uses informed judgment, objectivity, and individual competence as criteria when accepting assignments. The legal nurse consultant does not purport to be competent in matters in which he or she has limited knowledge or experience."[2]

Many legal nurse consultants agree that the relationships developed with experts is one of the most enriching aspects of the profession. Working with medical specialists, vocational rehabilitation experts, and others involves trust and respect, as well as excellent communication skills.

OTHER TYPES OF MEDICAL SUMMARIES

In addition to the previously mentioned tasks, legal nurse consultants may be asked to prepare customized summaries peculiar to a particular case. These summaries might include references to pleadings in a case or to discovery devices. Medical depositions may be indexed in relation to the medical records. The recollection of the client may be compared to the medical record for verification or for notation of discrepancy.

The attorney might ask the legal nurse consultant to do legal research or read case law on the appropriate informed consent rules in the state where the case is located and compare the prior rulings with the facts of the case at issue. When the medical expert who will be testifying for the other side is disclosed, the legal nurse consultant may be asked to collect any writings or other information about that expert and report her findings to the attorney. Where alteration of records is suspected, the attorney may ask the legal nurse consultant for a written explanation of why he or she, based on nursing experience, believes the records have been changed or falsified.

There is no end to the variety of medical summaries legal nurse consultants may be asked to prepare. It may be tempting, especially when time is of the essence, to skip over some of the details in the record. This should be avoided! What the legal nurse consultant fails to discover in the medical record will be discovered by the other side and may be used to the client's disadvantage. Professional integrity is always the most important component of the summaries prepared by the legal nurse consultant. It is far better to take extra time and present a thorough and professional product than to be caught off guard later.

CHAPTER SUMMARY

- Many of the summaries, chronologies, and evaluations of the legal nurse consultant will be considered attorney work product.
- The stages in the medical summary process include assembling the records, preparing a chronological overview, and drafting an analysis memo.
- Legal nurse consultants may be asked to follow up by locating experts, conducting medical research, or auditing medical bills.
- Summaries prepared by the legal nurse consultant may be formatted generally, or customized according to the needs of the case or the instructions of the attorney.

KEY TERMS

analysis memo   chronological overview   medical bill audit
attorney work product

REVIEW QUESTIONS

1. Why is it important to have some background information about the case before beginning the medical summary process?

2. What types of summaries, analyses, and reports may legal nurse consultants be asked to prepare?

3. Identify the stages in the medical summaries process and describe the activities that occur at each stage.

INTERNET EXERCISES

1. Access the web page for this textbook at *www.westlegalstudies.com*.

2. Click on the assignments page and complete the assignment(s) for Chapter Twenty-eight.

EXERCISES

1. Networking. Call a legal nurse consultant you have contacted previously who seems willing to share information with you. Ask about the types of summaries and reports prepared by the legal nurse consultant. If he or she is willing to share documentation, ask about a template chronology, analysis memo, or medical bill audit. Maintain these templates in your systems file, folder, or binder and organize or index them for easy reference.

2. Professional Portfolio. Photocopy the samples provided in this chapter and add them to your systems file, folder, or binder, organizing or indexing them for easy reference. When you have completed this study, you will be well prepared for a position in legal nurse consulting.

ENDNOTES

1. American Bar Association, *Annotated Model Rules of Professional Conduct,* (1999) 4th Edition Rule 1.16(a)(1). Copies of ABA *Model Code of Professional Responsibility, 1999 Edition* are available from Service Center, American Bar Association, 750 North Lake Shore Drive, Chicago, IL 60611-4997, 1-800-285-2221.

2. American Association of Legal Nurse Consultants, *AALNLC Code of Ethics and Conduct with Interpretive Discussion* (1997) Rule 3.

ADDITIONAL REFERENCES

AALNC Greater Detroit Chapter. "Chart Review: Allegations of Negligent Pain Management." *Journal of Legal Nurse Consulting* 10:4 (1999): 20, 24.

Mason-Kish, M., BS, RN, LNCC. "Finding the Needle in the Medical Records Haystack." *Legal Assistant Today* (March–April, 1993).

CHAPTER 29

MEDICAL BILL REVIEW

OBJECTIVES

In this chapter, you will discover

- what is meant by an audit of the medical bills

- how a medical bill audit may assist in developing the case

- how to organize a medical bill audit

- the format for medical bill reviews

OVERVIEW

Medical bills provide information that might substantiate or invalidate claims of damages and negligence. Legal nurse consultants may be asked to audit the medical bills. A **medical bill audit** may be used to verify damages, verify treatment, or verify services provided. Alternatively, a defense audit may be used to ascertain whether treatment was reasonable and necessary considering the injuries claimed, whether treatment was excessive or unusually costly, whether treatment was sought in a timely manner, and whether pre-existing conditions reduce plaintiff's claim for damages.

Medical bills should be collected at the same time as the medical records but should be maintained separately. Medical bills are essential for assessing damages, which is discussed in the next chapter. Additionally, medical bills should be cross referenced with the medical records to ascertain whether any records are missing, as where a procedure appears on the bill, but no record exists of that procedure, or whether the physician ordered the procedure.

Before beginning a medical bill audit, the legal nurse consultant should become familiar with the issues in the case. If the case involves personal injury resulting from an automobile accident, the medical bill review will be quite different from one that would be performed in a case involving a medical negligence claim.

USE OF MEDICAL BILL REVIEWS

Medical bill reviews are used for several purposes. If litigation is pending, the review might be used to verify the total medical damages. The legal nurse consultant may be asked to analyze the bills to determine whether the procedures identified were medically necessary and related to the injury claimed. Because the legal nurse consultant will be intimately familiar with the medical records, he or she can determine whether the billings are duplicates, whether the bills correspond with the records, and whether there were treatments indicated in the records for which there are no corresponding bills.

The medical bills can also provide the legal nurse consultant with insight into additional areas of liability. Scrutinizing the bills and corresponding records can alert the legal nurse consultant to omissions on the part of health care providers and can trigger research on specific standards of care. In situations where the procedure is documented in the record but not billed, the legal nurse consultant may become suspicious of the record, giving rise to a potential claim of falsified or altered documentation. This falsification or alteration of the record may indicate negligence.

Auditing the medical bills provided by the client or the insurance company may also alert the legal nurse consultant to health care providers not previously identified by the client. These records and related bills should be obtained, organized, and analyzed. Pharmacies maintain chronological information on drugs purchased by individuals. This record of prescriptions purchased by the client should be obtained and included in the medical bill audit. Similarly, bills and records for physical therapy, in outpatient facilities, and home health care providers should be obtained, organized, and analyzed.

If the medical bill audit is for the defense, it may be used to reduce the amount of damages. Legal nurse consultants will be able to separate related charges from unrelated charges such as annual physicals, visits for cold and flu symptoms, or injuries not resulting from the incident in question. The medical damages claimed may not be usual and customary considering the type and location of treatment and the provider of the treatment. Unnecessary and excessive charges may be reduced to values more consistent with typical charges. A legal nurse consultant working on the defense side of the claim may find that the medical bills are suspicious. If the frequency of diagnostic procedures seems unrealistic or the treatment unduly prolonged, the legal nurse consultant may be dealing with a fabricated or frivolous claim.

RESOURCES FOR MEDICAL BILL REVIEW

Before beginning a review of medical bills, several resources are recommended to assist the legal nurse consultant in understanding the bills and their relationship to the records. These resources are listed and described briefly in Figure 29-1.

Perhaps the two most important resources identified in Figure 29-1 are the *Physician's Current Procedural Terminology* (CPT) and *International Classification of Diseases—Clinical Modification* (ICD-9 CM). The CPT identifies five-digit codes for medical procedures and services accompanied by specific definitions and descriptions. Insurance carriers require these codes on bills submitted for payment, and the codes are used to determine the amount of allowable charges for that procedure or service. The CPT is compiled and published by the American Medical Association.

The ICD-9 is mandated by Medicare and lists three-digit number codes for various diagnoses. These three-digit codes may be modified for accuracy. The Healthcare Financing Administration (HCFA) form is used to submit charges and has become the industry standard.[1] It is consistent and clear. The information provided on the HCFA form expedites processing of claims through most carriers. ICD-9 codes are entered along with CPT codes and the charges for the procedure or service.

The list provided in Figure 29-1 is not exhaustive. The legal nurse consultant conducting the medical bill review will find medical and nursing textbooks helpful for referencing specific procedures, and the equipment and supplies needed. There are publications concerning fees (*Physician Fees, Fee Facts,* and *Cost of Injury*), procedures (*Diagnostic Procedure Handbook* and *Procedural/Utilization Facts*), and drugs (*Physician's Desk Reference* and *Physician's GenRX*), which might be of value if medical bill review becomes a routine task of the legal nurse consultant.

Net Results

Resources for Medical Billing Information

The Code of Federal Regulations is accessible online using the general law links described previously in this book: www.findlaw.com *and* www.law.cornell.edu. *Additionally, the Health Care Financing Administration may be accessed at* www.hcfa.gov. *Information about health care fraud and fraudulent billing may be accessed at the National Council for Reliable Health Information site (*www.ncrhi.org*) and at the National Health Care Anti-Fraud Association's web site (*www.nhcaa.org*).*

FIGURE 29-1　References Useful for Medical Bill Review	
Reference	**Description**
Code of Federal Regulations	Rules and regulations of the Department of Health and Human Services and the Health Care Financing Administration
Drug Topics Red Book	Medications by manufacturer, the forms in which medications are supplied, average wholesale price
Guidelines for Chiropractic Quality Assurance and Practice Parameters	Information concerning procedures, length of treatment, and standards of care
International Classification of Diseases—Clinical Modification	Lists of three-digit references for diagnoses used by the Health Care Financing Administration and for submission of claims to insurance carriers
Physician's Current Procedural Terminology	Annual publication of the American Medical Association classifying procedures and services in five-digit codes
Taber's Cyclopedic Medical Dictionary	Reference for understanding procedures and services with which the reviewer is unfamiliar

REVIEWING THE BILLS

There are three stages in the bill review process, with each stage containing several steps. These stages—organizing the bills, plotting the charges, and comparing the documents—and the steps involved are outlined in Figure 29-2.

Organizing the Bills

Once the bills have been collected, they must be organized in a way that will facilitate efficient review. It is recommended that the bills be separated by provider, then put in chronological order. The pages should be numbered sequentially for ease of reference. As the bills are organized, the legal nurse consultant should scan them for excessive quantities and for duplicate or sporadic entries. The bills may be maintained in three-ring binders or file folders secured by ACCO fasteners.

Plotting the Charges

Graphically displaying data provides a frame of reference that may not be seen in the narrative or in tables. Using calendars to show dates of treatment, medication, physical therapy, and so forth, helps the legal nurse consultant

---

FIGURE 29-2   Stages and Steps in Medical Bill Review

Stage	Steps
Organizing the review	• Separate bills by provider • Put in chronological order and paginate • Check for unusual entries
Plotting the charges	• Connect physician's order to bills • Identify unrelated charges
Comparing the documents	• Identify discrepancies • Determine whether items were medically necessary • Identify areas for review by medical experts

---

FIGURE 29-3   Sample Worksheet for Plotting Medical Charges

Description of Service	Ordered*	Location in Chart**	Date Billed	Date Submitted to Carrier	Amount	Amount Paid	Difference
Exam—orthopedics		G2000	03/25/—	03/25/—	55.00	55.00	0.00
Xray—humerus	X	G2015	03/25/—	03/24/—	78.88	78.88	0.00

*check if ordered
**identify the page number of the medical record where the procedure is documented

---

see the progress of the disease or frequency and type of medical intervention. Worksheets or computer spreadsheets may also be used. The dates and types of treatment or services should be related to the physician's orders. The legal nurse consultant should be alert to charges for procedures and services that are not a result of the injury at issue, especially if the injured party has preexisting conditions or is being treated for a chronic condition not related to the injury. Charges for these unrelated procedures and services should be subtracted from the total amount of the bill. A sample worksheet for plotting the medical charges is included in Figure 29-3.

Comparing the Documents

All billed services and procedures should also be documented in the medical record. The legal nurse consultant should cross reference the bills with the documentation and the physician's orders. Discrepancies in the orders, records, or bills should be noted for follow up. Suspicion as to whether or not a treatment was reasonable or necessary should be noted for additional research or for evaluation by the expert. Highlighting, in colors that are coded, the relevant portions of the plot, worksheet, or calendar identified in the previous section may assist other legal professionals in locating the items of discrepancy or suspicion.

WRITING THE REVIEW

The bill review must be communicated in a way that is clear and complete. A narrative summary may accompany a spreadsheet or worksheet. The summary may be enhanced by using headings, bolded information, or italics to identify areas where discrepancies appear or where research or investigation may be necessary.

The simplest form of medical bill review is the **medical expense summary.** A medical expense summary lists all the health care providers and their charges to date, and provides a detailed look at the medical specials. An example of a medical expense summary is included in Figure 29-4.

The medical expense summary may be expanded to include the dates bills were submitted to insurance carriers and the amount paid by those carriers. This will help the litigation team see the **subrogation** value, the amount that must be paid back to the insurance company if a favorable outcome is reached. The medical bill review may be used as an education tool for the litigation team and as an analytical tool for the legal nurse consultant. Additionally, this concise review and plot may be used in the evaluation of the medical specialist or expert on the case. The medical bills provide a valuable source for corroborating or discrediting claims of damages or negligence.

No specific qualifications are required to conduct medical bill reviews; the background and experience of the legal nurse consultant provides sufficient knowledge of the protocol of medical services. While it may take some experience to be able to identify what charges are reasonable, necessary, usual, or customary, these skills can greatly enhance the contribution of the legal nurse consultant.

FIGURE 29-4   Medical Expense Summary

SINCLAIR CONSULTING
Laura M. Sinclair, RN, BSN, LNC
1419 South Midpark Drive
Appleton, Wisconsin 54915
(920)954-6859

MEDICAL EXPENSE SUMMARY
(PATIENT NAME)
(CASE NUMBER)
(DATE OF INJURY/CLAIM/ACCIDENT)

Prepared by: L. Sinclair, RN, LNC   Date:

FACILITY:	EXPENSES
1. Mayo Clinic	5802.29
2. Howard Young Med. Ctr.	6073.08
3. Mayo Pharmacy	435.05
4. Park Pharmacy	537.49
5. P.C.S.	268.78
6. Flambeau Med. Ctr.	1810.25
7. St. Mary's Hospital	8208.76
8. Community Health Resources	5710.00
9. Health Management Consortium	559.13
10. Richard Steeves, MD	110.56
11. Marshfield Clinic	69.35
12. Northwoods Home Medical	30.77
13. Home Medical Products and Services	875.65
14. Herslof Opticians	406.25
15. Eye Institute of Central Kentucky	110.78
16. Eye Care of Lakeland	59.14
17. Brian F. Scott, MD	168.00
18. Ambu-Vans	396.50
19. Sawyer County Emergency Ambulance Service	292.50
20. Rite-Aid Pharmacy	22.59
Total medical expenses	**$31,946.92**

Reprinted by permission of Laura M. Sinclair, President, Sinclair Consulting.

CHAPTER SUMMARY

■ A medical bill review may validate medical expenses, corroborate medical treatment, and support or disprove claims of negligence.

■ Resources especially helpful for performing a medical bill review include the *Physician's Current Procedural Terminology* (CPT) and the *International Classification of Diseases—Clinical Modification* (ICD-9 CM).

■ There are three stages in the medical review process: organizing the bills, plotting the charges, and comparing the documentation.

■ The written review may be a simple medical expense summary or may include subrogated claims of insurance carriers. The medical review may also be used to detect suspicious or missing entries in the medical record.

KEY TERMS

medical bill audit   medical expense summary   subrogation

REVIEW QUESTIONS

1. Why is it important to review the medical bills?
2. Identify the stages in the medical bill review process and describe the steps that occur at each stage.

3. How can the medical bill review be used in the development of the case?

INTERNET EXERCISES

1. Access the web page for this textbook at *www.westlegalstudies.com.*

2. Click on the assignments section and complete the assignment(s) for Chapter Twenty-nine.

EXERCISES

1. Networking. In previous chapters, you have been assigned to go to the courthouse to review records of medical negligence claims. If the medical bills have been entered in evidence and are still available at the courthouse, use the file to prepare a medical expense summary. Note instances in the bills that appear to be unrelated to the claim of medical negligence.

2. Professional Portfolio. Photocopy the sample medical expense summary provided in this chapter. Adapt this summary to a summary that would include insurance payments on behalf of the injured party. Develop your own worksheets and/or calendars for comparing medical bills with medical records. Maintain these documents in your professional portfolio.

ENDNOTES

1. A. Grogan, RN, BS, "Health Care Bill Analysis and Audit," in *Legal Nurse Consulting: Principles and Practice,* ed. J. B. Bogart, RN, MN, (Boston: CRC Press, 1998).

2. American Bar Association, *Annotated Model Rules of Professional Conduct,* (1999) 4th Edition Rule 3.4(d). Copies of ABA *Model Code of Professional Responsibility, 1999 Edition* are available from Service Center, American Bar Association, 750 North Lake Shore Drive, Chicago, IL 60611-4497, 1-800-285-2221.

ADDITIONAL REFERENCES

AALNC Greater Detroit Chapter. "The LNC's Role in Healthcare Fraud and Abuse Cases. *Journal of Legal Nurse Consulting* 8:2 (1997): 17.

CHAPTER 30

DAMAGES AND LIFE-CARE PLANS

OBJECTIVES

In this chapter, you will discover

- the difference between general and special medical damages

- how to compute general damages

- how to establish a basis for punitive damages

- the process for developing a life-care plan

- the role of the legal nurse consultant and other experts in developing damages

OVERVIEW

In previous chapters, you have learned that negligence requires a relationship imposing a duty of care on the parties, a violation of that duty of care, causation, and injury. Without injury, the act or omission does not take on the character of a tort and no lawsuit would be permissible. Injuries are usually proved in court by establishing the medical nature of the harm done and the additional costs that those injuries have presented. These additional costs are referred to as damages. For an action in negligence to succeed, there must be an actual injury and actual, provable, damages.

The measure of compensatory damages in a personal injury action based on tort falls into one of three categories: past and future medical expenses, past and future lost wages, and past and future pain and suffering. You may recall from Chapter Nineteen that medical and income losses are referred to as **special damages** and noneconomic losses, such as pain and suffering and loss of enjoyment of life) are referred to as **general damages.** In order to recover for these losses, the plaintiff must prove them to a reasonable degree of certainty.

It is incumbent upon the legal team to calculate the damages in a way that is fair and just. The plaintiff's team will attempt to present a **damages package** that is as comprehensive as possible, while the defense's team will attempt to ensure that any damages for which the defendant would be liable are reasonable and are the natural and probable result of defendant's wrongful conduct.

DOCUMENTING PAST MEDICAL EXPENSES

Once a review of the medical records and medical bills has been made, it will be relatively easy to establish the medical expenses. (Please refer to Chapters Twenty-eight and Twenty-nine to review this procedure.) In addition to the medical expenses, other expenses related to medical injuries and treatment are available to the plaintiff. These related expenses include transportation to and from medical facilities and replacement costs.

Transportation to Medical Facilities

Since plaintiff would not have had to seek medical treatment but for the wrongful act that caused the injury, the court allows the plaintiff to recover for the reasonable and necessary costs involved in traveling back and forth to medical facilities. Travel to and from the clinic, doctor's office, and hospital are obviously allowed. Not so obvious are travel expenses to and from the pharmacy for medications; to and from the out-patient physical therapy, speech therapy, or occupational therapy facilities; and to and from psychological or mental health clinics. If an injured plaintiff must seek the care of a specialist or surgeon in a different city, the travel and overnight lodging, if required, are also recoverable expenses. Injured plaintiffs should be asked to

FIGURE 30-1	Sample Travel Expense Log				
Date	Facility	Mileage or Fare	Tools	Parking	Other

This chronology or log is maintained by the injured party and delivered to the litigation team for use in computing total medical damages.

maintain a log of travel expenses, including mileage, taxi fare, bus fare, tolls, parking fees, and any other travel expense involved in seeking medical treatment as a result of the incident in question. A sample travel expense log is included in Figure 30-1.

The travel costs reported by the injured plaintiff must correspond with records of medical treatment, dispensing of pharmaceuticals, or other services. The legal nurse consultant must be careful to cross check the travel expenses with the medical records and medical bills before including them in the damages package.

Replacement services include any expenses that may be incurred as a result of the incapacity of the injured party. Cleaning, cooking, transportation, child care, and laundry services are included in replacement damages. It is not relevant whether the injured party actually paid the expense in order to recover this cost. For example, a kind neighbor may gratuitously mow the lawn or shovel snow for an injured party who is incapable of engaging in that activity. Even though the injured party did not pay for this service, the reasonable value of that service is recoverable as a cost of the injury. If the kind neighbor moves away, the injured party will be forced to contract with a service for lawn care and snow removal. Expert testimony from economists may be required to prove the reasonable value of services for childcare and home management, and other services family members generally provide but are now unable to. Injured plaintiffs should maintain a log of replacement services, whether or not are paid for, and these services, if reasonable and necessary, should be included in the damages package. A sample form for keeping track of replacement services is included in Figure 30-2.

FIGURE 30-2 Sample Log of Replacement Services

Date	Description of Replacement Service	Cost or Time Involved

This chronology or log is maintained by the injured party and delivered to the litigation team for use in computing total medical damages.

SUPPORTING FUTURE MEDICAL EXPENSES

Whenever the injury requires continuing care, such as with amputations, burns, or excessive scarring, or is catastrophic, as in brain or spinal cord injuries, injuries at birth, or severe burns, future medical expenses must be calculated. Sometimes future medical expenses involve only the calculation for probable surgeries such as back surgery or plastic surgery, or for prosthetic replacement. Other times, the future medical expense calculation may be daunting. It may be based on the life expectancy of the injured party and involve several categories of expense, including physician services, hospitalizations, surgeries, pharmaceuticals, physical therapy, adaptive appliances, and rehabilitation.

Future medical expenses must be reduced to present values. To calculate present value, the future medical expenses are listed with their corresponding costs as if those costs were incurred today. An accountant or economist then takes the future medical expense and, employing sophisticated mathematical formulas based on the consumer price index and/or inflationary rates, reduces it to an amount that will, when invested, mature to the expected inflationary equivalent of the cost of that service when it is needed in the future.

To properly support and document future medical expenses, a worksheet or spreadsheet may be used. In situations involving extended or lifetime future medical expenses, a **life-care plan** should be developed. Life-care plans may be prepared by legal nurse consultants with the assistance of other professionals. To defend the life-care plan in court, the witness must be qualified to testify as an expert. The life-care plan developed by an in-house legal nurse consultant who is not expected to testify will be considered attorney work product and may not be discovered by the opposing party. If or when a life-care planning expert is hired to develop a new plan or to defend the plan developed in house, all portions of the plan and the information upon which it is based are discoverable. Similarly, if an independent legal nurse consultant is retained to develop the life-care plan and to defend it in court, all information used by the legal nurse consultant in preparing the plan, as well as the plan itself, is discoverable.

LIFE-CARE PLANS

A life-care plan presents a clear picture of what life will be like as a result of a catastrophic injury, the loss of a body part, or substantial impairment due to extensive burns or trauma. The intent of a life-care plan is to predict with reasonable certainty all future medical and living expenses that will be incurred as a result of the wrongful act causing injury. These must be expenses that would not ordinarily be incurred if the injured party had remained in his or her previous state of health.

Stages in Development of Life-Care Plans

There are several stages in the development of a life-care plan. Each stage of the plan must be thoroughly and comprehensively completed in order to present the most powerful picture of an injured client's future. The strategy of the attorney will play a role in the development of the life-care plan, and the legal nurse consultant should check with the attorney to determine if the attorney has any preferences concerning the nature of the plan. Additionally, because the case may not settle and the life-care plan may, as a result, be discoverable, the legal nurse consultant should use professional integrity to ensure that the plan is just, fair, and defensible. Painstakingly completing each step of the life-care planning process may forestall any potential challenges to the plan from the opposing side. A description of the stages and steps in the life-care planning process are included in the Figure 30-3.

FIGURE 30-3   Stages and Steps in the Life-Care Planning Process

Stage	Steps
Pre-plan investigating	• Review medical records and bills • Review reports from physicians and other health professionals • Interview client, family members, and others • Conduct on-site observations
Calculating the expenses	• Collect cost information • Identify topic areas for calculation • Prepare spreadsheet or worksheet • Extrapolate totals based on life expectancy
Supporting the plan	• Identify sources for medical needs • Cite medical literature for incidences of probable infection or medical complications • Cite legal authority for including potential medical treatments

Pre-plan Investigation. Prior to developing any portion of the life-care plan, the legal nurse consultant must perform some preliminary homework. This pre-plan investigation includes a review of the file to understand the incident causing injury; a review of the medical records, including pre-injury records, and medical bills to date; and examination of any medical reports concerning the client's condition. Once the legal nurse consultant is familiar with the medical facts of the case, a thorough analysis must be made of the human factors involved. This will involve assessment of the client, preferably at his or her home with family members and other caregivers, or at the institution where the client is receiving care. On-site observations are invaluable for understanding the significant details of the client's condition, preferences regarding vendors, and the home environment in general.

Assessment of the client should be comprehensive. It should include daily activities, living environment, transportation needs, thorough physiological evaluation, psychological issues, and all other health data that might be influenced by the illness or injury. Additionally, the legal nurse consultant should interview other professionals who have been working with the injured client. Before beginning the life-care plan, the legal nurse consultant should obtain the necessary consents and authorizations to release information that will enable a comprehensive study of the client's condition. Interviews should be conducted with family members, physicians, psychologists, school counselors, and others who may provide information concerning complications and frequency of incidents affecting the future care of the client.

Thorough investigation will provide the legal nurse consultant with insight into the components of the life-care plan and how it should be organized. After completing the interviews and reviewing the medical records, the legal nurse consultant might organize the plan by daily needs, monthly needs, annual needs, and long-term needs. Alternatively, results of the investigation may suggest that the plan be organized by type of expense, rather than frequency.

After the investigation, the legal nurse consultant will have a relatively clear idea of the equipment and supplies needed by the client. Collecting catalogs, brochures, and vendor information concerning those needs will aid the legal nurse consultant in completing the next stage of the life-care planning process.

Calculating the Expenses. Once the legal nurse consultant has a complete picture of the future needs of the client, these needs must be reduced to their dollar values. This is much like preparing a budget and may be done on a spreadsheet or other columnar worksheet. The cost for each item must be carefully identified. It has been suggested that a life-care planner average the most expensive and the least expensive prices for each item. It has also been suggested that the life-care planner use the cost of the item already used by the client. Allergies, sensitivities, and preferences of the client should be taken into consideration when identifying the cost of supplies needed for future care.

If medical interventions such as surgeries or hospitalizations are likely as a result of the injury, the legal nurse consultant must be careful to include all of the costs attendant to the probable intervention. Analgesics, antibiotics, additional pain medications, and the probability of complications from these interventions should be added. Review of the medical records will provide the legal nurse consultant with insight into frequency of infections, pneumonia, or surgical procedures, and the potential for successful outcomes.

The expenses should be categorized according to the topics identified in the pre-plan investigation. Totals should be extrapolated based on the life expectancy of the client.

Supporting the plan. Each of the expenses identified in the life-care plan is subject to challenge by the opposing side. Therefore, the legal nurse consultant may be asked to document a source or rationale for each item, for the frequency of the items, or for the probability of expected medical expenses. This may simply involve a cross reference to physician orders or a citation to an interview with family members, a school counselor, or a physician. Citation to medical literature that indicates the increased potential for infections or other medical complications will support the expenses attendant to anticipated infections or other complications. Additionally, legal citation can be used for items of potential medical expense for which precedence has been established.

Components of Life-Care Plans

Depending on the needs of the attorney, the life-care plan should be drafted in a way that presents future medical needs clearly and convincingly. While the legal nurse consultant or life-care planner may not take the position of patient advocate, the life-care plan should objectively portray the needs and potential difficulties of the patient, and the patient's family, as he or she lives with the catastrophic injury or illness.

At a minimum, the life-care plan should include a description of the injured client, a summary of the costs for future medical services, a detailed report supporting the summary of costs, a recitation of the information and investigation on which the life-care plan is based, and references, if any. It will be up to the attorney to decide how elaborate each of these components should be. The beginning legal nurse consultant should be as comprehensive as possible. Items in the plan can always be deleted; it will require much more time and investigation to include items originally left out. A sample life-care plan is included at the end of this chapter in Figure 30-6.

Description of the injured client. This section includes the name, birth date, sex, race, general health, and onset of the catastrophic injury or illness. These data provide the basis for life expectancy calculation. The legal nurse consultant may also include in this section a narrative summary of the medical records review completed during the pre-plan investigation, especially if the injured party has a history of low tolerance for or limited success with treatment. Providing this information will support future expenses for frequency of treatments or pain management.

Summary of the costs for future medical services. Because this is what everyone wants to know, the summary of costs for future medical needs should be

Net Results

Life Expectancy on the Internet

A life-care plan, by definition, is based on the life expectancy of the injured client. The web site for the Center for Disease Control includes considerable information, most of which is available on the Internet. Access this web site at www.cdc.gov. Other information can be found at federal depository libraries. Access life expectancy tables directly at www.cdc.gov/nchs/ about/major/dvs/ mortdata.htm.

relatively close to the beginning of the document. In the summary, the legal nurse consultant should identify the topics under which the detailed report is organized along with a description of the types of equipment, services, or treatments included under that topic. This document will be similar to a financial statement; it will display the subtotals for each topic and a total of all expected expenses and needs. Thus, legal and health professionals will be able to easily identify categories of anticipated expense, costs for those categories, and a grand total of expected medical costs based on the injured party's life expectancy.

Detailed report supporting the summary of costs. Following the summary of costs should be a detailed table or computer printout listing separate costs for each item claimed under the topics or categories of medical expense. A column in this table or computer printout may be used by the legal nurse consultant to cite sources supporting the expense. Additionally, if the legal nurse consultant averages costs, the maximum and minimum expense for each item should be included. If not the particular vendor's price favored by the injured party or the injured party's family.

Recitation of information and investigation on which the plan is based. To show that the life-care plan is based on the real needs of the injured party rather than a textbook case or hypothetical victim, the legal nurse consultant should include a section describing his or her investigation into the injured party's situation. Dates of observations, names of persons interviewed and dates of those interviews, and consultations with other professionals should support the topics identified and the medical needs outlined in the life-care plan.

References. In this section, the legal nurse consultant or life-care planner should identify any textbooks or medical literature from which information was obtained concerning the increased likelihood of infection or medical complications as a result of the catastrophic injury or illness. Additionally, catalogs, brochures, and other sources for the costs described in the plan should be noted. Even sources obtained via telephone conversations, such as conversations with personnel in orthopedic offices who provided the cost of specific treatments or surgeries, should be identified. Court opinions that establish precedent for inclusion of probable or potential future medical treatments should be cited.

SUPPORTING GENERAL DAMAGES

It is wise to research the law of the state to determine whether there are statutory caps for noneconomic damages. Both California and Wisconsin impose limits on noneconomic damages that can be recovered in health care negligence claims, and Wisconsin imposes a limit on noneconomic damages in wrongful death. It would not be expedient to spend a great deal of effort supporting general damages that would exceed the statutory limit.

Because general damages focus on losses that cannot be accurately measured, the legal nurse consultant should investigate general damages with a view toward a sympathetic jury. Support for general damages may be

---

FIGURE 30-4   General Damages

Type of Damage	Support for Damage Claim
Physical pain	• Medical records indicating complaints of physical pain • Pharmaceutical records showing prescriptions for pain medication • Records of pain management therapies • Medical literature indicating potential for future risks, pain, and complications
Emotional pain	• Diary entries of events causing emotional pain • Schedule of activities no longer engaged in as a result of humiliation or emotional plan • Visible scars or disfigurement
Indignity	• Records indicating functions that are limited or can no longer be performed independently • Diary entries, records, or reports of difficulties in personal relationships • Records of limitations on or inability to perform in chosen profession or work
Humiliation	• Views of the community concerning the injury, disability, or disfigurement • Diary entries of situations in which the injured party was ridiculed or subjected to ostracism

---

centered around the pain and indignity of the injured party. The table in Figure 30-4 displays examples of how general damages might be supported.

When developing general damages, the unique nature of the client should be considered. What the client was like before and after the injury are important indications of the pain and suffering experienced. Identifying how the injured client contributed to the welfare of the community, the family, or a church or charity, especially if the client is no longer capable of making those contributions, will provide the jury with insight into the degree of loss experienced as a result of the injury. If the client is a child, an on-site observation of the child at school may provide insight into the child's social difficulties and the emotional pain associated with being different.

DEVELOPING A BASIS FOR PUNITIVE DAMAGES

Besides compensatory damages, both special and general, the court may award punitive damages intended to punish the defendant for reckless disregard for the rights or safety of the plaintiff. There is little to guide the court in assessing punitive damages except the income and net worth of the defendant. To support punitive damages, the complaint must claim and the evidence must show that defendant's conduct was so reprehensible that the court must make an example of the defendant so that type of conduct does not recur. Punitive damages are, therefore, sometimes called exemplary damages.

What LNCs Say . . .

"Certification is becoming more important [for life-care planners]. However, there are other facts that are probably more important. This would include education specific to life-care planning. A comprehensive knowledge base is also important so that the life-care planner knows what someone with a catastrophic injury would typically need both short term and long term. There are also certain skills that are critical to a life-care planner. These would include the ability to interview clients and providers, collect data, organize data, explain the data to a jury, and to meet deadlines" LeaRae Keyes, BSN, PHN, CDMS, CCM, Minneapolis, MN, used with permission.

Tax returns, balance sheets, and other financial documents will provide evidence of the defendant's assets and economic situation. In a products liability action, the defendant manufacturer's current profit statements or annual reports will reveal its ability to pay punitive damages. Establishing the economic value of the defendant provides a base from which the jury may calculate an amount that will punish the defendant and deter other potential defendants from engaging in such reckless activities.

CALCULATING LOSS OF EARNINGS AND EARNING CAPACITY

You will recall that the measure of damages for personal injury actions includes past and future loss of income. Loss of past income may be documented with a letter from the employer identifying the job description, salary, and employer-paid benefits lost as a result of the injury. When the injured party is incapable of returning to work or may return to work only with workplace accommodations, it may be necessary to seek the services of a vocational expert to support the demand for lost future earnings and lost earning capacity. The legal nurse consultant may act as the liaison between the litigation team and the vocational expert.

Vocational damages include loss of earnings, loss of earning capacity, loss of recoverable employer-paid benefits, and retraining costs. Loss of earning capacity is the most difficult to assess and will depend on the injured plaintiff's prior employment history, education, and age, as well as economic indicators concerning employment opportunities and market trends. The injured party's willingness and ability to retrain will also be factors in determining loss of earning capacity.

To establish loss of earning capacity, the vocational expert will review records of past income and project what income the injured party could reasonably have expected if he or she had continued in the former profession until retirement. This projection is reduced by the amount of income, if any, the injured party is expected to receive after retraining. The accumulated difference will constitute the loss of earning capacity as a result of the injury. Loss of future earnings must be reduced to present value. This requires calculation by an economist or accountant applying mathematical formulas to the total value in a way that will reduce it to an amount that, when invested, would provide the anticipated future income.

THE ROLE OF THE LEGAL NURSE CONSULTANT IN DEVELOPMENT OF DAMAGES

The legal nurse consultant is actively involved in an assessment of the damages in a medical-legal claim. Preparing or critiquing a life-care plan, reviewing the medical expenses, and coordinating the location and use of experts to defend portions of the damages package are all duties of the legal nurse consultant. A damages worksheet should be employed to help develop damages and ensure that no item of damages has been overlooked. Several other worksheets, chronologies, or logs may be used to support the items included in the damages worksheet. A sample damages worksheet is included in Figure 30-5.[2]

FIGURE 30-5 Damage Summary and Worksheet

Plaintiff _____ Date of Accident _____

Case _____ v. _____ Case No. _____

Attorney _____ Prepared by _____

Date _____

I. Damage Totals

Special Damages _____

General Damages _____

Other Special and Exemplary Damages _____

_____

Total Damages _____

ITEMIZATION

II. Special Damages

A. Special Damages (Medical)

1. Ambulance Service: Name _____ Date _____

Amount _____

_____

2. Hospital: Name _____ Address _____

Date _____ Service, Test, or Treatment _____

Amount _____

Name _____ Address _____

Date _____ Service, Test, or Treatment _____

Amount _____

(add as needed)

3. Doctor: Name _____ Address _____ Date _____

Purpose or Treatment _____ Tests _____

Amount _____

(add as needed)

4. Pharmaceutical:

Pharmacy _____ Address _____ Date _____

Medication or Prosthetic Device _____ Purpose _____

Amount _____

Pharmacy _____ Address _____ Date _____

Medication or Prosthetic Device _____ Purpose _____

Amount _____

(add as needed)

continued

FIGURE 30-5 **Damage Summary and Worksheet** *continued*

5. Travel for Medical Purposes:
   Purpose _____ Date _____
   Mileage _____ × _____ ¢/mile = $_____ Lodging $_____
   Meals $ _____ Airfare, cabs, etc. $_____
   Amount _____
   (repeat as needed)

6. Home Care (Nurse or Attendant)
   Purpose _____ Date(s)_____
   Amount per day _____ × no. of days _____
   Amount _____
   (add as needed)

7. Psychologists and Physical Therapists
   Name _____ Address _____
   Purpose _____ Date _____
   Amount _____
   (add as needed)
   TOTALS: _____
   TOTAL PAST MEDICAL COSTS: _____

8. Future Medical Expenses
a. Special
   ☐ Hospitalization: no. of days _____ × cost _____ Amount _____
   ☐ Doctor: Purpose _____ $_____
   ☐ Surgery: Type _____ $_____
   ☐ Therapy: Type _____ no. _____ × cost _____ $_____
   ☐ Travel: Purpose _____ miles _____ × _____ ¢/mi. $_____
   Airfare, etc. _____ $_____
   ☐ Pharmacology: Nature _____ $_____
   ☐ Nurse: Cost/wk. _____ × no. of wks. _____ $_____
   ☐ Other: _____ $_____
b. Daily: Itemize current daily needs: nurse, equipment, medications, etc.
   Item: _____ Purpose: _____ Daily cost $_____
   Item: _____ Purpose: _____ Daily cost $_____
   _____ Total _____
   (add as needed)
   Total Daily Cost _____ × _____ Days/yr. × _____ Years + Special Costs
   + that figure × _____% for growth in medical costs = gross expenses × _____% for present cash value* = $_____
   TOTAL FUTURE MEDICAL EXPENSES $_____

*Present cash values (present value discount) reduces the future gross expense to a current lump sum, which if invested will provide for the total gross expenses when needed. The percentage of reduction is usually based on projected annuity tables or average yields for savings accounts or U.S. bonds over a reasonable historical period.

B. Special Damages (Economic Loss)

1. Current Wage _____ Date returned to work _____
2. Units (hours, days, months, etc.) or percentage of annual income lost _____
_____ Total wages lost to date _____
3. Lost Fringe Benefits, Bonuses, Perquisites _____
_____
(list if needed)   Total benefits lost to date _____
Total lost wages and benefits to date _____
4. Lost Household Services to Date:

  (Market value of household chores: bookkeeper, parent [care giver, tutor, chauffeur] maid, cook, decorator, gardener, etc.) $_____/wk. × no. of weeks _____ = $_____
5. Lost Other Considerations: _____
_____ $_____
                 Total Lost Wages, Benefits, Household Services to Date $_____
6. If the person's income is reduced by any disability, for example a need to change to a job with less pay, then that loss should also be added. $_____
7. Future Economic Loss

a. Future Wages (if complete disability or death):

Most recent normal year's wages $_____ × years of work expectancy**_____
(including any remaining portion of current year) + that figure × compounded annual growth rate***
of _____ % = gross wage loss $_____
Gross wage loss $_____ less _____ % reduction to present cash value =
                 $_____

☐ If the person has partial disability, gross wage loss can be computed by applying the same formula to the percentage of current yearly wage lost because of disability. If death, reduce gross wage loss by the percentage of annual wage actually consumed by that person. See family expenses over a period of several years.

**Years to age 65 or Department of Labor Statistics for work life in specific occupations or may be set by state law.
***Based on average % raise over same number of past years as work expectancy years for that person or industry standard. Consult Department of Labor statistics but usually between 4–8%. Adjust figure upward if raises show marked increase in recent years. Note: Provide alternative set of figures if promotion, career change, or other variable is likely.

b. Future Fringe Benefits:

Annual fringe benefit $_____ × _____ years of work expectancy + that figure × compounded annual growth rate for benefits of _____% = gross benefits loss
                 $_____
Gross benefits loss $_____ less _____ % reduction to present cash value =
                 $_____

☐ Annual growth rate for benefits is usually higher than wages. See Department of Labor statistics for occupation. Adjust if recent rise in %.

continued

FIGURE 30-5 Damage Summary and Worksheet *continued*

c. Future Investments (if applicable)
Amount of annual income placed in savings or other investments $_____ × compounded annual growth rate _____ % (based on average return over past years)

Total Lost Future Investment Income $_____
   (reduced to present cash value if necessary)
d. Future Household Services
   Annual Lost Market Value for each service (bookkeeper, cook, maid, painter, gardener, child-care giver, etc.) _____ Annual cost × _____ yrs. life expectancy[†] = $_____ + that figure × _____% annual growth rate in cost of household services[‡]=

Total Future Household Services $_____

[†]Life expectancy: based on readily accessible projections (consult reference librarian or insurance sources).
[‡]Annual growth rate for household services is often tied to projections based on history of consumer price index adjusted for any recent increases. The percentage usually ranges from 3–5%.

e. Adjustments for Income Taxes: Consult with Attorney
f. Adjustments for Inflation
   (Being allowed more frequently. See published reports from trustees of Federal Old Age and Survivors Insurance and Disability Insurance Trust Funds for inflation projections and what that means in real wage increases.)
Total Future Income Loss $_____ $_____
   C. Special Damages (Property)
1. Personal Property:
Item _____
Destroyed: Market Value $_____ less salvage $_____ = $_____
Damaged: Cost of restoration $_____ or if cannot be restored, value before damage
$_____ less value after damage $_____ plus costs to attempt to preserve or restore
$_____ = $_____
   Other Property:
List: Portraits, heirlooms, pets, etc., with appraiser's valuation or some other reasonable standard
$_____
Appliances, furniture, clothing, worth at time of loss $_____
2. Real Property (land, buildings)
Item _____
If permanent: value before damage $_____ less value after $_____ plus interest to date =
$_____
If temporary: reduction to rental or other profit value $_____ plus injury to crops, buildings, improvements $_____ plus restoration costs $_____ plus any applicable interest =
$_____
   (consult local law)
Total Property Damages $_____ $_____
Total Special Damages $_____

III. General Damages

　　Pain and Suffering: fear, humiliation, inconvenience, anxiety, horror of injury, pain, discomfort, loss of companionship, status, stimulation of job, enjoyment of life's experiences; and other subjective factors cause by injury. Briefly summarize: _____

_____

_____

_____

　　Standard: as estimated by party or reasonable person as fair.

Value per day $_____ × no. days/yr. _____ × yrs. of life expectancy _____

× _____% inflation factor if allowed =　　　　　　　$_____

Consortium: value per day $_____ × no. of days per year _____ × yrs. of life

expectancy × _____% inflation factor if allowed =　　　　$_____

Note: Review current jury verdicts for reasonable estimates. Check local statutes for any limits on awards. Most states do not require a reduction to present cash value for pain and suffering.

　　　　　　　　Total Pain and Suffering and General Damages $_____ $_____

IV. Other special and Exemplary Damages

1. Funeral Expenses　　　　$_____

2. Exemplary:

Punitive　　　　　　　　$_____

Attorney's

Fees　　　　　　　　　　$_____

3. Miscellaneous Damages　$_____

　　　　　　　Total of other Special and Exemplary Damages $_____ $_____

　　　　　　　　　　　　　　　TOTAL DAMAGES $_____

Reprinted with permission of James W. H. McCord. (1998). *The Litigation Paralegal,* West Publishing Company, 396–401.

　　Because many other experts and members of the litigation team may be involved in the calculation of damages, it is incumbent upon the legal nurse consultant to maintain an organized system for identifying and proving damages. A separate three-ring binder or file folder may be used for this purpose. The binder or folder may be tabbed to separate the components of the damages package. The medical expense summary would be filed behind the tab for past medical expenses, the life-care plan would be filed behind the tab for future medical expenses, the income tax returns and employer's report would be filed behind the tab for lost earnings, the report of the vocational expert would be filed behind the tab for loss of future earnings, and so forth.

FIGURE 30-6   Life-Care Plan

Don Adams
Adams Law Firm
123 Oak Street, Suite 300
Minneapolis, MN 55412

RE: Amy Smith
DOB: May 5, 1957
D.A.: October 9, 1998
Keyes & Associates, Ltd. #: 123

LIFE-CARE PLAN—AUGUST 15, 2000

I was asked to complete a life care plan involving projecting Amy Smith's medical costs for future medical care and treatment in present day dollars.

I met with Amy Smith, Judy Zimmerman (Amy Smith's sister), Dr. James South and Dr. Mark Adams. I also reviewed Ms. Smith's previous medical history and reports including medical records from First Health Clinic dated January 1999 to March 1999, medical records from Abbey Hospital dated February 9, 1999 to March 30, 1999, medical records from Neuro Associates dated January 1999 to November 1999, and Abbey Hospital medical records dated April 1999 to January 2000.

I have also met with Becky Anderson RN, with Ace County Public Health Nursing Service. As a result of these contacts and reviewing this information, I am completing a Life-Care Plan Table.

Background

I met with Ms. Smith and her sister, Judy Zimmerman, at North Nursing Home. Ms. Smith is a 43-year-old female. She was born on May 5, 1957. She has two children. Ms. Smith's children are 18 and 20 years of age. Ms. Smith graduated from North Senior High School after completing the 12th grade. Ms. Smith is 5'3" tall and weighs 150 pounds. In the past Ms. Smith has lived in a rented home in Sunnyvale, Minnesota. Her goal is to again live with her family in a home in Sunnyvale, Minnesota.

When I met with Ms. Smith, she was in a manual wheelchair. She indicated that this wheelchair was not hers and that it actually belonged to the facility. She also stated that she uses a walker at times, which she also does not own. Ms. Smith informed me that she is incontinent of bowel and bladder at times. She stated that she finds an indwelling catheter to be very uncomfortable and that she has gotten frequent urinary tract infections in the past with an indwelling catheter in place. She stated that essentially she has no bowel or bladder control.

Ms. Smith stated that she is unable to transfer independently. Ms. Smith has complained of tightness and edema particularly in her legs. She also reported that she is numb on her left side and that she is unable to sense hot and cold such as water and outdoor temperature.

Ms. Smith reported that she goes through phases and that there are times when she is able to do more for herself and that she goes through times when she is not able to do much of anything for herself. This was also verified by her sister and Dr. South. Ms. Smith indicated that, since about October of last year, she reports that she is unable to shower without a shower chair.

Medical History

Ms. Smith reports that in the past she has had a hysterectomy, right arthroscopic knee surgery for torn cartilage, and two caesarian sections.

Ms. Smith is a smoker and she reports that she smokes because she is nervous, in pain and bored.

Subjective Complaints

Ms. Smith indicates that her primary symptoms are weakness, pain, and pins and needles feeling, tiredness, and sleepiness. She states that she feels these symptoms throughout her body. She also reported increased pain in her neck and head. She reported that her legs hurt and they give out on her especially when she tries to walk.

Ms. Smith indicated that she now has difficulty sleeping through the night. She wakes during the night and has difficulty falling asleep again.

Functional Abilities

Ms. Smith indicated that she is able to feed herself although she has difficulty cutting food. She holds a cup with two hands. She cannot open things such as a yogurt container. She also stated that she is unable to get her arms above shoulder height. Ms. Smith indicated that sometimes, intermittently, she can support her weight on her legs. Ms. Smith is able to walk with two people holding on to a walking belt to support her. She has no grip strength on her left side and she may drop things that she is holding in her right hand. She reports having poor eyesight and good hearing. Ms. Smith reported having frequent vomiting and cramping. She also reports headaches and being sensitive to light and sound. She states that she has sharp pains in her head from her neck on up.

Ms. Smith indicated that she is unable to roll over in bed without help. She indicated that she has edema in both legs with the edema in her right leg and foot being more severe than on the left.

Ms. Smith indicated that she has a hard time swallowing and she also stated that she feels that her depression is worse now than prior to her injury and that her depression lasts longer than it did in the past.

Future Medical Care Routine

Dr. South has indicated that Ms. Smith needs to be followed by a physical medicine and rehabilitation physician four times per year. Ms. Smith will also need to be followed by Dr. Adams, a Psychiatrist. However, her need to see Dr. Adams and the frequency of visits has not changed as a result of her injury.

Projected Therapeutic Modalities

Dr. South has indicated that Ms. Smith will need to receive physical therapy two to three times per week for six week time periods, two to three more times during her lifetime. I have projected these sessions could occur in 2000, 2005, and 2010.

Wheelchair Mobility

Ms. Smith will need a manual wheelchair. This wheelchair will require ongoing maintenance. It is not believed that she will need a power wheelchair.

Aids for Independent Functioning

Ms. Smith has one reacher available to her. She has indicated that she would like additional reachers so that she does not have to carry her one and only reacher from room to room. Dr. South has indicated that he feels that three additional reachers would be appropriate for Ms. Smith.

continued

FIGURE 30-6 Life-Care Plan *continued*

Supplies

Ms. Smith needs adult diapers as she is incontinent, meaning she is unable to control her bowel and bladder functioning. She finds an indwelling catheter to be uncomfortable and she has a history of developing urinary tract infections. Ms. Smith is also in need of a plastic pad for her bed, a genital spray, and "Wet Ones." Her need for these products is also due to her incontinence and need for cleansing her genital area. She takes Ensure as a nutritional supplement.

Dr. South has indicated he feels that Ms. Smith may be in need of catheter equipment in the future. However, it is unknown if Ms. Smith's need for this equipment is definite. It is also unknown what equipment and how much Ms. Smith would need. Therefore, catheter supplies have not been included in the Life Care Plan Table.

Medications

Ms. Smith is currently on a medication regime which will remain basically unchanged. Her need for her psychiatric medications remains unchanged pre and post injury. Dr. South has indicated that she projects that Ms. Smith will need antibiotics two to three times per year throughout her lifetime.

Case Management Services

Dr. South has indicated that he believes that Ms. Smith will need case management services to coordinate her medical care. He has indicated that she will certainly need this if she were to be at home. The case management hours were based on four hours per month. I feel that four hours of case management services per month for Ms. Smith is a conservative number.

Leisure Time/Recreational

Dr. Adams has indicated that he feels that it would be therapeutic for Ms. Smith to have computer equipment available to her and to undergo some computer training. The goal of this activity would be as a recreational activity and not for gainful employment.

Home Health Care Services

Ms. Smith would like to return to Sunnyvale, Minnesota and live at home with her children. Her providers feel that it would be therapeutic for Ms. Smith to be at home. However, if she were to be at home, she would need a 24-hour home health aide. Dr. South has indicated that she feels that Ms. Smith would not only need someone with her 24 hours per day, but that she would need a number of care givers working with her who could rotate through her home. Dr. South did not believe that a live-in home health aide or PCA would be a reasonable alternative for Ms. Smith. Ms. Smith is totally dependent on her caregivers for transferring from bed to chair, chair to bed and transferring on and off the toilet. Since it would be unlikely that you could predict when Ms. Smith would need to be transferred on and off the toilet or other transfers it would seem unlikely that she could maintain with less than 24 hour per day care.

Ms. Smith is also receiving monthly RN visits for B-12 injections, so these visits have been included in the Life Care Plan Table.

Medical Equipment

Ms. Smith will need a room air conditioner and a shower chair.

Transportation

Ms. Smith would need a modified vehicle that she could access while in a wheelchair; however, this vehicle would not need to be modified with hand controls as it is not anticipated that Ms. Smith would be driving this vehicle. Ms. Smith would be very difficult to transfer in and out of a standard automobile.

Potential Complications

Dr. South indicated that Ms. Smith is at risk for blood clots, cardiovascular disease such as heart disease, contractures, and osteoporosis. No cost estimates are given for these potential complications. The likelihood of these complications for Ms. Smith is unknown. The cost would also depend on the severity and duration of each of these complications, should they occur.

Life Expectancy

According to the *"Expectations of Life and Expected Deaths, by Race, Sex, and Age: 1996"* table a white female who was 39 years old in 1996 would have a life expectancy of 42.0 additional years. This would calculate to the year 2038.

This data is published by the U.S. National Center for Health Statistics, Vital Statistics of the United States. I will use this only for the purpose of showing possible lifetime projected future medical costs for Ms. Smith. Dr. South has indicated that he believes that Ms. Smith would have a normal life expectancy.

Respectfully submitted,

LeaRae Keyes, RN, BSN, PHN, CDMS, CCM
Case Manager and Life-Care Planner

LRK/bjm

continued

FIGURE 30-6 Life-Care Plan *continued*

LeaRae Keyes, RN, BSN, PHN, CDMS, CCM
Keyes & Associates, Ltd.
4011 Genie Dr. NW
Andover, MN 55304
(763) 576-9570

DOB: May 5, 1997
D.A.: Oct. 9, 1998
Date Prepared: Aug. 15, 2000
Primary Disability: Quadripareses,
Chronic Pain, Neurogenic Bladder and Bowel, Depression

Life-Care Plan
Amy Smith

Future Medical Care Routine

Evaluations	Recommended by	Frequency	Number of Years Needed	Year Begin	Year End	Purpose	Annualized Costs	Vendors and Comments
Physical Medicine and Rehabilitation	Dr. James South	Four times per year	Lifetime	1999	2038	Management of medical care related to quadriparesis	$557.32	St. James University Minneapolis, Minnesota Penn Avenue Associates Minneapolis, Minnesota St. Mark's Hospital Minneapolis, Minnesota

Projected Therapeutic Modalities

Evaluations	Recommended by	Frequency	Number of Years Needed	Year Begin	Year End	Purpose	Annualized Costs	Vendors and Comments
Physical Therapy	Dr. James South	Two to three times per week for six weeks, two to three times during her lifetime (2000, 2005 and 2010)	One to three times during her lifetime	2000 2005 2010	2000 2005 2010	Therapeutic	$603.75	North Rehabilitation Minneapolis, Minnesota Access Rehab Minneapolis, Minnesota Infinity Rehab Minneapolis, Minnesota

Wheelchair(s) Mobility

Equipment	Recommended by	Frequency	Number of Years Needed	Year Begin	Year End	Purpose	Annualized Costs	Vendors and Comments
Manual Wheel Chair	Dr. James South	Every seven years	Lifetime	2000	2038	Mobility	$159.80	Home Medical Equipment Minneapolis, Minnesota Available Home Health Equipment Minneapolis, Minnesota Suitable Home Health Equipment Minneapolis, Minnesota
Wheel Chair Maintenance	Dr. James South	Yearly	Lifetime	2001	2038	Maintain wheelchair equipment	$125.00	Home Medical Equipment Minneapolis, Minnesota Available Home Health Equipment Minneapolis, Minnesota Suitable Home Health Equipment Minneapolis, Minnesota

Aids for Independent Function

Equipment	Recommended by	Frequency	Number of Years Needed	Year Begin	Year End	Purpose	Annualized Costs	Vendors and Comments
Reacher	Dr. James South	Needs three additional reachers Replace every 10 years	Lifetime	2000	2038	Activities of daily living	$5.58	Available Home Health Equipment Minneapolis, Minnesota Suitable Home Health Equipment Minneapolis, Minnesota Home Medical Equipment Minneapolis, Minnesota

continued

FIGURE 30-6 Life-Care Plan *continued*

Supplies

Supplies	Recommended by	Frequency	Number of Years Needed	Year Begin	Year End	Purpose	Annualized Costs	Vendors and Comments
Adult Diapers[1]	Dr. James South	Ongoing throughout her lifetime	Lifetime	2000	2038	Treatment of her urinary incontinence	$1,909.30	Affordable Pharmacy Minneapolis, Minnesota Merit Pharmacy Minneapolis, Minnesota Pharmacy Emporium Minneapolis, Minnesota
Nutritional Supplement one can twice daily between meals	Dr. James South	Twice daily	Lifetime	2000	2038	Nutritional Supplement	$921.91	Affordable Pharmacy Minneapolis, Minnesota Merit Pharmacy Minneapolis, Minnesota Pharmacy Emporium Minneapolis, Minnesota

[1]She has urgency and is not able to get to the bathroom quickly

Supplies

Equipment	Recommended by	Frequency	Number of Years Needed	Year Begin	Year End	Purpose	Annualized Costs	Vendors and Comments
Plastic under pad for her bed	Dr. James South	Ongoing throughout her lifetime	Lifetime	2000	2038	Treatment of her urinary incontinence	$434.76	Affordable Pharmacy Minneapolis, Minnesota Merit Pharmacy Minneapolis, Minnesota Pharmacy Emporium Minneapolis, Minnesota
Spray to clean genital area Prevents itching	Dr. James South	Ongoing throughout her lifetime	Lifetime	2000	2038	Cleaning	$58.80	Affordable Pharmacy Minneapolis, Minnesota Merit Pharmacy Minneapolis, Minnesota Pharmacy Emporium Minneapolis, Minnesota

Supplies

Equipment	Recommended by	Frequency	Number of Years Needed	Year Begin	Year End	Purpose	Annualized Costs	Vendors and Comments
"Wet Ones" to clean her genital area during diaper changes	Dr. James South	Ongoing throughout her lifetime	Lifetime	2000	2038	Cleansing	$69.93	Affordable Pharmacy Minneapolis, Minnesota Merit Pharmacy Minneaplis, Minnesota Pharmacy Emporium Minneapolis, Minnesota

Medications

Medications	Recommended by	Frequency	Number of Years Needed	Year Begin	Year End	Purpose	Annualized Costs	Vendors and Comments
Antibiotic such as Septra or Macrobid	Dr. James South says she may need this 2-3 times per year	2-3 times per year	Lifetime	2000	2038	Treatment for UTI	$84.73	Affordable Pharmacy Minneapolis, Minnesota Merit Pharmacy Minneapolis, Minnesota Pharmacy Emporium Minneapolis, Minnesota
Klor-Con 10 meq	Dr. James South	Daily	Lifetime	2000	2038	Potassium Supplement	$95.88	Affordable Pharmacy Minneapolis, Minnesota Merit Pharmacy Minneapolis, Minnesota Pharmacy Emporium Minneapolis, Minnesota

continued

FIGURE 30-6 Life-Care Plan *continued*

Medications

Medications	Recommended by	Frequency	Number of Years Needed	Year Begin	Year End	Purpose	Annualized Costs	Vendors and Comments
Neurotin 100 mg.	Dr. James South	Twice daily	Lifetime	2000	2038	Seizure Prevention	$95.88	Affordable Pharmacy Minneapolis, Minnesota Merit Pharmacy Minneapolis, Minnesota Pharmacy Emporium Minneapolis, Minnesota
Cyanoco-balamin 1000 mcg/ml 1M	Dr. James South	Daily	Lifetime	2000	2038	B-12 Supplement	$11.75	Affordable Pharmacy Minneapolis, Minnesota Merit Pharmacy Minneapolis, Minnesota Pharmacy Emporium Minneapolis, Minnesota

Medications

Medications	Recommended by	Frequency	Number of Years Needed	Year Begin	Year End	Purpose	Annualized Costs	Vendors and Comments
Premarin 0.625 mg	Dr. James South	Daily	Lifetime	2000	2038	Hormone Supplement	$201.48	Affordable Pharmacy Minneapolis, Minnesota Merit Pharmacy Minneapolis, Minnesota Pharmacy Emporium Minneapolis, Minnesota
Pepcid 20 mg. Daily	Dr. James South	Two Daily	Lifetime	2000	2038	Treatment of Gastritis	$1,123.08	Affordable Pharmacy Minneapolis, Minnesota Merit Pharmacy Minneapolis, Minnesota Pharmacy Emporium Minneapolis, Minnesota

Medications

Medications	Recommended by	Frequency	Number of Years Needed	Year Begin	Year End	Purpose	Annualized Costs	Vendors and Comments
Prenatal Plus Multivitamin 1 daily	Dr. James South	Daily	Lifetime	2000	2038	Vitamin Supplement	$165.48	Affordable Pharmacy Minneapolis, Minnesota Merit Pharmacy Minneapolis, Minnesota Pharmacy Emporium Minneapolis, Minnesota
Lorazepam 2 mg HS, 1 mg middle of night, 0.5 mg TID	Dr. James South	As needed	Lifetime	2000	2038	Anti-Anxiety	$1,034.04	Affordable Pharmacy Minneapolis, Minnesota Merit Pharmacy Minneapolis, Minnesota Pharmacy Emporium Minneapolis, Minnesota

Medications

Medications	Recommended by	Frequency	Number of Years Needed	Year Begin	Year End	Purpose	Annualized Costs	Vendors and Comments
Methadone 5 mg	Dr. James South	Four times daily	Lifetime	2000	2038	Pain control	$201.48	Affordable Pharmacy Minneapolis, Minnesota Merit Pharmacy Minneapolis, Minnesota Pharmacy Emporium Minneapolis, Minnesota
Senna Laxative 8.8 mg	Dr. James South	Daily	Lifetime	2000	2038	Constipation	$25.96	Affordable Pharmacy Minneapolis, Minnesota Merit Pharmacy Minneapolis, Minnesota Pharmacy Emporium Minneapolis, Minnesota

continued

FIGURE 30-6 Life-Care Plan *continued*

Medications

Medications	Recommended by	Frequency	Number of Years Needed	Year Begin	Year End	Purpose	Annualized Costs	Vendors and Comments
Hydrochlorothiazide 25 mg	Dr. James South	Daily	Lifetime	2000	2038	Diuretic	$77.88	Affordable Pharmacy Minneapolis, Minnesota Merit Pharmacy Minneapolis, Minnesota Pharmacy Emporium Minneapolis, Minnesota
Baclofen 10 mg	Dr. James South	Four times daily	Lifetime	2000	2038	Anti-spasm	$453.48	Affordable Pharmacy Minneapolis, Minnesota Merit Pharmacy Minneapolis, Minnesota Pharmacy Emporium Minneapolis, Minnesota

Medications

Medications	Recommended by	Frequency	Number of Years Needed	Year Begin	Year End	Purpose	Annualized Costs	Vendors and Comments
Detrol 2 mg	Dr. James South	Daily	Lifetime	2000	2038	Help control urinary incontinence or urgency	$659.88	Affordable Pharmacy Minneapolis, Minnesota Merit Pharmacy Minneapolis, Minnesota Pharmacy Emporium Minneapolis, Minnesota

Case Management Services

Case Management Services	Recommended by	Frequency	Number of Years Needed	Year Begin	Year End	Purpose	Annualized Costs	Vendors and Comments
Case Management Services	Dr. James South	Ongoing throughout her lifetime	Lifetime	2000	2038	Coordinate her medical care	$3,472.00	National Case Management St. Paul, Minnesota Star Case Management Minneapolis, Minnesota Quality Case Management Minneapolis, Minnesota

Leisure Time/Recreational

Equipment	Recommended by	Frequency	Number of Years Needed	Year Begin	Year End	Purpose	Annualized Costs	Vendors and Comments
Computer equipment	Dr. Adams	Every 5 years	Lifetime	2000	2038	Therapeutic	$766.66	Electronics Unlimited Minneapolis, Minnesota All Your Needs Electronics St. Paul, Minnesota Everyday Electronics Minneapolis, Minnesota
Computer training	Dr. Adams	One time training	One time training	2000	2000	Therapeutic, assist her to use computer equipment	$1,520.00	Technology Center St. Mark's Hospital Minneapolis, Minnesota Computer Resource Center Minneapolis, Minnesota

continued

FIGURE 30-6 Life-Care Plan *continued*

Home Health Care Services

Services	Recommended by	Frequency	Number of Years Needed	Year Begin	Year End	Purpose	Annualized Costs	Vendors and Comments
Home Health Aide 24 hours per day	Dr. James South	Ongoing throughout her lifetime	Lifetime	2000	2038	Home Health Care	$149,095.20	All Hours Home Care Minneapolis, Minnesota Superior Health Care Minneapolis, Minnesota Quality Home Care Minneapolis, Minnesota
RN Visits	Dr. James South	Ongoing throughout	Lifetime	2000	2038	B-12 Injection	$1,320.00	All Hours Home Care Minneapolis, Minnesota Superior Health Care Minneapolis, Minnesota Quality Home Care Minneapolis, Minnesota

Medical Equipment

Equipment	Recommended by	Frequency	Number of Years Needed	Year Begin	Year End	Purpose	Annualized Costs	Vendors and Comments
Air conditioning Room air conditioner (if she were to be at home)	Dr. James South	Replace every 15 years	Lifetime	2000	2038	Temperature control	$18.96	Electronics Unlimited Minneapolis, Minnesota All Your Needs Electronics St. Paul, Minnesota Everyday Electronics Minneapolis, Minnesota
Shower Chair	Dr. James South	Replace every 10 years	Lifetime	2000	2038	Bathing and showering	$41.88	Available Home Health Equipment Minneapolis, Minnesota Suitable Home Health Equipment Minneapolis, Minnesota Home Medical Equipment Minneapolis, Minnesota

Transportation

Equipment	Recommended by	Frequency	Number of Years Needed	Year Begin	Year End	Purpose	Annualized Costs	Vendors and Comments
Modified vehicle with air conditioning (if she were to be at home)	Dr. James South	Every 7 years	Lifetime	2000	2038	Transportation	$2,250.48	Adapting Vehicles Minneapolis, Minnesota Accessible Mobility Minneapolis, Minnesota Durable Mobility Minneapolis, Minnesota Park Chevrolet Minneapolis, Minnesota Nicollet Chevrolet Minneapolis, Minnesota Quality Ford Minneapolis, Minnesota

Potential Complications For information Purposes Only. No Prediction of Frequency of Occurrence Available.

Evaluations	Cost of Complications	Comment
Blood Clots	No cost information available	For information purposes only. Costs are not included in the Projected Future Medical Costs since frequency and duration of the complication cannot be predicted with any accuracy.
Cardiovascular (Heart Disease)	No cost information available	For information purposes only. Costs are not included in the Projected Future Medical Costs since frequency and duration of the complication cannot be predicted with any accuracy.
Contractures	No cost information available	For information purposes only. Costs are not included in the Projected Future Medical Costs since frequency and duration of the complication cannot be predicted with any accuracy.
Osteoporosis and risk or fractures	No cost information available	For information purposes only. Costs are not included in the Projected Future Medical Costs since frequency and duration of the complication cannot be predicted with any accuracy.

Reprinted with permission of LeaRae Keyes, Keyes & Associates, Ltd., Minneapolis, MN. For additional information on life-care plans, you may contact LeaRae Keyes at 763.576.9570.

Chapter Summary

- Compensatory damages in personal injury actions include special damages and general or noneconomic damages.

- A damages package is a comprehensive presentation of the injured party's losses.

- The measure of damages in personal injury claims is past and future medical expenses, past and future lost earnings, and past and future pain and suffering.

- In addition to medical expenses, injured plaintiffs are entitled to recover travel expenses to and from medical facilities and the cost of replacement services.

- A life-care plan is used to present the cost of anticipated future medical needs in cases involving catastrophic injury.

- The development of a life-care plan involves three stages: pre-plan investigation, calculating the expenses, and supporting the plan.

- A life-care plan should include a description of the injured client, a summary of the costs for future medical needs, a detailed report supporting the summary of costs, a recitation of the information and investigation on which the plan is based, and references.

- Future losses, medical expenses and earnings, must be reduced to present values.

- General damages may be supported by a review of the records concerning physical pain, emotional pain, indignity, and humiliation.

- Collecting information concerning the defendant's financial position will provide a basis for punitive damages.

- Vocational experts may be retained if the injured party is incapable of returning to his or her former employment or if the injured party may only return with workplace accommodations.

- The legal nurse consultant may direct, participate in, and organize the development of the damages package.

KEY TERMS

damages package	**life-care plan**	**special damages**
general damages		

REVIEW QUESTIONS

1. Explain the types of evidence that will support each item included in the measure of damages for personal injury actions.

2. What is a life-care plan and how is it used?
3. How can the legal nurse consultant assist in the development of the damages package?

INTERNET EXERCISES

1. Access the web page for this textbook at *www.westlegalstudies.com.*

2. Click on the assignments section and complete the assignment(s) for Chapter Thirty.

EXERCISES

1. Networking. Using the Yellow Pages, contact a vocational expert in your area. If the vocational expert is willing to share information with you, ask if he or she has ever testified in a personal injury action. Without violating confidentiality, ask the vocational expert to describe his or her role in the preparation of a report on lost earning capacity or in preparation of the damages package. Maintain this contact in your Rolodex or computer card file.

2. Professional Portfolio. Copy the forms provided in this chapter or prepare forms and worksheets of your own. Maintain these documents in your form file, computer database, or professional portfolio. You may want to make another trip to the courthouse and look through medical negligence files to see if a life-care plan was filed. If so, you may want to photocopy it to provide you with a sample document for future reference.

ENDNOTES

1. American Association of Legal Nurse Consultants, *Standards of Practice and Professional Performance* (1995) Standard II(2).

2. James W. H. McCord, *The Litigation Paralegal: A Systems Approach,* 3rd ed. (Albany, NY: West Thomson Learning, 1997).

ADDITIONAL REFERENCES

Barone, J. E., BS, RN. "Assessing Damages in a Case Involving a Brachial Plexus Injury." *Journal of Legal Nurse Consulting* 10:1 (1999): 3–4.

Bogart, J. B., RN, MN, ed. *Legal Nurse Consulting: Principles and Practice.* Boston: CRC Press, (1998).

Pinder, A. P., EdD, CVE, CRC, CIRC, ABVE, CCM. "How to Choose and Use a Vocational Expert." *Journal of Legal Nurse Consulting* 7:3 (1996): 8–10.

Thomas, R. L., PhD, CRC, CLCP, and L. D. Busby, MCP, CLCP. "Legal Nurse Consulting from a Life-Care Planning Perspective." *Journal of Legal Nurse Consulting* 7:4 (1996): 10–13.

CHAPTER 31

MEDICAL LITERATURE REVIEW

OBJECTIVES

In this chapter, you will discover

- sources for medical research and literature review

- a strategy for researching medical literature

- what is meant by "junk science"

- how use of the Internet enhances and expedites medical research

- the many ways that medical research results may be reported

OVERVIEW

Legal nurse consultants may be asked to perform medical research. The research may be for any of several reasons, some of which have been identified
in previous chapters. Legal nurse consultants may be asked to research the
credentials of an expert and any publications of that expert. Legal nurse consultants may be asked to check medical literature for standards of care and
medical protocol. Research may be needed to support future medical damages or disprove the necessity of claimed treatment. Medical research may
support or discredit claims of health care negligence.

Before embarking on medical research, the legal nurse consultant should
determine the purpose of the medical research and the medical issues in the
case. As with other legal nurse consulting activities, reviewing the file will provide insight into the background of the case, and a discussion with the attorney will help identify potential sources and constraints of the research project.

Constraints, particularly of time, may influence the legal nurse consultant's choice of sources. Additionally, the case at bar may not have sufficient
value to support exhaustive medical research. These initial considerations
should be ascertained by the legal nurse consultant before beginning a research assignment.

Once the background, purpose, and constraints of the project are identified, the legal nurse consultant must make determinations about where to locate the information requested, how to obtain complete information as
quickly and economically as possible, and how to ensure that the medical research results are valid and relevant to the date of the claimed injury.

SOURCES FOR MEDICAL RESEARCH

As with legal research, there are two sources of medical research: primary
and secondary. **Primary sources** are the experiments and observations conducted for research or scientific purposes, for dissertations, and on behalf of
funding agencies. These initial studies are difficult to obtain and most researchers rely on secondary reports of these studies in medical journals and
peer-reviewed publications.

Secondary sources interpret or explain primary research. Included in the
category of secondary sources are peer-reviewed journals, textbooks, medical periodicals, and online publications. The legal nurse consultant should
be cautious about the types of secondary sources relied upon. The attorney
may have a preference for scientific or medical journal research or authoritative textbooks. If the results of the research will be used in evidence, court
rules or precedent may impact the type of literature that can be admitted.

Medical and scientific journals that are peer reviewed are generally accepted as having greater influence than periodical publications. This is because the peer review prior to publication attempts to ensure that the
methodology, results, and conclusions of the experiment, observation, or

study are unbiased and meet criteria for scientific research. Questions regarding the **internal validity** (does it measure what it purports to measure?), **reliability** (if the study were replicated, would the same results be obtained?), and **external validity** (are the results applicable to daily practice?) of the study are taken into consideration in the peer-review process. For these reasons, peer-reviewed journal articles may be placed at the top of the hierarchy of secondary sources.

Some attorneys may prefer research from authoritative textbooks. Because the ultimate goal of case development is to clearly and convincingly present the medical facts and issues to a lay jury, attorneys may believe that jurors will feel more comfortable with textbooks than with high-brow journals. Authoritative textbooks are those that have been used in health care education for many years and have been produced in several editions since their first appearance on the market. They are published by reputable medical publishing houses, and are written by or contain contributions by medical professionals with considerable experience and expertise in the subject area of the textbook.

If the legal nurse consultant is uncertain about where to begin the legal research, a textbook provides quick reference and, very often, a general answer. Citations in the textbook may provide leads to additional sources of medical information. Where no textbook is available or where the medical issue being researched is completely new to the legal nurse consultant, resourcefulness and common sense will serve. Calling or e-mailing a colleague who has information about the medical issue often yields results. Entering a general search on the Internet might also provide enough introductory information to begin the medical research and to educate the legal nurse consultant on the terminology and procedures involved.

IDENTIFYING THE ISSUES TO RESEARCH

Before beginning any research project, the legal nurse consultant must employ analytical skills to identify the medical issues to be researched. The age, sex, and race of the injured party *at the time of injury* may be key to locating specific medical research. Particular facts concerning the client's health, medications being taken, and any other conditions that could have an impact on the medical issue should also be determined. The date of the occurrence and the state of medical science *at that time* will be critical in evaluating the results of the research.

While the research is progressing, or even after reviewing the file, the legal nurse consultant might find other medical issues that were not identified by the attorney. These issues should be documented and discussed to determine whether additional research should be conducted. Thus, the process of research is a spiral process. Information found in the medical literature often leads to more questions, which leads to additional research.

LOCATING APPROPRIATE MEDICAL SOURCES

The legal nurse consultant may consult any number of medical sources before determining which will provide the attorney with the most authoritative and objective information from which to draw a conclusion. Several sources, along with basic descriptions of the types of information contained in those sources, are listed in Figure 31-1.

Legal nurse consultants should also consider private organizations and public agencies in conducting medical research. Several nonprofit organizations such as the American Cancer Society, the American Red Cross, the American Heart Association, and the National Kidney Foundation provide information and statistics that may be of value. Federal agencies and quasi-government agencies such as the Food and Drug Administration, the Center for Disease Control, and the National Institute of Mental Health may provide additional information concerning medical issues. Many of these organizations and agencies are accessible via the Internet.

A medical library contains several other sources that may prove helpful. The *Encyclopedia of Medical Organizations and Agencies* provides information

FIGURE 31-1   Medical Research Sources

Publication Type	Description
Scientific and medical peer-reviewed journals	• Experiments, observations, and studies by reputable scientists and other professionals • Citations to other reports of scientific and medical significance
Authorative textbooks	• General standards of care • General protocols and procedures • Descriptions of cases
Association journals	• Emerging trends • Standards of care and legal issues • Ethics and reports on disciplinary actions • Association news • Practice and business articles
Medical periodicals	• Emerging trends and techniques • Prevailing philosophies on medical issues • Practice and business articles • Profiles of practitioners
Continuing education materials	• Emerging practices and protocols • Updates on medical issues • State of medical science at the time of the conference, seminar, or workshop

about more than 11,000 associations, foundations, and government agencies (both federal and state); research centers; and medical schools. The *Health Care Standards Directory* is useful for locating citations to health care standards, guidelines, and practices issued by professional associations, government agencies, and other health-related organizations.

How the legal nurse consultant conducts research is a personal matter. Many will find it easiest to start with textbooks while others may begin on the Internet. The search strategy is not as important as the results. Whatever strategy is employed, the legal nurse consultant will eventually arrive at the same sources that any other legal nurse consultant would arrive at given the same assignment. The critical aspect of research is evaluating which of these sources accurately and completely addresses the medical issue.

EVALUATING MEDICAL RESEARCH RESULTS

All research results are not equal. The legal nurse consultant must use discernment and analytical skills in determining how valid and on point the research results are. If the medical information is for educational purposes only, the research results may be acceptable regardless of their source. If, however, the medical information might be used in court, it is important to verify that the results meet statutory and common law guidelines for admission into evidence. (Please see Chapter Twenty-four for a review of evidence law, particularly the *Daubert* ruling and the learned treatise exception to hearsay.)

To evaluate medical research results, the legal nurse consultant should carefully examine the author's credentials and reputation; the reputation of the publishing house or publication; whether the author's study, article, report, or book is grounded in medical literature; and whether citations to related medical literature are provided. These criteria will help establish the credibility of the information contained in that medical source and forestall challenges to its admission in evidence or use as a learned treatise.

If textbook research is going to be used, the textbooks should be current and authoritative in nature. It has been suggested that three textbooks or other sources be used to fully corroborate that the medical issue described is generally accepted, or rejected, by medical experts.[1]

JUNK SCIENCE

Evidence that has been offered in evidence that purports to be scientific, but is not accepted in the medical or scientific community, has been termed **junk science.** The court has great discretion in admitting or disallowing expert, scientific, or medical information. To be authentic, many courts follow the *Daubert* rule. It requires that the scientific information offered must have been tested using acceptable scientific methodology, and that it must have been subjected to peer review.[2] Expert opinion and literature that is not based on these criteria may not be allowed in evidence in a court that follows *Daubert*.

Net Results

Medical Research on the Internet

Medical research is made convenient and user-friendly via the National Library of Medicine's MEDLINE access. MEDLINE links researchers with references and abstracts from 4300 biomedical journals. Searches may be made by author, journal, or MeSH (vocabulary of medical and scientific terms), and may be limited or expanded by using BOOLEAN connectors. Documents may be retrieved via LOANSOME DOC, a fee-based service. Access this web site at www.nlm.nih.gov.

Ethics Bookmark

Lawyers and Staff as Witnesses

The American Bar Association Model Rules prohibit a lawyer from serving as an "advocate at a trial in which the lawyer is likely to be a necessary witness" (ABA Annotated Model Rules of Professional Conduct, Fourth Edition, Rule 3.7(a), Copyright 1999.[3] *If the lawyer is a "necessary" witness, the lawyer is obligated to withdraw representation of the client. Whether in-house legal nurse consultants or other legal assistants fall within this prohibitive rule has not been tested. Since the legal nurse consultant does not act as "advocate" at the trial, he or she may potentially be called as a witness without jeopardizing the firm's representation. The legal nurse consultant would only be allowed to testify to facts; for example, the legal nurse consultant took photographs of the client or medicine bottles and testimony is required to authenticate those photographs.*
*American Bar Association. Reprinted by permission of the American Bar Association. American Bar Association, *Annotated Model Rules of Professional conduct,* 4th ed. (1999) Rule 3.7(a). Copies of Model Code of Professional Responsibility, 1999 edition are available from Service Center, American Bar Association, 750 North Lake Shore Drive, Chicago, IL 60611-4497, 1-800-285-2221.

RESEARCH STRATEGY USING PRINT MEDIA

Legal nurse consultants must have a general understanding of what medical and scientific resources are available and what information is contained in those resources. Using medical libraries is a traditional and accepted, albeit somewhat infrequent, component of nursing practice. For legal nurse consultants, the medical library is an integral part of the profession.

To use time wisely and efficiently in the medical library, legal nurse consultants should plan their research. The planning begins with a critical analysis of the medical issues and the purposes for the research. Several steps are involved in library research, which are outlined in a checklist in Figure 31-2.

The first step is to gather all of the relevant facts and define the medical issue, being certain to include the date of occurrence as a relevant fact. Draft a statement of the medical issue to guide the research. When the area of medicine has been identified, and if it is an area about which the legal nurse consultant is unfamiliar, textbook research and medical dictionaries will provide information on the vocabulary and generally accepted principles of that area. The legal nurse consultant should then target the sources that will serve the purpose of the research project. The card catalog should be consulted to determine if there are learned treatises on this area of medicine or if books have been written specifically about this topic. Using standard medical and nursing indexes to literature, the nurse should locate medical and scientific journals and peer-reviewed publications concerning the medical issue. After reading and evaluating these articles and reports, copies should be made of those that provide insight into the medical issue being researched. Results are then verified, or discredited, by locating corroborating, or contradictory, articles or reports. Throughout this process, the legal nurse consultant should main-

---

FIGURE 31-2   Checklist for Library Research

1. Gather and analyze relevant facts and define the medical issue.
2. Determine the area of medicine to be researched.
3. Use the online card catalog to locate learned treatises or books published on this issue and area of medicine.
4. Educate yourself on the area of medicine by using textbooks and medical dictionaries.
5. Locate scientific and medical journals and peer-reviewed publications that deal with this area of medicine by referencing medical indexes.
6. Verify that research is date-specific.
7. Summarize or photocopy relevant research.
8. Create a paper trail of research findings using appropriate citation techniques.

tain an accurate paper trail with appropriate citations to avoid a second trip to the library.

RESEARCH STRATEGY USING THE INTERNET

The comfort and convenience of medical research without leaving your office, home, or workstation is one advantage of using the Internet to research medical literature. Additionally, once skill has been acquired in Internet navigation, online research may be cost effective, efficient, and accurate, since most web sites update information frequently. The speed with which information can be obtained via the Internet is another great advantage.

Because anyone can publish online, it is critical for a legal nurse consultant to evaluate the results of a computer-based medical research project to determine whether the information will be acceptable to the medical and scientific communities and to the courts. If doubt exists about the validity of a particular search result, additional research should be conducted to corroborate or discredit it.

While the information available on the Internet seems limitless, and the speed and minimal expense of computer searches make them attractive, it is still wise to plan research so that time and resources are used productively. It is unfair to the attorney and the client to do otherwise. A checklist of the steps involved in researching medical literature using MEDLINE on the Internet is included in Figure 31-3.

The first step is still to analyze the facts and arrive at the medical issue. From the medical issue, key terms and phrases may be extracted. Using the MEDLINE database at www.nlm.nih.gov, select a search engine (PubMed or Grateful Med) and enter the key terms and phrases into the search dialogue box. The search may be expanded or limited by using BOOLEAN connectors, such as AND, OR, and NOT. Review the retrieved citations and abstracts to determine if they address the medical issue being researched. Select the citations

---

FIGURE 31-3   Checklist for Medical Research on the Internet

1. Gather and analyze relevant facts and define the medical issue.
2. Determine whether field searches can be used (e.g., author, journal).
3. Identify and enter MeSH terms if field searches are not appropriate.
4. Use BOOLEAN connectors to expand or limit the search.
5. Review citations and abstracts.
6. Mark the relevant citations.
7. Verify that research is date-specific.
8. Print the search results and locate the articles.
9. Order copies of the articles via LOANSOME DOC, the document retrieval system of the National Library of Medicine.

Net Results

Verifying Physician Credentials on the Internet

It is possible to verify the credentials of physicians on the Internet using the web site for the American Medical Association. This site provides primary source information concerning individual physicians, including medical school graduation, residency training, and board certification. Access this web site at www.ama-assn.org/ physdata/physrel/physrel. htm. Another web site with valuable information concerning physicians is Doctorline. Access this web site at http://doctorline. com/phystate.htm.

that appear to be the most relevant and print a list of them. Copies of articles can be obtained online using NLM's document retrieval system, LOANSOME DOC. There is a charge for this service.

The Internet places the world of medicine at the fingertips of the legal nurse consultant. The information that is accessible and the speed with which it can be obtained make Internet research of medical literature a compelling skill of the legal nurse consultant. A listing of the types of information available on the Internet and the URLs for obtaining that information is included in Figure 31-4.

RESEARCHING MEDICAL CREDENTIALS

Legal nurse consultants are often called upon to research the credentials of an expert. This may be easily accomplished by verifying the accuracy of the expert's curriculum vita[e]. Telephone calls to the universities from which the expert claims to have graduated or to medical facilities where the expert claims to be on staff will generally provide the needed information.

Other directories provide information concerning physician credentials, such as the *Official ABMS Directory of Board Certified Medical Specialists*, which lists physicians who are board certified. On the Internet, the American Medical Association's web site provides information for verifying physician credentials, including medical school graduation, residency training, and board certification by the National Committee for Quality Assurance. The Doctor Guide web site provides a quick reference resource of 796,000 doctors, dentists, hospitals, nursing homes, and pharmacies. The Doctorline Practice Profile provides even more detailed information about doctors and dentists in all fifty states and the District of Columbia.

FIGURE 31-4　Internet Sites for Medical Research

Site	URL
MEDLINE (Grateful Med)	igm.nl/m.nih.gov
American Medical Association	www.ama-assn.org
Joint Commission on Accreditation of Healthcare Organizations (JCAHO)	www.jcaho.org
American Cancer Society	www.cancer.org
Center for Disease Control	www.cdc.gov
Food and Drug Administration	www.fda.gov
American Heart Association	www.americanheart.org

Site	URL
Center for Substance Abuse Research (CESAR)	www.cesar.umd.edu
National Institute of Allergy and Infectious Diseases	www.niaid.nih.gov
Critical care	http://dacc.bsd.uchicago.edu
American Dental Association	www.ada.org
Americans with Disabilities Act Document Center (ADA)	http://janweb.icdi.wvu.edu/kinder
Emergency medicine	www.embbs.com
American Association of Clinical Endocrinologists (AACE)	www.aace.com
Agency for Toxic Substances and Disease Registry	http://atsdr1.atsdr.cdc.gov:8080/hazdat.html
Experts	www.expertpages.com
American Academy of Family Physicians (AAFP) - family medicine	www.aafp.org/family
Pediatrics	www.hopkinsmedicine.org/children.html
Consumer Product Safety Commission	www.cpsc.gov
Martindale's Virtual Nursing Center	www-sci.lib.uci.edu/~martindale/Nursing.html
American College of Forensic Examiners	www.acfe.com
Gastroenterology	http://cpmcnet.columbia.edu/dept/gi
Agency on Aging	www.aoa.dhhs.gov
The American Medical Women's Association	www.amwa-doc.org
ICD-9 Coding	www.eicd.com
American Society of Internal Medicine	www.acponline.org
American Association of Neuroscience Nurses	www.aann.org
American Association of Legal Nurse Consultants	www.aalnc.org
Boards of Nursing	www.ncsbn.org
Association of Reproductive Health Professionals	www.arhp.org
Occupational Safety and Health	www.osh.net
American Academy of Orthopaedic Surgeons	www.aaos.org
College of American Pathologists	www.cap.org

continued

FIGURE 31-4   Internet Sites for Medical Research   *continued*

Site	URL
Merck Manual	www.merck.com
Pharmaceutical	www.druginfonet.com
National Institute of Mental Health	www.nimh.nih.gov
Radiological Society of North America	www.rsna.org
National Rehabilitation Information Center	www.naric.com

CHAPTER SUMMARY

- Most medical research is done in secondary sources such as medical and scientific journals, textbooks, medical periodicals, and online publications.

- Medical research should be evaluated for its internal validity, reliability, and external validity.

- To research efficiently and effectively, the legal nurse consultant must gather facts concerning the injured party and the date of the occurrence.

- According to the *Daubert* rule, medical opinions sought to be admitted in evidence must be based on research using acceptable scientific methodology, and the results must have been subject to peer review.

- Junk science is information claiming to be scientific but lacking foundation.

- Before beginning research either in the library or online, the legal nurse consultant must develop a research strategy.

KEY TERMS

internal validity	junk science	reliability
external validity	primary sources	secondary sources

REVIEW QUESTIONS

1. What types of medical research might legal nurse consultants be asked to conduct?
2. How has the Internet made medical research easier?

3. Identify a research strategy that will work for you and will provide complete, accurate, and date-specific information.

INTERNET EXERCISES

1. Access the web page for this textbook at *www.westlegalstudies.com.*

2. Click on the assignments section and complete the assignment(s) for Chapter Thirty-one.

EXERCISES

1. Networking. Locate a nurse's association on the Internet from the list provided in Appendix D. Consider subscribing to the Listserv. Enter the chat room or post a message on the bulletin board asking if anyone in the organization has worked or is working as a legal nurse consultant. Maintain the names of the professionals who respond in your Rolodex or card file.
2. Professional Portfolio. Using the resources provided in this chapter, research the credentials of physicians with whom you have worked. Recall a medical event or situation that you thought was handled inappropriately. Develop a medical issues statement and conduct medical research concerning this procedure and the standard of care involved. Report your results in an interoffice memorandum. Maintain these documents as samples in your portfolio and add "knowledge of medical research" to your resume.

ENDNOTES

1. K.L. Wetther, "Literature Research," In *Legal Nurse Consulting: Principles and Practice,* ed. J.B. Bogart, MS, RN (Boston, MA: CRC Press, 1998), 459.
2. *Daubert v. Merrell Dow Pharmaceuticals, Inc.* 113 S. Ct. 2786, 125 L. Ed. 2d 469 (1993).

3. American Bar Association, *Annotated Model Rules of Professional Conduct,* (1999) 4th Edition Rule 3.7(a). Copies of ABA *Model Code of Professional Responsibility, 1999 Edition* are available from Service Center, American Bar Association, 750 North Lake Shore Drive, Chicago, IL 60611-4497, 1-800-285-2221.

ADDITIONAL REFERENCES

AALNC Greater Detroit Chapter. "How to Research Information about an Expert Witness." *Journal of Legal Nurse Consulting* 10:2 (1999): 29–30.

AALNC Greater Chicago Chapter. "Online Classes and Worthwhile Web Sites." *Journal of Legal Nurse Consulting.* 10:3 (1999): 23, 30.

McKinley, Linda, BSN, RN, CDMS, CCM, CLCP. "Medical Literature Research 2000." *Journal of Legal Nurse Consulting* 10:4 (1999): 26–27.

Newland, T., MS, RN. "References and Resources: World Wide Web Sites." *Journal of Legal Nurse Consulting* 9:4 (1998): 21.

CHAPTER 32

PREPARATION FOR TRIAL

OBJECTIVES

In this chapter, you will discover

■ how legal nurse consultants can help prepare for a trial

■ what a trial notebook is and how it is used

■ what a deposition summary is and how it is used

■ how legal nurse consultants can help prepare trial exhibits

■ the added value of having a legal nurse consultant assist at trial

OVERVIEW

Most lawsuits settle or are disposed of before they are taken to trial. However, all activities in the case—investigation, pleadings, settlement demands and negotiations, and discovery—are undertaken with a view toward preparation for trial, if necessary. The investigation and damages worksheet is preparation for the settlement demand and the pleadings, the pleadings provide the basis for discovery, and discovery provides the foundation for the pretrial conference.

Pretrial Conference

The **pretrial conference** is often placed on the calendar at the time of the scheduling conference. There, the attorneys for all sides meet with the judge to prepare an agenda for the trial and to handle several other issues as well:

- narrow issues of fact and law
- enter into stipulations on evidence
- agree on the number of potential jurors to impanel
- agree on the number of challenges to potential jurors
- agree on limitations on voir dire
- file and exchange pretrial briefs
- identify witness testimony and physical evidence expected to be brought
- identify and/or limit the number of expert witnesses

Many judges view the pretrial conference as a final opportunity to provide the parties with settlement options or **alternative dispute resolution.** At least one of the attorneys in attendance for each party must have the authority to settle on behalf of that party. Each jurisdiction has its own local rules concerning **pretrial briefs,** but generally some form of summary of the lawsuit must be provided to the court prior to the pretrial conference. The contents of a pretrial report are outlined in Figure 32-1.

The **pretrial order** includes the order of witnesses and exhibits. It is critical to include all potential witnesses and exhibits, since this will provide the basis for the pretrial order. Judges may demand that strict adherence to the pretrial order be observed, so if a witness is not identified in the pretrial report or brief, that witness may be barred from testimony. Conversely, if the witness is allowed to testify, it may provide grounds for mistrial or a motion for new trial if opposing counsel was not aware of the witness or prepared to rebut the evidence of the witness. Where medical issues are involved, legal nurse consultants may be called upon to assist in the development of the pretrial report. The pretrial order issued by the court after the pretrial conference guides all further preparations for trial.

FIGURE 32-1   Contents of Pretrial Report or Brief

Section	Explanation of Contents
Undisputed facts	A recitation, similar to the allegations in a complaint, of the facts that are not being contested at the trial.
Disputed facts	A recitation, similar to the allegations in a complaint, of the facts that plaintiff must prove.
Exhibits	A detailed list of the physical evidence, that will be introduced at trial, including any potential objections to each exhibit by opposing counsel.
Lay witnesses	A list of all lay witnesses who may be called at trial and the exhibits to which they are expected to testify.
Expert witnesses	A list of all expert witnesses who may be called at trial, their qualifications, and the exhibits to which they are expected to testify.
Testimony by deposition	Identification of any testimony that will be delivered via deposition and the specific pages within the deposition that will be entered as testimony.

RESPONSIBILITIES OF THE LEGAL NURSE CONSULTANT IN PREPARATION FOR TRIAL

Several activities may be delegated to the legal nurse consultant in preparation for trial. These include helping to develop the pretrial report, reviewing and summarizing litigation documents (if summaries have not already been prepared), using summaries to prepare witnesses and experts for testimony at trial, using summaries and records to assist in the development of trial exhibits, and helping to develop a trial notebook. Many of these activities have been discussed in previous chapters. This chapter will focus on trial notebooks, deposition summaries, and preparation of exhibits.

TRIAL NOTEBOOKS

Many attorneys like to use three-ring binders to organize for trial. Organization of case information into a binder ensures that the attorney will be able to locate critical information when it is needed at trial. If the **trial notebook** is prepared properly, it should contain or reference everything the attorney needs. Even when attorneys bring their laptop computers with sophisticated software programs organizing the information necessary for trial, notebooks should be prepared in the event of a crash.

Trial notebooks will always be customized to the preferences of the attorney and the needs of the case. The trial notebook can be thought of as the

What LNCs Say . . .

"Attorneys don't know what to ask for from legal nurse consultants. When we talked about medical-related cases, the attorney repeatedly said, 'Why don't you take this and see what you can do with it?' The attorney has to see what I can do in order to know what to ask for next time" Kay L. Scharn, RN, MSN, EdS, LNC, Eau Claire, WI, used with permission.

script. The first page will contain a cast of characters— that is the names of all the parties and their attorneys—and a brief description of the incident. Attorneys, like everyone else, occasionally suffer stage fright. It does not create a favorable impression when the attorney suddenly goes blank during the opening statements and cannot recall the plaintiff's name or the type of vehicle involved in the incident. Some attorneys prefer to have the names taped to the inside front cover of the three-ring binder.

It may be useful to use the pretrial order as the guiding organizational tool for the trial notebook. An index or table of contents should identify the contents of the trial notebook and each section should be tabbed for easy reference. Typical parts of a trial notebook include sections for the jury, pleadings, opening statements, proof chart, witnesses, expert witnesses, exhibits, authority, jury instructions, closing arguments, and notes.

Jury

The jury questionnaire obtained from the courthouse will be included in this section, along with any other jury investigation materials. A blank page is also inserted to write down the names and any pertinent information about potential jurors during the selection process. Once the jury is selected, a final jury chart is prepared with the names of each juror in each seat in the jury box. A potential jury chart is illustrated in Figure 32-2. Each box in the jury chart is just large enough for a small Post-it note. As each potential juror is called, his or her name and information is written on a Post-it note and the note is placed in the box where the potential juror is sitting. When the final

FIGURE 32-2   Sample Jury Chart

jury is selected, the names and information concerning each juror can be written directly on the chart.

Pleadings

The pleadings section should contain an index of the pleadings, copies of the complaint and answer, and any other important pleadings in the matter. This includes counterclaims, cross-claims, third-party complaints, and motions. These pleadings are tabbed or otherwise identified with reference to the index.

Opening Statements

In this section, the attorney will record any notes to assist in presenting opening statements. In addition, blank pages will be included for the attorney to make notes about the opposing counsel's opening statements.

Proof Chart

For each fact that must be proven at court, the **proof chart** will identify, in order, the fact, the witnesses who will testify to the fact, and the physical evidence that will be offered to prove the fact. The proof chart can be taken from the pretrial order, thereby providing an agenda for the trial. If the proof chart is properly prepared, no item of proof will be overlooked during the trial. The attorney checks off each item as it is brought forward. A sample proof chart is shown in Figure 32-3.

FIGURE 32-3 Sample Proof Chart

Proof Chart

Fact	Proof
1.	
2.	
3.	

Witnesses

For each witness who is expected to testify, a witness information form is completed. This form contains everything the attorney will need in order to elicit appropriate testimony from the witness. Copies of the witness's statements, or summaries of the witness's deposition may be included behind the witness information form. A sample witness information form is included in Figure 32-4.

Expert Witnesses

A separate expert witness information form, similar to the witness information form, should be completed for each expert. This form will include a summary of the expert's qualifications and opinion. Copies of the expert's re-

---

FIGURE 32-4   Sample Witness Information Form

Witness

Subpoena data: Witness No. _____

Issued: _____   Name _____

Served: _____   Address: _____

Deposition? _____   _____

Appearance? _____   Phone: _____

Appearance: Employer: _____

Date: _____   Address & Phone: _____

Time: _____   _____

Type of witness: _____

Questions: Exhibits

1. _____   _____

2. _____   _____

3. _____   _____

4. _____   _____

5. _____   _____

6. _____   _____

ports, summaries of the expert's deposition, and the expert's curriculum vitae may also be included in this section.

Exhibits

Each exhibit is identified in this section in the order in which the exhibits are expected to be produced at trial. Also included is who will testify to the exhibit, any potential objections to the exhibit, and potential authority for admission of the exhibit as evidence. As each exhibit is offered in evidence, it is checked on the exhibit list. A sample exhibit chronology is included in Figure 32-5.

Authority

Citations to any statutes, administrative rules and regulations, and case law that apply should be included here. Case briefs or copies of statutes may be included in this section and tabbed with reference to the index. Additionally, medical literature intended to be used during the trial may be included here.

Jury Instructions

Copies of the proposed jury instructions are included here. This allows the attorneys to review the instructions as they are given to the jury and to make notes for closing arguments.

Closing arguments

Throughout the trial, the attorneys make notes concerning their closing arguments. These notes, together with the notes taken during opening statements and during jury instructions, are valuable at the close evidence for impressing the jury with a summary of the proceedings.

FIGURE 32-5 Sample Exhibit Chronology

Exhibit No.	Description	Witness	Offered	Objection	Admitted

Net Results

Internet Searches

Numerous search engines are now available for locating people and information. Yahoo, Infoseek, and Lycos are common general search engines. Valuable information can be obtained, including maps for location of offices in other cities where depositions might be taken. Access these search engines by using their web sites at www.yahoo.com, www.infoseek.com, and www.lycos.com.

Note Pages

Every trial notebook should be equipped with plenty of blank pages for the attorney to take notes on the testimony and to make reminder notes for additional questioning. The trial notebook serves as a script and a checklist. As each item is entered into evidence in a logical and coherent manner, it is checked off the proof chart or witness information form. As the trial progresses, the attorney has a clear record of the proceedings at trial.

Occasionally the trial notebook will not be big enough to contain complete information. In those cases, bankers' boxes are often used. The trial notebook is tabbed or color-coded to reference the file folders in the bankers' boxes. For example, the testimony of an expert toxicologist may be identified as E4 and the tab may be color-coded purple. The purple file label (E4) will contain the information necessary to properly examine the expert toxicologist. In other purple-labeled file folders may be the expert's deposition, a summary of the deposition, the expert's curriculum vitae, the expert's report, the expert's bill, and miscellaneous correspondence with that expert.

The trial notebook is an efficient way to prepare for trial, and the legal nurse consultant may be called upon to assist in its development, especially if medical exhibits and expert medical testimony will be components of the trial notebook.

DEPOSITION SUMMARIES

Discovery results in the accumulation of massive amounts of information that must be organized so that the information will be accessible and useable. One way that legal nurse consultants assist in trial preparation is in the summarizing of discovery information.

Depositions are discovery devices that allow the attorneys to question witnesses under oath. The testimony of the witness (deponent) is recorded by a court reporter and transcribed into a document called a transcript of the deposition. Usually the original transcript is sealed in an envelope and filed with the court and may only be opened if the deposition is used in lieu of testimony at trial. Copies of the transcript are delivered to each party in the lawsuit.

Because deposition transcripts are often lengthy and the testimony may not seem to have any order, depositions must be summarized. There are several important reasons why depositions are summarized:

- to extract critical testimony
- to compare critical testimony with other documents and testimony in the lawsuit
- to condense the information into a useable format
- to provide quick access to the deposition testimony

If the testimony of a witness at trial is different from the testimony given at the deposition, the deposition testimony may be used to **impeach** that wit-

FIGURE 32-6 Deposition Summaries	
Deposition Summary	**Description**
Deposition digest	A deposition digest extracts testimony verbatim and identifies where that testimony appears in the deposition transcript.
Deposition index	A deposition index is similar to the index at the back of a book; it collects the important topics and identifies where testimony concerning those topics can be found in the deposition transcript.
Deposition summary	A deposition summary uses a standard format for paraphrasing the testimony of the witness and identifies where that testimony can be found in the deposition transcript.

ness. The attorney must be able to locate that testimony quickly, rather than page through a hundred-page deposition transcript, hoping to stumble onto the correct passage.

There are several terms used to describe deposition summaries. These terms are defined in Figure 32-6. Legal nurse consultants may be called upon to prepare any of these styles of deposition summaries and should be familiar with the terminology used for each.

If the attorney requires a deposition summary, the legal nurse consultant should be familiar with the various formats. A review of the file is critical to ensure that the information being extracted from the deposition transcript is the information that is relevant to the issues in the case. If the file is not available to the legal nurse consultant, a quick call to the attorney or the paralegal will provide the necessary background for effectively summarizing the deposition.

The formats that are generally used for deposition summaries include deponent summaries, chronological summaries, topical summaries, and special purpose summaries. It is always recommended that the complete deposition be read first to get a feel for the testimony and the issues raised before the more thorough review required to prepare a summary.

The attorney may not need a deposition summary, digest, or index at all, and may prefer to have the pages of the deposition tabbed to indicate critical testimony. Another inexpensive way to access deposition testimony is to locate the information and identify it with Post-it notes.

Deponent Summary

The most frequent type of deposition summary is the **deponent summary.** It calls for a summary of the testimony of a deponent beginning with the first page and ending with the last. The questions of the attorney are eliminated

FIGURE 32-7 Sample Deponent Summary	
Page:Line	**Summary**
1-5	Lance DuPont was born 01/08/58 (42), SS# 503-65-9659. He resides at 4000 Oakview Road, Minneapolis. He graduated from Randolf High School in 1976, received a BS in elementary education from the University of Minnesota in 1980. . . .

FIGURE 32-8 Sample Chronological Summary		
Date - Time	**Page:Line**	**Summary**
2/7/00-1:15 a	6:15	LD admitted to emergency room complaining of headache
1:27 a	7:08	Bradley Jones (BJ), RN, took history. . . .

and only the testimony is included. Deposition transcripts are printed on pages with line numbers in the left margin. These page and line numbers should precede the summarized information because they are critical for accessing the testimony in the transcript. A typical guideline for this type of summary is that ten pages of testimony may be summarized in one page.

Depending on the style requested by the attorney, the deponent summary might be paraphrased or use exact testimony. In either case, the summary should reference the page and line number on which that testimony appears. The beginning of a sample deponent summary is included in Figure 32-7.

Chronological Summary

Because the questioning and testimony during the deposition may not be in time-order, the attorney may request that the testimony be summarized using **chronological** order. In this case, reading the deposition transcript is necessary before beginning to summarize. The chronological summary includes the page and line number of the testimony along with the date or time. The beginning of a typical chronological summary is included in Figure 32-8.

Occasionally, the attorney will want a **collective deposition summary.** The testimony of several deponents may be matched by identifying the chronological order in which each party testified that events occurred. When a collective chronological summary is made, the headings in the summary will include the deponent, page number, line number, date or time, and the summary of his or her testimony as to what happened at that time. A sample collective chronological summary is included as Figure 32-9.

FIGURE 32-9   Sample Collective Deposition Summary

Date - Time	Deponent	Page:Line	Summary
2/7/00 - 1:27a	LD	6:15	BJ (RN) took history. . . .
1:20a	BJ	8:20	Took history, TPR. . . .

FIGURE 32-10   Sample Topical Summary

Topic	Page:Line	Summary
Background	1:1–20	DOB: 1/8/58; SS# 503-65-9659; Address: 4000 Oakview, Mpls; . . .

Topical Summary

Most people are trained to locate items by topic or subject matter. The attorney may request that the deposition be summarized using a subject matter or **topical summary.** This requires reading the deposition for a grasp of the subjects covered prior to actually preparing the summary. A topical summary will include topic headings followed by page and line numbers and a description of the testimony. Using a topical summary allows the attorney to locate all information concerning a particular event regardless of where that testimony appears in the deposition transcript. A sample topical summary is included in Figure 32-10.

Topical summaries should include a table of contents or index. The first page of the summary will include the items the testimony is collected under and the page number *of the summary* where that information is located. For example, the attorney may look for the testimony concerning a description of the incident and find that topic on page three of the summary. Page three of the summary provides the attorney with the page and line number of the exact testimony of the deponent in the deposition transcript. A sample table of contents for a topical deposition summary is included in Figure 32-11.

Attorneys may request that topical deposition summaries be collective or that a document be prepared containing all the deposition testimony on a particular topic. In this case, the deposition summary would have a topic heading, page and line numbers, identification of the deponent, and a summary of the testimony.

FIGURE 32-11   Sample Table of Contents

Deposition of XXX
Dated 00/00/00
Re: *Title of Case*

Table of Contents

Topic   *Page of Summary*

Background 1
Emergency Room..4

Special Purpose Summary

Attorneys may want to have specific testimony extracted from a deposition for **special purposes.** These may be to compare medical expert testimony to learned treatises or to publications or presentations made by the deponent or other experts. They might also be to cross reference the testimony with other documents or other testimony. A special purpose deposition summary is customized to the particular needs of the attorney and the case. Legal nurse consultants who obtain feedback concerning the type of deposition summary required can be sure that the work product they prepare matches the expectations of the attorney.

TRIAL STRATEGY

Before any trial, attorneys and the litigation team develop a **trial strategy.** In negligence cases, this is sometimes called the "three-legged stool" on which the case rests. The three legs are often described as duty, liability, and damages. For each of the legs, the litigation team tries to come up with a theme that will impress the jury. This theme must be something that the jury will understand and empathize with. For example, in a case involving repeated complaints of pain, the theme may be *listen to the patient.* The duty leg of the stool might include questioning witnesses to relate back to the obligation of a health care provider to *listen to the patient.*

Legal nurse consultants are invaluable members of the litigation team's strategy meetings. Because nurses have considerable experience in educating patients and others concerning health care matters, they are more likely to recognize what themes a jury will understand. Additionally, once the themes are developed, the legal nurse consultant will be better able to prepare exhibits that will educate, inform, and impress the jury, and continually reinforce the theme or strategy.

EXHIBITS

There are several watchwords to keep in mind when considering the preparation of exhibits for a trial:

- People remember more of what they hear *and* see than what they just hear.
- Visual aids assist the jury in understanding critical testimony.
- Visual aids should be simple.
- Visual aids should be memorable. This may be done simply by using color, as long as the color does not make the exhibit sensational and, thus, objectionable.

When preparing exhibits, it is important to keep in mind the layout of the courtroom. The jury, the witness, and the judge must all be able to see and appreciate the exhibit.

Legal nurse consultants may be asked to prepare simple exhibits; select records, graphic sheets, or x-rays for use as exhibits; or work with medical illustrators to prepare exhibits. Several computer programs allow interactive preparation of medical exhibits. Consulting firms provide videotape and computer simulation services that are valuable for educating a jury about surgical procedures, progression of disease, or circumstances of an incident.

Legal nurse consultants might be asked to develop timelines; photographs; graphs, charts, or tables; medical illustrations; or diagrams. These exhibits should be simple enough to reduce to transparencies and to copy for the jury in the event they want to have them available in the jury room. Thus, the 3-foot by 4-foot timeline produced on foam back as an exhibit for trial may be reproduced on letter-size paper for use by the attorney, the witness, opposing counsel, and the jury. Even when exhibits are computer designed, back-up copies should be made in case the equipment fails or the jury wishes to have the exhibit in the jury room.

Every exhibit, diagram, photograph, medical record, and so forth that is admitted into evidence must be proved to be the document it is claimed to be. Most exhibits require the testimony of someone who has knowledge of that exhibit. Certified copies of medical records need no authentication and are admissible without testimony. See Chapter Twenty-four for a discussion of evidence law. Another way that legal nurse consultants may help prepare for trial is by preparing witnesses to testify concerning the medical exhibits.

PREPARING WITNESSES AND CLIENTS TO TESTIFY

Clients and witnesses may be nervous about their testimony. It is helpful for the litigation team to calm them by reviewing the essential issues and facts in the claim. When the claim involves medical experts or health care liability issues, the legal nurse consultant may be called upon to prepare witnesses and clients for testifying.

At a minimum, clients and witnesses should be sent a letter reminding them of the trial date, suggesting that they visit the courtroom to get a feel for its layout, and enclosing copies of the documents they will be expected to testify about. This will serve to refresh the client's or witness's memory about the case.

Attorneys generally believe that clients, especially, should be prepared for trial by some simulation of direct examination and potential cross-examination. This may be as simple as sending a letter identifying the types of questions the client may expect, or as thorough as videotaping an actual rehearsal. The playback of the videotape will help identify gaps in the questioning and mannerisms of the client that might be distracting to the jury.

If the legal nurse consultant is involved in preparing witnesses or clients for testifying, it may be a good idea to develop a checklist to ensure that adequate preparation has been made. This checklist may include the following:

- reviewing the file to develop a list of topics each witness will be questioned about
- preparing questions that may be asked of each witness
- identifying documents and physical evidence that each witness may be asked about
- summarizing previous testimony (depositions) and information supplied by each witness
- comparing potential testimony of each witness with potential testimony of other witnesses
- preparing each witness for courtroom appearance
- preparing each witness for maintaining composure during examination on the witness stand

Clients may be anxious about what to wear to trial. Neat, conservative clothing is always appropriate. Jeans, cutoffs, shorts, halter tops or halter dresses, and see-through or clingy clothing are inappropriate. It is important to be cautious when advising clients about what to wear. The author has witnessed two separate situations in which the clients were told to wear their "best" clothes. In the first, a female client wore a lacy, very low-cut blouse, which was considered inappropriate for her trial. In the second, a young man's "best" were a t-shirt and jeans. The t-shirt proudly announced the name of a liquor company during his DUI trial! The trial does not get off to a good start when the attorney has to run home to find a shirt for the client to wear!

It is also important to make clients aware of ways that will help them remain composed during questioning. Some attorneys will be belligerent, firing questions at them. Others will seem nonchalant, even friendly. Both methods can be disconcerting. There are several instructions that help witnesses remain calm during questioning:

- Never guess at an answer.
- Do not allow the attorney to put words in your mouth.
- If you don't understand a question, ask that it be rephrased.
- If an attorney objects, stop! Wait for the judge to make a ruling on the objection. If the ruling allows the question, ask for it to be repeated.
- Do not overstate the case, or become antagonistic or impatient.
- Take all the time you need to formulate an answer. Do not allow the attorney to rush you.
- If the attorney interrupts your answer with another question, explain that you will finish answering the previous question, then respond to the interruption.
- Do not memorize answers.
- Always tell the truth.

Observing a trial will provide valuable insight into the process, the styles, and some of the common mistakes that are made during testimony. Legal nurse consultants who will be actively involved in trial preparation should sit in on other trials to observe directly the strategy and the proceedings. Whenever possible, legal nurse consultants should attend the trials they have helped prepare for. Their notes concerning the testimony and exhibits may be valuable for posttrial motions. The presence of the legal nurse consultant might also provide clients and witnesses with a calm, reassuring focus in the courtroom.

LEARNED TREATISE

The **learned treatise** rule of evidence allows the admission of a journal article, textbook, or book of specialized information without additional testimony if an expert testifies that it is commonly accepted as "truth" within the specialty. Legal nurse consultants who locate such learned treatises during the course of the medical literature review may save their clients and their attorneys considerable time and money. Before trial, these treatises should be brought to the attention of the attorney to determine whether the treatise will be used or whether the attorney prefers to have an expert testify to the facts or procedures contained in the treatise. Attorney strategy about what to present to the jury will always be controlling.

Ethics Bookmark

Solicitation

"A lawyer shall not by in-person or live telephone contact solicit professional employment from a prospective client with whom the lawyer has no family or prior professional relationship when a significant motive for the lawyer's doing so is the lawyer's pecuniary gain." Annotated Model Rules of Professional Conduct Fourth Edition Rule 7.3 Copyright 1999.*[1] There are stories about attorneys who are ambulance chasers. Fiction often describes attorneys hanging around in hospital waiting rooms handing out business cards. This type of conduct is unethical. Even more subtle solicitation must be avoided. If a legal nurse consultant hears about a legal problem and suggests that the person involved come to the law firm where he or she is employed, a potential for violation of this ethical rule exists.

*American Bar Association. Reprinted by permission of the American Bar Association. American Bar Association, *Annotated Model Rules of Professional conduct*, 4th ed. (1999) Rule 7.3. Copies of Model Code of Professional Responsibility, 1999 edition are available from Service Center, American Bar Association, 750 North Lake Shore Drive, Chicago, IL 60611-4497, 1-800-285-2221.

THE ROLE OF THE LEGAL NURSE CONSULTANT AT TRIAL

There are many reasons why the attorney might invite the legal nurse consultant to participate in trial. The legal nurse consultant might act as the record keeper and facilitate production of medical records and exhibits during the course of the trial. In addition, he or she may be asked to pay particular attention to the medical testimony and remind the attorney of questions that may not have been asked or information that needs follow-up. The legal nurse consultant may be asked to keep an eye on the jury to see if the jury seems to be understanding the themes presented during the course of the trial and whether they seem to react favorably or unfavorably to testimony or exhibits. Finally, a legal nurse consultant may be asked to read a medical deposition into the record. This simply involves sitting in the witness box and reading the answers to the questions the attorney reads aloud from the deposition transcript.

Note taking is a critical component of attendance at trial. If the trial is lengthy, everyone's notes are typed (or printed if prepared on laptops) and duplicated for the following morning's strategy meeting. At the strategy meeting, usually over breakfast, the attorneys discuss what points were made effectively and what needs additional emphasis. Note taking is also important for posttrial motions. Because it is difficult to obtain a transcript within the time provided for posttrial motions, usually 20 days, the notes of those attending the trial are relied upon for an explanation of the proceedings at the trial.

CHAPTER SUMMARY

- A pretrial conference is held to narrow the issues of fact and law and, among other things, to prepare an agenda for trial.
- The pretrial conference provides a basis for preparation of a trial notebook.
- A trial notebook is customized for each case and contains all materials and information the attorney may need at trial.
- Legal nurse consultants may be called upon to prepare summaries of depositions in preparation for trial.
- There are several types of deposition summaries, including deponent, chronological, topical, and special purpose summaries.
- Legal nurse consultants may assist in preparing trial exhibits and strategy, and preparing clients and witnesses for testimony.

KEY TERMS

alternative dispute resolution
chronological deposition
   summary
collective deposition summary
deponent summary
impeach

learned treatise
pretrial brief
pretrial conference
pretrial order
proof chart

special purpose deposition
   summary
topical deposition summary
trial notebook
trial strategy

REVIEW QUESTIONS

1. Identify the potential components of a trial notebook. Why is it beneficial to prepare a trial notebook?

2. Distinguish between deponent, chronological, topical, and special purpose deposition summaries.
3. How may legal nurse consultants assist in the development of trial exhibits and trial strategy?

INTERNET EXERCISES

1. Access the web page for this textbook at *www.westlegalstudies.com.*

2. Click on the assignments section and complete the assignment(s) for Chapter Thirty-two.

EXERCISES

1. Networking. Return to the county courthouse and to the file on the case of medical negligence that you reviewed earlier. Find any depositions that may have been filed with the case. Read through the deposition. Consider drafting a summary of the deposition or an index to it. Maintain this summary or index in your sys-tems file, folder, or binder, and organize or index it for easy reference.

2. Professional Portfolio. Photocopy the forms and samples provided in this chapter and main-tain them in your systems file, folder, or binder. Organizing the forms for easy reference will give you a competitive edge when interviewing or beginning a new position.

ENDNOTES

1. American Bar Association, *Annotated Model Rules of Professional Conduct,* (1999) 4th Edition Rule 7.3. Copies of ABA *Model Code of Professional Responsibility, 1999 Edition* are available from Service Center, American Bar Association, 750 North Lake Shore Drive, Chicago, IL 60611-4497, 1-800-285-2221.

ADDITIONAL REFERENCES

AALNC Greater Detroit Chapter. "Witness Lists." *Journal of Legal Nurse Consulting* 9:2 (1998): 13.

Kerley, P. N., J. B Hames, P. A. Sukys. *Civil Litigation,* 2nd ed. Albany, NY: West Thomson Learning, 1996.

McCord, J. W. H. *The Litigation Paralegal,* 3rd ed. St. Paul, MN: West Publishing Company, 1997.

Weishapple, Cynthia. "Deposition Summaries." *Journal of Legal Nurse Consulting* 3:14 (1998).

LEGAL NURSE CONSULTANT PROFILE

Franklin W. Wilson, Jr.

Independent Consulting—Medical Malpractice

Franklin W. Wilson, Jr., is past president of Legal Nurse Perspectives, Inc., of Reno, Nevada. Although he no longer works strictly as a legal nurse consultant, he still maintains an independent practice, primarily specializing in research. He received his associate degree in nursing from Truckee Meadows Community College in Reno, Nevada, and completed the basic legal nurse consulting program offered through Medical-Legal Consulting Institute of Houston, Texas. He is certified in basic life support and advanced cardiac life support. After eighteen years of hospital nursing, Frank opened Legal Nurse Perspectives, Inc., in 1997.

What do you like best about being a legal nurse consultant?

"Hands down, I would have to say it is the research I enjoy most. Each new case offers the opportunity to learn something different. During my time as a legal nurse consultant, I was able to add to my experience as a nurse and learn about the legal process as well."

What challenges do legal nurse consultants face in your area of law?

"It's a little easier for nurses in the area of medical malpractice. We are already familiar with practice standards and guidelines, and we are comfortable with medical records and review because of our own clinical nursing practice. The challenge comes with learning to market that talent and in becoming familiar enough with the legal process so we can interact easily with attorney clients."

What advice would you give nurses who are interested in legal nurse consulting?

"Don't be afraid to communicate with your attorney client. Make sure you both understand the duties and activities for which you are being hired. Good initial communication will help prevent misunderstandings later on.

"I feel that having a varied clinical background is important. When you bring a large pool of knowledge and clinical experience to your business, attorneys can come to you with all types of cases. You're less myopic in your clinical viewpoint and have a broader base of understanding in which to 'speak the language' of the healthcare system.

"Be assertive but also learn when to say 'I don't know.' No one is an expert on everything, and most people are wary of individuals who claim they are. Always seek to learn and add to your knowledge base. Strive to be open-minded. You never know when you might need that particular detail or newly acquired skill in your business."

What unique marketing strategy are you willing to share?

"Actually this marketing strategy is not unique; it's just something most people have forgotten while pursuing their own business goals in this so-called 'dog-eat-dog' world. It's this: treat others the way you want to be treated—pure and simple. Be honest about your capabilities and stick to your word. Don't be greedy. Avoid the 'what's in it for me' approach. Maintain high standards for yourself and your business. Ethics and integrity say volumes about you and your business and are more reliable than slick advertising could ever be."

> "Maintain high standards for yourself and your business. Ethics and integrity say volumes about you and your business and are more reliable than slick advertising could ever be."

Case Study IV

Clark v. Philadelphia College of Osteopathic Medicine, 693 A. 2d 202 (1999)

[The following case involves a rehabilitation nurse consultant. As you read through the court opinion, consider the following questions:

- Was this a civil or criminal matter? Explain.
- What role did the rehabilitation nurse consultant play in resolution of this matter?
- What credentials, experience, and education qualified the rehabilitation nurse consultant to play a role in resolution of this matter?
- What controversy, if any, existed concerning the rehabilitation nurse consultant's testimony?
- Consider making a diagram or process chart of the legal proceedings in this matter. Use your knowledge of legal procedure to fill in information not clearly specified in the court opinion; e.g., complaint served and filed, answer served and filed. Be as specific as possible by trying to identify what allegations might have been made in the complaint.
- Consider writing a case brief on this opinion using any of the formats outlined in Chapter Twelve.]

Cynthia CLARK, Appellee,

v.

PHILADELPHIA COLLEGE OF OSTEOPATHIC MEDICINE, Christine Viola, D.O., David A. Bevan, D.O.
Eugene Wyszynski, D.O., John Simelaro, D.O., Pete Hedrick, D.O.: Gail Shirley, D.O., Harold Tabaie, D.O.,
Edward Silverman, D.O., and Osteopathic Medical of Philadelphia Clinical Assocs.
Appeal of John SIMELARO, D.O. and Philadelphia College of Osteopathic Medicine.
Superior Court of Pennsylvania.
Argued Dec. 17, 1996.
Filed March 12, 1997.
Reargument Denied May 23, 1997.

MONTEMURO, J.
This is an appeal from a judgment for $1,582,789.38 plus interest entered in favor of Appellee in a medical malpractice case.
In June of 1990, Appellee instituted the instant negligence action against, inter alia, Drs. Christine Viola, John Simelaro, and Eugene Wyszynski, and the Pennsylvania College of Osteopathic Medicine (PCOM), [FN1] *204

claiming that as a result of unnecessarily protracted treatments with the corticosteroid prednisone administered for idiopathic thrombocytopenia purpura (ITP) and sarcoidosis, [FN2] Appellee developed avascular necrosis, a deterioration of the skeletal structure, particularly affecting the hips, shoulders, and knees. [FN3] After a three week trial, Dr. Viola, Appellee's family practitioner, was found not to have been negligent, and by agreement, the hospital accepted vicarious responsibility for Dr. Simelaro, Appellee's pulmonary specialist, and did not appear on the verdict sheet. Shortly before the verdict was rendered, a settlement was reached between Appellee and Dr. Wyszynski, the treating hematologist. The jury award, $4,100,000 equally apportioned between the two remaining defendants, was molded by the court to $1,582,789.38, including delay damages, plus interest. Appellants, Dr. Simelaro and PCOM, unsuccessfully moved for a new trial, disputing not Appellee's medical condition, but alleged errors committed by the court during the course of the trial. This appeal followed, raising five issues.

FN1. PCOM was substituted as a party in place of General Practice Associates of PCOM, Osteopathic Medical Center of Philadelphia, and Hospital of Philadelphia College of Osteopathic Medicine. Four additional defendants were dismissed prior to trial, and one settled separately.

FN2. ITP is a condition caused when antibodies attach to blood platelets, dragging them into the spleen, the liver and other tissues where they are then destroyed. The diminution in the number of platelets in turn causes, inter alia, mucosal, pulmonary and gastrointestinal hemorrhaging, and is fatal if left untreated.

Sarcoidosis is a condition in which granulomatous tissue forms, and can spread into lungs and chest cavity, bones, skin and eyes. It is life threatening only in a small percentage of cases.

continued

Clark v. Philadelphia College of Osteopathic Medicine   *continued*

FN3. Prednisone, a recognized treatment for both ITP and sarcoidosis, can, among other possible side effects, alter the way calcium is absorbed in the intestines and made available to the bones causing osteonecrosis. To minimize the occurrence of these reactions, attempts are made to keep dosages of the medication, which are variable from patient to patient, as low as the underlying disease process will allow, and administration time as short as possible.

[1][2] We note preliminarily the well-settled rule that the decision whether to grant a new trial is within the sound discretion of the trial court whose ruling will not be overturned on review absent a clear abuse of discretion or an error of law. *Chiaverini v. Sewickly Valley Hospital, 409 Pa.Super. 630, 598 A.2d 1021 (1991),* allocatur denied, *530 Pa. 659, 609 A.2d 167 (1992).*

[3] Appellants first argue that the court's adverse inference instruction to the jury concerning the absence of certain office notes from Appellee's file should not have been given and warrants retrial. Appellants contend that Dr. Simelaro's explanation for the missing documents was adequate to obviate the necessity for such an instruction, and, given the explanation, not only did the trial court abuse its discretion by failing to make the proper decision, but abdicated its responsibility altogether by allowing the jury to determine the propriety of the charge once given.

[4] The decision whether to tell the jury an unfavorable inference may be drawn from the failure of a party to produce some circumstance, witness, or document is also one which lies within the sound discretion of the trial court and which will not be reversed absent manifest abuse. *O'Rourke on Behalf of O'Rourke v. Rao, 411 Pa.Super. 609, 614, 602 A.2d 362, 364 (1992);* see also Wigmore, Evidence § 285, at 162 (1940 ed.). Appellant relies upon this court's decision in *Farley v. SEPTA, 279 Pa.Super. 570, 421 A.2d 346 (1980),* to support his assertion that the trial court in this case erroneously treated the jury's consideration of Appellant's justification for the missing documents as permissive rather than conclusive.

[5] The general rule is that:

[w]here evidence which would properly be part of a case is within the control of the party in whose interest it would naturally be to produce it, and, without satisfactory explanation he fails to do so, the jury may draw an inference that it would be unfavorable to him.

Haas v. Kasnot, 371 Pa. 580, 584–85, 92 A.2d 171, 173 (1952) (citation omitted). See also *Piwoz v. Iannacone, 406 Pa. 588, 178 A.2d 707 (1962); Davidson v. Davidson, 191 Pa.Super. 305, 156 A.2d 549 (1959).*

Farley, however, is distinguishable on its facts and of no assistance to Appellants here. There the missing evidence was testimony by the driver of a bus which had struck the rear ***205**

(Cite as: 693 A.2d 202, *205)

of the plaintiff's automobile at an intersection causing injuries. *Farley, 279 Pa.Super. at 574, 577, 421 A.2d at 348, 350.* The defendant bus company failed to produce the driver, explaining through witnesses that he had suffered a massive stroke, and was unable to speak intelligibly or to respond appropriately to simple questions. *Id. at 578–80, 421 A.2d at 350–51.* The trial court instructed the jury that if they found that the explanation given for his absence to be unsatisfactory, an adverse inference could be drawn. *Id. at 577, 421 A.2d at 350.* On review, this court ruled that because the reason given for the absence of the driver was both satisfactory and obviously so, treatment of the inference as permissive rather than conclusive was reversible error. *Id. at 580, 421 A.2d at 351.* This set of circumstances is not analogous to Appellants' situation.

Here, Dr. Simelaro offered two explanations for the absence of the notes. The first was provided during depositions when Dr. Simelaro testified that his office files were "thinned" every five years, that is, unimportant materials were removed, and such a procedure had been carried out in 1988. However, when Appellee received the file in its entirety during discovery in 1990 after suit had been initiated, no notes were to be found there. Appellant now concedes that the thinning process is irrelevant to the absence of the notes.

At trial, Appellant Simelaro repudiated his deposition testimony, effectively, as the trial court found, denying that he had taken any notes. He described having only scribbled "notations" (the distinction between this and notes is left unplumbed) from which he dictated a consultation letter in the presence of the patient. Along with this procedure, he currently asserts that the file was "tailored to and consistent with his role as a consultant" on Appellee's case rather than as her primary or treating physician. (Appellants' Brief at 14) (This distinction too is left unexplored).

Thus, of the theories offered by Appellant to account for the absence of the notes, the first is by his own admission inoperative, and the second neither satisfactory nor at all obvious. The trial court properly instructed the jury using the precise language of Standard Jury Instruction 5.06, and no error can be assigned to the decision to do so.

[6] Appellants next contend that the trial court criticized Dr. Viola for testifying in a manner favorable to Appellant Simelaro, and in so doing abused its discretion.

Both Dr. Simelaro, Appellee's pulmonary specialist, and Dr. Viola, Appellee's primary care physician, were represented by the same attorney. During his appearance, Dr. Simelaro testified that Dr. Viola had breached her duty of care toward Appellee. Dr. Viola, who testified later in the proceedings, however, made no corresponding accusation of negligence toward Dr. Simelaro, but rather defended him. During Dr. Viola's testimony, the court interrupted the proceedings, excused the jury and questioned counsel as to the inconsistencies, pointing out that the divergence in testimony could constitute a conflict of interest. Appellant Simelaro now complains that the court's actions, which are characterized as "chastising" the witness in an attempt to intimidate her, were not only an improper attempt to influence Dr. Viola's testimony, but also "signified a predisposition and bias against co-defendant Simelaro." (Appellant's Brief at 18). Appellants further accuse the court of gamesmanship in expressing its concerns, implying that the court is responsible for the jury's having found Dr. Simelaro, the accuser, and not Dr. Viola, the accused liable for Appellee's injuries.

Appellant provides us with no explanation of how the court's comments can have influenced the jury, which did not hear them. Moreover, Dr. Viola, was clearly not intimidated by the court's remarks since her testimony, once she resumed the stand, remained unaltered, a fact admitted by counsel during argument after the interruption. What Appellants proffer here is a nebulous assertion that, to some unknown extent and in some unknown way, the mere fact of the interruption communicated to the jury a lack of impartiality, thus influencing it to a degree neither actually measurable nor susceptible even to guess. However, no relief can be forthcoming for surmise; far less, as here, for wishful thinking.
***206**

[7] For their third assignment of error, Appellants claim that the trial court improperly allowed counsel to suggest a formula for pain and suffering during closing argument. Appellants refer to a drawing of a triangle with a horizontal line through it used by counsel during closing to suggest that Appellee's past and future medical expenses, wage loss and lost future earning capacity totalling over $2,000,000,

continued

Clark v. Philadelphia College of Osteopathic Medicine   *continued*

represented only the "tip of the iceberg," and that her pain and suffering were what remained below the horizontal "water line." Appellants claim that this schematic drawing contravenes the prohibition against estimating or suggesting to a jury the amount of damages to be awarded, especially for pain and suffering in a personal injury case. *Clark v. Essex Wire Corp., 361 Pa. 60, 63 A.2d 35 (1949); Atene v. Lawrence, 456 Pa. 541, 318 A.2d 695 (1974)*.

[8][9] The trial court, within whose discretion the presentation of closing speeches remains, *Catina v. Maree, 272 Pa.Super. 247, 415 A.2d 413 (1979),* rev'd. on other grounds, *498 Pa. 443, 447 A.2d 228 (1982),* overruled Appellants' objections and motions for mistrial, concluding that the objection was "specious, frivolous, and simply a reaction" to counsel's closing. (N.T. 10/13/94 at 74). It is well-settled that whether to declare a mistrial is yet another decision within the discretion of the trial court, whose vantage point enables it to evaluate the climate of the courtroom and the effect on the jury of closing arguments. *Speer v. Barry, 349 Pa.Super. 365, 503 A.2d 409 (1985).* The trial court in its Opinion observed that "[w]hether the tip of the iceberg argument is called rhetoric, analogy or metaphor, it was not a direct statement suggesting any specific sum or arbitrary amount." (Trial Ct. Op. at 25). We agree with this assessment, and find that as such, the drawing did not justify the declaration of a mistrial.

[10] Next, it is argued that there was reversible error in the trial court's refusal to allow certain questions to be posed on cross-examination to Appellee's life plan expert. This witness, Arlene Sloan, was a rehabilitation nurse whose area of expertise covered the requirements and costs of Appellee's projected life care management, that is, the types of physical objects and personal assistance necessitated by Appellee's physical condition both currently and in the future. Appellants wished to inquire of the witness whether and to what extent the effects of an automobile accident, which occurred subsequent to Appellant's medical treatment of Appellee, had been taken into account when Appellee's ←**life care plan**→ had been prepared. The trial court refused to allow the questions on the basis that they sought to explore causation, a matter both beyond the scope of direct examination and beyond the witness' area of expertise.

[11] Appellants state that their questions were occasioned because "the thrust of Nurse Sloan's testimony was that the items of equipment and personal assistance which she testified Ms. Clark would need were necessitated by the injuries resulting from her prednisone therapy." (Appellants' Brief at 31). However, the trial court points out that there was no testimony concerning causation, that is, the witness never rendered an opinion as to why Appellee was in her particular physical situation, and should not have done so. Decisions as to the permissible subjects of cross-examination are within the sound discretion of the trial court, *In re Townsend's Estate, 430 Pa. 318, 241 A.2d 534 (1968),* cert. denied, *Cochran v. Morris, 393 U.S. 934, 89 S.Ct. 293, 21 L.Ed.2d 270 (1968),* and we find no abuse of that discretion since Appellants have offered no convincing justification for introducing a subject outside the witness' expertise.

[12] Appellant's final assertion is that the trial court erred in its interpretation of a settlement agreement and joint tortfeasor release, resulting in an incorrectly molded verdict and a mistaken award of delay damages.

The agreement referred to was reached by Appellee, Dr. Wyszynski and the Medical Professional Liability Catastrophe (CAT) Fund, and provided that Appellee would receive $400,000 from the parties to the agreement. It also contained the following language:

It is understood that I am not hereby releasing any claims or demands that I have against Christine Viola, D.O., David ***207**

A. Bevan, D.O., John Simelaro, D.O., General Practice Associates of PCOM, Osteopathic Medical center of Philadelphia, and Hospital of Philadelphia College of Osteopathic Medicine (hereinafter referred to as "Non-Settling Defendants").

(Release at 3-4).

However, Dr. Simelaro, and PCOM having conceded its vicarious liability for Simelaro, moved that the verdict against Simelaro be molded to $200,000 , arguing that the following language was controlling: Additionally, for and in consideration of the monies promised to be paid, herein, by the Medical Professional Liability Catastrophe Loss Fund, the undersigned specifically waives the right to recover all monies in excess of $200,000 individual primary limits of the Non-Settling Defendants for which they may be found liable.

(Release at 5). (emphasis added).

[13][14] It is axiomatic that releases are construed in accordance with traditional principles of contract law, fundamental to which is the directive that "the effect of a release must be determined from the ordinary meaning of its language." *Buttermore v. Aliquippa Hospital, 522 Pa. 325, 328-29, 561 A.2d 733, 735 (1989)* (citations omitted). Here the wording of the release contains a reservation of rights against the non-settling defendants, but also limits the exercise of those rights to recovery of the $200,000 individual primary limits. Appellants are correct in assuming that the rationale for this restriction on damages was imposed by the CAT Fund, which drafted the agreement, to insulate itself from the statutory obligation to indemnify any non-settling defendants against whom a verdict larger than the individual limits might be brought in. To further buttress the CAT Fund's negotiated immunity, the agreement also promises to hold harmless any releasees from "any and all claims demands or actions . . . relating to or arising from" the underlying action. It cannot therefore be said that restraint on damages was not within the contemplation of the parties, only that it was not within Appellee's calculations. Moreover, as *Buttermore* observes, Parties with possible claims may settle their differences with each other upon such terms as are suitable to them . . . However improvident their agreement may be or subsequently prove for either party, their agreement, absent fraud, accident or mutual mistake, is the law of their case.

Id. at 328-29, 561 A.2d at 735.

[15] None of the exceptions is apparent here, or even alleged; thus we are compelled to restrict Appellee's recovery to the terms of the bargain she has made—$200,000 each from the two non-settling defendants, Appellants. [FN4]

> FN4. Appellants allege, without explanation, that there should be only one $200,000 recovery. However, both Dr. Simelaro and PCOM are named defendants, and while Dr. Simelaro was found liable by the jury, PCOM admitted vicarious liability, a separate and separately compensable matter.

As to Appellants' contention that delay damages were wrongly assessed, the waiver clause does, as Appellants' point out, operate to prevent the recovery of "all monies" over $200,000 regardless of classification.

Order denying Appellants' motion for a new trial is affirmed. Judgment awarding Appellee $1,582,789.38 is vacated, and case is remanded for entry of an order consistent with this Opinion.

ETHICS

Legal nurse consultants must be aware of the ethical constraints of the legal profession as well as the ethics of nursing and medical professions. In addition, professional growth and competence demand continuing learning and professional association. In this unit, you will find answers to these questions:

■ What ethical rules govern attorneys?

■ What ethical rules are proposed for legal nurse consultants?

■ What professional opportunities are available for growth and advancement in legal nurse consulting?

CHAPTER 33

ETHICS OF THE LEGAL PROFESSION

OBJECTIVES

In this chapter, you will discover

- the code of ethics under which attorneys practice

- how the code of ethics impacts all of the attorney's staff

- the ethical considerations about which legal nurse consultants must be keenly aware

- the ethical considerations that are specific to litigation

- why legal nurse consultants are bound by the code of ethics under which attorneys practice

OVERVIEW

The practice of law began when a party involved in a legal dispute was allowed to bring a friend or confidante to court who would be "of counsel" to the party in presenting and arguing the cases. As the field of legal representation emerged, it became apparent that certain regulations were necessary to protect the privacy of the parties and the integrity of the law.

Ethics are generally adopted by professions as a way to establish a standard of conduct and/or behavior for the members of the profession. In 1922, the Canons of Ethics were promulgated for lawyers. There were originally eleven canons designed to provide a minimum standard below which disciplinary action could be taken, and a high standard to which all attorneys should aspire. The canons were replaced with the Model Code of Professional Responsibility in 1969, which became the basis for the Model Rules of Professional Conduct in 1983. These ethical rules are advisory only and each state, through legislative action or through Supreme Court rule, establishes the ethical code with which lawyers licensed in that state must comply.

If a lawyer's conduct is suspect and a complaint is filed with the regulatory board, which is usually a Board of Inquiry, the proceedings do not take place in court. Members of the **inquiry board** will investigate the allegations of improper conduct against the attorney and will make a recommendation concerning disciplinary measures. The attorney in question may request a hearing before the board or before the Supreme Court, depending on the procedure within the state, prior to any disciplinary action being taken. Many state bar associations publish the names, the basis for the disciplinary proceedings, and the disciplinary measures taken in selected issues of the state bar journal.

SANCTIONS FOR UNETHICAL CONDUCT

If an attorney is found to have committed a crime, engaged in unethical conduct, or otherwise violated the rules of professional responsibility, there are several disciplinary sanctions that may be imposed upon the attorney. These sanctions are described in Figure 33-1.

Only attorneys may be sanctioned for ethical violations. Because the attorney will be responsible for the unethical conduct of lay staff, it is important for all those who work with attorneys to understand the ethical constraints of the legal profession.

MODEL RULES OF PROFESSIONAL CONDUCT

There are several important features of the Model Rules of Professional Conduct. Those features have been incorporated into each state's regulation of the practice of law. Several have already appeared in *Ethics Bookmarks* throughout this text.

Net Results

Ethics on the Internet

A site devoted to legal ethics is located at www.legalethics.com. *This site provides links to state legal ethics codes and ethics opinions, and names and addresses of members of the state boards of attorney professional responsibility. The American Society of Law, Medicine, and Ethics web site may be accessed at* www.aslme.org.

FIGURE 33-1 Disciplinary Sanctions for Attorney Unethical Conduct	
Sanction	**Description**
Private reprimand	A private reprimand may be delivered to the attorney when the unethical conduct is of a minor nature. This reprimand is not published and does not interfere with the attorney's right to continue practicing.
Public reprimand	Conversely, a public reprimand is a published notice of the unethical conduct of an attorney. This notice does not affect the attorney's right to practice.
Probation	An attorney may be placed on probation, which allows the attorney to continue practicing, so long as the attorney submits to certain conditions. These conditions may require attendance at ethics seminars, periodic audits, or compliance with other supervisory conditions imposed. Probationary status of the attorney is often published.
Suspension	An attorney whose license is suspended may not practice law during the period of the suspension. Following the period of suspension, the attorney's license is reinstated. Most states publish the names of attorneys whose licenses have been suspended.
Disbarment	Usually permanent, this sanction terminates the attorney's right to practice law and, thus, to be a member of the bar association. The names of attorneys who have been disbarred are usually published in the state bar journal.

Diligence and Promptness

An attorney is required to act with diligence and promptness when processing a claim on behalf of a client.[1] One of the most frequent complaints about the legal system is that the process is too lengthy. While attorneys may feel trapped into inactivity while waiting for additional documentation or investigation from an outside source, this does not relieve the attorney of acting with reasonable diligence and communicating the status of the case to the client.

Reasonable Fees

The hourly rate of an attorney will depend on many things, including the attorney's expertise, the geographical location of the office, the type of legal advice needed, and the client's ability to pay. Still, the Model Rules of Professional Conduct require that an attorney's fees be reasonable under the circumstances.[2]

Illegal or Fraudulent Conduct

An attorney may not engage in illegal or fraudulent conduct, even at the request of the client.[3] This includes fraudulent statements in legal documents, falsifying documents, pirating software, theft or embezzlement of client funds, and insider trading.

Obstructing Access to Evidence

Because the purpose of a legal claim is to arrive at the truth, it is unethical for an attorney to obstruct the opposing side's access to evidence.[4] This is part of the "fair play" concept of litigation.

Frivolous Claims

A **frivolous claim** is one that has no foundation in law or in fact. It is unethical and an abuse of legal process for an attorney to bring a claim for which there is no reasonable foundation.[5] Severe monetary sanctions may be applied against attorneys who use the courts for purposes other than justice.

Confidentiality

The relationship between the attorney and the client is **privileged;** that is, the information shared while in private consultation may not be disclosed without the permission of the parties.[6] An exception to this rule exists where the client makes a threat, which the attorney believes will be carried out.[7] The attorney has a duty to warn law enforcement or the threatened party if the attorney reasonably believes that the client will carry out the threat, and the threat involves death or serious bodily harm to another.

The rule of confidentiality is intended to facilitate the client's open and honest disclosure of all the facts, no matter how damaging they may be. The attorney needs to have complete information in order to represent the client. This privilege extends to the attorney's staff as well, when the client and the attorney's staff are engaged in private communications. If a conversation is held in the supermarket or via cellular phone, the privilege does not exist, as these conversations are not considered private.

Conflicts of Interest

The rule prohibiting **conflicts of interest** arises out of the **fiduciary duty** of the attorney.[8] If the attorney has a personal interest in both sides of a claim, his or her loyalty will be compromised. Avoiding conflicts of interest is intended to ensure that the client's best interest will be the motivating factor for the attorney's activities.

It is not always possible to completely avoid conflicts. An **ethical wall** may need to be erected in certain circumstances. For example, a legal nurse consultant previously worked at a health care facility that is the defendant in a law-suit. The legal nurse consultant is currently working for the law firm represent-ing the plaintiff in that action. In order to avoid a conflict of interest, the legal nurse consultant should stay behind the ethical wall and not be involved in the lawsuit or have any contact with the parties, witnesses, or others involved.

Property of Clients

Client funds are often deposited with an attorney pending the closing of a real estate transaction or for other purposes. Attorneys are required to maintain these funds separately from the operating funds of the law firm in an account called a trust account.[9] Commingling funds is an ethical violation for which the attorney will be sanctioned. Using client funds for purposes other than those authorized is betrayal of a trust. Frequently, clients are required to de-posit a **retainer** with the attorney to ensure representation on a particular matter. The retainer must be maintained in a separate account and may not be invaded until the attorney has actually expended funds on behalf of the client or provided services to the client. Even then, the amount withdrawn from the client's funds may not exceed the value of the services provided.

Withdrawal of Counsel

Attorneys are sometimes required to withdraw from representation of the client.[10] If any of the following circumstances exist, it is appropriate for the at-torney to resign:

- the client demands that the attorney engage in an illegal activity
- physical or mental condition impairs the lawyer in a way that inter-feres with the zealous representation of the client
- the client fires the attorney

Solicitation of Business

It is unethical for an attorney to solicit business from persons who are not al-ready clients. This is often referred to as **ambulance chasing.** Whenever the attorney directly or indirectly invites the legal business of a potential client, the attorney may be subject to disciplinary proceedings.[11]

Reporting Unethical Conduct of Others

Bar associations are self-policing. Each member is responsible for the con-duct of the other members and each is charged with reporting unethical con-duct when the conduct raises a substantial question about the attorney's hon-esty or fitness to practice.[12] This rule is intended to ensure that the ethical standards of the legal profession are honored and upheld.

Appearance of Impropriety

Because attorneys are charged with upholding the integrity of the law, the ethical rules demand a higher standard of conduct than that of other citizens. Thus, attorneys are admonished to avoid engaging in conduct that may have the appearance of being illegal or unethical.[13]

HOW LAWYERS MAY ADVERTISE

While it is ethically improper for attorneys to solicit business, attorneys may advertise their businesses to the public.[14] As long as the communication is not directed at a specific individual in an attempt to induce that individual to hire the attorney, and as long as the communication is not misleading, the advertisement is ethical. Therefore, an attorney may advertise with brochures, in newsletters, in telephone directories, in legal directories, in print, on the radio, on television, and on the Internet.

A question often arises about the message in an advertisement for personal injury representation stating that if the attorney does not win a verdict or settlement for the client, the client does not pay the attorney. It may not seem clear from this advertisement that the client remains responsible for all of the costs involved in the litigation. The only thing the client does not pay is the contingent fee to the attorney. Because the advertisement clearly states that the client does not pay *the attorney,* it is not considered misleading.

ETHICAL CODE RELATIVE TO LAY STAFF

The Model Rules of Professional Conduct allow delegation of tasks in processing a claim. Certain tasks, however, may not be delegated. A lawyer may never delegate an appearance at court to a nonlawyer, nor may a lawyer delegate the responsibility to provide legal advice or to enter into settlement negotiations on behalf of a client. Additionally, only an attorney may contract with a client for delivery of legal services. These specific duties are reserved for those who are licensed to practice law.

However, many of the tasks involved in daily legal proceedings are routine and do not require the specialized knowledge of the lawyer. These tasks may be delegated to nonlawyer staff under the following conditions:[15]

- The lawyer must maintain a relationship with the client.
- The lawyer must supervise the delegated work.
- The lawyer must remain accountable to the client for the quality of the work product.

Lawyers sometimes have sufficient faith in their staff to provide little direct supervision. Skilled and experienced nonlawyer staff generally know when it is necessary to call in the attorney for specific supervision and direction. Still, faith in the skill of the nonlawyer staff will not relieve the attorney of the responsibility for the work product. Supervision should be actively maintained in all proceedings.

LITIGATION ETHICS

There are some special ethical considerations that apply to attorneys and their staff while litigation is pending and during a trial. These ethical considerations fall within the realm of fair play, and ensure that each side is honest and aboveboard, and has access to all of the facts.

Ex parte Communications

An attorney is prohibited from entering into conversations with the judge who will be presiding over the trial if the opposing attorney is not privy to the conversation.[17] Engaging in one-sided conversations, called *ex parte,* has the appearance of influence and may be grounds for mistrial or a motion for new trial.

Ex parte Communications with Jurors

An attorney is prohibited from engaging in conversations with potential jurors or selected jurors who are serving on the attorney's trial.[18] In fact, any member of the law firm who engages in conversations with potential jurors or selected jurors may subject the law firm to disqualification or may provide the other side with grounds for a mistrial or a motion for new trial. Intent to influence the juror is not relevant. The appearance of influence is sufficient.

Reporting Improper Conduct Toward Jurors

Because the premise of a jury trial is an objective review of the facts by peers, any improper conduct by an attorney involved in the case that may have the appearance of influencing a juror must be reported. Failure to report unethical conduct toward jurors may result in disciplinary action against both the attorney engaging in unethical conduct toward a juror and the attorney who witnessed it and failed to report it.[19]

Communications with Parties Represented by Counsel

During the course of a lawsuit, investigation requires that several persons be interviewed regarding the circumstances giving rise to the lawsuit. Once the parties in the action have been identified, and those parties have retained attorneys, it is inappropriate to approach those parties.[20] Because attorneys stand in a fiduciary capacity, communication with the attorney represents communication with the party. In addition, it may be unethical to communicate with employees or expert witnesses hired by the party who is represented by an attorney.

UNAUTHORIZED PRACTICE OF LAW

Every state has adopted an unauthorized practice of law (UPL) statute. While these statutes vary somewhat as to penalties and specific language, there are generally three parallel themes in UPL statutes:

Ethics Bookmark

Honoring the Profession

"The legal nurse consultant maintains standards of personal conduct that reflect honorably upon the profession. The legal nurse consultant abides by all federal and state laws. The legal nurse consultant who knowingly becomes involved in unethical or illegal activities negates professional responsibility for personal interest or personal gain. Such activities jeopardize the public confidence and trust in the nursing profession"[16] AALNC Code of Ethics and Conduct with Interpretive Discussion (1997), Rule 4, used with permission.

- Nonlawyers may not give legal advice or instructions to clients concerning their rights.
- Nonlawyers may not prepare legal documents requiring knowledge of legal principles directly for clients, unless specifically authorized by law; for example, real estate brokers.
- Nonlawyers may not appear and represent clients at judicial proceedings.

In addition, most state statutes prohibiting the unauthorized practice of law include the use of attorney, lawyer, counselor at law, and similar terms by nonlawyers as a violation of the law. The unauthorized practice of law statute is designed to protect the public from persons who may misrepresent their qualifications and engage in practices that require the specialized knowledge and education of licensed members of the bar.

PROFESSIONALISM

Legal nurse consultants are not strangers to ethical restrictions. Because the potential exists for legal nurse consultants to be caught in conflicts of interest and because of the sensitive nature of the cases on which they may be working, it is always wise to review the ethical standards of the profession. To maintain integrity as a legal professional, the legal nurse consultant should remember the following:

- Understand the limitations in client interviews and refrain from giving legal advice or an evaluation of the claim.
- Research requirements of administrative agencies before appearing at administrative proceedings on behalf of a client. This might be unauthorized practice of law in some states.
- Strictly adhere to the Model Rules of Professional Conduct.
- Join professional associations and attend legal educational and ethical seminars and workshops.

A conscious choice to respect oneself and one's co-workers is the true mark of a professional. Engaging in conversations or conduct that is derogatory to co-workers, clients, or the legal profession speaks more about the person engaging in the conduct than it does about anyone else. Profanity and gossip are always inappropriate.

CHAPTER SUMMARY

- Each state, by legislation or Supreme Court rule, adopts ethical codes for evaluating the conduct of attorneys.
- Sanctions for violating ethical rules may range from private reprimand to disbarment.

- Legal nurse consultants should familiarize themselves with the ethical standards for lawyers in the states in which they practice.

- Attorneys may delegate tasks to nonlawyers as long as the attorney maintains a relationship with the client, supervises the work, and remains accountable for the work product of the nonlawyers.

- There are special ethical considerations for litigation practices.

- The unauthorized practice of law statute is intended to protect the public from persons who would misrepresent their qualifications to deliver legal services.

- Legal nurse consultants should strive for integrity and a high degree of professionalism in their practices.

KEY TERMS

ambulance chasing   *ex parte* communications   inquiry board
conflicts of interest   fiduciary duty   privilege
ethics   frivolous claims   retainer
ethical wall

REVIEW QUESTIONS

1. Identify and explain some of the major ethical standards to which attorneys must conform.
2. What is the ethical wall and how might it apply to legal nurse consultants?

3. What specific ethical standards apply to litigation?

INTERNET EXERCISES

1. Access the web page for this textbook at *www.westlegalstudies.com*.

2. Click on the assignments section and complete the assignment(s) for Chapter Thirty-three.

EXERCISES

1. Networking. In the library, collect several recent issues of the state bar journal. Find the department that discusses disciplinary actions against attorneys. Read through the articles and consider how a legal nurse consultant or specific management principles might have prevented this ethical violation. Consider whether you would wish to be retained by the attorneys identified.

2. Professional Portfolio. Make a list or chart of the ethical rules you think will be most important to you in your legal nurse consulting career. Maintain this list in your systems file, folder, or binder, and organize or index it for easy reference.

ENDNOTES

1. American Bar Association, *Annotated Model Rules of Professional Conduct,* (1999) 4th Edition Rule 1.3. Copies of ABA *Model Code of Professional Responsibility, 1999 Edition* are available from Service Center, American Bar Association, 750 North Lake Shore Drive, Chicago, IL 60611-4497, 1-800-285-2221.
2. Ibid. Rule 1.5.
3. Ibid. Rule 1.2(d).
4. Ibid. Rule 3.4(a).
5. Ibid. Rule 3.1.
6. Ibid. Rule 1.6
7. Ibid. Rule 1.6(b)(1).
8. Ibid. Rule 1.7.
9. Ibid. Rule 1.15.
10. Ibid. Rule 1.16.
11. Ibid. Rule 7.3.
12. Ibid. Rule 8.3.
13. Ibid. Rule 1.9.
14. Ibid. Rule 7.2.
15. Ibid. Rule 5.3.
16. American Association of Legal Nurse Consultants, *AALNC Code of Ethics and Conduct With Interpretive Discussion* (1997) Rule 4.
17. American Bar Association, *Annotated Model Rules of Professional Conduct* Fourth Edition (1999) Rule 3.5(b).
18. Ibid. Rule 3.5(a), (b).
19. American Bar Association, *Model Rules of Professional Conduct* (1967) DR7-108(G).
20. American Bar Association, *Annotated Model Rules of Professional Conduct* (1999) Rule 4.2.

ADDITIONAL REFERENCES

American Bar Association. *Annotated Model Rules of Professional Conduct,* 4th ed. Chicago, IL: American Bar Association, 1999.

Bogart, J. B., RN MN, ed. *Legal Nurse Consulting: Principles and Practice.* Boston: CRC Press, 1998.

Cannon, Therese. *Ethics and Professional Responsibility for Legal Assistants.* New York: Aspen Law and Business, 1999.

AMERICAN ASSOCIATION OF LEGAL NURSE CONSULTANTS

OBJECTIVES

In this chapter, you will discover

- the purposes for which the AALNC was organized

- The Code of Ethics adopted by the AALNC

- the Scope of Practice adopted by the AALNC

- certification requirements for the Legal Nurse Consultant Certified designation

- how membership in AALNC may benefit the practice of legal nurse consulting

OVERVIEW

The American Association of Legal Nurse Consultants was founded in 1989 with a membership of thirty. Today there are more than 3000 members in thirty-three chapters across the country. This association has done much to advance the profession of legal nurse consulting. They have published a core curriculum, *Legal Nurse Consulting: Principles and Practice;* adopted a Code of Ethics; and developed a certifying examination.

PURPOSES OF THE AMERICAN ASSOCIATION OF LEGAL NURSE CONSULTANTS

The AALNC was formed to advance the profession of legal nurse consulting, to provide a forum for disseminating information and educational opportunities for legal nurse consultants, and to promote communication and professional networking among legal nurse consultants.[1]

To further these purposes, AALNC publishes pamphlets and brochures explaining the role of the legal nurse consultant and offering practical tips for going into that business. The *Journal of Legal Nurse Consulting,* the official journal of AALNC, is published quarterly and provides topical articles on legal and medical issues affecting its readers. A separate quarterly publication, *Network News,* provides news and information concerning the organization and its chapters. National education seminars are presented annually providing tracks for novices and experienced legal nurse consultants. Nationally recognized speakers and specialists present trends in law and medicine that impact the practice of legal nurse consulting. To advance the profession, AALNC adopted a scope of practice, standards of practice, standards of performance, and code of ethics.

SCOPE OF PRACTICE

In April 1995 the AALNC approved the Scope of Practice for member legal nurse consultants. A professional association adopts a scope of practice in order to define the role of its member professionals and to distinguish its members from other professionals in the work environment. The Scope of Practice of the American Association of Legal Nurse Consultants is reproduced in its entirety in Figure 34-1.[2]

STANDARDS OF PRACTICE

In addition to adopting a Scope of Practice, AALNC approved a Standards of Professional Practice. Nurses are familiar with the concept of standards of practice. These guidelines are intended to establish criteria or baseline qualifications for those who enter and practice in the field of legal nurse consulting. The AALNC Standards of Legal Nurse Consulting Practice is reprinted in its entirety as Figure 34-2.[3]

Net Results

AALNC

One of the most useful sites on the internet for legal nurse consultants is the home page of the AALNC. It provides information concerning membership, educational seminars, certifying courses, and examinations. Links to legal and medical resources make it a site that every legal nurse consultant should bookmark. Access this site at www.aalnc.org.

FIGURE 34-1   Scope of Practice for the Legal Nurse Consultant[2]

Introduction

The legal nurse consultant is a licensed registered nurse who performs a critical analysis of health care facts and issues and their outcomes for the legal profession, health care professionals, and others, as appropriate. With a strong educational and experiential background, the legal nurse consultant is qualified to assess adherence to standards of health care practice as it applies to the nursing and health care professions.

This Scope of Practice for the Legal Nurse Consultant has been developed from data gathered by the American Association of Legal Nurse Consultants. The results reflect the diversity of practice settings of and services performed by legal nurse consultants nationwide. The American Association of Legal Nurse Consultants acknowledges the *American Association of Legal Nurse Consultants Code of Ethics* for legal nurse consultants, which provides the guidelines for professional performance and conduct for practice and affirms the values and practices of the American Nurses Association and the American Bar Association.

Practice Environment

The legal nurse consultant practices the art and science of his or her nursing specialty in a variety of settings, including law firms, government offices, insurance companies, hospital risk management departments, and as self-employed practitioners. The legal nurse consultant is a liaison between the legal and health care communities and provides consultation and education to legal, health care, and appropriate other professionals in areas such as personal injury, product liability, medical malpractice, workers' compensation, toxic torts, risk management, medical professional licensure investigation, and criminal law.

Role of the Legal Nurse Consultant

The primary role of the legal nurse consultant is to evaluate, analyze, and render informed opinions on the delivery of health care and the resulting outcomes. While the practice of each legal nurse consultant varies with respective practice opportunities and experience levels, certain commonalities prevail. Parameters of the practice may include, but are not limited to:

- Facilitating communications and thus strategizing with the legal professional for successful resolutions between parties involved in health care-related litigation or other medical-legal or health care-legal matters.
- Educating attorneys and/or others involved in the legal process regarding the health care facts and issues of a case or a claim.
- Researching and integrating health care and nursing literature as it relates to the health care facts and issues of a case or a claim.
- Reviewing, summarizing, and analyzing medical records and other pertinent health care and legal documents and comparing and correlating them to the allegations.
- Assessing issues of damages and causation relative to liability within the legal process.
- Identifying, locating, evaluating, and conferring with expert witnesses.

continued

FIGURE 34-1   Scope of Practice for the Legal Nurse Consultant[2]   *continued*

- Interviewing witnesses and parties pertinent to the health care issues in collaboration with legal professionals.
- Drafting legal documentations in medically related cases under the supervision of an attorney.
- Developing collaborative case strategies with those practicing within the legal system.
- Providing support during discovery, depositions, trial, and other legal proceedings.
- Supporting the process of adjudication of legal claims.

Summary

This document identifies the legal nurse consultant as a specialist unique in the profession of nursing and as someone whose practice is of value in the legal field. The intent of this document is to conceptualize the legal nurse consultant's practice as it exists today; it is limited only by the depth and breadth to which the nursing specialty has currently developed. It is anticipated that future studies will indicate expanded roles and practice environments for the legal nurse consultant.

Reprinted with permission of the American Association of Legal Nurse Consultants, 4700 W. Lake Avenue, Glenville, IL 60025-1485, Copyright 1995.

FIGURE 34-2   Standards of Legal Nurse Consulting Practice[3]

Section I: Standards of Practice

The legal nurse consultant has the knowledge and capability sufficient to conduct his or her practice in accordance with each of the standards set forth below.

Standard 1. Assessment.

   The legal nurse consultant collects data to support the systematic assessment of health care issues related to a case or claim.

Standard 2. Analysis and Issue Identification.

   The legal nurse consultant analyzes collected data to identify the health care issues related to a case or claim.

Standard 3. Outcome Identification.

   The legal nurse consultant identifies the desired outcome of his or her work product as related to the health care issues of a case or claim.

Standard 4. Planning.

   The legal nurse consultant formulates a plan of action to achieve the desired outcome.

Standard 5. Implementation.

   The legal nurse consultant implements the plan of action.

Standard 6. Evaluation.

   The legal nurse consultant evaluates the effectiveness of the plan of action in achieving the desired outcome.

Section II: Standards of Professional Performance

Standard 1. Quality of Practice.
The legal nurse consultant evaluates the quality and effectiveness of his or her practice.

Key Indicators
1. The LNC participates in quality of practice activities as appropriate to the individual's role, education, and practice environment.
2. The LNC uses the results of quality of practice activities to initiate changes in practice.

Standard 2. Performance Appraisal.
The legal nurse consultant evaluates his or her own practice in relation to professional practice standards and relevant statutes and regulations.

Key Indicators
1. The LNC engages in performance appraisal, identifying areas of strength as well as areas for professional practice developments.
2. The LNC seeks constructive feedback regarding his or her own practice.
3. The LNC takes action to achieve goals identified during performance appraisal.
4. The LNC participates in peer review, as appropriate.

Standard 3. Education.
The legal nurse consultant acquires and maintains current knowledge in nursing and health care issues.

Key Indicators
1. The LNC participates in ongoing educational activities pertaining to the health sciences and the law relevant to his or her practice areas.
2. The LNC seeks experiences necessary to maintain current licensure as a professional registered nurse.
3. The LNC seeks the knowledge and the skills that are appropriate to the LNC's practice setting.

Standard 4. Collegiality.
The legal nurse consultant contributes to the professional development of peers, colleagues, and others.

Key Indicators
1. The LNC shares knowledge and skills with colleagues and others.
2. The LNC provides peers with constructive feedback regarding their practice.
3. The LNC contributes to an environment that is conducive to the education of nurses entering the field of legal nurse consulting.
4. The LNC contributes to an environment that is conducive to the health science education of legal team members, as appropriate.
5. The LNC contributes to an environment that is conducive to the education of health care professionals regarding legal issues applicable to the health sciences.

Standard 5. Ethics.
The legal nurse consultant's decisions and actions are determined in an ethical manner.

continued

FIGURE 34-2   Standards of Legal Nurse Consulting Practice[3]   *continued*

Key Indicators
1. The LNC's practice is guided by the ANA's Code for Nurses with Interpretive Statements (1985) and the AALNC Code of Ethics.
2. The LNC's practice affirms the values, standards, and practices of professional nursing.
3. The LNC maintains confidentiality commensurate with the attorney-client privilege.
4. The LNC practices in a nonjudgmental and nondiscriminatory manner.
5. The LNC evaluates all cases and clients for potential conflicts of interest and declines when conflicts are evident.
6. The LNC seeks available resources to help formulate ethical decisions.
7. The LNC who testifies as an expert witness confines testimony to his or her area of expertise.

Standard 6. Collaboration.
The legal nurse consultant may collaborate with legal professionals, health care professionals, and others involved in the legal process.

Key Indicators
1. The LNC consults with legal professionals, health care professionals, and others, as appropriate.
2. The LNC makes referrals as needed.

Standard 7. Research.
The legal nurse consultant recognizes research as a methodology to further the legal nurse consultant's practice.

Key Indicators
1. The LNC takes action substantiated by research as appropriate to his or her role, education, and practice environment.
2. The LNC participates in research activities as appropriate to his or her role, education, and practice environment.

Standard 8. Resource Management.
The legal nurse consultant considers factors related to ethics, effectiveness, and cost in planning and delivering client service.

Key Indicators
1. The LNC selects expert assistance based on the needs of the case or the claim.
2. The LNC assigns tasks based on the knowledge and skill of the selected provider.
3. The LNC assists legal professionals and others in identifying and securing appropriate services available to address issues pertaining to the case or the claim.

Reprinted with permission of the American Association of Legal Nurses Consultant, 4700 W. Lake Avenue, Glenview, IL 60025-1485, copyright 1995.

CODE OF ETHICS

A code of ethics is one of the characteristics of a service profession. AALNC adopted its Code of Ethics in 1995. A statement of professional ethics provides a basis for disciplinary action in a certified profession and supports a certification examination. The AALNC Code of Ethics is reproduced in its entirety in Figure 34-3.[4]

FIGURE 34-3   Code of Ethics[4]

Preamble.

The Code of Ethics and Conduct of the American Association of Legal Nurse Consultants is based on beliefs about the nature of individuals and society. The code of professional and ethical conduct provides guidelines to its members for professional performance and behavior. The success of any professional organization results from the competence and integrity of its members. Our goal to those we serve is that they be assured of our accountability.

We recognize a responsibility to other professional organizations with which we are aligned, in particular, the American Nurses Association and the American Bar Association. We accept and abide by the principles of their codes of ethics and conduct. By our support of the Code of Ethics and Conduct of the American Association of Legal Nurse Consultants, we affirm that the rights and trust placed in us will not be violated.

1. The legal nurse consultant does not discriminate against any person based on race, creed, color, age, sex, national origin, social status, or disability and does not let personal attitudes interfere with professional performance.

Individual differences do not influence professional performance and practice. These factors are understood, considered, and respected when performing activities.

2. The legal nurse consultant performs as a consultant or an expert with the highest degree of integrity.

Integrity refers to uprightness, honesty, and sincerity. The legal nurse consultant directs those attributes to the requirements of the profession. Integrity is a personal and sacred trust and the standard against which the legal nurse consultant must ultimately test all decisions. Honest errors and differences of opinion may occur, but deceit, poor judgment, or lack of principles must not be tolerated.

3. The legal nurse consultant uses informed judgment, objectivity, and individual competence as criteria when accepting assignments.

The legal nurse consultant does not purport to be competent in matters in which he or she has limited knowledge or experience. Only services that meet high personal and professional standards are offered or performed.

4. The legal nurse consultant maintains standards of personal conduct that reflect honorably upon the profession.

The legal nurse consultant abides by all federal and state laws. The legal nurse consultant who knowingly becomes involved in unethical or illegal activities negates professional responsibility for personal interest or personal gain. Such activities jeopardize the public confidence and trust in the nursing profession.

continued

FIGURE 34-3   Code of Ethics[4]   *continued*

5. The legal nurse consultant provides professional services with objectivity.

The legal nurse consultant provides services free of personal prejudice and conflict of interest. The legal nurse consultant reflects on all current assignments and commitments before accepting assignments, making decisions, rendering opinions, or providing recommendations. Personal prejudices and conflicts of interest must be recognized, as they may interfere with objectivity and adversely affect performance.

6. The legal nurse consultant protects client privacy and confidentiality.

The legal nurse consultant uses confidential materials with discretion. The legal nurse consultant respects and protects the privacy of the client. The legal nurse consultant does not use any client information for personal gain.

7. The legal nurse consultant is accountable for responsibilities accepted and actions performed.

8. The legal nurse consultant maintains professional nursing competence.

The legal nurse consultant is a registered nurse and maintains an active nursing license. The legal nurse consultant is knowledgeable about the current scope of nursing practice and the standards of the profession. The legal nurse consultant does not practice law.

Conclusion

Each individual's personal commitment to the Code of Ethics and Conduct of the American Association of Legal Nurse Consultants is the ultimate regulator of his or her behavior. By adopting this Code of Ethics and Conduct, we affirm to those with whom we serve that they have the right to expect us to abide by this code.

As members of the American Association of Legal Nurse Consultants, we pledge to demonstrate to the public this commitment of integrity and professional excellence.

Reprinted with permission of the American Association of Legal Nurse Consultants, 4700 W. Lake Avenue, Glenview, IL 60025-1485, copyright 1992.

CERTIFICATION

AALNC has developed a certifying examination to promote recognition of legal nurse consulting as a distinct profession and to establish a level of competence to be attained by those practicing in the field. In order to include the **Legal Nurse Consultant Certified** (LNCC) designation among the qualifications of the legal nurse consultant, the he or she must have passed the AALNC certifying examination.

Prior to taking the certifying examination, the candidate for certification must make application. At the time of the application, the candidate must meet all of the following requirements:

- The candidate must possess a current full and unrestricted license as a registered nurse in the United States.
- The candidate must have a minimum of two years' experience as a registered nurse.

■ The candidate must have a bachelor's degree or the equivalent of five years' experience practicing as a legal nurse consultant.

■ The candidate must present evidence of 2000 hours of legal nurse consulting experience in a staff, administrative, teaching, or private practice capacity within the three years immediately preceding the application. (After 2003, all candidates will be required to present evidence of a minimum number of hours of continuing legal nurse consultant education within the two years immediately preceding the application.)[5]

Certifying examinations are conducted during the annual education seminar of the AALNC and during April and October of each year at specified test sites throughout the United States. The certification is valid for five years and may be renewed by examination or by continuing education.

The examination attempts to measure a legal nurse consultant's competence in the following areas:

■ investigating, collecting, and reviewing standards of care, medical literature, medical records, damages, legal causation, and more

■ evaluating standards of care, medical literature, medical records, damages, legal causation, and more, relative to a particular client's claim

■ communicating effectively with attorneys, clients, insurance personnel, investigators, expert witnesses, and others

■ drafting chronologies, analysis memos, timelines, and other documents that may be used as attorney work product or as evidence in cases involving medical-legal issues

■ educating attorneys, clients, and others on the medical issues in a case

■ participating in discovery, development of case strategy, and management of medical-legal cases

■ providing support for the resolution of medical-legal claims

■ testifying as a fact witness or as an expert witness[6]

A pilot examination was conducted at the annual education seminar in Dallas, Texas, in April 1998. The first certifying examination was given on October 24, 1998; 139 legal nurse consultants became Legal Nurse Consultant Certified.

PROFESSIONAL ASSOCIATION

There are many definitions of a profession. Authorities indicate that common features of all consulting professions include

■ extensive specialized training

■ the use of primarily intellectual skill to provide advice about matters not generally understood by the average person

■ the provision of an important service in society[7]

What LNCs Say . . .

"Be involved in professional organizations like the American Association of Legal Nurse Consultants, both at the national and the local chapter level. You can learn a great deal talking with your peers about legal nurse consulting. Many times jobs in legal nurse consulting, medical record summarization, or medical record abstracting are not advertised. Nurses get them through networking" James Fell, RN, BSN, MSN, MBA, LNC, Bay Village, OH, used with permission.

In addition, there are several features that describe consulting professions but are not common to all consulting professions. These include

- certification or licensure
- existence of an organization that represents the profession
- autonomy in one's work, including the independent exercise of judgment and the use of one's own discretion in carrying out the work
- the provision of important services to society by serving basic values
- the monopoly over the provision of services and an attempt to define the sphere of appropriate practice
- self-regulation or the absence of public or external control[9]

Clearly legal nurse consulting falls within the definition of a profession. The evolution of this alternative nursing career has provided many registered nurses with creative, meaningful, and responsible ways of using their education and expertise. To function effectively as a legal nurse consultant means all of the following:

- acquiring the knowledge of the profession and learning its disciplines
- learning to apply professional knowledge and skills effectively
- always putting the client's interests ahead of one's own interests and those of the group to which one belongs
- maintaining high standards for serving clients
- behaving at all times with a professional bearing[10]

The first step, acquiring the knowledge of the profession and learning its disciplines includes using resources such as this textbook, and affiliating with professional organizations such as the AALNC. Armed with medical education and experience and an understanding of legal principles, the legal nurse consultant is ready to assist and guide the resolution of medical-legal claims in the twenty-first century.

CHAPTER SUMMARY

- The AALNC has adopted a Scope of Practice, Standards of Practice, and a Code of Ethics.
- A certifying examination by AALNC allows successful candidates to include the LNCC (Legal Nurse Consultant Certified) with other professional qualifications.
- Legal nurse consulting is a profession that will grow in recognition and will enhance the delivery of legal services in the twenty-first century.

KEY TERM

Legal Nurse Consultant Certified

REVIEW QUESTIONS

1. How has the growth of the AALNC mirrored growth of the profession?
2. What characteristics set professions apart from occupations?
3. What does it mean to function effectively as a legal nurse consultant?

INTERNET EXERCISES

1. Access the web page for this textbook at *www.westlegalstudies.com*.
2. Click on the assignments section and complete the assignment(s) for Chapter Thirty-four.

EXERCISES

1. Networking. Consider joining the AALNC or other associations that will enhance your professionalism and put you in contact with other legal nurse consultants.
2. Professional portfolio. Make a list or chart of the most important features of the Scope of Practice, Standards of Practice, and Code of Ethics of the AALNC and include them in your systems file, folder, or binder. Organize or index them for easy reference. Commitment to professional ethics is highly regarded by legal professionals.

ENDNOTES

1. American Association of Legal Nurse Consultants, *The History of AALNC*. Fifth Annual Conference, Houston, TX, 1995.
2. J. B. Bogart, RN MN, ed, *Legal Nurse Consulting: Principles and Practice* (Boston: CRC Press, 1998): 16–18.
3. *Ibid,* 18–21.
4. *Ibid,* 23–24.
5. American Association of Legal Nurse Consultants, *Legal Nurse Consultant Certification Handbook* (1998–1999): 1.
6. *Ibid,* 3.
7. Bayles, 1981 *quoted in* W. Rothwell, R. Sullivan, and G. McLean, *Practicing Organization Development: A Guide for Consultants* (San Francisco: Jossey-Bass/Pfeiffer, 1995): 446.
8. American Bar Association, *Annotated Model Rules of Professional Conduct,* (1999) 4th Edition Rule 1.1. Copies of ABA *Model Code of Professional Responsibility, 1999 Edition* are available from Service Center, American Bar Association, 750 North Lake Shore Drive, Chicago, IL 60611-4497, 1-800-285-2221.

9. *Ibid,* 447.

10. Lippitt and Lippitt, 1978, *quoted in* W. Rothwell, R. Sullivan, and G. McLean. *Practicing Organiza-* *tion Development: A Guide for Consultants* (San Francisco: Jossey-Bass/Pfeiffer, 1978): 448.

ADDITIONAL REFERENCES

Miller, P.M., RN. "Ethical Dilemmas Faced by Legal Nurse Consultants." *Journal of Legal Nurse Consulting* 8:2 (1997): 12–13, 16.

APPENDIX A

The United States Constitution

[This text of the Constitution follows the engrossed copy signed by George Washington.]

We the People of the United States, in Order to form a more perfect Union, establish Justice, insure domestic Tranquility, provide for the common defence, promote the general Welfare, and secure the Blessings of Liberty to ourselves and our Posterity, do ordain and establish this Constitution for the United States of America.

ARTICLE I.

Section 1.

All legislative Powers herein granted shall be vested in a Congress of the United States, which shall consist of a Senate and House of Representatives.

Section 2.

Clause 1: The House of Representatives shall be composed of Members chosen every second Year by the People of the several States, and the Electors in each State shall have the Qualifications requisite for Electors of the most numerous Branch of the State Legislature.

Clause 2: No Person shall be a Representative who shall not have attained to the Age of twenty five Years, and been seven Years a Citizen of the United States, and who shall not, when elected, be an Inhabitant of that State in which he shall be chosen.

Clause 3: Representatives and direct Taxes shall be apportioned among the several States which may be included within this Union, according to their respective Numbers, which shall be determined by adding to the whole Number of free Persons, including those bound to Service for a Term of Years, and excluding Indians not taxed, three fifths of all other Persons. [The part of this Clause relating to the mode of apportionment of representatives among the several States has been affected by Section 2 of amendment XIV, and as to taxes on incomes without apportionment by amendment XVI.] The actual Enumeration shall be made within three Years after the first Meeting of the Congress of the United States, and within every subsequent Term of ten Years, in such Manner as they shall by Law direct. The Number of Representatives shall not exceed one for every thirty Thousand, but each State shall have at Least one Representative; and until such enumeration shall be made, the State of New Hampshire shall be entitled to chuse three, Massachusetts eight, Rhode-Island and Providence Plantations one, Connecticut five, New-York six, New Jersey four, Pennsylvania eight, Delaware one, Maryland six, Virginia ten, North Carolina five, South Carolina five, and Georgia three.

Clause 4: When vacancies happen in the Representation from any State, the Executive Authority thereof shall issue Writs of Election to fill such Vacancies.

Clause 5: The House of Representatives shall chuse their Speaker and other Officers; and shall have the sole Power of Impeachment.

Section 3.

Clause 1: The Senate of the United States shall be composed of two Senators from each State, chosen by the Legislature thereof, for six Years; and each Senator shall have one Vote. [This Clause has been affected by Clause 1 of amendment XVII.]

Clause 2: Immediately after they shall be assembled in Consequence of the first Election, they shall be divided as equally as may be into three Classes. The Seats of the Senators of the first Class shall be vacated at the Expiration of the second Year, of the second Class at the Expiration of the fourth Year, and of the third Class at the Expiration of the sixth Year, so that one third may be chosen every second Year; and if Vacancies happen by Resignation, or otherwise, during the Recess of the Legislature of any State, the Executive thereof may make temporary Appointments until the next Meeting of the Legislature, which shall then fill such Vacancies. [This Clause has been affected by Clause 2 of amendment XVIII.]

Clause 3: No Person shall be a Senator who shall not have attained to the Age of thirty Years, and been nine Years a Citizen of the United States, and who shall not, when elected, be an Inhabitant of that State for which he shall be chosen.

Clause 4: The Vice President of the United States shall be President of the Senate, but shall have no Vote, unless they be equally divided.

Clause 5: The Senate shall chuse their other Officers, and also a President pro tempore, in the Absence of the Vice President, or when he shall exercise the Office of President of the United States.

Clause 6: The Senate shall have the sole Power to try all Impeachments. When sitting for that Purpose, they shall be on Oath or Affirmation. When the President of the United States is tried, the Chief Justice shall preside: And no Person shall be convicted without the Concurrence of two thirds of the Members present.

Clause 7: Judgment in Cases of Impeachment shall not extend further than to removal from Office, and disqualification to hold and enjoy any Office of honor, Trust or Profit under the United States: but the Party convicted shall nevertheless be liable and subject to Indictment, Trial, Judgment and Punishment, according to Law.

Section 4.

Clause 1: The Times, Places and Manner of holding Elections for Senators and Representatives, shall be prescribed in each State by the Legislature thereof; but the Congress may at any time by Law make or alter such Regulations, except as to the Places of chusing Senators.

Clause 2: The Congress shall assemble at least once in every Year, and such Meeting shall be on the first Monday in December, unless they shall by Law appoint a different Day. [This Clause has been affected by amendment XX.]

Section 5.

Clause 1: Each House shall be the Judge of the Elections, Returns and Qualifications of its own Members, and a Majority of each shall constitute a Quorum to do Business; but a smaller Number may adjourn from day to day, and may be authorized to compel the Attendance of absent Members, in such Manner, and under such Penalties as each House may provide.

Clause 2: Each House may determine the Rules of its Proceedings, punish its Members for disorderly Behaviour, and, with the Concurrence of two thirds, expel a Member.

Clause 3: Each House shall keep a Journal of its Proceedings, and from time to time publish the same, excepting such Parts as may in their Judgment require Secrecy; and the Yeas and Nays of the Members of either House on any question shall, at the Desire of one fifth of those Present, be entered on the Journal.

Clause 4: Neither House, during the Session of Congress, shall, without the Consent of the other, adjourn for more than three days, nor to any other Place than that in which the two Houses shall be sitting.

Section 6.

Clause 1: The Senators and Representatives shall receive a Compensation for their Services, to be ascertained by Law, and paid out of the Treasury of the United States. [This Clause has been affected by amendment XXVII.] They shall in all Cases, except Treason, Felony and Breach of the Peace, be privileged from Arrest during their Attendance at the Session of their respective Houses, and in going to and returning from the same; and for any Speech or Debate in either House, they shall not be questioned in any other Place.

Clause 2: No Senator or Representative shall, during the Time for which he was elected, be appointed to any civil Office under the Authority of the United States, which shall have been created, or the Emoluments whereof shall have been encreased during such time; and no Person holding any Office under the United States, shall be a Member of either House during his Continuance in Office.

Section 7.

Clause 1: All Bills for raising Revenue shall originate in the House of Representatives; but the Senate may propose or concur with Amendments as on other Bills.

Clause 2: Every Bill which shall have passed the House of Representatives and the Senate, shall, before it become a Law, be presented to the President of the United States; If he approve he shall sign it, but if not he shall return it, with his Objections to that House in which it shall have originated, who shall enter the Objections at large on their Journal, and proceed to reconsider it. If after such Reconsideration two thirds of that House shall agree to pass the Bill, it shall be sent, together with the Objections, to the other House, by which it shall likewise be reconsidered, and if approved by two thirds of that House, it shall become a Law. But in all such Cases the Votes of both Houses shall be determined by Yeas and Nays, and the Names of the Persons voting for and against the Bill shall be entered on the Journal of each House respectively. If any Bill shall not be returned by the President within ten Days (Sundays excepted) after it shall have been presented to him, the Same shall be a Law, in like Manner as if he had signed it, unless the Congress by their Adjournment prevent its Return, in which Case it shall not be a Law.

Clause 3: Every Order, Resolution, or Vote to which the Concurrence of the Senate and House of Representatives may be necessary (except on a question of Adjournment) shall be presented to the President of the United States; and before the Same shall take Effect, shall be approved by him, or being disapproved by him, shall be repassed by two thirds of the Senate and House of Representatives, according to the Rules and Limitations prescribed in the Case of a Bill.

Section 8.

Clause 1:: The Congress shall have Power To lay and collect Taxes, Duties, Imposts and Excises, to pay the Debts and provide for the common Defence and general Welfare of the United States; but all Duties, Imposts and Excises shall be uniform throughout the United States;

Clause 2: To borrow Money on the credit of the United States;

Clause 3: To regulate Commerce with foreign Nations, and among the several States, and with the Indian Tribes;

Clause 4: To establish an uniform Rule of Naturalization, and uniform Laws on the subject of Bankruptcies throughout the United States;

Clause 5: To coin Money, regulate the Value thereof, and of foreign Coin, and fix the Standard of Weights and Measures;

Clause 6: To provide for the Punishment of counterfeiting the Securities and current Coin of the United States;

Clause 7: To establish Post Offices and post Roads;

Clause 8: To promote the Progress of Science and useful Arts, by securing for limited Times to Authors and Inventors the exclusive Right to their respective Writings and Discoveries;

Clause 9: To constitute Tribunals inferior to the supreme Court;

Clause 10: To define and punish Piracies and Felonies committed on the high Seas, and Offences against the Law of Nations;

Clause 11: To declare War, grant Letters of Marque and Reprisal, and make Rules concerning Captures on Land and Water;

Clause 12: To raise and support Armies, but no Appropriation of Money to that Use shall be for a longer Term than two Years;

Clause 13: To provide and maintain a Navy;

Clause 14: To make Rules for the Government and Regulation of the land and naval Forces;

Clause 15: To provide for calling forth the Militia to execute the Laws of the Union, suppress Insurrections and repel Invasions;

Clause 16: To provide for organizing, arming, and disciplining, the Militia, and for governing such Part of them as may be employed in the Service of the United States, reserving to the States respectively, the Appointment of the Officers, and the Authority of training the Militia according to the discipline prescribed by Congress;

Clause 17: To exercise exclusive Legislation in all Cases whatsoever, over such District (not exceeding ten Miles square) as may, by Cession of particular States, and the Acceptance of Congress, become the Seat of the Government of the United States, and to exercise like Authority over all Places purchased by the Consent of the Legislature of the State in which the Same shall be, for the Erection of Forts, Magazines, Arsenals, dock-Yards, and other needful Buildings;—And

Clause 18: To make all Laws which shall be necessary and proper for carrying into Execution the foregoing Powers, and all other Powers vested by this Constitution in the Government of the United States, or in any Department or Officer thereof.

Section 9.

Clause 1: The Migration or Importation of such Persons as any of the States now existing shall think proper to admit, shall not be prohibited by the Congress prior to the Year one thousand eight hundred and eight, but a Tax or duty may be imposed on such Importation, not exceeding ten dollars for each Person.

Clause 2: The Privilege of the Writ of Habeas Corpus shall not be suspended, unless when in Cases of Rebellion or Invasion the public Safety may require it.

Clause 3: No Bill of Attainder or ex post facto Law shall be passed.

Clause 4: No Capitation, or other direct, Tax shall be laid, unless in Proportion to the Census or Enumeration herein before directed to be taken. [This Clause has been affected by amendment XVI.]

Clause 5: No Tax or Duty shall be laid on Articles exported from any State.

Clause 6: No Preference shall be given by any Regulation of Commerce or Revenue to the Ports of one State over those of another: nor shall Vessels bound to, or from, one State, be obliged to enter, clear, or pay Duties in another.

Clause 7: No Money shall be drawn from the Treasury, but in Consequence of Appropriations made by Law; and a regular Statement and Account of the Receipts and Expenditures of all public Money shall be published from time to time.

Clause 8: No Title of Nobility shall be granted by the United States: And no Person holding any Office of Profit or Trust under them, shall, without the Consent of the Congress, accept of any present, Emolument, Office, or Title, of any kind whatever, from any King, Prince, or foreign State.

Section 10.

Clause 1: No State shall enter into any Treaty, Alliance, or Confederation; grant Letters of Marque and Reprisal; coin Money; emit Bills of Credit; make any Thing but gold and silver Coin a Tender in Payment of Debts; pass any Bill of Attainder, ex post facto Law, or Law impairing the Obligation of Contracts, or grant any Title of Nobility.

Clause 2: No State shall, without the Consent of the Congress, lay any Imposts or Duties on Imports or Exports, except what may be absolutely necessary for executing it's inspection Laws: and the net Produce of all Duties and Imposts, laid by any State on Imports or Exports, shall be for the Use of the Treasury of the United States; and all such Laws shall be subject to the Revision and Control of the Congress.

Clause 3: No State shall, without the Consent of Congress, lay any Duty of Tonnage, keep Troops, or Ships of War in time of Peace, enter into any Agreement or Compact with another State, or with a for-

eign Power, or engage in War, unless actually invaded, or in such imminent Danger as will not admit of delay.

ARTICLE II.

Section 1.

Clause 1: The executive Power shall be vested in a President of the United States of America. He shall hold his Office during the Term of four Years, and, together with the Vice President, chosen for the same Term, be elected, as follows

Clause 2: Each State shall appoint, in such Manner as the Legislature thereof may direct, a Number of Electors, equal to the whole Number of Senators and Representatives to which the State may be entitled in the Congress: but no Senator or Representative, or Person holding an Office of Trust or Profit under the United States, shall be appointed an Elector.

Clause 3: The Electors shall meet in their respective States, and vote by Ballot for two Persons, of whom one at least shall not be an Inhabitant of the same State with themselves. And they shall make a List of all the Persons voted for, and of the Number of Votes for each; which List they shall sign and certify, and transmit sealed to the Seat of the Government of the United States, directed to the President of the Senate. The President of the Senate shall, in the Presence of the Senate and House of Representatives, open all the Certificates, and the Votes shall then be counted. The Person having the greatest Number of Votes shall be the President, if such Number be a Majority of the whole Number of Electors appointed; and if there be more than one who have such Majority, and have an equal Number of Votes, then the House of Representatives shall immediately chuse by Ballot one of them for President; and if no Person have a Majority, then from the five highest on the List the said House shall in like Manner chuse the President. But in chusing the President, the Votes shall be taken by States, the Representation from each State having one Vote; A quorum for this Purpose shall consist of a Member or Members from two thirds of the States, and a Majority of all the States shall be necessary to a Choice. In every Case, after the Choice of the President, the Person having the greatest Number of Votes of the Electors shall be the Vice-President. But if there should remain two or more who have equal Votes, the Senate shall chuse from them by Ballot the Vice-President. [This Clause has been superseded by amendment XII.]

Clause 4: The Congress may determine the Time of chusing the Electors, and the Day on which they shall give their Votes; which Day shall be the same throughout the United States.

Clause 5: No Person except a natural born Citizen, or a Citizen of the United States, at the time of the Adoption of this Constitution, shall be eligible to the Office of President; neither shall any Person be eligible to that Office who shall not have attained to the Age of thirty five Years, and been fourteen Years a Resident within the United States.

Clause 6: In Case of the Removal of the President from Office, or of his Death, Resignation, or Inability to discharge the Powers and Duties of the said Office, the Same shall devolve on the Vice-President, and the Congress may by Law provide for the Case of Removal, Death, Resignation or Inability, both of the President and Vice President, declaring what Officer shall then act as President, and such Officer shall act accordingly, until the Disability be removed, or a President shall be elected. [This Clause has been affected by amendment XXV.]

Clause 7: The President shall, at stated Times, receive for his Services, a Compensation, which shall neither be encreased nor diminished during the Period for which he shall have been elected, and he shall not receive within that Period any other Emolument from the United States, or any of them.

Clause 8: Before he enter on the Execution of his Office, he shall take the following Oath or Affirmation:—

"I do solemnly swear (or affirm) that I will faithfully execute the Office of President of the United States, and will to the best of my Ability, preserve, protect and defend the Constitution of the United States."

Section 2.

Clause 1: The President shall be Commander in Chief of the Army and Navy of the United States, and of the Militia of the several States, when called into the actual Service of the United States; he may require the Opinion, in writing, of the principal Officer in each of the executive Departments, upon any Subject relating to the Duties of their respective Offices, and he shall have Power to grant Reprieves and Pardons for Offences against the United States, except in Cases of Impeachment.

Clause 2: He shall have Power, by and with the Advice and Consent of the Senate, to make Treaties, provided two thirds of the Senators present concur; and he shall nominate, and by and with the Advice and Consent of the Senate, shall appoint Ambassadors, other public Ministers and Consuls, Judges of the supreme Court, and all other Officers of the United States, whose Appointments are not herein otherwise provided for, and which shall be established by Law: but the Congress may by Law vest the Appointment of such inferior Officers, as they think proper, in the President alone, in the Courts of Law, or in the Heads of Departments.

Clause 3: The President shall have Power to fill up all Vacancies that may happen during the Recess of the Senate, by granting Commissions which shall expire at the End of their next Session.

Section 3.

He shall from time to time give to the Congress Information of the State of the Union, and recommend to their Consideration such Measures as he shall judge necessary and expedient; he may, on extraordinary Occasions, convene both Houses, or either of them, and in Case of Disagreement between them, with Respect to the Time of Adjournment, he may adjourn them to such Time as he shall think proper; he shall receive Ambassadors and other public Ministers; he shall take Care that the Laws be faithfully executed, and shall Commission all the Officers of the United States.

Section 4.

The President, Vice President and all civil Officers of the United States, shall be removed from Office on Impeachment for, and Conviction of, Treason, Bribery, or other high Crimes and Misdemeanors.

ARTICLE III.

Section 1.

The judicial Power of the United States, shall be vested in one supreme Court, and in such inferior Courts as the Congress may from time to time ordain and establish. The Judges, both of the supreme and inferior Courts, shall hold their Offices during good Behaviour, and shall, at stated Times, receive for their Services, a Compensation, which shall not be diminished during their Continuance in Office.

Section 2.

Clause 1: The judicial Power shall extend to all Cases, in Law and Equity, arising under this Constitution, the Laws of the United States, and Treaties made, or which shall be made, under their Authority;—to all Cases affecting Ambassadors, other public Ministers and Consuls;—to all Cases of admiralty and maritime Jurisdiction;—to Controversies to which the United States shall be a Party;—to Controversies between two or more States;—between a State and Citizens of another State;—between Citizens of different States,—between Citizens of the same State claiming Lands under Grants of different States, and between a State, or the Citizens thereof, and foreign States, Citizens or Subjects. [This Clause has been affected by amendment XI.]

Clause 2: In all Cases affecting Ambassadors, other public Ministers and Consuls, and those in which a State shall be Party, the supreme Court shall have original Jurisdiction. In all the other Cases before mentioned, the supreme Court shall have appellate Jurisdiction, both as to Law and Fact, with such Exceptions, and under such Regulations as the Congress shall make.

Clause 3: The Trial of all Crimes, except in Cases of Impeachment, shall be by Jury; and such Trial shall be held in the State where the said Crimes shall have been committed; but when not committed within any State, the Trial shall be at such Place or Places as the Congress may by Law have directed.

Section 3.

Clause 1: Treason against the United States, shall consist only in levying War against them, or in adhering to their Enemies, giving them Aid and Comfort. No Person shall be convicted of Treason unless on the Testimony of two Witnesses to the same overt Act, or on Confession in open Court.

Clause 2: The Congress shall have Power to declare the Punishment of Treason, but no Attainder of Treason shall work Corruption of Blood, or Forfeiture except during the Life of the Person attainted.

ARTICLE IV.

Section 1.

Full Faith and Credit shall be given in each State to the public Acts, Records, and judicial Proceedings of every other State. And the Congress may by general Laws prescribe the Manner in which such Acts, Records and Proceedings shall be proved, and the Effect thereof.

Section 2.

Clause 1: The Citizens of each State shall be entitled to all Privileges and Immunities of Citizens in the several States.

Clause 2: A Person charged in any State with Treason, Felony, or other Crime, who shall flee from Justice, and be found in another State, shall on Demand of the executive Authority of the State from which he fled, be delivered up, to be removed to the State having Jurisdiction of the Crime.

Clause 3: No Person held to Service or Labour in one State, under the Laws thereof, escaping into another, shall, in Consequence of any Law or Regulation therein, be discharged from such Service or Labour, but shall be delivered up on Claim of the Party to whom such Service or Labour may be due. [This Clause has been affected by amendment XIII.]

Section 3.

Clause 1: New States may be admitted by the Congress into this Union; but no new State shall be formed or erected within the Jurisdiction of any other State; nor any State be formed by the Junction of two or more States, or Parts of States, without the Consent of the Legislatures of the States concerned as well as of the Congress.

Clause 2: The Congress shall have Power to dispose of and make all needful Rules and Regulations respecting the Territory or other Property belonging to the United States; and nothing in this Constitution shall be so construed as to Prejudice any Claims of the United States, or of any particular State.

Section 4.

The United States shall guarantee to every State in this Union a Republican Form of Government, and shall protect each of them against Invasion; and on Application of the Legislature, or of the Executive (when the Legislature cannot be convened) against domestic Violence.

ARTICLE V.

The Congress, whenever two thirds of both Houses shall deem it necessary, shall propose Amendments to this Constitution, or, on the Application of the Legislatures of two thirds of the several States, shall call a Convention for proposing Amendments, which, in either Case, shall be valid to all Intents and Purposes, as Part of this Constitution, when ratified by the Legislatures of three fourths of the several States, or by Conventions in three fourths thereof, as the one or the other Mode of Ratification may be proposed by the Congress; Provided that no Amendment which may be made prior to the Year One thousand eight hundred and eight shall in any Manner affect the first and fourth Clauses in the Ninth Section of the first Article; and that no State, without its Consent, shall be deprived of its equal Suffrage in the Senate.

ARTICLE VI.

Clause 1: All Debts contracted and Engagements entered into, before the Adoption of this Constitution, shall be as valid against the United States under this Constitution, as under the Confederation.

Clause 2: This Constitution, and the Laws of the United States which shall be made in Pursuance thereof; and all Treaties made, or which shall be made, under the Authority of the United States, shall be the supreme Law of the Land; and the Judges in every State shall be bound thereby, any Thing in the Constitution or Laws of any State to the Contrary notwithstanding.

Clause 3: The Senators and Representatives before mentioned, and the Members of the several State Legislatures, and all executive and judicial Officers, both of the United States and of the several States, shall be bound by Oath or Affirmation, to support this Constitution; but no religious Test shall ever be required as a Qualification to any Office or public Trust under the United States.

ARTICLE VII.

The Ratification of the Conventions of nine States, shall be sufficient for the Establishment of this Constitution between the States so ratifying the Same.

ARTICLES IN ADDITION TO, AND AMENDMENTS OF, THE CONSTITUTION OF THE UNITED STATES OF AMERICA, PROPOSED BY CONGRESS, AND RATIFIED BY THE LEGISLATURES OF THE SEVERAL STATES, PURSUANT TO THE FIFTH ARTICLE OF THE ORIGINAL CONSTITUTION

ARTICLE I.

Congress shall make no law respecting an establishment of religion, or prohibiting the free exercise thereof; or abridging the freedom of speech, or of the press; or the right of the people peaceably to assemble, and to petition the government for a redress of grievances.

ARTICLE II.

A well regulated Militia, being necessary to the security of a free State, the right of the people to keep and bear Arms, shall not be infringed.

ARTICLE III.

No Soldier shall, in time of peace be quartered in any house, without the consent of the Owner, nor in time of war, but in a manner to be prescribed by law.

ARTICLE IV.

The right of the people to be secure in their persons, houses, papers, and effects, against unreasonable searches and seizures, shall not be violated, and no Warrants shall issue, but upon probable cause, supported by Oath or affirmation, and particularly describing the place to be searched, and the persons or things to be seized.

ARTICLE V.

No person shall be held to answer for a capital, or otherwise infamous crime, unless on a presentment or indictment of a Grand Jury, except in cases arising in the land or naval forces, or in the Militia, when in actual service in time of War or public danger; nor shall any person be subject for the same offence to be twice put in jeopardy of life or limb; nor shall be compelled in any criminal case to be a witness against himself, nor be deprived of life, liberty, or property, without due process of law; nor shall private property be taken for public use, without just compensation.

ARTICLE VI.

In all criminal prosecutions, the accused shall enjoy the right to a speedy and public trial, by an impartial jury of the State and district wherein the crime shall have been committed, which district shall have been previously ascertained by law, and to be informed of the nature and cause of the accusation; to be confronted with the witnesses against him; to have compulsory process for obtaining witnesses in his favor, and to have the Assistance of Counsel for his defence.

ARTICLE VII.

In Suits at common law, where the value in controversy shall exceed twenty dollars, the right of trial by jury shall be preserved, and no fact tried by a jury, shall be otherwise re-examined in any Court of the United States, than according to the rules of the common law.

ARTICLE VIII.

Excessive bail shall not be required, nor excessive fines imposed, nor cruel and unusual punishments inflicted.

ARTICLE IX.

The enumeration in the Constitution, of certain rights, shall not be construed to deny or disparage others retained by the people.

ARTICLE X.

The powers not delegated to the United States by the Constitution, nor prohibited by it to the States, are reserved to the States respectively, or to the people.

ARTICLE XI.

The Judicial power of the United States shall not be construed to extend to any suit in law or equity, commenced or prosecuted against one of the United States by Citizens of another State, or by Citizens or Subjects of any Foreign State.

ARTICLE XII.

The Electors shall meet in their respective states, and vote by ballot for President and Vice-President, one of whom, at least, shall not be an inhabitant of the same state with themselves; they shall name in their ballots the person voted for as President, and in distinct ballots the person voted for as Vice-President, and they shall make distinct lists of all persons voted for as President, and of all persons voted for as Vice-President, and of the number of votes for each, which lists they shall sign and certify, and transmit sealed to the seat of the government of the United States, directed to the President of the Senate;—The President of the Senate shall, in the presence of the Senate and House of Representatives, open all the certificates and the votes shall then be counted;—The person having the greatest number of votes for President, shall be the President, if such number be a majority of the whole number of Electors appointed; and if no person have such majority, then from the persons having the highest numbers not exceeding three on the list of those voted for as President, the House of Representatives shall choose immediately, by ballot, the President. But in choosing the President, the votes shall be taken by states, the representation from each state having one vote; a quorum for this purpose shall consist of a member or members from two-thirds of the states, and a majority of all the states shall be necessary to a choice. And if the House of Representatives shall not choose a President whenever the right of choice shall devolve upon them, before the fourth day of March next following, then the Vice-President shall act as President, as in the case of the death or other constitutional disability of the President.—The person having the greatest number of votes as Vice-President, shall be the Vice-President, if such number be a majority of the whole number of Electors appointed, and if no person have a majority, then from the two highest numbers on the list, the Senate shall choose the Vice-President; a quorum for the purpose shall consist of two-thirds of the whole number of Senators, and a majority of the whole number shall be necessary to a choice. But no person constitutionally ineligible to the office of President shall be eligible to that of Vice-President of the United States.

ARTICLE XIII.

Section 1.

Neither slavery nor involuntary servitude, except as a punishment for crime whereof the party shall have been duly convicted, shall exist within the United States, or any place subject to their jurisdiction.

Section 2.

Congress shall have power to enforce this article by appropriate legislation.

ARTICLE XIV.

Section 1.

All persons born or naturalized in the United States, and subject to the jurisdiction thereof, are citizens of the United States and of the State wherein they reside. No State shall make or enforce any law which shall abridge the privileges or immunities of citizens of the United States; nor shall any State deprive any person of life, liberty, or property, without due process of law; nor deny to any person within its jurisdiction the equal protection of the laws.

Section 2.

Representatives shall be apportioned among the several States according to their respective numbers, counting the whole number of persons in each State, excluding Indians not taxed. But when the right to vote at any election for the choice of electors for President and Vice President of the United States, Representatives in Congress, the Executive and Judicial officers of a State, or the members of the Legislature thereof, is denied to any of the male inhabitants of such State, being twenty-one years of age, and citizens of the United States, or in any way abridged, except for participation in rebellion, or other crime, the basis of representation therein shall be reduced in the proportion which the number of such male citizens shall bear to the whole number of male citizens twenty-one years of age in such State.

Section 3.

No person shall be a Senator or Representative in Congress, or elector of President and Vice President, or hold any office, civil or military, under the United States, or under any State, who, having previously taken an oath, as a member of Congress, or as an officer of the United States, or as a member of any State legislature, or as an executive or judicial officer of any State, to support the Constitution of the United States, shall have engaged in insurrection or rebellion against the same, or given aid or comfort to the enemies thereof. But Congress may by a vote of two-thirds of each House, remove such disability.

Section 4.

The validity of the public debt of the United States, authorized by law, including debts incurred for payment of pensions and bounties for services in suppressing insurrection or rebellion, shall not be questioned. But neither the United States nor any State shall assume or pay any debt or obligation incurred in aid of insurrection or rebellion against the United States, or any claim for the loss or emancipation of any slave; but all such debts, obligations and claims shall be held illegal and void.

Section 5.

The Congress shall have power to enforce, by appropriate legislation, the provisions of this article.

ARTICLE XV.

Section 1.

The right of citizens of the United States to vote shall not be denied or abridged by the United States or by any State on account of race, color, or previous condition of servitude.

Section 2.

The Congress shall have power to enforce this article by appropriate legislation.

ARTICLE XVI.

The Congress shall have power to lay and collect taxes on incomes, from whatever source derived, without apportionment among the several States, and without regard to any census or enumeration.

ARTICLE XVII.

The Senate of the United States shall be composed of two Senators from each State, elected by the people thereof, for six years; and each Senator shall have one vote. The electors in each State shall have the qualifications requisite for electors of the most numerous branch of the State legislatures.

When vacancies happen in the representation of any State in the Senate, the executive authority of such State shall issue writs of election to fill such vacancies: Provided, That the legislature of any State may empower the executive thereof to make temporary appointments until the people fill the vacancies by election as the legislature may direct.

This amendment shall not be so construed as to affect the election or term of any Senator chosen before it becomes valid as part of the Constitution.

ARTICLE XVIII.

Section 1.

After one year from the ratification of this article the manufacture, sale, or transportation of intoxicating liquors within, the importation thereof into, or the exportation thereof from the United States and all territory subject to the jurisdiction thereof for beverage purposes is hereby prohibited.

Section 2.

The Congress and the several States shall have concurrent power to enforce this article by appropriate legislation.

Section 3.

This article shall be inoperative unless it shall have been ratified as an amendment to the Constitution by the legislatures of the several States, as provided in the Constitution, within seven years from the date of the submission hereof to the States by the Congress.

ARTICLE XIX.

The right of citizens of the United States to vote shall not be denied or abridged by the United States or by any State on account of sex.

Congress shall have power to enforce this article by appropriate legislation.

ARTICLE XX.

Section 1.

The terms of the President and Vice President shall end at noon on the 20th day of January, and the terms of Senators and Representatives at noon on the 3d day of January, of the years in which such terms would have ended if this article had not been ratified; and the terms of their successors shall then begin.

Section 2.

The Congress shall assemble at least once in every year, and such meeting shall begin at noon on the 3d day of January, unless they shall by law appoint a different day.

Section 3.

If, at the time fixed for the beginning of the term of the President, the President elect shall have died, the Vice President elect shall become President. If a President shall not have been chosen before the time fixed for the beginning of his term, or if the President elect shall have failed to qualify, then the Vice President elect shall act as President until a President shall have qualified; and the Congress may by law provide for the case wherein neither a President elect nor a Vice President elect shall have qualified, declaring who shall then act as President, or the manner in which one who is to act shall be selected, and such person shall act accordingly until a President or Vice President shall have qualified.

Section 4.

The Congress may by law provide for the case of the death of any of the persons from whom the House of Representatives may choose a President whenever the right of choice shall have devolved upon them, and for the case of the death of any of the persons from whom the Senate may choose a Vice President whenever the right of choice shall have devolved upon them.

Section 5.

Sections 1 and 2 shall take effect on the 15th day of October following the ratification of this article.

Section 6.

This article shall be inoperative unless it shall have been ratified as an amendment to the Constitution by the legislatures of three-fourths of the several States within seven years from the date of its submission.

ARTICLE XXI.

Section 1.

The eighteenth article of amendment to the Constitution of the United States is hereby repealed.

Section 2.

The transportation or importation into any State, Territory, or possession of the United States for delivery or use therein of intoxicating liquors, in violation of the laws thereof, is hereby prohibited.

Section 3.

This article shall be inoperative unless it shall have been ratified as an amendment to the Constitution by conventions in the several States, as provided in the Constitution, within seven years from the date of the submission hereof to the States by the Congress.

AMENDMENT XXII

Section 1.

No person shall be elected to the office of the President more than twice, and no person who has held the office of President, or acted as President, for more than two years of a term to which some other person was elected President shall be elected to the office of the President more than once. But this article shall not apply to any person holding the office of President when this Article was proposed by the Congress, and shall not prevent any person who may be holding the office of President, or acting as President, during the term within which this article becomes operative from holding the office of President or acting as President during the remainder of such term.

Section 2.

This article shall be inoperative unless it shall have been ratified as an amendment to the Constitution by the legislatures of three-fourths of the several states within seven years from the date of its submission to the states by the Congress.

AMENDMENT XXIII

Section 1.

The District constituting the seat of government of the United States shall appoint in such manner as the Congress may direct:

A number of electors of President and Vice President equal to the whole number of Senators and Representatives in Congress to which the District would be entitled if it were a state, but in no event more than the least populous state; they shall be in addition to those appointed by the states, but they shall be considered, for the purposes of the election of President and Vice President, to be electors appointed by a state; and they shall meet in the District and perform such duties as provided by the twelfth article of amendment.

Section 2.

The Congress shall have power to enforce this article by appropriate legislation.

AMENDMENT XXIV

Section 1.

The right of citizens of the United States to vote in any primary or other election for President or Vice President, for electors for President or Vice President, or for Senator or Representative in Congress, shall not be denied or abridged by the United States or any state by reason of failure to pay any poll tax or other tax.

Section 2.

The Congress shall have power to enforce this article by appropriate legislation.

AMENDMENT XXV

Section 1.

In case of the removal of the President from office or of his death or resignation, the Vice President shall become President.

Section 2.

Whenever there is a vacancy in the office of the Vice President, the President shall nominate a Vice President who shall take office upon confirmation by a majority vote of both Houses of Congress.

Section 3.

Whenever the President transmits to the President pro tempore of the Senate and the Speaker of the House of Representatives his written declaration that he is unable to discharge the powers and duties of his office, and until he transmits to them a written declaration to the contrary, such powers and duties shall be discharged by the Vice President as Acting President.

Section 4.

Whenever the Vice President and a majority of either the principal officers of the executive departments or of such other body as Congress may by law provide, transmit to the President pro tempore of the Senate and the Speaker of the House of Representatives their written declaration that the President is unable to discharge the powers and duties of his office, the Vice President shall immediately assume the powers and duties of the office as Acting President.

Thereafter, when the President transmits to the President pro tempore of the Senate and the Speaker of the House of Representatives his written declaration that no inability exists, he shall resume the powers and duties of his office unless the Vice President and a majority of either the principal officers of the executive department or of such other body as Congress may by law provide, transmit within four days to the President pro tempore of the Senate and the Speaker of the House of Representatives their written declaration that the President is unable to discharge the powers and duties of his office. Thereupon Congress shall decide the issue, assembling within forty-eight hours for that purpose if not in session. If the Congress, within twenty-one days after receipt of the latter written declaration, or, if Congress is not in session, within twenty-one days after Congress is required to assemble, determines by two-thirds vote of both Houses that the President is unable to discharge the powers and duties of his office, the Vice President shall continue to discharge the same as Acting President; otherwise, the President shall resume the powers and duties of his office.

AMENDMENT XXVI

Section 1.

The right of citizens of the United States, who are 18 years of age or older, to vote, shall not be denied or abridged by the United States or any state on account of age.

Section 2.

The Congress shall have the power to enforce this article by appropriate legislation.

AMENDMENT XXVII

No law varying the compensation for the services of the Senators and Representatives shall take effect until an election of Representatives shall have intervened.

Chapters of the American Association of Legal Nurse Consultants

Headquarters

American Association of Legal Nurse Consultants
847–375–4713
4700 W. Lake Avenue
Glenview, IL 60025–14854
e mail: info@aalnc.org

If a state is not listed, contact AALNC or check the web site at www.aalnc.org for information about directors at large.

Alabama

Greater Birmingham Chapter
800–722–8407
2663 Valleydale Rd., Suite 292
Birmingham, AL 35244

Arizona

Phoenix Chapter
602–861–2705
P.O. Box 13441
Phoenix, AZ 85002

California

Bay Area of Northern California
877–545–6773
P.O. Box 3300
San Leandro, CA 94577–0300

Los Angeles Chapter
626–857–3206
P.O. Box 92226
City of Industry, CA 91715–2226

Orange County Chapter of Southern California
714–502–8106
3937 Garden Drive
San Bernardino, CA 92404

Greater Sacramento Area Chapter
916–783–7213
P.O. Box 660011
Sacramento, CA 95866–0011

San Diego Chapter
760–734–1584
1207 Fall River Way
San Marcos, CA 92069

Colorado

Denver CO Chapter
719–594–9994, ext. 1112
P.O. Box 480444
Denver, CO 80248–0444
e mail: coloradoaalnc@netscape.com

Delaware

Diamond State Chapter
302–368–0400
392 Papermill Road
Newark, DE 19711

Florida

Greater Fort Lauderdale Chapter
954–764–7150
P.O. Box 698
Fort Lauderdale, FL 33302

Greater Jacksonville Chapter
704–724–7067
PO Box 550853
Jacksonville, FL 32255–0853

Miami Chapter
305–253–2903
9820 SW 121st Street
Miami, FL 33176

Greater Orlando Chapter
407–843–0126
P.O. Box 3201
Orlando, FL 32802–3201

Greater Tampa Bay Chapter
813–877–0022
P.O. Box 22871
Tampa, FL 33622–2871

Georgia

Atlanta Chapter
770–888–8484
P.O. Box 55438
Atlanta, GA 30308

Illinois

Greater Chicago Chapter
847–604–1442
P.O. Box 3913–A
Chicago, IL 60690

Indiana

Greater Indianapolis Chapter
317–488–2000
P.O. Box 1702
Indianapolis, IN 46206–1702

Kentucky

Lexington Kentucky Chapter
502–484–3465
P.O. Box 490
Cynthiana, KY 41031–0490

Louisiana

Baton Rouge Chapter
877–371–0989
4434 Spain St.
New Orleans, LA 70122

Maryland

Greater Baltimore Area Chapter
410–296–9502
550 E Nicodemous Rd
Westminster, MD 21157

Michigan

Greater Detroit Chapter
248–642–2926
P.O. Box 1065
Bloomfield Hills, MI 48303–1065

Minnesota

Minneapolis Chapter
612–417–0632
10224 Windsor Lake Ln.
Minnetonka, MN 55305

Missouri

St. Louis Chapter
314–991–6177
P.O. Box 50166
Clayton, MO 63105
e-mail: AALNCSTL@juno.com

Greater Kansas City Chapter
913–383–4030
PO Box 7263
Kansas City, MO 64113

New Jersey

Morristown NJ Chapter
888–755–3771
470 Schooleys Mountain Rd.
Suite 8, Box 186
Hackettstown, NJ 07840

New York

Greater New York Metropolitan Chapter
718–573–1670
877–706–9666 (toll free)
PO Box 86–4108
Ridgewood, NY 11386

Rochester New York Chapter
716–244–6630
P.O. Box 92204
Rochester, NY 14692

Ohio

Cleveland/NEO Chapter
440–937–9474
P.O. Box 16532
Rocky River, OH 44116

Youngstown Ohio Chapter
330–539–0147
1024 Sodom Hutchings Rd. SE
PO Box 218
Vienna, OH 44473

Oregon

Greater Portland/Valley Chapter
503–293–7220
PO Box 3973
Portland, OR 97208–3973

Pennsylvania

Philadelphia Chapter
610–687–7771
175 Strafford Ave., Suite 1
Wayne, PA 19087

Pittsburgh Chapter
412–939–3426
P.O. Box 97104
Pittsburgh, PA 15229–0104

Rhode Island

Greater Providence Chapter
508–845–8882
6 Birch Brush Rd.
Shrewsbury, MA 01545

South Carolina

Columbia Chapter
843–521–1844
P.O. Box 12543
Columbia, SC 29211

Tennessee

Nashville TN Chapter
901–309–0733
PO Box 1082
Memphis, TN 38088–1082

Texas

Austin Chapter
512–708–9381
PO Box 5294
Austin, TX 78763
e mail: ghirsch@austin.rr.com

Dallas Chapter
972–874–2780
P.O. Box 224375
Dallas, TX 75222–4375

Fort Worth Chapter
817–326–4961
PO Box 866
Fort Worth, TX 76101–0866

Greater Houston Chapter
713–952–3620
7500 San Felipe, Suite 600
Houston, TX 77063

Virginia

National Capitol Area
804–224–5158
P.O. Box 337
Centreville, VA 20122

Washington

Puget Sound Chapter
206–440–0789
PO Box 2186
Lynnwood, WA 98036–2186

Wyoming

Western Casper Chapter
307–577–2538
3580 East 19th Street
Casper, WY 82609

APPENDIX C

Education Programs for Legal Nurse Consultants

[New education programs for legal nurse consultants and nurse paralegals begin in a variety of education settings, community colleges, technical colleges, private colleges, universities, and private vendors. Check with local postsecondary education facilities to see if a legal nurse or nurse paralegal program has been initiated in your area. Also check paralegal programs for certificate degrees which may complement your nursing background. If you are interested in risk management, case management, or life-care planning, check for these specific education resources near you.]

American Association of Legal Nurse Consultants
Professional Legal Nurse Consulting Course
4700 W. Lake Avenue
Glenview, IL 60025–2485
847–375–4713
www.aalnc.org

Baltimore City Community College
2901 Liberty Heights Avenue
Baltimore, MD 21215–7893
410–462–8005
www.bccc.state.md.us

California State University Hayward
25800 Carlos Bee Boulevard
Hayward, CA 94542–3024
510–885–3605
www.extension.scuhayward.edu

Canyon College
521 West Maple Street
Caldwell, ID 83605
208–455–0010
www.canyoncollege.edu

Cuyahoga Community College
2900 Community College Avenue
Cleveland, OH 44115
216–987–4000

Columbus State Community College
550 E. Spring St.
Columbus, OH 43215
614–287–5353
www.cscc.edu

Davidson County Community College
P.O. Box 1287
Lexington, NC 27293–2387
336–249–8186
www.davidson.cc.nc.us

Elms College
291 Springfield Street
Chicopee, MA 01013
413–594–2761
www.elms.edu

Fairleigh Dickinson University
Legal Nurse Consultant Program
285 Madison Avenue
Madison, NJ 07940
201–443–8990
www.fdu.edu

Florida Risk Management Institute
13575 58th Street North, Suite 127
Clearwater, FL 34620
813–538–4161

George Washington University
2121 Eye Street NW
Washington, DC 20052
202–994–1000
www.gwu.edu

Harper College
(William Rainey Harper College)
1200 W. Algonquin Road
Palatine, IL 60067–7398
847–925–6507
http://info2.harper.cc.il.us

Hofstra University
University College for Continuing Education
Republic Hall
Hempstead, NY 11549
516–463–5925
www.hofstra.edu

Johnson County Community College
12345 College Boulevard
Overland Park, KS 66210
914–469–8500 ext. 3184
www.jccc.net

Kaplan College
School of Legal Nurse Consulting
540 Madison Avenue, Fourth Floor
New York, NY 10022
212–446–2757
www.kaplancollege.com

Long Island University
School of Continuing Studies
C.W. Post Campus
720 Northern Blvd.
Brookville, NY 11548–1300
516–299–2236
www.liu.edu

Madonna University
36600 Schoolcraft Road
Livonia, MI 48150–1173
734–432–5549
ww3.munet.edu

Medical-Legal Consulting Institute, Inc.
2476 Bolsover, Suite 632
Houston, TX 77005
713–961–3078
http://nursing.education00.com

Medical-Legal Resources
7040 Avenida Encinas Ave. Suite 104–206
Carlsbad, CA 92009–4652
619–584–6489

National Center for Paralegal Training
Legal Nurse Consultant Program
400 Embassy Row, Suite 100
Atlanta, GA 30328
404–266–1060
www.ncpt.aii.edu

National Institute for Paralegal Arts and Sciences
School of Legal Nurse Consulting
164 W. Royal Palm Road
Boca Raton, FL 33432
561–368–2522

Northcentral Technical College
1000 W. Campus Drive
Wausau, WI 54401
715–675–3331 ext. 4004
www.northcentral.tec.wi.us

Northeastern University
Boston Main Campus
360 Huntington Avenue
Boston, MA 02115
617–373–7682
www.neu.edu

Ohio State University at Lima
4240 Campus Drive
Lima, OH 45804
419–995–8396
www.lima.ohio-state.edu

Pennsylvania College of Technology
One College Avenue
Williamsport, PA 17701
717–326–3761
www.pct.edu

San Francisco State University
College of Extended Learning
1600 Holloway Avenue
San Francisco, CA 94132
415–405–7700
www.cel.sfsu.edu

Spokane Community College
1810 N. Greene Street
Spokane, WA 99217–5399
509–533–7470
www.scc.spokane.cc.wa.us

Sullivan College
2659 Regency Rd.
Lexington, KY 40503
606–276–4357

University of California, Riverside
Extension Office
1200 University Avenue
Riverside, CA 92507–4596
909–787–4111 ext. 1616
www.uxweb.ucr.edu

University of California, San Diego
9500 Gilman Drive
La Jolla, CA 92093
858–534–2230
www.ucsd.edu

University of Cincinnati
College of Evening and Continuing Education
P.O. Box 210207
Cincinnati, OH 45221–0207
513–556–1731
www.uc.edu/cece

University of North Florida
Legal Studies Institute
4567 St. Johns Bluff Rd. South
Jacksonville, FL 32224–2645
904–620–1000
www.unf.edu

University of Florida
Rehabilitation Training Institute
Life Care Planning
2710 Rew Circle
Ocoee, FL 34761
800–431–6687

University of Pittsburgh
School of Nursing
3500 Victoria Street
Pittsburgh, PA 15261
412–624–4586
www.nursing.pitt.edu

University of Toledo
2801 W. Bankcroft St.
Toledo, OH 43606–3390
419–530–4242
www.utoledo.edu

Warren County Community College
475 Route 57 West
Washington, NJ 07882
908–689–1090
www.warren.cc.nj.us

William Rainey Harper College (see Harper
College)

Yavapai College
1100 E. Sheldon Street
Prescott, AZ 86301–3297
520–766–2343
www.yavapai.cc.az.us

APPENDIX D

Related Professional Associations

American Association for Paralegal Education
2965 Flowers Rd. S. Suite, 105
Atlanta, GA 30341
770–452–9877
www.aafpe.org

American Association of Critical Care Nurses
101 Columbia
Aliso Viejo, CA 92656
949–362–2000
www.aacn.org

American Association of Law Libraries
53 W. Jackson Blvd. Suite 940
Chicago, Il 60604
312–939–4764
aallhq@aol.com

American Association of Neuroscience Nurses
4700 W. Lake Avenue
Glenview, IL 60025
888–557–2266
www.aann.org

American Association of Nurse Anesthetists
222 S., Prospect Ave.
Park Ridge, IL 60068–4001
847–692–7050
www.aana.com

American Association of Nurse Life Care Planners
498 E. Golden Pheasant Drive
Draper, UT 84020
888–575–4047
www.aanlcp.com

American Association of Occupational Health Nurses
Suite 100, 2920 Brandywine Rd.
Atlanta, GA 30341
770–455–7757
www.aaohn.org

American Bar Association
750 N. Lake Shore Drive
Chicago, IL 60611
312–988–5000
www.abanet.org

American College of Nurse Practitioners
503 Capitol Ct. NE #300
Washington, DC 20002
202–546–4825
acnp@nurse.org

American Diabetes Association
1701 North Bouregard St.
Alexandria, VA 22311
800–342–2383
www.diabetes.org

American Health Information Management
Association
233 N. Michigan Ave., Suite 2150
Chicago, IL 60601–5800
312–233–1100
www.ahima.org

American Heart Association
7272 Greenville Avenue
Dallas, TX 75231
800–AHA–USA1
www.americanheart.org

American Medical Association
3115 Wacker Drive, Suite 5800
Chicago, IL 60606
800–AMA–1150
www.ama.org

American Medical Informatics Association
4915 St. Elmo Ave., Suite 401
Bethesda, MD 20814
301–657–1291
www.amia.org

American Medical Women's Association
801 N. Fairfax St. Suite 400
Alexandria, VA 22314
703–838–0500
www.amwa-doc.org

American Nurses Association
600 Maryland Ave. SW, Suite 100W
Washington, DC 20024
800–274–4ANA
www.ana.org

American Society for Healthcare Risk
Management
One North Franklin St.
Chicago, IL 60606
312–422–3980
ashrm@aha.org

American Society of PeriAnesthesia Nurses
10 Melrose Ave., Suite 110
Cherry Hill, NJ 08003–3696
877–737–9693
www.aspan.org

American Society of Questioned Document
Examiners
11420 SW 88th St. #206
Miami, FL 33176
703–285–2482

Association of Legal Administrators
175 E. Hawthorn Parkway, Suite 325
Vernon Hills, IL 66061–1428
847–816–1212

Association of Operating Room Nurses
2170 S. Parker Rd., Suite 300
Denver, CO 80231–5711
303–755–6304
www.aorn.org

Association of Pediatric Oncology Nurses
4700 W. Lake Avenue
Glenview, IL 60025
847–375–4724
www.apon.org

Association of Records Managers and
Administrators
4200 Somerset Dr., Suite 215
Prairie Village, KS 66208
913–341–3808

Association of Rehabilitation Nurses
4700 W. Lake Avenue
Glenview, IL 60025–1485
800–229–7530
www.rehabnurse.org

Association of Women's Health, Obstetric &
Neonatal Nurses
2000 L Street NW, Suite 720
Washington, DC 20036
800–673–8499
www.awhonn.org

Case Management Society of America
8201 Cantrel Rd. Suite 230
Little Rock, AR 72227
501–225–2229
www.csma.org

Emergency Nurses Association
915 Lee Street
Des Plaines, IL 60016–6569
800–243–8362
www.ena.org

Federal Administrative Law Judges Conference
2020 Penn. Ave. NW, Suite 717
Washington, DC 20006–8002
202–633–0042

Independent Association of Questioned
Document Examiners
403 W. Washington
Red Oak, IA 51566
712–623–9130

International Association of Forensic Nurses
East Holly Ave., Box 56
Pitman, NJ 08071–0056
856–256–2425
www.forensicnurse.org

Joint Commission on Accreditation of Healthcare
Organizations
One Renaissance Boulevard
Oakbrook Terrace, IL 60181
630–792–5000
www.jcaho.org

Legal Assistant Management Association
638 Prospect Ave.
Hartford, CT 06105–4250
860–586–7507
lamaoffice@aol.com

Legal Assistant Today
3520 Cadallac Ave., Suite E
Costa Mesa, CA 92626
714–7455–5450

Medical Library Association
6 N. Michigan Ave. Suite 300
Chicago, IL 60602–4895
312–419–9094

National Association of Document Examiners
20 Nassau St.
Princeton, NJ 08542
609–924–8193

National Association of Legal Assistants
1516 South Boston, Suite 200
Tulsa, OK 74119–4013
918–587–6828
nala@mail.webtek.com

National Association of Legal Investigators
P.O. Box 3254
Alton, IL 62002
618–465–4400

National Association of Orthopaedic Nurses
East Holly Avenue Box 56
Pitman, NJ 08071–0056
856–256–2310
naon@mail.ajj.com

National Federation of Paralegal Associations
32 West Bridlespur Terrace
PO Box 33108
Kansas City, MO 64114–0108
816–941–4000
infor@paralegals.org

National Institute of Nursing Research
Bethesda, MD 20892–2178
301–496–0207
www.nih.gov

National Library of Medicine
8600 Rockville Pike
Bethesda, MD 20894
www.nlm.nih.gov

National Organization of Social Security Claimants
Representatives
19 E. Central Ave., 2nd Floor
Pearl River, NY 10965
800–431–2804

National Paralegal Association
PO Box 406
Solebury, PA 18963
215–197–8333

National Resource Center for Consumers of Legal
Services
1444 Eye St. NW
Washington, DC 20005
202–842–3503

Oncology Nursing Society
P.O. Box 3575
Pittsburgh, PA 15230–3575
412–921–7373
www.ons.org

Society of Gastroenterology Nurses and
Associates
401 N. Michigan Ave
Chicago, IL 60611–4267
800–245–7462
www.sgna.org

Wound, Ostomy and Continence Nurses Society
1550 S. Coastal Highway, Suite 201
Laguna Beach, CA 92651
888–224–WOCN
www.wocn.org

GLOSSARY

Actions at law civil lawsuits that involved awards of money.

Actions in equity civil lawsuits that involved disputes where money awards would not protect the injured party.

Acts of God situations, such as hurricanes, high winds or freezing temperatures that provide a legal excuse or defense to a claim of injury.

Acts of nature a contemporary phrase for "acts of God."

Actus reus the conduct that violates law.

Ad damnum "to the damages," the part of the complaint that specifies the damages being sought by the plaintiff.

Adjudication the process of arriving at a judicial decision.

Administrative law the body of law that encompasses the rules and regulations made by and governing state and federal administrative agencies.

Administrative law judge a person qualified to hear reconsiderations and appeals of administrative decisions; in federal agencies, qualifications include being an attorney with seven years of experience.

Adverse medical examination an examination of the injured plaintiff by physicians selected by the defendant; sometimes called independent medical examination.

Affirmative defenses defenses that must be plead and proved by the defendant; defenses that will relieve defendant of liability.

Affirmed the appellate court agrees that the lower court correctly applied the law in the case.

Alternative dispute resolution processes for resolving legal claims without going through a courtroom trial.

Ambulance chasing a negative and unethical concept of taking advantage of people in the midst of a crisis.

Amicus curie brief a brief filed by a nonparty who may be impacted by the court's decision in an action that has been appealed.

Analysis memo an interoffice communication to the attorney relating the legal nurse consultant's preliminary evaluation concerning the medical issues.

Annotation essays regarding a particular rule of law that are thoroughly analyzed.

Answer a responsive pleading in which the defendant admits or denies the allegations of the complaint.

Appellant the party filing an appeal.

Appellate brief a written report submitted to an appeals court summarizing facts and legal issues that justify a change in the previous court's ruling.

Appellate jurisdiction the power of a court to review the decisions of other courts.

Appellate jurisdiction as a matter of right the appeals court has no discretion regarding cases that are appealed to it; the cases must be reviewed as part of due process protections.

Appellee the party responding to an appeal.

Arbiters the neutral third party or panel who makes the decision in an arbitration proceeding.

Arbitration the process in which a neutral third person or panel reviews the claim and makes a binding decision.

Arraignment the formal hearing at which the charges are read to the accused and the accused enters a plea.

As is a notice that the buyer is accepting the goods regardless of any defects that may be apparent or latent.

Assault a tort involving the creation of fear of harm by intentional menacing physical movements.

Assault and battery a tort involving intentional physical contact that is offensive or humiliating.

Assumption of risk a defense that claims plaintiff appreciated the danger and voluntarily proceeded to encounter it.

Attorney work product the theories, conclusions, and working papers prepared by the attorney on behalf of a client.

Attractive nuisance an artificial condition on land that is attractive to children and about which children cannot appreciate danger.

Authentication proof that an exhibit is what it is claimed to be.

Authority foundation for legal position, generally referring to legal sources.

Bad faith in tort constitutes a deliberate failure to complete a promise (although not a contract), upon which a person relies and is injured.

Bail an amount of money that is pledged to ensure that the accused appears for trial.

Battery a tort that arises when someone intentionally causes physical contact and physical harm to another without consent.

Bench trial trial without a jury.

Bicameral a legislature composed of two houses.

Binding authority sources of law that must be considered in arriving at a judicial decision.

Borrowed servants whenever employees are loaned to another for special purposes; the loaned employees are under the direct control of the temporary employer.

Breach of warranty a cause of action, like breach of contract, claiming that a promise about the product is untrue.

Brief a legal document that is used to summarize facts and law.

Burden of proof the requirement that the person who made the complaint prove the allegations made.

Business plan a written document that identifies what is necessary to start and manage a business.

Buy-sell agreement an agreement or a clause in an agreement that determines how an ownership share will be valued, distributed, paid for, or otherwise disposed of in the event of an owner's death, disability, or withdrawal from the business association.

By-laws the rules or regulations adopted by stockholders of a corporation that govern its operational structure.

Capital assets of value (money, property, equipment) invested in a business.

Captain of the ship a legal theory of responsibility, similar to that of the employer's vicarious liability for wrongful acts of employees, in situations other than employment.

Case brief a written report summarizing a court opinion.

Case law court opinions that create or interpret law.

Case reporters volumes in which decisions of courts are published.

Cash-flow how much money is taken in and paid out during a given time period.

Cause of action facts that support the elements of a legal theory (such as battery or negligence) and form the basis of a lawsuit.

Certiorari the process for requesting review by a discretionary appeals court.

Chain of custody tracing the possession and/or maintenance of an item to prove that it is the actual item claimed.

Charitable immunity historically, the doctrine that hospitals and other charitable organizations would be reluctant to provide "healing" services if they were subject to the costs of civil liability.

Chattels personal property.

Chronological overview a summary of the medical treatment of the client by date, treating facility, and treatment.

Chronological deposition summary a summary that arranges the testimony in time order.

Chronologies reports that condense numerous pieces of information from numerous sources into organized, chronological summaries.

Circumstantial evidence that which tends to prove a fact or occurrence.

Citators any of a variety of sources that provide judicial history and later treatment of a case.

Civil law body of law that deals with grievances one party may have against another that are not criminal or administrative in nature.

Class-action lawsuits multiple claimants having similar claims who are represented by one representative (because there are too many claimants to make them all parties in the lawsuit), so that the disputes may be resolved economically.

Closing arguments a summary presented to the jury by the attorneys emphasizing the evidence in favor of their respective clients.

Codified (Code) laws from a particular governmental entity that are collected and organized by subject matter.

Collateral materials documents, such as brochures, business cards, and flyers that support a business.

Collective deposition summary a summary containing the testimony of several deponents on key points in the case.

Common stock a share of stock for which no preference is given in the distribution of dividends.

Comparative negligence where plaintiff's damages will be reduced in proportion to plaintiff's fault.

Compensatory damages a money award intended to repay the injured party for expenses, pain, and suffering that would not have been incurred but for the wrongful conduct of the defendant.

Complaint the first document filed in a civil lawsuit, which outlines the facts and legal theories upon which the claim is based.

Complex litigation lawsuit involving many parties in numerous related cases pending in different jurisdictions.

Complimentary closing the part of a business letter that serves to end the communication.

Compulsory counterclaim a claim by the defendant against the plaintiff that arises out of the same circumstances that gave rise to plaintiff's claim; this claim must be joined in the lawsuit by plaintiff or be forever barred.

Concurrent jurisdiction where two or more courts have the power to make a determination in the legal matter.

Concurring opinion an opinion written by a judge who agrees with the majority but for different reasons.

Condition precedent a necessary prerequisite.

Conference committee a committee composed of members of both houses charged with compromising the different versions of a bill.

Conflicts of interest situations in which loyalty to the client may be jeopardized or compromised because of loyalty to other clients, previous employers, or to personal or financial interests.

Consent agreement that something shall happen.

Conservator a person appointed by the court to preserve and manage the property of another.

Constitution a founding set of principles approved by and for a group of people.

Contingency fee a fee constituting a percentage of the amount recovered and based on the successful outcome of a particular project.

Contributory negligence when plaintiff's conduct is a cause of all or a portion of plaintiff's injuries.

Conversion any unauthorized exercise of control over personal property of another.

Corporation an organization formed under state law. It is considered a separate legal entity (an artificial person) and is created for specific legal purposes. The legal process of forming a corporation is known as **incorporation.**

Counteranalysis examining a problem from various points of view, particularly the opposite point of view.

Counterclaim a claim made by the defendant against the plaintiff, which is joined in the lawsuit brought by plaintiff.

Crime conduct that has been declared by law to be opposed to the public good.

Criminal law the body of law that deals with making rules regarding conduct that is not in the public good and the procedures and punishments for violating those rules.

Cross examination the questioning of a witness by the adverse attorney.

Cross-claim a claim usually filed by one defendant against another defendant that alleges the wrongdoing was the responsibility of the other defendant.

Curriculum vita a summary of personal characteristics and professional qualifications.

Damages money awarded by a court or judicial tribunal to be paid to a party who has suffered injury or loss by the one responsible for the injuries. Damages may be compensatory or punitive. **Compensatory damages** are intended to compensate or pay the injured party for losses. **Punitive damages** are intended to punish the wrongdoer for conduct the court or jury finds outrageous.

Damages package a comprehensive presentation of damages used for settlement demand letters, settlement negotiations, and trial preparation.

Debenture bonds a loan to a corporation for which a document (bond) is given stating that the corporation will repay the debt with interest. A bond gives the bondholder no ownership in the corporation and is backed only by the general credit of the corporation.

Deductive reasoning a form of reasoning that relates one concept to another.

Defamation false statements about a person's character that harm the person's reputation.

Default judgment defendant makes no response to the complaint and the court grants judgment to plaintiff.

Defense of others force used to protect another from threatened bodily harm.

Defense of property force used to protect property after a warning has been ignored.

Demurrer a claim by defendant stating that even if plaintiff proved all of the allegations of the complaint, it would not establish liability against the defendant. Demurrers, as pleadings, have been abolished by federal court rules.

Deponent the person who is testifying at the deposition.

Deponent summary a summary of testimony starting from the first page and proceeding to the last.

Deposition testimony in answer to questions by the parties in a lawsuit (usually by their attorneys) that is made under oath and recorded by a court reporter.

Descriptive word index an index at the back of a series of legal sources that aids in accessing the information on a point of law.

Digests finding tools that collect the headnotes and organize them under topics in alphabetical order, so that researchers can locate additional sources on a point of law.

Direct evidence that which is observed by the witness or about which the witness has personal knowledge.

Direct examination the questioning of a witness by the attorney who called that witness.

Directed verdict when the judge, upon motion, grants verdict to a party (usually the defendant) because the other party has failed to establish with evidence a cause of action.

Disclaimer a denial or refusal to honor a warranty.

Disclosure court rules that require parties to voluntarily provide information to the other parties.

Discovery the portion of the litigation in which parties exchange information that is relevant to or will be presented at the trial of the matter.

Disparagement of goods false statements about the quality of goods that result in harm to the business.

Dispositive motions motions that dispose of all or a portion of the lawsuit before going to trial; e.g., motion to dismiss, motion for summary judgment.

Dissenting opinion an opinion written by a judge who disagrees with the majority.

Diversity jurisdiction the power of the federal courts to hear disputes between parties residing in different states when the amount in controversy exceeds $75,000.

Docket number the file number assigned to a case when it is first filed with the court; identifies the case as it progresses through the court system.

Doctrine of informed consent a professional's responsibility to disclose risks and alternatives so that the person contracting with the professional may make an informed decision about a course of action.

Elements the smallest parts of a law that must be proven with the facts to show that the law applies.

Enabling act legislation that creates an administrative agency, outlines its organizational structure, and defines the powers and duties of the officers of the agency.

Equitable remedies relief that is granted when money awards will not protect the injured party from harm.

Equity the value of an owner's interest in a business; that is, the assets minus the liabilities; actions in which the injury to plaintiff may not be satisfied or recompensed with an award of monetary damages.

Ergonomics a science that seeks to adapt working conditions to promote the health of the worker and/or prevent injury.

Ethical wall a process for shielding someone with a conflict of interest from engaging in work on the file when the conflict may compromise the client's interest.

Ethics standards of conduct to which a profession subscribes.

Ex parte communications one-sided conversations that have the appearance of attempting to influence an official at a trial.

Exclusive jurisdiction the power of the court is limited to one type of legal matter; no other court has the power to make a determination regarding this type of legal matter.

Executive agency one that is under the direct control of the president or governor.

Executive orders the rules made by the executive (president or governor) within the scope of the executive's authority.

Exemplary damages punitive damages.

Exhaust administrative remedies the requirement that the claimant pursue all available options within the administrative agency before bringing the action for judicial review.

Express warranties promises about the product that are communicated, directly or indirectly, to the consumer.

External validity a determination that the results of the experiment, observation, or study may be applied to actual practice settings.

False imprisonment unlawful, intentional detention or incarceration of another without consent.

False arrest a type of false imprisonment in which the detention results from an unauthorized use of authority.

Federal question jurisdiction the power of the federal courts to resolve disputes involving any federal law or Constitutional issue.

Felony a crime punishable by one year or more imprisonment.

Fiduciary responsibility a legal and ethical obligation to act in the best interests of someone else.

Focus groups a process in which a neutral panel reviews the evidence and provides information to the attorneys concerning the strengths and weaknesses of the case.

Foreseeability that which can be seen or known beforehand.

Fraud intentional false statements intended to induce a party to enter into a contract.

Frivolous claim a civil lawsuit that has no foundation in fact or law.

Full block a letter style in which all component parts are left justified.

General damages money damages that relate to pain and suffering and other damages that may not be subject to mathematical certainty.

General jurisdiction the power of a court to make a determination on any matter, civil or criminal, within its geographic territory.

General partnership a partnership in which all partners participate in running a business and sharing the income and losses.

Greater weight of the evidence sometimes called preponderance of the evidence, this standard of proof requires evidence to show that it is more likely than not that a particular event occurred in a particular way.

Guardian a person who has the responsibility of taking care of another person and that person's property because the other person is incapable of doing so. A guardian is appointed by the court in a guardianship proceeding.

Guardian ad litem a court-appointed representative charged with a fiduciary duty to another for the course of a lawsuit.

Headnotes numbered paragraphs preceding a court opinion that summarize the important facts and law in a case.

Hearsay evidence that is secondhand; something someone else said or otherwise communicated.

Hedonic damages a money award to compensate for the plaintiff's loss of enjoyment of life.

Hierarchy of authority a system for classifying which authority will have the greatest weight in the outcome of the matter.

Hire-a-judge similar to arbitration, a process in which a retired judge is retained to make a binding decision in the matter.

Hornbook refers to a series of textbooks for law school students.

IRAC a common acronym in law that stands for issue, rule, application, and conclusion.

Impeach to discredit a person's testimony; to cast doubt upon the credibility of the witness.

Implied warranties promises that exist as a matter of law.

Implied warranty of fitness for a particular purpose an implied warranty that a product will be fit for a particular purpose that the seller knows about and for which the seller recommends the product.

In rem jurisdiction the power of a court to make a determination concerning property located within its geographic territory.

Incorporate the legal process of forming a corporation.

Independent agency agencies that operate without direct control of the chief executive.

Independent contractor a person engaged by another to perform a particular service or do a particular job; the contractor is free to perform the work by his or her own methods and the person engaging the contractor has little control over how the work is completed.

Indices to law any of a series of finding tools that provide quick access to case law by topic; e.g., Words and Phrases.

Informatics the combination of knowledge and experience in a specific profession and knowledge of computer science, used for design and implementation of computer records management, retrieval, and database development specific to that profession.

Informed consent the duty of the professional to provide adequate information to the client or patient so the client or patient can make an informed decision about a course of action.

Initial appearance the requirement that the accused be brought before a judge or tribunal to know the reason for the arrest.

Injunction a court order prohibiting a certain activity or conduct.

Inquiry board a group of professionals charged with investigating complaints of unethical conduct.

Intent deliberate wrongful conduct directed toward someone that results in harm to that person.

Intent in tort acting with knowledge that someone will be impacted or harmed or with reasonable certainty that the consequences of that action will result in harm to someone.

Intentional infliction of emotional distress a tort involving intentional outrageous conduct that results in emotional suffering.

Intentional interference with contract a cause of action based upon a third party's inducement of a contract party to breach the contract.

Intentional tort a wrong acted out deliberately that causes harm to another.

Internal validity a determination that the experiment, observation, or study measures what it claims to measure.

International law body of law that is governed by treaties, customs, and practices between two or more nations.

Interpretive rules agency statements that outline how the agency intends to carry out the legislative intent.

Interrogatories written questions to a party that must be answered under oath.

Issues questions of law that arise when the facts do not exactly match the elements of the law.

Joined when the answer is served and filed and it is clear which allegations in the complaint must be proven.

Joining of issues a phrase that refers to the resulting requirements of proof that plaintiff must establish because of the denial of allegations in a complaint.

Joint tortfeasors two or more persons whose actions, when combined, cause harm to another.

Judgment notwithstanding the verdict an order of the court overturning the jury verdict where the verdict is not supported by the facts; also known as **judgment non obstante verdicto** and **JNOV.**

Judicial notice an evidentiary mechanism that allows admission of evidence without proof because the fact is readily verifiable.

Junk science information that claims to have scientific of medical merit but does not meet foundational tests.

Jurisdiction the authority of a court to make a determination in a legal matter.

Jury instructions the legal guidelines the jury must keep in mind when deliberating.

Key Number System an indexing system created by West Group that allows researchers to locate sources on a point of law using a topic and a "key" number.

Last clear chance historically a defense to negligence that provided for liability to attach to the person who had the last opportunity to prevent harm to plaintiff. This defense has been abolished or weakened in most states.

Lead counsel an attorney in a class action lawsuit appointed by the judge to develop positions on substantive and procedural issues.

Learned intermediary a doctrine providing that the manufacturer of drugs must provide warning information to the physician (the learned intermediary) who is in the best position to understand the risks to the patient.

Learned treatise scholarly work examining a particular topic written by an expert.

Legal citation a uniform system used for listing legal sources.

Legal digests a series of finding tools that collect and categorize headnotes and arrange them alphabetically as an index to case law.

Legal encyclopedias a series of volumes intended to comprehensively examine all areas of law.

Legal nurse consultant provides medical expertise to the legal community by evaluating, analyzing, and rendering opinions on the delivery of health care and resulting outcomes.

Legal Nurse Consultant Certified (LNCC) the designation achieved when a registered nurse has met the eligibility requirements and passed the examination administered by the American Association of Legal Nurse Consultants.

Legislative history documents generated during the legislative process that may be used to interpret the language of a statute and the intent of the lawmakers.

Liaison counsel an attorney in a class-action lawsuit appointed by the judge to perform administrative functions of the case management plan.

Libel defamation that may be reduced to writing regardless of how (television, radio, newsprint) it is communicated.

Life-care plan an itemization of all projected costs for care and medical treatment of an injured party who is not expected to recover complete self-care or vocational capability.

Limited jurisdiction the power of the court is restricted to only those cases that meet statutory guidelines.

Limited Liability Company an organization formed under state law to limit the liability of the member-owners for business debts. A limited liability company is considered a separate legal entity.

Limited Liability Partnership a special form of partnership designed to limit or negate the liability of one partner for the malpractice of other partners.

Limited partnership a partnership organized under state law in which one or more partners invests a specific amount of money and receives a specific share of the income. A limited partner does not participate in the business of the partnership and is not liable for losses, business debts, or judgments of the partnership that exceed that limited partner's investment.

Linear reasoning a process of reasoning that traces events to a logical conclusion.

Litigation the process of a lawsuit through adjudicatory channels.

Loss of companionship a separate claim brought by family members of an injured party to recover for the loss of support, comfort, affection, and familial services.

Majority opinion a court opinion written by one judge on behalf of the majority.

Mass tort claims multiple claims arising from a single incident, such as an explosion.

Mediation the process in which a neutral third party attempts to bring the parties to compromise.

Medical bill audit a review of the medical bills in relation to the medical records or to determine whether the treatment rendered was reasonable and necessary under the circumstances.

Medical expense summary a listing of the total expenses paid to various health care providers—useful for assessing past medical damages.

Memorandum of law a thorough research and analysis of legal principles pertaining to a particular point of law.

Memorandum opinion a short opinion that does not elaborate on the reasoning for the decision.

Mens rea the requirement for conviction of a crime that the actor intended to violate the law. Some crimes do not require intent, but may be based on conduct that is reckless or negligent.

Mini-trials any of a number of procedures in which a trial is simulated with the purpose of determining what the relative strength and weaknesses of the case may be.

Misdemeanor a crime punishable by less than one year imprisonment.

Misrepresentation in tort, constitutes negligently made statements upon which a person relies and is injured.

Modified block a letter style in which all components are left justified except the date, the complimentary close, and the signature, which begin in the center of the page.

Modified semi-block a letter style using the modified block, but indenting the reference line and all paragraphs approximately 1/2 inch from the left margin.

Motion for judgment on the pleadings a request to the court that the court review the documents filed and render judgment.

Motion for new trial a request for a new trial based on a prejudicial ruling of law; also called a motion for **trial de novo.**

Motion to dismiss responsive pleading requesting that the lawsuit be dismissed because of some legal defect.

Multidistrict litigation multiple claims in several judicial districts that are combined into one and litigated in one judicial district.

Municipal charter the legal document that creates a municipality, sets forth its organizational structure, and describes the powers and duties of municipal officials.

Natural and probable   that which is usual, normal, and foreseeable as a result of certain conduct.

Natural law   rights that are considered inherent to life as human beings.

Negligence   failure of reasonable care that results in harm to another.

Negligence per se   when violation of a statute is conclusive on the issue of negligence.

Nolo contendere   a plea that effectively states that the accused will not defend the charges but will accept punishment as if found guilty.

Official   (legal research) a publication of law required by statute.

Opening statements   comments to the jury preceding the admission of evidence that outline what the parties intend to prove.

Opt out   the right of any member of a class in a class-action lawsuit to choose not to participate in settlement.

Original jurisdiction   the power of a court to make the first determination on law and facts in a legal matter.

Parallel citations   the location of the same text in a different case reporter.

Parallel construction   describes the use of a consistent pattern for writing so that the reader is not distracted by lack of consistency.

Partnership   a business that is not incorporated and is owned by two or more persons. A partnership is created by a contract and is considered a separate legal entity from its owners.

Per curium   refers to an opinion of the entire court.

Permissive counterclaim   any claim defendant may have against plaintiff not barred by the statute of limitations; this claim may be brought in a separate lawsuit if not joined in the lawsuit by plaintiff.

Personal jurisdiction   the power of the court over the parties in the legal action; the power to enforce the decision of the court against the parties.

Personal property   generally all tangible, movable objects.

Personal recognizance   the oath of an accused who is not expected to flee the jurisdiction of the court.

Personal service   where delivery of the documents in the lawsuit is accomplished by handing the documents to the defendant.

Persuasive authority   sources of law that may be considered in arriving at a judicial decision.

Pied Piper cases   vendors and others who attract children for business are responsible for the safety of children who cannot appreciate danger.

Plain English   a movement away from legalese and toward drafting legal documents in language that is understandable by people who are not legal professionals.

Plain meaning   the concept that applies to interpretation of legal language so that it can be understood by ordinary people.

Plea bargaining   the negotiations between the prosecuting attorney and the defendant and/or defendant's attorney to dispose of the criminal action without a trial.

Pleadings   litigation documents that describe the cause of action and defenses.

Pocket parts   paper updates that are inserted into the back binding of a legal publication.

Pocket veto   the president's failure to sign a bill within ten days during which time the legislative session adjourns.

Power resume   a dynamic description of a person's qualifications, education, and experience.

Prayer for relief   sometimes called the ad damnum, or the Wherefore Clause, this part of the complaint identifies the damages or other remedy plaintiff is seeking.

Preamble   the introductory portion of a legal document that sets forth the purposes for which the document is intended.

Precedent   a rule of law established in a previous case.

Preferred stock   a share of stock in a corporation that receives a fixed rate of income (dividends) before distribution of income to common stocks.

Preliminary hearing a hearing at which the judge reviews the evidence to determine whether there is probable cause to charge the accused with a crime.

Presumption an evidentiary mechanism that conclusively establishes a fact by the proof of foundational facts.

Pretrial brief A written statement to the court summarizing the facts, legal issues, and evidence sought to be brought to court.

Pretrial conference a hearing attended by the attorneys for all parties at which the judge and the attorneys agree on matters for the efficient handling of the trial.

Pretrial order a court order that contains the information and procedure for orderly conduct of the trial.

Prima facie "on its face" the elements appear to be met.

Prima facie case where the evidence supports the allegations made so that it appears, on its face, to meet the elements of a cause of action.

Primary authority law made by those who are commissioned to make laws; e.g., legislatures, courts, administrative agencies.

Primary law the "letter of the law"; that which is made by governmental bodies such as legislatures, courts, and administrative agencies.

Primary sources (medical research) actual experiments, observations, and studies.

Private law law that deals with disputes involving rights of separate parties.

Private nuisance any thing or activity that unreasonably interferes with the use and enjoyment of land.

Privilege in evidence, a relationship in which communications between the parties are protected from disclosure without consent.

Probative value the weight or ability of the evidence to prove what it purports to prove.

Procedural law laws that detail the steps or processes that must be undertaken in order to preserve rights or enforce responsibilities.

Procedural rules agency rules dealing with the process that must be implemented to ensure rights and enforce responsibilities.

Products liability lawsuits against manufacturers of consumer products (and other entities) based on allegations that the products are inherently dangerous or fail to perform adequately and cause harm to the user of the product.

Promoter a person who arranges for the formation of a corporation.

Proof chart a system for identifying each fact that must be proven and the evidence that will be submitted to prove each fact.

Proximate cause the legal limit placed upon liability for consequences of a person's wrongful conduct. Proximate cause is a legal concept, rather than a fact concept.

Public law law to which the entire population or a significant portion of the population is subject.

Punitive damages a money award intended to punish the defendant for recklessly disregarding the safety of plaintiff; also known as exemplary damages.

Qualify the witness establish with evidence that the witness is an expert and capable of rendering an opinion on the facts.

Quasi contract a contract implied in law to prevent unjust enrichment.

Quasi in rem jurisdiction the power of a court to "attach" property within its geographic territory to satisfy a money judgment.

Question of fact disputes concerning what happened between the parties that gave rise to the legal conflict.

Question of law disputes concerning the legal proceedings, such as admission of evidence, that arise during the resolution of the legal conflict.

Real property land and anything affixed to the land.

Reasoning by analogy comparing the similarities and differences between cases to show that the same ruling should (or should not) apply.

Recuse when a judge voluntarily relinquishes the right to serve over a case.

Registered agent a person identified in the Articles of Incorporation who is authorized to receive documents on behalf of the corporation.

Regulatory agency an agency whose primary function is to manage and control activities.

Relevant that which tends to prove a material fact.

Reliability a general certainty that if the experiment, observation, or study were replicated, similar results would be obtained.

Remand the outcome of the lower court is overturned and the case is returned to the trial court level for further proceedings.

Request for production a discovery device used to obtain access to documents, land, and other physical evidence.

Request to admit a discovery device used to obtain agreement on facts or the genuineness of an article prior to trial.

Res gestae comments made immediately before, during, or after an incident that gives rise to a lawsuit.

Res ipsa loquitur "the thing speaks for itself"; a claim in negligence stating that the event causing injury could not have occurred if proper care had been taken; the fact of the incident gives rise to the presumption of negligence.

Reserve the amount of money set aside by an insurance company that represents the estimated sum required to settle a future claim.

Respondeat superior "let the master answer"; generally used in employment, a term that indicates the employer's responsibility for the actions of employees.

Retainer an amount of money delivered in advance for professional services and held in trust until those professional services are performed.

Reversed the outcome of the lower court is overturned.

Right to privacy in tort law includes the right to reasonable solitude, the right to be free of unreasonable publication of private facts, the right to one's image or likeness, and the right to be free of unreasonably offensive and false impressions.

Risk management anticipating and developing policies for prevention of, insuring against, investigating, managing, and assisting in settlement of a business's exposure to liability.

S Corporation a corporation whose stockholders have elected an IRS provision allowing income of the corporation to be taxed only once, when it is distributed to stockholders.

Salutation the part of a business letter that is used as a greeting to the recipient.

Scheduling conference a hearing usually attended by the attorneys for both sides at which time the judge and the attorneys agree upon a timeline for processing the lawsuit.

Seat belt defense the defense to damages that claim the plaintiff could have taken precautions to minimize injury and that failure to take those precautions enhanced the plaintiff's injuries.

Secondary authority sources that provide explanations and critiques of the primary law.

Secondary sources (legal research) legal sources that serve to explain and clarify the primary legal authority; (medical research) publications that explain or interpret primary sources.

Self-authenticating evidence that is admissible without proof that it is what it is claimed to be.

Self defense force used to protect oneself from threatened harm.

Service of process delivery of a legal document (usually a summons and complaint) to the defendant in a way that meets legal requirements.

Session laws the chronological publication of state statutes.

Settlement brochure an exhaustive and convincing presentation of the facts, liability, evidence, and authority that supports a plaintiff's claim for damages.

Shepard's Citations a widely used case verification system.

Shepardizing the process of verifying law using Shepard's Citations.

Sine qua non essential prerequisite; that without which.

Slander words or actions that constitute defamation.

Slander of title false statements about the title to goods that results in harm to a business.

Social welfare agency an agency dedicated to the health and well-being of the residents of the nation.

Sole proprietorship   a business that is not incorporated and is owned exclusively by one person.

Special damages   money damages that may be calculated with reasonable certainty.

Special purpose deposition summary   a summary that is customized to contain only requested testimony or that relates that testimony to other documents or research.

Specific performance   a court order compelling the completion of a contract for the transfer of unique property.

Stare decisis   the concept of following previously established precedent.

Statute law   law that is made by legislative bodies, including Acts of Congress, state legislation, and municipal ordinances.

Statute of limitations   a statutory time period within which a lawsuit must be brought based on a particular occurrence.

Statutes of repose   a law that limits the time within which a lawsuit may be brought based on the date of sale rather than the date of occurrence causing injury.

Steering committee   a team of attorneys and parties in a class-action lawsuit appointed by the judge to perform tasks assigned by the court and lead counsel.

Stream of commerce doctrine   a theory in products liability requiring that the manufacturer be accountable for products put into the stream of commerce in a dangerously defective condition.

Strict liability   situations in which the hazard is so great that the actor will be responsible for all consequences, regardless of due care and precautions to prevent harm.

Structured settlement   an annuity purchased for the purpose of providing regular payments to the injured party for life or for a specified period of time.

Subcontract   a legal relationship in which one party is engaged by contractor to perform a particular service or do a particular job, which is part of a larger project for which the independent contractor is responsible.

Subject matter jurisdiction   the power of a court to make a decision based on the type of controversy brought before it.

Subpoena   a court order requiring someone to appear and testify.

Subpoena duces tecum   a court order to appear and bring documents.

Subrogation   when one party with the right to collect a debt or obligation is substituted for another. When insurance companies pay medical bills that are later determined to be the responsibility of another wrongful party, the insurance company is entitled to reimbursement. The insurance company is substituted for the insured (on whose behalf payments were made) to recover the amount paid.

Substantive law   laws that deal with the theory of what is right and wrong.

Substantive rules   agency rules that deal with the rights and responsibilities of parties.

Substituted service   where delivery of the documents in a lawsuit is accomplished by delivering them to a person appointed as an agent by the defendant or where an agent exists by law.

Summary judgment   a court order disposing of all or a portion of a civil lawsuit before having to go to court.

Summation   when the attorneys present to the jury a review of the facts they believe were established with the evidence; sometimes called closing arguments.

Summons   the document that informs the defendant that a lawsuit has been brought and the time limit in which defendant must respond to the complaint.

Synopsis   a brief description of the facts and questions of law in the case, which precedes the court opinion.

Synthesis   the process of pulling together the information to create a logical and coherent whole.

Thesis statement   a proposition intended to be proved or disproved by the argument and research that follow it.

Third party complaint   a claim of responsibility against a party who is not already a party to the lawsuit.

Tickler system   a system (named after its inventor) for reminding people of important dates so that deadlines and other important matters are not missed or neglected.

Topical deposition summary   a summary organized in a way that collects all of the testimony on particular subjects.

Tort   a personal wrong that causes harm to another and for which the injured party may bring a lawsuit.

Tort reform   efforts of legislative interest groups to minimize the economic impact of personal injury litigation against manufacturers, health care providers, and insurance companies.

Tortfeasor   a person whose wrongful conduct (tort) has caused harm to another.

Toxic tort   a cause of action for a lawsuit seeking to recover for harm resulting from exposure to an inherently dangerous substance.

Trade libel   false statements about a business that result in harm to that business.

Transferred intent   when harm results to someone other than the person at whom the deliberate wrongful conduct was directed.

Transition sentence   a sentence that lends coherence from the preceding paragraph to the succeeding paragraph.

Trial strategy   the development of themes to which all of the evidence in the case will relate and that will be used to educate and impress the jury.

Treaties   agreements with other nations that govern transactions and the rights of parties involved in international commerce.

Treatises   a scholarly, comprehensive treatment of one subject by an expert.

Trespass   the unlawful, unpermitted entry onto land belonging to another.

Trespass to chattels   unauthorized invasion of the rights of an owner of personal property.

Trial brief   a written report submitted to the court summarizing the legal and factual issues that will be presented at trial.

Trial counsel   an attorney in a class-action lawsuit appointed by the judge to develop trial strategies and present evidence if trial becomes necessary.

Trial de novo   a new trial.

Trial notebook   a three-ring binder containing all the information needed by an attorney going to trial.

Unavoidable accident   one that cannot be predicted or prevented.

Unicameral   a legislature composed on one house or body.

Unintentional tort   a wrongful act that is not deliberate.

Unofficial   (legal research) a publication by a private vendor that publishes the law with additional editorial features.

Venue   the most convenient location for trial.

Vicarious liability   when one party is required to answer for the wrongful conduct of another.

Voir dire   questioning of the jury to ensure their impartiality.

Ward   a person placed under the care of another through a legal intervention (known as a guardianship proceeding) in which a guardian is appointed for that person.

Warranty   any statement of fact or promise concerning the quality or characteristics of goods.

Warranty of fitness for a particular purpose   an implied warranty that a product will be fit for a particular purpose about which the seller knows and for which the seller recommends the product.

Warranty of merchantability   an implied warranty that the goods are fit for their intended purpose.

Wrongful death   death caused by the wrongful act of another.

INDEX

duties of, 6–7
emergence of, 5–6
and evidence law, 400–401
future trends, 9–13
history of, 4–5
and legal correspondence, 477–479
marketing, 76–83
and medical negligence, 356–357
and products liability, 378–380
qualifications of, 7–8
role of, 207
and strict liability, 366–368
training programs, 8–9
and trial preparation, 563, 576
See also Employers; Employment; Independent
practice
Legal Nurse Consulting: Principles and Practice, 600
Legal periodicals, 284–285
Legal reasoning, 162–169, 202–205, 214, 217
Legal research, computerized, 290–291
Legal studies, 212
Legal writing, 450, 459
case briefs, 218–219
cautions concerning, 453–455
fundamentals, 455–458
and legal nurse consultants, 458–459
medical bill reviews, 512–513
stages of, 450–453
Legislative history, 287–288
Legislative tracking, 288
Letters, components of, 463–467
Letter styles, 467–470
Letter-writing tips, 471–472
Liability. *See specific types*
Liaison counsel, 386–387
Libel, 320
Library of Congress, 106
Licenses, 68
Licensing regulations, 348
Licensure, 45
Life-care planner, 22
Life-care plans, 22, 520
components of, 523–524
development of, 521–523
sample, 532–545
Life expectancy, on Internet, 523
Limitations on liability, 378

Limited jurisdiction, 124
Limited liability company, 62, 63, 66–67
Limited liability partnership, 62, 63, 65
Limited partnership, 64–65
Limiting-liability-to-risk theory, 338
Linear reasoning, 203
Literature. *See* Legal research; Medical research
Litigation, 120, 128–129
administrative, 120, 121
civil, 120, 121–124
complex, 384–389
criminal, 120, 121
federal court system, 126–128
jurisdiction, 124–126
remedies in, 123–124
state court systems, 128
See also specific types
Litigation ethics, 595
"Living document" interpretation, 115
Looseleaf services, 277, 285
Loss of companionship, 123

Magna Carta, 107
Majority opinion, 262
Malpractice, medical, 307
Manuals, 349
Manufacture defects, 375
Manufacturers' Directory, 45
Marketing, 42–43, 76–83
Marketing strategy, 73
Martindale-Hubbell Law Directory, 43
Mason-Kish, Marilyn, 221–222
Mass tort claims, 388
Mediation, 144
Medical authority, 567
Medical bill audits, 504, 508
Medical bill reviews, 508, 514
comparing documents, 512
organizing, 510
plotting charges, 510–511
resources for, 509
use of, 508–509
writing, 512–513
Medical credentials, 556
Medical expenses
documenting, 518–519
future, 520, 523–524